Rapid

Java

Application Development
Using JBuilder 3

Y. Daniel Liang
Purdue University at Fort Wayne
Department of Computer Science

An Alan R. Apt Book

Prentice Hall
Upper Saddle River, New Jersey 07458
http://www.prenhall.com

D1456590

Library of Congress Cataloging-in-Publication Data

Liang, Y. Daniel.
   Rapid Java application development using JBuilder3 / Y. Daniel Liang.
      p. cm.
   ISBN 0-13-026161-0
   1. Java (Computer program language)   2. Application software—Development. 3.
JBuilder. I. Title
QA76.73.J38 L534 2000
005.13'3—dc21
                                        99-053483
                                          CIP

Editor-in-chief: *Marcia Horton*
Publisher: *Alan Apt*
Project manager: *Ana Arias Terry*
Editorial assistant: *Toni Holm*
Marketing manager: *Jennie Burger*
Production editor: *Pine Tree Composition*
Executive managing editor: *Vince O'Brien*
Managing editor: *David A. George*
Art director: *Heather Scott*
Cover design: *John Christiana*
Manufacturing manager: *Trudy Pisciotti*
Manufacturing buyer: *Beth Sturla*
Assistant vice president of production and manufacturing: *David W. Riccardi*

© 2000 by Prentice-Hall, Inc.
Upper Saddle River, New Jersey

The author and publisher of this book have used their best efforts in preparing
this book. These efforts include the development, research, and testing of the
theories to determine their effectiveness.

Printed in the United States of America
10 9 8 7 6 5 4 3 2 1

ISBN 0-13-026161-0

Prentice-Hall International (UK) Limited, *London*
Prentice-Hall of Australia Pty. Limited, *Sydney*
Prentice-Hall Canada Inc., *Toronto*
Prentice-Hall Hispanoamericana, S.A., *Mexico*
Prentice-Hall of India Private Limited, *New Delhi*
Prentice-Hall of Japan, Inc., *Tokyo*
Pearson Education Asia Pte. Ltd., *Singapore*
Editora Prentice-Hall do Brasil, Ltda., *Rio de Janeiro*

ABOUT THE AUTHOR

Y. Daniel Liang holds B.S. and M.S. degrees in computer science from Fudan University in Shanghai and a Ph.D. degree in computer science from the University of Oklahoma. He is the author of four Java books. He has published numerous papers in international journals and has taught Java courses nationally and internationally. He has consulted in the areas of algorithm design, client/server computing, and database management.

Dr. Liang is currently an associate professor in the Department of Computer Science at Purdue University at Fort Wayne, where he twice received the Excellence in Research Award from the School of Engineering, Technology, and Computer Science. He can be reached via the Internet at **liangjava@yahoo.com**.

ACKNOWLEDGMENTS

I would like to congratulate the JBuilder development team for creating JBuilder 3, which is not only an excellent Java RAD tool for seasoned developers, but also a superior Java educational tool for learning rapid Java application development. I would like to thank Borland Education for providing me with early access to JBuilder 3.

I am grateful to the readers of the first and second edition of my *Introduction to Java Programming* text. Their enthusiastic support encouraged me to write an advanced Java text with emphasis on rapid Java application development.

Many students and colleagues offered comments and suggestions, which greatly improved the contents and presentation of the book. Michael Sunderman helped to correct some typos and errors in the early draft of the book.

I would like to thank Alan Apt, Ana Terry, Toni Holm, and their colleagues at Prentice Hall for organizing and managing this project, and thank Patty Donovan, Robert Milch, and Dan Boilard, and their colleagues at Pine Tree Composition for helping to produce the book.

As always, I am indebted to my wife, Samantha, for love, support, and encouragement.

*To Samantha, Michael, and Michelle,
with love*

INTRODUCTION

When I began writing my first introductory Java text in the summer of 1996, only a few schools were teaching Java. Today, Java has become the programming language of choice for many schools. The incorporation of Java into the computer science curriculum has increased the need for an advanced Java text. This book covers the advanced Java features that are needed to support upper-level CS courses, such as software engineering, graphics, database programming, and distributed programming. It can be used as a text for advanced Java programming or as a supplement for upper-level CS courses. In addition, it is perfectly suitable for Java programmers who want to learn rapid application development techniques using JBuilder.

In this book I introduce the concepts of JavaBeans, bean event model, model-view control, developing customized components, Swing components, creating custom layout managers, bean persistence, bound properties and constraint properties, bean introspection and customization, Java database programming, and distributed programming using remote method invocation or CORBA. The main thread of the book, however, is to promote rapid Java application development. Rapid application development, or RAD, is a software development technology for developing programs efficiently and effectively. This technology has been successfully implemented in Visual Basic, Delphi, Power Builder, Oracle Developer 2000, and many other program development tools. Using a RAD tool, projects can be developed quickly and efficiently with minimum coding. Projects developed using RAD are easy to modify and easy to maintain. The key elements in a RAD tool are the software components, such as buttons, labels, combo boxes, lists, check boxes, radio buttons, and menus. These components can be visually manipulated and tailored during design time in order to develop customized programs.

One of the central issues in software development is how to reuse programs effectively. Java is an object-oriented programming language that provides great flexibility, modularity, clarity, and reusability through method abstraction, class abstraction, and class inheritance. A Java program can be viewed as a collection of cooperating objects that are created during runtime. The JavaBeans technology is a significant extension and enhancement of the Java language that makes it possible for programmers to rapidly build applications by assembling objects and testing them during design time, thus making reuse of the software more productive.

To facilitate developing and managing Java programs, the book is aided by JBuilder. JBuilder is one of the best Java tools that rapidly simplify Java program development for maximum productivity. JBuilder provides a fully scalable, distributed, and cross-platform architecture for building reusable components. JBuilder provides a tightly integrated development environment that lets you visually design user interface and rapidly build applications with the UI Designer and Menu Designer. JBuilder BeansExpress makes it point-and-click easy to create standard JavaBeans. JBuilder also contains many intelligent wizards that are convenient to use to generate source code automatically.

Throughout the book there are numerous examples with step-by-step instructions that guide you in creating reusable components and using them to assemble large practical applications. It is assumed that you are familiar with the basics of Java programming, including creating graphical user interface using Swing, exception handling, internationalization, multithreads, IO streams, and networking. These topics are covered in my introductory Java text, *Introduction to Java Programming* (3rd edition), or in my *Introduction to Java Programming with JBuilder 3* (Prentice-Hall, © 2000).

One of the major considerations in choosing JBuilder to teach Rapid Java Application Development is the clarity of the JBuilder-generated source code. The source code generated by JBuilder UI Designer, Menu Designer, and various wizards does not contain any proprietary code. Thus, the JBuilder-generated source code is easy to read and to maintain. With JBuilder, students can not only develop Java programs more productively, but can also learn advanced Java programming more effectively by following the source code.

All the examples in the text are developed with JBuilder Standard Edition except those in Chapters 14 and 16. Chapter 14, "Applications Using JBuilder DataExpress and Data-Aware Components," creates database projects using the Java bean components provided by Borland, which are available in JBuilder Professional Edition. Chapter 16, "Multi-Tier Application Development Using CORBA," introduces VisiBroker, which is bundled in JBuilder Enterprise Edition. These two chapters are optional, and can be skipped.

Most of the examples in this book are Java applets. A main method is provided for each applet to enable it to run standalone. However, for the sake of brevity, the main method is not listed in source code in the text.

Pedagogical Features of this Book

Rapid Java Application Development Using JBuilder 3 uses the following elements to get the most out of the material:

- **Objectives** lists what students learn from the chapter. This helps students to determine whether they have met these objectives after completing the chapter.

- **Introduction** opens the discussion with a brief overview of what to expect from the chapter.

- Programming concepts are taught by representative **Examples**, carefully chosen and presented in an easy-to-follow style. Each example is described, and includes the source code, a sample run, and an example review. The source code of the examples is contained in the companion CD-ROM. Almost all of the examples can run in two modes: standalone application or applets. Each program is complete and ready to be compiled and executed. The sample run of the program is captured from the screen to give students a live presentation of the example. Reading these examples is much like entering and running them on a computer.

- **Chapter Summary** reviews the important subjects that students should understand and remember. It also helps students to reinforce the key concepts they have learned in the chapter.

- **Chapter Review** helps students to track their progress and evaluate their learning.

- **Programming Exercises** at the end of each chapter provide students opportunities to apply the skills on their own. The trick of learning programming is practice, practice, and practice. To that end, this book provides a large number of exercises.

- **Notes**, **Tips**, and **Cautions** are inserted throughout the text to offer students valuable advice and insight on important aspects of program development:

NOTE
Provides additional information on the subject and reinforces important concepts.

TIP
Teaches good programming style and practice.

CAUTION
Helps students steer away from the pitfalls of programming errors.

The Organization of This Book

Java is a comprehensive and powerful language with many evolving features. There is plenty of room for advanced Java text. This book, however, is centered on rapid Java application development. It is divided into five parts that, taken together, form a comprehensive course on rapid Java application development.

The early chapters introduce JavaBeans, which are the basis of rapid Java application development. Subsequent chapters apply Rapid Application Development techniques to build comprehensive, robust, and useful graphics applications, database and client/server applications, and distributed applications, with step-by-step instructions.

Part I: Introduction to JBuilder and JavaBeans

The first part of the book begins with an introduction to JBuilder 3, presents the concept of JavaBeans, discusses the bean event model, introduces the model-view architectures, and teaches developing and using beans in rapid Java application development.

Chapter 1, "Getting Started with JBuilder 3," gives an overview of JBuilder's integrated development environment. You will learn how to develop Java programs with a variety of JBuilder wizards for creating projects, applications, applets, and classes, and how to compile and run programs.

Chapter 2, "Introduction to JavaBeans," introduces the concept of JavaBeans. This chapter explains the relationship between JavaBeans and Java RAD builder tools, and shows you how to write simple JavaBeans and visually manipulate the beans in JBuilder.

Chapter 3, "Bean Events," covers the Java event delegation model, inner classes, and anonymous inner classes. You will learn how to develop source beans and listener beans and how to hook the source beans with the listener beans in JBuilder.

Chapter 4, "Developing and Using Components," discusses the differences between developing beans and using beans in rapid Java application development. This chapter introduces the model-view architecture. You will learn how to use the BeansExpress Wizard to create properties and events and the Deployment Wizard to deploy applications and applets.

Part II: Rapid Application Development with Swing Components

The book's second part covers Swing components and their use in rapid Java application development. You will learn how to use a variety of Swing components to develop Java projects using JBuilder 3.

Chapter 5, "Swing Components," introduces the concept of Swing components and discusses the differences between lightweight components and heavyweight components. You will learn how to use various Swing components in rapid application development.

Chapter 6, "Containers and Layout Managers," introduces Swing containers and layout managers, examines the structure of Swing containers, and studies the layout managers provided in JBuilder. You will learn how to create custom layout managers and install them in JBuilder. The components JTabbedPane, and JSplitPane are also covered in this chapter.

Chapter 7, "Menus, Toolbars, and Dialogs," introduces menus, popup menus, toolbars, JOptionPane dialogs, custom dialogs, JColorChooser, and JFileChooser. This chapter also teaches you how to use the Menu Designer to visually design menus and popup menus.

Chapter 8, "Advanced Swing Components," shows how to use several advanced Swing components, such as JList, JComboBox, JTable, and JTree, in rapid application development. You learn various data models, selection models, renderers, and editors for supporting these advanced components.

Part III: Bean Persistence, Interoperability, Introspection, and Customization

This part introduces the JavaBeans API. You will learn how to develop persistent beans, use bound and constraint properties, and create bean property editors.

Chapter 9, "Bean Persistence, Versioning, and Using Beans in Other Tools," introduces object serialization, which is a Java built-in mechanism for persistently storing and restoring beans. You will learn how to use Sun's Beanbox, a tool for testing beans, which can be used to verify bean persistence. You will also learn to customize serialization and bean versioning. Several examples that use JavaBeans in non-Java tools, such as Visual Basic and Word, will be demonstrated to give you a broad view of JavaBeans versatility.

Chapter 10, "Bound and Constraint Properties," introduces bound and constraint properties. A *bound property* of a component is one for which a property notification service is provided when the property changes. A *constraint property* allows the listener component to verify the property change to determine whether to accept or reject a change. These properties are useful for creating custom property editors.

Chapter 11, "Bean Introspection and Customization," takes an in-depth look at how builder tools learn bean information through introspection. You will learn how to create and deploy custom editors.

Part IV: Java Database Programming

This part of the book is devoted to developing database projects using Java. You will learn the Java database programming interface, handle database metadata, create and process SQL statements, and use JBuilder database beans for rapidly developing Java database applications.

Chapter 12, "Introduction to Java Database Programming," begins with an overview of the JDBC interface for accessing relational database from Java. A thorough introduction to the four types of the JDBC drivers is presented through examples of the use of MS Access, Oracle, and InterBase.

Chapter 13, "Metadata and Statements," gives a comprehensive treatment of obtaining database metadata, and processing statements, prepared statements, and callable statements.

Chapter 14, "Applications Using JBuilder DataExpress and Data-Aware Components," teaches you how to use JBuilder's powerful data access beans and data-aware Swing components for rapidly developing database applications.

Part V: Distributed Java Programming

The book's final part introduces the development of distributed projects using Java. You will learn how to use Remote Method Invocation (RMI) and CORBA to develop distributed applications using JBuilder.

Chapter 15, "Distributed Programming Using Java Remote Method Invocation," introduces Remote Method Invocation, a technology providing a framework for building distributed Java systems. You will learn how to use it to create useful distributed applications.

Chapter 16, "Multi-Tier Application Development Using CORBA," introduces *Common Object Request Broker Architecture*, a technology for creating interoperable distributed object systems. You will learn how to create distributed applications using VisiBroker, a product by Inprise that implements the CORBA technology using Java.

CONTENTS AT A GLANCE

PART I	**INTRODUCTION TO JBUILDER AND JAVABEANS**	**1**
Chapter 1.	Getting Started with JBuilder 3	3
Chapter 2.	Introduction to JavaBeans	49
Chapter 3.	Bean Events	75
Chapter 4.	Developing and Using Components	109

PART II	**RAPID APPLICATION DEVELOPMENT USING SWING COMPONENTS**	**159**
Chapter 5.	Swing Components	161
Chapter 6.	Containers and Layout Managers	215
Chapter 7.	Menus, Toolbars, and Dialogs	261
Chapter 8.	Advanced Swing Components	313

PART III	**BEAN PERSISTENCE, INTEROPERABILITY, INTROSPECTION, AND CUSTOMIZATON**	**385**
Chapter 9.	Bean Persistence, Versioning, and Using Beans in Other Tools	387
Chapter 10.	Bound and Constraint Properties	427
Chapter 11.	Bean Introspection and Customization	461

PART IV	**JAVA DATABASE PROGRAMMING**	**513**
Chapter 12.	Introduction to Java Database Programming	515
Chapter 13.	Metadata and Statements	553
Chapter 14.	Applications Using JBuilder DataExpress and Data-Aware Components	603

PART V	**DISTRIBUTED JAVA PROGRAMMING**	**641**
Chapter 15.	Distributed Programming Using Java Remote Method Invocation	643
Chapter 16.	Multi-Tier Application Development Using CORBA	683
	Index	723

Table of Contents

PART I INTRODUCTION TO JBUILDER AND JAVABEANS 1

CHAPTER 1 Getting Started with JBuilder 3 3

Objectives 3

Introduction 4

Starting JBuilder 3 5

    The Main Window 6

    The AppBrowser Window 7

    Compiling and Running the Projects 10

    Running the Exercises in This Book 11

Creating and Managing Projects 13

    Setting Project Properties 13

    Creating a New Project 18

Creating Java Programs 19

    The Application Class 21

    The Frame Class 22

    Modifying the Code in the Frame Class 24

    Using the Applet Wizard 27

    Modifying the Generated Applet Class 31

Designing User Interfaces Using the UI Designer 34

Customizing JBuilder Environments 41

Getting Online Help from JBuilder 45

Chapter Summary 46

Chapter Review 46

Programming Exercises 47

CHAPTER 2 Introduction to JavaBeans 49

Objectives 49

Introduction 50

Beans and Objects 50

JavaBeans and Java Builder Tools 55

Using JavaBeans in JBuilder 56

    Adding a Bean to the Component Palette 56

    Using Beans in JBuilder 59

Bean Properties 65

    Property Naming Patterns 65

    Properties and Data Members 66

    Property Types 66

Property Editors 67

Chapter Summary 73

Chapter Review 73

Programming Exercises 73

CHAPTER 3 | **Bean Events** **75**

Objectives 75

Introduction 76

Java Event Model 76

Event Objects 77

Source Components 78

Event Listener Interface 78

Listener Components 78

Review of the JButton Component 78

Creating Custom Event Sets and Source Components 79

Creating Listener Components 86

Event Adapters 89

Using Adapters in JBuilder 90

Inner Classes and Anonymous Inner Classes 97

Working with Existing Event Sets 101

Chapter Summary 106

Chapter Review 106

Programming Exercises 107

CHAPTER 4 | **Developing and Using Components** **109**

Objectives 109

Introduction 110

Developing Beans versus Using Beans 110

Component Development Process 111

Using the BeansExpress Wizard to Create Properties 112

Using the Bean Designer to Create Events 124

Developing Components Using the Model-View Approach 131

Rapid Application Development Process 142

Packaging and Deploying Java Projects in JBuilder 149

Packaging Projects Using the Deployment Wizard 150

The Manifest File 151

Running Archived Applications and Applets 152

Chapter Summary 153

Chapter Review 154

Programming Exercises 154

**PART II RAPID APPLICATION DEVELOPMENT
WITH SWING COMPONENTS**   **159**

| CHAPTER 5 | **Swing Components** | **161** |

Objectives	161
Introduction	162
Lightweight Component Framework	162
The Swing Model-View Architecture	163
Pluggable Look-and-feel	164
Overview of the Swing Classes	167
The JComponent Class	169
Keystroke Handling	170
Action Objects	170
JComponent Properties	170
The SwingSet Demo	172
JButton	173
JToggleButton	175
JCheckBox	176
JRadioButton	176
Border	177
JLabel	189
JScrollPane	190
JTextField	195
JTextArea	196
JEditorPane	197
JScrollBar	200
JSlider	205
JProgressBar	207
Chapter Summary	212
Chapter Review	212
Programming Exercises	212

| CHAPTER 6 | **Containers and Layout Managers** | **215** |

Objectives	215
Introduction	216
About Containers	216
JFrame	217
JApplet	218
JPanel	218
Layout Managers	219

Working with Layout Managers 221

BorderLayout 222

FlowLayout 222

GridLayout 222

CardLayout 222

GridBagLayout 223

Null 225

BoxLayout and Box Class 225

BoxLayout2 227

XYLayout 227

OverlayLayout2 228

PaneLayout 228

VerticalFlowLayout 229

How Does a Layout Manager Lay Out Components? 240

Creating Custom Layout Managers 242

JTabbedPane 247

JSplitPane 251

Chapter Review 256

Chapter Summary 256

Programming Exercises 257

CHAPTER 7   **Menus, Toolbars, and Dialogs** 261

Objectives 261

Introduction 262

Menus 262

Image Icons, Keyboard Mnemonics,
and Keyboard Accelerators 265

Using the JBuilder Menu Designer 266

Popup Menus 273

JToolBar 277

JOptionPane Dialogs 281

Message Dialogs 282

Confirmation Dialogs 283

Input Dialogs 284

Option Dialogs 286

Creating Custom Dialogs 293

JColorChooser 300

JFileChooser 302

Chapter Review 310

Chapter Summary 310

Programming Exercises 310

CHAPTER 8 | **Advanced Swing Components** **313**

Objectives 313

Introduction 313

JList 313

List Models 319

List Selection Models 324

List Cell Renderers 325

JComboBox 332

Editing Combo Boxes 338

JTable 342

JTable Properties 343

Table Models 350

Table Column Models 351

The TableColumn Class 351

Table Renderers and Editors 358

Custom Table Renderers and Editors 362

Table Events 365

JTree 370

Creating Trees 372

Processing Tree Nodes 375

Tree Node Rendering and Editing 380

Tree Events 381

Chapter Summary 382

Chapter Review 382

Programming Exercises 383

PART III BEAN PERSISTENCE, INTEROPERABILITY, INTROSPECTION, AND CUSTOMIZATION **385**

CHAPTER 9 | **Bean Persistence, Versioning, and Using Beans in Other Tools** **387**

Objectives 387

Introduction 388

Object Serialization and Deserialization 388

The transient Keyword 395

Instantiating Serialized Beans 396

The BeanBox 401

Customizing Serialization 409

Bean Versioning   412

JavaBeans Bridge for ActiveX   417

   Converting JavaBeans Components
   to ActiveX Components   417

Chapter Summary   425

Chapter Review   425

Programming Exercises   425

CHAPTER 10   **Bound and Constraint Properties**   **427**

Objectives   427

Introduction   428

Implementing Bound Properties   428

The `PropertyChangeSupport` Class   437

Using the Bean Designer to Create Bound Properties   438

Implementing Constraint Properties   445

Implementing Model-View Components Using Bound
and Constraint Properties   450

Chapter Summary   460

Chapter Review   460

Programming Exercises   460

CHAPTER 11   **Bean Introspection and Customization**   **461**

Objectives   461

Introduction   462

Creating `BeanInfo` Classes   462

   The `PropertyDescriptor` Class   464

   The `EventSetDescriptor` Class   465

   The `MethodDescriptor` Class   465

   Specifying Image Icons   465

Inspecting Bean Components   470

Using the BeanInsight Wizard   475

Customizing Property Editors   476

   Displaying Property Values   477

   Editing Property Values   477

   Creating Property Editors   477

The FeatureDescriptor Class   484

Using the Bean Designer to Create Property Editors
and Generate BeanInfo Classes   485

Creating GUI Custom Editors   492

Creating Component Customizers   501

Chapter Summary   509

Chapter Review 509

Programming Exercises 510

PART IV   JAVA DATABASE PROGRAMMING 513

CHAPTER 12   Introduction to Java Database Programming 515

Objectives 515

Introduction 516

Overview of the JDBC API 517

Developing JDBC Applications 518

The Driver Interface 520

The DriverManager Class 520

The DriverPropertyInfo Class 521

The Connection Interface 521

The Statement, PreparedStatement, and CallableStatement Interfaces 521

The ResultSet Interface 522

The SQL Exception Classes 522

The DatabaseMetaData Interface 522

The ResultSetMetaData Interface 523

The JDBC Support Classes 523

JDBC Drivers 523

Type 1: JDBC-ODBC Bridge Driver 524

Type 2: Native-API Driver 524

Type 3: Middle-Tier Driver 525

Type 4: Native-Protocol Driver 526

Connecting to Databases Using JDBC Drivers 526

JDBC URL Naming Conventions 527

Using the JDBC-ODBC Driver 528

Using the Native-API Driver 533

Using the Native-Protocol Driver 536

Using the Middle-Tier Driver 540

Chapter Summary 551

Chapter Review 551

Programming Exercises 552

CHAPTER 13   Metadata and Statements 553

Objectives 553

Introduction 554

Getting Database MetaData 554

Statement   578

    The execute(), executeQuery(),
    and executeUpdate() Methods   579

PreparedStatement   590

CallableStatement   596

Chapter Review   601

Chapter Summary   601

Programming Exercises   601

CHAPTER 14 | **Applications Using JBuilder DataExpress and
Data-Aware Components**   **603**

Objectives   603

Introduction   604

DataExpress API   604

Data-Aware Components   614

Master-Detail Relationship   622

Data Modules   627

Chapter Summary   638

Chapter Review   638

Programming Examples   639

PART V   DISTRIBUTED JAVA PROGRAMMING   **641**

CHAPTER 15 | **Distributed Programming Using Java Remote
Method Invocation**   **643**

Objectives   643

Introduction   644

RMI Basics   644

    How Does RMI Work?   644

    Passing Parameters   646

Developing RMI Applications   646

RMI vs. Socket-Level Programming   656

Developing Three-Tier Applications Using RMI   661

RMI Callbacks   666

Chapter Summary   679

Chapter Review   680

Programming Exercises   680

CHAPTER 16 | **Multi-Tier Application Development Using CORBA**   **683**

Objectives   683

Introduction   684

Introduction to CORBA   684

CORBA Is Distributed   684
Interface Definition Language   685
Object Request Broker   685
Basic Object Adapter   685
Internet Inter-ORB Protocol   685
The IDL Compiler and Its Generated Files   686
Developing CORBA Applications   691
VisiBroker Smart Agent   701
Location Services   701
Fault Tolerance   702
Load Balancing   703
Configuring osagent   703
The osfind Utility   704
VisiBroker Gatekeeper   704
Developing Three-Tier Applications Using CORBA   705
CORBA Callbacks   708
Chapter Summary   720
Chapter Review   720
Programming Exercises   721
INDEX   **723**

INTRODUCTION TO JBUILDER AND JAVABEANS

You have heard a lot about Java and its Rapid Application Development capability. You are anxious to start rapid Java development. The first part of the book is a stepping stone that will prepare you to embark on the journey of rapid Java application development using JBuilder. You will begin to learn JBuilder 3, the concept of JavaBeans, and the bean event model, and to develop and use beans in rapid Java application development.

CHAPTER 1   GETTING STARTED WITH JBUILDER 3

CHAPTER 2   INTRODUCTION TO JAVABEANS

CHAPTER 3   BEAN EVENTS

CHAPTER 4   DEVELOPING AND USING COMPONENTS

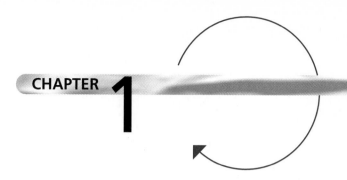

GETTING STARTED WITH JBUILDER 3

Objectives

- ◉ Get a quick start on JBuilder 3.
- ◉ Understand project properties and know how to set them.
- ◉ Become familiar with the wizards in Object Gallery.
- ◉ Create projects using the Project Wizard.
- ◉ Create applications using the Application Wizard.
- ◉ Create applets using the Applet Wizard.
- ◉ Learn to use the UI Designer to create user interfaces.
- ◉ Customize JBuilder Environments.
- ◉ Get Online Help from JBuilder.

Introduction

JBuilder 3, released in May 1999 by Borland (a division of Inprise Corporation), is a premier Java development tool for developing Java programs. Borland products are known to be "best of breed" in the Rapid Application Development tool market. Over the years, Borland has led the charge to create visual development tools like Delphi and C++ Builder. And now Borland is leading the way in Java development tools with JBuilder. JBuilder is endorsed by major information technology companies, such as IBM, which also makes its own Java IDE tool, *Visual Age for Java*.

JBuilder provides a fully scalable, distributed, and cross-platform architecture for building reusable components. JBuilder provides a tightly integrated development environment that lets you visually design user interfaces and rapidly build applications with the UI Designer and Menu Designer. JBuilder BeansExpress makes it point-and-click easy to create standard Java bean components. JBuilder also comes with many intelligent wizards that are convenient to use for generating source code automatically. With JBuilder, you can create Java programs with minimum coding for maximum productivity.

JBuilder 3 is available in four versions: JBuilder University Edition, JBuilder Standard Edition, JBuilder Professional Edition, and JBuilder Enterprise Edition. The University Edition is ideal for students to learn the basics of Java programming without the need to create JavaBeans or use visual design tools. The University Edition is free for educational use. The Standard Edition is a lean package that contains all the essential components for developing Java applications and applets. It is a perfect development tool for Java beginners who want to learn and explore Java visual design capabilities. The Professional Edition contains the components in JBuilder Standard, plus the components for developing database applications. The Enterprise Edition contains all the components in JBuilder professional, plus components used to write middle-tier programs to serve clients with various database servers. The companion CD-ROM in this book contains JBuilder University Edition and JBuilder Enterprise 60-day Trial Edition.

NOTE

All the chapters in this book are based on JBuilder Standard Edition except Chapters 14 and 16. Chapter 14, Applications Using JBuilder DataExpress and Data-Aware Components," creates database projects using the Java bean components provided by Borland, which are available in JBuilder Professional Edition. Chapter 16, "Multi-Tier Application Development Using CORBA," introduces VisiBroker, which is bundled in JBuilder Enterprise Edition.

Most of the examples in this book are JAVA applets. To view Java 2 platform applets from a Web browser, use the HTML converter to convert the applet's HTML file into the HTML file using the JAVA Plug-In. For more information, please refer to my *Introduction to Java Programming with JBuilder 3.*

Starting JBuilder 3

Assume you have successfully installed JBuilder 3 Standard Edition on your machine. To start JBuilder, click the Windows Start button and choose Programs, Borland JBuilder 3 Standard, JBuilder 3. The main JBuilder user interface appears, as shown in Figure 1.1. If you don't see the Welcome project, choose Welcome Project (Sample) from the Help menu.

TIP

I recommend that you install JBuilder 3 with the default options. With the default installation, you can download the projects in this book and run them without modifications.

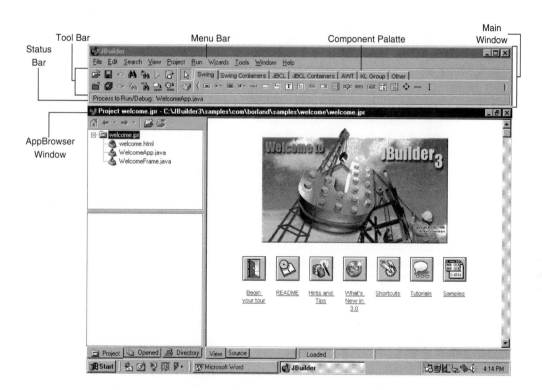

Figure 1.1   *The JBuilder user interface consists of the main window and the AppBrowser window.*

> ■■■ **Tip**
>
> The critical problem facing Java is its sluggish performance. The Java HotSpot Performance Engine is a product developed by Sun to resolve the problem. The performance of JBuilder and your Java programs can be improved significantly if this product is plugged into JBuilder 3. The Java HotSpot Performance Engine speeds up execution by identifying the "hotspots", the parts of the application where the most time is spent executing bytecode, and accelerating the rate of execution for this performance-critical code. The Java HotSpot Performance Engine can be downloaded from **www.javasoft.com/products/ hotspot/index.html**. To plug the HotSpot Performance Engine to JBuilder 3, create a directory named hotspot under the jbuilder3\java\jre\bin and copy jvm.dll to the hotspot directory. When you type c:\jbuilder3\java\bin\java -version, you should see the following message to indicate that the HotSpot Performance Engine is correctly installed.
>
> ```
> java version "1.2"
> HotSpot VM (1.0.1, mixed, build g)
> ```

The user interface consists of the main window and the AppBrowser window. The main window is at the top of the screen when you start JBuilder. It serves as the development control center, consisting of the menu bar, the toolbar, the Component palette, and the status bar. The AppBrowser window (below the main window) is used to perform all the usual development functions, such as creating and editing programs, designing user interfaces, compiling and running programs, and debugging programs.

The Main Window

The main window consists of the menu bar, toolbar, Component palette, and status bar. The *menu bar* provides most of the commands you need to use JBuilder, including those for creating programs, editing programs, compiling, running, and debugging programs.

The *toolbar* provides buttons for several frequently used commands on the menu bar. Clicking a toolbar button is faster than using the menu bar. For some commands, you also can use function keys or keyboard shortcuts. For example, you can save a file in three ways:

- Select File, Save from the menu bar.
- Click the Save (⊞) toolbar button.
- Use the keyboard shortcut Ctrl+S.

> ■■■ **Tip**
>
> You can display a label for a button by pointing the mouse to the button without clicking.

The *Component palette* contains visual components for Rapid Application Development. The components are grouped into nine groups with the tab names Swing, Swing Containers, JBCL, JBCL Containers, AWT, KL Group, and Other. You can see the components in a group by clicking the group's tab. JBuilder has intelligent click-and-drop capability that enables you to click a component, such as a JButton, from the Swing group, then drop it into the user interface for Rapid Java Application Development.

The *status bar* displays a message to alert users of the operation status, such as "file saved" for the Save file command, and "compilation successful" for the Compilation command.

The AppBrowser Window

Traditional IDE tools use many windows to accommodate various development tasks, such as editing, debugging, and browsing information. As a result, it is often difficult to find the window you need. Because it is easy to get lost, beginners may be intimidated. For this reason, some new programmers prefer to use separate utilities, such as the JDK command line tools, for developing programs.

Borland is aware of the usability problem and has made significant efforts to simplify JBuilder user interface. JBuilder introduces an AppBrowser window that enables you to explore, edit, design, and debug projects all in one unified window.

An AppBrowser contains three panes: the Navigation pane (upper left), the Content pane (right side), and the Structure pane (bottom left), as shown in Figure 1.2.

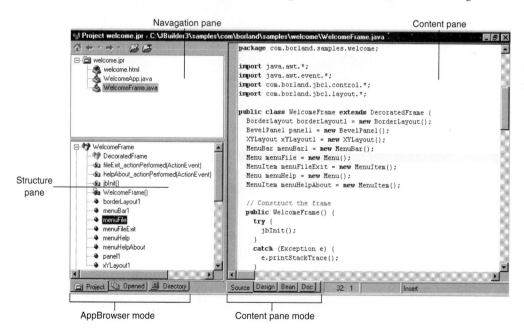

Figure 1.2   *The AppBrowser Window consists of a Navigation pane, Content pane, and Structure pane.*

The Navigation Pane

The Navigation pane shows a list of one or more files. In the case of the Project browser, you will see the project (.jpr) file first. Attached to that is a list of the files in the project. The list can include .java, .html, text, or image files. Packages can also be added to the list. You can select a file in the Navigation pane by clicking it. The Content pane and the Structure pane display information about the selected file. As you select different files in the Navigation pane, each one will be represented in the Content and Structure panes. If you select WelcomeFrame.java in the Navigation pane, you will see the corresponding contents in the Structure pane and the Content pane, as shown in Figure 1.2.

There are three tabs (Project, Opened, and Directory), known as AppBrowser modes, below the Structure pane. These allow you to navigate through the project, the opened files, and files in the directory, respectively. For example, if you choose the Directory tab, you will see the directories in the Navigation pane (see Figure 1.3).

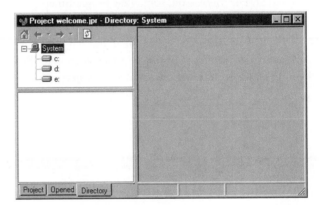

Figure 1.3   *Choosing the Directory tab enables you to navigate through the directories and files.*

If you choose the Project tab, you will see five buttons above the Navigation pane. You can see the tool tip of the button by pointing the mouse on the button. The first three buttons are for navigating through the browser, and the last two are for adding files to the project or removing files from the project.

The Content Pane

The Content pane displays the detailed content of the file selected in the Navigation pane. The editor or viewer used is determined by the file's extension. If you click the WelcomeFrame.java file in the Navigation pane, for example, you will see four tabs (Source, Design, Bean, and Doc) on the bottom of the Content pane (see Figure 1.2). If you select the Source tab, you will see the JBuilder Java Source Code Editor. This is a full-featured, syntax-highlighted programming editor.

If you select welcome.html in the Navigation pane, the Content pane becomes an HTML browser. If you choose the Source tab, you can edit the HTML file in the Content pane. You can also view the image files in the Content pane. To view an image file, first use the Add button to add it to the project if it is not in the Navigation pane, and choose the image file in the Navigation pane to view the image in the Content pane (see Figure 1.4).

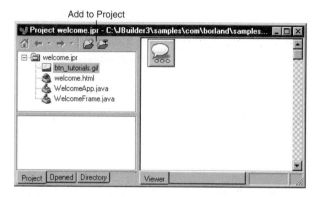

Figure 1.4   *You can view image files in the Content pane.*

With WelcomeFrame.java selected in the Navigation pane, if you select the Design tab in the Content pane, you will see the JBuilder UI Designer in the Content pane (see Figure 1.5). The designer shows you what the UI appearance of this class

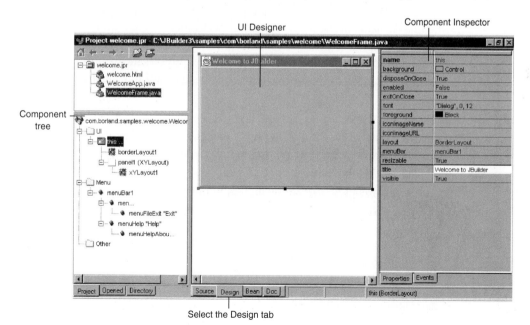

Figure 1.5   *When you select the Design tab, the AppBrowser window shows the component structure in the Structure pane, the UI Designer, and the Component Inspector in the Content pane.*

will be at runtime, and enables you to visually construct and develop your UI with minimum coding. You also can see that the Structure pane has changed to show the UI items in the code. On the right of the UI Designer is the Component Inspector, which enables you to set the component's properties or associate events to it. For example, if you select `this` in the Structure pane, you will see the Component Inspector for the frame. If you change the `title` property to "Welcome to JBuilder 3," you will see the new title in the UI Designer. JBuilder automatically modifies the source code to reflect the change. You can see the source code by choosing the Source tab and searching for the `setTitle` method to see the change.

NOTE

JBuilder synchronizes visual designing with the source code. Any changes you make in the designer are automatically reflected in the source code. Likewise, any changes made to the source code that affect the visual interface are reflected in the visual designer. This synchronization enables you to build applications by editing the source code or using the visual designer, whichever is more convenient.

The Structure Pane

The Structure pane displays structural information about the files you selected in the Navigation pane. All the items displayed in the Structure pane are in the form of a hierarchical indexed list. The + symbol in front of an item indicates that the item contains subitems. You can see the subitems by clicking the + symbol.

You can use the Structure pane as a quick navigational tool to locate the various structural elements in the file. If you select WelcomeFrame.java in the Navigation pane, for example, you will see classes, variables, and methods in the Structure pane (see Figure 1.2). You can then click on any of the elements in the Structure pane, and the Content pane will move to that element, and highlight it in the source code.

If you click on the `menuFile` item in the Structure pane, as shown in Figure 1.2, the Content pane moves to and highlights the statement that defines the `menuFile` data field. This provides a much faster way to browse and find the elements of a .java file than scrolling through it.

When you select a .java file and then choose the Design tab in the Content pane, the Structure pane will display the designable objects in the file, and how they are nested and interrelated (see Figure 1.5). This view is known as the *Component tree*.

Compiling and Running the Projects

The Welcome project is already created as a sample in JBuilder. To run it, use one of the following methods:

- Select Run, Run "WelcomeApp.java" from the menu bar.
- Click the Run ( ) toolbar button.

- Point to WelcomeApp.java in the Navigation pane, right-click the mouse button to display a popup menu (see Figure 1.6), and choose Run from the menu.

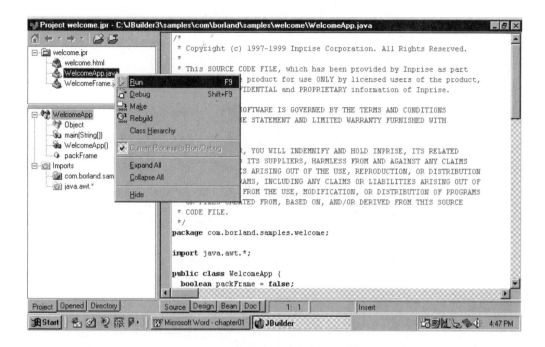

Figure 1.6 *Point the mouse to the file in the Navigation pane and right-click it to display a popup menu that contains the commands for processing the file.*

NOTE
The Run command invokes the Compile command if the program is not compiled or if it was modified after the last compilation.

Running the Exercises in This Book

A good way to learn programming is through examples. There are abundant examples in this book. The examples can be downloaded at **www.prenhall.com/liang/LiangBook.zip**.

Assume that you have successfully uncompressed the projects and stored the source code in c:\LiangBook. Here are the steps to run the ClockDemo project in Example 4.1, "Creating a Clock Component," in Chapter 4, "Developing and Using Components."

1. Choose File, Open to bring up the File Open dialog box, as shown in Figure 1.7.

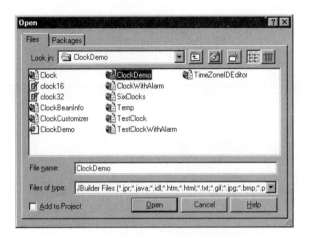

Figure 1.7 *The Open dialog box allows you to open files from a file directory or from a package.*

2. Choose or type ClockDemo.jpr in C:\LiangBook\ClockDemo in the Open/Create dialog box. A new AppBrowser window appears on the screen for the project, as shown in Figure 1.8. Note that the icon for a Java project file in JBuilder is (⬛).

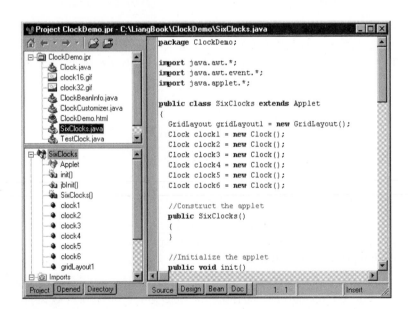

Figure 1.8 *JBuilder creates a new AppBrowser window when you open a project file.*

3. Run SixClocks.java. Figure 1.9 is a sample run of the program.

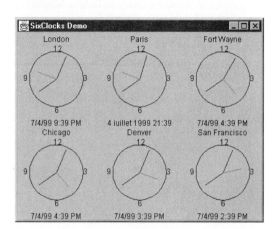

Figure 1.9 *The program displays six running clocks.*

■■■■ NOTE

If you open a nonproject file, it will be added to the project in the active App-Browser.

Creating and Managing Projects

To develop programs in the JBuilder environment, you should first create a JBuilder project. A *project* acts like a holder to tie the relevant files together. Information about each JBuilder project is stored in a project file with a .jpr file extension. The project file contains a list of all the files, project settings, and properties in the project. JBuilder uses this information to load and save all the files in the project and to compile and run the programs.

You cannot edit the project file manually; it is modified automatically, however, whenever you add or remove files from the project or set project options. You can see the project file as a node at the top of the project tree in the Navigation pane (see Welcome.jpr in Figure 1.5). JBuilder uses a Project Properties dialog box to set project properties and provides a Project Wizard to facilitate creating projects.

Setting Project Properties

JBuilder uses the Default Project Properties dialog box to set default properties for all the projects. An individual project has its own Project Properties dialog box, which can be used to set project-specific properties.

To display the default Project Properties dialog box, choose Project, Default Properties, as shown in Figure 1.10. To display the Project Properties dialog box for the current project, choose Project, Properties, as shown in Figure 1.11. You can also

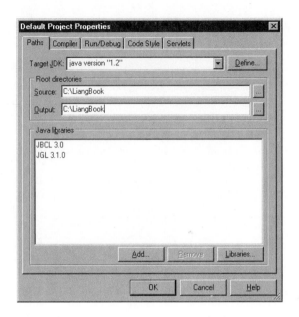

Figure 1.10 *The Default Project Properties dialog box enables you to set default properties to cover all the projects.*

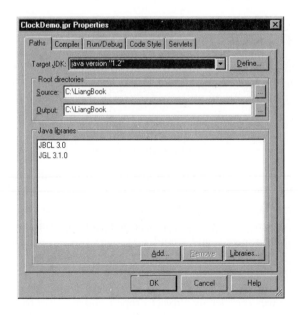

Figure 1.11 *Each project keeps its own project properties.*

right-click the project file in the Navigation pane and choose the Properties command to display the Project Properties dialog box.

The Default Project Properties dialog box (Figure 1.10) and the Project Properties dialog box (Figure 1.11) look the same except that they have different titles. Both dialog boxes contain Paths, Compiler, Code Style, Run/Debug, and Servlets tabs. You can set options in these pages for the current project or the default project, depending on whether the dialog box is for the current project or for the default project. JBuilder Professional and JBuilder Enterprise Edition have more options in the Project Properties dialog box.

The Paths Page

The Paths page of the Project Properties dialog box sets the following options:

- JDK version to compile against.
- Source root directories where the source code is located.
- Output root directory where the compilation output is stored.
- Java libraries to use for compiling and running.

JBuilder can compile and run against JDK 1.1 or JDK 1.2. To set up the list of available JDKs, click the Define button to display the Available JDK Versions dialog for adding new JDK compilers.

Setting proper paths is necessary for JBuilder to locate the associate files in the right directory for compiling and running the programs in the project. The Source root directories field enables you to specify one or more paths (separated with semicolons) for the source file. A warning message would be reported if the source file is not in one of the Source root directories. The Output root directory specifies the path in which the compiler places the .class files. Files are placed in a directory tree based on the package structure. For example, if the Output root directory is c:\JBuilder3\myclasses, and the package statement in the Java source code is

```
package Demo;
```

JBuilder will store the class file in the c:\JBuilder3\myclasses\Demo directory.

All the libraries you need for this book are already taken care of. If you need to add custom libraries to the project, click the Add button. To remove a library, click the Remove button. To switch the order of libraries, drag and drop them. To change the list of available libraries, choose the Libraries button to display the Available Java Libraries dialog.

The Compiler Page

The Compiler page of the Project Properties dialog box (see Figure 1.12) sets compiler options. The options are applied to all the files in the project, as well as to files referenced by these files, stopping at packages marked "stable."

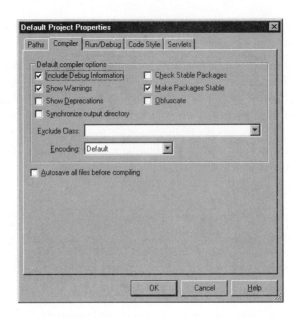

Figure 1.12 *The Compiler page of the Project Properties dialog box sets compiler options for the project.*

The option "Include Debug Information" includes symbolic debug information in the .class file when you make, or rebuild a node. The option "Show Warnings" displays compiler warning messages. The option "Show Deprecations" displays all deprecated classes, methods, properties, events, and variables used in the API. The option "Synchronize output directory" deletes class files on the output path for which you don't have source files before compiling.

The Option "Check Stable Packages" checks files in the packages marked "stable" to see whether they and their imported classes need to be recompiled. Unchecking this option shortens the edit/recompile cycle by not rechecking stable packages.

The option "Make Package Stable" checks all the classes of a package on the first build and marks the package "stable." If this option is unchecked, only the referenced classes of this package will be compiled, and the package will not be marked "stable." This option should be unchecked when working with partial projects. It is especially useful for working with a library of classes with no source code.

The option "Obfuscate" makes your programs less vulnerable to decompiling. Decompiling means to translate the Java bytecode to Java source code. After decompiling your obfuscated code, the generated source code contains altered symbol names for private symbols.

The "Exclude Class" choice lets you specify that a .class file is excluded from being compiled. The "Encoding" choice menu specifies the encoding that controls how the compiler interprets characters beyond the ASCII character set. If no setting is specified, the default native-encoding converter for the platform is used.

The option "Autosave all files before compiling" automatically saves all files in the project before each compile.

The option "Generate source to output path" is applicable only to RMI and IDL files. These files are used in multi-tier Java applications, introduced in Chapter 15, "Distributed Programming Using Java Remote Method Invocation," and in Chapter 16, "Multi-Tier Application Development Using CORBA."

The Code Style Page

The Code Style page of the Project Properties dialog box (see Figure 1.13) enables you to specify the code style of the program generated by JBuilder.

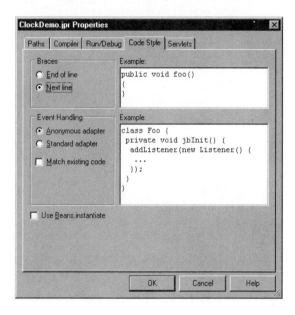

Figure 1.13   *The Code Style page of the Project Properties dialog box sets the options for the code style of the program generated by JBuilder.*

With the option "End of line" selected, JBuilder will generate the code with opening braces inserted at the end of the line; otherwise, the opening braces are inserted at the beginning of the line. All the code generated in this book uses the New Line style.

In the Event Handling section, you can choose one of the options to tell JBuilder to generate event-handling code using anonymous adapter, standard adapter, or by matching the existing style of event-handling code. The adapters will be introduced in Chapter 3, "Bean Events."

The option "Use Beans.instantiate" tells JBuilder to instantiate objects using Beans.instantiate() instead of using the new operator. Using the Beans.instantiate() method to create objects will be introduced in Chapter 9, "Bean Persistence, Versioning, and Using Beans in Other Tools."

The Run/Debug Page

The Run/Debug Properties page of the Project Properties dialog box (see Figure 1.14) lets you enter command-line arguments to pass your application or applet at runtime. You also can use this page to set Debugger options. You can send the output either to the console or to the Execution Log in the Console I/O section. You can view the Execution Log by choosing View, Execution Log. If the option "Close Console Window on exit" is selected, the console window is closed when the application's main method is completely executed.

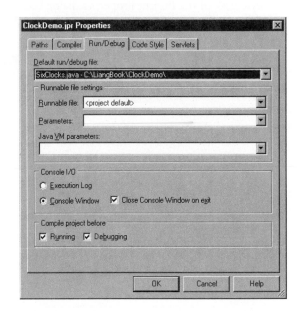

Figure 1.14 *The Run/Debug page of the Project Properties dialog box allows you to set execution and debugging options.*

Creating a New Project

Assume that you have set the Source root directories and Output root directory to C:\LiangBook in the Default Project Properties dialog box. To create a new project, follow the steps below.

1. Choose File, New Project to bring up the Project Wizard dialog box, as shown in Figure 1.15.

2. Type C:\LiangBook\Welcome\Welcome.jpr in the File field.

3. Fill in the title, author, company, and description fields. These optional fields provide a description for the project.

4. Click Finish. The new project is displayed in a new AppBrowser.

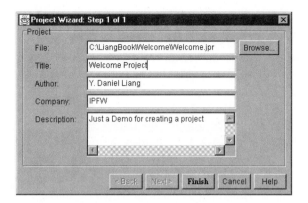

Figure 1.15   *You must use the Project Wizard to create a project file.*

The Project Wizard generates a project file with a .jpr extension and a .html file with the same name as the project file. The HTML file contains default project information. You can edit this file in the Content pane to record any pertinent information about the project that you want to display. The contents of this file always are displayed in the Content pane when the project file is selected, even if this file is removed from the project.

Creating Java Programs

JBuilder provides numerous wizards for generating templates that you can use to speed up your development of applications, applets, beans, dialogs, etc. These wizards are contained in the Object Gallery (see Figure 1.16), which is accessible by

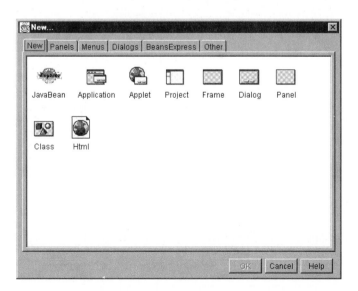

Figure 1.16   *The Object Gallery contains many wizards for creating applications, applets, beans, dialogs, etc.*

choosing File, New from the menu bar. You can use the Application Wizard to generate the class templates for your application.

This section shows you how to create Java applications using the Application Wizard. You will write an application that adds two integers and displays the sum. (See Figure 1.17.)

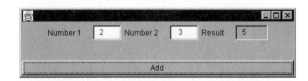

Figure 1.17   *The program adds the numbers from Number 1 and Number 2 and displays the result.*

Here are the steps to complete the project:

1. Create a new project.

   1.1. Choose File, New Project to bring up the Project Wizard.

   1.2. Edit the File field to read:

           `C:\LiangBook\ApplicationDemo\ApplicationDemo.jpr`

   1.3. Choose Finish.

NOTE

All the examples in this book assume that the source root directories and output root directory are set to C:\LiangBook.

---

2. Create a new application.

   2.1. Choose File, New to display the Object Gallery (i.e., The New dialog box, as shown in Figure 1.16).

   2.2. Click the Application icon to bring up the Application Wizard, as shown in Figure 1.18. Make sure to check the option "Use only core JDK and Swing classes."

   2.3. Type TestApplication in the Class field of Application Wizard's Step 1 of 2, and click Next to display Application Wizard's Step 2 of 2, as shown in Figure 1.19.

   2.4. Click Finish.

The Application Wizard creates the following two files:

- TestApplication.java, referred to as the *application class*.
- TestFrame.java, referred to as the *frame class*.

one class per file?

Figure 1.18   *The Application Wizard's Step 1 of 2 dialog box prompts you to enter a package name and an application main class name.*

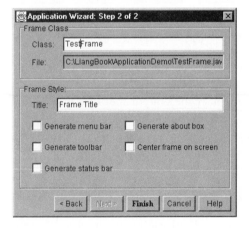

Figure 1.19   *The Application Wizard's Step 2 of 2 dialog box prompts you to enter the frame class name and to specify frame style.*

The Java interpreter executes the project starting from the application class. The frame class creates the user interface and performs the actual operations.

The Application Class

The application class contains a constructor and a main method, as shown in Figure 1.20. The constructor creates an instance for the frame class and makes it visible. The main() method is called by the Java interpreter to start the application class. You can navigate through the Structure pane to show these two methods in the Content pane. If you highlight TestApplication.java in the Navigation pane, for example, and then highlight its constructor in the Structure pane, you will see the source code for the constructor in the Content pane.

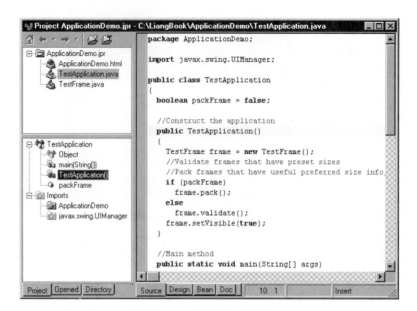

Figure 1.20   *The application class contains a main method and a constructor.*

The statement package ApplicationDemo in the first line tells JBuilder that the compiled bytecode of the application class will be saved in the ApplicationDemo subdirectory under the Output root directory. Since the Output root directory is set to c:\LiangBook, the .class files will be stored in c:\LiangBook\Application-Demo when the class is compiled. Recall that the Output root directory is defined at the Project Properties dialog box and can be modified by choosing Project, Project Properties, or right-click the .jpr file in the Navigation pane.

Normally you should not add any code in the Application class except to set a different look-and-feel in the main method or to set the packFrame variable to false or true. The look and feel will be discussed in Chapter 5, "Swing Components." If packFrame is set to true, the frame's pack() method will be invoked to set the initial size for the frame. Often you need to modify the frame class to write the code for creating the user interface and carrying out operations for the project.

The Frame Class

Before modifying the frame class, let us take a look at the contents generated by the Application Wizard. Highlighting TestFrame.java in the Navigation pane displays the structure of the source code in the Structure pane and the source code itself in the Content pane (see Figure 1.21).

The import statements import Java packages used in this file. You can import additional packages if needed when you modify the code in the frame class. Since you check the option "Use only core JDK and Swing classes" in Figure 1.18, the generated TestFrame class extends JFrame. You may click on JFrame in the Structure pane to browse the source code for JFrame, as shown in Figure 1.22. You can see the

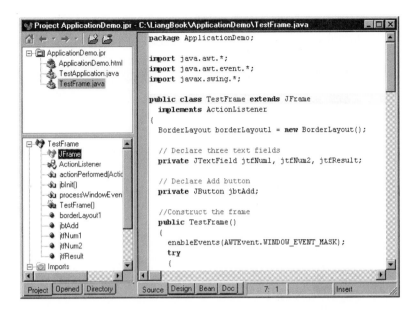

Figure 1.21   *The frame class contains the code that creates the user interface and carries out actual operations.*

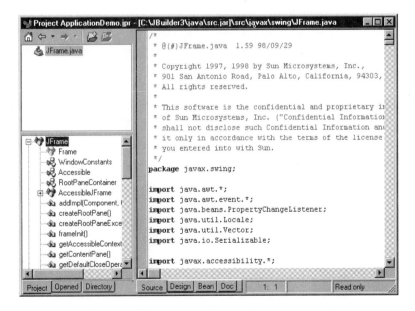

Figure 1.22   *You can browse the Java files you imported to your class in the AppBrowser.*

documentation of JFrame by clicking the Doc tab in the Content pane, as shown in Figure 1.23.

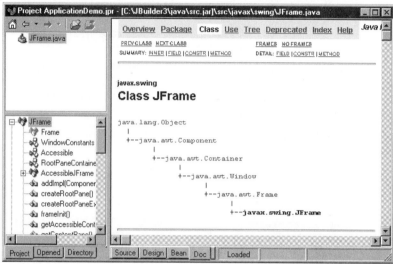

Figure 1.23   *You can browse the documentation of the Java class by clicking the Doc tab in the Content pane.*

TestFrame has a method jbInit() and a constructor. The jbInit() method sets the frame's initial size, title, and the layout style. You also can modify or add new code in this method. The constructor uses the enableEvents() method to enable window events and invokes the jbInit() method. The processWindowEvent() is overridden so that the program exits when the window is closed.

If you run the program now, you will see a blank frame.

Modifying the Code in the Frame Class

By now you know the files generated by the Application Wizard as well as their contents. The Application Wizard cannot generate everything you need in the project. To make the program work, you will have to modify the TestFrame class as follows:

1. Add implements ActionListener in the class heading because TestFrame needs to listen to button actions and add import java.awt.event.*. (Alternatively, you can use the Implement Interface Wizard to implement the ActionListener automatically from the Wizards menu.)

2. Add the code in the data declaration part of the program to declare instances of JTextField named jtfNum1, jtfNum2, and jtfResult, and an instance of JButton named jbtAdd, as shown in Listing 1.1.

3. Add the code in the jbInit() method to create the user interface, and register the listener for jbtAdd, as shown in Listing 1.1.

4. Implement the `actionPerformed()` method to add the numbers, and display the result, as shown in Listing 1.1.

5. Run the program. A sample run is shown in Figure 1.17.

```java
package ApplicationDemo;

import java.awt.*;
import java.awt.event.*;
import javax.swing.*;

public class TestFrame extends JFrame
  implements ActionListener
{
  BorderLayout borderLayout1 = new BorderLayout();

  // Declare three text fields
  private JTextField jtfNum1, jtfNum2, jtfResult;

  // Declare Add button
  private JButton jbtAdd;

  // Construct the frame
  public TestFrame()
  {
    enableEvents(AWTEvent.WINDOW_EVENT_MASK);
    try
    {
      jbInit();
    }
    catch(Exception e)
    {
      e.printStackTrace();
    }
  }

  // Component initialization
  private void jbInit() throws Exception
  {
    this.getContentPane().setLayout(borderLayout1);
    this.setSize(new Dimension(400, 300));
    this.setTitle("Frame Title");

    // Place labels and text fields in a panel
    JPanel p1 = new JPanel();
    p1.setLayout(new FlowLayout());
    p1.add(new JLabel("Number 1"));
    p1.add(jtfNum1 = new JTextField(3));
    p1.add(new JLabel("Number 2"));
    p1.add(jtfNum2 = new JTextField(3));
    p1.add(new JLabel("Result"));
    p1.add(jtfResult = new JTextField(4));
    jtfResult.setEditable(false);  // Set it noneditable

    // Add the panel and the Add button in the frame
    this.getContentPane().add(p1, BorderLayout.CENTER);
    this.getContentPane().add(jbtAdd = new JButton("Add"),
      BorderLayout.SOUTH);

    // Register listener
    jbtAdd.addActionListener(this);
  }
```

Listing 1.1   *TestFrame.java*

```java
  // Overridden so we can exit on System Close
  protected void processWindowEvent(WindowEvent e)
  {
    super.processWindowEvent(e);
    if(e.getID() == WindowEvent.WINDOW CLOSING)
    {
      System.exit(0);
    }
  }

  // Handle add button action
  public void actionPerformed(ActionEvent e)
  {
    int num1 =
      (Integer.valueOf(jtfNum1.getText().trim())).intValue();
    int num2 =
      (Integer.valueOf(jtfNum2.getText().trim())).intValue();
    int result = num1 + num2;

    // Display result
    jtfResult.setText(String.valueOf(result));
  }
}
```

Listing 1.1   *Continued*

■■■ TIP

You can use JBuilder's Code Insight to display a context-sensitive popup window within the Editor, as shown in Figure 1.24. Code Insight helps you to complete the code. To adjust the option settings for Code Insight, choose Tools, Environment Options and click the Code Insight tab.

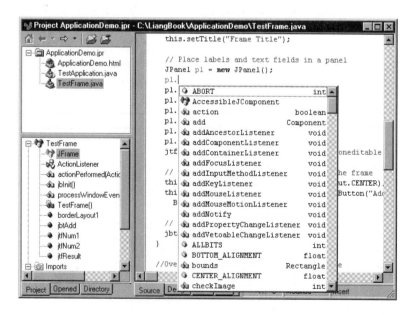

Figure 1.24   *The Code Insight provides code completion and parameter lists for the methods.*

> **NOTE**
> All the applications will be created in the same way as TestApplication and TestFrame in this book, with the same options checked in the Application Wizard unless explicitly noted otherwise.

Creating Java Applets

This section shows you how to create Java applets using the Applet Wizard. You will write an applet to display a message on the applet at a specified location. The message and the location are passed as parameters using the <param> tag in HTML.

The Applet Wizard uses three dialog boxes to collect applet information from the user, and it generates two files: an HTML file and an applet file. You can modify these two files if necessary to make them work for your project.

Using the Applet Wizard

Before starting to create a new project for the applet, close all projects by choosing File, Close All (if any are open). The following steps create several template files for a new applet project.

> **NOTE**
> If you did not close all the projects, the following steps will not work correctly. When creating an applet or an application with all the projects closed, JBuilder automatically displays the Project Wizard to generate a new project for the application or applet. Of course, you can first create a new project using the Project Wizard, then use the Applet Wizard or the Application Wizard to create applets or applications.

1. Create a new project and an applet in one step.

    1.1. Choose File, New to display the Object Gallery. Double-click the Applet icon. The Project Wizard dialog (for the Applet Wizard) appears on-screen, as shown in Figure 1.25.

    1.2. Edit the File field to read

    ```
    c:\LiangBook\AppletDemo\AppletDemo.jpr
    ```

    1.3. Choose Finish. You will see the Applet Wizard now.

2. Complete the Applet Wizard (Step 1 of 3).

    2.1. Edit the Class field to DisplayMessageApplet, as shown in Figure 1.26.

    2.2. Check the options "Use only JDK and Swing classes" and "Can run standalone."

    2.3. Click Next. You will see Step 2 of 3 of Applet Wizard, as shown in Figure 1.27.

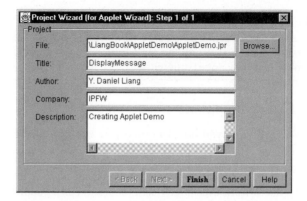

Figure 1.25 *The Project Wizard window (for the Applet Wizard) helps you to create a project for applets.*

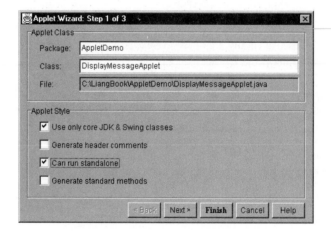

Figure 1.26 *Applet Wizard Step 1 of 3 prompts you to enter the package name, the applet class name, and other optional information.*

3. Complete Step 2 of 3 in the Applet Wizard. This step enables you to define parameters in the HTML file to be passed to your applets. Each parameter is defined in one line. The Name column specifies the name in the <param> tag. The Variable column specifies the variable for the parameter in the program. The Type column specifies the variable type in the program. The Default column specifies the value of the parameter passed from the HTML file. The Description column gives an explanatory description of the parameter.

3.1. Add three parameters in the window, as shown in Figure 1.27. Click the Add Parameter button to start a new parameter line when adding a new parameter.

3.2. Click Next. You will see Step 3 of 3 of Applet Wizard, as shown in Figure 1.28.

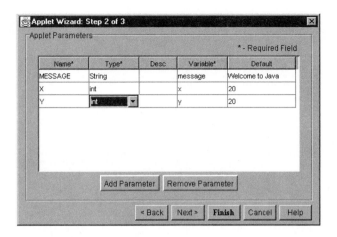

Figure 1.27   *The Applet Wizard Step 2 of 3 dialog box enables you to enter HTML parameters to be passed to the applet.*

4. Complete Step 3 of 3 in Applet Wizard. This step gives you the option to generate an HTML file for the applet.

   4.1. Check "Generate HTML page." If you check it, the Applet Wizard will generate an HTML file. If you don't check it, you have to create an HTML file manually for this applet. If you checked it, you can specify the width and height of the applet viewing area.

   4.2. Fill other fields, as shown in Figure 1.28.

   4.3. Click Finish.

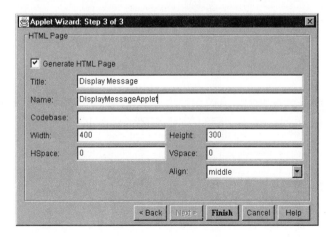

Figure 1.28   *The Applet Wizard Step 3 of 3 dialog box enables you to specify the applet viewing-area size and other properties for the HTML page.*

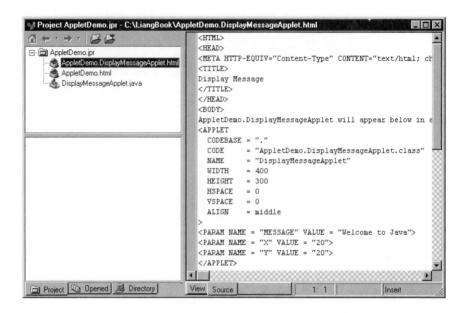

Figure 1.29   *The source code of DisplayMessageApplet.html is shown in the AppBrowser.*

The Applet Wizard generates DisplayMessageApplet.html and DisplayMessage-Applet.java. The source code for DisplayMessageApplet.html is shown in the Content pane in the AppBrowser in Figure 1.29, and the source code of DisplayMessageApplet.java is shown in Figure 1.30.

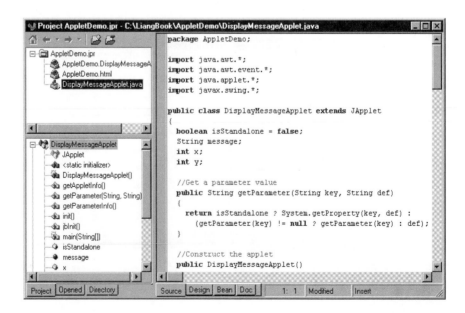

Figure 1.30   *The source code of* DisplayMessageApplet.java *is shown in the AppBrowser.*

Modifying the Generated Applet Class

The Applet Wizard creates the following two files:

- DisplayMessageApplet.html — contains an APPLET tag referencing your applet class. This is the file you should select to run or debug your applet. This file is stored in the output root directory.

- DisplayMessageApplet.java —this is your applet, which extends the JApplet class. This file is stored in the AppletDemo directory under the output root directory.

Although the Application Wizard generates two .java files, the Applet Wizard generates just one. In this example, the file is DisplayMessageApplet.java. The DisplayMessageApplet class contains a constructor, and a main method, and five methods: getAppletInfo(), getParameter(), getParameterInfo(), init(), and jbInit(). Since you checked the standalone option in Step 1 of 3 of the Applet Wizard, JBuilder generates a main method for running the applet as a standalone application.

The methods getAppletInfo(), getParameterInfo(), and init() are defined in the java.applet.Applet class and are overridden in the DisplayMessageApplet class with concrete contents. The jbInit() method initializes the applet user interface; this method is called by init(). The getParameter() method in this class has the same method name as the getParameter() method in the Applet class, but these two methods have different signatures. The getParameter() method in DisplayMessageApplet returns a specified default value if the parameter does not exist in the HTML file.

NOTE
You will have more methods and varying implementations of the methods if you check certain options in Step 1 of 3 of the Applet Wizard.

The variables message, x and y were generated because you declared them in Step 2 of 3 of the Applet Wizard, when specifying the HTML parameters.

To make the applet display a message, you need to add the paint() method, as shown in Listing 1.2.

```
package AppletDemo;

import java.awt.*;
import java.awt.event.*;
import java.applet.*;
import javax.swing.*;
```

Listing 1.2 *DisplayMessageApplet.java*

```java
public class DisplayMessageApplet extends JApplet
{
  boolean isStandalone = false;
  String message;
  int x;
  int y;

  // Get a parameter value
  public String getParameter(String key, String def)
  {
    return isStandalone ? System.getProperty(key, def) :
      (getParameter(key) != null ? getParameter(key) : def);
  }

  // Construct the applet
  public DisplayMessageApplet()
  {
  }

  // Initialize the applet
  public void init()
  {
    try { message = this.getParameter("MESSAGE", "Welcome to Java"); }
    catch (Exception e) { e.printStackTrace(); }
    try { x = Integer.parseInt(this.getParameter("X", "20")); }
    catch (Exception e) { e.printStackTrace(); }

    try { y = Integer.parseInt(this.getParameter("Y", "20")); }
    catch (Exception e) { e.printStackTrace(); }

    try
    {
      jbInit();
    }
    catch(Exception e)
    {
      e.printStackTrace();
    }
  }

  // Component initialization
  private void jbInit() throws Exception
  {
    this.setSize(new Dimension(400,300));
  }

  // Get Applet information
  public String getAppletInfo()
  {
    return "Applet Information";
  }

  // Get parameter info
  public String[][] getParameterInfo()
  {
    String[][] pinfo =
    {
      {"MESSAGE", "String", ""},
      {"X", "int", ""},
      {"Y", "int", ""},
    };
    return pinfo;
  }
```

Listing 1.2   *Continued*

```
// Main method
public static void main(String[] args)
{
  DisplayMessageApplet applet = new DisplayMessageApplet();
  applet.isStandalone = true;
  JFrame frame = new JFrame();
  frame.setTitle("Applet Frame");
  frame.getContentPane().add(applet, BorderLayout.CENTER);
  applet.init();
  applet.start();
  frame.setSize(400,320);
  Dimension d = Toolkit.getDefaultToolkit().getScreenSize();
  frame.setLocation((d.width - frame.getSize().width) / 2,
    (d.height - frame.getSize().height) / 2);
  frame.setVisible(true);
}

// static initializer for setting look & feel
static {
  try
  {
    UIManager.setLookAndFeel(
      UIManager.getSystemLookAndFeelClassName());
    //UIManager.setLookAndFeel(
        UIManager.getCrossPlatformLookAndFeelClassName());
  }
  catch (Exception e) {}
}

// Display message on the applet. This is the code you write
public void paint(Graphics g)
{
  g.drawString(message, x, y);
}
}
```

Listing 1.2   *Continued*

Run DisplayMessageApplet.java as an applet or as an application. Figure 1.31 shows the output as an applet.

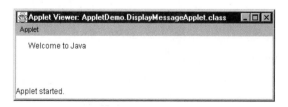

Figure 1.31   *The DisplayMessageApplet displays "Welcome to Java."*

▬▬ TIP
You may need to close some applications to make more memory space available to JBuilder if your program is compiled properly but cannot run.

> **NOTE**
> Most of the examples in this book will be created using the Applet Wizard.
> When using the Applet Wizard, the options "Use only JDK and Swing classes"
> and "Can run standalone" are always checked. For brevity, the methods
> `main()`, `getAppletInfo()`, `getParameter()`, and `getParameterInfo()` will not
> be listed in the future examples. The static block in the applet that specifies
> the look and feel of Motif, Metal, or Windows will not be listed either, for the
> same reason.

Designing User Interfaces Using the UI Designer

JBuilder provides tools for visually designing and programming Java classes. This
enables you to quickly and easily assemble the elements of a user interface (UI) for
a Java application or applet. You can construct the UI with various building blocks
chosen from the Component palette that contains such components as buttons,
text areas, lists, dialogs, and menus. Then you set the values of the component
properties and attach event-handler code to the component events, telling the program how to respond to UI events.

The JBuilder's visual tools make programming in Java easier and more productive.
No tools, however, can accomplish everything you need. You have to modify the
program produced by the tools. Thus, it is imperative to know the basic concept of
Java graphics programming before starting to use the visual tools. This book assumes that you have a basic knowledge of Java. Now you can use the UI Designer
to make programming more productive.

This section demonstrates using visual design tools to create the same program that
you manually coded in the section, "Creating Java Applications."

JBuilder's visual tools are designed to work well with the class templates created
from the wizards. To use the UI Designer, you should use the wizards in the Object Gallery to create classes.

Follow the steps below to create a new application to demonstrate the UI Designer
in the ApplicationDemo project.

1. Choose File, Reopen to display a popup menu that includes a list of recently
   opened projects. Double-click ApplicationDemo.jpr on the list to open it. If
   it is not on the list, choose File, Open to open it.

2. Create a new application class named `TestUIApplication` and its associated
   frame class named `TestUIFrame` using the Application Wizard.

You wrote the code to create the UI in TestFrame.java. Now you will learn how to
use the UI Designer to create the user interface in TestUIFrame.java. The following are the steps to complete the example:

1. With TestUIFrame.java selected in the Navigation pane, choose the Design tab in the Content pane to switch to the UI Designer, as shown in Figure 1.32.

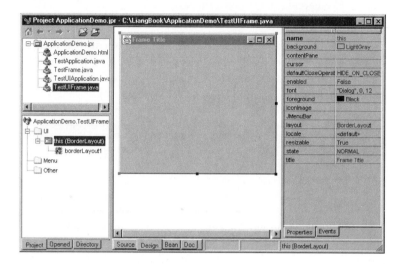

Figure 1.32   *The UI Designer is shown in the Content pane, and the Component tree is shown in the Structure pane.*

2. Click JPanel in the Swing Containers page of the Component palette and drop it to the center of the UI Designer or to the Component tree. A new object named jPanel1 is created. You can see it in the Component tree under the this node (see Figure 1.33).

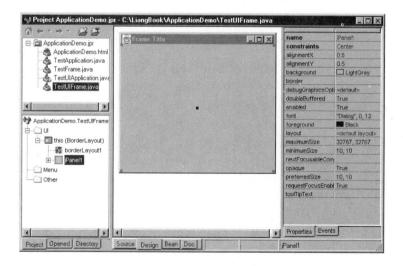

Figure 1.33   *The view of the AppBrowser is shown here after* jPanel1 *is created.*

3. Select jPanel1 in the Component tree. In the Inspector of jPanel1, set its constraints property to Center if it is not Center, set its layout property to FlowLayout. (By default, the layout of a JPanel is FlowLayout.) If the Inspector is not on-screen, choose View, Show Inspector to display it.

4. With the this node selected in the Component tree, click JButton from the Swing page of the Component palette and drop it to the south of the frame. An object named jButton1 is created. You can see the object under the this Node in the Component tree (see Figure 1.34).

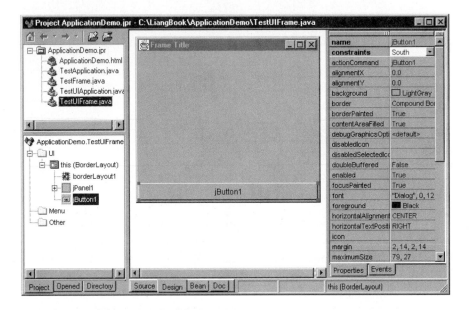

Figure 1.34   *The view of the AppBrowser is shown here after* jButton1 *is created.*

5. Select jButton1 in the Component tree. In the Inspector of jButton1, change its name property to jbtAdd, set its constraints to South, and change its text to Add. Whenever you make changes in the Inspector, you will see their effects in the UI and in the Component tree (see Figure 1.35) as well as in the source code (see Figure 1.36).

6. With jPanel1 selected in the Component tree, drop a JLabel, a JTextField, a JLabel, a JTextField, a JLabel, a JTextField from the Swing page of the Component palette into jPanel1 to create objects named jLabel1, jTextField1, jLabel2, jTextField2, jLabel3, and jTextField3, as shown in Figure 1.37.

7. In the Inspector of jLabel1, change its name to jlblNum1 and its text property to Number 1. Similarly, change jLabel2's name to jlblNum2 and its text to Number 2, and jLabel3's name to jlblResult and text to Result.

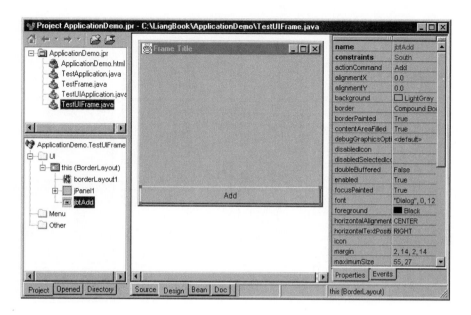

Figure 1.35   *The view of the AppBrowser is shown here after modifications of* jbtAdd*'s properties.*

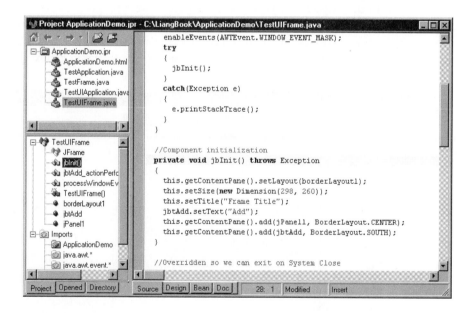

Figure 1.36   *The source code is synchronized with the UI Designer.*

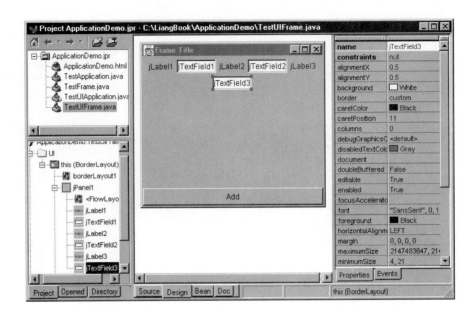

Figure 1.37   *The view of the AppBrowser is shown here after labels and text fields were created.*

8. In the Inspector of jTextField1, change its name property to jtfNum1, set its text property to empty, and its columns to 3. Similarly, set jTextField2's name to jtfNum2, text to empty and columns to 3, and jTextField3's name to jtfResult, text to empty, and columns to 4, as shown in Figure 1.38.

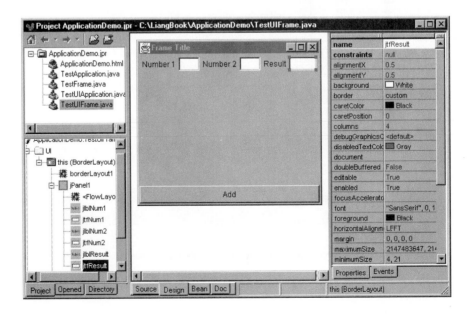

Figure 1.38   *The view of the AppBrowser is shown here after modifications of the properties of labels and text fields.*

TIP

You can set properties for multiple components. When more than one component is selected, the Component Inspector displays only the properties they have in common that you can edit. When the values for the shared property differ among the selected components, the property value displayed is either the default or the value of the first component selected. When you change any of the shared properties in the Component Inspector, the property value changes to the new value in all the selected components. To select multiple components, hold down the Shift key and select each of the components in the UI Designer.

---

9. By now you have created the user interface. You are ready to implement the code for handling the Add button action. Use one of the following two approaches to generate the even handling code:

   ■ Double-click the Add button, or

   ■ In the Events page of the Inspector for the Add button, double-click the value field of `actionPerformed`.

   Either of the above actions will cause JBuilder to generate the following code:

   ➤ The line `import java.awt.event.*;` was inserted.

   ➤ A listener was created and registered with `jbtAdd` using the anonymous adapter as follows.

   ```
   jbtAdd.addActionListener(new java.awt.event.ActionListener()
   {
     public void actionPerformed(ActionEvent e)
     {
       jbtAdd_actionPerformed(e);
     }
   });
   ```

NOTE

The standard adapter would be generated if you selected the standard adapter option in the Code Style page of the Project Properties dialog box. Various adapters will be introduced in Chapter 3.

   ➤ The method `jbtAdd_actionPerformed()` for handling the action event is created. You need to fill in the code to carry out the actual action.

10. Implement `jbtAdd_actionPerformed` using the same code as in the `actionPerformed()` method in TestFrame.java. The complete code for TestUIFrame.java is shown in Listing 1.3.

```java
package ApplicationDemo;

import java.awt.*;
import java.awt.event.*;
import javax.swing.*;

public class TestUIFrame extends JFrame
{
  BorderLayout borderLayout1 = new BorderLayout();
  JPanel jPanel1 = new JPanel();
  JLabel jlblNum1 = new JLabel();
  JTextField jtfNum1 = new JTextField();
  JLabel jlblNum2 = new JLabel();
  JTextField jtfNum2 = new JTextField();
  JLabel jlblResult = new JLabel();
  JTextField jtfResult = new JTextField();
  JButton jbtAdd = new JButton();

  // Construct the frame
  public TestUIFrame()
  {
    enableEvents(AWTEvent.WINDOW_EVENT_MASK);
    try
    {
      jbInit();
    }
    catch(Exception e)
    {
      e.printStackTrace();
    }
  }

  // Component initialization
  private void jbInit() throws Exception
  {
    this.getContentPane().setLayout(borderLayout1);
    this.setSize(new Dimension(286, 254));
    this.setTitle("Frame Title");
    jlblNum1.setText("Number 1");
    jtfNum1.setColumns(3);
    jlblNum2.setText("Number 2");
    jlblResult.setText("Result");
    jtfNum2.setColumns(3);
    jtfResult.setColumns(4);
    jbtAdd.setText("Add");
    jbtAdd.addActionListener(new java.awt.event.ActionListener()
    {
      public void actionPerformed(ActionEvent e)
      {
        jbtAdd_actionPerformed(e);
      }
    });
    this.getContentPane().add(jPanel1, BorderLayout.CENTER);
    jPanel1.add(jlblNum1, null);
    jPanel1.add(jtfNum1, null);
    jPanel1.add(jlblNum2, null);
    jPanel1.add(jtfNum2, null);
    jPanel1.add(jlblResult, null);
    jPanel1.add(jtfResult, null);
    this.getContentPane().add(jbtAdd, BorderLayout.SOUTH);
  }
```

Listing 1.3 *TestUIFrame.java*

```
      // Overridden so we can exit on System Close
      protected void processWindowEvent(WindowEvent e)
      {
        super.processWindowEvent(e);
        if(e.getID() == WindowEvent.WINDOW CLOSING)
        {
          System.exit(0);
        }
      }

      void jbtAdd_actionPerformed(ActionEvent e)
      {
        int num1 =
          (Integer.valueOf(jtfNum1.getText().trim())).intValue();
        int num2 =
          (Integer.valueOf(jtfNum2.getText().trim())).intValue();
        int result = num1 + num2;

        // Display result
        jtfResult.setText(String.valueOf(result));
      }
    }
```

Listing 1.3   *Continued*

All the code in TestUIFrame.java was automatically generated except the body of
the btAdd_actionPerformed() method. The UI Designer enables you to rapidly develop Java programs with minimum coding. All the components in the Component palette are JavaBeans components. JavaBeans provides the foundations for
Rapid Application Development in Java. The rest of the book is centered on creating JavaBeans components and using the beans in Rapid Application Development.

Customizing JBuilder Environments

JBuilder allows you to customize your development environment by changing various environment options. Certain options, such as syntax highlighting, can make
your programs easy to read and help you to spot errors.

To set environment options, choose Tools, Environment Options to display the
Environment Options dialog box, as shown in Figure 1.39. The dialog box contains five pages: Editor, Display, Colors, AppBrowser, and Code Insight.

The Editor page enables you to customize editing behavior in the Source pane.
You can set the editor's handling of text using editor options, such as Auto indent
mode, Use tab character, and Use syntax highlight. Selecting the Auto indent
mode positions the cursor under the first non-blank character of the preceding
non-blank line when you press Enter. Selecting the Use tab character option inserts
a tab character when you press the Tab key instead of using spaces to fill the gap.
Selecting the Use syntax highlight option activates syntax highlighting preferences.
Use the options on the Colors page of the environment Options dialog box to set
the colors for highlighted syntax.

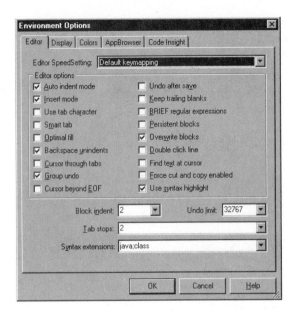

Figure 1.39   *The Environment Options dialog box enables you to set the environment, such as Editor, Display, Color, AppBrowser, and Code Insight.*

The Display page (see Figure 1.40) enables you to select display and font options and other miscellaneous Editor-related features for the Source pane. You can set the display and file options, such as BRIEF cursor shape, Create backup file, Preserve line ends, and Zoom to full screen. For example, selecting the BRIEF cursor

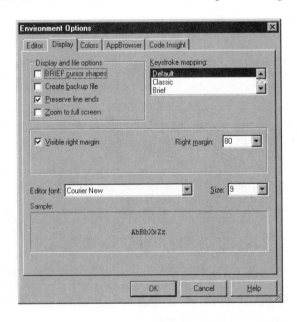

Figure 1.40   *You can customize display, and fonts for the code in the source pane.*

shape option uses a small bold square for blank spaces and a bold underline for non-blank spaces, selecting the Creates a backup file option creates a file that replaces the first letter of the extension with a tilde (~) when you save the file, and selecting the Zoom to full screen maximizes the Source pane to fill the entire screen. When this option is off, the Source pane does not cover the JBuilder Main window when maximized.

The Colors page (see Figure 1.41) specifies the colors of the different elements of your code in the Source pane. You can specify foreground and background colors for the elements, such as Comment, Reserved word, String, Symbol, and Error line, in the Element list. The sample code at the bottom of the dialog box shows how your settings will appear in the Source pane. You must select Use syntax highlight on the Editor page for the setting in the Colors page to be effective.

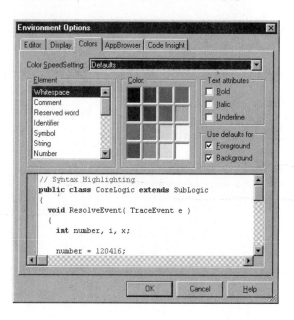

Figure 1.41   *You can customize colors for different elements of the source code.*

The AppBrowser page (see Figure 1.42) enables you to configure the behavior of the AppBrowser. You can control how data members and methods are grouped, how accessors, such as public and private, are used to sort the display, how properties, methods, events, and data members are grouped, and how the Inspector is displayed. You can also specify whether to reload the last opened project when JBuilder restarts.

The Code Insight page (see Figure 1.43) enables you to configure Code Insight (Code completion assistant). JBuilder's Code Insight enhancements display context-sensitive popup windows within the Editor. Code Insight provides code completion, and parameter lists for the methods. Code Insight highlights illegal class references and statements that import packages not in the Class Path.

Figure 1.42   *You can customize AppBrowser for Inspector and for grouping data and methods based on access modifiers.*

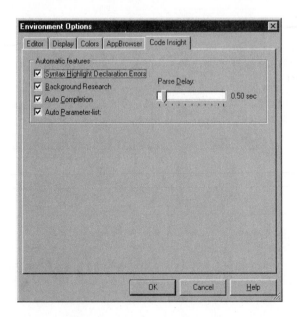

Figure 1.43   *You can specify whether to use Code Insight and how Code Insight is used on the Code Insight page of the Environment Options dialog box.*

> **TIP**
>
> You can restore all the JBuilder environment settings to the default values by deleting the file jbuilder3\bin\jbuilder.ini. When JBuilder is restarted, a new jbuilder.ini file will be created.

Getting Online Help from JBuilder

JBuilder provides a large number of documents online, giving you a great deal of information on a variety of topics related to the use of JBuilder and Java in general.

To access online help, choose Help, Help Topics to display JBuilder Help, as shown in Figure 1.44. Alternatively, you can get Help Viewer by pressing F1 with the main menu focused.

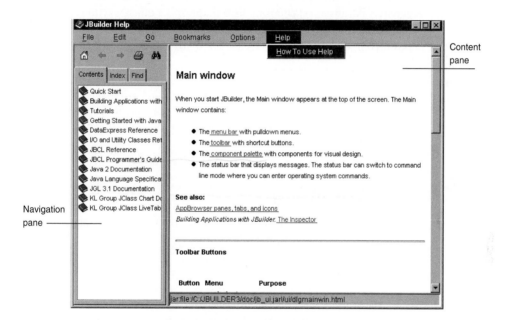

Figure 1.44   *All help documents are displayed in JBuilder Help.*

JBuilder Help behaves like a Web browser and contains the main menus, the Navigation pane, and the Content pane. From the main menus, you can open a URL from the File menu, add bookmarks from the Bookmarks menu, and get help on using JBuilder Help from the Help menu.

The Navigation pane contains five action buttons on top of the three tabs. The buttons are Home, Previous, Next, Print, and Find in Page. The Home, Previous, and Next buttons take you, respectively, to the first, previous, and next topic in the history list. The Print button prints the document in the content pane. The Find in Page button enables you to search the current topic.

The three tabs are **Contents**, **Index**, and **Find**. The Contents tab displays available documents. The table of contents of the document is displayed in a treelike list in the Navigation pane. To view a given topic, select the node in the tree associated with the topic. JBuilder Help displays the document for the topic in the Content pane.

The Index tab shows the index entries for the current document. The Find page shows the combined index entries for all the available documents in JBuilder. To display the index, simply type the first few letters in the entry. As you start typing, the index scrolls, doing an incremental search on the index entries to find the closest match. Select and double-click the index in the entry to display the document for the entry in the Content pane.

In addition to Help Topics, the Help menu also contains the menu items for directly accessing the JBuilder online documentation set on BeansExpress and Java Reference. For instance, choosing BeansExpress is a quick way to get the document on BeansExpress in Help Viewer. You can link to the Borland Online Web site by choosing borland.com Home Page.

TIP

The Help menu is not the only way to get help. There are many ways to get help on a topic when you are using JBuilder. For example, if you want to find out what a particular menu item does, highlight it on a pull-down menu without out activating it and press F1.

Chapter Summary

This chapter gave you a quick start on using JBuilder to develop Java programs. JBuilder contains numerous wizards in the Object Gallery that can be used to create program templates. You learned how to use the Project Wizard, the Application Wizard, and the Applet Wizard to create projects, applications, and applets. You also learned how to customize project properties, including how to modify Source root directories and the Output root directory, how to set compiler options, how to specify the code style, how to customize environments, and how to get online help in JBuilder. Finally, you learned how to use the UI Designer for creating user interfaces and generating event-handling code with minimum coding.

Chapter Review

1.1. How do you create a Java project in JBuilder?

1.2. How do you compile a Java program in JBuilder?

1.3. How do you run a Java application in JBuilder?

1.4. How do you create a Java applet in JBuilder?

1.5. Where is the .class file stored after successful compilation in JBuilder?

1.6. What would happen if a Java source file was not in one of the Source root directories?

1.7. How do you add a file to an existing project or remove one from a project? How do you add (or remove) a package to (or from) a project? Does removing a file from the project cause the file to be deleted from the disk?

1.8. How do you browse .java files that are not part of your project, but are referred to in the class you are editing?

1.9. How do you control how properties, methods, events, and data members are grouped in the AppBrowser?

1.10. How do you set the option to enable JBuilder to save the files before compiling?

1.11. How do you set the option to enable JBuilder to generate the code with the new-line brace style?

1.12. How do you set the environment option not to save backup files?

1.13. How do you set the option so that the Java keywords are displayed in red in the Content pane?

1.14. How do you turn off the Code Insight?

1.15. How do you open the UI Designer? How do you set properties for a component? How do you set properties for multiple components at the same time?

1.16. If the Component Inspector is not displayed, how do you show it?

1.17. Show at least two ways to display online documentation for JBuilder compiler options.

Programming Exercises

1.1. Use the Application Wizard and UI Designer to create a project that converts a Celsius temperature to a Fahrenheit temperature with the following requirements:

- Create a project file named Conversion.jpr using the Project Wizard.

- Create an application class named `ConvApplication` and a frame class named `ConvFrame` using the Application Wizard.

- Use the UI Designer to create the user interface, as shown in Figure 1.45.

- Implement the code that converts the temperature when the Convert button is clicked and displays the resulting Fahrenheit temperature.

- The formula for converting Celsius to Fahrenheit is as follows:

```
fahrenheit = (9.0/5.0)*celsius + 32.0
```

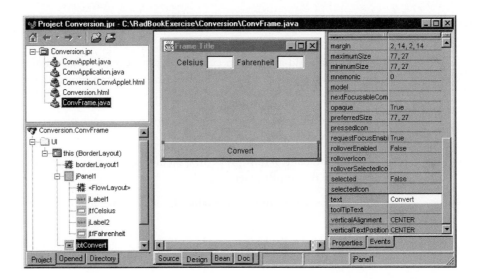

Figure 1.45   *The user enters a temperature in Celsius and clicks the Convert button to display the corresponding temperature in Fahrenheit.*

1.2. Use the Applet Wizard and UI Designer to create an applet that converts a Celsius temperature to a Fahrenheit temperature with the following requirements:

■ Reopen the project Conversion.jpr that was created in the previous exercise.

■ Create an applet named ConvApplet using the Applet Wizard.

■ Use the UI Designer to create the user interface, as shown in Figure 1.45.

■ Implement the code that converts the temperature when the Convert button is clicked and displays the resulting Fahrenheit temperature.

CHAPTER 2

INTRODUCTION TO JAVABEANS

Objectives

- Know what a JavaBeans component is.

- Discover the similarities and differences between beans and regular objects.

- Learn how to create JavaBeans components in JBuilder and install them in the Component palette.

- Understand JavaBeans properties and their naming patterns.

- Become familiar with JavaBeans property types.

- Know how to use the property editors in JBuilder.

Introduction

The JavaBeans technology is a significant extension and enhancement of the Java language. This technology enables programmers to rapidly build applications by assembling objects and testing them during design time. It is the foundation for the Java builder tools that support rapid Java application development.

JavaBeans are 100% pure Java programs. They are simple to develop and easy to use. JavaBeans are a special kind of Java classes. If you know Java, you may have already developed JavaBeans. In fact, all the AWT and Swing user interface classes are JavaBeans components. With JavaBeans, you can create new applications by connecting various off-the-shelf software components using a builder tool, such as JBuilder, with minimum coding. The JavaBeans technology ushers in a new era of component computing. An application can be viewed as a framework consisting of various software components that can be added, removed, or customized, as needed.

This chapter introduces the concept of JavaBeans and the relationship between JavaBeans and Java RAD builder tools. You will begin to write simple JavaBeans and use them in JBuilder.

Beans and Objects

JavaBeans is a software component architecture that extends the power of the Java language to enable well-formed objects to be manipulated visually in a builder tool like JBuilder during design time. Such well-formed objects are referred to as *Java beans* or simply *beans*. The classes that define the beans, referred to as *JavaBeans components* or *bean components*, or simply *components*, must conform to the Java-Beans component model with the following requirements:

- A bean must be a public class.

- A bean must have a public default constructor (one that takes no arguments), although it can have other constructors, if needed. For example, a bean named `MyBean` must either have a constructor with the signature

  ```
  public MyBean();
  ```

  or have no constructor if its superclass has a default constructor.

- A bean must implement the `Serializable` or `Externalizable` interface to ensure persistent state. JavaBeans can be used in a wide variety of tools, such as Lotus, Delphi, MS Visual Basic, and MS Word. Bean persistence may be required when JavaBeans are used in other tools. Some tools need to save the beans and restore them later. Bean persistence ensures that the tools can reconstruct the properties and consistent behaviors of the bean to the state in which it was saved. Persistence and serialization will be further discussed in Chapter 9, "Bean Persistence, Versioning, and Using Beans in Other Tools."

■ A bean usually has properties with correctly constructed public accessor methods to enable them to be seen and updated visually by a builder tool. To enable the properties to be manipulated, the accessor methods must conform to the naming patterns or be specified explicitly, using the `BeanInfo` interface. According to the accessor method naming pattern, the method must be named `get<PropertyName>()` for getting the property value and `set<PropertyName>()` for setting the property value. The naming patterns of properties and their accessor methods will be discussed in detail in the section "Bean Properties." The `BeanInfo` interface will be introduced in Chapter 11, "Bean Introspection and Customization."

■ A bean may have events with correctly constructed public registration methods to enable the bean to add and remove listeners. If the bean plays a role as the source of events, it must provide registration methods. This will be discussed in depth in Chapter 3, "Bean Events."

The first three requirements must be observed by all beans, and therefore are referred to as the *minimum JavaBeans component requirements*. The last two requirements are dependent on implementations. It is possible to write a bean without accessor methods and event registration methods.

A JavaBeans component is a special kind of Java class. The relationship of a Java-Beans component and a Java class is illustrated in Figure 2.1.

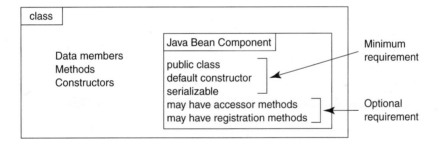

Figure 2.1   *A Java bean component is a serializable public class with a default constructor.*

Example 2.1 Writing a Simple Java Bean Component

In this example, you will learn how to write a simple Java bean component that displays a message on the panel.

To see the development in action, follow these steps:

1. Create a new project named MessagePanelDemo.jpr.

2. Choose File, New to bring up the Object Gallery, as shown in Figure 1.16. Click the Class icon to display the New Java File dialog box, as shown in Figure 2.2.

continues

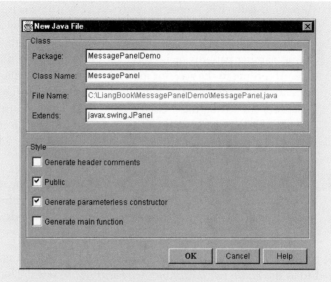

Figure 2.2 *You can create a new Java class using the New Java Class Wizard.*

3. Type MessagePanel as Class Name and type javax.swing.JPanel in the Extends field. Choose Public and "Generate parameterless constructor" in the Style section.

4. Click OK to generate a template for MessagePanel.java, as shown in Figure 2.3.

5. Complete the following class MessagePanel, as shown in Listing 2.1.

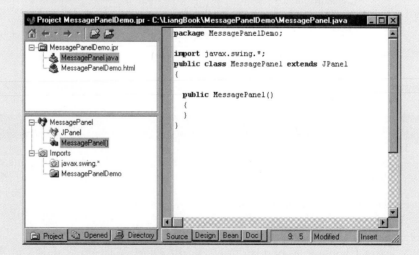

Figure 2.3 *The New Java Class Wizard generates a Java class template.*

```
package MessagePanelDemo;

import javax.swing.*;
import java.awt.*;

public class MessagePanel extends JPanel
{
  private String message = "Welcome to Java"; // Message to display

  // (x, y) coordinates where the message is displayed
  private int xCoordinate = 20;
  private int yCoordinate = 20;

  // Indicating whether the message is displayed in the center
  private boolean centered;

  // Default constructor
  public MessagePanel()
  {
    repaint();
  }

  // Contructor with a message parameter
  public MessagePanel(String message)
  {
    this.message = message;
    repaint();
  }

  public String getMessage()
  {
    return message;
  }

  public void setMessage(String message)
  {
    this.message = message;
  }

  public int getXCoordinate()
  {
    return xCoordinate;
  }

  public void setXCoordinate(int x)
  {
    this.xCoordinate = x;
  }

  public int getYCoordinate()
  {
    return yCoordinate;
  }

  public void setYCoordinate(int y)
  {
    this.yCoordinate = y;
  }
```

continues

Listing 2.1   *MessagePanel.java*

```java
    public boolean isCentered()
    {
      return centered;
    }

    public void setCentered(boolean centered)
    {
      this.centered = centered;
    }

    // Display the message at specified location
    public void paintComponent(Graphics g)
    {
      super.paintComponent(g);

      if (centered)
      {
        // Get font metrics for the font
        FontMetrics fm = g.getFontMetrics(getFont());

        // Find the center location to display
        int w = fm.stringWidth(message);  // Get the string width
        int h = fm.getAscent(); // Get the string height
        xCoordinate = (getSize().width-w)/2;
        yCoordinate = (getSize().height+h)/2;
      }

      g.drawString(message, xCoordinate, yCoordinate);
    }

    public Dimension getPreferredSize()
    {
      return new Dimension(200, 100);
    }

    public Dimension getMinimumSize()
    {
      return new Dimension(200, 100);
    }

    // Move the message in the pane to the left
    public void moveLeft()
    {
      if (getXCoordinate() > 10)
      {
        // Shift the message to the left
        setXCoordinate(getXCoordinate()-10);
        repaint();
      }
    }

    // Move the message in the panel to the right
    public void moveRight()
    {
      if (getXCoordinate() < getSize().width - 20)
      {
        // Shift the message to the right
        setXCoordinate(getXCoordinate()+10);
        repaint();
      }
    }
  }
```

Listing 2.1 *Continued*

Example Review

Since `javax.awt.Component` implements `Serializable`, and `MessagePanel` is a subclass of `JPanel`, which is a subclass of `Component`, `MessagePanel` also implements `Serializable`.

The `MessagePanel` class is a public class with a default constructor `MessagePanel()`. Since `MessagePanel` is a serializable public class with a default constructor, it is a JavaBeans component.

The `MessagePanel` class has properties `message`, `xCoordinate`, `yCoordinate`, and `centered`. The `getMessage()`, `getXCoordinate()`, `getYCoordinate()`, and `isCentered()` methods read the properties `message`, `xCoordinate`, `yCoordinate`, and `centered`, respectively; and `setMessage()`, `setXCoordinate()`, `setYCoordinate()`, and `setCentered()` methods update these properties. The message is painted on the panel starting at the position specified by coordinates `xCoordinate` and `yCoordinate`.

The `getPreferredSize()` and `getMinimumSize()` methods are overridden to specify the `preferredSize` and `minimumSize` properties for instances of `MessagePanel`. The `MessagePanel` class also contains two methods `moveLeft()` and `moveRight()` for moving the message to the left and to the right on the panel.

JavaBeans and Java Builder Tools

Since a JavaBeans component is a Java class, it can be used wherever a class is applicable. You can create a JavaBeans component, access its properties, and invoke its methods in a scripting environment, just as you use regular classes. Nevertheless, JavaBeans components are specially designed for use in a builder tool that enables the bean user to visually manipulate the beans during design time. The builder tools may be a Java IDE like JBuilder or Symantec Visual Café, a non-Java IDE like Microsoft Visual Basic or Borland Delphi, a Web page builder like Microsoft FrontPage, or even a word processor like Microsoft Word.

A builder tool can discover the contents (properties, methods, and events) and expose them to the bean user for visual manipulation during design time. The contents are presented on a user interface, referred to as a *Component Inspector* in JBuilder, on which the user can update property values and register events of the bean. The JavaBeans architecture provides a core API to support builder tools that find out what is inside the beans. The process of discovering and analyzing a bean, referred to as *bean introspection*, will be covered in Chapter 11, "Bean Introspection and Customization."

A builder tool usually has a component, referred to as a *Reflector,* that is responsible for communication between the bean and the Component Inspector during design time. The Reflector analyzes the bean and presents its properties and events on the

Component Inspector. When the bean user modifies the properties, the Reflector applies the changes to the bean by invoking the setter method of the properties. The relationship of Component Inspector, Reflector, and bean is illustrated in Figure 2.4.

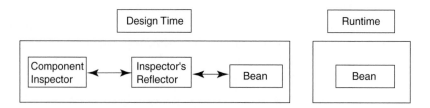

Figure 2.4   *During design time, the user interacts with the Inspector, and the Reflector controls the execution of the bean. During runtime, the bean runs just like a regular object.*

■■■ **NOTE**
The Component Inspector and the Reflector are used during design time and play no role at runtime.

If the bean follows the naming patterns for properties and events, the Reflector will automatically recognize and present it on the Component Inspector. If not, you have to provide a bean information class that implements the `BeanInfo` interface to describe the properties and events of the bean to the Reflector in order for the Inspector to reveal the properties and events to the user. How to write such a description class will be introduced in Chapter 11.

Using JavaBeans in JBuilder

One of the major applications of JavaBeans is for Rapid Application Development, or RAD, a powerful feature used in software development tools for visual programming. RAD allows you to select a component and drop it to a desired location. The click-and-drop capability enables you to write programs with little or no coding, thereby greatly improving software reusability and productivity.

The RAD in JBuilder is completely based on JavaBeans, and each RAD component in JBuilder is a bean accessible from the Component palette in the App-Browser. In this section, you will learn how to add a bean to the Component palette and utilize it in the applications, using the example of the `MessagePanel` bean presented in Example 2.1.

Adding a Bean to the Component Palette

All the classes in AWT and Swing are already beans. Some of them, such as `JButton`, `JCheckBox`, `JComboBox`, `JLabel`, `JList`, `JRadioButton`, `JTextArea`, `JTextField`, `JMenuBar`, `JPopupMenu`, `JScrollbar`, `JPanel`, and `JScrollPanel`, are already added into the Swing page and Swing Containers group in the Component palette. The other groups are JBCL, JBCL Containers, AWT, KL Group, and Others. The Swing and Swing Containers are Swing components. The components in JBCL and JBCL Containers are provided by Borland. The KL group contains the beans licensed from the KL group, which is a third-party vendor for Java products. The JBCL (JavaBeans Component Library) was developed before Swing was introduced. With the arrival of Swing release, JBCL has become obsolete, as are AWT components. This book uses Swing components to create graphics user interfaces. The necessary basic knowledge of Swing components is covered in my *Introduction to Java Programming with JBuilder 3*. More detailed information on Swing components will be provided in Part II, "Rapid Application Development with Swing Components."

Suppose you want to use the `MessagePanel` bean in the JBuilder visual environment. First you must add it to the Component palette following the steps below.

1. Choose Tools, Configure Palette or right-click anywhere in the Component palette and choose Properties. The Palette Properties dialog box appears as shown in Figure 2.5.

Figure 2.5   *The Palette Property dialog box lets you add beans to the Component palette.*

2. Select the Pages tab and choose the page on the Component palette on which you want the component to appear. Optionally, you may create a new page by clicking the Add button and entering the page name in the Add Page dialog box.

3. Suppose you want to add the `MessagePanel` bean to the `Other` group. Select `Other` in the page Column.

4. Select the class name for the component from either the Add from Archive page or the Add from Package page.

If you deployed your component as a .JAR or .ZIP file, use the Add from Archive page.

If you are still developing your component and haven't placed the classes into a .JAR or .ZIP file yet, use the Add from Package page.

Since `MessagePanel` has not been deployed in a compressed file, choose Add from Package and click the Browse button to locate and select Message Panel.class in the directory C.\LiangBook\MessagePanelDemo as shown in Figure 2.6.

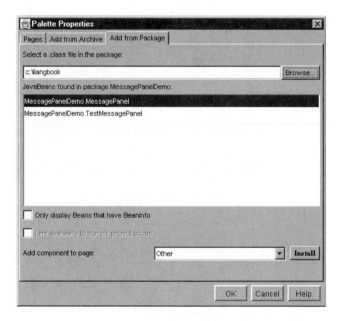

Figure 2.6   *You can add bean components from archive files or packages to the Component palette.*

Highlight `MessagePanel` in the package and choose Install when you are finished.

5. Optionally you may specify an image to represent the bean on the Component palette. If you don't specify an image, the default image icon is used. The image icon must be a .GIF file of either 16 or 32 pixels square. To specify an image, highlight MessagePanelDemo.MessagePanel in the Palette Properties dialog box and click the Property button to bring up the Item Properties dialog box as shown in Figure 2.7. Click Browse to locate and select the image you want to represent the bean.

6. Choose OK to close the dialog box.

Figure 2.7 *The Item Property dialog box lets you choose an image icon for representing the bean in the Component palette.*

Using Beans in JBuilder

You are now ready to test the `MessagePanel` bean you just added to the Component palette. Open project MessagePanelDemo.jpr that was created in Example 2.1 and create a new applet named `TestMessagePanel` using the Applet Wizard. In Step 1 of 3 of the Applet Wizard, check "Can run standalone" to generate the applet that can also run as application, check "Use only core JDK and Swing classes," and click Finish. TestMessagePanel.java is created and added in the AppBrowser for the MessagePanelDemo project, as shown in Figure 2.8.

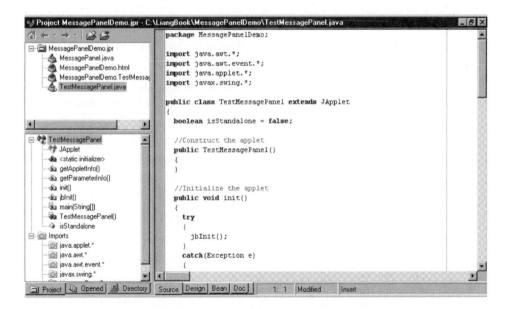

Figure 2.8 *TestMessagePanel.java is created to test the* `MessagePanel` *bean.*

You can now add `MessagePanel` bean to `TestMessagePanel`. Highlight TestMessagePanel.java in the Navigation pane and choose the Design tab in the Content pane to switch to the UI designer, as shown in Figure 2.9.

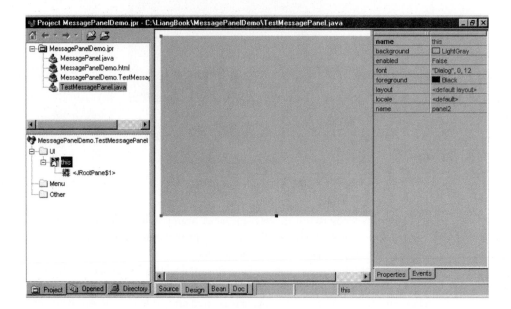

Figure 2.9 `TestMessagePanel` *is visually displayed in the Content pane of the AppBrowser window during design.*

`TestMessagePanel` itself is a bean component. You can visually inspect and update its properties through the Component Inspector.

To add a `MessagePanel` bean, first choose `TestMessagePanel` in the Component tree, then click the `MessagePanel` component from the Other group in the Component palette and drop it to the center of the applet, as shown in Figure 2.10.

JBuilder generates a bean named `messagePanel1`. You can change the bean's properties, including its name, from the Inspector window. To reveal the Inspector window for `messagePanel1`, highlight `messagePanel1` in the Component tree and choose View, Show Inspector. The Inspector window is embedded inside the App-Browser shown in Figure 2.10.

NOTE

JBuilder generates the source code to carry out all the changes made in the UI Designer. For example, if you drop a bean into the UI Designer, JBuilder generates the code to declare and create an instance of the bean; if you change a property value, JBuilder generates the code that invokes the property's setter method to update the value.

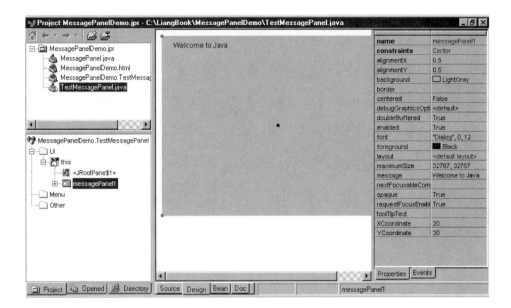

Figure 2.10   *A* MessagePanel *bean is placed inside* TestMessagePanel.

The name and constraints properties are highlighted in the Component Inspector. These two properties do not belong to a bean. JBuilder uses them to support the UI Designer. The name property is for identifying the bean, and the constraints property is for locating the bean in its parent container.

▓▓▓▓ TIP
You can move the Inspector out of the AppBrowser by setting the Inspector option to Floating in the Environment Options dialog box, as shown in Figure 2.11.

The Inspector contains a property sheet and an event sheet that can be selected by choosing the Properties tab or the Events tab on the bottom of Component Inspector.

The name property is for naming the bean; you may change it to a name of your choice. The properties message, xCoordinate, yCoordinate, and centered are defined in MessagePanel and all the other properties are defined in the superclasses of MessagePanel. Type "Welcome to JavaBeans" in the message property and press the Enter key to let the change take effect. You will see "Welcome to JavaBeans" displayed on the panel. You don't need to run the program to see the changes. The changes can be verified instantaneously, since the bean is live during design time.

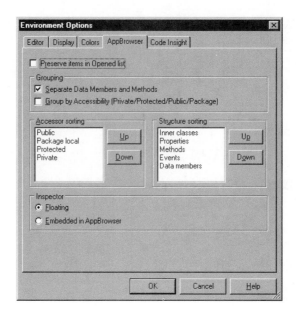

Figure 2.11   *You can choose Floating or Embedded in AppBrowser for Component Inspector in the Environment Options dialog box.*

NOTE

If you change the `centered` property to True, the message is supposed to appear centered in the applet, but this does not happen, because the panel is not repainted by this property change. To repaint the panel, add the `repaint()` method in the `setCentered()` method body or double-click `messagePanel1` to redisplay `messagePanel1`, which would cause the panel to be repainted.

NOTE

When a nondefault value is assigned to the property from the Inspector, the setter method is created in the source code to synchronize the change. When a default value is assigned to the property, the setter method is deleted from the source code, so that the default value can take effect.

You have learned how to create a simple bean component, install it in the Component palette, and manipulate it in the UI Designer. Below, you will see an example that uses the `MessagePanel` in a project with other beans.

Example 2.2 Moving Message on a Panel

This example involves a MessagePanel bean and two JButton beans. The MessagePanel bean displays a message and two JButton beans for moving the message to the left and right, respectively. A sample run of the program is shown in Figure 2.12.

Figure 2.12   *You can use the buttons to move the message to the left and the right.*

Here are the steps to complete the example.

1. Reopen project MessagePanelDemo.jpr created in Example 2.1 and use the Applet Wizard to create a new Java applet named MovingMessage.

2. With MovingMessage.java selected in the Navigation pane, choose the Design tab in the Content pane to start the UI Designer. Drop a MessagePanel from the Component palette to the center of the applet to create an instance of MessagePanel, named messagePanel1. Verify messagePanel1's constraints property and set it to Center, if it is not Center.

3. Drop JPanel from the Swing Containers page in the Component palette to the south of the applet to create an instance of JPanel, named jPanel1. Verify jPanel1's constraint property and set it to South, if it is not South. jPanel1 may appear very small now, but its size will change after buttons are added to the panel.

4. Drop a JButton from the Swing page of the Component palette to jPanel1 twice to create jButton1 and jButton2. In the Component Inspector, change their names to jbtLeft and jbtRight, change their text properties to <= and =>, respectively. If the text is not displayed, double-click jPanel1. Usually, if the components are not displayed correctly, you can double-click the container of the components in the Component tree to redisplay the components.

5. Double-click the <= button in the UI Designer to generate the handler for the jbtLeft button. Implement the handler jbtLeft actionPerformed (ActionEvent e) to move the message to the left, as shown in Listing 2.2.

continues

6. Double-click the => button in the UI Designer to generate the handler for the `jbtRight` button. Implement the handler `jbtRight actionPerformed(ActionEvent e)` to move the message to the right, as shown in Listing 2.2.

```java
package MessagePanelDemo;

import java.awt.*;
import java.awt.event.*;
import java.applet.*;
import javax.swing.*;

public class MovingMessage extends JApplet
{
  boolean isStandalone = false;
  MessagePanel messagePanel1 = new MessagePanel();
  JPanel jPanel1 = new JPanel();
  JButton jbtLeft = new JButton();
  JButton jbtRight = new JButton();

  // Construct the applet
  public MovingMessage()
  {
  }

  // Initialize the applet
  public void init()
  {
    try
    {
      jbInit();
    }
    catch(Exception e)
    {
      e.printStackTrace();
    }
  }

  // Component initialization
  private void jbInit() throws Exception
  {
    this.setSize(new Dimension(400,300));
    jbtLeft.setText("<=");
    jbtRight.setText("=>");
    this.getContentPane().add(messagePanel1, BorderLayout.CENTER);
    this.getContentPane().add(jPanel1, BorderLayout.SOUTH);
    jPanel1.add(jbtLeft, null);
    jPanel1.add(jbtRight, null);
  }
}
```

Listing 2.2   *MovingMessage.java*

Example Review

When the <= button is clicked, the messagePanel1's moveLeft() method is invoked to move the message to the left if there is room for the move. When the => button is clicked, the messagePanel1's moveRight() method is invoked to move the message to the right if there is room for the move.

During design time, you can set properties for each bean and generate handlers for bean events. You cannot test how beans interact with one another, however. For example, you cannot see the effect of clicking a button at design time. You will only see it at runtime.

Bean Properties

Properties are discrete, named attributes of a Java bean that can affect its appearance or behavior. They are often data fields of a bean. For example, the MessagePanel component has a property named message that represents the message to be displayed on the panel. Private data fields are often used to hide specific implementations from the user and prevent the user from accidentally corrupting the properties. Accessor methods are provided instead to let the user read and write the properties. To enable properties to be accessed from a builder tool, either the signatures of the accessor methods must conform to the accessor method naming pattern or the properties and their accessor methods have to be explicitly specified using the BeanInfo interface.

Property Naming Patterns

The bean property naming pattern is a mechanism of the JavaBeans component model that simplifies the bean developer's task of presenting properties for inspection in a builder tool. A property can be a primitive data type or an object type. The property type dictates the signature of the accessor methods and determines how the user edits the property in the Component Inspector window.

In general, the getter method is named get<PropertyName>(), which takes no parameters and returns an object of the type identical to the property type. For example,

```
public String getMessage() { }

public int getXCoordinate() { }

public int getYCoordinate() { }
```

For a property of boolean type, the getter method should be named is<PropertyName>(), which returns a boolean value. For example,

```
public boolean isCentered() { }
```

The setter method should be named set<PropertyName>(), which takes a single parameter identical to the property type and returns void. For example,

```
public void setMessage(String s) { }

public void setXCoordinate(int x) { }

public void setYCoordinate(int y) { }

public void setCentered(boolean centered) { }
```

> **NOTE**
> A property may be read-only with a getter method but no setter method, or write-only with a setter method but no getter method. However, JBuilder cannot expose the property in the Component Inspector unless its getter and setter methods are both provided in the component.

Properties and Data Members

Properties describe the state of the bean. Naturally, data members are used to store properties. However, a bean property is not necessarily a data field. For example, you may create a new property named messageLength that represents the number of the characters in message. The getter method for the property may be defined as follows.

```
public int getMessageLength()
{
  return message.length();
}
```

To enable the property to be seen in the JBuilder's Component Inspector window, both the getter and setter methods must be provided. Since the messageLength property has no setter method, you would not see it in the Component Inspector. To be able to see it, you can provide a setter method with a dummy parameter that does nothing, as follows:

```
public void setMessageLength(int dummy) { }
```

> **NOTE**
> You may have multiple getter and setter methods, but there must be one getter or setter method with a signature conforming to the accessor method patterns. Any other methods are for programmatic use, and are not available to the visual designer.

Property Types

Properties can have any legitimate data type, including primitive data types, arrays, and objects. Properties can be classified into four types: *simple*, *indexed*, *bound*, and *constraint*.

A *simple property* represents a single value of primitive data types or object types. A pair of getter and setter methods defines the simple property. The getter method is constructed as `get<Property>` or `is<Property>` for `boolean` values. The setter method is constructed as `set<Property>`.

An *indexed property* or array property represents an array of elements. The property supports getting and setting the entire array at once. Some builder tools may also support getting and setting individual elements. JBuilder provides a built-in editor for arrays of strings. The signatures of the accessor methods are:

```
public PropertyType[] get<Property>() { }

public void set<Property>(PropertyType[] a) { }
```

JavaBeans provides support for bound and constraint properties. A *bound property* of a component is one for which a notification service is provided when the property changes. The components interested in the property receive the notification and perform operations in response to the property change. These components are related through the bound property. Sometimes, when a property change occurs, the listener component for the bound property may wish to validate the change and reject it if it is inappropriate. Such a property is referred to as *constraint property*. These properties will be introduced in Chapter 10, "Bound and Constraint Properties."

Property Editors

The Inspector uses property editors to update property values. JBuilder provides standard editors for the properties of primitive data types, array of strings and several commonly used object types such as Color and Font. The standard editors can be classified into *simple editor, array editor, choice-menu editor,* and *object editor* according to their appearance in the Inspector.

- A simple editor edits a single value, such as a number, a character, or a string. The user edits the value of the property directly in the Component Inspector window. For example, the property editors for `message`, `xCoordinate`, and `yCoordinate` in the `MessagePanel` component are examples of simple editors.

- An array editor edits an array of elements. The elements may be of any legitimate data type. The Inspector has no built-in support for editing array properties except for arrays of strings. The component developer has to provide a property editor for manipulating the array property.

- A choice-menu editor edits the value as numbers, characters, or strings, with all possible values enumerated in a choice menu. A `boolean` property is of the enumerated type with the values True and False, which is built into JBuilder. The component developer has to provide a property editor for any other choice-menu editors.

■ An object editor edits an instance of the object. Properties of the object type must have their own property editors, except for several standard Java classes, such as Color and Font, whose editors are predefined in JBuilder.

The editors of array properties and object properties appear in the Inspector with an ellipsis (...) at the right of the value when the property is selected. The user clicks the ellipsis to bring up the property editor.

The following example demonstrates the use of JBuilder's built-in property editors to manipulate array properties, enumerated type properties, and object properties. In Chapter 11, you will learn how to write your own property editors.

Example 2.3   Using Editors for Array, Enumerated, and Object Properties

This example creates a bean to display a single message or a composite message. The composite message is constructed from an array of strings. The bean uses a boolean property displayed to turn the display on or off and another boolean property showingSingleMessage to determine whether a single message or a composite message is shown on the panel when displayed is true.

Follow the steps below to complete the example.

1. Reopen the project MessagePanelDemo.jpr and create a new class for the NewMessagePanel component using the New Java Class Wizard that extends MessagePanel. Complete NewMessagePanel as shown in Listing 2.3. Compile it and install it in the Component palette.

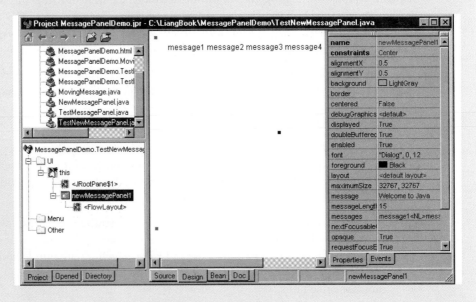

Figure 2.13 *A* NewMessagePanel *bean is placed into the applet.*

2. Create an applet named TestNewMessagePanel.java using the Applet Wizard. With TestNewMessagePanel.java selected in the Navigation pane, click the Design tab to display the UI Designer.

3. Select `NewMessagePanel` from the Component palette and drop it into TestNewMessagePanel to the applet to create `newMessagePanel1`. The AppBrowser for the project is shown in Figure 2.13.

```
package MessagePanelDemo;

import java.awt.*;

public class NewMessagePanel extends MessagePanel
{
  private String[] messages =
    {"message1", "message2", "message3", "message4"};
  private boolean displayed = true;
  private boolean showingSingleMessage = false;

  public NewMessagePanel()
  {
  }

  public boolean isDisplayed()
  {
    return displayed;
  }

  public void setDisplayed(boolean displayed)
  {
    this.displayed = displayed;
  }

  public int getMessageLength()
  {
    return getMessage().length();
  }

  public void setMessageLength(int dummy)
  {
  }

  public boolean isShowingSingleMessage()
  {
    return showingSingleMessage;
  }

  public void setShowingSingleMessage(boolean b)
  {
    this.showingSingleMessage = b;
  }

  public String[] getMessages()
  {
    return messages;
  }
```

continues

Listing 2.3 *NewMessagePanel.java*

```
              public void setMessages(String[] messages)
              {
                System.arraycopy(messages, 0, this.messages, 0, messages.length);
                repaint();
              }

              public void paintComponent(Graphics g)
              {
                // Clear the panel
                g.clearRect(0, 0, getSize().width, getSize().height);

                // Things to display
                String thingsToDisplay = new String();

                if (displayed)
                {
                  if (showingSingleMessage)
                    thingsToDisplay = getMessage();
                  else
                  {
                    for (int i=0; i<messages.length; i++)
                      thingsToDisplay += messages[i] + " ";
                  }
                }

                if (isCentered())
                {
                  // Get font metrics for the font
                  FontMetrics fm = g.getFontMetrics(getFont());

                  // Find the center location to display
                  int w = fm.stringWidth(ThingsToDisplay); // Get the width
                  int h = fm.getAscent(); // Get the string height
                  setXCoordinate((getSize().width-w)/2);
                  setYCoordinate((getSize().height+h)/2);
                }

                g.drawString(thingsToDisplay, getXCoordinate(),
                  getYCoordinate());
              }
          }
```

Listing 2.3   *Continued*

Example Review

The `NewMessagePanel` class extends the `MessagePanel` class created in Example 2.1.

The `showingSingleMessage` is a `boolean` property that determines whether a single message or a composite message is displayed. By default, it is false, indicating that a composite message is displayed. If you change the property to True in the Inspector window and double-click `newMessagePanel1`, you would see a single message "Welcome to Java" displayed. The `boolean` property is an enumeration type with two values, True and False, for selection in a choice menu. Double-clicking `newMessagePanel1` in the Component tree causes the `paintComponent()` method to be executed. When you set the `showingSingleMessage` property, the `paintComponent()` method is not invoked.

The `messageLength` property represents the number of characters in `message`. It is worth noting that it is not a data member in the `NewMessagePanel` component. The setter method of the property does nothing, and its presence in the component is for the property to be read during design, since JBuilder requires both getter and setter methods to be present for the property to be shown in the Inspector.

The `messages` property is an array property, consisting of four strings with initial values "message1," "message2," "message3," and "message4." The strings in the array are separated by <NL>, the new line symbol, as shown in the Inspector window in Figure 2.14. Click the ellipsis to bring up the property editor shown in Figure 2.15. Change the strings to "Welcome," "to," "Java," "!!!"; and click OK to finish editing. You will see "Welcome to Java !!!" displayed on the panel, if the `showingSingleMessage` property is false.

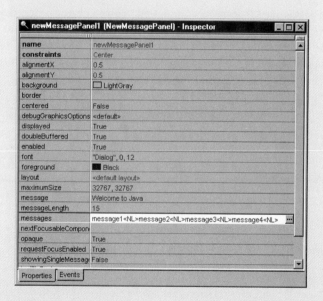

Figure 2.14   *You may edit an array of strings from the Inspector window using a standard editor built into JBuilder.*

continues

71

Figure 2.15   *JBuilder has a built-in property editor for manipulating an array of strings.*

TIP

In order for the change to take effect, you need to press the Enter key on the line where changes are made in the array property editor.

The background, foreground, and font are the object properties. They are defined in java.awt.Component and inherited by NewMessagePanel. JBuilder provides built-in editors for the Color class and the Font class, respectively. For example, you can click the ellipsis on the font property to bring up the font property editor, as shown in Figure 2.16.

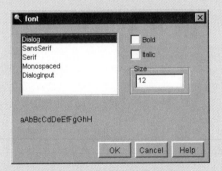

Figure 2.16   *The* Font *class property editor lets you choose desired type, style, and size for the font.*

Chapter Summary

In this chapter, you learned that a JavaBeans component is simply a Java class that is public and serializable and has a default constructor. Beans are especially useful in builder tools that enable programmers to visually manipulate them through Component Inspector during design time. You learned how to write simple beans, install beans in the Component palette in JBuilder, and update bean properties during design time.

Chapter Review

2.1. What are the minimum requirements for a bean component? Is a bean component a Java class? Is a Java class a bean component?

2.2. How do you install a bean component into the Component palette in JBuilder? How do you specify an icon to represent the bean in the Component palette?

2.3. How do you display a separate window for the Component Inspector?

2.4. How do you name a getter method for a non-boolean property? How do you name a getter method for a boolean property? How do you name a setter method for a property?

2.5. List the types of properties.

2.6. Is a property always a data member of the class?

2.7. Some Java builder tools can work with read-only properties. Can JBuilder display read-only properties in the Inspector?

2.8. If a superclass is not a bean component, can a subclass be a bean component?

2.9. Is a bean component always a GUI component?

Programming Exercises

2.1. Add a button labeled Up and a button labeled Down in Example 2.2 to move the message upward and downward.

2.2. Create a bean component named `Circle`, which displays a circle in the center of the panel. The `Circle` component has a property named `radius`, which determines the size of the circle, and it also contains a method for computing the area of the circle. Install the component in the Component palette and use it to create an applet that enables the user to set the radius and displays the area of the circle. A sample run of the applet is shown in Figure 2.17.

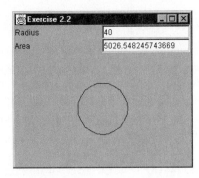

Figure 2.17   *You can set the radius of the circle and display its area.*

2.3. Create a bean component named `MessageControl`, which controls how a message is displayed. The message can blink or move from right to left circularly, or both at the same time. The properties of `MessageControl` are as follows:

- `message`: A string for the message to be displayed.

- `blinking`: a `boolean` value indicating whether the message should blink.

- `moving`: a `boolean` value indicating whether the message moves.

2.4. Create a bean component named `ImageControl`, which displays an image for a specified image file. The properties of `ImageControl` are as follows:

- `filename`: the name of the file containing the image.

- `stretched`: a `boolean` value indicating whether the image is stretched to fill the entire view area.

BEAN EVENTS

Objectives

- Review the Java event delegation model.
- Create a new event class and listener interface.
- Develop source components using new event sets or existing event sets.
- Make source components from scratch or from existing components.
- Implement listener components.
- Become familiar with adapters, inner classes, and anonymous classes.
- Learn how to hook up source components with listener components in JBuilder.

Introduction

A bean may communicate with other beans. The Java event delegation model provides the foundation for beans to send, receive, and handle events. When something happens to a bean, such as a mouse click on a `javax.swing.JButton` bean, an event object is created that encapsulates information pertaining to the event. The bean passes the event object to the interested beans for the event to be processed.

Events are typically generated by Java GUI components, such as `javax.swing.JButton`, but are not limited to GUI components. This chapter introduces the development of beans that can generate events and beans that listen for events. You will learn how to create custom events and link the beans via events in JBuilder.

Java Event Model

The Java event model consists of the following four types of classes, whose relationship is illustrated in Figure 3.1.

- The event object
- The event source
- The event listener interface
- The event listener

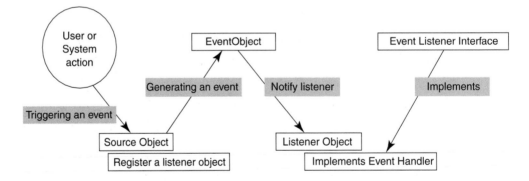

Figure 3.1   *An event is triggered by user actions on the source object, and the source object "fires" the event and invokes the handler of the listener object to process the event.*

An *event* is a type of signal to the program that something has happened. It can be generated by external user actions, such as mouse movements, mouse button clicks, and keystrokes, or by the operating system, such as a timer. An *event object* contains the information that describes the event. A *source object* is where the event originates. When an event occurs on the source object, an event object is created. An object interested in the event receives the event. Such an object is called a *listener*. Not all objects can receive events. To become a listener, the object must be registered as a listener by the source object. The source object maintains a list of listeners and notifies all the registered listeners by invoking the event-handling method implemented on the listener object. The handlers are defined in the class known as the *event listener interface*. Each class of an event object has a corresponding event listener interface.

NOTE
The Java event model is referred to as a *delegation-based model* simply because the source object delegates the event to the listeners for processing.

Event Objects

The Java event model is essential to Java graphics programming. Each GUI component is associated with one or more events, as shown in Figure 3.2.

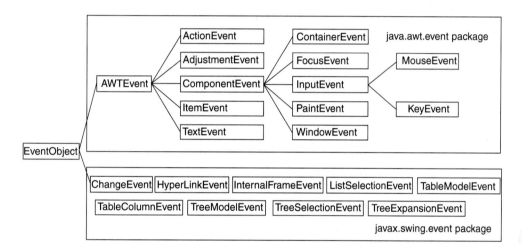

Figure 3.2   *The* java.util.EventObject *class is the root of all Java event classes.*

The event classes introduced in JDK 1.1 are grouped in the java.awt.event package. These classes were originally designed for AWT components, but many Swing components generate these events. The events in the javax.swing.event package are only applicable to Swing components.

The event class contains whatever data values and methods are pertinent to the particular event type. For example, the KeyEvent class describes the data values related to a key event and contains the methods, such as getKeyChar(), for retrieving the key associated with the event.

All the event classes extend EventObject. You will learn to create custom event classes by extending EventObject in the section, "Creating Custom Events."

Source Components

The component on which an event is generated is referred to as an *event source*. Each Java AWT and Swing user interface component is an *event source*. For example, JButton is an event source because it generates an java.awt.event.ActionEvent when a button object is clicked.

The source component contains the code that detects an external or internal action that triggers the event. Upon detecting the action, the source should fire an event to the listeners by invoking their event handler. The source component must also contain methods for registering and deregistering listeners.

Event Listener Interface

Each event class is associated with an event listener interface that defines one or more methods, referred to as *handlers*. The handlers are implemented by the listener components. The source component invokes the listeners' handlers when the event is detected.

Since an event class and its listener interface are coexistent, they are often referred to as an *event set* or *event pair*. The event listener interface must be named as *X*Listener for the *X*Event. For example, the listener interface for ActionEvent is ActionListener.

Listener Components

A listener component for an event must implement the event listener interface. The object of the listener component cannot receive event notifications from a source component unless the object is registered as a listener of the source.

A listener component may implement any number of listener interfaces to listen to several types of events. A source component and a listener component may be the same.

Review of the JButton Component

To further explain how to create custom event sets and your own source components, let us take a look at the JButton component and its associated event set and listener component.

TIP
You can find the source code of a class by choosing Search, Browse Symbol to bring up a dialog box in which you can type a fully qualified class name to review its source code.

---

java.awt.event.ActionEvent   extends   java.awt.AWTEvent,   which   extends java.util.EventObject. ActionEvent contains two constructors as follows:

```
public ActionEvent(Object source, int id, String command)
public ActionEvent(Object source, int id, String command,
int modifiers)
```

These constructors can be used by source components to create event objects.

`java.awt.event.ActionListener` extends `java.util.EventListener`. `ActionListener` simply contains the `actionPerformed` method, which must be implemented by the listener component that responds to `ActionEvent`.

The `JButton` is a subclass of `AbstractButton`. The `fireActionPerformed()` method defined in `AbstractButton` is invoked when an external user action is detected on a `JButton` object. This method invokes the registered listener's `actionPerformed` handler.

The `AbstractButton` class also provides registration methods `addActionListener` and `removeActionListener` for listeners. These methods are defined as follows.

```
public synchronized void addActionListener(ActionListener l)
public synchronized void removeActionListener(ActionListener l)
```

As shown in Figure 3.3, a listener component implements the `ActionListener` interface and provides the actual code for handling the event in the `actionPerformed` method. The Application class creates an instance of `JButton` and an instance of the listener component, and registers the listener with the source. When an `ActionEvent` occurs on a button, the button object invokes the listener's `actionPerformed` method to deal with the event.

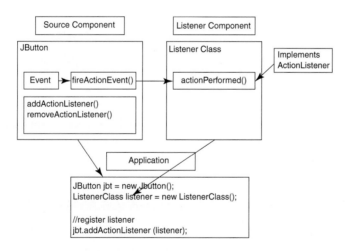

Figure 3.3   *The source component invokes the listener's handler to process the events.*

Creating Custom Event Sets and Source Components

You have already used event sets and event source components in Java graphics programming, since certain event sets and source components are provided as part of the Java API. In this section, you will learn how to create custom event sets and develop your own source components. By developing your own event sets and source components, you will gain a better understanding of the Java event model.

A custom event class must extend `java.util.EventObject` or a subclass of `java.util.EventObject`. Additionally, you need to provide data members and methods to describe and process the event.

A custom event listener interface must always extend `java.util.EventListener`. You need to define the signature of the handlers for the event. The listener interface should be named *<Event>*Listener for a builder tool to recognize it during design time.

A source component must have the following two essential contents:

- The appropriate registration methods for adding and removing listeners. To enable a builder tool to recognize events, the registration methods must conform to the registration method naming patterns. Events can be unicasted (only one object is notified of the event) or multicasted (each object in a list of listeners is notified of the event). The naming pattern for adding a unicast listener is

  ```
  public void add<Event>Listener(<Event>Listener l) throws
     TooManyListenersException;
  ```

  The naming pattern for adding a multicast listener is the same, except that it does not throw the `TooManyListenersException`.

  ```
  public void add<Event>Listener(<Event>Listener l)
  ```

- The naming pattern for removing a listener (either unicast or multicast) is:

  ```
  public void remove<Event>Listener(<Event>Listener l)
  ```

  It contains the code that creates an event object and passes it to the listening components by calling a method in the listener's event listener interface. You may use a standard Java event class like `ActionEvent` to create event objects or may define your own event classes if necessary.

Example 3.1   Creating a Custom Event Set and a Source Component

This example creates a custom event set named `TickEvent` and `TickListener` for describing tick events, and develops a source component that generates a tick event at every specified time interval in milliseconds. The event class shown in Listing 3.1 contains the information on tick count and tick interval.

```
package EventDemo;

public class TickEvent extends java.util.EventObject
{
  // Properties for TickEvent
  private long tickCount, tickInterval;
```

Listing 3.1   *TickEvent.java*

```
    // Constructor
    public TickEvent(Object o)
    {
      super(o);
    }

    public long getTickCount()
    {
      return tickCount;
    }

    public void setTickCount(long tickCount)
    {
      this.tickCount = tickCount;
    }

    public long getTickInterval()
    {
      return tickInterval;
    }

    public void setTickInterval(long milliseconds)
    {
      tickInterval = milliseconds;
    }
}
```

Listing 3.1   *Continued*

An event listener interface must be defined for each new event class. The listener interface for `TickEvent` presented in Listing 3.2 contains a method `handleTick()` that will be implemented by the listeners of `TickEvent`.

```
package EventDemo;

import EventDemo.TickEvent;

public interface TickListener extends java.util.EventListener
{
  // Handler for TickEvent
  public void handleTick(TickEvent e);
}
```

Listing 3.2   *TickListener.java*

The source component is responsible for registering listeners, generating events, and notifying listeners by invoking the methods defined in the listeners' interfaces. The `Tick` component presented in Listing 3.3 is capable of registering multiple listeners, generating a `TickEvent` object at every specified time interval, and notifying the listeners by invoking the listeners' `handleTick()` method.

Follow the steps below to complete the project:

1. Create a new project named EventDemo.jpr and create an applet named TestTick using the Applet Wizard. Create classes for `TickEvent`, `TickListener`, and `Tick` in the project, compile the classes, and install the `Tick` component into the Component palette.

continues

```
package EventDemo;

import EventDemo.*;
import java.util.Vector;

public class Tick implements Runnable
{
  // A thread to control tick
  protected Thread thread = null;

  // Whether the thread is suspended
  private boolean suspended;

  // Store Tick listeners in a vector
  private Vector tickListenerList = new Vector();

  // Tick event
  private TickEvent e;

  // Tick count and Tick interval
  private long tickCount = 0;
  private long tickInterval = 1000;

  // Default constructor
  public Tick()
  {
    // Create a TickEvent
    e = new TickEvent(this);

    // Create and start the thread
    thread = new Thread( this );
    thread.start( );
  }

  public long getTickInterval( )
  {
    return tickInterval;
  }

  public void setTickInterval(long interval)
  {
    tickInterval = interval;
  }

  // Run the thread
  public void run()
  {
    while (true)
    {
      try
      {
        Thread.sleep(tickInterval);
        synchronized (this)
        {
          while (suspended)
            wait();
        }
      }
      catch (InterruptedException e)
      {  }

      // Adjust Tick count and interval
      e.setTickCount(tickCount++);
```

Listing 3.3 *Tick.java*

```
            e.setTickInterval(tickInterval);

            // Fire TickEvent
            processEvent(e);
        }
    }

    public synchronized void resume()
    {
        if (suspended)
        {
            suspended = false;
            notify();
        }
    }

    public synchronized void suspend()
    {
        suspended = true;
    }

    public synchronized void addTickListener(TickListener l)
    {
        tickListenerList.addElement(l);
    }

    public synchronized void removeTickListener(TickListener l)
    {
        tickListenerList.removeElement(l);
    }

    // Fire TickEvent
    public void processEvent(TickEvent e)
    {
        Vector v;

        synchronized (this)
        {
            v = (Vector)tickListenerList.clone();
        }

        for (int i=0; i < v.size(); i++)
        {
            TickListener listener = (TickListener)v.elementAt(i);
            listener.handleTick(e);
        }
    }
}
```

Listing 3.3 *Continued*

2. Click Tick from the Component palette and drop it in the UI designer, as shown in Figure 3.4. Since Tick is not a UI component, it is not seen in the UI designer, but in the Component tree you can see a bean named tick1 whose properties and event handler can be visually manipulated in the Component Inspector. The Inspector window in Figure 3.4 shows the bean property. To reveal the bean event handlers, choose the Event tab at the bottom of the Component Inspector, as shown in Figure 3.5. You will learn how to link the source component with listeners by implementing

continues

the handlers using JBuilder's visual designer in the section, "Linking Components via Events in JBuilder."

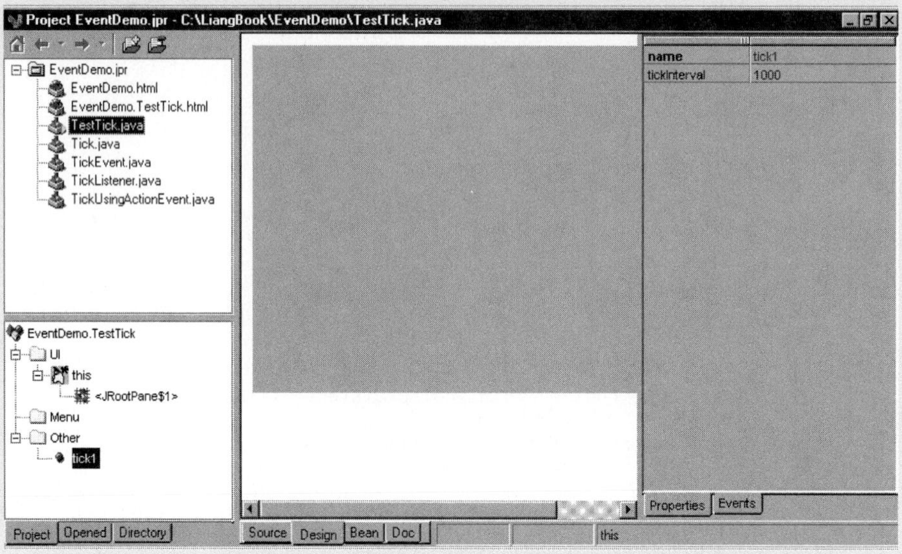

Figure 3.4   *You can add a non-UI JavaBeans component into the designer and manipulate its properties and event handlers from the Component Inspector.*

Figure 3.5   *The* handleTick *handler is shown in the Component Inspector, where you can link the source component to a listener in JBuilder.*

Example Review

The Tick class is a JavaBeans component; however, TickEvent and TickListener are not components. Therefore, Tick can be installed in the Component palette, but not TickEvent and TickListener.

The suspend() and resume() methods are for suspending and resuming ticking. Their implementation is compatible with the JDK 1.2 requirements. The suspend() and resume() methods in the Thread class in JDK 1.1 are deprecated because they are known to be deadlock-prone. Therefore, instead of using the suspend() method, the wait() method is used, along with a boolean variable, to indicate whether a thread is suspended.

TickEvent is a new-event class. Most of the time you don't need to create your own event classes unless you want to encapsulate information not available in the existing event classes, as in the case of the TickEvent class that contains tick count and tick interval. In this case, you need to write an event set that includes the event class and its listener interface.

Since the source component Tick is designed for multiple listeners, a java.util.Vector instance tickListenerList is used to hold all the listeners for the source component. The data type of the elements in the vector is Object. To add a listener l to the tickListenerList vector, use

```
tickListenerList.addElement(l);
```

To remove a listener l from tickListenerList, use

```
tickListenerList.removeElement(l);
```

The addTickListener() and removeTickListener() methods are synchronized to prevent data corruption on tickListenerList when attempting to register multiple listeners concurrently.

The processEvent() method is invoked at every tickInterval in milliseconds. This notifies the listeners in the tickListenerList vector by calling each listener's handleTick() method to process the event. It is possible that a new listener may be added or an existing listener may be removed when proecessEvent() is running. To avoid corruption on tickListenerList, a clone v of tickListenerList is created for use to notify listeners. To avoid corruption when creating the clone, all the methods of the object are synchronized as follows:

```
synchronized (this)
{
  v = (Vector)tickListenerList.clone();
}
```

The Tick component is created from scratch. If you build a new component that extends a component capable of generating events, the new component inherits the ability to generate the same type of events. For example, the MessagePanel component is derived from javax.swing.JPanel, which is a subclass of java.awt.Component. The MessagePanel component can detect and generate a number of events, such as key and mouse events. You don't need to write the code to generate these events and register listeners for them, since the code is already given in the superclass. However, you still need to write the code to make your component capable of firing events not supported in the superclass.

continues

Creating Listener Components

If a component is to be a listener for an event, it must implement the event listener interface and be registered with a source object. For example, to listen for TickEvent, the listener component must implement TickListener, and must be registered with an instance of a source component, such as Tick.

A builder tool can help to automate the process of creating a listener and registering it with a source. For example, in JBuilder, the code can be generated by selecting and pressing the event handler in the Component Inspector. To further show how JBuilder generates listeners, let us first look at the following example, which creates a listener manually.

Example 3.2   Writing a Listener Component Manually

In this example, a hand-coded program is given to display the tick count and tick interval when a tick event occurs. The display is shown in a MessagePanel bean placed on an instance of JFrame, which is a subclass of the java.awt.Frame bean. The MessagePanel component was presented in Example 2.1. A Tick bean is used to generate tick events. The JFrame bean is the listener for tick events.

Follow the steps below to complete the example:

1. Reopen project EventDemo.jpr and create a class named ShowTick that extends JFrame using the New Class Wizard. In the New Class Wizard, check the options "Public," "Generate parameterless constructor," and "Generate main function," as shown in Figure 3.6.

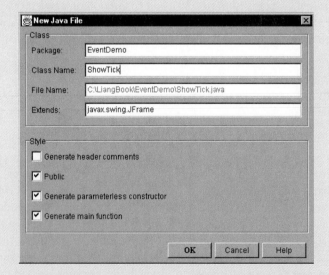

Figure 3.6   *You can use the New Java File Wizard to create a template for the* ShowTick *class.*

2. Choose Wizards, Implement Interface to bring up the Implement Interface Wizard, as shown in Figure 3.7. Expand `EventDemo.*` to select the `EventDemo.TickListener` interface. Click OK to let JBuilder generate the code for implementing the interface in ShowTick.java.

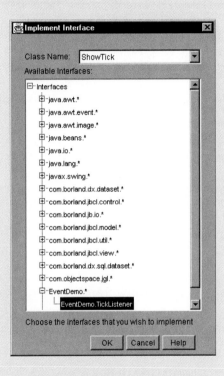

Figure 3.7   *The Implement Interface Wizard can help you to implement all the handlers in an interface.*

3. Complete the code as shown in Listing 3.4. A sample run of the program is shown in Figure 3.8.

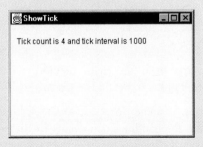

Figure 3.8   *The tick count is updated every 1 second.*

continues

```
package EventDemo;

import javax.swing.*;
import MessagePanelDemo.MessagePanel;
import java.awt.*;

public class ShowTick extends JFrame implements TickListener
{
  private Tick tick;
  private MessagePanel messagePanel;

  // Constructor
  public ShowTick()
  {
    // Create a Tick event instance and set tick interval to 1000
    Tick tick = new Tick();
    tick.setTickInterval(1000);

    // Create a message panel instance
    messagePanel = new MessagePanel();

    // Place the message canvas to the frame
    this.getContentPane().setLayout(new BorderLayout());
    this.getContentPane().add(messagePanel);
    setTitle("ShowTick");

    // Register listener
    tick.addTickListener(this);
  }

  // Main method
  public static void main(String[] args)
  {
    ShowTick showTick = new ShowTick();
    showTick.setSize(100, 100);
    showTick.setVisible(true);
  }

  public void handleTick(TickEvent e)
  {
    //TODO: implement this EventDemo.TickListener method;
    messagePanel.setMessage("Tick count is " + e.getTickCount() +
      " and tick interval is " + e.getTickInterval());
  }
}
```

Listing 3.4 *ShowTick.java*

Example Review

The program starts from the main method, which creates an instance of ShowTick and displays the frame on the screen.

To make ShowTick a listener for Tick, ShowTick implements TickListener and provides the code for handling tick events in the handleTick() method. You should also register the listener by invoking TickListener's add listener method as follows:

```
tick.addTickListener(this);
```

When an event occurs in tick, the processEvent() method is invoked to notify the listener ShowTick by invoking its handleTick() method. The flow of the event processing from the source to the listener is shown in Figure 3.9.

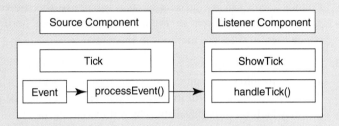

Figure 3.9   *When a Tick event occurs, the* processEvent() *method is invoked, which invokes the* handleTick() *method defined in the listener's interface and implemented in the listener.*

Event Adapters

The Java event model shown in Figure 3.1 is flexible, allowing modifications and variations. One useful variation of the model is the addition of adapters, as shown in Figure 3.10. When an event occurs, the source object notifies the adapter. The adapter then delegates the handling of the event to the real listener object, which is referred to as a *target*.

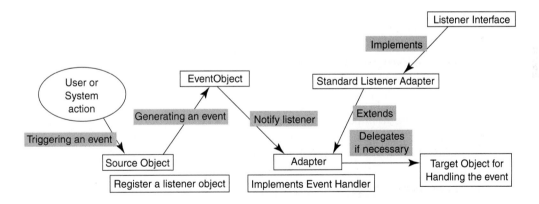

Figure 3.10   *The adapter listens for events and delegates handling to the actual listener (target).*

The adapter is a service object that provides a level of indirection between the source and the target. It is registered as a listener for the source event. Instead of passing the event object to the target, the source passes the event object to the adapter and lets it delegate to the target handler.

At first glance, the advantages of using adapters are not apparent. Adapters seem to make things more complex, but they are valuable in many situations. Here are some examples:

■ If you need to hook a source to an existing bean that cannot be modified or extended, you can use an adapter as a listener to the source and register it with the source. When an event occurs, the source notifies the adapter, which then invokes the methods in the target.

■ You can use an adapter to place all the event notifications from the source in a queue to allow the source object to resume execution without blocking. This is particularly useful in a distributed environment where the target object may be busy or not available when the event occurs.

■ You can create a generic adapter to listen for all types of events from all sources, then deliver them to one or multiple targets. This generic adapter can be used as a filter for the events before they are delegated out to the targets. You can apply all kinds of business rules and logic to the delivery of events and sort the events by priority.

An adapter usually extends a convenience listener adapter. A *convenience listener adapter* is a support class that provides default implementations for all the methods in the listener interface. The default implementation is usually an empty body. Java provides convenience listener adapters for all the AWT listener interfaces except the `ActionListener`. A convenience listener adapter is named *X*Adapter for *X*Listener. For example, `MouseAdapter` is a standard listener adapter for `MouseListener`.

A listener interface may contain many methods for handling various types of actions of an event. For example, `MouseListener` contains `mouseClicked()`, `mousePressed()`, `mouseReleased()`, `mouseEntered()`, and `mouseExited()`. The convenience listener adapter is convenient because a listener class may simply extend the adapter and implement only the method for the intended type of action instead of all the methods of the listener interface.

Adapters are an important addition to the Java event model. You will see more examples and different ways of using adapters. In the next section, you will see how adapters can make builder tools more efficient.

Using Adapters in JBuilder

A builder tool like JBuilder uses adapters to delegate handling events to the target objects. For example, suppose a target object is a listener for two buttons named Ok and Cancel, respectively. JBuilder generates an adapter for the Ok button and an adapter for the Cancel button, as shown in Figure 3.11. The target object contains a method (say `ok_actionPerformed()`) for handling the Ok button and a separate method (say `cancel_actionPerformed()`) for handling the Cancel button. When you click on the Ok button, it fires the `ActionEvent` to the Ok adapter, which then delegates the event to `ok_actionPerformed`.

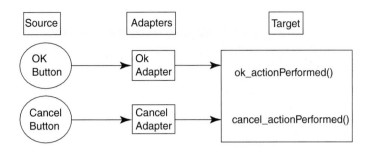

Figure 3.11   *JBuilder uses adapters to hook up source components with listeners.*

JBuilder greatly simplifies the task of creating listeners. It automatically registers listeners and provides an empty method for the user to fill in the code for handling the event. JBuilder can generate anonymous adapters or standard adapters. In the following example, you will learn how to use JBuilder's UI Designer to link source components and listeners via standard adapters. Anonymous adapters will be introduced in the section, "Inner Classes and Anonymous Inner Classes."

Example 3.3   Creating a Listener Component Using JBuilder

This exercise uses JBuilder's visual designer to develop the same program as in Example 3.2. Additionally, the program stops the tick when the mouse is pressed, and the tick resumes when the mouse is released. Suppose that the `MessagePanel` and `Tick` components are already placed in the Component palette. To see the development in action, follow these steps:

1. Reopen the project EventDemo.jpr and create an applet named ShowTickWithStandardAdapter using the Applet Wizard.

2. Choose Project, Project Properties to bring up the EventDemo.jpr Properties dialog box, as shown in Figure 3.12. Make sure you select Standard adapter for the event handling in the Code Style page of the dialog box. With this selection, JBuilder will generate standard adapters.

3. With ShowTickWithStandardAdapter.java selected in the Navigation pane, choose the Design tab to display the UI Designer. Drop a `Message Panel` component to the center of the applet to create `messagePanel1`. Set its `background` to Cyan and `yCoordinate` to 30 in the Component Inspector.

4. Drop a `Tick` component to the frame. You will see `tick1` in the Component tree under the node Other.

5. With `tick1` selected in the Component tree, switch to the Events page of the Component Inspector. Select the `handleTick` event and double-click its value field in the Component Inspector. The following code is automatically generated.

continues

91

Figure 3.12   *You may choose an event-handling style from the Project Properties dialog.*

➤ The following line was added into the jbInit() method to register the listener for TickEvent.

```
tick1.addTickListener(new
  ShowTickWithStandardAdapter_tick1_tickAdapter(this));
```

➤ An empty handler method is created for you to fill in the code for handling the TickEvent.

```
void tick1_handleTick(TickEvent e)
{ }
```

➤ A new event listener adapter class was created as follows.

```
class ShowTickWithStandardAdapter_tick1_tickAdapter
  implements EventDemo.TickListener
{
  ShowTickWithStandardAdapter adaptee;

ShowTickWithStandardAdapter_tick1_tickAdapter(
  ShowTickWithStandardAdapter adaptee)
  {
    this.adaptee = adaptee;
  }

  public void handleTick(TickEvent e)
  {
    adaptee.tick1_handleTick(e);
  }
}
```

7. Fill in the following code in the method `tick1_handleTick` to handle the tick event.

```
void tick1_handleTick(TickEvent e)
{
  messagePanel1.setMessage("Tick count is "+
    e.getTickCount()+" and tick interval is " +
      e.getTickInterval());
}
```

8. We now turn our attention to creating the code for handling the mouse events. In the Events page of the Component Inspector for `messagePanel1`, double-click the value field of the `mousePressed` event. The following code is automatically generated.

   ➤ The following line is added into the `jbInit()` method to register the listener for `MouseEvent`.

   ```
   this.addMouseListener(new
     ShowTickWithStandardAdapter_this_mouseAdapter(this));
   ```

   ➤ An empty handler method was created for you to fill in the code for handling the `mousePressed` event.

   ```
   void messagePanel1_mousePressed(MouseEvent e)
   { }
   ```

   ➤ A new event listener adapter class was created as follows.

   ```
   class ShowTickWithStandardAdapter_messagePanel1_mouseAdapter
     extends java.awt.event.MouseAdapter
   {
     ShowTickWithStandardAdapter adaptee;

     ShowTickWithStandardAdapter_messagePanel1_mouseAdapter
       (ShowTickWithStandardAdapter adaptee)
     {
       this.adaptee = adaptee;
     }

     public void mousePressed(MouseEvent e)
     {
       adaptee.messagePanel1_mousePressed(e);
     }
   }
   ```

9. Fill in the following code in the method `messagePanel1_mousePressed` to suspend the tick when the mouse is pressed.

   ```
   void messagePanel1_mousePressed(MouseEvent e)
   {
     tick1.suspend();
   }
   ```

10. To generate the code for handling the `mouseReleased` event, click the value field of `mouseReleased` in the Events page for `messagePanel1`. Since the

continues

adapter for the MouseEvent was already created and is registered with the source as a MouseEvent listener, this code will not regenerated. Instead the following code was generated.

➤ An empty handler method was created for you to fill in the code for handling the mouseReleased event.

```
void messagePanel1_mouseReleased(MouseEvent e)
{ }
```

➤ A handler for the mouseReleased event was added to adapter.

```
public void mouseReleased(MouseEvent e)
{
  adaptee.messagePanel1_mouseReleased(e);
}
```

11. Fill in the following code in the method messagePanel1_mouseReleased to resume the tick when the mouse is pressed.

```
void messagePanel1_mouseReleased(MouseEvent e)
{
  tick1.resume();
}
```

12. The ShowTickWithStandardAdapter.java code generated by JBuilder is shown in Listing 3.5. Run ShowTickWithStandardAdapter.java in the project to test the program. The output of a sample run is shown in Figure 3.8, which is the same as in Example 3.1.

```
package EventDemo;

import java.awt.*;
import java.awt.event.*;
import java.applet.*;
import javax.swing.*;
import MessagePanelDemo.*;

public class ShowTickWithStandardAdapter extends JApplet
{
  boolean isStandalone = false;
  MessagePanel messagePanel1 = new MessagePanel();
  Tick tick1 = new Tick();

  // Construct the applet
  public ShowTickWithStandardAdapter()
  {
  }

  // Initialize the applet
  public void init()
  {
    try
    {
```

Listing 3.5   *ShowTickWithStandardAdapter.java*

```
      jbInit();
    }
    catch(Exception e)
    {
      e.printStackTrace();
    }
  }

  // Component initialization
  private void jbInit() throws Exception
  {
    this.setSize(new Dimension(400,300));
    messagePanel1.setBackground(Color.cyan);
    messagePanel1.setYCoordinate(30);
    messagePanel1.addMouseListener(new
      ShowTickWithStandardAdapter_messagePanel1_mouseAdapter(this));
    tick1.addTickListener
      (new ShowTickWithStandardAdapter_tick1_tickAdapter(this));
    this.getContentPane().add(messagePanel1, BorderLayout.CENTER);
  }

  void tick1_handleTick(TickEvent e)
  {
    messagePanel1.setMessage("Tick count is " + e.getTickCount() +
      " and tick interval is " + e.getTickInterval());
  }

  void messagePanel1_mousePressed(MouseEvent e)
  {
    tick1.suspend();
  }

  void messagePanel1_mouseReleased(MouseEvent e)
  {
    tick1.resume();
  }
}

class ShowTickWithStandardAdapter_tick1_tickAdapter
  implements EventDemo.TickListener
{
  ShowTickWithStandardAdapter adaptee;

  ShowTickWithStandardAdapter_tick1_tickAdapter
    (ShowTickWithStandardAdapter adaptee)
  {
    this.adaptee = adaptee;
  }

  public void handleTick(TickEvent e)
  {
    adaptee.tick1_handleTick(e);
  }
}

class ShowTickWithStandardAdapter_messagePanel1_mouseAdapter
  extends java.awt.event.MouseAdapter
{
  ShowTickWithStandardAdapter adaptee;
```

continues

Listing 3.5 *Continued*

```
ShowTickWithStandardAdapter_messagePanel1_mouseAdapter
  (ShowTickWithStandardAdapter adaptee)
{
  this.adaptee = adaptee;
}

public void mousePressed(MouseEvent e)
{
  adaptee.messagePanel1_mousePressed(e);
}

public void mouseReleased(MouseEvent e)
{
  adaptee.messagePanel1_mouseReleased(e);
}
}
```

Listing 3.5   *Continued*

Example Review

The `Tick` component can generate `TickEvent`. `MessagePanel` is a subclass of `java.awt.Component`. Since the `Component` class can generate `MouseEvent`, `MessagePanel` is a source for `MouseEvent`.

JBuilder uses a listener adapter as an intermediary class interposed between an event source and the real listener, as shown in Figure 3.13 for the `TickEvent`, and in Figure 3.14 for the `MouseEvent`. The adapter plays the role to pair a source event with a listener. When a `TickEvent` occurs, the `processEvent()` method in the event source invokes the `handleTick()` method in the adapter, which then invokes the real handler `tick1_handleTick()` in the target component.

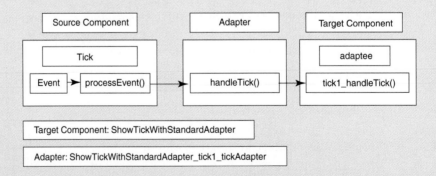

Figure 3.13   *When a* `TickEvent` *occurs, the* `processEvent()` *method is invoked, which invokes the* `handleTick()` *method in the adapter, which in turn invokes the real handler,* `handleTick()`.

When a `MouseEvent` occurs, the `processMouseEvent()` method in the event source invokes one of the five mouse events (`mousePressed`, `mouseReleased`, `mouseClicked`, `mouseEntered`, and `mouseExited`). Which of the five events

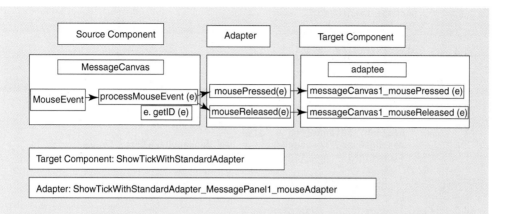

Figure 3.14   *When a* MouseEvent *occurs, the* processMouseEvent() *method is invoked, which invokes the* mousePressed() *method or* mouseReleased() *method in the adapter, and then the real handler* messagePanel1_mousePressed() *or* messagePanel1_mouseReleased().

is processed depends on the event ID. For the detailed code of the processMouseEvent method, please refer to java.awt.Component. Since you are only interested in the mousePressed and mouseReleased events, these two handlers are provided in the adapter. When one of these two handlers is invoked in the adapter, the corresponding real handler in the target component is invoked.

The adapter for the TickEvent implements the TickListener interface and the adapter for the MouseEvent extends the MouseAdapter convenience listener adapter class. JBuilder creates adapters by extending the listener interface's convenience adapter class, if the convenience adapter exists.

 TIP
To delete an existing event handler, highlight the entire value field of the event handler in the Events page, press the Delete key, and then press the Enter key. JBuilder automatically deletes the adapter class and the registration method from the source code. The associated event-handling method is also deleted if it is empty.

Inner Classes and Anonymous Inner Classes

As you have just learned, JBuilder generates an event adapter for every type of event from the source in which the target is interested. Consequently, there are usually many classes in the project. You can use inner classes to reduce the proliferation of adapter classes and to shorten the program.

An *inner class* is a class defined within the scope of another class. Here is an example (see Listing 3.6) of rewriting ShowTickWithStandardAdapter.java using inner classes.

```java
package EventDemo;

import java.awt.*;
import java.awt.event.*;
import java.applet.*;
import javax.swing.*;
import MessagePanelDemo.*;

public class ShowTickWithInnerClass extends JApplet
{
  boolean isStandalone = false;
  MessagePanel messagePanel1 = new MessagePanel();
  Tick tick1 = new Tick();

  // Construct the applet
  public ShowTickWithInnerClass()
  {
  }

  // Initialize the applet
  public void init()
  {
    try
    {
      jbInit();
    }
    catch(Exception e)
    {
      e.printStackTrace();
    }
  }

  // Component initialization
  private void jbInit() throws Exception
  {
    this.setSize(new Dimension(400,300));
    messagePanel1.setBackground(Color.cyan);
    messagePanel1.setYCoordinate(30);
    messagePanel1.addMouseListener (new
      ShowTickWithStandardAdapter_messagePanel1_mouseAdapter());
    tick1.addTickListener (new
      ShowTickWithStandardAdapter_tick1_tickAdapter());
    this.getContentPane().add(messagePanel1, BorderLayout.CENTER);
  }

  void tick1_handleTick(TickEvent e)
  {
    messagePanel1.setMessage("Tick count is " + e.getTickCount() +
      " and tick interval is " + e.getTickInterval());
  }

  void messagePanel1_mousePressed(MouseEvent e)
  {
    tick1.suspend();
  }

  void messagePanel1_mouseReleased(MouseEvent e)
  {
    tick1.resume();
  }
```

Listing 3.6   *ShowTickWithInnerClass.java.*

```
class ShowTickWithStandardAdapter_tick1_tickAdapter
  implements EventDemo.TickListener
{
  public void handleTick(TickEvent e)
  {
    tick1_handleTick(e);
  }
}

class ShowTickWithStandardAdapter_messagePanel1_mouseAdapter
  extends java.awt.event.MouseAdapter
{
  public void mousePressed(MouseEvent e)
  {
    messagePanel1_mousePressed(e);
  }

  public void mouseReleased(MouseEvent e)
  {
    messagePanel1_mouseReleased(e);
  }
}
}
```

Listing 3.6   *Continued*

The adapters are simplified inside `ShowTickWithInnerClass` using inner classes. Inner classes are just like any regular classes with the following features:

■ An inner class can reference the data and methods defined in its parent class so that you do not need to pass the reference of the parent class to the constructor of the inner class. Therefore, the constructors of the adapters are eliminated and the `handleTick()` method invokes `tick1_handleTick()`, which is defined in `ShowTickWithInnerClass`.

■ Inner classes make programs simple and concise. As you can see, the new class is shorter and leaner.

■ An inner class is only for supporting the work of its containing outer class, and it is compiled into a class named *OutClassName*$*InnerClassName*.class. For example, the inner class `ShowTickWithStandardAdapter_tick1_tick-Adapter` in `ShowTickWithInnerClass` is compiled into

    ShowTickWithInnerClass$ShowTickWithStandardAdapter_tick1_tick-
    Adapter.class.

The inner class can be further shortened by using an anonymous inner class. An *anonymous inner class* is an inner class without a name. An anonymous inner class combines declaring an inner class and creating an instance of the class in one step. JBuilder lets you choose either anonymous adapters or standard adapters. If you checked the option "Anonymous adapter" for event handling in the project property dialog box in Figure 3.14, and repeat the same steps in Example 3.3 using new file named ShowTickWithAnonymousAdapter.java, ShowTickWithAnonymous-Adapter.java can be generated as shown in Listing 3.7.

In `messagePanel1.addMouseListener()`, the anonymous class extends `MouseAdapter` convenience adapter class and implements the `mousePressed` and `mouseReleased`

```
package EventDemo;

import java.awt.*;
import java.awt.event.*;
import java.applet.*;
import javax.swing.*;
import MessagePanelDemo.*;

public class ShowTickWithAnonymousAdapter extends JApplet
{
  boolean isStandalone = false;
  MessagePanel messagePanel1 = new MessagePanel();
  Tick tick1 = new Tick();

  // Construct the applet
  public ShowTickWithAnonymousAdapter()
  {
  }

  // Initialize the applet
  public void init()
  {
    try
    {
      jbInit();
    }
    catch(Exception e)
    {
      e.printStackTrace();
    }
  }

  // Component initialization
  private void jbInit() throws Exception
  {
    this.setSize(new Dimension(400,300));
    messagePanel1.setBackground(Color.cyan);
    messagePanel1.setYCoordinate(30);
    messagePanel1.addMouseListener(new java.awt.event.MouseAdapter()
    {
      public void mousePressed(MouseEvent e)
      {
        messagePanel1_mousePressed(e);
      }

      public void mouseReleased(MouseEvent e)
      {
        messagePanel1_mouseReleased(e);
      }
    });
    tick1.addTickListener(new EventDemo.TickListener()
    {
      public void handleTick(TickEvent e)
      {
        tick1_handleTick(e);
      }
    });
    this.getContentPane().add(messagePanel1, BorderLayout.CENTER);
  }
```

Listing 3.7   *ShowTickWithAnonymousAdapter.java*

```
void tick1_handleTick(TickEvent e)
{
  messagePanel1.setMessage("Tick count is " + e.getTickCount() +
    " and tick interval is " + e.getTickInterval());
}

void messagePanel1_mousePressed(MouseEvent e)
{
  tick1.suspend();
}

void messagePanel1_mouseReleased(MouseEvent e)
{
  tick1.resume();
}
}
```

Listing 3.7   *Continued*

handlers. In `tick1.addTickListener()`, the anonymous class implements the `TickListener` interface and the `handleTick` handler. These adapters were completely generated by JBuilder.

TIP

Reload the project to ensure that the changes in the Code Style page of the Project Properties dialog take effect in JBuilder 3.

NOTE

Since anonymous inner classes make the code condensed, from now on all the projects will use anonymous adapters for event handling.

Working with Existing Event Sets

You created `TickEvent` and `TickListener` in the section "Creating Custom Event Sets and Source Components." Most of the time you will not need to create event sets from scratch, since you will be able to use existing event sets. For example, suppose you don't need the tick count and tick interval contained in the Tick event. There is no need to create a `TickEvent` class; instead you can use `ActionEvent` and let the Tick generate an `ActionEvent` instance when a tick event occurs.

Example 3.4   Developing a Source Component Using Existing Event Sets

This example presents a new component that generates an `ActionEvent` when a tick event occurs. The new source component named `TickUsingActionEvent` is created as shown in Listing 3.8.

continues

```
package EventDemo;

import java.util.Vector;
import java.awt.event.*;

public class TickUsingActionEvent implements Runnable
{
  // A thread to control tick
  protected Thread thread = null;

  // Whether the thread is suspended
  private boolean suspended;

  // Store Tick listeners in a vector
  private Vector tickListenerList = new Vector();

  // Tick count and Tick interval
  private long tickCount = 0;
  private long tickInterval = 1000;

  public TickUsingActionEvent ()
  {
    thread = new Thread(this);
    thread.start();
  }

  public long getTickCount()
  {
    return tickCount;
  }

  public long getTickInterval()
  {
    return tickInterval;
  }

  public void setTickInterval(long interval)
  {
    tickInterval = interval;
  }

  // Run the thread
  public void run()
  {
    while (true)
    {
      try
      {
        Thread.sleep(tickInterval);
        synchronized (this)
        {
          while (suspended)
            wait();
        }
      }
      catch (InterruptedException e)
      { }
```

Listing 3.8   *TickUsingActionEvent.java*

```
      // Adjust Tick count
      tickCount++;

      // Fire TickEvent
      processEvent(new ActionEvent(this,
        ActionEvent.ACTION_PERFORMED, null));
    }
  }

  public synchronized void resume()
  {
    if (suspended)
    {
      suspended = false;
      notify();
    }
  }

  public synchronized void suspend()
  {
    suspended = true;
  }

  public synchronized void addActionListener(ActionListener l)
  {
    tickListenerList.addElement(l);
  }

  public synchronized void removeActionListener(ActionListener l)
  {
    tickListenerList.removeElement(l);
  }

  public void processEvent(ActionEvent e)
  {
    Vector v;

    synchronized (this)
    {
      v = (Vector)tickListenerList.clone();
    }

    for (int i=0; i < v.size(); i++)
    {
      ActionListener listener = (ActionListener)v.elementAt(i);
      listener.actionPerformed(e);
    }
  }
}
```

Follow the steps below to complete the example.

1. Reopen the project EventDemo.jpr and create ShowTickUsingActionEvent using the Applet Wizard.

2. Create TickUsingActionEvent as shown in Listing 3.8, compile, and place it in the Component palette.

continues

3. With ShowTickUsingActionEvent.java selected in the Navigation pane, choose the Design tab to display the UI Designer. Drop a `MessagePanel` component into the center of the applet to create `messagePanel1`. Change `messagePanel1`'s background to Cyan and `yCoordinate` to 30 in the Inspector.

4. Drop the `TickUsingActionEvent` component on the frame. You will see `tickUsingActionEvent1` created in the Component tree under the node Other.

5. With `tickUsingActionEvent1` selected in the Component tree, switch to the Events page of the Component Inspector. Select the `actionPerformed` event and double-click its value field in the Component Inspector. JBuilder generates the adapter and an empty event-handling method `tickUsingActionEvent1_actionPerformed()`. Fill in the following code in this method:

```
void tickUsingActionEvent1_actionPerformed(ActionEvent e)
{
    messagePanel1.setMessage("Tick count is " +
      tickUsingActionEvent1.getTickCount() +
       "and tick interval is "
      +tickUsingActionEvent1.getTickInterval());
}
```

TIP

The adapter for `ActionEvent` of a source object can be generated by double-clicking the object in the UI Designer. This is quicker than generating the adapter from the Inspector.

6. ShowTickUsingActionEvent.java is shown in Listing 3.9. Run ShowTickUsingActionEvent.java in the project to test the program. This program should run in the same way as Example 3.1.

```
package EventDemo;

import java.awt.*;
import java.awt.event.*;
import java.applet.*;
import javax.swing.*;
import MessagePanelDemo.*;

public class ShowTickUsingActionEven extends JApplet
{
  boolean isStandalone = false;
  MessagePanel messagePanel1 = new MessagePanel();
  TickUsingActionEvent tickUsingActionEvent1 =
    new TickUsingActionEvent();
```

Listing 3.9 *ShowTickUsingActionEvent.java*

```
      // Construct the applet
      public ShowTickUsingActionEven()
      {
      }

      // Initialize the applet
      public void init()
      {
        try
        {
          jbInit();
        }
        catch(Exception e)
        {
          e.printStackTrace();
        }
      }

      // Component initialization
      private void jbInit() throws Exception
      {
        this.setSize(new Dimension(400,300));
        messagePanel1.setBackground(Color.cyan);
        messagePanel1.setYCoordinate(30);
        tickUsingActionEvent1.addActionListener
          (new java.awt.event.ActionListener()
        {
          public void actionPerformed(ActionEvent e)
          {
            tickUsingActionEvent1_actionPerformed(e);
          }
        });
        this.getContentPane().add(messagePanel1, BorderLayout.CENTER);
      }

      void tickUsingActionEvent1_actionPerformed(ActionEvent e)
      {
        messagePanel1.setMessage("Tick count is " +
          tickUsingActionEvent1.getTickCount() + " and tick interval is "
          +tickUsingActionEvent1.getTickInterval());
      }
    }
```

Listing 3.9 *Continued*

Example Review

TickUsingActionEvent is very similar to the Tick component presented in Example 3.1 except that it utilizes ActionEvent to generate events and register listeners. Invoking the following constructor generates an ActionEvent.

```
new ActionEvent(this, ActionEvent.ACTION_PERFORMED, null);
```

The listener interface for ActionEvent is an ActionListener that contains a handler actionPerformed for the listener to implement. The registration methods addActionListener() and removeActionListener() are defined in the component for adding and removing listeners.

continues

The `TickEvent` class contains methods `getTickCount()` and `getTickInterval()`, but the `ActionEvent` class does not contain these methods. Therefore, when processing the event using `actionPerformed(ActionEvent e)` handler, you cannot get tick count or tick interval from e. To enable the listener to obtain tick count and tick interval, `getTickCount()` and `getTickInterval()` are defined in the `TickUsingActionEvent` class. Since `tickUsingActionEvent1` is an instance of `TickUsingActionEvent`, you can get tick count and tick interval from `tickUsing-ActionEvent1`.

Chapter Summary

This chapter took you inside the Java delegation model and showed you the basics on event sets, source components, and listener components. The event delegation model separates the tasks of generating events from handling events, thus making it possible to develop source components and listener components independently. Adapters are used to listen for events and delegate them to the right components for handling them.

You learned how to create a custom event like `TickEvent` by extending `java.util.EventObject` and an event listener interface like `TickListner` by extending `java.util.EventListener`. You can use custom event sets to create a source component like `Tick` and Java-provided event sets to create a source component like `TickUsingActionEvent`.

Chapter Review

3.1. If an event class is named *X*Event, what should you name its associated listener class? If an event listener interface is named *X*Listener, what should you name the registration methods in the source component?

3.2. Is an event class a subclass of `java.util.EventObject`? Is an event listener interface a subclass of `java.util.EventListener`?

3.3. Show the code that generates and fires the event in the `Tick` component in Listing 3.3.

3.4. How do you register events for multicasting or for unicasting?

3.5. How are the listeners notified of the events?

3.6. How do you use the Implement Interface Wizard?

3.7. What is a convenience adapter? What are the benefits of convenience adapters?

3.8. How do you set the Project Properties to generate anonymous adapters or standard adapters?

3.9. What does JBuilder generate for handling a button click action using standard adapters? What does JBuilder generate for handling a button click action using anonymous adapters?

3.10. The new operator cannot be used to create an instance of an interface. Why does JBuilder generate the anonymous adapter using new TickListener() in Listing 3.7?

3.11. How do you construct an ActionEvent?

Programming Exercises

3.1. Develop a project that meets the following requirements:

- Create a source component named MemoryWatch for monitoring memory. The component generates a MemoryEvent when the free memory space exceeds a specified highLimit or is below a specified lowLimit. The highLimit and lowLimit are customizable properties in MemoryWatch.

- Create an event set named MemoryEvent and MemoryListener. The MemoryEvent simply extends java.util.EventObject and contains two methods, freeMemory and totalMemory, which return the free memory and total memory of the system. The MemoryListener interface contains two handlers: sufficientMemory and insufficientMemory. The sufficientMemory method is invoked when the free memory space exceeds the specified high limit, and the insufficientMemory is invoked when the free memory space is lower than the specified low limit.

- Develop a listener component that displays free memory, total memory, and whether the memory is sufficient or insufficient when a MemoryEvent occurs.

DEVELOPING AND USING COMPONENTS

Objectives

- Understand the differences between writing components and using components.

- Become familiar with the component development process.

- Develop bean components using JBuilder's Bean Designer.

- Use the model-view approach to separate data and logic from the presentation of the data.

- Understand the application development process.

- Use JBuilder Deployment Wizard to deploy applications and applets.

Introduction

We developed the components `MessagePanel` and `NewMessagePanel` in Chapter 2, "Introduction to JavaBeans," and the components `Tick` and `TickUsingActionEvent` in Chapter 3, "Bean Events." From these examples, you learned the techniques of writing components. The techniques are not new. Developing bean components is nothing more than writing Java classes that follow some fairly strict naming conventions for accessor methods and event registration methods. There are, however, differences between developing components and using components. This chapter explores these differences, and, through comprehensive examples, introduces the process of developing beans and using them in rapid Java application development. You will learn how to use JBuilder's visual Bean Designer to rapidly develop bean components and create components using the model-view approach.

Developing Beans versus Using Beans

Throughout the book, you will develop beans and use beans to build projects. Sometimes, you will play the role of both bean writer and bean user. It is important to note the differences between developing beans and using beans.

From a user's perspective, a bean is an object that consists of properties, methods, and events. The user may use it in a builder tool or in scripting programming. The user creates a bean and customizes its behavior by changing properties and writing code to carry out responses to events.

From a writer's perspective, a bean is designed for use in a visual environment, where the bean properties and events are exposed during design time. In order to expose the properties and events of the bean in a builder tool, the bean writer must follow property and event design patterns.

There are three major differences between developing beans and using beans.

- A bean is a black box to the bean user. The user manipulates the bean through public accessor methods and events without knowing the implementation of the bean. However, the bean writer knows all the details of the bean if the bean is created from scratch. If the bean is derived from an existing bean, the writer has access to all the protected data fields and methods of the superclasses.

- Beans are usually designed for use by many different customers. To make your beans useful in a wide range of applications, they should provide a variety of ways for customization through properties, methods, and events.

- Beans are designed for reuse. Users can incorporate beans in many different combinations, orders, and environments. Therefore, you should design a bean that imposes no restrictions on what or when the user can do with it, design the properties to ensure that the user can set properties in any order, with any combination of values, and design events and methods to function independently of their order of occurrence at runtime.

Component Development Process

As in the development of any software, developing bean components requires an engineering approach that involves the following steps:

1. Understand the requirements of the bean and determine the functions it requires.

2. Design the properties, methods, and events to support the functions required by the bean.

3. Based on the requirements, decide whether to create a UI component or a non-UI component. A UI component must extend `java.awt.Component` or its subclass. A non-UI component can extend any appropriate class. A UI component can have drawings on it and can become part of the user interface of the application. A non-UI component is invisible on the UI Designer, but generally provides encapsulated functionality to interact with the UI components. The `MessagePanel` component in Example 2.1, "Writing a Simple Java Bean Component," is a UI component, but the `Tick` component in Example 3.1, "Creating a Custom Event Set and a Source Component," is a non-UI component.

4. Create properties. Choose the names for properties to follow the bean property naming convention. Decide whether to use the default property editor or a customized property editor. Creating a customized property editor will be introduced in Chapter 11, "Bean Introspection and Customization."

5. Create the customized events your component needs by writing their event classes and event listener interfaces.

6. Implement the code that generates and fires events. Implement event registration methods and choose the names according to the naming conventions.

7. Implement public methods. Component methods encapsulate the behavior of the component. They are standard Java methods, which can be called from other components. Unlike accessor methods, component methods cannot change the behavior of the bean during design time. The component methods are available only at runtime.

8. Create a `BeanInfo` class for the component to customize the exposure of the bean's properties and events, if necessary. How to create a component's `BeanInfo` class will be introduced in Chapter 11.

9. Compile, install the component in the Component palette, and test the component.

NOTE

The development process is cyclic. If the requirements are changed, you will have to redevelop or modify the component following the development process.

Components can be efficiently created using JBuilder's BeansExpress Wizard. In the following section, you will apply the development process and use the Beans-Express Wizard to create a component for an analog clock.

Using the BeansExpress Wizard to Create Properties

The BeansExpress Wizard is a visual bean designer that helps to create the Java-Beans component without writing extensive code. To activate the BeansExpress Wizard, select the Bean tab in the Content pane from the AppBrowser, as shown in Figure 4.1. The BeansExpress Wizard contains the following tabs:

- General: Displays general information about the bean. You can set the options for specifying "Use only core JDK and Swing classes" and "Support serialization."

- Properties: You can use the property designer to add or remove properties.

- BeanInfo: You can use the BeanInfo designer to customize the exposure of properties and events to the component users.

- Events: You can use the event designer to add or remove events that your component may generate.

- Property Editors: You can create customized property editors.

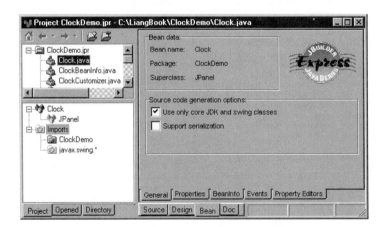

Figure 4.1   *You can use JBuilder's BeansExpress to assist in creating the bean component.*

You will learn how to use the property designer to create properties in Example 4.1, and how to use the event designer in Example 4.2. In Chapter 11, you will learn how to use the BeanInfo designer and the property editor designer to generate BeanInfo classes and custom property editors.

Example 4.1 Creating a Clock Component

This example creates a useful bean for displaying an analog clock. This bean allows the user to customize a clock through the following properties:

- secondHandColor: The color of the second hand.

- minuteHandColor: The color of the minute hand.

- hourHandColor: The color of the hour hand.

- headerColor: The color of header. Header is an optional title for the clock, displayed above the analog clock.

- digitalDateTimeColor: The color of the optional digital time, displayed below the analog clock.

- header: The contents of the header (a string).

- showingHeader: A boolean value indicating whether the header is displayed.

- showingDigitalDateTime: A boolean value indicating whether the digital time is displayed.

- dateStyle: An int value representing four formats for displaying date. The values are DateFormat.FULL (0), DateFormat.LONG (1), DateFormat.MEDIUM (2), DateFormat.SHORT (3).

- timeStyle: An int value representing four formats for displaying time. The values are DateFormat.FULL (0), DateFormat.LONG (1), DateFormat.MEDIUM (2), DateFormat.SHORT (3).

- usingTimeZoneID: A boolean value indicating whether the timeZoneID property is used to set the timeZoneOffset property.

- timeZoneID: A string representing a valid time zone. All the time zone IDs can be obtained in TimeZone.getAvailableIDs().

- timeZoneOffset: An int value representing a time zone offset from GMT. The valid values are between -12 and 12.

- running: A boolean value indicating whether the clock is running.

Figure 4.2 shows the properties of a Clock bean in the Component Inspector.

The Clock component also provides two public methods start() and stop() to let the component user start and stop the clock.

This example demonstrates how BeansExpress can be used to create the properties. Here are the steps in creating the component:

1. Create a new project named ClockDemo.jpr and create a Java class named Clock that extends javax.swing.JPanel using the New Java File Wizard.

continues

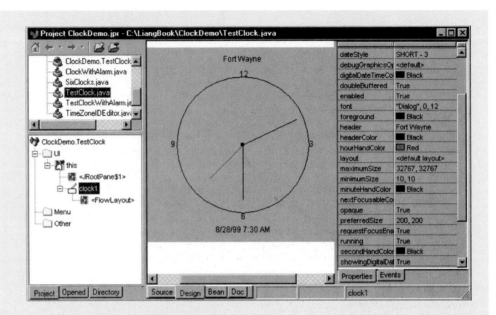

Figure 4.2   *When using the Clock bean, you can customize it to suit your needs with a variety of properties provided by the component.*

2. With Clock.java selected in the Navigation pane, choose the Bean tab in the Content pane to switch to Bean Designer, as shown in Figure 4.1.

3. Choose the Properties tab at the bottom of the Bean Designer to switch to the Properties page, as shown in Figure 4.3.

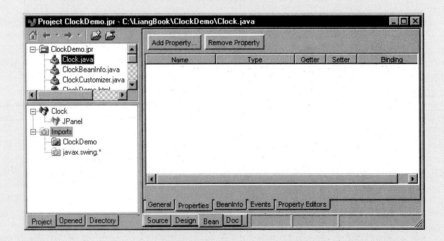

Figure 4.3   *You can add or remove properties from the Properties page in Bean Designer.*

4. Click the Add Property button to bring up the New Property dialog box, as shown in Figure 4.4. Enter `secondHandColor` in the Property Name

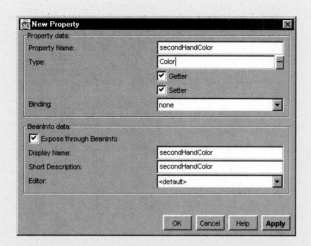

Figure 4.4   *The New Property dialog box lets you specify the property information, such as name, type, and editor.*

field and Color in the Type field. Press Apply to let JBuilder generate the source code for the property. If you choose the Source tab in the Content pane, you will see that the data member and the accessor methods were automatically generated.

5. Repeatedly apply Step 4 to add additional properties `minuteHandColor`, `hourHandColor`, `digitalTimeColor`, `headerColor`, `running`, `showingDigitalTime`, `showingHeader`, `header`, `timeZoneID`, `timeZoneOffset`, and `usingTimeZoneID`. The Properties page of the Bean Designer is shown in Figure 4.5.

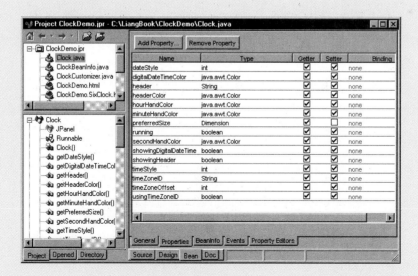

Figure 4.5   *The properties are displayed in the Properties page of the BeansExpress Wizard.*

continues

6. Modify the default implementation for the `setRunning()` method and set the default values of the properties as shown in Listing 4.1.

TIP

I recommend providing default values for properties for the following three reasons:

■ A default value gives the user an example of the property value.

■ Some builder tools do not display the property unless a default value is provided for it.

■ Using default values helps avoid runtime errors. For example, when using a property of object type, a null pointer exception would occur if the property were not initialized.

---

7. Choose Wizards, Implements to bring up the Implements Interface dialog box. Choose and click `java.lang.Runnable` from the dialog box to generate code for implementing this interface.

8. Declare an instance of `Thread`, named `thread`, for running the clock and drawing it.

9. Override the `paintComponent()` method to paint the clock every second as shown in Listing 4.1.

10. Create public methods `start()` and `stop()` for starting and stopping the clock as shown in Listing 4.1.

```java
package ClockDemo;

import java.awt.*;
import javax.swing.*;
import java.lang.Runnable;
import java.util.*;
import java.text.*;

public class Clock extends JPanel implements Runnable
{
  // Create a thread to control clock running
  protected transient Thread thread;
  private java.awt.Color secondHandColor = Color.black;
  private java.awt.Color minuteHandColor = Color.black;
  private java.awt.Color hourHandColor = Color.red;
  private java.awt.Color digitalDateTimeColor = Color.black;
  private java.awt.Color headerColor = Color.black;
  private boolean running;
  private boolean showingDigitalDateTime = true;
  // TimeStyle 0-FULL, 1-LONG, 2-MEDIUM, 3-SHORT
  private int timeStyle = 3;
  // DateStyle 0-FULL, 1-LONG, 2-MEDIUM, 3-SHORT
  private int dateStyle = 3;
  private boolean showingHeader = true;
```

Listing 4.1   *Clock.java*

```
private java.lang.String header = "Fort Wayne";
private java.lang.String timeZoneID = "CST";
private int timeZoneOffset;
private boolean usingTimeZoneID = true;

// Create TimeZone
protected TimeZone tz = TimeZone.getDefault();

public Clock()
{
  // Start clock
  setRunning(true);
}

public java.awt.Color getSecondHandColor()
{
  return secondHandColor;
}

public void setSecondHandColor(java.awt.Color newSecondHandColor)
{
  secondHandColor = newSecondHandColor;
}

public void setMinuteHandColor(java.awt.Color newMinuteHandColor)
{
  minuteHandColor = newMinuteHandColor;
}

public java.awt.Color getMinuteHandColor()
{
  return minuteHandColor;
}

public void setHourHandColor(java.awt.Color newHourHandColor)
{
  hourHandColor = newHourHandColor;
}

public java.awt.Color getHourHandColor()
{
  return hourHandColor;
}

public void setDigitalDateTimeColor
  (java.awt.Color newDigitalDateTimeColor)
{
  digitalDateTimeColor = newDigitalDateTimeColor;
}

public java.awt.Color getDigitalDateTimeColor()
{
  return digitalDateTimeColor;
}

public void setHeaderColor(java.awt.Color newHeaderColor)
{
  headerColor = newHeaderColor;
}
```

continues

```
        public java.awt.Color getHeaderColor()
        {
          return headerColor;
        }

        // Start the clock
        public void setRunning(boolean newRunning)
        {
          running = newRunning;
          if (running)
            start();
          else
            stop();
        }

        public boolean isRunning()
        {
          return running;
        }

        public void setShowingDigitalDateTime
          (boolean newShowingDigitalDateTime)
        {
          showingDigitalDateTime = newShowingDigitalDateTime;
        }

        public boolean isShowingDigitalDateTime()
        {
          return showingDigitalDateTime;
        }

        public void setTimeStyle(int newtimeStyle)
        {
          timeStyle = newtimeStyle;
        }

        public int getTimeStyle()
        {
          return timeStyle;
        }

        public void setDateStyle(int newDateStyle)
        {
          dateStyle = newDateStyle;
        }

        public int getDateStyle()
        {
          return dateStyle;
        }

        public void setShowingHeader(boolean newShowingHeader)
        {
          showingHeader = newShowingHeader;
        }

        public boolean isShowingHeader()
        {
          return showingHeader;
        }
```

Listing 4.1   *Continued*

```
public void setHeader(java.lang.String newHeader)
{
  header = newHeader;
}

public java.lang.String getHeader()
{
  return header;
}

public void setTimeZoneID(java.lang.String newTimeZoneID)
{
  timeZoneID = newTimeZoneID;
}

public java.lang.String getTimeZoneID()
{
  return timeZoneID;
}

public void setTimeZoneOffset(int newTimeZoneOffset)
{
  timeZoneOffset = newTimeZoneOffset;
}

public int getTimeZoneOffset()
{
  return tz.getRawOffset()/(1000*3600);
}

public void setUsingTimeZoneID(boolean newUsingTimeZoneID)
{
  usingTimeZoneID = newUsingTimeZoneID;
}

public boolean isUsingTimeZoneID()
{
  return usingTimeZoneID;
}

// Display the clock
public void paintComponent(Graphics g)
{
  super.paintComponent(g);

  int clockRadius =
    (int)(Math.min(getSize().width,getSize().height)*0.7*0.5);
  int centerx = (getSize().width)/2;
  int centery = (getSize().height)/2;

  // Draw circle
  g.setColor(Color.black);
  g.drawOval(centerx - clockRadius, centery - clockRadius,
    2*clockRadius, 2*clockRadius);
  g.drawString("12",centerx-5, centery-clockRadius);
  g.drawString("9",centerx-clockRadius-10,centery+3);
  g.drawString("3",centerx+clockRadius,centery+3);
  g.drawString("6",centerx-3,centery+clockRadius+10);
```

continues

```
            if (usingTimeZoneID)
              tz = TimeZone.getTimeZone(timeZoneID);
            else
              tz.setRawOffset(timeZoneOffset*1000*3600);

            // Get current time using GregorianCalendar
            GregorianCalendar cal = new GregorianCalendar(tz);

            // Draw second hand
            int s = (int)cal.get(GregorianCalendar.SECOND);
            int sLength = (int)(clockRadius*0.9);
            int secondx =
              (int)(centerx + sLength*Math.sin(s*(2*Math.PI/60)));
            int secondy =
              (int)(centery - sLength*Math.cos(s*(2*Math.PI/60)));
            g.setColor(secondHandColor);
            g.drawLine(centerx, centery, secondx, secondy);

            // Draw minute hand
            int m = (int)cal.get(GregorianCalendar.MINUTE);
            int mLength = (int)(clockRadius*0.8);
            int minutex =
              (int)(centerx + mLength*Math.sin(m*(2*Math.PI/60)));
            int minutey =
              (int)(centery - mLength*Math.cos(m*(2*Math.PI/60)));
            g.setColor(minuteHandColor);
            g.drawLine(centerx, centery, minutex, minutey);

            // Draw hour hand
            int h = (int)cal.get(GregorianCalendar.HOUR_OF_DAY);
            int hLength = (int)(clockRadius*0.7);
            int hourx =
              (int)(centerx + hLength*Math.sin((h+m/60.0)*(2*Math.PI/12)));
            int houry =
              (int)(centery - hLength*Math.cos((h+m/60.0)*(2*Math.PI/12)));
            g.setColor(hourHandColor);
            g.drawLine(centerx, centery, hourx, houry);

            if (showingHeader)
            {
              // Display header
              FontMetrics fm = g.getFontMetrics();
              g.setColor(headerColor);
              g.drawString(header, (getSize().width -
                fm.stringWidth(header))/2, (centery-clockRadius)/2);
            }

            if (showingDigitalDateTime)
            {
              // Set display format in specified style, locale and timezone
              DateFormat myFormat = DateFormat.getDateTimeInstance
                (dateStyle, timeStyle, getLocale());
              myFormat.setTimeZone(tz);

              // Display time
              String today = myFormat.format(cal.getTime());
              FontMetrics fm = g.getFontMetrics();
              g.setColor(digitalDateTimeColor);
              g.drawString(today, (getSize().width -
                fm.stringWidth(today))/2, centery+clockRadius+30);
            }
          }
```

Listing 4.1 *Continued*

```
      // Run the clock
      public void run()
      {
        // TODO: implement this java.lang.Runnable method;
        while (true)
        {
          if (thread == null) return;

          try
          {
            thread.sleep(1000);
          }
          catch (InterruptedException e)
          {}
          repaint();
        }
      }

      // Start the clock
      public void start()
      {
        if (thread == null)
        {
          thread = new Thread(this);
          thread.start();
        }
      }

      // Stop the clock
      public void stop()
      {
        if (thread != null)
        {
          thread = null;
        }
      }

      // Set the preferred size for the clock
      public Dimension getPreferredSize()
      {
        return new Dimension(200, 200);
      }
    }
```

Listing 4.1 *Continued*

To test the component, compile Clock.java and install it in the Component palette. You may simply drop the bean on the UI Designer, change its properties from the Component Inspector, and see how the bean responds to the changes. Below you will use it to develop a program that shows a set of clocks for displaying the time in London, Paris, Fort Wayne, Chicago, Denver, and San Francisco.

Here are the steps to complete the project.

1. Create a new applet named SixClocks in the ClockDemo project using the Applet Wizard. With SixClocks.java selected in the Navigation pane, switch to the UI Designer. Set layout of the applet to GridLayout. In the

continues

Component Inspector of gridLayout1, set rows to 2, hgap to 10, and vgap to 10, so as to have three clocks in one row and three in the other row, with a 10-pixel gap horizontally and vertically.

2. Add six clocks to the applet. Set the appropriate header and time zone ID for each clock. The generated source code for SixClocks.java is shown in Listing 4.2. Figure 4.6 contains a sample run of the program.

```java
package ClockDemo;

import java.awt.*;
import java.awt.event.*;
import java.applet.*;
import javax.swing.*;
import java.util.Locale;

public class SixClocks extends JApplet
{
  boolean isStandalone = false;
  GridLayout gridLayout1 = new GridLayout();
  Clock clock1 = new Clock();
  Clock clock2 = new Clock();
  Clock clock3 = new Clock();
  Clock clock4 = new Clock();
  Clock clock5 = new Clock();
  Clock clock6 = new Clock();

  // Construct the applet
  public SixClocks()
  {
  }

  // Initialize the applet
  public void init()
  {
    try
    {
      jbInit();
    }
    catch(Exception e)
    {
      e.printStackTrace();
    }
  }

  // Component initialization
  private void jbInit() throws Exception
  {
    this.setSize(new Dimension(400,300));
    this.getContentPane().setLayout(gridLayout1);
    gridLayout1.setHgap(10);
    gridLayout1.setRows(2);
    gridLayout1.setVgap(10);
    clock1.setHeader("London");
    clock1.setTimeZoneID("GMT");
    clock2.setLocale(Locale.FRANCE);
    clock2.setDateStyle(1);
```

Listing 4.2   *SixClocks.java*

```
            clock2.setHeader("Paris");
            clock2.setTimeZoneID("GMT");
            clock3.setTimeZoneID("IET");
            clock4.setHeader("Chicago");
            clock5.setTimeZoneID("MST");
            clock6.setTimeZoneID("PST");
            clock6.setHeader("San Francisco");
            clock5.setHeader("Denver");
            this.getContentPane().add(clock1, null);
            this.getContentPane().add(clock2, null);
            this.getContentPane().add(clock3, null);
            this.getContentPane().add(clock4, null);
            this.getContentPane().add(clock5, null);
            this.getContentPane().add(clock6, null);
        }
    }
```

Listing 4.2 *Continued*

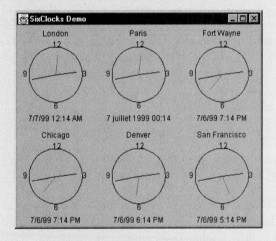

Figure 4.6 *The Clock bean is used to develop a set of six clocks.*

Example Review

In the `Clock` component, `thread` is an instance of `Thread`. Since it cannot be serialized, the `transient` modifier was used to mark it so that `thread` is not stored when a `Clock` object is stored. If `transient` was not used, this example would work fine, because no objects are stored during design time in JBuilder. However, it might be erroneous if it is used in another development tool. To ensure portability, make your beans serializable by marking `transient` on all nonserializable data fields. Bean serialization will be covered in Chapter 9, "Bean Persistence, Versioning, and Using Beans in Other Tools."

Since the `Thread thread` is `protected` rather than `private`, `thread` can be referenced in a subclass of `Clock` in Example 9.4, "Making the Clock Component Persistent," and in Example 9.5, "Using the `Externalizable` Interface," of Chapter 9.

continues

To make the bean versatile and useful, a variety of properties are provided in Clock. For instance, you can set the clock using the time zone ID or using the offset to the GMT time, whichever is convenient.

NOTE

The timeZoneOffset value is automatically adjusted when timeZoneID is changed. However, the reversal is not true. A time zone may have several IDs. For instance, IET (Indiana Eastern Time) and CST are the same during summer, and IET and EST are the same during winter. Therefore, when you set the timeZoneOffset property, the timezoneID property cannot be automatically adjusted.

TIP

When adding components to a container of GridLayout, add them column by column. For instance, when dropping the second Clock into the applet, place it into the second row rather than the first. If you want the second clock to appear in the same row next to the first clock, modify the source code after all six clocks are created, so that the following two lines appear together in this order:

```
this.add(clock1, null);
this.add(clock2, null);
```

Using the Bean Designer to Create Events

In the preceding example you created a Clock component. Now your customers want to have an alarm clock. In this section, you will learn how to use the Bean Designer to help develop a new clock component that fires an ActionEvent for the alarm.

Example 4.2 Creating an Alarm Clock

This example creates an alarm clock, named ClockWithAlarm, that extends the Clock component built in Example 4.1. This component contains two new properties:

- alarmDate: is a string consisting of year, month, and day, separated by commas. For example, 1998,5,13 represents the year 1998, month 5, and day 13.

- alarmTime: is a string consisting of hour, minute, and second, separated by commas. For example, 10,45,2 represents 10 hours, 45 minutes, and 2 seconds.

When the clock time matches the alarm time, `ClockWithAlarm` fires an `ActionEvent`.

Follow the steps below to create the `ClockWithAlarm` component.

1. Reopen the ClockDemo project created in Example 4.1. Create a new class `ClockWithAlarm` that extends `Clock` using the New Java File Wizard.

2. With ClockWithAlarm.java selected in the Navigation pane, choose the Bean tab in the Content pane to switch to the Bean Designer. Add properties `alarmDate` and `alarmTime` using the Properties page in the Bean Designer.

3. Choose the Events tab in the Bean Designer to switch to the Events page, as shown in Figure 4.7. Check the box for Action in the "Fires these types of events" column. Checking it triggers JBuilder to automatically generate the event registration methods and the code for firing the `ActionEvent`. Unchecking the box would remove the code.

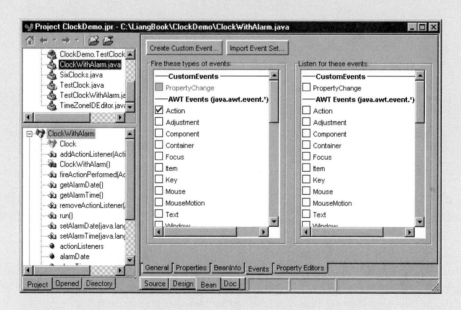

Figure 4.7   *You can use the Bean Designer to generate event registration methods and the code for firing events.*

4. Initialize `alarmTime` and `alarmDate` in the `ClockWithAlarm` constructor, and override the `run()` method to run the clock and fire the `ActionEvent` when the clock matches the alarm time, as shown in Listing 4.3.

```java
package ClockDemo;

import java.awt.*;
import java.util.*;
import java.awt.event.*;

public class ClockWithAlarm extends Clock
{
  private java.lang.String alarmDate;
  private java.lang.String alarmTime;
  private transient Vector actionListeners;

  public ClockWithAlarm()
  {
    super();

    // Get initial date and time
    GregorianCalendar cal = new GregorianCalendar(tz);

    // Initialize alarm date, which consists of
    // year, month, and date, separated by commas.
    alarmDate = cal.get(cal.YEAR) + "," + cal.get(cal.MONTH)
      + "," + cal.get(cal.DATE);

    // Initialize alarm time, which consists of
    // hour, minute, and second, separated by commas.
    alarmTime = cal.get(cal.HOUR) + "," + cal.get(cal.MINUTE)
      + "," + cal.get(cal.SECOND);
  }

  public void run()
  {
    while (true)
    {
      try
      {
        thread.sleep(1000);
      }
      catch (InterruptedException e)
      {}
      repaint();

      // Fire tick event if the current time matches alarm time
      GregorianCalendar rightNow = new GregorianCalendar(tz);
      String rightNowDate = rightNow.get(rightNow.YEAR)
        + "," + rightNow.get(rightNow.MONTH) + "," +
        rightNow.get(rightNow.DATE);
      String rightNowTime = rightNow.get(rightNow.HOUR)
        + "," + rightNow.get(rightNow.MINUTE) + "," +
        rightNow.get(rightNow.SECOND);
      if (rightNowDate.equals(alarmDate)
        && rightNowTime.equals(alarmTime))
        fireActionPerformed(new ActionEvent
          (this, ActionEvent.ACTION_PERFORMED, null));
    }
  }
```

Listing 4.3   *ClockWithAlarm.java*

```
      public void setAlarmDate(java.lang.String newAlarmDate)
      {
        alarmDate = newAlarmDate;
      }

      public java.lang.String getAlarmDate()
      {
        return alarmDate;
      }

      public void setAlarmTime(java.lang.String newAlarmTime)
      {
        alarmTime = newAlarmTime;
      }

      public java.lang.String getAlarmTime()
      {
        return alarmTime;
      }

      // Generated by JBuilder
      public synchronized void removeActionListener(ActionListener l)
      {
        if (actionListeners != null && actionListeners.contains(l))
        {
          Vector v = (Vector) actionListeners.clone();
          v.removeElement(l);
          actionListeners = v;
        }
      }

      // Generated by JBuilder
      public synchronized void addActionListener(ActionListener l)
      {
        Vector v = actionListeners ==
          null ? new Vector(2) : (Vector) actionListeners.clone();
        if (!v.contains(l))
        {
          v.addElement(l);
          actionListeners = v;
        }
      }

      // Generated by JBuilder
      protected void fireActionPerformed(ActionEvent e)
      {
        if (actionListeners != null)
        {
          Vector listeners = actionListeners;
          int count = listeners.size();
          for (int i = 0; i < count; i++)
            ((ActionListener) listeners.elementAt(i)).actionPerformed(e);
        }
      }
    }
```

Listing 4.3 *Continued*

To test the ClockWithAlarm component, follow the steps below to create an applet that makes a sound when the clock alarms.

continues

1. Compile `ClockWithAlarm` and install it in the Component palette. Create an applet named `TestClockWithAlarm` using the Applet Wizard.

2. With TestClockWithAlarm.java selected in the Navigation pane, switch to the UI Designer in the Content pane. Set the `layout` to `BorderLayout` for the applet. Drop a `ClockWithAlarm` to the applet to create `clockWithAlarm1` and set its `alarmDate` and `alarmTime` to a later time, as shown in Figure 4.8.

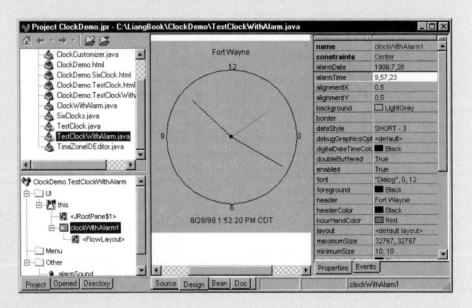

Figure 4.8   `alarmDate` *and* `alarmTime` *are the two new properties in the* `ClockWithAlarm` *component.*

3. Double-click `clockWithAlarm1` in the UI Designer to generate the handler for handling the alarm event.

4. Declare an `AudioClip` instance named `alarmSound` for playing sound file alarmSound.au, create the audio clip in the `jbInit()` method, and complete the `clockWithAlarm1_actionPerformed` handler, as shown in Listing 4.4.

```
package ClockDemo;

import java.awt.*;
import java.awt.event.*;
import java.applet.*;
import javax.swing.*;
import java.net.URL;
```

Listing 4.4   *TestClockWithAlarm.java*

```java
public class TestClockWithAlarm extends JApplet
{
  boolean isStandalone = false;
  ClockWithAlarm clockWithAlarm1 = new ClockWithAlarm();

  // Declare audio clip for alarm sound
  AudioClip alarmSound;

  // Construct the applet
  public TestClockWithAlarm()
  {
  }

  // Initialize the applet
  public void init()
  {
    try
    {
      jbInit();
    }
    catch(Exception e)
    {
      e.printStackTrace();
    }
  }

  // Component initialization
  private void jbInit() throws Exception
  {
    this.setSize(new Dimension(400,300));
    clockWithAlarm1.addActionListener
      (new java.awt.event.ActionListener()
    {
      public void actionPerformed(ActionEvent e)
      {
        clockWithAlarm1_actionPerformed(e);
      }
    });
    clockWithAlarm1.setTimeStyle(0);
    clockWithAlarm1.setAlarmTime("9,57,23");
    this.getContentPane().add(clockWithAlarm1, BorderLayout.CENTER);

    // Get the URL for the file name
    URL url = this.getClass().getResource("alarmSound.au");

    // Get the audio clip
    alarmSound = Applet.newAudioClip(url);
  }

  // Main method
  public static void main(String[] args)
  {
    TestClockWithAlarm applet = new TestClockWithAlarm();
    applet.isStandalone = true;
    JFrame frame = new JFrame();
    frame.setTitle("Applet Frame");
    frame.getContentPane().add(applet, BorderLayout.CENTER);
    applet.init();
    applet.start();
    frame.setSize(400,320);
```

continues

```
          Dimension d = Toolkit.getDefaultToolkit().getScreenSize();
          frame.setLocation((d.width - frame.getSize().width) / 2,
              (d.height - frame.getSize().height) / 2);
          frame.setVisible(true);
      }

      void clockWithAlarm1_actionPerformed(ActionEvent e)
      {
          // Play alarm sound
          alarmSound.play();
      }
  }
```

Listing 4.4   *Continued*

Example Review

When designing a component, you may have two conflicting objectives. On the one hand, you want the bean to be simple, so that it will not intimidate an inexperienced user; on the other hand, you want the bean to be comprehensive, so that it will meet the needs of a variety of customers in various applications. The only way to resolve the conflict is to make several versions of the component available, and let each user choose the one that suits his needs. As in the case of the clock, if you don't need the alarm function, you could simply choose Clock rather than ClockWithAlarm.

ClockWithAlarm extends Clock with the capability of firing an ActionEvent when the clock time matches the alarm time. The run() method is overridden to repaint the clock every second and check to see whether the current time matches the alarm time. When they match, an ActionEvent is fired.

The Bean Designer generates the event registration methods and the code for firing ActionEvent. In Example 3.1, "Creating Custom Event Sets and a Source Component," and Example 3.4, "Developing Source Component Using Existing Event Sets," you hand-coded the registration methods and the events firing methods for the Tick component and the TickUsingActionEvent component. The Bean Designer makes creating beans easy.

The test program makes a sound for the alarm. If you wish to embed the task of playing the audio in the ClockWithAlarm component, declare and create an AudioClip instance, say alarmSound, for alarmSound.au, in the ClockWithAlarm class. Play the alarmSound when the current time matches the specified alarm time.

The test program can run as an applet as well as an application. The newAudio-Clip(url) method is a new static method in the Applet class in Java 2 for creating an AudioClip in an applet or in an application.

There is an annoying problem in this example. When the alarm starts, the clock pauses. The clock resumes only after the audio clip finishes playing. To fix this problem, play the audio clip on a separate thread, as suggested in Exercise 3 of this chapter.

NOTE
When entering `alarmDate` and `alarmTime`, you must follow the pattern. Do not pad zeros before the number. For example, use 4 rather than 04 for number 4.

Developing Components Using the Model-View Approach

The model-view approach is a way of developing components by separating data storage and handling from the visual representation of the data. The component for storing and handling data, known as a *model*, contains the actual contents of the component. The component for presenting the data, known as a *view*, handles all essential component behaviors. It is the view that comes to mind when you think of the component. It does all the displaying of the components.

The major benefits of separating a component into a model and a view are the following:

- It makes multiple views possible so that data can be shared through the same model. For example, a model storing student names can simultaneously be displayed in a combo box or in a list box.

- It simplifies the task of writing complex applications and makes system maintenance easier. Changes can be made to the view without affecting the model, and vice versa.

A model contains data, whereas a view makes the information accessible and may allow the data to be modified. Once a view is associated with a model, it immediately displays updates to the model. This ensures that all the views of the model display the same data consistently. To achieve consistency and synchronize the model with its dependent views, the model should notify the views when there is a change in a property in the model that is used in the view. In response to a change notification, the view is responsible for redisplaying the viewing area affected by the property change.

Prior to JDK 1.1, you have to create a model by extending the `java.util.Observable` class and create a view by implementing the `java.util.Observer` interface. There are many drawbacks to developing components with `Observable` and `Observer`:

1. `Observable` and `Observer` were introduced in JDK 1.0 and their use is not consistent with the JDK 1.1 event model.

2. The `Observable/Observer` pair architecture is inflexible. You need a third class, referred to as *controller*, which attaches the model to a view. You can attach a model to multiple views, but it is difficult to attach multiple models to a view.

With the arrival of the new Java event delegation model, using `Observable` and `Observer` is obsolete. The JDK event delegation model provides a superior architecture for supporting model-view component development. The model can be implemented as a source with appropriate event and event listener registration methods. The view can be implemented as a listener. To enable the selection of the model during design time in a builder tool, simply add the model as a property in the view. You can easily create a property for each kind of model in the view with the event delegation model, but this task would be difficult with the Observable/Observer architecture.

Example 4.3 Developing Model-View Components

This example demonstrates the development of components using the model-view approach with the event delegation model. The example creates a model named `CircleModel`, and its two dependent views, named `CircleView` and `CircleEditor`. `CircleView` draws a circle according to the properties of the circle and enables changes that increase the circle's radius by a left mouse click and changes that decrease it by a right mouse click. `CircleEditor` enables editing of the `radius` property in a text field. An applet is created to host the instances of `CircleModel`, `CircleView`, and `CircleEditor` and test the interaction among these instances. A sample run of the applet is shown in Figure 4.9.

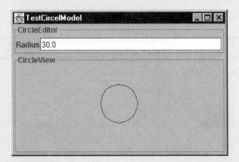

Figure 4.9   *A* `CircleEditor` *is shown on the north, and a* `CircleView` *is shown in the center of the applet. A* `CircleModel` *is shared by both* `CircleEditor` *and* `CircleView`.

The `CircleModel` contains the following properties:

- radius: The radius of the circle.
- filled: A boolean value indicating whether the circle is filled with a color.
- color: The color used to fill in the circle.

When a property value is changed, the `CircleModel` generates an `ActionEvent` and notifies its views of the associated change. Here are the steps in creating `CircleModel`:

1. Create a project named ModelViewDemo.jpr. Use the New Java File Wizard to create a template for CircleModel.java.

2. With CircleModel.java selected in the Navigation pane, choose the Bean tab in the Content pane to start the Bean Designer. In the Properties page of the Bean Designer, click the Add Property button to add properties `radius`, `filled`, and `color`.

3. In the Events page of the Bean Designer, check Action in the section "Fire these types of events" to generate the code for firing and registering `ActionEvent`.

4. Modify `setRadius()`, `setFilled()`, and `setColor()` methods to invoke the `fireActionPerformed()` method upon a property change, as shown in Listing 4.5.

```
package ModelViewDemo;

import java.awt.event.*;
import java.util.*;

public class CircleModel
{
  private double radius = 20;
  private boolean filled;
  private java.awt.Color color;

  private transient Vector actionListeners;

  public CircleModel()
  {
  }

  public double getRadius()
  {
    return radius;
  }

  public void setRadius(double newRadius)
  {
    radius = newRadius;
```

continues

Listing 4.5   *CircleModel.java*

```
      // Notify the listener for the change on radius
      fireActionPerformed(
        new ActionEvent(this, ActionEvent.ACTION_PERFORMED, "radius"));
    }

    public void setFilled(boolean newFilled)
    {
      filled = newFilled;

      // Notify the listener for the change on filled
      fireActionPerformed(
        new ActionEvent(this, ActionEvent.ACTION_PERFORMED, "filled"));
    }

    public boolean isFilled()
    {
      return filled;
    }

    public void setColor(java.awt.Color newColor)
    {
      color = newColor;

      // Notify the listener for the change on color
      fireActionPerformed(
        new ActionEvent(this, ActionEvent.ACTION_PERFORMED, "color"));
    }

    public java.awt.Color getColor()
    {
      return color;
    }

    public synchronized void removeActionListener(ActionListener l)
    {
      if (actionListeners != null && actionListeners.contains(l))
      {
        Vector v = (Vector) actionListeners.clone();
        v.removeElement(l);
        actionListeners = v;
      }
    }

    public synchronized void addActionListener(ActionListener l)
    {
      Vector v = actionListeners ==
        null ? new Vector(2) : (Vector) actionListeners.clone();
      if (!v.contains(l))
      {
        v.addElement(l);
        actionListeners = v;
      }
    }

    protected void fireActionPerformed(ActionEvent e)
    {
      if (actionListeners != null)
      {
        Vector listeners = actionListeners;
        int count = listeners.size();
        for (int i = 0; i < count; i++)
          ((ActionListener) listeners.elementAt(i)).actionPerformed(e);
      }
    }
  }
```

Listing 4.5   *Continued*

134

Follow the steps below to create the `CircleView` component.

1. Choose File, New to display the Object Gallery. Click the JavaBean icon in the Object Gallery to display the JavaBean Wizard. Create `CircleView` that extends `javax.swing.JPanel` using this wizard. The generated JavaBean uses the `BoderLayout` in the panel.

2. With CircleView.java selected in the Navigation pane, choose the Bean tab in the Content pane to start the Bean Designer. In the Properties page of the Bean Designer, add a property named `model` with type `CircleModel`.

3. In the Event page, check the Action box in the section "Listen for these events" to implement the `ActionListener` for `CircleView`, as shown in Figure 4.10. You could equally well use the Implement Interface Wizard to generate the code for implementing the `ActionListener` interface, but using the Bean Designer is more convenient.

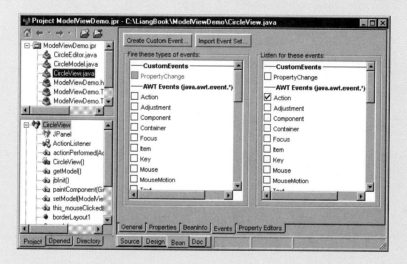

Figure 4.10   *You can generate the code for implementing an event listener interface from the Bean Designer.*

NOTE
The "listen for these events" wizard in Bean Designer only generates listeners for an event listener interface, while the Implement Interface Wizard can generate the code for implementing all kinds of interfaces.

4. Implement the `actionPerformed()` method to add the `repaint()` method to repaint the circle upon receiving a property change notification from the model. Implement the `paintComponent()` method to paint the circle in the center of the panel.

continues

5. Implement the `setModel()` method to set the new model and register the view with the model, as shown in Listing 4.6.

6. Choose the Design tab to switch to the UI Designer. In the Events page of `CircleView`, double-click the value field of the `mouseClicked()` handler to generate the code for handling mouse-clicked events. Implement the `mouseClicked()` method to handle the right-button click for increasing radius and the left-button click for decreasing radius, as shown in Listing 4.6.

```java
package ModelViewDemo;

import java.awt.*;
import javax.swing.JPanel;
import java.awt.event.*;

public class CircleView extends JPanel implements ActionListener
{
  BorderLayout borderLayout1 = new BorderLayout();
  private ModelViewDemo.CircleModel model;

  public CircleView()
  {
    try
    {
      jbInit();
    }
    catch(Exception ex)
    {
      ex.printStackTrace();
    }
  }

  private void jbInit() throws Exception
  {
    this.addMouseListener(new java.awt.event.MouseAdapter()
    {

      public void mouseClicked(MouseEvent e)
      {
        this_mouseClicked(e);
      }
    });
    this.setLayout(borderLayout1);
  }

  // Set the model
  public void setModel(ModelViewDemo.CircleModel newModel)
  {
    model = newModel;

    if (model != null)
    {
      // Register the view as listener for the model
      model.addActionListener(this);
    }
    else
    {
      model.removeActionListener(this);
    }
```

Listing 4.6   *CircleView.java*

```java
      repaint();
    }

    public ModelViewDemo.CircleModel getModel()
    {
      return model;
    }

    public void actionPerformed(ActionEvent e)
    {
      repaint();
    }

    public void paintComponent(Graphics g)
    {
      super.paintComponent(g);

      if (model == null) return;

      g.setColor(model.getColor());

      int xCenter = getSize().width/2;
      int yCenter = getSize().height/2;
      int radius = (int)model.getRadius();

      if (model.isFilled())
      {
        g.fillOval(xCenter - radius, yCenter - radius,
          2*radius, 2*radius);
      }
      else
      {
        g.drawOval(xCenter - radius, yCenter - radius,
          2*radius, 2*radius);
      }
    }

    void this_mouseClicked(MouseEvent e)
    {
      if (model == null) return;

      if (e.isMetaDown())
        model.setRadius(model.getRadius()-5);
      else
        model.setRadius(model.getRadius()+5);
    }
  }
```

Listing 4.6   *Continued*

Follow the steps below to create the CircleEditor component.

1. Use the JavaBean Wizard to create a CircleEditor that extends javax.swing.JPanel.

2. With CircleEditor.java selected in the Navigation pane, choose the Design tab to switch to the UI Designer. Drop a JLabel to the west of CircleEditor, and change the text of the label to Radius. Drop a JTextField to the center of CircleEditor and rename it jtfRadius.

continues

137

3. Choose the Bean tab to switch to the Bean Designer. Add a property named model with type CircleModel. In the Events page of the Bean Designer, check Action in the section "Listen for these events" to generate code for implementing ActionListener. Modify the setModel() method to register the view with the model, as shown in Listing 4.7, and implement the actionPerformed() method to set the radius from the model.

4. To enable CircleEditor to edit the radius in the jtfRadius text field, switch to the UI Designer and double-click jtfRadius to generate jtfRadius_actionPerformed() method and its associated event adapter. Implement jtfRadius_actionPerformed() to set a new radius in the model, as shown in Listing 4.7.

```java
package ModelViewDemo;

import java.awt.*;
import javax.swing.*;
import java.awt.event.*;

public class CircleEditor extends JPanel implements ActionListener
{
  BorderLayout borderLayout1 = new BorderLayout();
  JLabel jLabel1 = new JLabel();
  JTextField jtfRadius = new JTextField();
  private ModelViewDemo.CircleModel model;

  public CircleEditor()
  {
    try
    {
      jbInit();
    }
    catch(Exception ex)
    {
      ex.printStackTrace();
    }
  }

  private void jbInit() throws Exception
  {
    jLabel1.setText("Radius");
    this.setLayout(borderLayout1);
    jtfRadius.addActionListener(new java.awt.event.ActionListener()
    {
      public void actionPerformed(ActionEvent e)
      {
        jtfRadius_actionPerformed(e);
      }
    });
    this.add(jLabel1, BorderLayout.WEST);
    this.add(jtfRadius, BorderLayout.CENTER);
  }

  public void setModel(ModelViewDemo.CircleModel newModel)
  {
```

Listing 4.7   *CircleEditor.java*

```
        model = newModel;

        if (model != null)
        {
          // Register the view as listener for the model
          model.addActionListener(this);
        }
        else
        {
          model.removeActionListener(this);
        }
      }

      public ModelViewDemo.CircleModel getModel()
      {
        return model;
      }

      public void actionPerformed(ActionEvent e)
      {
        if (model != null)
          if (e.getActionCommand().equals("radius"))
            jtfRadius.setText(
              new Double(model.getRadius()).toString());
      }

      void jtfRadius_actionPerformed(ActionEvent e)
      {
        model.setRadius(
          new Double(jtfRadius.getText()).doubleValue());
      }
    }
```

Listing 4.7 *Continued*

After creating a model and two views, you are ready to put them together in an applet. Here are the steps in creating this applet:

1. Create an applet named TestCircleModel using the Applet Wizard.

2. Install CircleModel, CircleView, and CircleEditor to the Component palette. In the UI Designer for TestCircleModel.java, drop a CircleView to the center of the applet to create circleView1, and drop a CircleEditor to the north of the applet to create circleEditor1.

3. Set the border property for circleEditor to Titled to create titleBorder1. You will see titledBorder1 in the Component tree. Set the title of titledBorder1 to CircleEditor. Similarly, create a title named CircleView for circleView1.

4. Set the model property of circleView1 and circleEditor1 to circleModel1, as shown in Figure 4.11.

5. In the Inspector for circleModel1, change radius to 40, color to Blue, and filled to True. You will see a circle to be drawn accordingly in circleView1, as shown in Figure 4.12. The code for TestCircleModel is shown in Listing 4.8.

continues

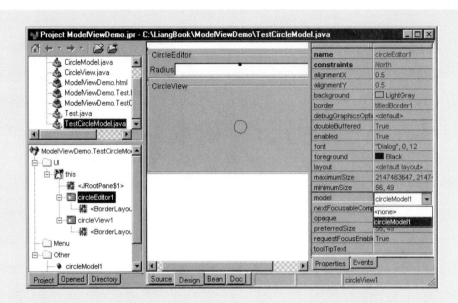

Figure 4.11   `circleModel1` *appears in the combo box of the* `model` *property in the Inspector for* `circleEditor1`.

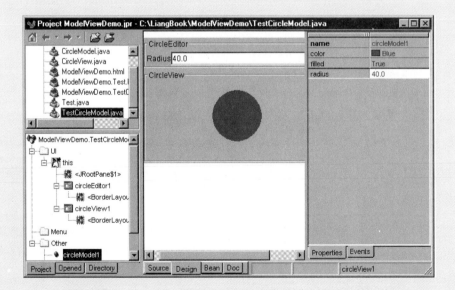

Figure 4.12   *Updates of* `circleModel1` *are immediately shown in* `circleView1` *in the App-Browser.*

```
            package ModelViewDemo;

            import java.awt.*;
            import java.awt.event.*;
            import java.applet.*;
            import javax.swing.*;
            import javax.swing.border.*;

            public class TestCircleModel extends JApplet
            {
              boolean isStandalone = false;
              CircleModel circleModel1 = new CircleModel();
              CircleEditor circleEditor1 = new CircleEditor();
              CircleView circleView1 = new CircleView();
              TitledBorder titledBorder1;
              TitledBorder titledBorder2;

              // Construct the applet
              public TestCircleModel()
              {
              }

              // Initialize the applet
              public void init()
              {
                try
                {
                  jbInit();
                }
                catch(Exception e)
                {
                  e.printStackTrace();
                }
              }

              // Component initialization
              private void jbInit() throws Exception
              {
                titledBorder1 = new TitledBorder("");
                titledBorder2 = new TitledBorder("");
                this.setSize(new Dimension(400,300));
                circleView1.setBorder(titledBorder2);
                circleView1.setModel(circleModel1);
                circleEditor1.setBorder(titledBorder1);
                circleEditor1.setModel(circleModel1);
                circleModel1.setRadius(40.0);
                circleModel1.setFilled(true);
                circleModel1.setColor(Color.blue);
                titledBorder1.setTitle("CircleEditor");
                titledBorder2.setTitle("CircleView");
                this.getContentPane().add(circleEditor1, BorderLayout.NORTH);
                this.getContentPane().add(circleView1, BorderLayout.CENTER);
              }
            }
```

Listing 4.8   *TestCircleModel.java*

continues

Example Review

The model stores and handles data, and the view is responsible for presenting data. The fundamental issue in the model-view approach is to ensure consistency between the views and the model. Any change in the model should be notified to the dependent views, and all the views should display the same data consistently. You can change the radius either by entering a value in the radius text field in `circleEditor1` or by clicking the left or right mouse button to increase or decrease it in `circleView1`. Both views will display the same radius at the same time.

All the code in CircleModel.java was automatically generated by JBuilder except that you added the code in `setRadius()`, `setFilled()`, and `setColor()` to invoke the `fireActionPerformed()` method. All the code in `CircleView` and `CircleEditor` was automatically generated except that you modified the `setModel()` method and the methods for handling mouse-click events in `CircleView` and action events in `CircleEditor`. Finally, all the code in TestCircle.java was automatically generated.

The `setModel()` method in `CircleView` and `CircleEditor` set a new model and registered the view with the model by invoking the model's `addActionListener` method. This is the preferred approach to implementing the view. It simplifies the use of the model-view components. If registration were not done in the `setModel()` method, you would have to attach the view to the model in `TestCircle`.

Rapid Application Development Process

Rapid Application Development, or RAD, is a software development technology introduced in the 1980s by researchers at the Xerox Palo Alto Research Lab. This technology for developing programs efficiently and effectively has been successfully implemented in program development tools like Visual Basic, Delphi, Power Builder, and Oracle Developer 2000, among many others. Using a RAD tool, projects can be developed quickly and efficiently with minimum coding. Projects developed using RAD are easy to modify and easy to maintain. The key elements in a Java RAD tool are the JavaBeans components. These components can be visually manipulated and tailored during design time for developing customized programs.

The application development process is similar to the component development process in many ways. Developing a software project is an engineering process. Software products, no matter how large or how small, have the same developmental phases: requirement specification, analysis, design, implementation, testing, deployment, and maintenance, as shown in Figure 4.13.

Requirements specification is a formal process that seeks to understand the problem and document in detail what it needs to do. This phase involves close interaction between users and designers. Most of the examples in this book are simple, and

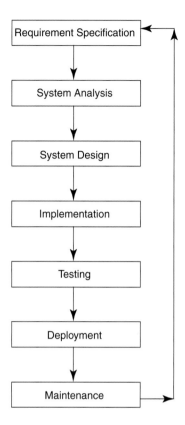

Figure 4.13   *Developing a project involves requirements specification, system analysis, system design, implementation, testing, deployment, and maintenance.*

their requirements are clearly stated. In the real world, however, problems are not well defined. You need to study a problem carefully to identify its requirements.

System analysis seeks to analyze the business process in terms of data flow, and to identify the system's input and output.

System design is the process of designing the system's components. This phase involves the use of many levels of abstraction to decompose the problem into manageable components and design algorithms for each of them.

Implementation is the process of translating the system design into programs. A program is written for each component, and they are put to work together. This phase requires the use of a specific programming language.

Testing ensures the code to meet the requirements specification and weed out bugs. An independent team of software engineers not involved in design and implementation of the project usually conducts such testing.

Deployment makes the project available for use. For a Java applet, this means installing it on a Web server. For a Java application, install it on the client's computer. The project usually consists of many classes. An effective approach for deployment is to package all the classes into a Java archive file, which is introduced in the section, " Packaging and Deploying Java Projects in JBuilder."

Maintenance is concerned with changing and improving the product. A software product must continue to perform and improve in a changing environment. This requires periodic upgrades of the product to fix newly discovered bugs and to incorporate changes.

The development phases are cyclic. You can use a CASE (Computer Aided Software Engineering) tool to aid software development. Requirements specification, analysis, and design are usually taught in a software engineering course. This chapter focuses on creating a project using Rapid Application Development.

When writing a project using a RAD tool, you should first carefully plan the project before implementing it. The major part of the planning involves designing the user interface. You may draw a sketch of the screens that shows all the visible beans you plan to use. Indicate the layout for the containers, and identify all the objects with appropriate names.

The implementation is a two-step process that involves creating user interfaces and writing code. To create a user interface, click-and-drop the bean components, such as buttons, labels, combo boxes, lists, and text fields, from the Component palette to the UI Designer, and set the beans properties in the Inspector.

After the user interface is created, you will add event handlers and write the code to carry out the actions for the associated events.

The following example illustrates the process for rapid Java application development.

Example 4.4 Developing a Mortgage Calculator

This example creates a mortgage calculator for computing mortgage payments, as shown in Figure 4.14. The mortgage calculator lets the user enter Loan Amount, Interest Rate, and Years, and click the Compute button to display monthly pay and total pay.

Figure 4.14   *The Mortgage Calculator gets input on Loan Amount, Interest Rate, and Year, and computes Monthly Pay and Total Pay.*

Here are the steps to complete the project:

1. It is often useful to draw a sketch of a complex user interface, as shown in Figure 4.15.

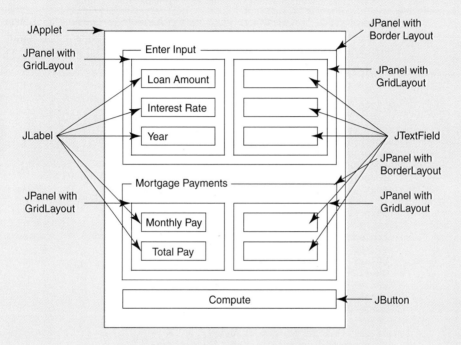

Figure 4.15   *The labels, text fields, borders, and a button are placed in the applet.*

2. Create a new project named MortgageDemo.jpr and create an applet named `ComputeMortgage` using the Applet Wizard.

3. In the UI Designer of ComputeMortgage.java, drop a `JPanel` to the north of the applet to create `jpInput`, and drop a `JPanel` to the center of the applet to create `jpResults`. Drop a `JButton` to the south of the applet to create `jbtCompute` with text Compute.

4. Set the `layout` of `jpInput` to `BorderLayout`. Drop a `JPanel` to the west of jpInput to create `jpInputLabels`, and drop a `JPanel` to the center of jpIn-put to create `jpInputTextFields`.

5. Set the `layout` of `jpInputLabels` to `GridLayout` with three rows, and drop three labels with text "Loan Amount," "Interest Rate," and "Years." Set the `layout` of `jpInputTextFields` to `GridLayout` with three rows, and drop three text fields to create `jtfLoanAmount`, `jtfInterestRate`, and `jtfYears`.

6. Set the `layout` of `jpResults` to `BorderLayout`. Drop a `JPanel` to the west of jpResults to create `jpResultLabels`, and drop a `JPanel` to the center of jpResults to create `jpResultTextFields`.

continues

7. Set the `layout` of `jpResultLabels` to `GridLayout` with two rows, and drop three labels with text "Monthly Pay" and "Total Pay." Set the `layout` of `jpResultTextFields` to `GridLayout` with two rows, and drop two text fields to create `jtfMonthlyPay` and `jtfTotalPay`.

8. Double click `jbtCompute` to generate the handler `jbtCompute_actionPer-formed` for handling the button-click event. Fill in the code in this handler to read the input, compute, and display monthly pay and total pay. The code can be found in Listing 4.9.

```java
package MortgageDemo;

import java.awt.*;
import java.awt.event.*;
import java.applet.*;
import javax.swing.*;
import javax.swing.border.*;
import java.text.*;

public class ComputeMortgage extends JApplet
{
  boolean isStandalone = false;
  JPanel jpInput = new JPanel();
  JPanel jpResults = new JPanel();
  JButton jbtCompute = new JButton();
  JPanel jpInputLabels = new JPanel();
  JLabel jlblLoanAmount = new JLabel();
  BorderLayout borderLayout1 = new BorderLayout();
  JLabel jlblInterestRate = new JLabel();
  JLabel jlblYears = new JLabel();
  GridLayout gridLayout1 = new GridLayout();
  JPanel jpInputTextFields = new JPanel();
  JTextField jtfLoanAmount = new JTextField();
  JTextField jtfInterestRate = new JTextField();
  JTextField jtfYears = new JTextField();
  GridLayout gridLayout2 = new GridLayout();
  TitledBorder titledBorder1;
  JPanel jpResultLabels = new JPanel();
  BorderLayout borderLayout2 = new BorderLayout();
  JLabel jlbMonthlyPay = new JLabel();
  JLabel jlblTotalPay = new JLabel();
  GridLayout gridLayout3 = new GridLayout();
  JPanel jpResultTextFields = new JPanel();
  JTextField jtfMonthlyPay = new JTextField();
  JTextField jtfTotalPay = new JTextField();
  GridLayout gridLayout4 = new GridLayout();
  TitledBorder titledBorder2;

  // Construct the applet
  public ComputeMortgage()
  {
  }
```

Listing 4.9 *MortgageApplet.java.*

146

```java
// Initialize the applet
public void init()
{
  try
  {
    jbInit();
  }
  catch(Exception e)
  {
    e.printStackTrace();
  }
}

// Component initialization
private void jbInit() throws Exception
{
  titledBorder1 = new TitledBorder("");
  titledBorder2 = new TitledBorder("");
  this.setSize(new Dimension(400,300));
  jbtCompute.setText("Compute");
  jbtCompute.addActionListener(new java.awt.event.ActionListener()
  {
    public void actionPerformed(ActionEvent e)
    {
      jbtCompute_actionPerformed(e);
    }
  });
  jlblLoanAmount.setText("Loan Amount");
  jpInput.setLayout(borderLayout1);
  jlblInterestRate.setText("Interest Rate");
  jlblYears.setText("Years");
  jpInputLabels.setLayout(gridLayout1);
  gridLayout1.setRows(3);
  jpInputTextFields.setLayout(gridLayout2);
  gridLayout2.setRows(3);
  borderLayout1.setHgap(10);
  borderLayout1.setVgap(10);
  jpInput.setBorder(titledBorder1);
  titledBorder1.setTitle
    ("Enter Loan Amount, Interest Rate, and Years");
  jpResults.setLayout(borderLayout2);
  jlbMonthlyPay.setText("Monthly Pay");
  jlblTotalPay.setText("Total Pay");
  jpResultLabels.setLayout(gridLayout3);
  gridLayout3.setRows(2);
  jpResultTextFields.setLayout(gridLayout4);
  gridLayout4.setRows(2);
  borderLayout2.setHgap(10);
  borderLayout2.setVgap(10);
  jpResults.setBorder(titledBorder2);
  titledBorder2.setTitle("Mortgage Payments");
  jtfLoanAmount.setHorizontalAlignment(SwingConstants.RIGHT);
  jtfInterestRate.setHorizontalAlignment(SwingConstants.RIGHT);
  jtfYears.setHorizontalAlignment(SwingConstants.RIGHT);
  jtfMonthlyPay.setEditable(false);
  jtfMonthlyPay.setHorizontalAlignment(SwingConstants.RIGHT);
  jtfTotalPay.setEditable(false);
  jtfTotalPay.setHorizontalAlignment(SwingConstants.RIGHT);
  this.getContentPane().add(jpInput, BorderLayout.NORTH);
  jpInput.add(jpInputLabels, BorderLayout.WEST);
```

continues

147

```
            jpInputLabels.add(jlblLoanAmount, null);
            jpInputLabels.add(jlblInterestRate, null);
            jpInputLabels.add(jlblYears, null);
            jpInput.add(jpInputTextFields, BorderLayout.CENTER);
            jpInputTextFields.add(jtfLoanAmount, null);
            jpInputTextFields.add(jtfInterestRate, null);
            jpInputTextFields.add(jtfYears, null);
            this.getContentPane().add(jpResults, BorderLayout.CENTER);
            jpResults.add(jpResultLabels, BorderLayout.WEST);
            jpResultLabels.add(jlbMonthlyPay, null);
            jpResultLabels.add(jlblTotalPay, null);
            jpResults.add(jpResultTextFields, BorderLayout.CENTER);
            jpResultTextFields.add(jtfMonthlyPay, null);
            jpResultTextFields.add(jtfTotalPay, null);
            this.getContentPane().add(jbtCompute, BorderLayout.SOUTH);
        }

        // Compute mortgage payments
        void jbtCompute_actionPerformed(ActionEvent e)
        {
            // Retrieve input from user
            double loan = new Double(jtfLoanAmount.getText()).doubleValue();
            double interestRate =
              new Double(jtfInterestRate.getText()).doubleValue()/1200;
            int year = new Integer(jtfYears.getText()).intValue();

            // Calculate payment
            double monthlyPay =
            loan*interestRate/(1-(Math.pow(1/(1+interestRate),year*12)));
            double totalPay = monthlyPay*year*12;

            // Display results in currency format
            NumberFormat nf = NumberFormat.getCurrencyInstance(getLocale());
            jtfMonthlyPay.setText(nf.format(monthlyPay));
            jtfTotalPay.setText(nf.format(totalPay));
        }
    }
```

Listing 4.9 *Continued*

Example Review

This example uses many panels to group components in order to achieve the desired layout. Creating UI interfaces using Java is more complex than using Visual Basic or Delphi, mainly because Java has a variety of layout styles. However, VB uses the fixed position layout. Chapter 6, "Containers and Layout Managers," presents a thorough discussion of Java layout managers.

The program displays monthly pay and total pay in locale-sensitive format. An instance, named nf, of NumberFormat is created to format the number in the applet's locale. The format() method in nf is used to format the number into a locale-sensitive string. For more information on number formatting, please refer to Chapter 12, "Internationalization," in my *Introduction to Java Programming with JBuilder 3*.

You created the user interface with labels, text fields, and a button. The default name for an object is *xi*, where *x* stands for the name of the bean, and *i* is an integer indicating that it is the *i*th object created for the same type of bean. There are five labels named jLable1, jLabel2, jLable3, jLabel4, and jLable5. For better identification, these names were changed to jlblLoanAmount, jlblInterest-Rate, jlblYears, jlblMonthlyPay, and jlblTotalPay. For the same reason, five text fields were renamed jtfLoanAmount, jtfInterestRate, jtfYears, jtfMonthlyPay, and jtfTotalPay.

TIP

I recommend replacing the default names of multiple objects of the same type with more descriptive names to help identify them. It is not necessary to rename the objects, however, if they are not used in hand-written codes. For example, the five text fields are used in the hand-written code; thus renaming them makes referencing easier. But since the five labels are not referenced in the code, it is not necessary to rename them.

Packaging and Deploying Java Projects in JBuilder

Your project may consist of many classes and supporting files, such as image files and audio files. To make your programs run on an end-user side, you need to provide end-users with all these files. For convenience, Java supports an archive file that can be used to group all the project files in a compressed file.

The Java archive file format (JAR) is based on the popular ZIP file format. Although JAR can be used as a general archiving tool, the primary motivation for its development was so that Java applications, applets, and their requisite components (.class files, images, and sounds) could be transported in a single file.

This single file can be deployed on an end-user's machine as an application. It also can be downloaded to a browser in a single HTTP transaction, rather than opening a new connection for each piece. This greatly simplifies application deployment and improves the speed with which an applet can be loaded onto a Web page and begin functioning. The JAR format also supports compression, which reduces the size of the file and improves download time still further. Additionally, individual entries in a JAR file can be digitally signed by the applet author to authenticate their origin.

You can create an archive file using the JDK *jar* command or using the JBuilder Deployment Wizard. The following command creates an archive file named Des.jar for classes A1 and A2.

```
jar -cf des.jar A1.class A2.class
```

Packaging Projects Using the Deployment Wizard

With the jar command, you have to manually identify the dependent files. JBuilder provides a Deployment Wizard to gather all the classes your program depends on into one JAR archive that includes image and audio files.

Let us use the ComputeMortgage class in the previous example to demonstrate packaging projects. The following are the steps to generate the archive file:

1. Open the MortgageDemo project. Make sure that ComputeMortage.java appears in the Navigation pane.

2. Choose Wizards, Deployment Wizards to open the Deployment Wizard, as shown in Figure 4.16. Check "Extract generated manifest file to project." This option adds the new manifest file to your project and displays it in the Navigation pane. This allows you to make additional changes to the manifest file for inclusion in the archive.

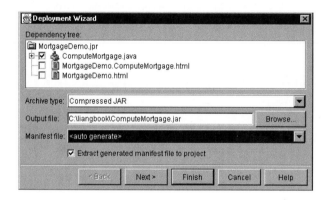

Figure 4.16   *You can use the Deployment Wizard to create an archive file for the project.*

3. Check the box for ComputeMortgage.java and leave all others unchecked. Choose Compress JAR as archive type and enter C:\LiangBook\Compute-Mortgage.jar in the Output file field. Click Next to let JBuilder automatically identify all the dependent files and display them in Figure 4.17.

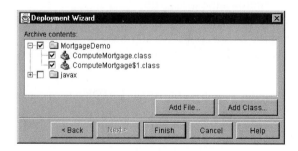

Figure 4.17   *The JBuilder Deployment Wizard finds all the dependent classes needed to run the project.*

4. Assume that the target machine supports Java 2. Thus you don't need to include any Swing components in the archive. Uncheck the box for javax in Figure 4.17. If there are any files or classes you need to run the project, but not shown in Figure 4.17, use the Add Class or Add File button to add them.

5. Press Finish to generate the archive file ComputeMortgage.jar.

■■■ NOTE

You can view the contents of a .JAR file using WinZip32, a popular compression utility for Windows 95 and Windows NT, as shown in Figure 4.18.

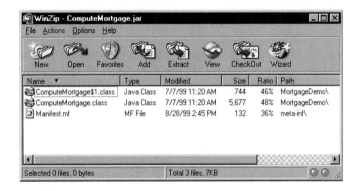

Figure 4.18 *You can view the files contained in the archive file using the WinZip utility.*

The Manifest File

As shown in Figure 4.18, a manifest file was created with the path name `meta-inf\`. The manifest is a special file that contains information about the files packaged in a JAR file. For instance, the manifest file in Figure 4.18 contains the following information as shown in Figure 4.19.

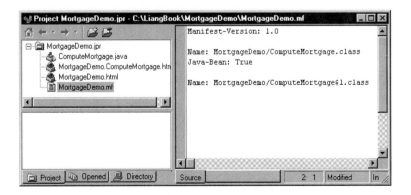

Figure 4.19 *The manifest file is added to the project because you check the option "Extract generated manifest file to project" in Figure 4.16.*

You can modify the information contained in the manifest file to enable the JAR file to be used for a variety of purposes. For instance, you can add information to specify a main class to run an application using the .jar file.

Running Archived Applications and Applets

The Deployment Wizard packages all the class files and dependent resource files into an archive file that can be distributed to the end-user. If the project is a Java application, the user should have a Java Running Environment already installed. If it is not installed, the user can download Java Runtime Environment (JRE) from JavaSoft at **www.javasoft.com** and install it.

NOTE

The Java Runtime Environment is the minimum standard Java platform for running Java programs. It contains the Java interpreter, Java core classes, and supporting files. The JRE does not contain any of the development tools (such as Applet Viewer or javac) or classes that pertain only to a development environment. The JRE is a subset of JDK.

To run ComputeMortgage as an application, take the following steps:

1. Update the manifest file to insert an entry for the main class, as shown in Figure 4.20.

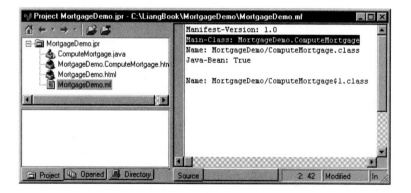

Figure 4.20   *You need to specify a main class in the JAR file to run an application in the JAR file.*

2. Run the Deployment Wizard again and choose MortgageDemo.mf as the manifest file, as shown in Figure 4.21.

3. Run the .jar file using the java command from the directory that contains ComputerMortgage.jar, as follows:

```
java -jar ComputeMortgage.jar
```

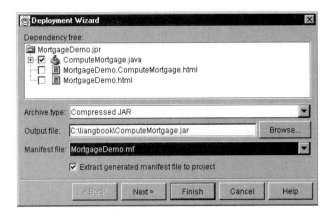

Figure 4.21   *You can specify a manifest file to be added in the JAR file.*

TIP
You can write an installation procedure that creates the necessary directories and subdirectories on the end-user's computer. The installation can also create an icon that the end-user can double-click to start the program.

To run ComputeMortgage as an applet, you need to modify the <APPLET> tag in the HTML file to include an ARCHIVE attribute. The ARCHIVE attribute specifies the archive file in which the applet is contained. For example, the HTML file for running the ComputeMortgage can be modified as follows:

```
<APPLET
  CODE    = "MortgageDemo.ComputeMortgage.class"
  ARCHIVE = "ComputeMortgage.jar"
  WIDTH   = 400
  HEIGHT  = 300
  HSPACE  = 0
  VSPACE  = 0
  ALIGN   = Middle
>
</APPLET>
```

Chapter Summary

This chapter introduced the process of developing bean components and developing applications using beans, the model-view approach, and JBuilder's powerful Bean Designer for creating bean properties and events with minimum coding. You learned the difference between a bean developer and a bean user, and learned how to apply the bean development process to create bean components. You used the Bean Designer to create bean properties in the Clock component, and to create bean events in the ClockWithAlarm component. You learned how to develop components using the model-view approach.

Finally, you learned to package and deploy Java Projects Using JBuilder's Deployment Wizard.

Chapter Review

4.1. Describe the differences between developing beans and using beans.

4.2. Describe the component development process.

4.3. How do you start the BeansExpress Wizard? How do you add or remove a property? How do you add or delete the code for generating and firing events? How do you add or delete the code for listening to events?

4.4. What are the differences between the Implement Interface Wizard and the "listen for these events" wizard in BeansExpress?

4.5. What is the model-view approach? What are advantages of developing components using the model-view approach? How do you implement the model and the view so that they are synchronized when a property is changed?

4.6. Describe the project development process.

4.7. Describe the steps in developing projects using RAD.

4.8. Describe the preinstall components in JBuilder's Component palette.

4.9. How do you use the Deployment Wizard to package a Java project? How do you execute an application from an archive, and how do you specify an applet in an archive file?

Programming Exercises

4.1. Use the Clock component to develop an applet, as shown in Figure 4.22, which can display the time in London, New York, Fort Wayne, Chicago, Denver, and San Francisco.

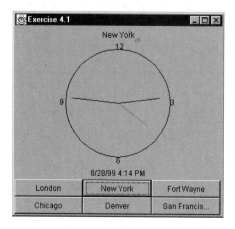

Figure 4.22   *The applet displays the clock for one of the six cities.*

4.2. Create a program that displays three clocks in a group. Each clock has individual Resume and Suspend control buttons. You can also resume or suspend all the clocks by using group control Resume All and Suspend All buttons, as shown in Figure 4.23.

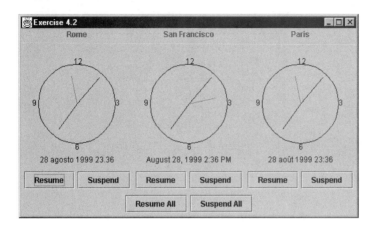

Figure 4.23   *Three clocks run independently with individual control and group control.*

4.3. Modify TestClockWithAlarm in Example 4.2 to play the alarm audio clip on a separate thread, so as to avoid interfering with repainting of the clock.

4.4. Develop a model, named `Rectangle`, for describing rectangles. `Rectangle` contains the properties `width`, `height`, `color`, and `filled` and the methods `findArea` and `findPerimeter` for computing the area and the perimeter of the rectangle. Develop a view that displays the rectangle as a figure, and develop another view like a Component Inspector that displays all the properties of the rectangle.

4.5. Create a model, named `Student`, for storing student information, including SSN, LastName, FirstName, MI, StreetAddress, City, State, Phone, and ImageFileName (for photo). Develop the following three views for `Student`:

- A panel that is similar to a component inspector to display the student's information and enable editing properties.

- A panel that displays a mailing label.

- A component (like an ID card) that contains the photo and other essential information on the card.

4.6. Create a project that meets the following requirements:

- Develop a `CalendarControl` bean with properties `month`, `year`, and `showHeader`, as shown in Figure 4.24.

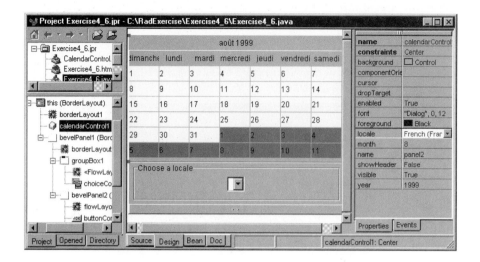

Figure 4.24   *An instance of* `CalendarControl` *is shown in the UI Designer.*

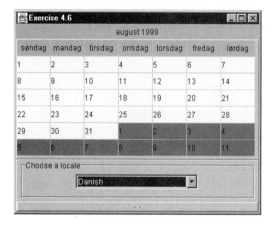

Figure 4.25   *The calendar applet displays the calendar with the Danish locale.*

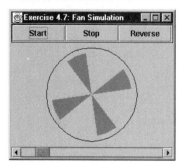

Figure 4.26   *The program simulates a running fan.*

■ Use the bean to create a program that displays the calendar based on the specified locale, as shown in Figures 4.25. The user can specify a locale from a combo box that consists of a list of all the available locales supported by the system.

4.7. Create a project that meets the following requirements:

■ Develop a `Fan` bean component that displays a fan with properties `running`, `speed`, and `reversed`.

■ Use the bean component to create a program that displays and controls the fan, as shown in Figures 4.26.

PART II

RAPID APPLICATION DEVELOPMENT WITH SWING COMPONENTS

Swing components are the essential elements in rapid Java application development. This part of the book covers Swing components and uses them in rapid Java application development. You will learn how to use a variety of Swing components to develop Java projects with JBuilder 3.

CHAPTER 5   SWING COMPONENTS

CHAPTER 6   CONTAINERS AND LAYOUT MANAGERS

CHAPTER 7   MENUS, TOOLBARS, AND DIALOGS

CHAPTER 8   ADVANCED SWING COMPONENTS

SWING COMPONENTS

Objectives

- Know the differences between Swing components and AWT components.
- Understand Swing model-view architecture.
- Use the pluggable look-and-feel features of Swing components in JBuilder.
- Become familiar with the basic features of JComponent.
- Create projects using the Swing components JButton, JRadioButton, JToggleButton, JCheckBox, JLabel, JTextField, JTextArea, JEditorPane, JScrollPane, JScrollBar, JSlider, and JProgressBar.

Introduction

When Java was introduced, the graphics components were bundled in a library known as *Abstract Window Toolkit,* or *AWT.* For each platform on which Java runs, the AWT components are automatically mapped to the platform-specific components through their respective agents, known as *peers.* AWT is fine for developing simple GUI applications, but it is inadequate for developing comprehensive GUI applications. Besides, AWT is prone to platform-specific bugs, because its peer-based approach relies heavily on the underlying platform. With the release of JDK 1.2, the AWT user interface components were replaced by a more robust, versatile, and flexible set of a library known as the *Swing components.* Most Swing components are painted directly on canvases using Java code, except for components that are subclasses of `java.awt.Window` or `java.awt.Panel`, which must be drawn using native GUI on a specific platform. Swing components are less dependent on the target platform and use fewer native GUI resources. For this reason, Swing components are referred to as *lightweight components,* and AWT components are referred to as *heavyweight components.* Although AWT components are still supported in Java 2, I recommend that you learn to program with the Swing components, because the AWT user interface components will eventually fade away. That is why this book uses Swing components exclusively.

Java provides a rich set of classes to help you build graphical user interfaces. You can use various GUI-building classes, such as frames, panels, labels, buttons, text fields, text areas, combo boxes, check boxes, radio buttons, menus, scroll bars, scroll panes, and tabbed panes, to construct user interfaces. This chapter introduces the basic Swing components. You will learn how to use them in Rapid Application Development.

Lightweight Component Framework

Swing components are lightweight. To understand what a lightweight component is, it is necessary to review the design of the AWT components. AWT provides a platform-independent interface to develop visual programs and graphical user interfaces. For each platform on which Java runs, the AWT components are automatically mapped to the platform-specific components. These platform-specific mappings, called *peers,* are defined in `java.awt.peer` package. The user interface components (`java.awt.Button`, `java.awt.Canvas`, `java.awt.Label`, etc.), `java.awt.Window`, and `java.awt.Panel` all have their supporting peers, named *X*peer for component *X.* For example, the button peer is named `ButtonPeer`. Since the peers enable the user applications to be consistent with other applications running on the same platform, a Java user interface on Windows has the same look-and-feel as other Windows applications.

Peer architecture has the obvious advantage of simultaneously preserving the look-and-feel of each platform on which Java runs and maintaining a platform-independent API that can be used on all platforms. This architecture has two drawbacks, however.

- The peer architecture consumes a lot of resources. To create a new GUI class, you must subclass `java.awt.Canvas` or `java.awt.Panel`. Components that extend these classes have their own native windows. These native windows, the peers, exist along with the components you are creating. In essence, creating one component using this peer model consumes the resources of two. For this reason, the component with an underlying peer is referred to as *heavyweight*.

- The native windows are also opaque (nontransparent). This means that a window onscreen covers any other windows behind it; you can't "see through" such windows.

To alleviate these problems, Swing components with no native peer were introduced. These components are completely implemented in Java without an underlying native peer. Because they don't require native data structures or peer classes, they are indeed "lighter" in their consumption of resources. For this reason, they are referred to as *lightweight*.

Lightweight components extend `java.awt.Component` and `java.awt.Container` classes instead. As a result, these components no longer have native windows associated with them. Also, lightweight components need not be opaque. They can have transparent parts if their paint methods do not render these areas.

CAUTION

Do not mix AWT peer components with Swing Components. Mixing them may cause problems. This book uses only Swing components.

The Swing Model-View Architecture

In Chapter 4, "Developing and Using Components," you learned how to use the model-view approach in developing models and views that separate data storage and handling from the visual representation of the data. The model-view approach is the backbone of the Swing architecture. Most Swing user interface components are implemented using a variation of the classic model-view approach known as *Swing Model-View Architecture*.

A Swing user interface component usually consists of the following objects:

- A component, such as `JButton`, which extends `JComponent`.

- A UI delegate, such as `BasicButtonUI`, which is responsible for displaying the component.

- A model, such as `ButtonModel`, which maintains a component's data.

Swing components delegate visual presentation to their respective UI delegates. A UI delegate plays the role of the view in the classic model-view architecture. Programmers use Swing components to create user interfaces. Components indirectly create their UI delegates. The UI delegates work behind the scenes to paint the components whenever the models change. The UI delegates can be plugged into a component when the components are constructed. The major benefit of delegating painting to the UI delegates is for implementing pluggable look-and-feel, which is introduced in the next section.

Each UI delegate listens for the model change. The change listeners are implemented as inner classes for most of the UI delegates. A few listeners, such as ButtonUIListener, are implemented as separate classes, because ButtonUIListener is shared by JButton, JToggleButton, JCheckBox, and JRadioButton.

The models for most components are implemented by interfaces whose names end with Model. For example, the model for button component is ButtonModel; its default implementation is DefaultButtonModel. For convenience, most Swing components contain some properties of their models, and these properties can be modified directly from the component without knowing the existence of the model. Some Swing models even contain properties that are not stored in the model, but are used by the UI delegate for painting the component. In any case, all the data are synchronized behind the scenes. For instance, when one of its properties changes, the component notifies the model, and the model sends the change to the UI delegate. The UI delegate then repaints the component.

Most Swing user interface components have a property named model that enables programmers to access and manipulate the model through the component. When you create a Swing user interface component, a default model is assigned to the model property. For simple components like JButton, JToggleButton, JCheckBox, JRadioButton, JTextField, and JTextArea, you need not be concerned about the models. For advanced components like JList, JComboBox, JTable, and JTree, you have to work with their models directly and access the components through the models.

Pluggable Look-and-feel

Lightweight components consume fewer resources and can be transparent, but they lack the AWT's platform-specific look-and-feel advantage. To address this problem, a new pluggable look-and-feel feature was introduced in Java.

The pluggable look-and-feel feature lets you design a single set of GUI components that can automatically have the look-and-feel of any OS platform. The implementation of this feature is independent of the underlying native GUI, yet it can imitate the native behavior of the native GUI.

Currently, Java supports the following three look-and-feel styles:

- Metal
- Motif
- Windows

JavaSoft provides an example to demonstrate these three styles. To run this example, open the project C:\JBuilder3\samples\jdk\demo\jfc\Simple\SimpleExample.jpr and execute SimpleExample.java. Figure 5.1 shows three sample runs of the example.

Figure 5.1   *The SimpleExample demonstrates three look-and-feel styles.*

The Metal style, also known as the *Java style*, gives you a consistent look regardless of operating systems. The Windows style is currently only available on Windows due to Windows copyright restrictions. The Motif style is used on Unix operating systems.

The `javax.swing.UIManager` class manages the look-and-feel of the user interface. You can use one of the following three methods to set the look-and-feel for Metal, Motif, and Windows:

```
UIManager.setLookAndFeel(
   UIManager.getCrossPlatformLookAndFeelClassName());
UIManager.setLookAndFeel(
   new javax.swing.plaf.motif.MotifLookAndFeel());
UIManager.setLookAndFeel(
   new javax.swing.plaf.windows.WindowsLookAndFeel());
```

The `setLookAndFeel()` method throws `UnsupportedLookAndFeelException`, so you have to put the method inside the `try`/`catch` block for it to compile.

The look-and-feel can be plugged during design time or at runtime, but mostly you set a look-and-feel during design time. To ensure that the setting takes effect, the `setLookAndFeel()` method should be executed before any of the components are instantiated. Thus, you need to place the code in the beginning of the `main()` method for applications and in the beginning of the `init()` method for applets. Alternatively, you can put the code in an anonymous static block. The anonymous static block is always executed when the class is instantiated.

When you create an application with JBuilder's Application Wizard, the following `main()` method is automatically generated in the application class. The `getSystemLookAndFeelClassName()` method returns the name of the `LookAndFeel` class that implements the native systems look-and-feel if there is one; otherwise the name of the default cross platform `LookAndFeel` class is returned.

```
// Main method
public static void main(String[] args)
{
  try
  {
    UIManager.setLookAndFeel(
      UIManager.getSystemLookAndFeelClassName());
  }
  catch(Exception e)
  {
  }
  new Application1();
}
```

When you create an applet with JBuilder's Applet Wizard, the following anonymous static block is automatically generated in the applet class, which sets the system default look-and-feel style.

```
static
{
  try
  {
    UIManager.setLookAndFeel(
      UIManager.getSystemLookAndFeelClassName());
    //UIManager.setLookAndFeel(
    //  UIManager.getCrossPlatformLookAndFeelClassName());
  }
  catch (Exception e) {}
}
```

NOTE

For simplicity, I deliberately deleted the static block in the code generated by
the Applet Wizard. Thus this block is not shown in the source code listing in
the text.

TIP

You can preview a particular look-and-feel in your UI design from the UI Designer in JBuilder as follows:

1. Right-click in the UI Designer and choose Look and Feel.

2. Select the look you want from the menu list, as shown in Figure 5.2.

The UI Designer repaints the components to display the selected look-and-feel.
Note that the preview does not set the look-and-feel for the runtime.

NOTE

By default, the Windows look-and-feel is used in the UI Designer for the Windows version of JBuilder during design time. If a look-and-feel is not explicitly
specified in the program, the Metal look-and-feel is used.

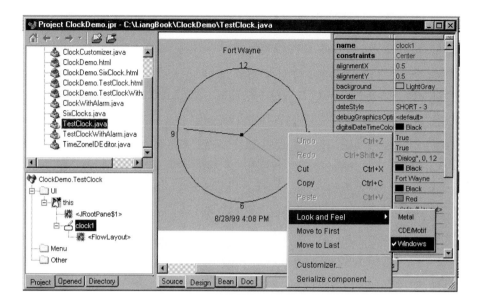

Figure 5.2 *You can review look-and-feel in the UI Designer.*

Overview of the Swing Classes

The Swing classes are extensions of and enhancements to the Java API. There are more than 250 Swing classes grouped in the following packages:

- javax.swing—Contains the lightweight user interface components, including pure Java implementation of the standard AWT components, such as JButton for java.awt.Button, JLabel for java.awt.Label, and JPanel for java.awt.Panel, plus a rich set of advanced components, such as JProgressBar, JTree, and JTable.

- javax.swing.border—Contains classes that describes the borders of the Swing components. You can use the border styles, such as BevelBorder, SoftBevelBorder, EtchedBorder, LineBorder, TitledBorder, and MatBorder, to create a (decorated or plain) area around the edge of a component with optional titles.

- javax.swing.event—Contains the event sets (the event classes and their listeners) for Swing components. Swing components use the event sets in the java.awt.event package as well as in the javax.swing.event package.

- javax.swing.text—Contains the classes for viewing and editing text.

- javax.swing.text.html—Contains the HTMLEditorKit class. This is the default implementation of HTML editing functionality. The primary goal here is to be small but flexible. It is not intended to be a full-fledged HTML implementation, but it meets modest needs, with the idea that more substantial needs can be met with alternative implementations.

- `javax.swing.text.html.parser`—Contains the parser classes for HTML files.

- `javax.swing.text.rtf`—Contains the `RTFEditorKit` class. This is the default implementation of RTF editing functionality.

- `javax.swing.undo`—Contains the classes for supporting the cut, copy, and paste operations.

- `javax.accessibility`—Swing has built-in support for developers to make products that are compatible with Assistive Technologies (for alternative interfaces like Braille). All of the Swing components implement interface `Accessible`, which is the main interface for the accessibility package.

- `javax.swing.table`—Contains the classes for supporting `JTable`. `JTable` is a user interface component that presents data in a two-dimensional table format.

- `javax.swing.tree`—Contains the classes for supporting `JTree`. `JTree` is a user interface component that presents a set of hierarchical data as an outline.

- `javax.swing.colorchooser`—Contains support classes and interfaces for the `javax.swing.JColorChooser` component.

- `javax.swing.filechooser`—Contains support classes and interfaces for the `javax.swing.JFileChooser` component.

- `javax.swing.plaf`—Contains one interface and many abstract classes that Swing uses to provide its pluggable look-and-feel capabilities.

- `javax.swing.plaf.basic`—Provides user interface objects built according to the basic look-and-feel.

- `javax.swing.plaf.metal`—Provides user interface objects built according to the Metal look-and-feel.

Figures 5.3 and 5.4 illustrate the hierarchical relationship of Swing classes.

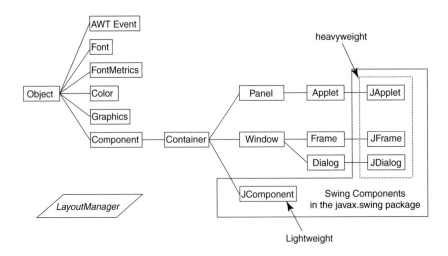

Figure 5.3 *Java graphics programming utilizes the classes shown in this hierarchical diagram.*

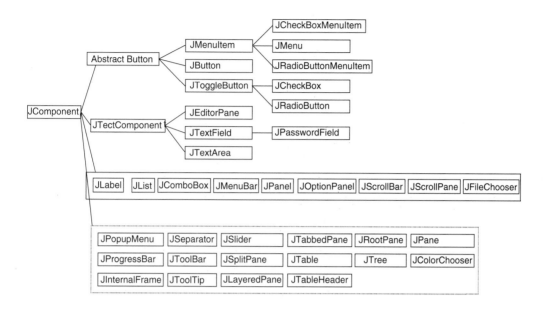

Figure 5.4 *The* JComponent *and its subclasses are the basic elements for building graphical user interfaces.*

The JComponent Class

All Swing components preinstalled in the Swing page and the Swing Containers page in the Component palette extend javax.swing.JComponent or a subclass of JComponent. JComponent is derived from java.awt.Container. JComponent provides the following basic features of Swing components:

- A pluggable look-and-feel feature that can be specified by the programmer or (optionally) selected by the user at runtime.

- Comprehensive keystroke handling that works with nested components.

- Action objects for single-point control of program actions initiated by multiple components.

- Support for accessibility. Accessibility involves magnifying fonts for sight-impaired users or displaying captions associated with sounds for hearing-impaired users.

- Support for international localization. Each swing component has a locale property that encapsulates information about a specific locale. A locale determines how locale-sensitive information like date, time, and number is displayed, and how locale-sensitive operations like sorting strings are performed. Swing components can also display Unicode characters.

Keystroke Handling

The `JComponent` architecture makes it easy to handle keyboard events in nested components. You can register interest in a particular combination of keystrokes by creating a `KeyStroke` object and registering it with the component. When you register the keystroke combination and its associated action, you also specify one of the following conditions to determine when the action is initiated:

- The component has the focus.

- A child or grandchild of the component has the focus.

You can use this capability to define global actions for a composite component. For example, a tree control could act on the Plus key to expand all elements in the tree, as long as any component in the tree has the focus.

The window in which the component is located has the focus. In other words, if the component is a child or grandchild of a window, and any component in the window has the focus, then the component receives the event. You can use this capability to direct the keystroke combination Alt+C to the Cancel button in a dialog, for example, as long any component in the dialog has the focus.

Action Objects

Action-interface objects provide a single point of control for program actions. For example, a toolbar icon and a menu item can reference the same action object. When the action object is disabled, the GUI items that reference it are automatically disabled. The `Action` interface extends `java.awt.event.ActionListener`, specifying an `enabled` property as well as properties for text descriptions and graphic icons.

JComponent Properties

Figure 5.5 shows the `JComponent` properties in the Component Inspector. Since these properties are inherited by subclasses of `JComponent`, it is important to understand them.

- `alignmentX`: The preferred horizontal alignment of the component, which specifies how the component would like to be aligned relative to other components along the x-axis. The value should be a number between 0 and 1, where 0 represents alignment along the origin, 1 is aligned the farthest away from the origin, 0.5 is centered, etc. This property is used with the `BoxLayout`, which is introduced in Chapter 6, "Containers and Layout Managers."

- `alignmentY`: The preferred vertical alignment of the component, which specifies how the component would like to be aligned relative to other components along the y-axis. The value should be a number between 0 and 1, where 0 represents alignment along the origin, 1 is aligned the farthest away from the origin, 0.5 is centered, etc. This property is used with the `BoxLayout`.

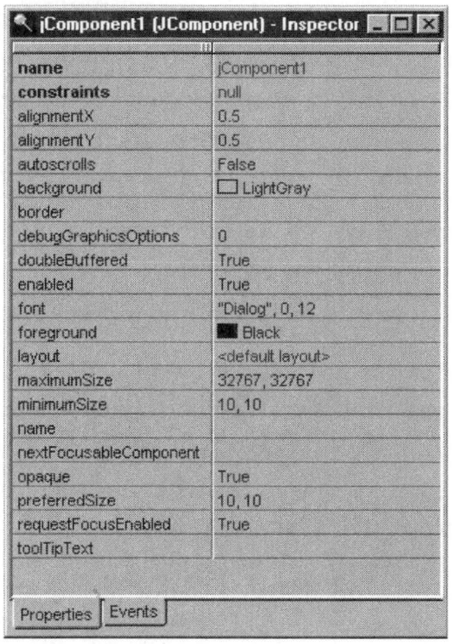

Figure 5.5 *The properties of a* JComponent *object are shown in the Component Inspector.*

■ autoscrolls: A boolean property to enable automatic scrolling in a list, table, or tree that occurs when the user is dragging the mouse. By default, it is false.

■ border: Specifies a border of the component with an optional title. Many types of border styles are available, and they can be combined to create compound borders.

■ debugGraphicsOption: Allows you to set slow-motion graphics rendering, so that you can see what is being displayed on screen and whether or not it is being overwritten. This feature is useful in debugging.

■ doubleBuffered: Specifies whether the component is painted using double-buffering. This is a technique for reducing flickering. In AWT programming, you have to manually implement this technique in the program. With Swing, this capability is automatically supported if the doubleBuffered property is set to true. By default, it is true.

■ enabled: Determines whether the component is enabled. An enabled component can respond to user input and generate events. By default, enabled is true.

■ font: The font used to display text on the component.

■ foreground: The foreground color of the component.

■ background: The background color of the component.

■ layout: Specifies a layout manager used when the component is a container, such as JPanel.

- `maximumSize`: Specifies the maximum size the component needs so that the layout manager won't waste space giving it to a component that does not need it. For instance, `BorderLayout` could limit the center component's size to its maximum size, and then either give the space to edge components or limit the size of the outer window when resized.

- `minimumSize`: Specifies the minimum size for the component to be useful. For most Swing components, `minimumSize` is the same as `preferredSize`. Layout managers generally respect `minimumSize` rather than `preferredSize`.

- `preferredSize`: Indicates the ideal size for the component to look best. This property may or may not be considered by some layout managers, depending on their rules. For example, a component uses its preferred size in a container with a `FlowLayout` manager, but its preferred size may be ignored if it is placed in a container with a `GridLayout` manager.

- `nextFocusableComponent`: Specifies the next focusable component or null if the focus manager should choose the next focusable component automatically.

- `requestFocusEnabled`: Determines whether the receiving component can obtain the focus by calling the `requestFocus()` method. The default value is true.

- `opaque`: Specify whether the component is opaque. By default it is true.

- `toolTipText`: The text displayed when the mouse points on the component without clicking. This text is usually used to give the user a tip about the function of the component.

- `visible`: A `boolean` value indicating whether the component is visible.

- `size`: The size of the component displayed. This property's type is `java.awt.Dimension`.

The `background`, `enabled`, `font`, `foreground`, `maximumSize`, `minimunSize`, and `preferredSize` properties are defined in `java.awt.Component`, and the `alignmentX`, `alignmentY`, and `layout` properties are defined in `java.awt.Container`.

The SwingSet Demo

Swing comes with a variety of samples that demonstrate various aspects of the Swing components. By far the most interesting of all the samples is the SwingSet example, which is an excellent demonstration of many important and useful features of Swing components. To run the example, open c:\JBuilder3\samples\jdk\jfc\swingset\SwingSet.jpr and execute SwingSet.html or SwingSet.java. A sample run of the example is shown in Figure 5.6.

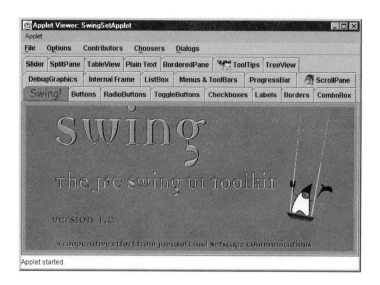

Figure 5.6   *The SwingSet applet is a comprehensive example that demonstrates many interesting features of the Swing components.*

JButton

JButton is the Swing version of a button component. You can have either a text or an image icon on the button, or both a text and an image icon at the same time. You can have a pressed icon, which appears when the button is pressed. You can have a rollover icon, which appears when the mouse points to the button without clicking. Figure 5.7 shows buttons in the SwingSet demo.

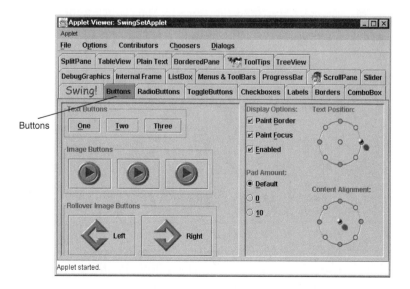

Figure 5.7   *The Buttons panel in the SwingSet demo demonstrates the features of JButton.*

JButton is a subclass of AbstractButton, which defines the common behaviors for the JButton, JToggleButton, JCheckBox, and JRadioButton. All the properties of JButton are defined in its superclass, such as JComponent and AbstractButton.

The following priorities are defined in the AbstractButton class.

- text: The label on the button. You can set a label using the setText() method.

- horizontalAlignment: One of the three values, SwingConstants.LEFT, SwingConstants.CENTER, and SwingConstants.RIGHT, to specify how the text is placed horizontally on a button. The default alignment is SwingConstants.CENTER.

- horizontalTextPosition: One of the five values, SwingConstants.LEFT, SwingConstants.CENTER, SwingConstants.RIGHT, SwingConstants.LEADING, and SwingConstants.TRAILLING, to specify horizontal position of the text relative to the icon. The default alignment is SwingConstants.RIGHT.

- verticalAlignment: One of the three values, SwingConstants.TOP, SwingConstants.CENTER, and SwingConstants.BOTTOM, to specify how the label is placed vertically on a button. The default alignment is SwingConstants.CENTER.

- verticalTextPosition: One of the three values, SwingConstants.TOP, SwingConstants.CENTER, and SwingConstants.BOTTOM, to specify vertical position of the text relative to the icon. The default alignment is SwingConstants.CENTER.

- actionCommand: Specifies an action command string associated with the button. By default, the action command is the same as the button text. The action command string is passed to the ActionEvent when an ActionEvent is generated on the button.

- mnemonic: Specifies a shortcut key. You can select the button by pressing the ALT key and the mnemonic key at the same time. As shown in Figure 5.7, the text buttons are One, Two, and Three, which implies that the buttons can be accessed using Alt+O, Alt+T, and Alt+H.

- disabledIcon: The icon displayed when the button is disabled. You can set a disabled icon using the setDisableIcon() method.

- icon: The image icon on the button. You can set an icon using the setIcon() method.

- pressedIcon: An icon that is displayed when a button is pressed.

- rolloverIcon: An icon that is displayed when the mouse points to the button without clicking. To see a rollover icon, the rolloverEnabled property must be true.

- rolloverEnabled: Determines whether rollover is enabled. By default, it is true. When you set a rollover icon in the Component Inspector, the rolloverEnabled property is automatically set to true.

- **borderPainted**: Determines whether the button border is painted. By default, it is true.

- **contentAreaFilled**: Determines whether the button should paint the content area or leave it transparent. By default, the content area is painted.

- **focusPainted**: Determines whether a focus indicator is painted when a button has the focus. By default, it is true.

- **margin**: The space between the button's border and its content. The margin property type is `java.awt.Insets`.

- **model**: Model that a button represents. Rarely used with buttons.

- **selected**: This property, inherited from `AbstractButton`, has no meaning in `JButton`. It is used in `JRadioButton`, `JCheckBox`, and `JToggleButton`.

- **selectedIcon**: This property, inherited from `AbstractButton`, has no meaning in `JButton`. It is used in `JRadioButton`, `JCheckBox`, and `JToggleButton`.

Buttons can generate many types of events, but often you use the `ActionEvent` to respond to button-click action. Most of the events are inherited from `JButton`'s superclass.

JToggleButton

Toggle buttons are buttons that have two states: selected and deselected. `JToggleButton` is a subclass of `AbstractButton` and a superclass of `JRadioButton` and `JCheckBox`. `JToggleButton` provides an implementation of a two-state button, which is the basis for `JRadioButton` and `JCheckBox`. Figure 5.8 demonstrates using `JToggleButton` in the SwingSet demo. As you see in this demo, when the button is clicked, the button appears toggled.

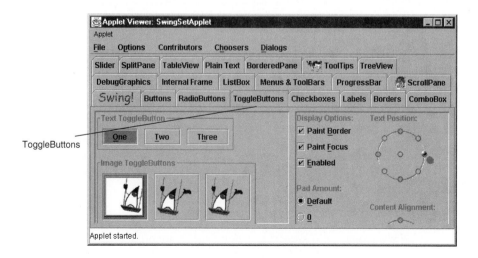

Figure 5.8   *The ToggleButtons panel in the SwingSet demo demonstrates the features of* `JToggleButton`.

All the properties of the JToggleButton class are inherited from its superclass. These properties are the same as the properties of JButton. JToggleButton can fire all the events that can be generated by a JButton object. Whenever a button is clicked, an ActionEvent and an ItemEvent are generated.

JCheckBox

A check box is a component that enables the user to toggle a choice on or off, like a light switch. Check boxes are usually displayed in a group and allow multiple selections. Figure 5.9 shows using JCheckBox in the SwingSet demo.

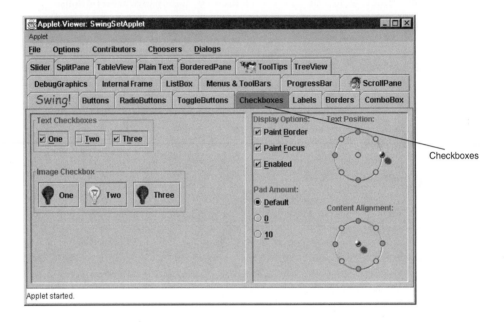

Figure 5.9   *The Checkboxes panel in the SwingSet demo demonstrates the features of* JCheckBox.

JCheckBox is a subclass of JToggleButton. All the properties of JCheckBox are inherited from its superclasses. These properties are the same as the properties in JToggleButton, but the default values may be different. By default, borderPainted is false for a JCheckBox object. If an image icon is used, the image icon replaces the check box indicator.

JCheckBox can fire all the events that can be generated by its superclass. Whenever a check box is checked or unchecked, an ActionEvent and an ItemEvent are generated.

JRadioButton

Radio buttons, also known as *option buttons*, are often used to choose one item exclusively from a list of choices. In appearance they are similar to check boxes. A check box displays a square that is either checked or blank, and a radio button displays a circle that is either filled (if selected) or blank (if not selected). Figure 5.10 demonstrates using JRadioButton in the SwingSet demo.

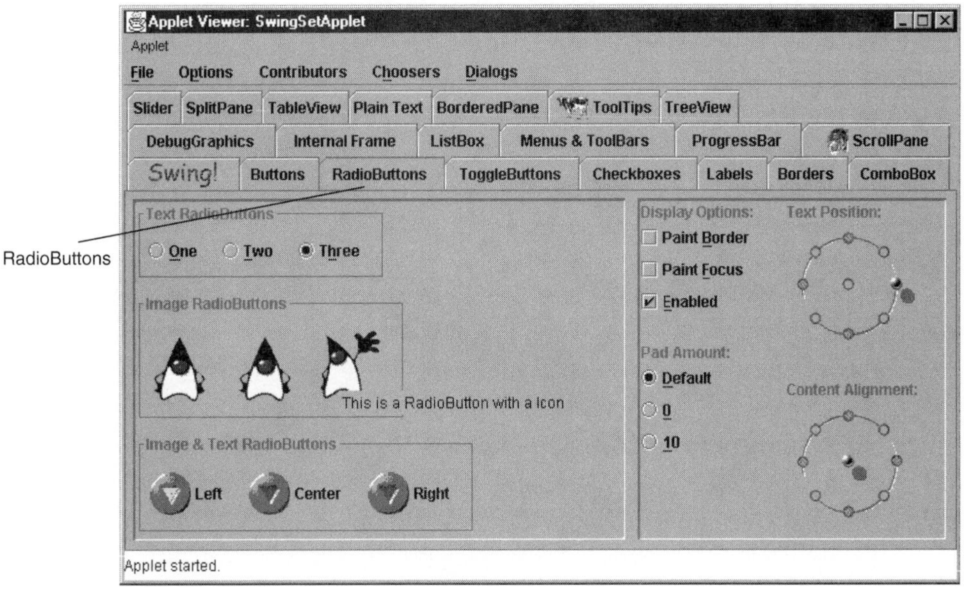

Figure 5.10   *The RadioButtons panel in the SwingSet demo demonstrates the features of* JRadioButton.

JRadioButton is a subclass of JToggleButton. All the properties of JRadioButton are inherited from its superclasses. These properties are the same as the properties in JToggleButton, but the default values may be different. By default, borderPainted is false for a JRadioButton object. If an image icon is used, the image icon replaces the radio button indicator.

JRadioButton can fire all the events that can be generated by its superclass. Whenever a radio button is checked or unchecked, an ActionEvent and an ItemEvent are generated.

To group radio buttons, create an instance of ButtonGroup and place the radio buttons into the group using the add() method. For example, the following statements group radio button jrb1, jrb2, and jrb3:

```
ButtonGroup btg = new ButtonGroup();
btg.add(jrb1);
btg.add(jrb2);
btg.add(jrb3);
```

Border

Border, one of the interesting new Swing components features, renders a border around the edges of a Swing component. The BevelBorder, SoftBevelBorder, EtchedBorder, LineBorder, TitledBorder, and MatBorder classes are used to create specific border styles. You can use `EmptyBorder` to create a plain border, and `CompoundBorder` to nest multiple border objects, creating a single, combined border. Figure 5.11 shows various types of borders in the SwingSet demo.

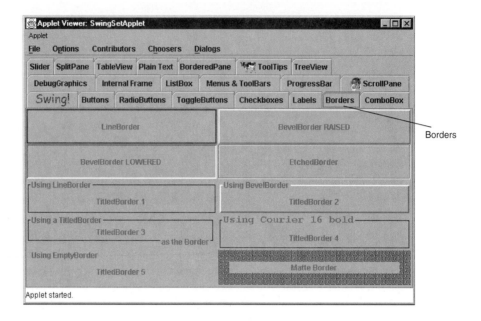

Figure 5.11   *The Borders panel in the SwingSet demo demonstrates the features of* `Border`.

To create a titled border, simply use the following statement:

```
Border titledBorder = new TitledBorder("A Title");
```

`Border` is the interface for all types of borders. `TitledBorder` is an implementation of `Border` with a title. You can create a desired border using the following properties:

- `title`: The title of the border.

- `titleColor`: The color of the title.

- `titleFont`: The font of the title.

- `titleJustification`: Specifies `Border.LEFT`, `Border.CENTER`, or `Border.RIGHT` for left, center, or right title justification.

- `titlePosition`: One of the six values (`Border.ABOVE_TOP`, `Border.TOP`, `Border.BELOW_TOP`, `Border.ABOVE_BOTTOM`, `Border.BOTTOM`, `Border.BELOW_BOTTOM`) to specify the title position above the border line, on the border line, or below the border line.

- `border`: The `TitledBorder` itself has the `border` property for building composite borders.

The other types of borders can be created using the following classes:

- `BevelBorder`: Creates a border with a 3-D look that can be lowered or raised. To construct a `BevelBorder`, use the following constructor, which creates a `BevelBorder` with the specified `bevelType` (`BevelBorder.LOWERED` or `BevelBorder.BevelBorder`).

  `public BevelBorder(int bevelType)`

- `EtchedBorder`: Creates an etched border which can either be etched-in or etched-out. You can use its default constructor to construct an `EtchedBorder` with lowered border. `EtchedBorder` has a property `etchType` with values `LOWERED` or `RAISED`.

- `LineBorder`: Creates a line border of arbitrary thickness in a single color. To create a `LineBorder`, use the following constructor:

  `public LineBorder(Color c, int thickness)`

- `MatteBorder`: Creates a matte-like border padded with icon images. To create a `MatteBorder`, use the following constructor:

  `public MatteBorder(Icon tileIcon)`

- `EmptyBorder`: Creates a border with border space but no drawings. To create an `EmptyBorder`, use the following constructor:

  `public EmptyBorder(int top, int left, int bottom, int right)`

NOTE

All the border classes and interfaces are grouped in the `javax.swing.border` package.

Swing also provides the `javax.swing.BorderFactory` class, which contains static methods for creating borders. Some of the static methods are:

- `public static TitledBorder createTitledBorder(String title)`

- `public static Border createLoweredBevelBorder()`

- `public static Border createRaisedBevelBorder()`

- `public static Border createLineBorder(Color color)`

- `public static Border createLineBorder(Color color, int thickness)`

- `public static Border createEtchedBorder()`

- `public static Border createEtchedBorder(Color highlight, Color shadow)`

- `public static Border createEmptyBorder()`

- `public static MatteBorder createEmptyBorder(int top, int left, int bottom, int right)`

- ◼ `public static MatteBorder createMatteBorder(int top, int left, int bottom, int right, Color color)`

- ◼ `public static MatteBorder createMatteBorder(int top, int left, int bottom, int right, Icon tileIcon)`

- ◼ `public static Border createCompoundBorder(Border outsideBorder, Border insideBorder)`

For example, to create an etched border, simply use the following statement:

```
Border border = BorderFactory.createEtchedBorder();
```

`Border` instances can be shared. Rather than create a new border object using one of the border classes, you can create a shared instance of the common border types. You can also create a custom border class, which inherits `AbstractBorder`.

Example 5.1 Using **JButton, JToggleButton, JCheckBox, JRadioButton**, and Border

This example demonstrates using `JButton`, `JToggleButton`, `JCheckBox`, `JRadioButton`, and borders. A sample run of the example is shown in Figure 5.12. The program enables you to dynamically set the properties of `JButton`, `JToggleButton`, `JCheckBox`, and `JRadioButton` at runtime.

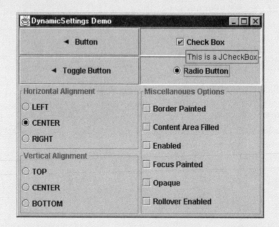

Figure 5.12   *You can set the properties of the button, toggle button, check box, and radio button dynamically.*

Here are the steps to complete the project:

1. Create a new project named DynamicSettingsDemo.jpr and an applet named DynamicSettings.java using the Applet Wizard.

2. Select DynamicSettings.java in the Navigation pane, and choose the Design tab in the Content pane to switch to the UI Designer. Drop a `JPanel`

into the center of the applet and rename it jpButtons. Drop a JPanel into the south of the applet and rename it jpSettings.

3. Drop a JButton, a JToggleButton, a JCheckBox, and a JRadioButton into jpButtons, and rename them jbt, jtb, jchk, and jrb. Set their texts to Button, Toggle Button, Check Box, and Radio Button, and tooltip to appropriate strings. Set the layout property of jpButtons to GridLayout, and set the row and column of the GridLayout to 2.

4. Set the layout of jpSettings to GridLayout. Drop a JPanel twice into jpSettings to create two panels, and rename them jpAlignment, and jpMiscSettings.

5. Set the layout of jpAlignment to GridLayout and set the row of the GridLayout to 2. Drop a JPanel twice into jpAlignment to create two panels named jpHorizontalAlignment and jpVerticalAlignment.

6. Drop a JRadioButton three times into jpHorizontalAlignment to create three radio buttons named jrbLeft, jrbCenter, and jrbRight with text set to LEFT, CENTER, and RIGHT. Set the layout of jpHorizontalAlignment to GridLayout with the row property set to 3.

7. Drop a JRadioButton three times into jpVerticalAlignment to create three radio buttons named jrbTop, jrbVCenter, and jrbBottom with text set to TOP, CENTER, and BOTTOM. Set the layout of jpVerticalAlignment to GridLayout with the row property set to 3.

8. Drop a JCheckBox six times into jpMiscSettings to create six check boxes named jchkBorderPainted, jchkContentAreaFilled, jchkEnabled, jchkFocusPainted, jchkOpaqued, and jchkRolloverEnabled with text set to Border Painted, Content Area Filled, Enabled, Focus Painted, Opaque, and Rollover Enabled. Set the layout of jpMiscSettings to GridLayout with the row property set to 6.

9. To set the borders, choose titled in the border property of jpHorizontalAlignment to create titledBorder1. Select titledBorder1 in the Other node in the Component tree and set the title property to "Horizontal Alignment." Similarly, you can create a titled border for jpVerticalAlignmnment, and jpMiscSettings.

10. Declare three image icons named icon1, icon2, and icon3 as members of the applet. Create the image icons in the jbInit method, as shown in Listing 5.1.

11. Choose icon1 in the icon property of jtb, jtb, jchk, and jrb, choose icon2 in the pressedIcon property of jtb, jtb, jchk, and jrb, and choose icon3 in the rolloverIcon property of jtb, jtb, jchk, and jrb.

continues

12. Declare two `ButtonGroup` instances named `btg1` and `btg2`, and write the code to add the radio buttons for horizontal alignment to `btg1`, and the radio buttons for vertical alignment to `btg2` in the `jbInit()` method.

13. Generate action events for the radio buttons in the `jpHorizontalAlignment` panel, in the `jpVerticalAlignment` panel, and in the `jpMiscSettings` panel, and implement these handlers for setting the properties of the buttons in the `jpButtons` panel, as shown in Listing 5.1.

```java
package DynamicSettingsDemo;

import java.awt.*;
import java.awt.event.*;
import java.applet.*;
import javax.swing.*;
import javax.swing.border.*;
import java.net.URL;

public class DynamicSettings extends JApplet
{
  // Create button group
  ButtonGroup btg1 = new ButtonGroup();
  ButtonGroup btg2 = new ButtonGroup();

  // Create image icons
  ImageIcon icon1;
  ImageIcon icon2;
  ImageIcon icon3;

  // Generated by JBuilder
  boolean isStandalone = false;
  JPanel jpButtons = new JPanel();
  JPanel jpSettings = new JPanel();
  JPanel jpAlignment = new JPanel();
  GridLayout gridLayout1 = new GridLayout();
  JButton jbt = new JButton();
  JToggleButton jtb = new JToggleButton();
  JCheckBox jchk = new JCheckBox();
  JRadioButton jrb = new JRadioButton();
  TitledBorder titledBorder1;
  TitledBorder titledBorder3;
  JPanel jpMiscSettings = new JPanel();
  JCheckBox jchkBorderPainted = new JCheckBox();
  JCheckBox jchkContentAreaFilled = new JCheckBox();
  JCheckBox jchkEnabled = new JCheckBox();
  JCheckBox jchkFocusPainted = new JCheckBox();
  JCheckBox jchkOpaque = new JCheckBox();
  JCheckBox jchkRolloverEnabled = new JCheckBox();
  GridLayout gridLayout4 = new GridLayout();
  JRadioButton jrbLeft = new JRadioButton();
  JRadioButton jrbRight = new JRadioButton();
  JRadioButton jrbCenter = new JRadioButton();
  GridLayout gridLayout3 = new GridLayout();
  GridLayout gridLayout2 = new GridLayout();
  JPanel jpHorizontalAlignment = new JPanel();
  JPanel jpVerticalAlignment = new JPanel();
```

Listing 5.1 *DynamicSettings.java*

```
    GridLayout gridLayout5 = new GridLayout();
    BorderLayout borderLayout1 = new BorderLayout();
    JRadioButton jrbTop = new JRadioButton();
    JRadioButton jrbVCenter = new JRadioButton();
    JRadioButton jrbBottom = new JRadioButton();
    TitledBorder titledBorder2;
    GridLayout gridLayout6 = new GridLayout();

    // Construct the applet
    public DynamicSettings()
    {
    }

    // Initialize the applet
    public void init()
    {
      try
      {
        jbInit();
      }
      catch(Exception e)
      {
        e.printStackTrace();
      }
    }

    // Component initialization
    private void jbInit() throws Exception
    {
      // Load images using URLs
      Toolkit toolkit = Toolkit.getDefaultToolkit();
      URL url = this.getClass().getResource("images/prior.gif");
      icon1 = new ImageIcon(toolkit.getImage(url));

      url = this.getClass().getResource("images/next.gif");
      icon2 = new ImageIcon(toolkit.getImage(url));

      url = this.getClass().getResource("images/home.gif");
      icon3 = new ImageIcon(toolkit.getImage(url));

      //  Generated by JBuilder
      titledBorder1 = new TitledBorder("");
      titledBorder3 = new TitledBorder("");
      titledBorder2 = new TitledBorder("");
      this.setSize(new Dimension(400,300));
      this.getContentPane().setLayout(borderLayout1);
      jpButtons.setLayout(gridLayout1);
      jbt.setToolTipText("This is a JButton");
      jbt.setIcon(icon1);
      jbt.setPressedIcon(icon2);
      jbt.setRolloverIcon(icon3);
      jbt.setText("Button");
      jtb.setIcon(icon1);
      jtb.setToolTipText("This is a JToggleButton");
      jtb.setRolloverIcon(icon3);
      jtb.setPressedIcon(icon2);
      jtb.setText("Toggle Button");
      jchk.setToolTipText("This is a JCheckBox");
      jchk.setRolloverIcon(icon3);
      jchk.setBorderPainted(true);
```

continues

183

```
                    jchk.setPressedIcon(icon2);
                    jchk.setText("Check Box");
                    jrb.setToolTipText("This is a radio button");
                    jrb.setRolloverIcon(icon3);
                    jrb.setBorderPainted(true);
                    jrb.setPressedIcon(icon2);
                    jrb.setText("Radio Button");
                    gridLayout1.setRows(2);
                    titledBorder1.setTitle("Horizontal Alignment");
                    jpAlignment.setLayout(gridLayout3);
                    jpMiscSettings.setBorder(titledBorder3);
                    jpMiscSettings.setLayout(gridLayout4);
                    titledBorder3.setTitle("Miscellanoues Options");
                    jchkBorderPainted.setText("Border Painted");
                    jchkBorderPainted.addActionListener(
                      new java.awt.event.ActionListener()
                    {
                      public void actionPerformed(ActionEvent e)
                      {
                        jchkBorderPainted_actionPerformed(e);
                      }
                    });
                    jchkContentAreaFilled.setText("Content Area Filled");
                    jchkContentAreaFilled.addActionListener(
                      new java.awt.event.ActionListener()
                    {
                      public void actionPerformed(ActionEvent e)
                      {
                        jchkContentAreaFilled_actionPerformed(e);
                      }
                    });
                    jchkEnabled.setText("Enabled");
                    jchkEnabled.addActionListener(new java.awt.event.ActionListener()
                    {
                      public void actionPerformed(ActionEvent e)
                      {
                        jchkEnabled_actionPerformed(e);
                      }
                    });
                    jchkFocusPainted.setText("Focus Painted");
                    jchkFocusPainted.addActionListener(
                      new java.awt.event.ActionListener()
                    {
                      public void actionPerformed(ActionEvent e)
                      {
                        jchkFocusPainted_actionPerformed(e);
                      }
                    });
                    jchkOpaque.setText("Opaque");
                    jchkOpaque.addActionListener(new java.awt.event.ActionListener()
                    {
                      public void actionPerformed(ActionEvent e)
                      {
                        jchkOpaque_actionPerformed(e);
                      }
                    });
                    jchkRolloverEnabled.setText("Rollover Enabled");
                    jchkRolloverEnabled.addActionListener(
                      new java.awt.event.ActionListener()
```

Listing 5.1 *Continued*

```
{
  public void actionPerformed(ActionEvent e)
  {
    jchkRolloverEnabled_actionPerformed(e);
  }
});
gridLayout4.setRows(6);
jrbLeft.setText("LEFT");
jrbLeft.addActionListener(new java.awt.event.ActionListener()
{
  public void actionPerformed(ActionEvent e)
  {
    jrbLeft_actionPerformed(e);
  }
});
jrbRight.setText("RIGHT");
jrbRight.addActionListener(new java.awt.event.ActionListener()
{
  public void actionPerformed(ActionEvent e)
  {
    jrbRight_actionPerformed(e);
  }
});
jrbCenter.setText("CENTER");
jrbCenter.addActionListener(new java.awt.event.ActionListener()
{
  public void actionPerformed(ActionEvent e)
  {
    jrbCenter_actionPerformed(e);
  }
});
gridLayout3.setRows(2);
jpHorizontalAlignment.setLayout(gridLayout5);
gridLayout5.setRows(3);
jpHorizontalAlignment.setBorder(titledBorder1);
jrbTop.setText("TOP");
jrbTop.addActionListener(new java.awt.event.ActionListener()
{
  public void actionPerformed(ActionEvent e)
  {
    jrbTop_actionPerformed(e);
  }
});
jrbVCenter.setText("CENTER");
jrbVCenter.addActionListener(new java.awt.event.ActionListener()
{
  public void actionPerformed(ActionEvent e)
  {
    jrbVCenter_actionPerformed(e);
  }
});
jrbBottom.setText("BOTTOM");
jrbBottom.addActionListener(new java.awt.event.ActionListener()
{
  public void actionPerformed(ActionEvent e)
  {
    jrbBottom_actionPerformed(e);
  }
});
```

continues

```
            jpVerticalAlignment.setBorder(titledBorder2);
            jpVerticalAlignment.setLayout(gridLayout6);
            gridLayout6.setRows(3);
            titledBorder2.setTitle("Vertical Alignment");
            this.getContentPane().add(jpButtons, BorderLayout.CENTER);
            jpButtons.add(jbt, null);
            jpButtons.add(jchk, null);
            jpButtons.add(jtb, null);
            jpButtons.add(jrb, null);
            this.getContentPane().add(jpSettings, BorderLayout.SOUTH);
            jpSettings.setLayout(gridLayout2);
            jpSettings.add(jpAlignment, null);
            jpAlignment.add(jpHorizontalAlignment, null);
            jpHorizontalAlignment.add(jrbLeft, null);
            jpHorizontalAlignment.add(jrbCenter, null);
            jpHorizontalAlignment.add(jrbRight, null);
            jpAlignment.add(jpVerticalAlignment, null);
            jpVerticalAlignment.add(jrbTop, null);
            jpVerticalAlignment.add(jrbVCenter, null);
            jpVerticalAlignment.add(jrbBottom, null);
            jpSettings.add(jpMiscSettings, null);
            jpMiscSettings.add(jchkBorderPainted, null);
            jpMiscSettings.add(jchkContentAreaFilled, null);
            jpMiscSettings.add(jchkEnabled, null);
            jpMiscSettings.add(jchkFocusPainted, null);
            jpMiscSettings.add(jchkOpaque, null);
            jpMiscSettings.add(jchkRolloverEnabled, null);

            // Group radio buttons for setting horizontal alignment
            btg1.add(jrbLeft);
            btg1.add(jrbCenter);
            btg1.add(jrbRight);

            // Group radio buttons for setting horizontal alignment
            btg2.add(jrbTop);
            btg2.add(jrbVCenter);
            btg2.add(jrbBottom);
        }

        // Handler for check box borderPainted
        void jchkBorderPainted_actionPerformed(ActionEvent e)
        {
          jbt.setBorderPainted(jchkBorderPainted.isSelected());
          jtb.setBorderPainted(jchkBorderPainted.isSelected());
          jchk.setBorderPainted(jchkBorderPainted.isSelected());
          jrb.setBorderPainted(jchkBorderPainted.isSelected());
        }

        // Handler for check box contentAreaFilled
        void jchkContentAreaFilled_actionPerformed(ActionEvent e)
        {
          jbt.setContentAreaFilled(jchkContentAreaFilled.isSelected());
          jtb.setContentAreaFilled(jchkContentAreaFilled.isSelected());
          jchk.setContentAreaFilled(jchkContentAreaFilled.isSelected());
          jrb.setContentAreaFilled(jchkContentAreaFilled.isSelected());
        }

        // Handler for check box enabled
        void jchkEnabled_actionPerformed(ActionEvent e)
        {
```

Listing 5.1   *Continued*

```
    jbt.setEnabled(jchkEnabled.isSelected());
    jtb.setEnabled(jchkEnabled.isSelected());
    jchk.setEnabled(jchkEnabled.isSelected());
    jrb.setEnabled(jchkEnabled.isSelected());
  }

  // Handler for check box focusPainted
  void jchkFocusPainted_actionPerformed(ActionEvent e)
  {
    jbt.setFocusPainted(jchkFocusPainted.isSelected());
    jtb.setFocusPainted(jchkFocusPainted.isSelected());
    jchk.setFocusPainted(jchkFocusPainted.isSelected());
    jrb.setFocusPainted(jchkFocusPainted.isSelected());
  }

  // Handler for check box opaque
  void jchkOpaque_actionPerformed(ActionEvent e)
  {
    jbt.setOpaque(jchkOpaque.isSelected());
    jtb.setOpaque(jchkOpaque.isSelected());
    jchk.setOpaque(jchkOpaque.isSelected());
    jrb.setOpaque(jchkOpaque.isSelected());
  }

  // Handler for check box rolloverEnabled
  void jchkRolloverEnabled_actionPerformed(ActionEvent e)
  {
    jbt.setRolloverEnabled(jchkRolloverEnabled.isSelected());
    jtb.setRolloverEnabled(jchkRolloverEnabled.isSelected());
    jchk.setRolloverEnabled(jchkRolloverEnabled.isSelected());
    jrb.setRolloverEnabled(jchkRolloverEnabled.isSelected());
  }

  // Handler for the radio button to set left horizontal alignment
  void jrbLeft_actionPerformed(ActionEvent e)
  {
    if (jrbLeft.isSelected())
      setHorizontalAlignment(SwingConstants.LEFT);
  }

  // Handler for the radio button to set center horizontal alignment
  void jrbCenter_actionPerformed(ActionEvent e)
  {
    if (jrbCenter.isSelected())
      setHorizontalAlignment(SwingConstants.CENTER);
  }

  // Handler for the radio button to set right horizontal alignment
  void jrbRight_actionPerformed(ActionEvent e)
  {
    if (jrbRight.isSelected())
      setHorizontalAlignment(SwingConstants.RIGHT);
  }

  // Handler for the radio button to set top vertical alignment
  void jrbTop_actionPerformed(ActionEvent e)
  {
    if (jrbTop.isSelected())
      setVerticalAlignment(SwingConstants.TOP);
  }
```

continues

```
     // Handler for the radio button to set center vertical alignment
     void jrbVCenter_actionPerformed(ActionEvent e)
     {
       if (jrbVCenter.isSelected())
         setVerticalAlignment(SwingConstants.CENTER);
     }

     // Handler for the radio button to set bottom vertical alignment
     void jrbBottom_actionPerformed(ActionEvent e)
     {
       if (jrbBottom.isSelected())
         setVerticalAlignment(SwingConstants.BOTTOM);
     }

     // Set horizontal alignment
     private void setHorizontalAlignment(int alignment)
     {
       jbt.setHorizontalAlignment(alignment);
       jtb.setHorizontalAlignment(alignment);
       jchk.setHorizontalAlignment(alignment);
       jrb.setHorizontalAlignment(alignment);
     }

     // Set vertical alignment
     private void setVerticalAlignment(int alignment)
     {
       jbt.setVerticalAlignment(alignment);
       jtb.setVerticalAlignment(alignment);
       jchk.setVerticalAlignment(alignment);
       jrb.setVerticalAlignment(alignment);
     }
   }
```

Listing 5.1 *Continued*

Example Review

Each button has an icon, a pressed icon, and a rollover icon. When you point the mouse to the button, the rollover icon is displayed if the Rollover Enabled option box is checked. When you press the button, the pressed icon is displayed. Using the radio buttons in the Horizontal Alignment and Vertical Alignment panels, you can set the horizontal alignment and vertical alignment of the icon and the button.

By default, the border of JButton and JToggleButton is painted and the border of JCheckBox and JRadioButton is not painted. You can use the borderPainted property to specify a border. When an icon is associated with JCheckBox or JRadioButton, the check box or the radio button is replaced by the icon.

The icons and borders can be shared. As seen in this example, the icons are shared by button, toggle button, check box, and radio button. If two components have the same border, they can share it. In this example, no two borders are the same.

The program contains over 400 lines of code, but most of the code is generated automatically by JBuilder. The code is easy to read and easy to maintain. This example and many other examples in this book demonstrate the power of rapid Java application development.

You may create an image icon using the filename as follows:

```
ImageIcon icon1 = new ImageIcon("/images/prior.gif");
```

This approach is simple, but it works only with standalone applications. To load images in Java applets, you have to obtain the URL of the image and load the image through it. This approach works for both Java applications and applets.

JLabel

JLabel is a Swing implementation of a java.awt.Label. A JLabel object can display text, an image, or both. An example of using JLabel is shown in Figure 5.13.

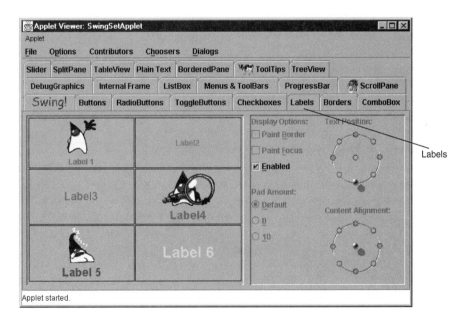

Figure 5.13 *The Labels panel in the SwingSet demo demonstrates the features of* JLabel.

JLabel inherits all the properties from JComponent and shares many properties, such as text, icon, horizontalAlignment, and verticalAlignment, with JButton. Setting the vertical and horizontal alignments specifies the label's location. By default, labels are vertically centered in their display area, text-only labels are left aligned, and image-only labels are horizontally centered. You can also specify the position of the text relative to the image. By default, text is to the right of the image, with the text and image vertically aligned.

JScrollPane

JScrollPane is a component that supports *automatically* scrolling without coding. You can add a component to a scroll pane. The scroll pane takes care of scrolling.

A scroll pane can be viewed as a specialized container with a view port for displaying the contained component. In addition to horizontal and vertical scroll bars, a JScrollPane can have a column header, a row header, and corners, as shown in Figure 5.14.

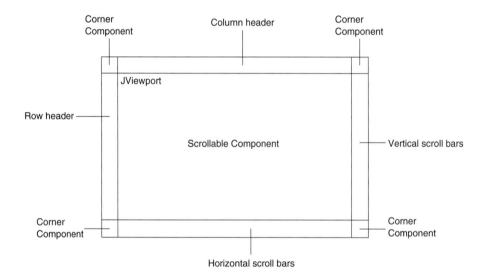

Figure 5.14 *A* JScrollPane *has a view port, optional horizontal and vertical bars, optional column and row headers, and optional corners.*

The view port is an instance of JViewport through which a scrollable component is displayed. Adding a component to the scroll pane actually places it in the scroll pane's view port.

The following properties of JScrollPane are often useful:

- horizontalScrollBarPolicy: Determines when the horizontal scrollbar appears in the scroll pane.

- verticalScrollBarPolicy: Determines when the vertical scrollbar appears in the scroll pane.

- viewportView: Specifies the component to be viewed in the view port.

- viewportBorder: Specifies a border around the view port in the scroll pane.

■ rowHeaderView: Specifies the row-header view component to be used in the scroll pane.

■ columnHeaderView: Specifies the column-header view component to be used in the scroll pane.

To set a corner component, use the following method:

```
public void setCorner(String key,
                      Component corner)
```

Legal values for the key are the following:

■ JScrollPane.LOWER_LEFT_CORNER

■ JScrollPane.LOWER_RIGHT_CORNER

■ JScrollPane.UPPER_LEFT_CORNER

■ JScrollPane.UPPER_RIGHT_CORNER

Example 5.2 Using Labels and Scroll Panes

This example uses a scroll pane to browse large maps. The program lets the user choose a map from a radio button and displays the map in the scroll pane, as shown in Figure 5.15.

Figure 5.15 *You can choose a map from a radio button and display it in a scroll pane.*

continues

191

Here are the steps to complete the example:

1. Create a new project named DisplayMapDemo.jpr and an applet named DisplayMap.java using the Applet Wizard.

2. Create a class named CornerPanel for displaying scroll pane corners, as shown in Listing 5.3. This class extends JPanel and draws simple lines on a panel for decorating scroll pane corners.

3. With DisplayMap.java selected in the Navigation pane, choose the Design tab in the Content pane to display the UI Designer. Drop a JScrollPane to the center of the applet and rename it jspMap. Drop a JPanel to the north of the applet and rename it jpSelection.

4. Drop a JRadioButton twice into jpSelection to create jrbMap1 and jrbMap2. Set the text property of these two radio buttons "Indiana" and "Ohio."

5. Drop a JLabel to jspMap and rename it jlblMap.

6. Declare and create two image icons named map1 and map2 for two image maps. Load the images using the URLs as shown in Listing 5.2. Set row header, column header, and corner header in the jbInit() method.

7. Generate action-event handlers for the two radio buttons, and implement the handlers for map selections, as shown in Listing 5.2.

```java
// DisplayMap.java: Display maps in a label placed in a scroll pane
package DisplayMapDemo;

import java.awt.*;
import java.awt.event.*;
import java.applet.*;
import javax.swing.*;
import javax.swing.border.*;
import java.net.URL;

public class DisplayMap extends JApplet
{
  // Create image icons for maps
  ImageIcon map1;
  ImageIcon map2;

  // Create a button group
  ButtonGroup btg = new ButtonGroup();

  // Generated by JBuilder
  boolean isStandalone = false;
  JScrollPane jspMap = new JScrollPane();
  JLabel jlblMap = new JLabel();
  JPanel jpSelection = new JPanel();
  JRadioButton jrbMap2 = new JRadioButton();
  JRadioButton jrbMap1 = new JRadioButton();
  FlowLayout flowLayout1 = new FlowLayout();
  TitledBorder titledBorder1;
```

Listing 5.2 *DisplayMap.java*

```
//Construct the applet
public DisplayMap()
{
}

//Initialize the applet
public void init()
{
  try
  {
    jbInit();
  }
  catch(Exception e)
  {
    e.printStackTrace();
  }
}

//Component initialization
private void jbInit() throws Exception
{
  // Load images
  Toolkit toolkit = Toolkit.getDefaultToolkit();
  URL url = this.getClass().getResource("images/indianaMap.gif");
  map1 = new ImageIcon(toolkit.getImage(url));

  url = this.getClass().getResource("images/ohioMap.gif");
  map2 = new ImageIcon(toolkit.getImage(url));

  url = this.getClass().getResource("images/horizontalRuler.gif");
  ImageIcon hRuler = new ImageIcon(toolkit.getImage(url));

  url = this.getClass().getResource("images/verticalRuler.gif");
  ImageIcon vRuler = new ImageIcon(toolkit.getImage(url));

  titledBorder1 = new TitledBorder("");
  this.setSize(new Dimension(400,300));
  jpSelection.setLayout(flowLayout1);
  jrbMap1.setText("Indiana");
  jrbMap1.addActionListener(new java.awt.event.ActionListener()
  {
    public void actionPerformed(ActionEvent e)
    {
      jrbMap1_actionPerformed(e);
    }
  });
  jrbMap2.setText("Ohio");
  jrbMap2.addActionListener(new java.awt.event.ActionListener()
  {
    public void actionPerformed(ActionEvent e)
    {
      jrbMap2_actionPerformed(e);
    }
  });
  jpSelection.setBorder(titledBorder1);
  titledBorder1.setTitle("Select a Map");
  this.getContentPane().add(jspMap, BorderLayout.CENTER);
  this.getContentPane().add(jpSelection, BorderLayout.NORTH);
  jpSelection.add(jrbMap1, null);
  jpSelection.add(jrbMap2, null);
  jspMap.getViewport().add(jlblMap, null);
```

continues

```java
        // Set row header, column header and corner header
        jspMap.setColumnHeaderView(new JLabel(hRuler));
          jspMap.setRowHeaderView(new JLabel(vRuler));
        jspMap.setCorner(JScrollPane.UPPER_LEFT_CORNER,
          new CornerPanel(JScrollPane.UPPER_LEFT_CORNER));
        jspMap.setCorner(ScrollPaneConstants.UPPER_RIGHT_CORNER,
          new CornerPanel(JScrollPane.UPPER_RIGHT_CORNER));
        jspMap.setCorner(JScrollPane.LOWER_RIGHT_CORNER,
          new CornerPanel(JScrollPane.LOWER_RIGHT_CORNER));
        jspMap.setCorner(JScrollPane.LOWER_LEFT_CORNER,
          new CornerPanel(JScrollPane.LOWER_LEFT_CORNER));

        // Group buttons
        btg.add(jrbMap1);
        btg.add(jrbMap2);
      }

      void jrbMap1_actionPerformed(ActionEvent e)
      {
        if (jrbMap1.isSelected())
        {
          jlblMap.setIcon(map1);
        }
      }

      void jrbMap2_actionPerformed(ActionEvent e)
      {
        if (jrbMap2.isSelected())
        {
          jlblMap.setIcon(map2);
        }
      }
    }
```

Listing 5.2   *Continued*

```java
    // CornerPanel.java: A panel displaying a line used for scroll
    // pane corner
    package DisplayMapDemo;

    import javax.swing.*;
    import java.awt.*;

    public class CornerPanel extends JPanel
      implements ScrollPaneConstants
    {
      // Line location
      private String location;

      // Constructor
      public CornerPanel(String location)
      {
        this.location = location;
      }

      // Draw a line depending on the location
      public void paintComponent(Graphics g)
      {
        super.paintComponents(g);
```

Listing 5.3   *CornerPanel.java*

```
            if (location == "UPPER_LEFT_CORNER")
              g.drawLine(0, getSize().height, getSize().width, 0);
            else if (location == "UPPER_RIGHT_CORNER")
              g.drawLine(0, 0, getSize().width, getSize().height);
            else if (location == "LOWER_RIGHT_CORNER")
              g.drawLine(0, getSize().height, getSize().width, 0);
            else if (location == "LOWER_LEFT_CORNER")
              g.drawLine(0, 0, getSize().width, getSize().height);
        }
      }
```

Example Review

JLabel can be used to display images as well as text. The program displays an image map in a label, and places the label in the scroll pane. You cannot directly place an image into a scroll pane, because an image is not a component.

The scroll pane holds a label in its view port. Choosing a radio button causes an image icon to be set in the label and displayed in the view port. The scroll pane has the row header, column header, and corners. The row header, column header, and corners can be any components. The program places a label with a horizontal-ruler image as the row header, and another label with a vertical ruler as the column header. The corners are the instances of CornerPanel. The CornerPanel class is a subclass of JPanel, which draws simple lines on the panel.

JTextField

JTextField is a Swing implementation of java.awt.TextField that allows the editing of a single line of text. The setEchoChar() and getEchoChar() methods in TextField are not provided in JTextField in order to avoid a new implementation of a pluggable look-and-feel inadvertently exposing password characters. To provide password-like services, a separate class, JPasswordField, extends JTextField to provide this service with an independently pluggable look-and-feel. An example of using JTextField is shown in Figure 5.16.

JTextField has capabilities not found in TextField. For example, the horizontal alignment of JTextField can be set to be left-justified, centered, or right-justified if the required size of the field text is smaller than the size allocated to it. This is determined by the horizontalAlignment property. The default is to be left-justified.

In addition to properties like text and horizontalAlignment, JTextField has the following useful properties:

- actionCommand: Specifies an action command string associated with the text. By default, the action command is the same as the text. The action command string is passed to the ActionEvent when an ActionEvent is generated on the button.

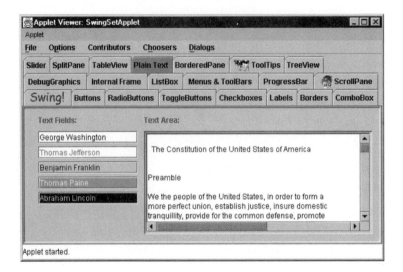

Figure 5.16   *The Plain Text panel in the SwingSet demo demonstrates the features of* JTextField *and* JTextArea.

- ■ editable: A boolean property indicating whether the text field can be edited by the user.

- ■ columns: The width of the text field.

JTextField can fire ActionEvent and ItemEvent among many other events. Pressing Enter in a text field triggers the ActionEvent. Changing contents in a text field triggers the TextEvent.

JTextArea

JTextArea is a Swing implementation of java.awt.TextArea—a multi-line area that displays plain text. JTextArea and JTextField are subclasses of JTextComponent. In addition to properties like text, editable, and columns shared with JTextField. JTextArea has the following properties:

- ■ lineWrap: A boolean property indicating whether the line in the text area is automatically wrapped.

- ■ wrapStyleWord: A boolean property indicating whether the line is wrapped on word or character. The default value is false, which indicates that the line is wrapped on character boundaries.

- ■ rows: The number of lines in the text area.

- ■ lineCount: The number of lines in the text.

- ■ tabSize: The number of characters inserted when the Tab key is pressed.

You can use the following methods to insert, append, and replace text:

■ public void insert(String s, int pos)

This inserts string s in the specified position in the text area.

■ public void append(String s)

This appends string s to the end of the text.

■ public void replaceRange(String s, int start, int end)

This replaces partial texts in the range from position start to position end with string s.

JTextArea does not handle scrolling, but you can create a JScrollPane object to hold an instance of JTextArea and let the scroll pane handle scrolling for JTextArea, as shown in Figure 5.16.

JEditorPane

Swing provides a new component named javax.swing.JEditorPane, which can be used to display HTML files. JEditorPane is a subclass of JTextArea. Thus it inherits all the behavior and properties from JTextArea. Additionally, it is capable of rendering an HTML file with a given URL. The URL is specified in the page property, whose setter method is defined as follows:

```
public void setPage(URL url) IOException
```

JEditorPane generates javax.swing.event.HyperlinkEvent when a hyperlink in the editor pane is clicked. Through this event, you can get the URL of the hyperlink and display the content again using the setPage(url) method.

Example 5.3 Using JEditorPane

This example creates a simple Web browser to render HTML files. The program lets the user enter an HTML file in a text field and press the Enter key to display the HTML file in an editor pane, as shown in Figure 5.17.

Here are the steps to complete the project:

1. Create a new project named ViewHTMLDemo.jpr and an applet named ViewHTML.java using the Applet Wizard.

2. With ViewHTML.java selected in the Navigation pane, choose the Design tab to display the UI Designer. Drop a JScrollPane to the center of the applet, and drop a JEditorPane to the scroll pane and rename it jep. Drop a JPanel to the north of the applet and rename it jpURL.

continues

197

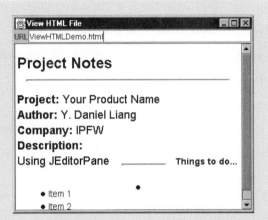

Figure 5.17   *You can specify a URL in the text field and display the HTML file in an editor pane.*

3. Set the layout of jpURL to BorderLayout. Drop a JLabel to the west of jpURL and a JTextField to the center of jpURL and rename it jtfURL.

4. Generate an action-event handler for the text field, and implement the handler for displaying the URL in the editor pane, as shown in Listing 5.4.

5. Generate a hyperlink event handler for the editor pane, and implement it to display the content of the hyperlink in the editor pane, as shown in Listing 5.4.

```java
// ViewHTML.java: Display HTML file in JEditorPane
package ViewHTMLDemo;

import java.awt.*;
import java.awt.event.*;
import java.applet.*;
import javax.swing.*;
import java.net.URL;
import javax.swing.event.*;
import java.io.*;

public class ViewHTML extends JApplet
{
  boolean isStandalone = false;
  JScrollPane jScrollPane1 = new JScrollPane();
  JEditorPane jep = new JEditorPane();
  JPanel jpURL = new JPanel();
  JLabel jLabel1 = new JLabel();
  BorderLayout borderLayout1 = new BorderLayout();
  JTextField jtfURL = new JTextField();
```

Listing 5.4   *ViewHTML.java*

```java
// Construct the applet
public ViewHTML()
{
}

// Initialize the applet
public void init()
{
  try
  {
    jbInit();
  }
  catch(Exception e)
  {
    e.printStackTrace();
  }
}

// Component initialization
private void jbInit() throws Exception
{
  this.setSize(new Dimension(400,300));
  jep.setEditable(false);
  jep.addHyperlinkListener(
    new javax.swing.event.HyperlinkListener()
  {
    public void hyperlinkUpdate(HyperlinkEvent e)
    {
      jep_hyperlinkUpdate(e);
    }
  });
  jLabel1.setText("URL");
  jpURL.setLayout(borderLayout1);
  jtfURL.addActionListener(new java.awt.event.ActionListener()
  {
    public void actionPerformed(ActionEvent e)
    {
      jtfURL_actionPerformed(e);
    }
  });
  this.getContentPane().add(jScrollPane1, BorderLayout.CENTER);
  this.getContentPane().add(jpURL, BorderLayout.NORTH);
  jpURL.add(jLabel1, BorderLayout.WEST);
  jpURL.add(jtfURL, BorderLayout.CENTER);
  jScrollPane1.getViewport().add(jep, null);
}

void jep_hyperlinkUpdate(HyperlinkEvent e)
{
  try
  {
    jep.setPage(e.getURL());
  }
  catch (IOException ex)
  {
    System.out.println(ex);
  }
}
```

continues

```
        void jtfURL_actionPerformed(ActionEvent e)
        {
          // Get the URL of the HTML file
          URL url = this.getClass().getResource(
            jtfURL.getText().trim());

          try
          {
            // Display the HTML file
            jep.setPage(url);
          }
          catch (IOException ex)
          {
            System.out.println(ex);
          }
        }
      }
```

Listing 5.4   *Continued*

Example Review

In this example, a simple Web browser is created using the JEditorPane class. JEditorPane is capable of displaying files in the HTML format or in the RTF format. To enable scrolling, the editor pane is placed inside a scroll pane.

The user enters a URL of the HTML file in the text field and presses the Enter key to fire an action event to display the URL in the editor pane. To display the URL in the editor pane, simply set the URL in the page property of the editor pane.

The editor pane does not have all the functions of a commercial Web browser, but it is convenient for displaying HTML files, including embedded images.

JScrollBar

You used scroll panes to view large contents with automatically scrolling. In many cases, a scroll pane is simple, convenient, and sufficient to provide scrolling functions, but occasionally you need to use scroll bars to manually control scrolling. A *scroll bar* is a control that enables the user to select from a range of values. The scroll bar appears in two styles, *horizontal* and *vertical*, as shown in Figure 5.18.

The JScrollBar has the following properties.

- orientation: Specifies horizontal or vertical style, with 0 for horizontal and 1 for vertical.

- maximum: The maximum value the scroll bar represents when the bubble reaches to the right end of the scroll bar for horizontal style or to the bottom of the scroll bar for vertical style.

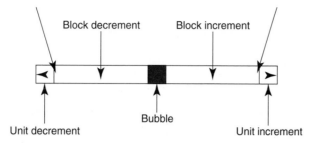

Figure 5.18 *A scroll bar represents a range of values graphically.*

- minimum: The minimum value the scroll bar represents when the bubble reaches to the left end of the scroll bar for horizontal style or to the top of the scroll bar for vertical style.

- visibleAmount: The relative width of the scroll bar's bubble. The actual width appearing on the screen is determined by the maximum value and the value of visibleAmount.

- value: Represents the current value of the scroll bar. Normally, a program should change a scroll bar's value by calling the setValue() method. The setValue() method simultaneously and synchronously sets the minimum, maximum, visible amount, and value properties of a scroll bar, so that they are mutually consistent.

- blockIncrement: The value that is added (subtracted) when the user activates the block increment (decrement) area of the scroll bar, as shown in Figure 9.27. The blockIncrement property, which is new in JDK 1.1, supersedes the pageIncrement property used in JDK 1.02.

- unitIncrement: The value that is added (subtracted) when the user activates the unit increment (decrement) area of the scroll bar, as shown in Figure 9.27. The unitIncrement property, which is new in JDK 1.1, supersedes the lineIncrement property used in JDK 1.02.

NOTE

The actual width of the scroll bar's track is maximum+visibleAmount. When the scroll bar is set to its maximum value, the left side of the bubble is at maximum, and the right side is at maximum+visibleAmount.

Normally, the user changes the value of the scroll bar by making a gesture with the mouse. For example, the user can drag the scroll bar's bubble up and down or click in the scroll bar's unit increment or block increment area. Keyboard gestures can also be mapped to the scroll bar. By convention, the Page Up and Page Down keys are equivalent to clicking in the scroll bar's block increment and block decrement areas.

When the user changes the value of the scroll bar, the scroll bar generates an instance of `AdjustmentEvent`, which is passed to any registered listeners. Any object that wishes to be notified of changes to the scroll bar's value should implement `adjustmentValueChanged()` method in the `AdjustmentListener` interface defined in the package `java.awt.event`.

Example 5.4 Using Scroll Bars

This example uses three scroll bars to specify the red, green, and blue components of a color and set the color as the background color for a panel, as shown in Figure 5.19.

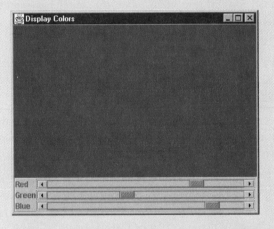

Figure 5.19   *The background color of the panel changes as you adjust the scroll bars.*

Here are the steps to complete the project:

1. Create a new project named DisplayColorDemo.jpr and a new applet named DisplayColor.java using the Applet Wizard.

2. In the UI Designer for DisplayColor.java, drop a `JPanel` to the center of the applet and rename it `jpColor`, and drop a `JPanel` to the south of the applet and rename it `jpSelections`.

3. Set the `layout` of `jpSelections` to `BorderLayout`. Drop a `JPanel` to the west of `jpSelections` and rename it `jpLabels`, and drop a `JPanel` to the Center of `jpSelections` and rename it `jpScrollBars`.

4. Set the `layout` of `jpLabels` to `GridLayout` and set the `row` property of the `GridLayout` to 3. Drop a `JLabel` three times into `jpLabels`, and set the text of the labels to Red, Green and Blue.

5. Set the `layout` of `jpScrollBars` to `GridLayout`, and set the `row` property of the `GridLayout` to 3. Drop a `JScrollBar` three times and rename them

`jscbRed`, `jscbGreen`, and `jscbBlue`. Set orientation and maximum of each scroll bar to VERTICAL and 128.

6. Declare variables redValue, greenValue, and blueValue for representing the red, green, and blue components of the color. Generate adjustment-event handlers for the scroll bars, and implement these handlers to adjust these variables and update the background color in the panel jpColor, as shown in Listing 5.5.

```java
// DisplayColor.java: Use scroll bars to select colors and
// display colors in a panel
package DisplayColorDemo;

import java.awt.*;
import java.awt.event.*;
import java.applet.*;
import javax.swing.*;

public class DisplayColor extends JApplet
{
  // Declare color component values
  int redValue, greenValue, blueValue;
  Color color;

  boolean isStandalone = false;
  JPanel jpColor = new JPanel();
  JPanel jpSelections = new JPanel();
  JPanel jpLabels = new JPanel();
  JPanel jpScrollBars = new JPanel();
  JLabel jLabel1 = new JLabel();
  BorderLayout borderLayout1 = new BorderLayout();
  JLabel jLabel2 = new JLabel();
  JLabel jLabel3 = new JLabel();
  GridLayout gridLayout1 = new GridLayout();
  JScrollBar jscbRed = new JScrollBar();
  JScrollBar jscbGreen = new JScrollBar();
  JScrollBar jscbBlue = new JScrollBar();
  GridLayout gridLayout2 = new GridLayout();

  // Construct the applet
  public DisplayColor()
  {
  }

  // Initialize the applet
  public void init()
  {
    try
    {
      jbInit();
    }
    catch(Exception e)
    {
      e.printStackTrace();
    }
  }
```

Listing 5.5   *DisplayColor.java*

```
// Component initialization
private void jbInit() throws Exception
{
  this.setSize(new Dimension(400,300));
  jLabel1.setText("Red");
  jpSelections.setLayout(borderLayout1);
  jLabel2.setText("Green");
  jLabel3.setText("Blue");
  jpLabels.setLayout(gridLayout1);
  gridLayout1.setRows(3);
  jscbRed.setOrientation(JScrollBar.HORIZONTAL);
  jscbRed.setMaximum(128);
  jscbRed.setBorder(BorderFactory.createEtchedBorder());
  jscbRed.addAdjustmentListener(
    new java.awt.event.AdjustmentListener()
  {
    public void adjustmentValueChanged(AdjustmentEvent e)
    {
      jscbRed_adjustmentValueChanged(e);
    }
  });
  jscbBlue.setOrientation(JScrollBar.HORIZONTAL);
  jscbBlue.setMaximum(128);
  jscbBlue.setBorder(BorderFactory.createEtchedBorder());
  jscbBlue.addAdjustmentListener(
    new java.awt.event.AdjustmentListener()
  {
    public void adjustmentValueChanged(AdjustmentEvent e)
    {
      jscbBlue_adjustmentValueChanged(e);
    }
  });
  jscbGreen.setOrientation(JScrollBar.HORIZONTAL);
  jscbGreen.setMaximum(128);
  jscbGreen.setBorder(BorderFactory.createEtchedBorder());
  jscbGreen.addAdjustmentListener(
    new java.awt.event.AdjustmentListener()
  {
    public void adjustmentValueChanged(AdjustmentEvent e)
    {
      jscbGreen_adjustmentValueChanged(e);
    }
  });
  jpScrollBars.setLayout(gridLayout2);
  gridLayout2.setRows(3);
  jpSelections.setBorder(BorderFactory.createEtchedBorder());
  this.getContentPane().add(jpColor, BorderLayout.CENTER);
  this.getContentPane().add(jpSelections, BorderLayout.SOUTH);
  jpSelections.add(jpLabels, BorderLayout.WEST);
  jpLabels.add(jLabel1, null);
  jpLabels.add(jLabel2, null);
  jpLabels.add(jLabel3, null);
  jpSelections.add(jpScrollBars, BorderLayout.CENTER);
  jpScrollBars.add(jscbRed, null);
  jpScrollBars.add(jscbGreen, null);
  jpScrollBars.add(jscbBlue, null);
}

// Handler for jscbRed
void jscbRed_adjustmentValueChanged(AdjustmentEvent e)
{
```

continues

204

```
                redValue = jscbRed.getValue();
                updateColor();
              }

              // Handler for jscbGreen
              void jscbGreen_adjustmentValueChanged(AdjustmentEvent e)
              {
                greenValue = jscbGreen.getValue();
                updateColor();
              }

              // Handler for jscbBlue
              void jscbBlue_adjustmentValueChanged(AdjustmentEvent e)
              {
                blueValue = jscbBlue.getValue();
                updateColor();
              }

              void updateColor()
              {
                color = new Color(redValue, greenValue, blueValue);
                jpColor.setBackground(color);
              }
            }
          }
```

Listing 5.5 *Continued*

Example Review

The color of the panel above the scroll bars changes as you adjust the scroll bars. The colors are determined by the values represented in the scroll bars. Since the red, green, and blue component values range from 0 to 128, the maximum values of the scroll bars are set at 128.

Whenever the user adjusts a scroll bar, an AdjustmentEvent is fired. The event handler obtains the current value of the color and updates the background color of the panel.

JSlider

JSlider is similar to JScrollBar in the sense that both can be used to represent a range of values, but JSlider has more properties than JScrollBar and can appear in many forms and styles, as shown in Figure 5.20.

JSlider lets the user graphically select a value by sliding a knob within a bounded interval. The slider can show both major tick marks and minor tick marks between them. The number of pixels between the tick marks is controlled with setMajorTickSpacing and setMinorTickSpacing. Sliders can be displayed horizontally or vertically, with or without ticks, and with or without labels.

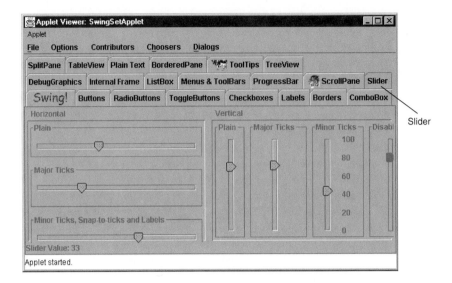

Figure 5.20   *The Slider panel in the SwingSet demo demonstrates the features of* `JSlider`.

The following priorities are defined in the `JSlider` class.

- `extend`: The size of the range covered by the knob. Default value is 0.

- `inverted`: A `boolean` value. If `true`, indicating values increase from right to left or from top to bottom. If `false`, indicating values increase from left to right or from bottom to top. The default value is `false`.

- `maximum`: The maximum value the slider represents. The default value is 100.

- `minimum`: The minimum value the slider represents. The default value is 0.

- `majorTickSpacing`: The number of units between major ticks. The default value is 0.

- `minorTickSpacing`: The number of units between minor ticks. The default value is 0.

- `orientation`: The orientation of the slider, either `HORIZONTAL` or `VERTICAL`. The default value is `HORIZONTAL`.

- `paintLabels`: A `boolean` value indicating whether the labels are painted at tick marks. The default value is `false`, which indicates that the labels are not painted.

- `paintTicks`: A `boolean` value indicating whether the tick marks are painted. The default value is `false`, which indicates that the tick marks are not painted.

- `paintTrack`: A `boolean` value indicating whether the track is painted. The default value is true, which indicates that the track is painted.

- `value`: The current value of the slider. The default value is 50.

■ valueIsAdjusting: A `boolean` value indicating whether the knob is being dragged. The default value is `false`.

When the user changes the value of the slider, the slider generates an instance of `javax.swing.event.ChangeEvent`, which is passed to any registered listeners. Any object that wishes to be notified of changes to the slider's value should implement `stateChanged()` method in the `ChangeListener` interface defined in the package `javax.swing.event`.

JProgressBar

`JProgressBar` is a component that displays a value graphically within a bounded interval. A progress bar is typically used to show the percentage of completion of a lengthy operation; it comprises a rectangular bar that is "filled in" from left to right horizontally or from bottom to top vertically as the operation is being performed. It provides the user with feedback as to the progress of a particular operation. For example, when a file is being read, it alerts the user to the progress of the operation, thereby keeping the user attentive.

You can choose the ProgressBar tab to see the demo for using `JProgressBar` in the SwingDemo project, as shown in Figure 5.21.

Figure 5.21   *The ProgressBar panel demonstrates the features of using* `JProgressBar`.

When the SwingSet demo starts, a progress bar displays the loading status of all the panels. The progress bar can be displayed horizontally or vertically, as determined by its `orientation` property. The `minimum`, `value`, and `maximum` properties determine the minimum, current, and maximum length on the progress bar.

Example 5.5 Using the Progress Bar

This example creates a program that lets you copy files. A progress bar is used to show the progress of the copying operation, as shown in Figure 5.22.

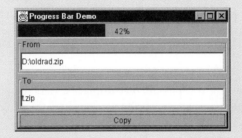

Figure 5.22   *The user enters the files in the text fields and clicks the Copy button to start copying files.*

Here are the steps to complete the project.

1. Create a new project named ProgressBarDemo.jpr. Use the Application Wizard to create an application class named `TestProgressBarApplication` and a frame class named `TestProgressBarFrame`.

2. In the UI Designer of TestProgressBarFrame.java, drop a `JProgressBar` from the Swing page to the north of the frame, a `JButton` to the south of the frame, and a `JPanel` to the center of the frame. Rename the generated objects jpb, jbtCopy, and jpFiles.

3. Set the `stringPainted` property of jpb to True, so that the percentage of completion will be displayed in the progress bar.

4. Set the `layout` of jpFiles to `GridLayout` with two rows. Drop a `JPanel` twice into jpFiles to create jpFromFile and jpToFile. Set the border with title "From" for jpFromFile and the border with title "To" for jpToFile.

5. Set the layout of jpFromFile and jpToFile to `BorderLayout`. Drop a `JTextField` to the center of jpFromFile and the center of jpToFile to create jtfFrom and jtfTo.

6. Generate and implement the code for handling the Copy button, as shown in Listing 5.6.

7. Create a thread class for copying files and updating the progress bar.

```
package ProgressBarDemo;

import java.awt.*;
import java.awt.event.*;
```

Listing 5.6   *TestProgressBarFrame.java*

```
import javax.swing.*;
import javax.swing.border.*;
import java.io.*;

public class TestProgressBarFrame extends JFrame
{
  BorderLayout borderLayout1 = new BorderLayout();
  JProgressBar jpb = new JProgressBar();
  JPanel jPanel1 = new JPanel();
  JButton jbtCopy = new JButton();
  JPanel jPanel2 = new JPanel();
  JPanel jPanel3 = new JPanel();
  GridLayout gridLayout1 = new GridLayout();
  TitledBorder titledBorder1;
  TitledBorder titledBorder2;
  JTextField jtfFrom = new JTextField();
  JTextField jtfTo = new JTextField();
  BorderLayout borderLayout2 = new BorderLayout();
  BorderLayout borderLayout3 = new BorderLayout();

  // Construct the frame
  public TestProgressBarFrame()
  {
    enableEvents(AWTEvent.WINDOW_EVENT_MASK);
    try
    {
      jbInit();
    }
    catch(Exception e)
    {
      e.printStackTrace();
    }
  }

  // Component initialization
  private void jbInit() throws Exception
  {
    titledBorder1 = new TitledBorder("");
    titledBorder2 = new TitledBorder("");
    this.getContentPane().setLayout(borderLayout1);
    this.setSize(new Dimension(348, 193));
    this.setTitle("Progress Bar Demo");
    jbtCopy.setText("Copy");
    jbtCopy.addActionListener(new java.awt.event.ActionListener()
    {

      public void actionPerformed(ActionEvent e)
      {
        jbtCopy_actionPerformed(e);
      }
    });
    jPanel1.setLayout(gridLayout1);
    gridLayout1.setRows(2);
    jPanel2.setBorder(titledBorder1);
    jPanel2.setLayout(borderLayout2);
    jPanel3.setBorder(titledBorder2);
    jPanel3.setLayout(borderLayout3);
    titledBorder1.setTitle("From");
    titledBorder2.setTitle("To");
    jpb.setStringPainted(true);
```

continues

209

```java
      this.getContentPane().add(jpb, BorderLayout.NORTH);
      this.getContentPane().add(jPanel1, BorderLayout.CENTER);
      jPanel1.add(jPanel2, null);
      jPanel2.add(jtfFrom, BorderLayout.CENTER);
      jPanel1.add(jPanel3, null);
      jPanel3.add(jtfTo, BorderLayout.CENTER);
      this.getContentPane().add(jbtCopy, BorderLayout.SOUTH);
  }

  // Overridden so we can exit on System Close
  protected void processWindowEvent(WindowEvent e)
  {
    super.processWindowEvent(e);
    if(e.getID() == WindowEvent.WINDOW_CLOSING)
    {
      System.exit(0);
    }
  }

  void jbtCopy_actionPerformed(ActionEvent e)
  {
    // Create a thread for copying files
    CopyFileThread thread = new CopyFileThread(this);
    thread.start();
  }
}

// Copy file and update progress bar in a separate thread
class CopyFileThread extends Thread
{
  int currentValue;
  Runnable updateProgressBar;
  TestProgressBarFrame frame;

  public CopyFileThread(final TestProgressBarFrame frame)
  {
    this.frame = frame;

    updateProgressBar = new Runnable()
    {
      public void run()
      {
        JProgressBar jpb = frame.jpb;
        jpb.setValue(currentValue);
      }
    }
  }

  public void run()
  {
    try
    {
      // Create file input stream
      File inFile = new File(frame.jtfFrom.getText().trim());
      BufferedInputStream in = new BufferedInputStream
        (new FileInputStream(inFile));

      // Create file output stream
      File outFile = new File(frame.jtfTo.getText());
      BufferedOutputStream out =  new BufferedOutputStream
```

Listing 5.6   *TestProgressBarFrame.java*

```
            (new FileOutputStream(outFile));

        // Get total bytes in the file
        long totalBytes = in.available();

        // Start progress meter bar
        frame.jpb.setValue(0);
        frame.jpb.setMaximum(100);

        int r;
        long bytesRead = 0;
        byte[] b = new byte[512];
        while ((r = in.read(b, 0, b.length)) != -1)
        {
          out.write(b, 0, r);
          bytesRead += r;
          currentValue = (int)(bytesRead*100/totalBytes);

          // Update the progress bar
          SwingUtilities.invokeLater(updateProgressBar);
        }

        System.out.println("Completed");
        in.close();
        out.close();
      }
      catch (FileNotFoundException ex)
      {
        System.out.println(ex);
      }
      catch (IOException ex)
      {
        System.out.println(ex);
      }
    }
  }
```

Example Review

Since the project involves accessing local files, it creates a standalone application rather than an applet. For security reasons, an applet cannot access local files.

Swing components are not thread-safe, meaning that they can only be accessed from the event dispatch thread once they are displayed. The event dispatch thread is the thread that invokes callback methods like update() and paint() as well as the event handlers in the event listener interface. Occasionally, you need to update GUI components from a nonstandard event, as in this case, where the progress bar is repainted in the thread that copies files. To ensure that the progress bar is updated in the event dispatch thread, you need to use the SwingUtilities's invokeLater() method to invoke the thread for updating the progress bar.

Chapter Summary

Swing lightweight components are written in Java, without window-system-specific code. This facilitates a customizable look-and-feel without relying on the native windowing system, and simplifies the deployment of applications. Swing also supports a pluggable look-and-feel architecture. Thanks to this feature, users can switch the look-and-feel of an application or an applet without restarting it and without the developer having to subclass the entire component set.

This chapter introduced the basic features of Swing components. You learned to create projects using the components JButton, JRadioButton, JToggleButton, JCheckBox, Border, JLabel, JScrollPane, JTextField, JTextArea, JEditorPane, JScrollBar, JSlider, and JProgressBar in JBuilder.

Chapter Review

5.1. Why are AWT user interface components considered heavyweight? Why are Swing user interface components considered lightweight?

5.2. Describe the Swing model-view architecture.

5.3. How do you specify a particular look-and-feel in Java programs?

5.4. How do you preview a particular look-and-feel in JBuilder?

5.5. Describe the properties of JComponent.

5.6. Describe the properties of AbstractionButton.

5.7. How do you create a scrollable text area?

5.8. How do you display an HTML page in a JEditorPane?

5.9. Describe the similarities and differences between JScrollPane and JScrollBar.

5.10. Describe the similarities and differences between JScrollBar and JSlider.

5.11. Why is it necessary to use the invokeLater() method in Example 5.5? What is the property that displays the percentage of work completed in JProgressBar?

Programming Exercises

5.1. Develop a program to set the horizontal alignment and column size properties of a text field dynamically, as shown in Figure 5.23.

5.2. Create a program that demonstrates the wrapping styles of the text area. The program uses a check box to indicate whether the text area is wrapped. In the case where the text area is wrapped, you need to specify whether it is wrapped by characters or by words, as shown in Figure 5.24.

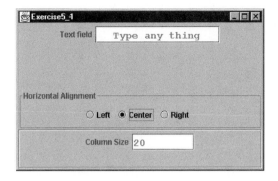

Figure 5.23   *You can set the horizontal alignment and column size properties of a text field dynamically.*

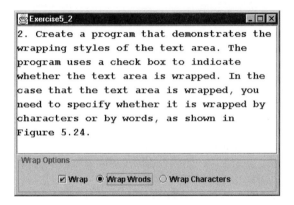

Figure 5.24   *You can set the options to wrap a text area by characters or by words dynamically.*

5.3. Modify Example 5.4 and use the `JSlider` to select colors instead of using `JScrollBar`.

5.4. Create a program that displays an instance of `JProgressBar` and sets its `value` property randomly every 500 milliseconds infinitely.

CONTAINERS AND LAYOUT MANAGERS

Objectives

- Know the structures of the Swing container.

- Understand how a layout manager works in Java.

- Examine the layout managers provided in JBuilder.

- Create custom layout managers and install custom layout managers in JBuilder.

- Use `JTabbedPane` to create tabbed panes.

- Use `JSplitPane` to create split panes.

Introduction

If you have used a Windows-based RAD tool like Visual Basic, you know that it is easier to create user interfaces with Visual Basic than with a Java RAD tool like JBuilder. This is mainly because the components are placed in absolute positions and sizes in Visual Basic, whereas they are placed in containers using a variety of layout managers in Java. Using absolute positions and sizes is fine if the application is developed and deployed on the same platform, but what looks fine on the development system may not look right on a deployment system on a different platform. To solve this problem, Java provides a set of layout managers that place the components in containers in a way that is independent of fonts, screen resolutions, and platform differences.

A container is an object that holds and groups components. A *layout manager* is a special object used to place the components in a container. Containers and layout managers play a crucial role in creating user interfaces. This chapter presents a conceptual overview of containers, reviews the layout managers in Java, and introduces new layout managers provided by JBuilder. You will also learn how to create your own layout manager and install it in JBuilder.

About Containers

User interface components like `JButton` cannot be displayed without being placed in a container. A container is a component that is capable of containing other components. You do not display a user interface component; you place it in a container, and the container displays the components it contains.

The base class for all containers is `java.awt.Container`, which is a subclass of `java.awt.Component`. The `Container` class has the following essential functions:

- Add and remove components using various `add()` and `remove()` methods.

- Maintain a `layout` property for specifying a layout manager that is used to lay out components in the container.

- Provide registration methods for the `java.awt.event.ContainerEvent`.

In AWT programming, the `java.awt.Frame` class is used as a top-level container for Java applications, and `java.awt.Applet` class is used for all Java applets. These classes do not work with Swing lightweight components. Special versions of `Frame` and `Applet` named `JFrame` and `JApplet` are developed to accommodate Swing components. `JFrame` is a subclass of `Frame`, and `JApplet` is a subclass of `Applet`. The Swing containers inherit all the functions of their heavyweight counterparts, but they have a more complex internal structure with several layered panes, as shown in Figure 6.1.

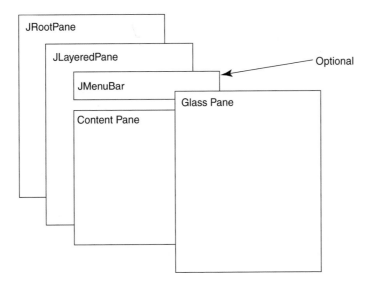

Figure 6.1   *Swing containers use layers of panes to group lightweight components and make them work properly.*

javax.swing.JRootPane is a container that is contained in all of Swing's top-level containers, such as JFrame and JDialog. javax.swing.JLayeredPane is a container that manages the optional menu bar and the content pane. The content pane is an instance of Container with default BorderLayout. This is the container where the user interface components are added. To obtain the content pane in a JFrame or in a JApplet, use the getContentPane() method. The glass pane floats on top of everything and allows you to intercept mouse events.

Now let us review the three most frequently used Swing containers: JFrame, JApplet, and JPanel.

JFrame

JFrame, a Swing version of Frame, is a top-level container for Java graphics applications. Like Frame, JFrame is displayed as a standalone window with a title bar and a border. The following properties are often useful in JFrame.

■ contentPane: The content pane of the frame.

■ iconImage: The image that represents the frame. This image replaces the default Java image on the frame's title bar and is also displayed when the frame is minimized. This property type is Image. You can get an image using the Toolkit class or using the ImageIcon class, as follows:

```
Image image = (new ImageIcon(filename)).getImage();
```

■ jMenuBar: The optional menu bar for the frame.

217

- layout: This property is inherited from Frame, but is not used in JFrame because the components are not directly placed in the frame; instead they are placed in the content pane. In JBuilder 3, this property is associated with the content pane of the frame. When you set a new layout, JBuilder sets the layout in the content pane of JFrame.

- resizable: A boolean value indicating whether the frame is resizable. The default value is true.

- title: The title of the frame.

All the above properties are inherited from Frame except contentPane and jMenuBar.

JApplet

JApplet is a Swing version of Applet. Since it is a subclass of Applet, it has all the functions required by the Web browser. Here are the four essential methods defined in Applet:

```
// Called by the browser when the Web page containing
// this applet is initially loaded.
public void init()

// Called by the browser after the init() method and
// every time the Web page is visited.
public void start()

// Called by the browser when the page containing this
// applet becomes inactive.
public void stop()

// Called by the browser when the Web browser exits.
public void destroy()

// Called by the browser when the Web browser exits.
public void destroy()
```

Additionally, JApplet has the contentPane and jMenuBar property, among others. As with JFrame, you do not place components directly into JApplet; instead you place them into the content pane of the applet. The Applet class cannot have the menu bar, but the JApplet class allows you to set the menu bar using the setJMenuBar() method.

TIP

The contentPane and jMenuBar are hidden properties in JApplet. By default, these properties do not appear in the Inspector. To display hidden properties, right-click the Inspector, choose Property Exposure Level, hidden.

JPanel

Panels act as smaller containers for grouping user interface components. javax.swing.JPanel is different from JFrame and JApplet. First, JPanel is not a top-level container; it must be placed inside another container, and it can be placed inside another JPanel. Second, since JPanel is a subclass of JComponent, JPanel is a lightweight component, but JFrame and JApplet are heavyweight components.

JPanel is a Swing version of Panel, but it is not a subclass of Panel. Nevertheless, you can use JPanel the same way you use Panel. As a subclass of JComponent, JPanel can take advantage of JComponent, such as double buffering and borders. You should draw on JPanel rather than JFrame or JApplet because JPanel supports double buffering, which is the technique for eliminating flickers.

Layout Managers

Every container has a layout manager that is responsible for arranging the components in the container. The container's setLayout() method can be used to set a layout manager. Certain types of containers have default layout managers. For instance, the content pane of JFrame or JApplet uses BorderLayout, and JPanel uses FlowLayout.

A container's layout property appears in the Inspector for the container, as shown in Figure 6.2. You can specify a layout manager for a container by selecting one from a list of available layout managers. JBuilder automatically updates the container's call to setLayout().

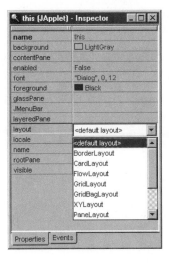

Figure 6.2   *Every container has a* layout *property. You can choose a layout from a drop-down list of layout managers in JBuilder.*

The layout manager places the components in accordance with its own rules and property settings, and with the constraints associated with each component.

Every layout manager has its own specific set of rules. For example, the FlowLayout manager places components in rows from left to right and starts a new row when the previous row is filled. The BorderLayout manager places components in the north, south, east, west, or center of the container. The GridLayout manager places components in a grid of cells in rows and columns from left to right in order.

Some layout managers have properties that can affect the sizing and location of the components in the container. For example, BorderLayout has properties called hgap (horizontal gap) and vgap (vertical gap) that determine the distance between components horizontally and vertically. FlowLayout has properties that can be used to specify the alignment (left, center, right) of the components and properties for specifying the horizontal or vertical gap between the components. GridLayout has properties that can be used to specify the horizontal or vertical gap between columns and rows and the properties for specifying the number of rows and columns. These properties can be viewed and edited in the Inspector when the layout manager is selected in the Component tree. As shown in Figure 6.3, the layout manager is displayed as an item in the Tree just below the container to which it is attached.

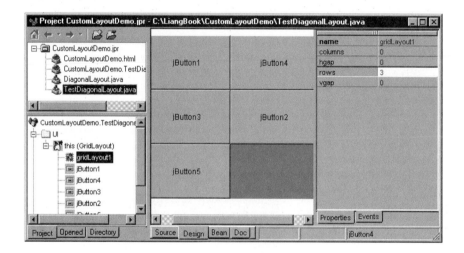

Figure 6.3   *You can view and edit the properties of a layout manager in the UI Designer.*

For each component you drop into a container, JBuilder uses the *constraints* property to provide additional information about how the layout manager should locate and size this specific object. For example, a component added to a container with BorderLayout has the constraints property with selectable values North, South, East, West, and Center. When a component is created, an initial value is assigned to constraints depending on where this component is placed in the container. The constraints value of a component added to a container with FlowLayout is always null. The constraints property is associated with a component, but it is not specified until the component is added to a container.

> ■■■■ NOTE
>
> The `constraints` property is JBuilder-specific, and is created for every object that is added to a container. This property can be viewed and edited in the Inspector. The type of object or value created depends on the type of layout manager being used. Modifications of the `constraints` property are synchronized with the updates of the container's `add()` method in the source code.

The size of a component in a container is determined by many factors, such as:

- The type of layout manager used by the container.

- The layout constraints associated with each component.

- The size of the container.

- Certain properties common to all components (such as `preferredSize`, `minimumSize`, `maximumSize`, `alignmentX`, and `alignmentY`).

The `preferredSize` property indicates the ideal size for the component to look best. Depending on the rules of the particular layout manager, this property may or may not be considered. For example, the preferred size of a component is used in a container with a `FlowLayout` manager, but ignored if it is placed in a container with a `BorderLayout` manager.

The `minimumSize` property specifies the minimum size for the component to be useful. For most GUI components, `minimumSize` is the same as `preferredSize`. Layout managers generally respect `minimumSize` more than `preferredSize`.

The `maximumSize` property specifies the maximum size needed by a component, so that the layout manager won't wastefully give space to a component that does not need it. For instance, `BorderLayout` could limit the center component's size to its maximum size, and then either give the space to edge components or limit the size of the outer window when resized.

The `alignmentX` property specifies how the component would like to be aligned relative to other components along the x-axis. This value should be a number between 0 and 1, where 0 represents alignment along the origin, 1 is aligned the farthest away from the origin, 0.5 is centered, etc.

The `alignmentY` property specifies how the component would like to be aligned relative to other components along the y-axis. The value should be a number between 0 and 1, where 0 represents alignment along the origin, 1 is aligned the farthest away from the origin, 0.5 is centered, etc.

Working with Layout Managers

Java provides a variety of layout managers. In addition, you can create custom layout managers. `BorderLayout`, `FlowLayout`, `GridLayout`, `CardLayout`, `GridBagLayout`, and `Null` were introduced with Java AWT. `BoxLayout` and `OverlayLayout` were introduced in Swing. `BoxLayout2`, `OverlayLayout2`, `XYLayout`, `PaneLayout`, and `VerticalLayout` are custom layout managers provided by JBuilder.

BorderLayout

BorderLayout arranges and resizes its components to fit in five regions: North, South, East, West, and Center. The components are laid out according to their preferred sizes and constraints. The North and South components may be stretched horizontally; the East and West components may be stretched vertically; the Center component may stretch both horizontally and vertically to fill any space left over.

By default, a BorderLayout puts no gap between the components in the container. However, you can specify the horizontal gap (hgap) and the vertical gap (hgap) in the Inspector.

BorderLayout is ideal for docking components to one or more edges of a container, and for filling up the center of the container with a component. Use BorderLayout if you want a single component to occupy the entire container.

FlowLayout

FlowLayout arranges components according to their preferredSize in a left-to-right flow, much like lines of text in a paragraph.

You can choose how to place components in the rows by specifying an alignment justification of left, right, or center on the alignment property in the Inspector for the layout manager. You can also specify the size of the horizontal or vertical gap between the components, using the hgap and vgap properties. By default, the gap is 5 pixels.

GridLayout

GridLayout arranges components in a rectangular grid of cells. The container is divided into equal-sized rectangles, and one component is placed in each rectangle. GridLayout expands each component to fill the entire cell.

You can specify the number of columns and rows in the grid; one of these can be zero, but at least one must be nonzero. For example, if you specify four columns and zero rows, GridLayout creates a grid with four columns and a variant number of rows depending on the number of components that are added to the container. You can also specify the gap between rows and columns. By default, the gap is 0.

GridLayout is ideal when you want the components in a container to be the same size. In Example 4.1, "Creating a Clock Component," you put six clocks in the applet using GridLayout to ensure that all the clocks were the same size.

CardLayout

CardLayout places components in the container as cards. Only one card is visible at a time, and the container acts as a stack of cards. The ordering of cards is determined by the container's own internal ordering of its component objects. CardLayout defines a set of methods that allow an application to flip through the cards sequentially or to show a specified card directly.

You can specify the size of the horizontal and vertical gap surrounding a stack of components in a CardLayout manager.

CardLayout is ideal when you need to manage two or more panels that have to share the same display area. In many situations, CardLayout can be replaced by JTabbedPane, which is introduced later in this chapter.

GridBagLayout

GridBagLayout is the most flexible and the most complex. It is similar to GridLayout in the sense that both layout managers arrange components in a grid. However, in GridBagLayout the components can vary in size and can be added in any order.

GridBagLayout uses a dynamic rectangular grid of cells, with each component occupying one or more cells called its *display area*. Each component managed by a GridBagLayout manager is associated with a GridBagConstraints instance that specifies how the component is laid out within its display area. How a GridBagLayout places a set of components depends on each component's GridBagConstraints and minimum size, as well as the preferred size of the components' container.

To use GridBagLayout effectively, you must customize one or more of its components' GridBagConstraints. You customize a GridBagConstraints object by setting one or more of its instance variables:

- gridx and gridy: Specify the cell at the upper left of the component's display area, where the upper-left-most cell has address gridx=0, gridy=0. Note that gridx specifies the column in which the component will be placed, and gridy specifies the row in which the component will be placed.

- gridwidth and gridheight: Specify the number of cells in a row (for gridwidth) or column (for gridheight) in the component's display area. The default value is 1.

- weightx and weighty: Specify the extra space to allocate the component horizontally and vertically when the window is resized. Unless you specify a weight for at least one component in a row (weightx) and column (weighty), all the components clump together in the center of their container. This is because when the weight is zero (the default), the GridBagLayout puts any extra space between its grid of cells and the edges of the container.

- fill: Specifies how the component should be resized if its viewing area is larger than its current size. Valid values are GridBagConstraints.NONE (the default), GridBagConstraints.HORIZONTAL (make the component wide enough to fill its display area horizontally, but don't change its height), GridBagConstraints.VERTICAL (make the component tall enough to fill its display area vertically, but don't change its width), and GridBagConstraints.BOTH (make the component fill its display area entirely).

■ anchor: Specifies where the component is placed in the area when it does not fill in the entire area. Valid values are GridBagConstraints.CENTER (the default), GridBagConstraints.NORTH, GridBagConstraints.NORTHEAST, GridBag-Constraints.EAST, GridBagConstraints.SOUTHEAST, GridBagConstraints.SOUTH, GridBagConstraints.SOUTHWEST, GridBagConstraints.WEST, and GridBagConstraints.NORTHWEST.

■ insets: Specify the minimum amount of external space (padding) in pixels between the component and the edges of its display area.

The fill and anchor parameters deal with how to fill and place the component when the viewing area is larger than the requested area. The fill and anchor parameters are class variables, while gridx, gridy, width, height, weightx, and weighty are instance variables.

GridBagLayout is a complex layout manager that many people find difficult to use. JBuilder greatly simplifies the use of GridBagLayout with a Constraint property editor. The Constraint property editor enables you to edit all the GridBagConstraints values, as shown in Figure 6.4. To open the editor, either right-click the component in the UI Designer and choose Constraints or select the constraints property in the Inspector and click the ellipsis button.

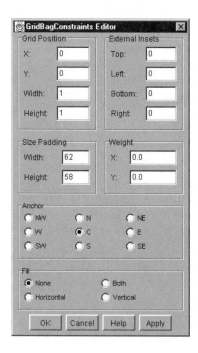

Figure 6.4   *The* GridBagConstraints *property editor lets you edit all the properties of a component's constraints.*

By right-clicking on a component and choosing Show Grid, you can display a grid on the UI Designer that lets you see exactly where and how components are placed in the container. The grid is only visible when a component inside a GridBagLayout is selected. When you right-click on a component, you also see other choices on the popup menu, and these let you quickly set or remove certain constraints without using the Constraint property editor, as shown in Figure 6.5.

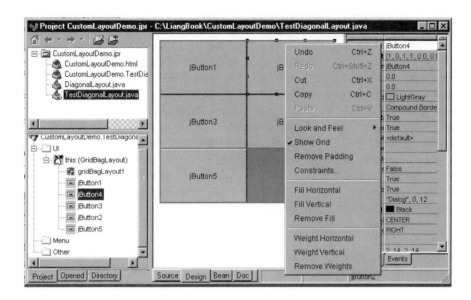

Figure 6.5   *You can set the constraints of a component with* GridBagLayout *in a popup menu in the UI Designer.*

TIP
While GridBagLayout can accommodate a complex grid, it behaves more predictably if you organize your components into smaller panels, nested inside the GridBagLayout container. These nested panels can use other layouts and can contain additional panels if necessary.

Null

Null means that no layout manager is assigned to the container. You should use XYLayout, which is similar to Null layout but provides more controls for the components.

BoxLayout and Box Class

BoxLayout is a Swing layout manager that arranges components in a row or a column. The JToolBar component introduced in Chapter 7, "Menus, Toolbars, and Dialogs," uses BoxLayout. You can use BoxLayout in any container, but it is simpler to use the `Box` class, which is a container of `BoxLayout`. To create a `Box` container, use one of the following two static methods:

```
Box box1 = Box.createHorizontalBox();
Box box2 = Box.createVerticalBox();
```

The former creates a box that contains components horizontally, and the latter creates a box that contains components vertically. These two types of boxes are preinstalled in the Swing Containers page of the Component palette in JBuilder. So you can create horizontal or vertical boxes using JBuilder's UI Designer.

You can add components to a box programmatically in the same way as you add them to the containers of `FlowLayout` or `GridLayout` using the `add()` method as follows:

```
box1.add(new JButton("A Button"));
```

You can drop components to a box in the same way as you drop components to a container. The components are laid left to right in a horizontal box, and top to bottom in a vertical box.

`BoxLayout` is similar to `GridLayout` but `BoxLayout` has many unique features.

First, `BoxLayout` respects a component's preferred size, maximum size, and minimum size. If the total preferred size of all the components in the box is greater than the box size, then the components are expanded up to their maximum size. If the total preferred size of all the components in the box is less than the box size, then the components are shrunk down to their minimum size. If the components do not fit at their minimum width, some of them will not be shown. In the `GridLayout`, the container is divided into cells of equal size, and the components are fit in regardless of their preferred, maximum or minimum size.

Second, unlike other layout managers, `BoxLayout` considers the component's `alignmentX` or `alignmentY` property. The `alignmentX` property is used to place the component in a vertical box layout, and the `alignmentY` property is used to place it in a horizontal box layout.

Third, `BoxLayout` does not have gaps between the components, but you can use fillers to separate components. A filler is an invisible component. There are three kinds of fillers: *struts*, *rigid areas*, and *glues*.

A strut simply adds some space between components. You can use the static method `createHorizontalStrut()` in the `Box` class to create a horizontal strut, or use the static method `createVerticalStrut()` to create a vertical strut. For example, the following code adds a vertical strut of 8 pixels between two buttons in a vertical box.

```
box2.add(new JButton("Button 1"));
box2.add(Box.createVerticalStrut(8));
box2.add(new JButton("Button 2"));
```

A rigid area is a two-dimensional space that can be created using the static method `createRigidArea(dimension)` in the `Box` class. For example, the following code adds a rigid area 10 pixels wide and 20 pixels high into a box.

```
box2.add(Box.createRigidArea(new Dimension(10, 20));
```

A glue separates components as much as possible. For example, by adding a glue between two components in a horizontal box, you place one component at the left end and the other at the right end. A glue can be created using the `Box.createGlue()` method.

JBuilder installs three fillers in the Swing page of the Component palette. These three fillers are the following:

- ■ ⬦ `Box.createGlue()`

- ■ ⊢ `Box.createHorizontalStrut(8)`

- ■ I `Box.createVerticalStrut(8)`

BoxLayout2

`BoxLayout2`, a Borland custom layout manager, is a Swing `BoxLayout` wrapped as a bean so that it can be selected as a layout in the Inspector. `BoxLayout2` places components in a row or a column and expands them to fill the available space in the container.

You can choose whether the components are placed in a row or in a column by specifying the axis of `x-axis` or `y-axis` in the Inspector of the layout manager.

XYLayout

`XYLayout` arranges components in absolute positions and sizes. It is easy to use, but lacks portability, because when you resize a container, the components do not reposition or resize. You should avoid using `XYLayout` for cross-platform projects.

You can modify the `constraints` property to set the location and size for the component. This can also be done by using the mouse. You can align the components and make them of the same width and height. To perform the alignment operations, select the components you want to align, right-click in the UI Designer, and select the desired operations from the popup menu, as shown in Figure 6.6.

`XYLayout` is very useful for prototyping UI design. You can use `XYLayout` to design complex UI with multiple, nested panels, then convert the design using portable layout managers. It is particularly convenient to use `XYLayout` for prototyping designs involving `GridBagLayout`. This can help speed up your design work. JBuilder intelligently converts the layout to `GridBagLayout`.

■■■ CAUTION
Save the source code before converting from one layout to the other. It is possible that the conversion may distort the UI design and make it unusable.

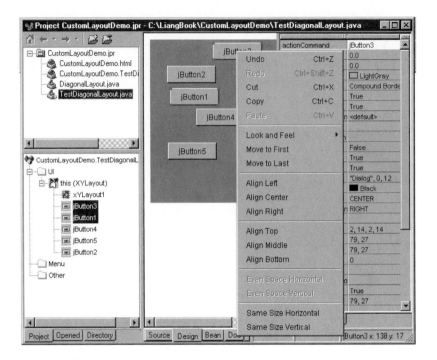

Figure 6.6   *The alignment operations make it easy to organize components in a clean look.*

■■■ TIP

When prototyping with XYLayout, use XYLayout for all the nested containers. When converting the design, start from the inner containers.

OverlayLayout2

OverlayLayout2, a Borland custom layout manager, is Swing's OverlayLayout wrapped as a bean so that it can be selected as a layout in the Inspector. It is similar to CardLayout in that it places the components on top of one other. Unlike CardLayout, where only one component is visible at a time, the components can be visible at the same time if you make each component in the container transparent. For example, to make a composite graphics, you could overlay multiple transparent images on top of one other in the container.

PaneLayout

PaneLayout is a Borland custom layout manager that lets you specify the size of a component in relation to its sibling components. PaneLayout was introduced before the Swing components were proposed. The usefulness of PaneLayout has diminished with the introduction of JSplitPane. JSplitPane is more versatile and flexible than PaneLayout. I recommend the use of JSplitPane to create split panes. JSplitPane is covered later in this chapter.

VerticalFlowLayout

`VerticalFlowLayout` is a Borland custom layout manager. While `FlowLayout` arranges components in a left-to-right flow, `VerticalFlowLayout` arranges components in columns from top to bottom, then left to right, based on the components' `preferredSize`.

Like `FlowLayout`, you can specify alignment and horizontal and vertical gaps in `VerticalFlowLayout`. You can also specify whether all the components are placed in one column using the `horizontalFill` property and whether the last component fills the remaining height of the container using the `verticalFill` property. By default, `horizontalFill` is true, and `verticalFill` is false.

■■■■ TIP

The standard Java layout managers are sufficient in most situations. I recommend that you avoid using the layout managers provided in JBuilder. Although the JBuilder layout managers are 100% pure Java, you need to import them to your project and package them for deployment.

The following example demonstrates the use of a variety of Swing containers and layout managers to create projects in JBuilder.

Example 6.1 Choosing Colors

This example creates a project that selects a standard color from a combo box or selects any color by specifying an RGB value or an HSB value. A sample run of the project is shown in Figure 6.7.

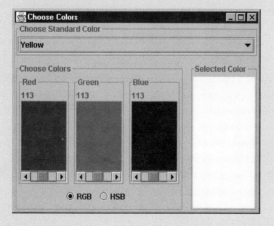

Figure 6.7   *You can choose a standard color from the combo box or choose any color by specifying either RGB or HSB values.*

continues

229

The three color-selection panels titled Red, Green, and Blue in the Choose color panel have similar functions. This makes it ideal to create a bean component for modeling these panels. Let the bean component be named SingleColorPanel. This component generates an ActionEvent to notify listeners whenever the color value changes in the panel.

Here are the steps in creating SingleColorPanel.

1. Create a new project named ChooseColorDemo.jpr, choose File, and create a bean named SingleColorPanel using the JavaBeans Wizard that extends JPanel.

2. Click the Bean tab in the Content pane to switch to BeansExpress. Choose Properties to add three properties: colorType (a string of value either RGB or HSB), currentValue (an int value) and title (a string for the title on the border of the panel).

3. Choose the Events tab in the BeansExpress and check Action to enable the bean to fire Action events. The Action event is needed to notify the listeners that a new color has been selected.

4. Click the Design tab to switch to the UI Designer. Set layout of the panel to BorderLayout. Set the border to titled to create titledBorder1. Drop a JLabel to the north, a JTextField to the Center and a JScrollBar to the South of the panel. Rename these components jlblColor, jtfColor, and jscbColor. The UI layout of SingleColorPanel is shown in Figure 6.8.

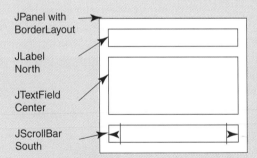

JPanel with
BorderLayout

JLabel
North

JTextField
Center

JScrollBar
South

Figure 6.8   *The* SingleColorPanel *consists of a* JScrollBar *for selecting values, a* JTextField *for showing the color, and a* JLabel *for displaying the value.*

5. In the Events page of jscbColor, click the value field of adjustmentValueChanged to generate the code for handling the adjustment value change of the scroll bar. Fill in the code as shown in Listing 6.1.

6. Modify the getTitle() method and setTitle() method to get the title from titledBorder1 and set the title to titledBorder1. Delete the declara-

tion for the `title` variable, since it is not used to maintain the `title` property.

7. Install `SingleColorPanel` in the Component palette for use in the `ChooseColor` class.

```java
package ChooseColorDemo;

import java.awt.*;
import javax.swing.*;
import javax.swing.border.*;
import java.awt.event.*;
import java.util.*;

public class SingleColorPanel extends JPanel
  implements com.borland.jbcl.util.BlackBox
{
  BorderLayout borderLayout1 = new BorderLayout();
  JScrollBar jscbColor = new JScrollBar();
  JTextField jtfColor = new JTextField();
  JLabel jlblColorValue = new JLabel();

  private String colorType = "Red";
  private String buttonType = "RGB";
  private int colorValue = 0;

  private transient Vector actionListeners;
  TitledBorder titledBorder1;

  // Constructor
  public SingleColorPanel()
  {
    try
    {
      jbInit();
    }
    catch (Exception ex)
    {
      ex.printStackTrace();
    }
  }

  // Component initialization
  private void jbInit() throws Exception
  {
    titledBorder1 = new TitledBorder("");
    jscbColor.addAdjustmentListener(
      new java.awt.event.AdjustmentListener()
    {
      public void adjustmentValueChanged(AdjustmentEvent e)
      {
        jscbColor_adjustmentValueChanged(e);
      }
    });
    jscbColor.setOrientation(JScrollBar.HORIZONTAL);
    jtfColor.setEditable(false);
```

continues

Listing 6.1   *SingleColorPanel.java*

```
                    jlblColorValue.setText("jLabel1");
                    this.setLayout(borderLayout1);
                    this.setBorder(titledBorder1);
                    this.add(jscbColor, BorderLayout.SOUTH);
                    this.add(jtfColor, BorderLayout.CENTER);
                    this.add(jlblColorValue, BorderLayout.NORTH);

                    setTitle("Color type");
                  }

                  // Setter method for the colorType property
                  public void setColorType(String newColorType)
                  {
                    colorType = newColorType;
                  }

                  // Getter method for the colorType property
                  public String getColorType()
                  {
                    return colorType;
                  }

                  // Getter method for the colorValue property
                  public int getColorValue()
                  {
                    return colorValue;
                  }

                  // Setter method for the title property
                  public void setTitle(String newTitle)
                  {
                    titledBorder1.setTitle(newTitle);
                  }

                  // Getter method for the title property
                  public String getTitle()
                  {
                    return titledBorder1.getTitle();
                  }

                  void jscbColor_adjustmentValueChanged(AdjustmentEvent e)
                  {
                    colorValue = jscbColor.getValue();
                    jlblColorValue.setText(colorValue+"");

                    if (buttonType.equals("RGB"))
                    {
                      if (colorType.equals("Red"))
                        jtfColor.setBackground(new Color(colorValue, 0, 0));
                      else if (colorType.equals("Green"))
                        jtfColor.setBackground(new Color(0, colorValue, 0));
                      else if (colorType.equals("Blue"))
                        jtfColor.setBackground(new Color(0, 0, colorValue));

                      jtfColor.repaint();
                    }

                    fireActionPerformed(
                      new ActionEvent(this, ActionEvent.ACTION_PERFORMED, null));
                  }
```

Listing 6.1   *Continued*

```java
    public void switchButton(String s)
    {
      if (s.equals("RGB"))
        jscbColor.setMaximum(255);
      else if (s.equals("HSB"))
        jscbColor.setMaximum(100);

      jtfColor.setBackground(Color.white);
      jtfColor.repaint();
      jscbColor.setValue(0);

      this.repaint();

      buttonType = s;
    }

    // Remove listener. Generated by JBuilder
    public synchronized void removeActionListener(ActionListener l)
    {
      if (actionListeners != null && actionListeners.contains(l))
      {
        Vector v = (Vector) actionListeners.clone();
        v.removeElement(l);
        actionListeners = v;
      }
    }

    // Add listener. Generated by JBuilder
    public synchronized void addActionListener(ActionListener l)
    {
      Vector v = actionListeners ==
        null ? new Vector(2) : (Vector) actionListeners.clone();
      if (!v.contains(l))
      {
        v.addElement(l);
        actionListeners = v;
      }
    }

    // Fire ActionEvent. Generated by JBuilder
    protected void fireActionPerformed(ActionEvent e)
    {
      if (actionListeners != null)
      {
        Vector listeners = actionListeners;
        int count = listeners.size();
        for (int i = 0; i < count; i++)
          ((ActionListener) listeners.elementAt(i)).actionPerformed(e);
      }
    }
  }
```

TIP

The SingleColorPanel class implements borland.jbcl.util.BlackBox, which is an empty interface that signals that the component is a noncontainer, i.e., that no objects can be added into it. This useful interface prevents clients from mistakenly adding objects to the bean.

---

continues

Let us turn our attention to the main part of this example for creating the ChooseColor class as follows:

1. Use the Applet wizard to create the ChooseColor class. With ChooseColor.java selected in the Navigation pane, switch to the UI Designer and create the UI as shown in Figure 6.9.

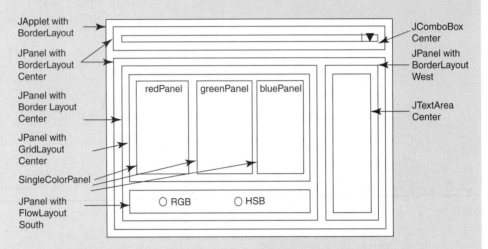

Figure 6.9   *The user interface employs nested panels to group the components in order to achieve the desired layout.*

2. Drop a JPanel to the north of the applet and rename it jpStandardColor. Set the layout of jpStandardColor to BorderLayout; drop a JComboBox to the center of jpStandardColor and rename it jcboStandardColor. Drop a JPanel to the Center of the applet and rename it jpSelection.

3. Set the layout of jpSelection to BorderLayout. Drop a JPanel to the center and a JPanel to the east of jpSelection, and rename them jpSelectColor and jpSelectedColor.

4. Set the layout of jpSelectedColor to BorderLayout, and the width (the first argument) of the preferredSize property to 80. Drop a JTextArea to the center of jpSelectedColor and rename it jtaSelectedColor.

5. Set the layout of jpSelectColor to BorderLayout. Drop a JPanel to the center and drop a JPanel to the south of jpSelectColor. Rename them jpColors and jpRadioButtons.

6. Set the layout of jpColors to GridLayout and drop a SingleColorPanel to jpColors three times to create redPanel, greenPanel, and bluePanel. Set the title properties of these three panels to "Red," "Green," and "Blue," receptively.

7. Drop a JRadioButtons into jpRadioButtons to create jrbRGB, and set its text to RGB. Drop a JRadioButton into jpRadioButtons to create jrbHSB, and set its text to HSB.

8. Set a border with title "Choose Standard Color" in jpStandardColor, a border with title "Choose Colors" in jpSelection, a border with title "Selected Color" in jpSelectedColor.

9. Add items "Red," "Green," "Blue," and "Yellow" into the combo box jcboStandardColor in the jbInit() method, as shown in Listing 6.2.

10. Declare an instance of ButtoGroup, named btg, for grouping the RGB and HSB radio buttons.

11. Double-click jcboStandardColor to generate the code for handling combo item selection. Implement the handler to display the selected color in jtaSelectedColor, as shown in Listing 6.2.

12. In the Events page of redPanel, click the value field of actionPerformed to generate the code for handling the color value change action. This action is generated when the color value changes. Implement the handler to display the selected color in jtaSelectedColor, as shown in Listing 6.2. Similarly, create the code for handling actions from greenPanel and bluePanel.

13. Double-click on jrbRGB to generate the code for handling the radio button switch. Implement the handler to switch the RGB mode for selecting colors, as shown in Listing 6.2. Similarly, generate and implement the code for handling the HSB radio button.

```
package ChooseColorDemo;

import java.awt.*;
import java.awt.event.*;
import java.applet.*;
import javax.swing.*;
import javax.swing.border.*;

public class ChooseColor extends JApplet
{
  boolean isStandalone = false;
  BorderLayout borderLayout1 = new BorderLayout();
  JPanel jpSelection = new JPanel();
  BorderLayout borderLayout2 = new BorderLayout();
  JPanel jpSelectColor = new JPanel();
  BorderLayout borderLayout4 = new BorderLayout();
  JPanel jpColors = new JPanel();
  JPanel jpRadioButtons = new JPanel();
  GridLayout gridLayout2 = new GridLayout();
  JRadioButton jrbRGB = new JRadioButton();
  JRadioButton jrbHSB = new JRadioButton();
  SingleColorPanel redPanel = new SingleColorPanel();
```

continues

Listing 6.2 *ChooseColor.java*

```java
      SingleColorPanel greenPanel = new SingleColorPanel();
      SingleColorPanel bluePanel = new SingleColorPanel();
      JPanel jpStandardColor = new JPanel();
      BorderLayout borderLayout5 = new BorderLayout();
      JComboBox jcboStandardColor = new JComboBox();
      JPanel jpSelectedColor = new JPanel();
      BorderLayout borderLayout3 = new BorderLayout();

      JTextArea jtaSelectedColor = new JTextArea();
      TitledBorder titledBorder1;
      TitledBorder titledBorder2;
      TitledBorder titledBorder3;

      // Declare a ButtonGroup for grouping RGB and HSB radio buttons
      ButtonGroup btg = new ButtonGroup();

      // Construct the applet
      public ChooseColor()
      {
      }

      // Initialize the applet
      public void init()
      {
        try
        {
          jbInit();
        }
        catch (Exception e)
        {
          e.printStackTrace();
        }
      }

      // Component initialization
      private void jbInit() throws Exception
      {
        titledBorder1 = new TitledBorder("");
        titledBorder2 = new TitledBorder("");
        titledBorder3 = new TitledBorder("");
        this.getContentPane().setLayout(borderLayout1);
        this.setSize(400,300);
        jpSelection.setLayout(borderLayout2);
        borderLayout1.setVgap(10);
        borderLayout1.setHgap(10);
        borderLayout2.setVgap(10);
        borderLayout2.setHgap(10);
        gridLayout2.setHgap(5);
        gridLayout2.setColumns(3);
        jrbRGB.setText("RGB");
        jrbRGB.setSelected(true);
        jrbRGB.addActionListener(new java.awt.event.ActionListener()
        {
          public void actionPerformed(ActionEvent e)
          {
            jrbRGB_actionPerformed(e);
          }
        });
```

Listing 6.2   *Continued*

236

```
jrbHSB.setText("HSB");
jrbHSB.addActionListener(new java.awt.event.ActionListener()
{
  public void actionPerformed(ActionEvent e)
  {
    jrbHSB_actionPerformed(e);
  }
});
redPanel.setTitle("Red");
redPanel.addActionListener(new java.awt.event.ActionListener()
{
  public void actionPerformed(ActionEvent e)
  {
    redPanel_actionPerformed(e);
  }
});
greenPanel.setColorType("Green");
greenPanel.setTitle("Green");
greenPanel.addActionListener(new java.awt.event.ActionListener()
{
  public void actionPerformed(ActionEvent e)
  {
    greenPanel_actionPerformed(e);
  }
});
bluePanel.setColorType("Blue");
bluePanel.setTitle("Blue");
jcboStandardColor.setToolTipText(
  "You may choose a standard color from here");
jcboStandardColor.addActionListener(
  new java.awt.event.ActionListener()
{
  public void actionPerformed(ActionEvent e)
  {
    jcboStandardColor_actionPerformed(e);
  }
});
bluePanel.addActionListener(new java.awt.event.ActionListener()
{
  public void actionPerformed(ActionEvent e)
  {
    bluePanel_actionPerformed(e);
  }
});
jpSelectedColor.setLayout(borderLayout3);
jpStandardColor.setLayout(borderLayout5);
jpColors.setLayout(gridLayout2);
jpSelectColor.setLayout(borderLayout4);
jtaSelectedColor.setPreferredSize(new Dimension(100, 18));
jpStandardColor.setBorder(titledBorder1);
titledBorder1.setTitle("Choose Standard Color");
jpSelectColor.setBorder(titledBorder2);
titledBorder2.setTitle("Choose Colors");
jpSelectedColor.setBorder(titledBorder3);
titledBorder3.setTitle("Selected Color");
this.getContentPane().add(jpSelection, BorderLayout.CENTER);
jpSelection.add(jpSelectColor, BorderLayout.CENTER);
jpSelectColor.add(jpColors, BorderLayout.CENTER);
jpColors.add(redPanel, null);
jpColors.add(greenPanel, null);
```

continues

237

```
      jpColors.add(bluePanel, null);
      jpSelectColor.add(jpRadioButtons, BorderLayout.SOUTH);
      jpRadioButtons.add(jrbRGB, null);
      jpRadioButtons.add(jrbHSB, null);
      jpSelection.add(jpSelectedColor, BorderLayout.EAST);
      jpSelectedColor.add(jtaSelectedColor, BorderLayout.CENTER);
      this.getContentPane().add(jpStandardColor, BorderLayout.NORTH);
      jpStandardColor.add(jcboStandardColor, BorderLayout.CENTER);

      // Intialize combo box
      jcboStandardColor.addItem("Red");
      jcboStandardColor.addItem("Green");
      jcboStandardColor.addItem("Blue");
      jcboStandardColor.addItem("Yellow");

      // Group radio buttons
      btg.add(jrbRGB);
      btg.add(jrbHSB);

      // Set RGB radio button by default
      switchButton("RGB");
    }

    // Handler for jrbRGB
    void jrbRGB_actionPerformed(ActionEvent e)
    {
      switchButton("RGB");
    }

    // Handler for jrbHSB
    void jrbHSB_actionPerformed(ActionEvent e)
    {
      switchButton("HSB");
    }

    // Switch to RGB or HSB for selecting colors
    private void switchButton(String radioButtonName)
    {
      if (radioButtonName.equals("RGB"))
      {
        redPanel.setTitle("Red");
        redPanel.setToolTipText("Specify red component of the color");
        greenPanel.setTitle("Green");
        greenPanel.setToolTipText(
          "Specify green component of the color");
        bluePanel.setTitle("Blue");
        bluePanel.setToolTipText(
          "Specify blue component of the color");
      }
      else
      {
        redPanel.setTitle("Hue");
        redPanel.setToolTipText("Specify hue of the color");
        greenPanel.setTitle("Saturation");
        greenPanel.setToolTipText("Specify saturation of the color");
        bluePanel.setTitle("Brightness");
        bluePanel.setToolTipText("Specify brightness of the color");
      }
```

Listing 6.2   *Continued*

```java
    redPanel.switchButton(radioButtonName);
    greenPanel.switchButton(radioButtonName);
    bluePanel.switchButton(radioButtonName);
  }

  // Handler for red color change in redPanel
  void redPanel_actionPerformed(ActionEvent e)
  {
    showSelectedColor();
  }

  // Handler for green color change in greenPanel
  void greenPanel_actionPerformed(ActionEvent e)
  {
    showSelectedColor();
  }

  // Handler for blue color change in bluePanel
  void bluePanel_actionPerformed(ActionEvent e)
  {
    showSelectedColor();
  }

  // Get selected colors and display it in the text area
  private void showSelectedColor()
  {
    if (jrbRGB.isSelected())
    {
      Color c = new Color(redPanel.getColorValue(),
        greenPanel.getColorValue(),
      bluePanel.getColorValue());
      jtaSelectedColor.setBackground(c);
    }
    else
    {
      Color c = Color.getHSBColor(redPanel.getColorValue(),
        greenPanel.getColorValue(),
      bluePanel.getColorValue());
      jtaSelectedColor.setBackground(c);
    }
  }

  // Handler for selecting a standard color in the combo box
  void jcboStandardColor_actionPerformed(ActionEvent e)
  {
    String s = (String)jcboStandardColor.getSelectedItem();
    if (s.equals("Red"))
      jtaSelectedColor.setBackground(Color.red);
    else if (s.equals("Green"))
      jtaSelectedColor.setBackground(Color.green);
    else if (s.equals("Blue"))
      jtaSelectedColor.setBackground(Color.blue);
    else if (s.equals("Yellow"))
      jtaSelectedColor.setBackground(Color.yellow);
  }
}
```

continues

239

Example Review

You can choose a color either by using the scroll bar to specify the red, green, and blue components of the color or by selecting a standard color from the combo box. The selected color is displayed as the background of the text area. This program does not synchronize the color selected in the combo box with the color displayed in the jpColors panel. You can fix the problem by adding a setter method for the colorValue property in the SingleColorPanel class and set the red, green, and blue components in the redPanel, greenPanel, and bluePanel to match the selected color in the combo box. See Exercise 6.4 for more details.

This is a quite sophisticated project with pages of source code, but the amount of the code you hand-wrote is very small. Most of the code was generated automatically by JBuilder. Once again, this demonstrates that you can develop powerful programs in Java using JBuilder with minimum coding.

To use the Swing components in an applet, the applet must extend JApplet instead of Applet. To use the Swing components in an application, the application must extend JFrame or a subclass of JFrame.

TIP

You can nest panels within other panels to gain more control over the placement of components. Each panel may use a different layout manager to achieve the desired look.

TIP

Sometimes it is very difficult to put a component into a small or obscured container in the UI Designer. In these situations, drop the component on the container displayed in the Component tree. To do so, select the component in the Component palette, then click the container in the Component tree.

How Does a Layout Manager Lay Out Components?

A container's setLayout() method specifies a layout manager for the container. The layout manager is responsible for laying out the components and displaying them in a desired location with an appropriate size. Many introductory Java texts state that once a layout manager is selected for a container, it works dutifully behind the scenes to place the components in the right place and display them in the right size automatically. This statement is true, but it does not explain how a layout manager works and interacts with the components. This section will help you understand the nuts and bolts of the layout managers so that you can create your own custom layout managers in the next section, "Creating Custom Layout Managers."

Every layout manager must directly or indirectly implement the `LayoutManager` interface. For instance, `FlowLayout` directly implements `LayoutManager`, and `BorderLayout` implements `LayoutManager2`, which implements `LayoutManager`. The `LayoutManager` interface provides the following methods for laying out components in a container:

- `public void addLayoutComponent(String name, Component comp)`

  Adds the specified component with the specified name to the container.

- `public void layoutContainer(Container parent)`

  Lays out the components in the specified container. You should provide concrete instructions in this method to specify where the components are to be placed.

- `public Dimension minimumLayoutSize(Container parent)`

  Calculates the minimum size dimensions for the specified panel, given the components in the specified parent container.

- `public Dimension preferredLayoutSize(Container parent)`

  Calculates the preferred size dimensions for the specified panel, given the components in the specified parent container.

- `public void removeLayoutComponent(Component comp)`

  Removes the specified component from the layout.

These methods in `LayoutManager` are invoked by the methods in the `java.awt.Container` class through the layout manager in the container. `Container` contains a property named `layout` (an instance of `LayoutManager`) and the methods for adding and removing components from the container. There are five overloading `add()` methods defined in `Container` for adding components with various options. The `remove()` method simply removes a component from the container. The `add()` method invokes `addImpl()`, which then invokes the `addLayoutComponent()` method defined in the `LayoutManager` interface. The `layoutContainer()` method in the `LayoutManager` interface is indirectly invoked by `validate()` through several calls. The `remove()` method invokes `removeLayoutComponent` in `LayoutManager`. The `validate()` method is invoked to refresh the container after the components it contains have been added to or modified. The relationship of `Container` and `LayoutManager` is shown in Figure 6.10.

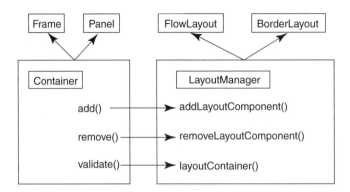

Figure 6.10   *The* add(), remove(), *and* validate() *methods in* Container *invoke the methods defined in the* LayoutManager *interface.*

Creating Custom Layout Managers

Besides the layout managers provided in JBuilder, you can create your own layout managers. The ability to create custom layout managers truly demonstrates Java's flexibility. The custom layout manager can be installed in JBuilder. This feature shows JBuilder's extensibility.

A custom layout manager can be created by simply implementing the LayoutManager interface. In the following example, you will learn how to create a custom layout manager and install it in JBuilder.

Example 6.2 Creating a Custom Layout Manager

This example creates a layout manager named DiagonalLayout that places the components in a diagonal, as shown in Figure 6.11.

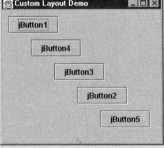

Figure 6.11   *The* DiagonalLayout *manager places the components in a diagonal in the container.*

The `DiagonalLayout` class is similar to `FlowLayout` and `VerticalFlowLayout`. `DiagonalLayout` arranges components along a diagonal using each component's natural `preferredSize`. It contains three constraints: `gap`, `lastFill`, and `majorDiagonal`.

- `gap`: Specifies the gap between the components.

- `lastFill`: Specifies whether the last component in the container is stretched to fill the rest of the space.

- `majorDiagonal`: Specifies whether components are placed along the major diagonal or the subdiagonal.

Here are the steps to complete the project.

1. Create a new project named CustomLayoutDemo.jpr and a JavaBean named `DiagonalLayout` using the JavaBean Wizard.

2. With DiagonalLayout.java selected in the Navigation pane, choose Wizard, Implement Interface to bring up the Implement Interface wizard. Select `LayoutManager` under `java.awt`, and click OK to generate code for implementing the methods in the `LayoutManager` interface.

3. Choose the Bean tab to start BeansExpress for creating properties `gap`, `lastFill`, and `majorDiagonal`, as shown in Figure 6.12.

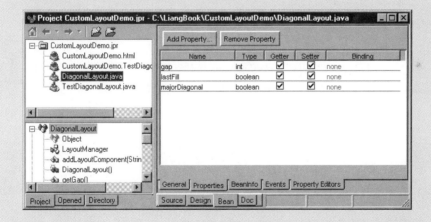

Figure 6.12 *You use the BeansExpress to create three properties:* `gap`, `lastFill`, *and* `majorDiagonal`.

4. Implement `preferredLayoutSize()`, `minimumLayoutSize()`, and `layoutContainer()`, as shown in Listing 6.3. Compile DiagonalLayout.java.

5. To install `DiagonalLayout` in JBuilder, you need to exit JBuilder and add the following line to c:\JBuilder3\lib\jbuilder.properties:

continues

```
jbuilder.uiassistant.CustomLayoutDemo.DiagonalLayout=com.borland.
jbuilder.uidesigner.BasicLayoutAssistant
```

Also add C:\LiangBook on the Djava.class.path as defined in JBuilder3\bin\JBuilder.ini, so that the class `CustomLayoutDemo.Diagonal-Layout` is available in JBuilder IDE.

6. Now use the `DiagonalLayout` layout manager in JBuilder. Restart JBuilder. Reopen CustomLayoutDemo.jpr. Use the Applet Wizard to create an applet named `TestDiagonalLayout`.

7. With TestDiagonalLayout.java selected, click the Design tab to switch to the UI Designer in the Content pane. Change the layout to `DiagonalLayout`. Drop a `JButton` from the Swing page five times to the applet. You will see the buttons placed in a diagonal in the applet.

```java
package CustomLayoutDemo;

import java.awt.*;

public class DiagonalLayout implements LayoutManager
{
  // The properties of DiagonalLayout
  private int gap = 10;
  private boolean majorDiagonal = true;
  private boolean lastFill = false;

  // Constructor
  public DiagonalLayout()
  {
  }

  public void addLayoutComponent(String name, Component comp)
  {
    //TODO: implement this java.awt.LayoutManager method;
  }

  public void removeLayoutComponent(Component comp)
  {
    //TODO: implement this java.awt.LayoutManager method;
  }

  public Dimension preferredLayoutSize(Container parent)
  {
    //TODO: implement this java.awt.LayoutManager method;
    return minimumLayoutSize(parent);
  }

  public Dimension minimumLayoutSize(Container parent)
  {
    //TODO: implement this java.awt.LayoutManager method;
    return new Dimension(0, 0);
  }
```

Listing 6.3   *DiagonalLayout.java*

```java
public void layoutContainer(Container parent)
{
  //TODO: implement this java.awt.LayoutManager method;
  int numberOfComponents = parent.getComponentCount();

  Insets insets = parent.getInsets();
  int w = parent.getSize().width - insets.left - insets.right;
  int h = parent.getSize().height - insets.bottom - insets.top;

  if (majorDiagonal)
  {
    int x = 10, y = 10;

    for (int j=0; j<numberOfComponents; j++)
    {
      Component c = parent.getComponent(j);
      Dimension d = c.getPreferredSize();

      if (c.isVisible())
        if (lastFill && (j == numberOfComponents -1))
          c.setBounds(x, y, w-x, h-y);
        else
          c.setBounds(x, y, d.width, d.height);
      x += d.height+gap;
      y += d.height+gap;
    }
  }
  else // It is subdiagonal
  {
    int x = w-10, y = 10;

    for (int j=0; j<numberOfComponents; j++)
    {
      Component c = parent.getComponent(j);
      Dimension d = c.getPreferredSize();

      if (c.isVisible())
        if (lastFill & (j == numberOfComponents -1))
          c.setBounds(0, y, x, h-y);
        else
          c.setBounds(x-d.width, y, d.width, d.height);

      x -= (d.height+gap);
      y += d.height+gap;
    }
  }
}

public int getGap()
{
  return gap;
}

public void setGap(int gap)
{
  this.gap = gap;
}

public void setMajorDiagonal(boolean newMajorDiagonal)
{
```

continues

245

```
        majorDiagonal = newMajorDiagonal;
      }

      public boolean isMajorDiagonal()
      {
        return majorDiagonal;
      }

      public void setLastFill(boolean newLastFill)
      {
        lastFill = newLastFill;
      }

      public boolean isLastFill()
      {
        return lastFill;
      }
    }
```

Listing 6.3   *Continued*

Example Review

When you change the layout of a container to DiagonalLayout, an object named
diagonalLayout1 is created, and this object appears under the container's name
in the Component tree. You can modify three parameters gap, lastFill, and
majorDiagonal in the property editor of the Inspector for diagonalLayout1, as
shown in Figure 6.13.

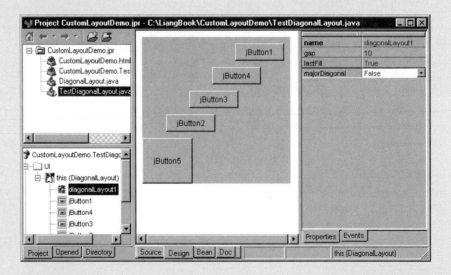

Figure 6.13   *You can modify the parameters* gap, lastFill, *and* majorDiagonal *in the In-spector for an object of* DiagonalLayout.

The modification of the parameters is reflected in the source code, but no immediate changes are taken in the UI Designer. This is because the container's `validate()` method was not invoked. To force `validate()` to be invoked, double-click `diagonalLayout1` in the Component tree. The `validate()` method invokes the `layoutContainer()` method in the `DiagonalLayout` class to display the components.

The `Insets` class describes the size of the borders of a container. It contains the variables `left`, `right`, `bottom`, and `top`, which correspond to the measurements for the *left border*, *right border*, *top border*, and *bottom border*.

The `Dimension` class encapsulates the width and height of a component in a single object. The class is associated with certain properties of components. Several methods defined by the `Component` class and the `LayoutManager` interface return a `Dimension` object.

JTabbedPane

`JTabbedPane` is a useful Swing container that provides a set of mutually exclusive tabs for accessing multiple components. Usually you place the panels inside a `JTabbedPane` and associate a tab with each panel. `JTabbedPane` is easy to use, since the selection of the panel is handled automatically by clicking the corresponding tab. You can switch between a group of panels by clicking on a tab with a given title and/or icon.

`JTabbedPane` has the following useful properties:

- `selectedComponent`: The component that is currently selected.

- `selectedIndex`: The index of the currently selected tab.

- `tabPlacement`: The location of the tabs. Valid values are `JTabbedPane.TOP`, `JTabbedPane.LEFT`, `JTabbedPane.BOTTOM`, and `JTabbedPane.RIGHT`.

The following methods in the `JTabbedPane` class are often useful:

- `public void setIconAt(int index, Icon icon)`

  Set icon at the tab with the specified index.

- `public int getTabCount()`

  Return the number of tabs in the tabbed pane.

- `public void setTitleAt(int index, Icon icon)`

  Set title at the tab with the specified index.

Example 6.3 Using JTabbedPane

This example uses a tabbed pane with four tabs to display four types of figures: Square, Rectangle, Circle, and Oval. You can select a figure to display by clicking the corresponding tab, as shown in Figure 6.14.

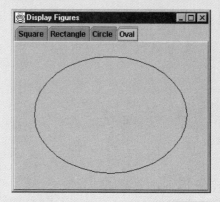

Figure 6.14 *The tabbed pane lets you select figure panels with tabs automatically.*

The figures are displayed in a panel, which is created as follows:

1. Create a new project named DisplayFigureDemo.jpr, and create a Java-Bean component named `FigurePanel` that extends `JPanel` using the Java-Bean Wizard.

2. Select FigurePanel.java in the Navigation pane, and choose the Bean tab in the Content pane to start BeansExpress. Click the Properties tab in the BeansExpress to add a new `int` property named `figureType` to represent figure types: 1 for Square, 2 for Rectangle, 3 for Circle, 4 for Oval.

3. Override the `paintComponent()` method, as shown in Listing 6.4.

4. Compile and install `FigurePanel` in the Component palette.

```
package DisplayFigureDemo;

import java.awt.*;
import javax.swing.JPanel;

public class FigurePanel extends JPanel
{
  BorderLayout borderLayout1 = new BorderLayout();
  private int figureType = 1;

  // Constructor
  public FigurePanel()
  {
```

Listing 6.4 *FigurePanel.java*

```java
      try
      {
        jbInit();
      }
      catch(Exception ex)
      {
        ex.printStackTrace();
      }
    }

    // Initialize component
    private void jbInit() throws Exception
    {
      this.setLayout(borderLayout1);
    }

    // Draw a figure on the panel
    public void paintComponent(Graphics g)
    {
      super.paintComponent(g);

      // Get the appropriate size for the figure
      int width = getSize().width;
      int height = getSize().height;
      int side = (int)(0.80*Math.min(width, height));

      switch (figureType)
      {
        case 1: // Display a square
          g.drawRect((width-side)/2, (height-side)/2, side, side);
          break;
        case 2: // Display a rectangle
          g.drawRect((int)(0.1*width), (int)(0.1*height),
            (int)(0.8*width), (int)(0.8*height));
          break;
        case 3: // Display a circle
          g.drawOval((width-side)/2, (height-side)/2, side, side);
          break;
        case 4: // Display an oval
          g.drawOval((int)(0.1*width), (int)(0.1*height),
            (int)(0.8*width), (int)(0.8*height));
          break;
      }
    }

    // Setter method for figureType
    public void setFigureType(int newFigureType)
    {
      figureType = newFigureType;
    }

    // Getter method for figureType
    public int getFigureType()
    {
      return figureType;
    }

    // Specify preferred size
    public Dimension getPreferredSize()
    {
      return new Dimension(80, 80);
    }
  }
```

continues

Now turn your attention to the main program that creates a tabbed pane and places the figure panels in the tabbed pane, as follows:

1. Create a new Java applet named DisplayFigure.java using the Applet Wizard.

2. In the UI Designer for DisplayFigure, drop a JTabbedPane from the Swing Containers page and rename it jtpFigures.

3. Drop a FigurePanel four times to jtpFigures and rename them squarePanel, rectanglePanel, circlePanel, and ovalPanel. Set the figureType property to 1 for squarePanel, 2 for rectanglePanel, 3 for circlePanel, and 4 for ovalPanel.

4. The tabs are created with default name, which is the same as the component's name. To change the name, you need to modify the constraints property for the panel in the Inspector. For example, to set the tab name for ovalPanel, change the constraints property to Oval in the Inspector for ovalPanel. The source code for DisplayFigure.java is shown in Listing 6.5.

```java
package DisplayFigureDemo;

import java.awt.*;
import java.awt.event.*;
import java.applet.*;
import javax.swing.*;

public class DisplayFigure extends JApplet
{
  boolean isStandalone = false;
  JTabbedPane jtpFigures = new JTabbedPane();
  FigurePanel squarePanel = new FigurePanel();
  FigurePanel rectanglePanel = new FigurePanel();
  FigurePanel circlePanel = new FigurePanel();
  FigurePanel ovalPanel = new FigurePanel();

  // Construct the applet
  public DisplayFigure()
  {
  }

  // Initialize the applet
  public void init()
  {
    try
    {
      jbInit();
    }
    catch(Exception e)
    {
      e.printStackTrace();
    }
  }
```

Listing 6.5 *DisplayFigure.java*

```
      // Component initialization
      private void jbInit() throws Exception
      {
        this.setSize(new Dimension(400,300));
        squarePanel.setFigureType(1);
        rectanglePanel.setFigureType(2);
        circlePanel.setFigureType(3);
        ovalPanel.setFigureType(4);
        this.getContentPane().add(jtpFigures, BorderLayout.CENTER);
        jtpFigures.add(squarePanel, "Square");
        jtpFigures.add(rectanglePanel, "Rectangle");
        jtpFigures.add(circlePanel, "Circle");
        jtpFigures.add(ovalPanel, "Oval");
      }
    }
```

Example Review

The program creates a tabbed pane to hold four panels, each of which displays a figure. A panel is associated with a tab. Tabs are titled Square, Rectangle, Circle, and Oval, which can be set using the `constraints` property.

By default, the tabs are placed at the top of the tabbed pane. You can select a different placement using the `tabPlacement` property.

JSplitPane

`JSplitPane` is a convenient Swing container that contains two components with a separate bar known as a *divider*. The bar can divide the container horizontally or vertically, and can be dragged to change the amount of space occupied by each component.

`JSplitPane` has the following useful properties:

- `bottomComponent`: The component to the left or below the divider.

- `continousLayout`: A boolean value indicating whether the components in the split pane are continuously resized and repainted as the bar moves. By default, it is `false`.

- `dividerLocation`: An `int` value that specifies the location of the divider from the top or left edge of the split pane in pixels.

- `dividerSize`: The size of the divider in pixels.

- `lastDividerLocation`: The previous location of the divider.

- `leftComponent`: The component to the left of or above the divider.

- `oneTouchExpandable`: If `true`, the divider has an expanding and contracting look, and it can expand and contract with one touch. The default value is `false`.

- orientation: Specify whether the container is divided horizontally or vertically. The possible values are JSplitPane.HORIZONTAL_SPILT and JSplitPane.VERTICAL_SPLIT. The default value is HORIZONTAL, which divides the container into a left part and a right part.

- rightComponent: Same as bottomComponent.

- topComponent: Same as leftComponent.

You can also set the divider location as a percentage of JSplitPane's size using the following method:

```
public void setDividerLocation(double proportionalLocation)
```

where proportionalLocation is a value between 0.0 and 1.0.

Example 6.4 Using JSplitPane

This example demonstrates the use of split panes. It lets the user select a layout manager dynamically and use the layout manager to show buttons in a panel. The usage of the layout manager is displayed in an instance of JEditorPane at the same time. A sample run of the program is shown in Figure 6.15.

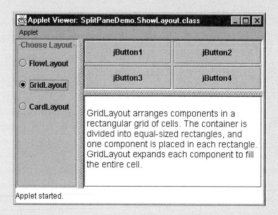

Figure 6.15   *The split pane lets you adjust the component size in the split panes.*

Here are the steps to complete the project:

1. Create a new project named SplitPaneDemo.jpr and a Java applet named ShowLayout.java using the Applet Wizard.

2. In the UI Designer for ShowLayout.java, drop a JSplitPane from the Swing Containers page to create jSplitPane1. Drop a JPanel to the left part of jSplitPane1 to create jpChooseLayout and drop a JSplitPane to the right part of jSplitPane1 to create jSplitPane2.

3. Set the orientation of jSplitPane2 to VERTICAL_SPLIT. Drop a JPanel to the top part of jSplitPane2 to create jpComponents, and drop a JScrollPane to the bottom part of jSplitPane2 to create jScrollPane1.

4. Drop a JButton four times to jpComponents to create jButton1, jButton2, jButton3, and jButton4.

5. Set the layout of jpChooseLayout to GridLayout with three rows. Drop a JRadionButton three times to jpChooseLayout to create jrbFlowLayout, jrbGridLayout, and jrbCardLayout, and set the text of radio buttons to FlowLayout, GridLayout, and CardLayout.

6. Drop a JEditorPane to jScrollPane1 to create jEditorPane1. Set the editable property of jEditorPane1 to false.

7. Create an instance of ButtonGroup to group the radio buttons. Generate handlers for three radio buttons, and implement the handlers, as shown in Listing 6.6.

```java
package SplitPaneDemo;

import java.awt.*;
import java.awt.event.*;
import java.applet.*;
import javax.swing.*;
import javax.swing.border.*;
import java.net.URL;
import java.io.*;

public class ShowLayout extends JApplet
{
  boolean isStandalone = false;
  JSplitPane jSplitPane1 = new JSplitPane();
  JSplitPane jSplitPane2 = new JSplitPane();
  JPanel jpChooseLayout = new JPanel();
  JRadioButton jrbFlowLayout = new JRadioButton();
  JRadioButton jrbGridLayout = new JRadioButton();
  JRadioButton jrbCardLayout = new JRadioButton();
  TitledBorder titledBorder1;
  GridLayout gridLayout1 = new GridLayout();
  JPanel jpComponents = new JPanel();
  JButton jButton1 = new JButton();
  JButton jButton2 = new JButton();
  JButton jButton3 = new JButton();
  JButton jButton4 = new JButton();
  JScrollPane jScrollPane1 = new JScrollPane();
  JEditorPane jEditorPane1 = new JEditorPane();

  // Create a button group
  ButtonGroup btg = new ButtonGroup();

  // Create layout managers
  FlowLayout flowLayout = new FlowLayout();
```

continues

Listing 6.6   *ShowLayout.java*

```
         GridLayout gridLayout = new GridLayout(2, 2, 3, 3);
         CardLayout cardLayout = new CardLayout();

         // get the url for HTML files
         URL urlFlowLayoutHTML =
           this.getClass().getResource("FlowLayout.html");
         URL urlGridLayoutHTML =
           this.getClass().getResource("GridLayout.html");
         URL urlCardLayoutHTML =
           this.getClass().getResource("CardLayout.html");

         // Construct the applet
         public ShowLayout()
         {
         }

         // Initialize the applet
         public void init()
         {
           try
           {
             jbInit();
           }
           catch(Exception e)
           {
             e.printStackTrace();
           }
         }

         // Component initialization
         private void jbInit() throws Exception
         {
           titledBorder1 = new TitledBorder("");
           this.setSize(new Dimension(400,300));
           jSplitPane2.setOrientation(JSplitPane.VERTICAL_SPLIT);
           jrbFlowLayout.setText("FlowLayout");
           jrbFlowLayout.addActionListener(
             new java.awt.event.ActionListener()
           {
             public void actionPerformed(ActionEvent e)
             {
               jrbFlowLayout_actionPerformed(e);
             }
           });
           jrbGridLayout.setText("GridLayout");
           jrbGridLayout.addActionListener(
             new java.awt.event.ActionListener()
           {
             public void actionPerformed(ActionEvent e)
             {
               jrbGridLayout_actionPerformed(e);
             }
           });
           jrbCardLayout.setText("CardLayout");
           jrbCardLayout.addActionListener(
             new java.awt.event.ActionListener()
           {
             public void actionPerformed(ActionEvent e)
             {
```

Listing 6.6   *Continued*

254

```
        jrbCardLayout_actionPerformed(e);
      }
    });
    jpChooseLayout.setBorder(titledBorder1);
    jpChooseLayout.setLayout(gridLayout1);
    titledBorder1.setTitle("Choose Layout");
    gridLayout1.setRows(6);
    jButton1.setText("jButton1");
    jButton2.setText("jButton2");
    jButton3.setText("jButton3");
    jButton4.setText("jButton4");
    jEditorPane1.setText("jEditorPane1");
    jEditorPane1.setEditable(false);
    this.getContentPane().add(jSplitPane1, BorderLayout.CENTER);
    jSplitPane1.add(jSplitPane2, JSplitPane.RIGHT);
    jSplitPane2.add(jpComponents, JSplitPane.TOP);
    jpComponents.add(jButton1, null);
    jpComponents.add(jButton2, null);
    jpComponents.add(jButton3, null);
    jpComponents.add(jButton4, null);
    jSplitPane2.add(jScrollPane1, JSplitPane.BOTTOM);
    jScrollPane1.getViewport().add(jEditorPane1, null);
    jSplitPane1.add(jpChooseLayout, JSplitPane.LEFT);
    jpChooseLayout.add(jrbFlowLayout, null);
    jpChooseLayout.add(jrbGridLayout, null);
    jpChooseLayout.add(jrbCardLayout, null);

    // Group radio buttons
    btg.add(jrbFlowLayout);
    btg.add(jrbGridLayout);
    btg.add(jrbCardLayout);
  }

  // Handler for using FlowLayout
  void jrbFlowLayout_actionPerformed(ActionEvent e)
  {
    jpComponents.setLayout(flowLayout);
    jpComponents.doLayout();
    displayHTML(urlFlowLayoutHTML);
  }

  // Handler for using GridLayout
  void jrbGridLayout_actionPerformed(ActionEvent e)
  {
    jpComponents.setLayout(gridLayout);
    jpComponents.doLayout();
    displayHTML(urlGridLayoutHTML);
  }

  // Handler for using CardLayout
  void jrbCardLayout_actionPerformed(ActionEvent e)
  {
    jpComponents.setLayout(cardLayout);
    jpComponents.doLayout();
    displayHTML(urlCardLayoutHTML);
  }

  // Display an HTML file in EditorPane
  void displayHTML(URL url)
  {
```

continues

```
        try
        {
          // Render the HTML file
          jEditorPane1.setPage(url);
        }
        catch (IOException ex)
        {
          System.out.println(ex);
        }
      }
    }
```

Listing 6.6   *Continued*

Example Review

Split panes can be embedded. Adding a split pane to an existing split results in three split panes. The program creates two split panes to hold a panel for radio buttons, a panel for buttons, and a scroll pane.

The radio buttons are used to select layout managers. A selected layout manager is used in the panel for laying out the buttons. The scroll pane contains a JeditorPane for displaying the HTML file that describes the selected layout manager.

The HTML files are preloaded using the getResource() method in the Class class. The displayHTML() method is invoked by the radio button handler for displaying a specified HTML file in the JEditorPane.

Chapter Summary

A Java container is an object that holds and groups user interface components. A *layout manager* is a special object used to manage how the components in the container are displayed. Java provides a set of layout managers that you can use to intelligently place components that are independent of fonts, screen resolutions, and platform. This chapter discussed Swing containers and reviewed the layout managers provided in JBuilder. You learned how to use two useful Swing containers, JTabbedPane and JSplitPane. You also learned how to create custom layout managers and install them in JBuilder.

Chapter Review

6.1. How does the layout in Java differ from the ones in Visual Basic or Delphi?

6.2. Are the following statements correct?

■ Each layout has a set of properties applied to all the components in the container.

■ The constraints property is associated with a component.

6.3. Describe the various preinstalled layout managers in JBuilder.

6.4. When should `OverlayLayout` be used?

6.5. How do you use `JTabbedPane` and `JSplitPane`? Can you specify a layout manager in these two containers?

6.6. How do you create a custom layout manager and install it in JBuilder?

Programming Exercises

6.1. Create a program that enables the user to set the properties of a `FlowLayout` manager dynamically, as shown in Figure 6.16. The `FlowLayout` manager is used to place 15 components in a panel. You can set the `alignment`, `hgap`, and `vhap` properties of the `FlowLayout` dynamically.

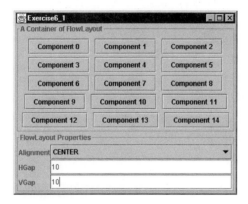

Figure 6.16 *The program enables you to set the properties of a* `FlowLayout` *manager dynamically.*

6.2. Create a program that enables the user to set the properties of a `GridLayout` manager dynamically, as shown in Figure 6.17. The `GridLayout` manager is

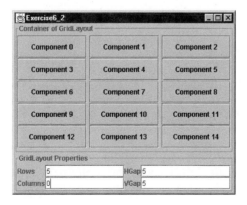

Figure 6.17 *The program enables you to set the properties of a* `GridLayout` *manager dynamically.*

257

used to place 15 components in a panel. You can set the rows, columns, hgap, and vhap properties of the GridLayout dynamically.

6.3. Create a program that uses OverlayLayout to display two overlaid labels with images and texts in a panel, as shown in Figure 6.18.

Figure 6.18   *You can display components transparently at the same time using* OverlayLayout.

6.4. Modify Example 6.1 to set the red, green, and blue components in the redPanel, greenPanel, and bluePanel to match the selected color in the combo box.

6.5. Create a program that displays four figures in split panes, as shown in Figure 6.19. The figures are defined in the FigurePanel class defined in Example 6.3.

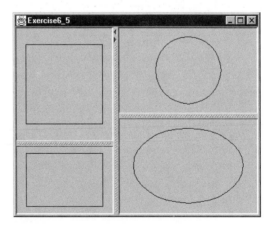

Figure 6.19   *Four figures are displayed in split panes.*

6.6. Modify Example 6.3 to add a panel of radio buttons for specifying the tab placement of the tabbed pane, as shown in Figure 6.20.

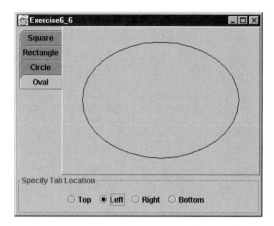

Figure 6.20 *The radio buttons let you choose the tab placement of the tabbed pane.*

6.7. Create a program that enables the user to set the properties of a split pane dynamically, as shown in Figure 6.21.

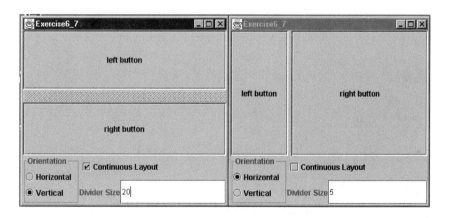

Figure 6.21 *The program enables you to set the properties of a split pane dynamically.*

CHAPTER 7

MENUS, TOOLBARS, AND DIALOGS

Objectives

- ❂ Learn how to use the menu components `JMenuBar`, `JMenu`, `JPopupMenu`, `JMenuItem`, `JCheckBoxMenuItem`, and `JRadioButtonMenuItem`.

- ❂ Create menus and popup menus using the Menu Designer.

- ❂ Use `JToolBar` to create tool bars.

- ❂ Learn how to create standard dialogs using the `JOptionPane` class.

- ❂ Extend the `JDialog` class to create custom dialogs.

- ❂ Select colors using `JColorChooser`.

- ❂ Use `JFileChooser` to display Open and Save file dialogs.

Introduction

In the preceding two chapters, you learned how to use Swing components, containers, and layout managers. This chapter introduces menus, popup menus, tool bars, and dialogs. Using these components effectively can greatly boost your programming productivity.

Menus

Menus make selection easier, and are widely used in Windows applications. Java provides five classes, JMenuBar, JMenu, JMenuItem, JCheckBoxMenuItem, and JRadioButtonMenuItem, to implement menus.

JMenuBar, the top-level menu component, is used to hold the menus. Menus consist of *menu items* that the user can select (or toggle on or off). Menu items can be an instance of JMenuItem, JCheckBoxMenuItem, or JRadioButtonMenuItem.

The sequence of implementing menus in Java is as follows:

1. Create a menu bar and associate it with a frame.

```
JFrame frame = new JFrame();
frame.setSize(300, 200);
frame.setVisible(true);
JMenuBar jmb = new JMenuBar();
frame.setJMenuBar(jmb);  // Attach a menu bar to a frame
```

This code creates a frame and a menu bar, and sets the menu bar in the frame.

2. Create menus.

You can use the following constructor to create a menu:

```
public JMenu(String label)
```

The following is an example of creating menus:

```
JMenu fileMenu = new JMenu("File");
JMenu helpMenu = new JMenu("Help");
jmb.add(fileMenu);
jmb.add(helpMenu);
```

This creates two menus labeled File and Help, as shown in Figure 7.1. The menus will not be seen until they are added to JMenuBar.

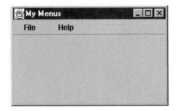

Figure 7.1 *The menu bar appears below the title bar on the frame.*

3. Create menu items and add them to menus.

```
fileMenu.add(new JMenuItem("New"));
fileMenu.add(new JMenuItem("Open"));
fileMenu.addSeparator();
fileMenu.add(new JMenuItem("Print"));
fileMenu.addSeparator();
fileMenu.add(new JMenuItem("Exit"));
```

This code adds the menu items New, Open, a separator bar, Print, another separator bar, and Exit in this order into the File menu, as shown in Figure 7.2.

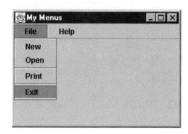

Figure 7.2   *Clicking a menu on the menu bar reveals the items under the menu.*

The addSeparator() method adds a separate bar in the menu.

You can also embed menus inside menus so that the embedded menus become submenus. Here is an example:

```
JMenu softwareHelpSubMenu = new JMenu("Software");
JMenu hardwareHelpSubMenu = new JMenu("Hardware");
helpMenu.add(softwareHelpSubMenu);
helpMenu.add(hardwareHelpSubMenu);
softwareHelpSubMenu.add(new JMenuItem("Unix"));
softwareHelpSubMenu.add(new JMenuItem("NT"));
softwareHelpSubMenu.add(new JMenuItem("Win95"));
```

This code adds two submenus: softwareHelpMenu and hardwareHelpMenu in helpMenu. The menu items Unix, NT, and Win95 are added into softwareHelp-Menu (see Figure 7.3).

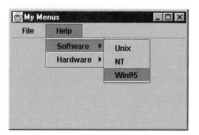

Figure 7.3   *Clicking a menu item reveals the secondary items under the menu item.*

263

You can also add a `JCheckBoxMenuItem` to a `JMenu`. `JCheckBoxMenuItem` is a subclass of `JMenuItem` that adds a `boolean` state to the `JMenuItem`, and displays a check when its state is true. You can click the menu item to turn it on and off. For example, the following statement adds the check box menu item `Check it` (see Figure 7.4).

```
helpMenu.add(new JCheckBoxMenuItem("Check it"));
```

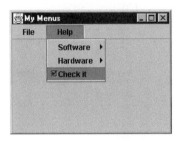

Figure 7.4   *A check box menu item, just like a check box, lets you check or uncheck a menu item.*

You can also add radio buttons in a menu using the `JRadioButtonMenuItem` class. This is often useful when you have a group of mutually exclusive choices in the menu. For example, the following statements add a submenu named Color and a set of radio buttons for choosing a color (see Figure 7.5).

```
JMenu colorHelpSubMenu = new JMenu("Color");
helpMenu.add(colorHelpSubMenu);

JRadioButtonMenuItem jrbmiBlue, jrbmiYellow, jrbmiRed;
colorHelpSubMenu.add(jrbmiBlue = new
  JRadioButtonMenuItem("Blue"));
colorHelpSubMenu.add(jrbmiYellow =
  new JRadioButtonMenuItem("Yellow"));
colorHelpSubMenu.add(jrbmiRed = new JRadioButtonMenuItem("Red"));

ButtonGroup btg = new ButtonGroup();
btg.add(jrbmiBlue);
btg.add(jrbmiYellow);
btg.add(jrbmiRed);
```

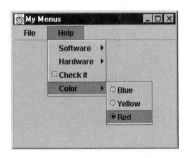

Figure 7.5   *You can use* `JRadioButtonMenuItem` *to choose a mutually exclusive menu choice.*

4. The menu items generate `ActionEvent`. Your program must implement the `actionPerformed` handler to respond to the menu selection. The following is an example:

```java
public void actionPerformed(ActionEvent e)
{
  String actionCommand = e.getActionCommand();

  // Make sure the source is JMenuItem
  if (e.getSource() instanceof JMenuItem)
    if ("New".equals(actionCommand))
      respondeToNew();
}
```

This code executes the method `respondToNew()` when the menu item labeled New is selected.

Image Icons, Keyboard Mnemonics, and Keyboard Accelerators

The menu components `JMenu`, `JMenuItem`, `JCheckBoxMenuItem`, and `JRadioButtonMenuItem` have `icon` and `mnemonic` properties. For example, you can set icons for the New and Open menu items and set keyboard mnemonic for File, Help, New, and Open using the following code:

```java
JMenuItem jmiNew, jmiOpen;
fileMenu.add(jmiNew = new JMenuItem("New"));
fileMenu.add(jmiOpen = new JMenuItem("Open"));
jmiNew.setIcon(new ImageIcon("images/new.gif"));
jmiOpen.setIcon(new ImageIcon("images/open.gif"));
helpMenu.setMnemonic('H');
fileMenu.setMnemonic('F');
jmiNew.setMnemonic('N');
jmiOpen.setMnemonic('O');
```

The new icons and mnemonics are shown in Figure 7.6. You can also use `JMenuItem` constructors like the following to construct and set an icon or a mnemonic in one statement.

```java
public JMenuItem(String label, Icon icon);
```

```java
public JMenuItem(String label, int mnemonic);
```

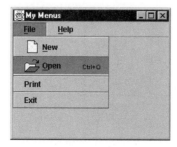

Figure 7.6   *You can set image icons, keyboard mnemonics, and keyboard accelerators in menus.*

To select a menu, press the ALT key and the mnemonic key. For example, press ALT+F to select the File menu. You can then press ALT+O to select the Open menu item. Keyboard mnemonics are useful, but they only let you select menu items from the currently open menu. Key accelerators, however, let you select a menu item directly by pressing the CTRL key and the accelerator key. For example, you can attach the accelerator key CTRL+O to the Open menu item using the following code:

```
jmiOpen.setAccelerator(KeyStroke.getKeyStroke
  (KeyEvent.VK_O, ActionEvent.CTRL_MASK));
```

The setAccelerator() method takes an object of the KeyStroke class. The static method getKeyStoke() in the KeyStroke class creates an instance of the key stroke. VK_O is a constant representing the O key, and CTRL_MASK is a constant indicating that the CTRL key is associated with the keystroke.

Using the JBuilder Menu Designer

JBuilder has a Menu Designer that can be used to simplify the task of designing menus. This section demonstrates the use of the Menu Designer with simple examples.

Example 7.1 Using JBuilder Menu Designer

This example demonstrates how to create menus using JBuilder Menu Designer, as shown in Figure 7.6. You will learn how to add and remove menus, menu items, separator bars, submenus, check box menus, and radio button menus.

Here are the steps to complete the project.

1. Create a new project named MenuDemo.jpr and create an applet named TestMenuDesigner using the Applet Wizard.

2. With TestMenuDesigner.java selected in the Navigation pane, switch to the UI Designer. Drop a JMenuBar in the Swing Containers page to the UI Designer to create jMenuBar1.

3. To activate the Menu Designer, double-click on jMenuBar1 under the Menu node in the Component tree, as shown in Figure 7.7.

4. You are going to create a new menu named File and add four menu items named New, Open, Print, and Exit into the File menu. Add a separator bar between Open and Print, and another separator between Print and Exit as follows:

   4.1. Click the empty menu, type **File**, then press the Enter key.

   4.2. The first menu item under File is automatically highlighted. Type **New** and press Enter.

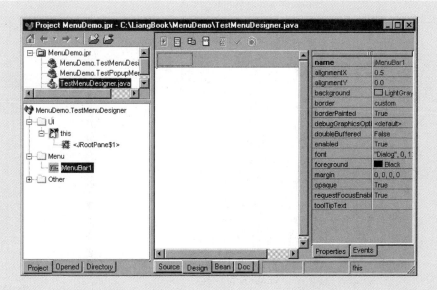

Figure 7.7   *You can visually add and remove menus, menu items, separator bars, submenus, check box menus, and radio button menus.*

4.3. The next menu item after New is automatically highlighted. Type **Open** and press Enter.

4.4. The next menu item after Open is now highlighted, click the Insert Separator button (the second button on the top of the menu) to create a separator bar.

4.5. The next menu item after the separator is highlighted. Type Print and press Enter.

4.6. The next menu item after Print is now highlighted, click the Insert Separator button to create a separator bar.

4.7. The next menu item after the separator is highlighted. Type **Exit** and press Enter.

5. You are going to create a new menu named Help after the File menu and create submenus, check box menu items and radio button menu items under Help, as follows:

5.1. Click the empty menu on the right of the File menu, type **Help**, then press the Enter key.

5.2. The first menu item under Help is automatically highlighted. Type **Software** and press Enter to create a menu item for Software. Select Software and right-click the mouse to display a popup menu, as

continues

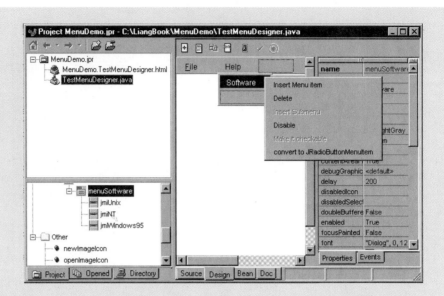

Figure 7.8 *The popup menu gives you the options for inserting menu items, deleting menu items, inserting submenus, disabling menu items, creating check box menu items, or creating radio button menu items.*

shown in Figure 7.8. Choose Insert Submenu to create three submenu items named Unix, NT, and Windows 95, as shown in Figure 7.9. Note that the Software menu item is converted to a Software menu automatically.

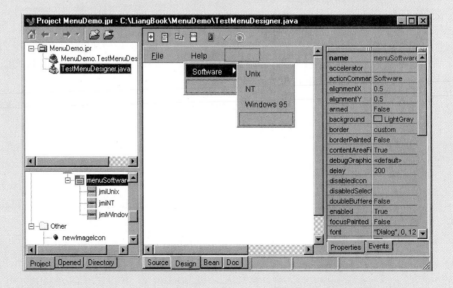

Figure 7.9 *Three submenu items are created in the Software menu.*

5.3. Highlight the next menu item below Software, type **Hardware**, and press Enter.

5.4. The next menu item after Hardware is now highlighted, type **Check It** and press Enter to create a menu item for Check It. Select Check It and choose Make it checkable in the popup menu. The menu item for Check It is converted to a check box menu item.

5.5. Highlight the next menu item after Check It. Type **Color** and press Enter to create a menu item for Color. Select Color and choose Convert to JRadioButtonMenuItem in the popup menu. The menu item for Color is converted to a menu. Add three radio buttons named Blue, Yellow, and Red in the Color menu, as shown in Figure 7.10.

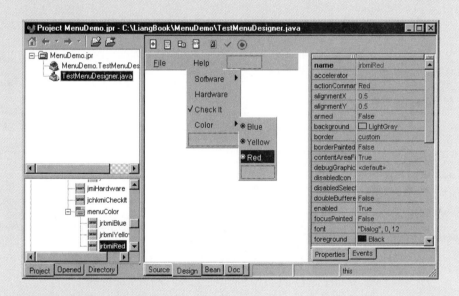

Figure 7.10   *Three radio button menu items are created in the Color menu.*

6. Rename the menus and menu items to menuFile, jmiNew, jmiOpen, jmiPrint, jmiExit, menuHelp, menuSoftware, jmiHardware, jchkmiCheckIt, menuColor, jrbmiBlue, jrbmiYellow, and jrbmiRed.

7. Create an instance of ButtonGroup to group the radio buttons, as shown in Listing 7.1.

8. Declare three image icons named newImageIcon, openImageIcon, and printImageIcon, and load the image icons, as shown in Listing 7.1. In the Menu Designer, set the icon properties of jmiNew, jmiOpen, and jmiPrint to newImageIcon, openImageIcon, and printImageIcon, respectively.

continues

9. Set the mnemonic properties of menuFile, jmiNew, jmiOpen, jmiPrint, and jmiExit to F, N, O, P, and E, respectively.

10. Declare and create a keystroke for the Open menu named openKeyStroke, and set the accelerator property of jmiOpen to openKeyStroke.

11. Switch the UI Designer by clicking the this under the UI node. Right-click the Inspector for the applet to display hidden properties. Set the JMenuBar property to jMenuBar1 to attach the menu bar to the applet.

12. In the Events page of the Inspector for jmiEixt, double-click the value field of actionPerformed to generate the code for handling the Exit menu item. Add the code to terminate the program in the handler, as shown in Listing 7.1.

```
package MenuDemo;

import java.awt.*;
import java.awt.event.*;
import java.applet.*;
import javax.swing.*;
import java.net.URL;

public class TestMenuDesigner extends JApplet
{
  boolean isStandalone = false;
  JMenuBar jMenuBar1 = new JMenuBar();
  JMenu menuFile = new JMenu();
  JMenuItem jmiNew = new JMenuItem();
  JMenuItem jmiOpen = new JMenuItem();
  JMenuItem jmiPrint = new JMenuItem();
  JMenuItem jmiExit = new JMenuItem();
  JMenu menuHelp = new JMenu();
  JMenu menuSoftware = new JMenu();
  JMenuItem jmiUnix = new JMenuItem();
  JMenuItem jmiNT = new JMenuItem();
  JMenuItem jmiWindows95 = new JMenuItem();
  JMenu menuColor = new JMenu();
  JRadioButtonMenuItem jrbmiBlue = new JRadioButtonMenuItem();
  JRadioButtonMenuItem jrbmiYellow = new JRadioButtonMenuItem();
  JRadioButtonMenuItem jrbmiRed = new JRadioButtonMenuItem();
  JCheckBoxMenuItem jchkmiCheckIt = new JCheckBoxMenuItem();
  JMenuItem jmiHardware = new JMenuItem();

  // Declare image icons
  ImageIcon newImageIcon;
  ImageIcon openImageIcon;
  ImageIcon printImageIcon;

  // Create key stroke for the Open menu itme
  KeyStroke openKeyStroke =
    KeyStroke.getKeyStroke(KeyEvent.VK_O, ActionEvent.CTRL_MASK);

  //Construct the applet
  public TestMenuDesigner()
```

Listing 7.1   *TestMenuDesigner.java*

```
  {
  }

  // Initialize the applet
  public void init()
  {
    try
    {
      jbInit();
    }
    catch(Exception e)
    {
      e.printStackTrace();
    }
  }

  // Component initialization
  private void jbInit() throws Exception
  {
    // Create image icons
    Toolkit toolkit = Toolkit.getDefaultToolkit();
    Class appletClass = this.getClass();
    newImageIcon = new ImageIcon(toolkit.getImage(
      appletClass.getResource("images/new.gif")));
    openImageIcon = new ImageIcon(toolkit.getImage(
      appletClass.getResource("images/open.gif")));
    printImageIcon = new ImageIcon(toolkit.getImage(
      appletClass.getResource("images/print.gif")));

    // Set menu bar in the applet
    this.setJMenuBar(jMenuBar1);

    // Code generated by JBuilder
    this.setSize(new Dimension(400,300));
    menuFile.setMnemonic('F');
    menuFile.setText("File");
    jmiNew.setIcon(newImageIcon);
    jmiNew.setMnemonic('N');
    jmiNew.setText("New");
    jmiOpen.setAccelerator(openKeyStroke);
    jmiOpen.setIcon(openImageIcon);
    jmiOpen.setMnemonic('O');
    jmiOpen.setText("Open");
    jmiPrint.setIcon(printImageIcon);
    jmiPrint.setMnemonic('P');
    jmiPrint.setText("Print");
    jmiExit.setMnemonic('E');
    jmiExit.setText("Exit");
    jmiExit.addActionListener(new java.awt.event.ActionListener()
    {
      public void actionPerformed(ActionEvent e)
      {
        jmiExit_actionPerformed(e);
      }
    });
    menuHelp.setText("Help");
    menuSoftware.setText("Software");
    jmiUnix.setText("Unix");
    jmiNT.setText("NT");
    jmiWindows95.setText("Windows 95");
```

continues

```
            menuColor.setText("Color");
            jrbmiBlue.setText("Blue");
            jrbmiYellow.setText("Yellow");
            jrbmiRed.setText("Red");
            jchkmiCheckIt.setText("Check It");
            jmiHardware.setText("Hardware");
            jMenuBar1.add(menuFile);
            jMenuBar1.add(menuHelp);
            menuFile.add(jmiNew);
            menuFile.add(jmiOpen);
            menuFile.addSeparator();
            menuFile.add(jmiPrint);
            menuFile.addSeparator();
            menuFile.add(jmiExit);
            menuHelp.add(menuSoftware);
            menuHelp.add(jmiHardware);
            menuHelp.add(jchkmiCheckIt);
            menuHelp.add(menuColor);
            menuSoftware.add(jmiUnix);
            menuSoftware.add(jmiNT);
            menuSoftware.add(jmiWindows95);
            menuColor.add(jrbmiBlue);
            menuColor.add(jrbmiYellow);
            menuColor.add(jrbmiRed);

            // Group radio button menu items
            ButtonGroup btg = new ButtonGroup();
            btg.add(jrbmiBlue);
            btg.add(jrbmiYellow);
            btg.add(jrbmiRed);
        }

        // Handler for the Exit menu
        void jmiExit_actionPerformed(ActionEvent e)
        {
            System.exit(0);
        }
    }
```

Listing 7.1 *Continued*

Example Review

Before starting the Menu Designer, you need to create an instance of JMenuBar by dropping it to the UI Designer from the Swing Containers page in the Component palette.

The Menu Designer appears in the Content pane of the AppBrowser when a menu item in the Component tree is double-clicked. It has its own toolbar and recognizes keystrokes such as the navigation cursors and the *INS* and *DEL* keys.

JBuilder IDE maintains everything in sync as you work. As you edit menu items in the Menu Designer, all changes are reflected immediately to the AppBrowser and the Inspector. When you make changes to the menus in the source code or the Inspector, they are reflected in the Menu Designer, and vice versa.

The program exits when you click the Exit menu item. Exit command is ignored if the applet runs from a Web browser.

NOTE

The menu bar is usually attached to the window using the `setJMenuBar()` method. However, it can be placed in a container like any other component. For instance, you can place a menu bar in the south of the container with `BorderLayout`.

TIP

To switch to the Menu Designer, click any item under the node Menu. To switch back to the UI Designer, click any item under the Node this.

Popup Menus

A popup menu, also known as *a context menu*, is like a regular menu, but does not have a menu bar and can float anywhere on the screen. You create a popup menu the same way you create a regular menu using JBuilder's Menu Designer.

A regular menu is always attached to a menu bar using the `setJMenuBar()` method, but a popup menu is associated with a parent component and is displayed using the `show()` method in the `JPopupMenu` class. You specify the parent component and the location of the popup menu, using the coordinate system of the parent like this:

```
popupMenu.show(component, x, y);
```

The popup menu usually contains the commands for an object. Customarily, you display a popup menu by pointing to the object and clicking a certain mouse button, the so-called *popup trigger*. Popup triggers are system-dependent. In Windows, the popup menu is displayed when the right mouse button is released. In Motif, the popup menu is displayed when the third mouse button is pressed and held down.

Example 7.2 Using Popup Menus

This example demonstrates creating popup menus using JBuilder Menu Designer. The program creates a text area in a scroll pane. The popup menu is displayed when the mouse pointed to the text area triggers the popup menu, as shown in Figure 7.11.

Here are the steps to complete the project.

1. Reopen project MenuDemo.jpr and create an applet named `TestPopupMenu` using the Applet Wizard.

continues

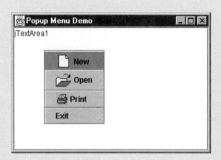

Figure 7.11   *A popup menu is displayed when the popup trigger is issued on the text area.*

2. In the UI Designer of TestPopupMenu.java, drop a JScrollPane to the center of the applet, and drop a JTextArea into the scroll pane to create jTextArea1.

3. Drop a JPopupMenu from the Swing Containers page to the applet to create jPopupMenu1. Double-click jPopupMenu1 in the Component tree to switch to the Menu Designer, as shown in Figure 7.12.

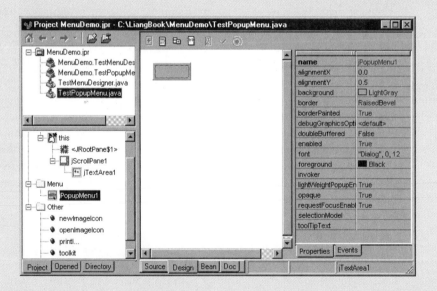

Figure 7.12   *You can design popup menus the same way you design regular menus in the Menu Designer.*

4. Create menu items New, Open, a separator, a menu item Print, a separator, and a menu item Exit in the popup menu. Rename the menu items jmiNew, jmiOpen, jmiPrint, and jmiExit.

5. Generate and implement the handler for the Exit menu to exit the program.

6. Declare and create image icons and set the image icons for jmiNew, jmiOpen, and jmiPrint, the same as in the previous example.

7. Switch to the UI Designer by double-clicking jTextArea1. In the Events page of jTextArea1, double-click the value field of mousePressed and mouseReleased to generate the code for displaying the popup menu, as shown in Listing 7.2.

```java
package MenuDemo;

import java.awt.*;
import java.awt.event.*;
import java.applet.*;
import javax.swing.*;

public class TestPopupMenu extends JApplet
{
  boolean isStandalone = false;
  JPopupMenu jPopupMenu1 = new JPopupMenu();
  JMenuItem jmiNew = new JMenuItem();
  JMenuItem jmiOpen = new JMenuItem();
  JMenuItem jmiPrint = new JMenuItem();
  JMenuItem jmiExit = new JMenuItem();
  JScrollPane jScrollPane1 = new JScrollPane();
  JTextArea jTextArea1 = new JTextArea();

  // Construct the applet
  public TestPopupMenu()
  {
  }

  // Initialize the applet
  public void init()
  {
    try
    {
      jbInit();
    }
    catch(Exception e)
    {
      e.printStackTrace();
    }
  }

  // Component initialization
  private void jbInit() throws Exception
  {
    this.setSize(new Dimension(400,300));
    jmiNew.setText("New");
    jmiOpen.setText("Open");
    jmiPrint.setText("Print");
    jmiExit.setText("Exit");
```

continues

Listing 7.2   *TestPopupMenu.java*

```java
      jmiExit.addActionListener(new java.awt.event.ActionListener()
      {
        public void actionPerformed(ActionEvent e)
        {
          jmiExit_actionPerformed(e);
        }
      });
      jTextArea1.setText("jTextArea1");
      jTextArea1.addMouseListener(new java.awt.event.MouseAdapter()
      {
        public void mousePressed(MouseEvent e)
        {
          jTextArea1_mousePressed(e);
        }

        public void mouseReleased(MouseEvent e)
        {
          jTextArea1_mouseReleased(e);
        }
      });
      jPopupMenu1.add(jmiNew);
      jPopupMenu1.add(jmiOpen);
      jPopupMenu1.addSeparator();
      jPopupMenu1.add(jmiPrint);
      jPopupMenu1.addSeparator();
      jPopupMenu1.add(jmiExit);
      this.getContentPane().add(jScrollPane1, BorderLayout.CENTER);
      jScrollPane1.getViewport().add(jTextArea1, null);
    }

    // Display popup menu for Motif
    void jTextArea1_mousePressed(MouseEvent e)
    {
      showPopup(e);
    }

    // Display popup menu for Windows
    void jTextArea1_mouseReleased(MouseEvent e)
    {
      showPopup(e);
    }

    // Display popup menu when triggered
    void showPopup(MouseEvent e)
    {
      if (e.isPopupTrigger())
        jPopupMenu1.show(e.getComponent(), e.getX(), e.getY());
    }

    // Exit the program
    void jmiExit_actionPerformed(ActionEvent e)
    {
      System.exit(0);
    }
  }
```

Listing 7.2   *Continued*

Example Review

The process of creating popup menus is the same as for creating regular menus. To create a popup menu, drop a JPopupMenu from the Component palette to the UI Designer to create an instance of JPopupMenu. You can start the Menu Designer by double-clicking the instance under the Menu node in the Component tree.

To show a popup menu, the applet uses the show() method by specifying the parent component and the location for the popup menu. The show() method is invoked when the popup menu is triggered by a particular mouse click on the text area. Popup triggers are system-dependent. This program implements the mouseReleased() handler for displaying the popup menu in the Windows and the mousePressed() handler for displaying the popup menu in the Motif.

JToolBar

In windowing systems, a toolbar is often used to hold commands that also appear in the menus. The frequently used commands are placed in a toolbar for quick access. Instead of choosing the commands from the menu, clicking the command in the toolbar is faster.

Swing provides the JToolBar class as the container to hold tool bar components. JToolBar uses BoxLayout to manage components. The components usually appear as icons. Since icons are not components, they cannot be placed into a tool bar directly. Instead you place buttons into the tool bar and set the icons on the buttons. An instance of JToolBar is like a regular container. Often it is placed in the north, west, or east of a container of BorderLayout.

The following properties in the JToolBar class are often useful:

- orientation: Specifies whether the items in the tool bar appear horizontally or vertically. The possible values are JToolBar.HORIZONTAL and JToolBar.VERTICAL. The default value is JToolBar.HORIZONTAL.

- floatable: A boolean value that specifies whether the tool bar can be floated. By default, the tool bar is floatable.

Example 7.3 Creating Tool Bars

This example demonstrates creating a tool bar for the commands New, Open, and Print, as shown in Figure 7.13.

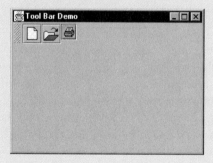

Figure 7.13   *The tool bar contains the icons representing the commands New, Open, and Print.*

Here are the steps to complete the example:

1. Create a new project named ToolBarDemo.jpr and an applet named TestToolBar using the Applet Wizard.

2. In the UI Designer of TestToolBar.java, drop a JToolBar from the Swing Containers page into the north of the applet to create jToolBar1.

3. Drop a JButton three times into jToolBar1 and name the buttons jbtNew, jbtOpen, and jbtPrint.

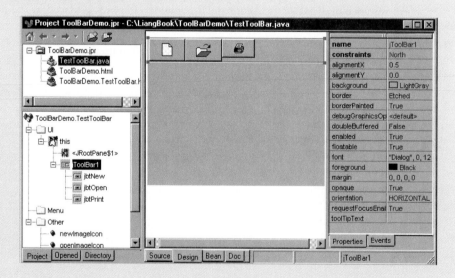

Figure 7.14   *The buttons are added to the tool bar, and the icons are set on the buttons.*

4. Switch to the source code. Declare and create image icons named `newImageIcon`, `openImageIcon`, and `printImageIcon` for New, Open, and Print, as shown in Listing 7.3.

5. Switch to the UI Designer. Set the `icon` property of `jbtNew`, `jbtOpen`, and `jbtPrint` to `newImageIcon`, `openImageIcon`, and `printImageIcon`, as shown in Figure 7.14.

```java
package ToolBarDemo;

import java.awt.*;
import java.awt.event.*;
import java.applet.*;
import javax.swing.*;

public class TestToolBar extends JApplet
{
  boolean isStandalone = false;
  JToolBar jToolBar1 = new JToolBar();
  JButton jbtNew = new JButton();
  JButton jbtOpen = new JButton();
  JButton jbtPrint = new JButton();

  // Declare image icons
  ImageIcon newImageIcon; // = new ImageIcon("images/new.gif");
  ImageIcon openImageIcon; // = new ImageIcon("images/open.gif");
  ImageIcon printImageIcon; // = new ImageIcon("images/print.gif");

  // Construct the applet
  public TestToolBar()
  {
  }

  // Initialize the applet
  public void init()
  {
    try
    {
      jbInit();
    }
    catch(Exception e)
    {
      e.printStackTrace();
    }
  }

  // Component initialization
  private void jbInit() throws Exception
  {
    // Create image icons
    Toolkit toolkit = Toolkit.getDefaultToolkit();
    Class appletClass = this.getClass();
    newImageIcon = new ImageIcon(toolkit.getImage(
      appletClass.getResource("images/new.gif")));
    openImageIcon = new ImageIcon(toolkit.getImage(
```

continues

Listing 7.3   *TestToolBar.java*

```
          appletClass.getResource("images/open.gif")));
      printImageIcon = new ImageIcon(toolkit.getImage(
          appletClass.getResource("images/print.gif")));

      // Code generated by JBuilder
      this.setSize(new Dimension(366, 300));
      jbtNew.setToolTipText("New");
      jbtNew.setIcon(newImageIcon);
      jbtOpen.setIcon(openImageIcon);
      jbtPrint.setIcon(printImageIcon);
      this.getContentPane().add(jToolBar1, BorderLayout.NORTH);
      jToolBar1.add(jbtNew, null);
      jToolBar1.add(jbtOpen, null);
      jToolBar1.add(jbtPrint, null);
    }
  }
```

Listing 7.3   *Continued*

Example Review

The tool bar is a container with BoxLayout. The layout is fixed and cannot be changed. Using the orientation property, you can specify whether components in the tool bar are organized horizontally or vertically.

By default, the tool bar is floatable, and a floatable controller is displayed in front of its components. You can drag the floatable controller to move the tool bar to different locations of the window or can show the tool bar in a separate window, as shown in Figure 7.15.

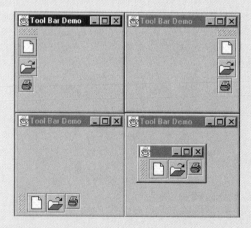

Figure 7.15   *The buttons are added to the tool bar, and the icons are set on the buttons.*

JOptionPane Dialogs

A *dialog box* is normally used as a temporary window to receive additional information from the user or to provide notification that some event has occurred. Java provides the JOptionPane class, which can be used to create standard dialogs. You can also build custom dialogs by extending the JDialog class.

The JOptionPane class can be used to create four kinds of standard dialogs:

- Message dialog: Shows a message and waits for the user to click OK.

- Confirmation dialog: Shows a question and asks for confirmation, such as OK and Cancel.

- Input dialog: Shows a question and gets the user's input from a text field, combo box, or list.

- Option dialog: Shows a question and gets the user's answer from a set of options.

These dialogs are created using the static methods showXxxDialog() and generally appear as shown in Figure 7.16.

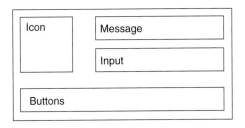

Figure 7.16   *A standard dialog can display an icon, a message, an input, and option buttons.*

For example, you can use the following method to create a message dialog box, as shown in Figure 7.17.

```
JOptionPane.showMessageDialog(this, "SSN not found",
   "For Your Information", JOptionPane.INFORMATION_MESSAGE);
```

Figure 7.17   *The Message dialog displays a message and waits for the user to click OK.*

Message Dialogs

A *message dialog* box simply displays a message to alert the user and waits for the user to click the OK button to close the dialog. The methods for creating message dialogs are as follows:

```
public static void showMessageDialog(Component parentComponent,
                                     Object message)
public static void showMessageDialog(Component parentComponent,
                                     Object message,
                                     String title,
                                     int messageType)
public static void showMessageDialog(Component parentComponent,
                                     Object message,
                                     String title,
                                     int messageType,
                                     Icon icon)
```

The parentComponent can be any component. The message is an object, but often a string is used. These two parameters must always be specified. The title is a string displayed in the title bar of the dialog with default value "Message."

The messageType is one of the following constants:

- JOptionPane.ERROR_MESSAGE

- JOptionPane.INFORMATION_MESSAGE

- JOptionPane.PLAIN_MESSAGE

- JOptionPane.WARNING_MESSAGE

- JOptionPane.QUESTION_MESSAGE

By default, messageType is JOptionPane.INFORMATION_MESSAGE. Each type has an associated icon except the PLAIN_MESSAGE type, as shown in Figure 7.18. You can also supply your own icon in the icon parameter.

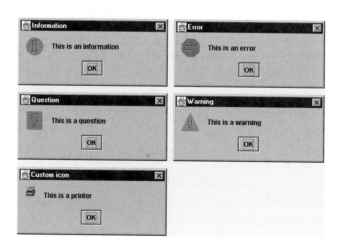

Figure 7.18   *The Message dialog can appear in various forms.*

The message parameter is an object. If it is a GUI component, the component is displayed. If it is a non-GUI component, the string representation of the object is displayed. For example, the following statement displays a clock in a message dialog, as shown in Figure 7.19.

```
JOptionPane.showMessageDialog(this, new Clock(),
    "Current Time", JOptionPane.PLAIN_MESSAGE);
```

Figure 7.19   *A clock is displayed in a message dialog.*

Confirmation Dialogs

A message dialog box displays a message and waits for the user to click the OK button to dismiss the dialog. The message dialog does not return any value. A *confirmation dialog* asks a question and requires the user to respond with an appropriate button. The confirmation dialog returns a value that corresponds to a selected button.

The methods for creating confirmation dialogs are as follows:

```
public static int showConfirmDialog(Component parentComponent,
                                    Object message)
public static int showConfirmDialog(Component parentComponent,
                                    Object message,
                                    String title,
                                    int optionType)
public static int showConfirmDialog(Component parentComponent,
                                    Object message,
                                    String title,
                                    int optionType,
                                    int messageType)
public static int showConfirmDialog(Component parentComponent,
                                    Object message,
                                    String title,
                                    int optionType,
                                    int messageType,
                                    Icon icon)
```

The parameters `parentComponent`, `message`, `title`, `icon`, and `messageType` are the same as in the `showMessageDialog()` method. The default value for `title` is "Select an Option" and for `messageType` is `QUESTION_MESSAGE`. The `optionType` determines which buttons are displayed in the dialog. The possible values are as follows:

- `JOptionPane.YES_NO_OPTION`
- `JOptionPane.YES_NO_CANCEL_OPTION`
- `JOptionPane.OK_CANCEL_OPTION`

Figure 7.20 shows the confirmation dialogs with these options.

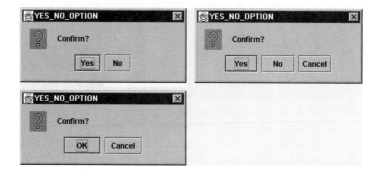

Figure 7.20   *The confirmation dialog displays a question and three types of option buttons, and requires responses from the user.*

The `showConfirmDialog()` method returns one of the following `int` values corresponding to the selected option.

- `JOptionPane.YES_OPTION`
- `JOptionPane.NO_OPTION`
- `JOptionPane.CANCEL_OPTION`
- `JOptionPane.OK_OPTION`
- `JOptionPane.CLOSED_OPTION`

These options correspond to the button that was activated, except for the `CLOSE_OPTION`, which implies that the dialog box is closed with buttons activated.

Input Dialogs

An *input dialog* box is used to receive input from the user. The input can be entered from a text field or selected from a combo box or a list. Selectable values can be specified in an array, and a particular value can be designated as the initial selected value. If no selectable value is specified when an input dialog is created, a text field is used for entering input. If fewer than 20 selection values are specified, a combo box is displayed in the input dialog. If 20 or more than 20 selection values are specified, a list is used in the input dialog.

The methods for creating input dialogs are as follows:

```
public static String showInputDialog(Object message)
public static String showInputDialog(Component parentComponent,
                                     Object message)
public static String showInputDialog(Component parentComponent,
                                     Object message,
                                     String title,
                                     int messageType)
public static Object showInputDialog(Component parentComponent,
                                     Object message,
                                     int messageType,
                                     Icon icon,
                                     Object[] selectionValues,
                                     Object initialSelectionValue)
```

The first three methods listed above use text field for input, as shown in Figure 7.21. The last method listed above specifies an array of `Object` type as selection values in addition to an object that is specified as an initial selection. The first three methods return a `String` that is entered from the text field in the input dialog. The last method returns an `Object` selected from a combo box or a list. The input dialog displays a combo box if the selection values are fewer than 20, as shown in Figure 7.22; it displays a list if the selection values are 20 or more, as shown in Figure 7.23.

Figure 7.21   *When creating an input dialog without specifying selection values, the input dialog displays a text field for data entry.*

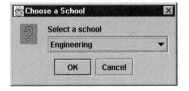

Figure 7.22   *When creating an input dialog with selection values, the input dialog displays a combo box if the selection values are fewer than 20.*

285

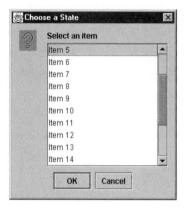

Figure 7.23   *When creating an input dialog with selection values, the input dialog displays a list if the selection values are 20 or more.*

■■■ NOTE

The showInputDialog() method does not have the optionType parameter. The buttons for input dialog are not configurable. The OK and Cancel buttons are always used.

Option Dialogs

An *option dialog* allows you to create custom buttons. You can create an option dialog using the following method:

```
public static int showOptionDialog(Component parentComponent,
                                   Object message,
                                   String title,
                                   int optionType,
                                   int messageType,
                                   Icon icon,
                                   Object[] options,
                                   Object intialValue)
```

The buttons are specified using the options parameter. The intialValue parameter allows you to specify a button to receive initial focus. The showOptionDialog() method returns an int value indicating the button that was activated. For example, the following code creates an option dialog as shown in Figure 7.24.

```
int value =
  JOptionPane.showOptionDialog(this, "Select a button",
    "Option Dialog", JOptionPane.DEFAULT_OPTION,
    JOptionPane.PLAIN_MESSAGE, null,
    new Object[]{"Button 0", "Button 1", "Button 2"}, "Button 1");
```

Figure 7.24 *The option dialog displays the custom buttons.*

Example 7.4 Creating Standard Dialogs

This example demonstrates creating message dialogs, confirmation dialogs, input dialogs, and option dialogs. The example uses menus to display the dialogs, as shown in Figure 7.25.

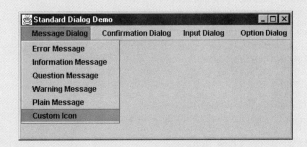

Figure 7.25 *You can display a dialog box by clicking a menu item.*

Here are the steps to complete the project:

1. Create a new project named DialogDemo.jpr and an applet named TestStandardDialog using the Applet Wizard.

2. In the UI Designer of TestStandardDialog.java, drop a JLabel to the center of the applet to create jlblStatus. Set the horizontalAlignment property of jlblStatus to center.

3. Drop a JMenuBar to the applet to create jMenuBar1. Double-click jMenuBar1 to switch to the Menu Designer. Add menus Message Dialog, Confirmation Dialog, Input Dialog, and Option Dialog, and their appropriate menu items.

4. Generate and implement the handlers for the menu items to display dialog boxes, as shown in Listing 7.4.

5. Attach jMenuBar1 to the applet by setting the applet's JMenuBar property to jMenuBar1.

continues

```
package DialogDemo;

import java.awt.*;
import java.awt.event.*;
import java.applet.*;
import javax.swing.*;
import ClockDemo.Clock;

public class TestStandardDialog extends JApplet
{
  boolean isStandalone = false;
  JMenuBar jMenuBar1 = new JMenuBar();
  JMenu jMenu1 = new JMenu();
  JMenuItem jmiErrorMessage = new JMenuItem();
  JMenuItem jmiInformationMessage = new JMenuItem();
  JMenuItem jmiQuestionMessage = new JMenuItem();
  JMenuItem jmiWarningMessage = new JMenuItem();
  JMenuItem jmiPlainMessage = new JMenuItem();
  JMenuItem jmiCustomIcon = new JMenuItem();
  JMenu jMenu2 = new JMenu();
  JMenuItem jmiYesNo = new JMenuItem();
  JMenuItem jmiYesNoCancel = new JMenuItem();
  JMenuItem jmiOkCancel = new JMenuItem();
  JLabel jlblStatus = new JLabel();
  JMenu jMenu3 = new JMenu();
  JMenuItem jmiTfInput = new JMenuItem();
  JMenuItem jmiCboInput = new JMenuItem();
  JMenuItem jmiLstInput = new JMenuItem();
  JMenu jMenu4 = new JMenu();
  JMenuItem jmiCustomOption = new JMenuItem();

  // Construct the applet
  public TestStandardDialog()
  {
  }

  // Initialize the applet
  public void init()
  {
    try
    {
      jbInit();
    }
    catch(Exception e)
    {
      e.printStackTrace();
    }
  }

  // Component initialization
  private void jbInit() throws Exception
  {
    this.setSize(new Dimension(400, 298));
    jMenu1.setText("Message Dialog");
    jmiErrorMessage.setText("Error Message");
    jmiErrorMessage.addActionListener(
      new java.awt.event.ActionListener()
    {
```

Listing 7.4   *TestStandardDialog.java*

```
      public void actionPerformed(ActionEvent e)
      {
        jmiErrorMessage_actionPerformed(e);
      }
    });
    jmiInformationMessage.setText("Information Message");
    jmiInformationMessage.addActionListener(
      new java.awt.event.ActionListener()
    {
      public void actionPerformed(ActionEvent e)
      {
        jmiInformationMessage_actionPerformed(e);
      }
    });
    jmiQuestionMessage.setText("Question Message");
    jmiQuestionMessage.addActionListener(
      new java.awt.event.ActionListener()
    {
      public void actionPerformed(ActionEvent e)
      {
        jmiQuestionMessage_actionPerformed(e);
      }
    });
    jmiWarningMessage.setText("Warning Message");
    jmiWarningMessage.addActionListener(
      new java.awt.event.ActionListener()
    {
      public void actionPerformed(ActionEvent e)
      {
        jmiWarningMessage_actionPerformed(e);
      }
    });
    jmiPlainMessage.setText("Plain Message");
    jmiPlainMessage.addActionListener(
      new java.awt.event.ActionListener()
    {
      public void actionPerformed(ActionEvent e)
      {
        jmiPlainMessage_actionPerformed(e);
      }
    });
    jmiCustomIcon.setText("Custom Icon");
    jmiCustomIcon.addActionListener(
      new java.awt.event.ActionListener()
    {
      public void actionPerformed(ActionEvent e)
      {
        jmiCustomIcon_actionPerformed(e);
      }
    });
    jMenu2.setText("Confirmation Dialog");
    jmiYesNo.setText("YES_NO_OPTION");
    jmiYesNo.addActionListener(new java.awt.event.ActionListener()
    {
      public void actionPerformed(ActionEvent e)
      {
        jmiYesNo_actionPerformed(e);
      }
    });
```

continues

```
jmiYesNoCancel.setText("YES_NO_CANCEL_OPTION");
jmiYesNoCancel.addActionListener(
  new java.awt.event.ActionListener()
{
  public void actionPerformed(ActionEvent e)
  {
    jmiYesNoCancel_actionPerformed(e);
  }
});
jmiOkCancel.setText("OK_CANCEL_OPTION");
jmiOkCancel.addActionListener(new java.awt.event.ActionListener()
{
  public void actionPerformed(ActionEvent e)
  {
    jmiOkCancel_actionPerformed(e);
  }
});
jlblStatus.setHorizontalAlignment(SwingConstants.CENTER);
jMenu3.setText("Input Dialog");
jmiTfInput.setText("TextField Input");
jmiTfInput.addActionListener(new java.awt.event.ActionListener()
{
  public void actionPerformed(ActionEvent e)
  {
    jmiTfInput_actionPerformed(e);
  }
});
jmiCboInput.setText("ComboBox Input");
jmiCboInput.addActionListener(new java.awt.event.ActionListener()
{
  public void actionPerformed(ActionEvent e)
  {
    jmiCboInput_actionPerformed(e);
  }
});
jmiLstInput.setText("List Input");
jmiLstInput.addActionListener(new java.awt.event.ActionListener()
{
  public void actionPerformed(ActionEvent e)
  {
    jmiLstInput_actionPerformed(e);
  }
});
jMenu4.setText("Option Dialog");
jmiCustomOption.setText("Custom Option");
jmiCustomOption.addActionListener(
  new java.awt.event.ActionListener()
{
  public void actionPerformed(ActionEvent e)
  {
    jmiCustomOption_actionPerformed(e);
  }
});
jMenuBar1.add(jMenu1);
jMenuBar1.add(jMenu2);
jMenuBar1.add(jMenu3);
jMenuBar1.add(jMenu4);
jMenu1.add(jmiErrorMessage);
jMenu1.add(jmiInformationMessage);
jMenu1.add(jmiQuestionMessage);
```

Listing 7.4   *Continued*

```
        jMenu1.add(jmiWarningMessage);
        jMenu1.add(jmiPlainMessage);
        jMenu1.add(jmiCustomIcon);
        jMenu2.add(jmiYesNo);
        jMenu2.add(jmiYesNoCancel);
        jMenu2.add(jmiOkCancel);
        this.getContentPane().add(jlblStatus, BorderLayout.CENTER);
        jMenu3.add(jmiTfInput);
        jMenu3.add(jmiCboInput);
        jMenu3.add(jmiLstInput);
        jMenu4.add(jmiCustomOption);

        // Attach the menu bar to the applet
        this.setJMenuBar(jMenuBar1);
    }

    void jmiErrorMessage_actionPerformed(ActionEvent e)
    {
      JOptionPane.showMessageDialog(this, "This is an error",
        "Error", JOptionPane.ERROR_MESSAGE);
    }

    void jmiInformationMessage_actionPerformed(ActionEvent e)
    {
      JOptionPane.showMessageDialog(this, "This is an information",
        "Information", JOptionPane.INFORMATION_MESSAGE);
    }

    void jmiQuestionMessage_actionPerformed(ActionEvent e)
    {
      JOptionPane.showMessageDialog(this, "This is a question",
        "Question", JOptionPane.QUESTION_MESSAGE);
    }

    void jmiWarningMessage_actionPerformed(ActionEvent e)
    {
      JOptionPane.showMessageDialog(this, "This is a warning",
        "Warning", JOptionPane.WARNING_MESSAGE);
    }

    void jmiPlainMessage_actionPerformed(ActionEvent e)
    {
      JOptionPane.showMessageDialog(this, new Clock(),
        "Current Time", JOptionPane.PLAIN_MESSAGE);
    }

    void jmiCustomIcon_actionPerformed(ActionEvent e)
    {
      JOptionPane.showMessageDialog(this, "This is a printer",
        "Custom icon", JOptionPane.INFORMATION_MESSAGE,
        new ImageIcon("images/print.gif"));
    }

    void jmiYesNo_actionPerformed(ActionEvent e)
    {
      int selectedOption =
        JOptionPane.showConfirmDialog(
          this, "Confirm?", "YES_NO_OPTION",
          JOptionPane.YES_NO_OPTION, JOptionPane.QUESTION_MESSAGE);
      jlblStatus.setText("Option " + selectedOption + " selected");
    }
```

continues

```
void jmiYesNoCancel_actionPerformed(ActionEvent e)
{
  int selectedOption =
    JOptionPane.showConfirmDialog(
      this, "Confirm?", "YES_NO_OPTION",
      JOptionPane.YES_NO_CANCEL_OPTION,
      JOptionPane.QUESTION_MESSAGE);
  jlblStatus.setText("Option " + selectedOption + " selected");
}

void jmiOkCancel_actionPerformed(ActionEvent e)
{
  int selectedOption =
    JOptionPane.showConfirmDialog(
      this, "Confirm?", "YES_NO_OPTION",
      JOptionPane.OK_CANCEL_OPTION, JOptionPane.QUESTION_MESSAGE);
  jlblStatus.setText("Option " + selectedOption + " selected");
}

void jmiTfInput_actionPerformed(ActionEvent e)
{
  String input =
    JOptionPane.showInputDialog(this, "Enter your name");
  jlblStatus.setText("Input is " + input);
}

void jmiCboInput_actionPerformed(ActionEvent e)
{
  Object input =
    JOptionPane.showInputDialog(this, "Select a school",
      "Choose a School", JOptionPane.QUESTION_MESSAGE, null,
      new String[]{"Arts and Science", "Engineering", "Education"},
      "Engineering");
  jlblStatus.setText("Input is " + input);
}

void jmiLstInput_actionPerformed(ActionEvent e)
{
  Object input =
    JOptionPane.showInputDialog(this, "Select an item",
      "Choose a State", JOptionPane.QUESTION_MESSAGE, null,
      new String[]{"Item 1", "Item 2", "Item 3", "Item 4",
        "Item 5", "Item 6", "Item 7", "Item 8", "Item 9",
        "Item 10", "Item 11", "Item 12", "Item 13", "Item 14",
        "Item 15", "Item 16", "Item 17", "Item 18", "Item 19",
        "Item 20"},
      "Item 5");
  jlblStatus.setText("Input is " + input);
}

void jmiCustomOption_actionPerformed(ActionEvent e)
{
  int value =
    JOptionPane.showOptionDialog(this, "Select a button",
      "Option Dialog", JOptionPane.DEFAULT_OPTION,
      JOptionPane.PLAIN_MESSAGE, null,
      new Object[]{"Button 0", "Button 1", "Button 2"},
      "Button 1");
  jlblStatus.setText("Value is " + value);
}
}
```

Listing 7.4   *Continued*

Example Review

There are four types of standard dialog boxes: Message, Confirmation, Input, and Option. Use the message dialog if you want to display a message to the user. Use the confirmation dialog if you want the user to confirm the question. Use the input dialog if you want input from the user. Use the option dialog if you want custom buttons in the dialog.

The standard dialogs can be easily created using the methods `showMessageDialog()`, `showConfirmDialog()`, `showInputDialog()`, and `showOptionDialog()`. These methods use the parameters `parentComponent`, `message`, `title`, `optionType`, `messageType`, `options`, and `initialValue`. The `message` is usually a string, but it can be a GUI component. The `optionType` specifies the buttons. The message dialog has a fixed OK button, and the input dialog has two fixed buttons, OK and Cancel. Therefore, the `optionType` parameter is not used in the message and input dialogs.

Creating Custom Dialogs

Standard dialogs are sufficient in most cases. Occasionally, you need to create custom dialogs. Swing has the `JDialog` class. You can create custom dialogs by extending the `JDialog` class. JBuilder provides the Dialog Wizard, which can be used to generate a dialog class.

`JDialog` is a subclass of `java.awt.Dialog` fitted with an instance of `JRootPane`. As with `JFrame`, components are added to the `contentPane` of `JDialog`. Creating a custom dialog usually involves laying out user interface components in the dialog, adding buttons for dismissing the dialog, and installing listeners that respond to button actions.

The standard dialogs are modal, but the custom dialogs derived from the `JDialog` are not modal by default. To make the dialog modal, set its `modal` property to `true`. To display an instance of `JDialog`, set its `visible` property to `true`.

Example 7.5 Creating Custom Dialogs

This example demonstrates creating custom dialogs using the Dialog Wizard in JBuilder. The example creates a button. When you click the button, a dialog for selecting colors is displayed, as shown in Figure 7.26.

continues

Figure 7.26   *The custom dialog allows you to choose the color from the button's foreground.*

The color dialog can be created as follows:

1. Reopen the project DialogDemo.jpr and double-click the Dialog icon in the Object Gallery to display the Dialog Wizard, as shown in Figure 7.27. Enter ColorDialog in the Name field, and click OK to generate Color-Dialog.java.

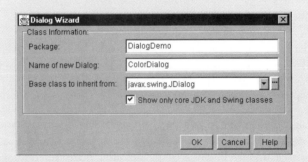

Figure 7.27   *The Dialog Wizard can be used to generate custom dialogs.*

2. Select ColorDialog.java in the Navigation pane, click the Design tab to switch to the UI Designer. You will see panel1 in the UI in Component tree. panel1 was created and added to the dialog by the Dialog Wizard.

3. Drop a JPanel to the center of panel1 to create jpColor, and set its layout to BorderLayout. Drop a JPanel to the south of panel to create jpButtons, and set its layout to FlowLayout with left alignment.

4. Drop a JPanel to the center of jpColor to create jpSelectedColor, and drop a JPanel to the south of jpColor to create jpSelectColor. Set the layout of jpSelectColor to BorderLayout. Set the border property of jpSelectColor to titledBorder to create titledBorder1, and set the title of titledBorder1 to "Select Color."

5. Drop a JPanel to the west of jpSelectColor to create jpLabels. Drop a JPanel to the center of jpSelectColor to create jpScrollBars.

6. Set the layout of jpLabels and jpScrollBar to GridLayout with three rows. Drop three labels to jpLabels and three scroll bars to jpScrollBar. Rename the scroll bars jscbRed, jscbGreen, and jscbBlue.

7. Declare a variable named color of the Color type for the currently selected color. Declare variables named redValue, greenValue, and blueValue for the currently selected red, green, and blue colors.

8. Generate and implement the handlers for handling the adjustment ValueChanged event in the scroll bars. Generate and implement the handlers for handling the action event in the buttons, as shown in Listing 7.5.

```java
package DialogDemo;

import java.awt.*;
import javax.swing.*;
import javax.swing.border.*;
import java.awt.event.*;

public class ColorDialog extends JDialog
{
  JPanel panel1 = new JPanel();
  BorderLayout borderLayout1 = new BorderLayout();
  JPanel jpSelectedColor = new JPanel();
  JPanel jpSelectColor = new JPanel();
  TitledBorder titledBorder1;
  BorderLayout borderLayout2 = new BorderLayout();
  JPanel jpLabels = new JPanel();
  JLabel jLabel1 = new JLabel();
  JLabel jLabel2 = new JLabel();
  JLabel jLabel3 = new JLabel();
  GridLayout gridLayout1 = new GridLayout();
  JPanel jpScrollBars = new JPanel();
  JScrollBar jscbRed = new JScrollBar();
  JScrollBar jscbGreen = new JScrollBar();
  JScrollBar jscbBlue = new JScrollBar();
  GridLayout gridLayout2 = new GridLayout();
  JPanel jpColor = new JPanel();
  BorderLayout borderLayout3 = new BorderLayout();
  JPanel jpButtons = new JPanel();
  JButton jbOK = new JButton();
  JButton jbCancel = new JButton();
  FlowLayout flowLayout1 = new FlowLayout();

  // Declare color component values and selected color
  int redValue, greenValue, blueValue;
  Color color = null;

  public ColorDialog(Frame frame, String title, boolean modal)
  {
    super(frame, title, modal);
```

continues

Listing 7.5   *ColorDialog.java*

```
            try
            {
               jbInit();
               pack();
            }
            catch(Exception ex)
            {
               ex.printStackTrace();
            }
         }

         public ColorDialog()
         {
            this(null, "", false);
         }

         void jbInit() throws Exception
         {
            titledBorder1 = new TitledBorder("");
            panel1.setLayout(borderLayout1);
            jpSelectColor.setBorder(titledBorder1);
            jpSelectColor.setLayout(borderLayout2);
            titledBorder1.setTitle("Select Color");
            jLabel1.setText("Red");
            jLabel2.setText("Green");
            jLabel3.setText("Blue");
            jpLabels.setLayout(gridLayout1);
            gridLayout1.setRows(3);
            jscbRed.setOrientation(JScrollBar.HORIZONTAL);
            jscbRed.addAdjustmentListener(
               new java.awt.event.AdjustmentListener()
            {
               public void adjustmentValueChanged(AdjustmentEvent e)
               {
                  jscbRed_adjustmentValueChanged(e);
               }
            });
            jscbGreen.setOrientation(JScrollBar.HORIZONTAL);
            jscbGreen.addAdjustmentListener(
               new java.awt.event.AdjustmentListener()
            {
               public void adjustmentValueChanged(AdjustmentEvent e)
               {
                  jscbGreen_adjustmentValueChanged(e);
               }
            });
            jscbBlue.setOrientation(JScrollBar.HORIZONTAL);
            jscbBlue.addAdjustmentListener(
               new java.awt.event.AdjustmentListener()
            {
               public void adjustmentValueChanged(AdjustmentEvent e)
               {
                  jscbBlue_adjustmentValueChanged(e);
               }
            });
            jpScrollBars.setLayout(gridLayout2);
            gridLayout2.setRows(3);
            jpColor.setLayout(borderLayout3);
            jbOK.setText("OK");
            jbOK.addActionListener(new java.awt.event.ActionListener()
            {
```

Listing 7.5   *Continued*

```
      public void actionPerformed(ActionEvent e)
      {
        jbOK_actionPerformed(e);
      }
  });
  jbCancel.setText("Cancel");
  jbCancel.addActionListener(new java.awt.event.ActionListener()
  {
      public void actionPerformed(ActionEvent e)
      {
        jbCancel_actionPerformed(e);
      }
  });
  jpButtons.setLayout(flowLayout1);
  getContentPane().add(panel1);
  panel1.add(jpColor, BorderLayout.CENTER);
  jpColor.add(jpSelectedColor, BorderLayout.CENTER);
  jpColor.add(jpSelectColor, BorderLayout.SOUTH);
  jpSelectColor.add(jpLabels, BorderLayout.WEST);
  jpLabels.add(jLabel1, null);
  jpLabels.add(jLabel2, null);
  jpLabels.add(jLabel3, null);
  jpSelectColor.add(jpScrollBars, BorderLayout.CENTER);
  jpScrollBars.add(jscbRed, null);
  jpScrollBars.add(jscbGreen, null);
  jpScrollBars.add(jscbBlue, null);
  panel1.add(jpButtons, BorderLayout.SOUTH);
  jpButtons.add(jbOK, null);
  jpButtons.add(jbCancel, null);
}

void jscbRed_adjustmentValueChanged(AdjustmentEvent e)
{
  redValue = jscbRed.getValue();
  color = new Color(redValue, greenValue, blueValue);
  jpSelectedColor.setBackground(color);
}

void jscbGreen_adjustmentValueChanged(AdjustmentEvent e)
{
  greenValue = jscbGreen.getValue();
  color = new Color(redValue, greenValue, blueValue);
  jpSelectedColor.setBackground(color);
}

void jscbBlue_adjustmentValueChanged(AdjustmentEvent e)
{
  blueValue = jscbBlue.getValue();
  color = new Color(redValue, greenValue, blueValue);
  jpSelectedColor.setBackground(color);
}

void jbOK_actionPerformed(ActionEvent e)
{
  setVisible(false);
}

void jbCancel_actionPerformed(ActionEvent e)
{
  color = null;
  setVisible(false);
}
```

continues

297

```
      public Dimension getPreferredSize()
      {
        return new Dimension(200, 200);
      }
    }
```

Listing 7.5   *Continued*

Now you create a test class to use the color dialog, as follows:

1. Reopen the project DialogDemo.jpr and create an applet named `TestCustomDialog` using the Applet Wizard.

2. In the UI Designer of `TestCustomDialog`, set the `layout` of the applet to `FlowLayout`. Drop a `JButton` in the applet to create `jbtChangeColor`. Set the `text` of the button to "Change Button Text Color."

3. Install `ColorDialog` to the Component palette and drop a `ColorDialog` to the applet to create `colorDialog1`. Set the `modal` property of the dialog to `True`.

4. Generate and implement the handler for the button to show the dialog, as shown in Listing 7.6.

```
package DialogDemo;

import java.awt.*;
import java.awt.event.*;
import java.applet.*;
import javax.swing.*;

public class TestCustomDialog extends JApplet
{
  boolean isStandalone = false;
  FlowLayout flowLayout1 = new FlowLayout();
  JButton jbtChangeColor = new JButton();
  ColorDialog colorDialog1 = new ColorDialog();

  // Construct the applet
  public TestCustomDialog()
  {
  }

  // Initialize the applet
  public void init()
  {
    try
    {
      jbInit();
    }
```

Listing 7.6   *TestCustomDialog.java*

```
          catch(Exception e)
          {
            e.printStackTrace();
          }
        }

        // Component initialization
        private void jbInit() throws Exception
        {
          jbtChangeColor.setText("Change Button Text Color");
          jbtChangeColor.addActionListener(
            new java.awt.event.ActionListener()
          {
            public void actionPerformed(ActionEvent e)
            {
              jbtChangeColor_actionPerformed(e);
            }
          });
          this.setSize(new Dimension(400,300));
          this.getContentPane().setLayout(flowLayout1);
          colorDialog1.setModal(true);
          this.getContentPane().add(jbtChangeColor, null);
        }

        void jbtChangeColor_actionPerformed(ActionEvent e)
        {
          colorDialog1.setVisible(true);

          if (colorDialog1.color != null)
            jbtChangeColor.setForeground(colorDialog1.color);
        }
      }
```

Listing 7.6 *Continued*

Example Review

The custom dialog box allows the user to use the scroll bars to select colors. The selected color is stored in the `color` variable. When the user clicks the Cancel button, color becomes `null`, which implies that no selection has been made.

The dialog box is displayed when the user clicks the "Change Button Text Color" button and is closed when the OK or the Cancel button is clicked.

TIP

Not setting the dialog modal when needed is a common mistake. In this example, if the dialog is not modal, all the statements in the "Change Button Text Color" button handler are executed before the color is selected from the dialog box.

JColorChooser

You created a color dialog in the previous example. This dialog is a subclass of JDialog, which is a subclass of java.awt.Dialog. Therefore, it cannot be added to a container as a component. Color dialogs are commonly used in graphics programming. Swing provides a convenient and versatile color dialog named javax.swing.JColorChooser. Like JOptionPane, JColorChooser is a lightweight component inherited from JComponent. It can be added to any container if desired. Figure 7.28 shows a JColorChooser in an applet.

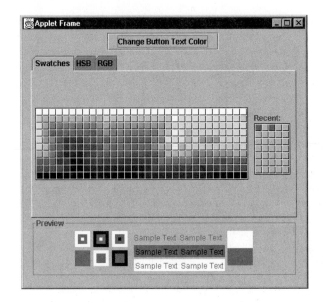

Figure 7.28   *An instance of* JColorChooser *is displayed in an applet.*

Often you add an instance of JColorChooser to a dialog window to display a color dialog. To display color chooser in a dialog box, use JColorChooser's static showDialog() method as follows:

```
public static Color showDialog(Component parentComponent,
                               String title,
                               Color initialColor)
```

This method creates an instance of JDialog with three buttons, OK, Cancel, and Reset, to hold a JColorChooser object, as shown in Figure 7.29. The method displays a modal dialog. If the user clicks the OK button, this method dismisses the dialog and returns the selected color. If the user clicks the Cancel button or closes the dialog, this method dismisses the dialog and returns null.

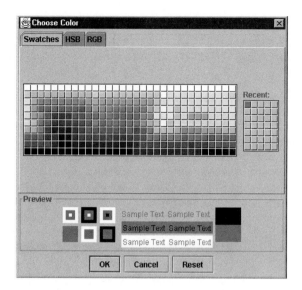

Figure 7.29 *An instance of* JColorChooser *is displayed in a dialog box with the OK, Cancel, and Reset buttons.*

JColorChooser consists of a tabbed pane and a color preview panel. The tabbed pane has three tabs for choosing colors using Swatches, HSB, and RGB, as shown in Figure 7.30. The preview panel shows the effect of the selected color.

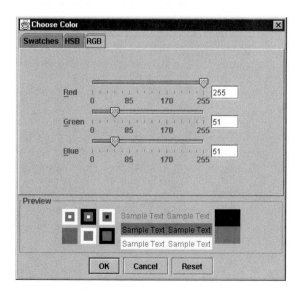

Figure 7.30 *The* JColorChooser *class contains a tabbed pane with three tabs for selecting colors using Swatches, HSB, and RGB.*

■■■ NOTE

JColorChooser is very flexible. It allows you to replace the tabbed pane or the color preview panel with custom components. The default tabbed pane and the color preview panel are sufficient. You rarely need to use custom components.

JFileChooser

Swing provides the javax.swing.JFileChooser class that displays a dialog box from which the user can navigate through the file system and select files for loading or saving, as shown in Figure 7.31.

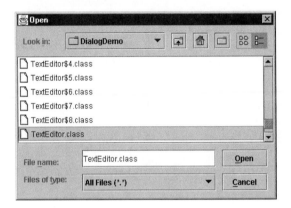

Figure 7.31   *The Swing* JFileChooser *shows files and directories, and enables the user to navigate through the file system visually.*

Like JColorChooser, JFileChooser is a lightweight component inherited from JComponent. It can be added to any container if desired, but often you create an instance of JFileChooser and display it standalone.

JFileChooser is a subclass of JComponent. There are several ways to construct a file dialog box. The simplest is to use the JFileChooser's default constructor.

The file dialog box can appear in two types: *open* and *save*. The *open type* is for opening a file, and the *save type* is for storing a file. To create an open file dialog, use the following method:

```
public int showOpenDialog(Component parent)
```

This method creates a dialog box that contains an instance of JFileChooser for opening a file. The method returns an int value APPROVE_OPTION or CANCEL_OPTION, which indicates whether the OK button or the Cancel button was clicked.

Similarly, you can use the following method to create a dialog for saving files.

```
public int showSaveDialog(Component parent)
```

The file dialog box created with the showOpenDialog() or showSaveDialog() is modal. The JFileChooser class has the properties inherited from JComponent. Additionally, it has the following useful properties:

- **dialogType**: The type of this dialog. Use OPEN_DIALOG when you want to bring up a file chooser that the user can use to open a file. Likewise, use SAVE_DIALOG to let the user choose a file for saving.

- **dialogTitle**: The string that is displayed in the title bar of the dialog box.

- **currentDirectory**: The current directory of the file. The type of this property is java.io.File. If you want the current directory to be used, use setCurrentDirectory(new File(".")).

- **selectedFile**: The selected file. You can use getSelectedFile() to return the selected file from the dialog box. The type of this property is java.io.File. If you have a default file name that you expect to use, use setSelectedFile(new File(filename)).

- **selectedFiles**: A list of selected files if the file chooser is set to allow multi-selection. The type of this property is File[].

- **multiSelectionEnabled**: A boolean value indicating whether multiple files can be selected. By default, it is false.

Example 7.6 Creating a Text Editor

This example uses Swing menus, tool bar, file chooser, and color chooser to create a simple text editor, as shown in Figure 7.32, which allows the user to open and save text files, clear text, and change the color and font of the text.

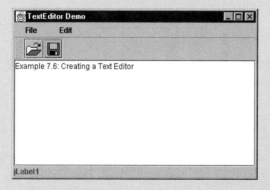

Figure 7.32 *The editor enables you to open and save text files from the File menu or from the tool bar, and to change the color and font of the text from the Edit menu.*

continues

Follow the steps below to complete the project.

1. Reopen the project DialogDemo.jpr and create an applet named `TextEditor` using the Applet Wizard.

2. With TextEditor.java selected in the Navigation pane, switch to the UI Designer in the Content pane. Drop a `JScrollPane` to the center of the applet, and drop a `JTextArea` to the scroll pane named it `jta`.

3. Drop a `JToolBar` to the north of the applet to create `jToolBar1`. Drop a `JButton` twice to `jToolBar1` to create `jbtOpen` and `jbtSave`. Drop a `JLabel` to the south of the applet to create `jlblStatus`.

4. Select the UI node and drop a `JFileChooser` from the Swing Containers page to the UI node to create an instance of `jFileChooser1`.

5. Drop a `JMenuBar` to the applet to create `jMenuBar1`. Right-click the Inspector for the applet to display hidden properties. Set the `JMenuBar` property to `jMenuBar1`.

6. Double click `jMenuBar1` to switch to the Menu Designer. Add menus File and Edit. In the File menu, add menu items Open, Save, and Clear. In the Edit menu, add menu items Foreground Color and Background Color. Rename the menu items `jmiOpen`, `jmiSave`, `jmiClear`, `jmiExit`, `jmiForeground`, and `jmiBackground`.

7. Switch to the source code editor, declare and create image icons named `openImageIcon` and `saveImageIcon`. Set the `icon` property of `jtbOpen` and `jmiOpen` to `openImageIcon`, and the `icon` property of `jtbSave` and `jmiSave` to `saveImageIcon`.

8. Generate the action event handlers for buttons and menu items. Implement the handlers as shown in Listing 7.7.

```
package DialogDemo;

import java.awt.*;
import java.awt.event.*;
import java.applet.*;
import javax.swing.*;
import java.io.*;

public class TextEditor extends JApplet
{
  boolean isStandalone = false;
  JToolBar jToolBar1 = new JToolBar();
  JButton jbtOpen = new JButton();
  JButton jbtSave = new JButton();
  JScrollPane jScrollPane1 = new JScrollPane();
  JTextArea jta = new JTextArea();
```

Listing 7.7   *TextEditor.java*

```java
// Declare image icons
ImageIcon openImageIcon; // = new ImageIcon("images/open.gif");
ImageIcon saveImageIcon;
JMenuBar jMenuBar1 = new JMenuBar();
JMenu jMenu1 = new JMenu();
JMenuItem jmiOpen = new JMenuItem();
JMenuItem jmiSave = new JMenuItem();
JMenuItem jmiClear = new JMenuItem();
JMenuItem jmiExit = new JMenuItem();
JMenu jMenu2 = new JMenu();
JMenuItem jmiForeground = new JMenuItem();
JMenuItem jmiBackground = new JMenuItem();
JFileChooser jFileChooser1 = new JFileChooser();
JLabel jlblStatus = new JLabel();

// Construct the applet
public TextEditor()
{
}

// Initialize the applet
public void init()
{
  try
  {
    jbInit();
  }
  catch(Exception e)
  {
    e.printStackTrace();
  }
}

// Component initialization
private void jbInit() throws Exception
{
  // Create image icons
  Toolkit toolkit = Toolkit.getDefaultToolkit();
  Class appletClass = this.getClass();
  openImageIcon = new ImageIcon(toolkit.getImage(
    appletClass.getResource("images/open.gif")));
  saveImageIcon = new ImageIcon(toolkit.getImage(
    appletClass.getResource("images/save.gif")));

  this.setJMenuBar(jMenuBar1);
  this.setSize(new Dimension(400,300));
  jta.setText("jTextArea1");
  jbtOpen.setIcon(openImageIcon);
  jbtOpen.addActionListener(new java.awt.event.ActionListener()
  {
    public void actionPerformed(ActionEvent e)
    {
      jbtOpen_actionPerformed(e);
    }
  });
  jbtSave.setIcon(saveImageIcon);
  jbtSave.addActionListener(new java.awt.event.ActionListener()
  {
    public void actionPerformed(ActionEvent e)
    {
```

continues

```
          jbtSave_actionPerformed(e);
        }
      });
      jMenu1.setText("File");
      jmiOpen.setIcon(openImageIcon);
      jmiOpen.setText("Open");
      jmiOpen.addActionListener(new java.awt.event.ActionListener()
      {
        public void actionPerformed(ActionEvent e)
        {
          jmiOpen_actionPerformed(e);
        }
      });
      jmiSave.setIcon(saveImageIcon);
      jmiSave.setText("Save");
      jmiSave.addActionListener(new java.awt.event.ActionListener()
      {
        public void actionPerformed(ActionEvent e)
        {
          jmiSave_actionPerformed(e);
        }
      });
      jmiClear.setText("Clear");
      jmiClear.addActionListener(new java.awt.event.ActionListener()
      {
        public void actionPerformed(ActionEvent e)
        {
          jmiClear_actionPerformed(e);
        }
      });
      jmiExit.setText("Exit");
      jmiExit.addActionListener(new java.awt.event.ActionListener()
      {
        public void actionPerformed(ActionEvent e)
        {
          jmiExit_actionPerformed(e);
        }
      });
      jMenu2.setText("Edit");
      jmiForeground.setText("Foreground Color");
      jmiForeground.addActionListener(
        new java.awt.event.ActionListener()
      {
        public void actionPerformed(ActionEvent e)
        {
          jmiForeground_actionPerformed(e);
        }
      });
      jmiBackground.setText("Background Color");
      jmiBackground.addActionListener(
        new java.awt.event.ActionListener()
      {
        public void actionPerformed(ActionEvent e)
        {
          jmiBackground_actionPerformed(e);
        }
      });
      jlblStatus.setText("jLabel1");
```

Listing 7.7   *Continued*

```java
    this.getContentPane().add(jToolBar1, BorderLayout.NORTH);
    jToolBar1.add(jbtOpen, null);
    jToolBar1.add(jbtSave, null);
    this.getContentPane().add(jScrollPane1, BorderLayout.CENTER);
    this.getContentPane().add(jlblStatus, BorderLayout.SOUTH);
    jScrollPane1.getViewport().add(jta, null);
    jMenuBar1.add(jMenu1);
    jMenuBar1.add(jMenu2);
    jMenu1.add(jmiOpen);
    jMenu1.add(jmiSave);
    jMenu1.add(jmiClear);
    jMenu1.addSeparator();
    jMenu1.add(jmiExit);
    jMenu2.add(jmiForeground);
    jMenu2.add(jmiBackground);

    // Set current directory
    jFileChooser1.setCurrentDirectory(new File("."));
  }

  void jmiOpen_actionPerformed(ActionEvent e)
  {
    open();
  }

  void jbtOpen_actionPerformed(ActionEvent e)
  {
    open();
  }

  void jmiSave_actionPerformed(ActionEvent e)
  {
    save();
  }

  void jmiClear_actionPerformed(ActionEvent e)
  {
    jta.setText(null);
  }

  void jmiExit_actionPerformed(ActionEvent e)
  {
    System.exit(0);
  }

  void jbtSave_actionPerformed(ActionEvent e)
  {
    save();
  }

  void jmiForeground_actionPerformed(ActionEvent e)
  {
    Color selectedColor =
      JColorChooser.showDialog(this, "Choose Foreground Color",
        jta.getForeground());

    if (selectedColor != null)
      jta.setForeground(selectedColor);
  }
```

continues

307

```
            void jmiBackground_actionPerformed(ActionEvent e)
            {
              Color selectedColor =
                JColorChooser.showDialog(this, "Choose Background Color",
                  jta.getForeground());

              if (selectedColor != null)
                jta.setBackground(selectedColor);
            }

            // Open file
            private void open()
            {
              if (jFileChooser1.showOpenDialog(this) ==
                JFileChooser.APPROVE_OPTION)
              {
                open(jFileChooser1.getSelectedFile());
              }
            }

            // Open file with the specified File instance
            private void open(File file)
            {
              try
              {
                // Read from the specified file and store it in jta
                BufferedInputStream in = new BufferedInputStream(
                  new FileInputStream(file));
                byte[] b = new byte[in.available()];
                in.read(b, 0, b.length);
                jta.append(new String(b, 0, b.length));
                in.close();

                // Display the status of the Open file operation in jlblStatus
                jlblStatus.setText(file.getName() + " Opened");
              }
              catch (IOException ex)
              {
                jlblStatus.setText("Error opening " + file.getName());
              }
            }

            // Save file
            private void save()
            {
              if (jFileChooser1.showSaveDialog(this) ==
                JFileChooser.APPROVE_OPTION)
              {
                save(jFileChooser1.getSelectedFile());
              }
            }

            // Save file with specified File instance
            private void save(File file)
            {
              try
              {
                // Write the text in jta to the specified file
                BufferedOutputStream out = new BufferedOutputStream(
                  new FileOutputStream(file));
```

Listing 7.7   *Continued*

```
            byte[] b = (jta.getText()).getBytes();
            out.write(b, 0, b.length);
            out.close();

            // Display the status of the save file operation in jlblStatus
            jlblStatus.setText(file.getName()  + " Saved ");
          }
          catch (IOException ex)
          {
            jlblStatus.setText("Error saving " + file.getName());
          }
        }
      }
    }
```

Listing 7.7   *Continued*

Example Review

The program creates the File and Edit menus. The File menu contains menu commands Open for loading a file, Save for saving a file, Clear for clearing the text editor, and Exit for terminating the program. The Edit menu contains menu commands Foreground Color and Background Color for setting foreground color and background color in the text. The Open and Save menu commands can also be accessed by the tool bar. The status of executing Open and Save is displayed in the status label.

An instance jFileChooser1 of JFileChooser is created for displaying the file dialog box to open and save files. The setCurrentDirectory(new File(".")) method is used to set the current directory to the directory where the class is stored.

The open() method is invoked when the user clicks the Open menu command. The showOpenDialog() method displays an Open dialog box, as shown in Figure 7.31. Upon receiving the selected file, the method open(file) is invoked to load the file to the text area using a BufferedInputStream wrapped on a FileInputStream.

The save() method is invoked when the user clicks the Save menu command. The showSaveDialog() method displays a Save dialog box. Upon receiving the selected file, the method save(file) is invoked to save the contents from the text area to the file using a BufferedOutputStream wrapped on a FileOutputStream.

The color dialog is displayed using the static method showDialog() of JColorChooser. So, you don't need to create an instance of JFileChooser. The showDialog() method returns the selected color if the OK button is clicked after a color is selected.

Chapter Summary

You learned how to create menus visually using JBuilder's Menu Designer and how to create tool bars using JToolBar. You learned how to display standard dialogs using JOptionPane, how to create custom dialog by directly extending the JDialog class, and how to use JColorChooser and JFileChooser for selecting colors and files.

Chapter Review

7.1. How do you display the Menu Designer? How do you switch to the UI Designer from the Menu Designer?

7.2. How do you create a submenu? How do you create a check box menu item? How do you create a radio button menu item?

7.3. How do you display the JMenuBar property of JFrame, JApplet, or JDialog in the Inspector?

7.4. How do you create a popup menu in JBuilder? How do you show a popup menu? Describe popup trigger.

7.5. Describe the standard dialog boxes created using the JOptionPane class.

7.6. How do you create a message dialog? What are the message types? What is the button in the message dialog?

7.7. How do you create a confirmation dialog? What are button option types?

7.8. How do you create an input dialog with a text field for entering input? How do you create a combo box dialog for selecting values as input? How do you create a list dialog for selecting values as input?

7.9. How do you show an instance of JDialog? Is an instance of JOptionPane modal? Is an instance of JDialog modal?

7.10. How do you display an instance of JColorChooser? Is an instance of JColorChooser modal? How do you obtain the selected color?

7.11. How do you display an instance of JFileChooser? Is an instance of JFileChooser modal? How do you obtain the selected file?

Programming Exercises

7.1. Write a program to calculate the future value of an investment at a given interest rate for a specified number of years. The formula for the calculation is as follows:

```
futureValue = investmentAmount * (1 + interestRate)years
```

Use text fields for interest rate, investment amount, and years. Display the future amount in a text field when the user clicks the Calculate button or chooses Calculate from the Operation menu (see Figure 7.33). Show a message dialog box when the user clicks the About menu item from the Help menu.

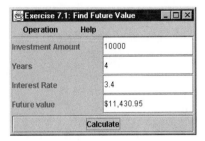

Figure 7.33 *The user enters the investment amount, years, and interest rate to compute future value.*

7.2. Write a program to emulate a paint utility. Your program should enable the user to choose options and draw shapes or get characters from the keyboard based on the selected options (see Figure 7.34). The options are displayed in a tool bar. To draw a line, the user first clicks the line icon in the tool bar and then uses the mouse to draw a line in the same way you would draw using Microsoft Paint.

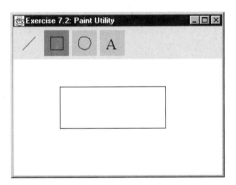

Figure 7.34 *This exercise produces a prototype drawing utility that enables you to draw lines, rectangles, ovals, and characters.*

7.3. JBuilder displays a dialog for choosing fonts when you click the `font` property in the Inspector, as shown in Figure 7.35. Create this dialog as an exercise.

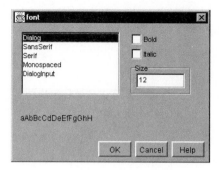

Figure 7.35   *The font dialog box allows you to choose a font by specifying font name, font style, and font size.*

ADVANCED SWING COMPONENTS

Objectives

- ℮ Use JList to select single or multiple items in a list.
- ℮ Use JComboBox to select a single item from a combo box.
- ℮ Use JTable to display and process tables.
- ℮ Use JTree to display data in a tree hierarchy.
- ℮ Learn how to create custom renderers for JList, JComboBox, JTable, and JTree.
- ℮ Learn how to create custom editors for JComboBox, JTable, and JTree.

Introduction

In the preceding three chapters, you learned how to use Swing components, containers, layout managers, menus, tool bars, and dialog boxes. This chapter will show you how to work with some of the complex Swing components. You will learn how to use JList, JComboBox, JTable, and JTree to create advanced graphical user interfaces.

JList

A *list* is a component that enables you to choose one or more items. It is useful in limiting a range of choices and avoids the cumbersome validation of data input. JList is the Swing version of list. Functionally it is similar to a set of check boxes or radio buttons, but the selectable items are placed in a list and are chosen by clicking on the items themselves. Figure 8.1 shows an example of JList.

JList doesn't support scrolling directly. To create a scrollable list, you need to create a JScrollPane and add an instance of JList to the scroll pane. An instance of JList can be created using its default constructor or one of the following three constructors:

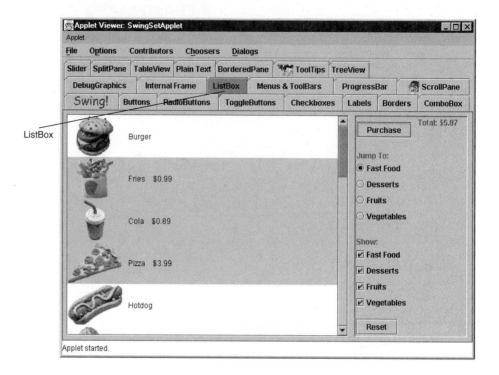

ListBox

Figure 8.1   *The ListBox panel in the SwingSet demo demonstrates the features of* JList.

■   public JList(ListModel dataModel)

■   public JList(Object[] listData)

■   public JList(Vector listData)

If you have a list of a fixed number of string items, you can simply create it as follows:

```
String[] listData = {"Item 1", "Item 2", "Item 3"};
JList jlst = new JList(listData);
```

JList supports three selection modes: *single selection*, *single-interval selection*, and *multiple-interval selection*. Single selection allows only one item to be selected. Single-interval selection allows multiple selections, but the selected items must be contiguous. Multiple-interval selection is the most flexible, because it allows selections of any items at a given time.

JList has the following useful properties:

■   cellRenderer: An object used to render the cells in a list. By default, an instance of DefaultListCellRenderer is used to display items in a list that can display strings or icons. Using custom cell renderer is introduced in the section, "List Cell Renderers."

- **listData**: A write-only property used to set an array or a vector of objects for the list.

- **fixedCellHeight**: The height of a list cell. All the cells in a list have the same height. If this property is not specified, the tallest item in the list dictates the cell height for all the cells.

- **fixedCellWidth**: The width of a list cell. All the cells in a list have the same width. If this property is not specified, the widest item in the list dictates the cell width for all the cells.

- **model**: An object that maintains the data for the list. List models must be used explicitly when adding or deleting items in a list. List models are introduced in the section "List Models."

- **prototypeCellValue**: An object whose cell size dictates the cell size of the list.

- **selectedIndex**: An int value indicating the index of the selected item in the list.

- **selectedIndices**: An array of int values representing the indices of the selected items in the list.

- **selectedValue**: The first selected value in the list.

- **selectedValues**: An array of objects representing selected values in the list. This property is read-only.

- **selectionBackground**: The background color for selected cells.

- **selectionForeground**: The foreground color for selected cells.

- **selectionMode**: One of the three values (SINGLE_SELECTION, SINGLE_INTERVAL_SELECTION, MULTIPLE_INTERVAL_SELECTION) that indicate whether single items, single-interval items, or multiple-interval items can be selected.

- **selectionModel**: An object that tracks list selection. List-selection models are rarely used explicitly. List-selection models are discussed in the section "List-Selection Models."

- **visibleRowCount**: The preferred number of rows in the list that can be displayed without a scroll bar. The default value is 8.

JList generates javax.swing.event.ListSelectionEvent to notify the listeners of the selections. The listener must implement the valueChanged() handler to process the event.

Example 8.1 Simple List Demo

This example creates a list of a fixed number of items displayed as strings. The example allows you to set a selection mode dynamically from a combo box, as shown in Figure 8.2. When you select an item or multiple items, the item values are displayed in a status label below the list.

Figure 8.2 *You can choose single selection, single-interval selection, or multiple-interval selection in a list.*

Here are the steps to complete the project:

1. Create a new project named ListDemo.jpr and a new applet named TestList.java using the Applet Wizard.

2. In the UI Designer of TestList.java, drop a `JPanel` to the north of the applet to create `jpSelectionMode`. Drop a `JScrollPane` to the center of the applet, and drop a `JList` to the scroll pane to crate `jList1`. Drop a `JLabel` to the south of the applet to create `jlblStatus`.

3. Set `layout` of `jpSelectionMode` to `BorderLayout`. Drop a `JLabel` and a `JComboBox` to `jpSelectionMode`, and rename the combo box to `jcboSelectionMode`.

4. Create an array of strings named `countries` for the names of several countries. Add countries to the list using the following method:

   ```
   jList1.setListData(countries);
   ```

5. Add three items "SINGLE_SELECTION," "SINGLE_INTERVAL_ SELECTION," and "MULTIPLE_INTERVAL_SELECTION" to the combo box using the `addItem()` method.

6. Generate the `ActionEvent` handler for the combo box, and implement it to set a selection mode for the list, as shown in Listing 8.1.

7. Generate the `ListSelectionEvent` handler for the list, and implement it to display the selected items in the label, as shown in Listing 8.1.

```java
package ListDemo;

import java.awt.*;
import java.awt.event.*;
import javax.swing.*;
import javax.swing.event.*;

public class TestList extends JApplet
{
  boolean isStandalone = false;
  JScrollPane jScrollPane1 = new JScrollPane();
  JList jList1 = new JList();

  JPanel jpSelectionMode = new JPanel();
  JComboBox jcboSelectionMode = new JComboBox();
  JLabel jlblStatus = new JLabel();

  JLabel jLabel1 = new JLabel();
  BorderLayout borderLayout1 = new BorderLayout();

  // Create an array of strings for country names
  String[] countries = {"United States", "United Kingdom", "China",
    "Germany", "France", "Canada"};

  // Construct the applet
  public TestList()
  {
  }

  // Initialize the applet
  public void init()
  {
    try
    {
      jbInit();
    }
    catch(Exception e)
    {
      e.printStackTrace();
    }
  }

  // Component initialization
  private void jbInit() throws Exception
  {
    this.setSize(new Dimension(400, 300));

    jList1.setListData(countries);
    jList1.addListSelectionListener(
      new javax.swing.event.ListSelectionListener()
    {
      public void valueChanged(ListSelectionEvent e)
      {
        jList1_valueChanged(e);
      }
```

continues

Listing 8.1 *TestList.java*

```java
        });
        jpSelectionMode.setLayout(borderLayout1);
        jcboSelectionMode.addActionListener(
          new java.awt.event.ActionListener()
          {
            public void actionPerformed(ActionEvent e)
            {
              jcboSelectionMode_actionPerformed(e);
            }
        });
        jlblStatus.setText("Status");
        jLabel1.setText("Choose Selection Mode");
        this.getContentPane().add(jScrollPane1, BorderLayout.CENTER);
        jScrollPane1.getViewport().add(jList1, null);
        this.getContentPane().add(jpSelectionMode, BorderLayout.NORTH);
        jpSelectionMode.add(jLabel1, BorderLayout.WEST);
        jpSelectionMode.add(jcboSelectionMode, BorderLayout.CENTER);
        this.getContentPane().add(jlblStatus, BorderLayout.SOUTH);

        // Add selection modes to the combo box
        jcboSelectionMode.addItem("SINGLE_SELECTION");
        jcboSelectionMode.addItem("SINGLE_INTERVAL_SELECTION");
        jcboSelectionMode.addItem("MULTIPLE_INTERVAL_SELECTION");
    }

    // Handler for selecting items from a combo box
    void jcboSelectionMode_actionPerformed(ActionEvent e)
    {
        String selectedMode =
          (String)jcboSelectionMode.getSelectedItem();

        if (selectedMode.equals("SINGLE_SELECTION"))
          jList1.setSelectionMode(ListSelectionModel.SINGLE_SELECTION);
        else if (selectedMode.equals("SINGLE_INTERVAL_SELECTION"))
          jList1.setSelectionMode(
            ListSelectionModel.SINGLE_INTERVAL_SELECTION);
        if (selectedMode.equals("MULTIPLE_INTERVAL_SELECTION"))
          jList1.setSelectionMode(
            ListSelectionModel.MULTIPLE_INTERVAL_SELECTION);
    }

    // Handler for item selection in the list
    void jList1_valueChanged(ListSelectionEvent e)
    {
        int[] indices = jList1.getSelectedIndices();
        Object[] selectedItems = jList1.getSelectedValues();
        String display = "";

        for (int i=0; i<indices.length; i++)
        {
          display += (String)selectedItems[i] + " ";
        }

        jlblStatus.setText(display);
    }
}
```

Listing 8.1   *Continued*

Example Review

The program creates an array of strings and sets the array as `listData` in the list. The list is placed in a scroll pane so that you can scroll it when the number of items in the list exceeds the viewing area.

When the user selects an item in the list, the `valueChanged` handler is executed, which gets the selected items and displays all the items in the label.

The example enables you to specify selection mode from a combo box. When you choose SINGLE_SELECTION, only one item can be selected at a given time. When you choose SINGLE_INTERVAL_SELECTION, multiple consecutive items can be selected all together by holding down the SHIFT key. When you choose MULTIPLE_INTERVAL_SELECTION, you can choose any number of items anywhere in the list by holding down the CTRL key.

List Models

The previous example constructs a list with a fixed set of strings. If you want to add new items or delete existing items from the list, you have to use the model of list. This section introduces list models.

The `JList` class delegates the responsibilities of storing and maintaining data to its data model. The `JList` class itself does not have the methods for adding or removing items from the list. These methods are supported in the list model.

All list models implement the `ListModel` interface, which defines the registration methods for `ListDataEvent`. The instances of `ListDataListener` are notified when the items in the list are modified. `ListModel` also defines the methods `getSize()` and `getElementAt()`. The `getSize()` method returns the length of the list, and the `getElementAt()` method returns the element at the specified index.

`AbstractListModel` implements the `ListModel` and `Serializable` interfaces. `AbstractListModel` implements the registration methods in the `ListModel`, but does not implement the methods `getSize()` and `getElementAt()`.

`DefaultListModel` extends `AbstractListModel` and implements the two methods `getSize()` and `getElementAt()`, which are not implemented by `AbstractListModel`. The methods in `DefaultListModel` are similar to those in the `Vector` class. In fact, the `DefaultListModel` stores data in an instance of `java.uitl.Vector`. The following methods in `DefaultListModel` are often useful:

- `public void add(int index, element)`

  Inserts the specified element at the specified position in this list.

- `public void addElement(obj)`

  Adds the specified component to the end of this list.

■ `public void clear()`

Removes all of the elements from this list.

■ `public boolean contains(elem)`

Tests whether the specified object is a component in this list.

■ `public int getSize()`

Returns the number of components in this list.

■ `public getElementAt(int index)`

Returns the component at the specified index.

■ `public void removeElementAt(int index)`

Deletes the component at the specified index.

■ `public void setElementAt(obj, int index)`

Sets the component at the specified index of this list to be the specified object. The previous component at that position is discarded.

Example 8.2 List Model Demo

This example creates a list using a list model and allows the user to add and delete items in the list. A sample run of the program is shown in Figure 8.3.

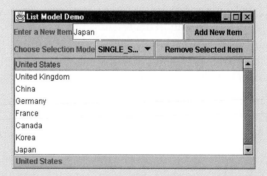

Figure 8.3   *You can add elements and remove elements in a list using list models.*

Here are the steps to complete the project:

1. Reopen project ListDemo.jpr and create a new applet named TestList-Model.java using the Applet Wizard.

2. In the UI Designer of TestListModel.java, drop a `JPanel` to the north of the applet to create jpSettings. Drop a `JScrollPane` to the center of the

applet, and drop a JList to the scroll pane to create jList1. Drop a JLabel to the south of the applet to create jlblStatus.

3. Set layout of jpSettings to BorderLayout, and drop a JPanel to the north and a JPanel to the south of jpSettings to create jpAdd and jpRemove. Set layout of jpAdd and jpRemove to BorderLayout. Drop a JLabel, a JTextField, and a JButton to the east, center, and west of jpAdd, and re-name the text field and button to jtfNewItem and jbtAdd. Drop a JLabel, a JComboBox, and a JButton to the east, center, and west of jpRemove, and rename the combo box and button to jcboSelectionMode and jbtRemove.

4. Switch to the source pane to create an instance of DefaultListModel named listModel, and add items to the model using listModel.add Element(), as shown in Listing 8.2. Add three items "SINGLE_SELECTION," SINGLE_INTERVAL_SELECTION," and "MULTIPLE_INTERVAL_SELECTION" to the combo box jcboSelectionMode.

5. Switch to the UI Designer and set the model property of jList1 to listModel.

6. Generate the ActionEvent handlers for the combo box, the Add New Item button, and the Remove Selected Item button, and implement these han-dlers for setting a selection mode, adding a new element, and deleting ele-ments in the list, as shown in Listing 8.2.

7. Generate the ListSelectionEvent handler for the list and implement it to display the selected items in the label, as shown in Listing 8.2.

```
package ListDemo;

import java.awt.*;
import java.awt.event.*;
import javax.swing.*;
import javax.swing.event.*;

public class TestListModel extends JApplet
{
  boolean isStandalone = false;
  JScrollPane jScrollPane1 = new JScrollPane();
  JList jList1 = new JList();
  JPanel jpSettings = new JPanel();
  JLabel jLabel1 = new JLabel();
  JTextField jtfNewItem = new JTextField();
  JButton jbtAdd = new JButton();
  JButton jbtRemove = new JButton();
  JPanel jpAdd = new JPanel();
  JPanel jpRemove = new JPanel();
  JComboBox jcboSelectionMode = new JComboBox();
  BorderLayout borderLayout1 = new BorderLayout();
  BorderLayout borderLayout2 = new BorderLayout();
```

continues

Listing 8.2 *TestListModel.java*

```
            BorderLayout borderLayout3 = new BorderLayout();
            JLabel jlblStatus = new JLabel();
            JLabel jLabel2 = new JLabel();

            // Create a list model
            DefaultListModel listModel = new DefaultListModel();

            // Construct the applet
            public TestListModel()
            {
            }

            // Initialize the applet
            public void init()
            {
              try
              {
                jbInit();
              }
              catch(Exception e)
              {
                e.printStackTrace();
              }
            }

            // Component initialization
            private void jbInit() throws Exception
            {
              this.setSize(new Dimension(400, 300));
              jLabel1.setText("Enter a New Item");
              jbtAdd.setText("Add New Item");
              jbtAdd.addActionListener(new java.awt.event.ActionListener()
              {
                public void actionPerformed(ActionEvent e)
                {
                  jbtAdd_actionPerformed(e);
                }
              });
              jbtRemove.setText("Remove Selected Item");
              jbtRemove.addActionListener(new java.awt.event.ActionListener()
              {
                public void actionPerformed(ActionEvent e)
                {
                  jbtRemove_actionPerformed(e);
                }
              });

              jList1.setModel(listModel);
              jList1.addListSelectionListener(
                new javax.swing.event.ListSelectionListener()
              {
                public void valueChanged(ListSelectionEvent e)
                {
                  jList1_valueChanged(e);
                }
              });
              jpAdd.setLayout(borderLayout1);
              jpSettings.setLayout(borderLayout2);
```

Listing 8.2 *Continued*

```
      jpRemove.setLayout(borderLayout3);
      jcboSelectionMode.addActionListener(
        new java.awt.event.ActionListener()
      {
        public void actionPerformed(ActionEvent e)
        {
          jcboSelectionMode_actionPerformed(e);
        }
      });
      jlblStatus.setText("Status");
      jLabel2.setText("Choose Selection Mode");
      this.getContentPane().add(jScrollPane1, BorderLayout.CENTER);
      jScrollPane1.getViewport().add(jList1, null);
      this.getContentPane().add(jpSettings, BorderLayout.NORTH);
      jpSettings.add(jpRemove, BorderLayout.SOUTH);
      jpRemove.add(jcboSelectionMode, BorderLayout.CENTER);
      jpRemove.add(jbtRemove, BorderLayout.EAST);
      jpRemove.add(jLabel2, BorderLayout.WEST);
      jpSettings.add(jpAdd, BorderLayout.NORTH);
      jpAdd.add(jLabel1, BorderLayout.WEST);
      jpAdd.add(jtfNewItem, BorderLayout.CENTER);
      jpAdd.add(jbtAdd, BorderLayout.EAST);
      this.getContentPane().add(jlblStatus, BorderLayout.SOUTH);

      // Add items to the list model
      listModel.addElement("United States");
      listModel.addElement("United Kingdom");
      listModel.addElement("China");
      listModel.addElement("Germany");
      listModel.addElement("France");
      listModel.addElement("Canada");

      // Add selection modes to the combo box
      jcboSelectionMode.addItem("SINGLE_SELECTION");
      jcboSelectionMode.addItem("SINGLE_INTERVAL_SELECTION");
      jcboSelectionMode.addItem("MULTIPLE_INTERVAL_SELECTION");
    }

    // Handler for adding an element to the list
    void jbtAdd_actionPerformed(ActionEvent e)
    {
      listModel.addElement(jtfNewItem.getText());
    }

    // Handler for removing elements from the list
    void jbtRemove_actionPerformed(ActionEvent e)
    {
      int selectedIndices[] = jList1.getSelectedIndices();

      for (int i=0; i<selectedIndices.length; i++)
      {
        listModel.removeElementAt(selectedIndices[i] - i);
      }
    }

    // Handler for choosing a selection mode
    void jcboSelectionMode_actionPerformed(ActionEvent e)
    {
      String selectedMode =
        (String)jcboSelectionMode.getSelectedItem();
```

continues

```
            if (selectedMode.equals("SINGLE_SELECTION"))
              jList1.setSelectionMode(ListSelectionModel.SINGLE_SELECTION);
            else if (selectedMode.equals("SINGLE_INTERVAL_SELECTION"))
              jList1.setSelectionMode(
                ListSelectionModel.SINGLE_INTERVAL_SELECTION);
            if (selectedMode.equals("MULTIPLE_INTERVAL_SELECTION"))
              jList1.setSelectionMode(
                ListSelectionModel.MULTIPLE_INTERVAL_SELECTION);
          }

          // Handler for selecting items in the list
          void jList1_valueChanged(ListSelectionEvent e)
          {
            int[] indices = jList1.getSelectedIndices();
            Object[] selectedItems = jList1.getSelectedValues();
            String display = "";

            for (int i=0; i<indices.length; i++)
            {
              display += " " + (String)selectedItems[i];
            }

            jlblStatus.setText(display);
          }
        }
```

Listing 8.2   *Continued*

Example Review

The program creates `listModel`, which is an instance of `DefaultListModel` and uses the model to manipulate data in the list. The model enables you to add and remove items in the list.

To add an element, the user enters the new element in the text field, and clicks the Add New Item button to add the element to the model. The model notifies the list's UI delegate to display the new element in the list.

To remove elements, the user specifies a selection mode, selects the elements, and clicks the Remove Selected Item to remove the item(s) from the model. The `getSelectedIndices()` method returns the indices of all selected items in strict order. Whenever an item is removed from the list, the indices of the items are immediately rearranged. Thus, the current index of *i*th item to remove is `selectedIndices[i] - i`, as shown in Listing 8.2.

List Selection Models

Unlike most Swing components, `JList` has two models: a list model and a list selection model. List models handle data management, and list selection models deal with data selection. A list selection model must implement the `ListModelSelection` interface, which defines constants for three selection modes (SINGLE_SELECTION, SINGLE_INTERVAL_SELECTION, and MULTIPLE_INTERVAL_SELECTION), and registration methods for ListSectionListener. It also defines the methods for adding and removing selection intervals, and the access methods for the properties, such as selectionMode, anchorSelectionIndex, leadSelectionIndex, and valueIsAdjusting.

By default, an instance of JList uses DefaultListSelectionModel, which is a concrete implementation of ListSelectionModel. Usually, you do not need to provide custom list selection model, because the DefaultListSelectionModel class is sufficient in most cases. Unlike the list data model, you do not need to access the list selection model directly, because most of the methods you need from the list selection model are also defined in Jlist.

List Cell Renderers

The previous example displays items as strings in a list. JList is very flexible and versatile, and it can be used to display images and drawings in addition to simple texts. This section introduces list cell renderers for displaying items in any desired form.

In addition to delegating data storage and processing to list models, JList delegates the rendering of the list cells to list cell renderers. All list cell renderers implement the ListCellRenderer interface, which defines a single method getListCellRendererComponent() as follows:

```
public Component getListCellRendererComponent
  (JList list, Object value, int index, boolean isSelected,
   boolean cellHasFocus)
```

This method is passed with a list, the value associated with the cell, the index of the value, and the information regarding whether the value is selected and the cell has the focus. The component returned from the method is painted on the cell in the list.

By default, JList uses DefaultListCellRenderer to render its cells. The DefaultListCellRenderer class implements ListCellRenderer, extends JLabel, and can display either a string or an icon, but not both in the same cell. You can create custom renderer by implementing ListCellRenderer.

Example 8.3 List Cell Renderer Demo

This example creates a list of countries and displays the country flag and the country name in the list, as shown in Figure 8.4. When a country is selected in the list, its flag is displayed in a panel next to the list.

The program requires a custom list cell renderer to display an image and a text in the same cell. Often you need to create a new list model that provides additional information for rendering the cell. In this example, each item has an

continues

325

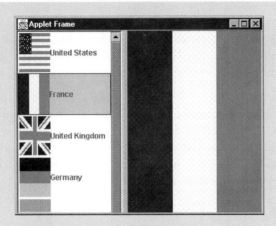

Figure 8.4   *The image and the text are displayed in the list cell.*

image and a label, which should be stored in the list model for use by the list cell renderer as well as by the users of the list. The new list model named MyListModel is given in Listing 8.3.

```java
package ListDemo;

import javax.swing.*;
import java.awt.*;

public class MyListModel extends DefaultListModel
{
  public MyListModel(String[] name, Image[] image)
  {
    for (int i=0; i<name.length; i++)
    {
      addElement(new Object[] {name[i], image[i]});
    }
  }

  public String getName(Object value)
  {
    Object[] array = (Object[])value;
    return (String)array[0];
  }

  public Image getImage(Object value)
  {
    Object[] array = (Object[])value;
    return (Image)array[1];
  }
}
```

Listing 8.3   *MyListModel.java*

The `MyListModel` class extends `DefaultListModel` and is constructed with an array of country names and country flag images. Each pair consisting of a country name and a country flag image is stored as an array object in the list model. The `getName(value)` method returns the country name for the specified object value, and the `getImage(value)` method returns the country flag image for the specified object value. These two methods are used by the list cell renderer to obtain the name and image of the value of the cell.

The custom list cell renderer that displays the image and the name is given in Listing 8.4.

```java
package ListDemo;

import java.awt.*;
import javax.swing.*;
import javax.swing.border.*;

public class MyListCellRenderer implements ListCellRenderer
{
  JPanel listCellPanel = new JPanel();
  ImagePanel imagePanel = new ImagePanel();
  JLabel jlbl = new JLabel(" ", JLabel.LEFT);
  Border lineBorder =
    BorderFactory.createLineBorder(Color.black, 1);
  Border emptyBorder =
    BorderFactory.createEmptyBorder(2, 2, 2, 2);

  public MyListCellRenderer()
  {
    listCellPanel.setOpaque(true);
    imagePanel.setPreferredSize(new Dimension(60, 60));
    listCellPanel.setLayout(new BorderLayout());
    listCellPanel.add(imagePanel, BorderLayout.WEST);
    listCellPanel.add(jlbl, BorderLayout.CENTER);
  }

  public Component getListCellRendererComponent
    (JList list, Object value, int index, boolean isSelected,
      boolean cellHasFocus)
  {
    // TODO: implement this javax.swing.ListCellRenderer method;
    MyListModel listModel =
      (MyListModel)list.getModel();
    String country = listModel.getName(value);
    Image image = listModel.getImage(value);
    jlbl.setText(country);
    imagePanel.showImage(image);

    if (isSelected)
    {
      listCellPanel.setForeground(list.getSelectionForeground());
      listCellPanel.setBackground(list.getSelectionBackground());
    }
    else
    {
```

continues

Listing 8.4 *MyListCellRenderer.java*

```
              listCellPanel.setForeground(list.getForeground());
              listCellPanel.setBackground(list.getBackground());
          }

          if (cellHasFocus)
            listCellPanel.setBorder(lineBorder);
          else
            listCellPanel.setBorder(emptyBorder);

          return listCellPanel;
      }
    }
```

Listing 8.4 *Continued*

The MyListCellRenderer class implements the getListCellRendererComponent()
method in the ListCellRenderer interface. The getListCellRendererComponent()
method obtains the list model of list, and obtains the name and image of
the cell value through the list model. It then displays the image in an image
panel and the name in a label. The image panel and the label are placed
in a panel (listCellPanel) that is the returned component of the
getListCellRendererComponent() method.

The ImagePanel class extends JPanel and provides the showImage(image)
method for displaying a specified image, as shown in Listing 8.5.

```java
// ImagePanel.java: Define the panel for showing an image
package ListDemo;

import java.awt.*;
import javax.swing.*;

public class ImagePanel extends JPanel
{
  // Image filename
  private String filename;

  // Image instance
  private Image image = null;

  // Default constructor
  public ImagePanel()
  {
  }

  // Set image and show it
  public void showImage(Image image)
  {
    this.image = image;
    repaint();
  }
```

Listing 8.5 *ImagePanel.java*

```
    // Draw image on the panel
    public void paintComponent(Graphics g)
    {
      super.paintComponent(g);

      if (image != null)
        g.drawImage(image, 0, 0,
          getSize().width, getSize().height, this);
    }
  }
}
```

Listing 8.5 *Continued*

Finally, let us construct the main program that utilizes the custom list model and custom list cell renderer in a list. Here are the steps to complete the project:

1. Reopen project ListDemo.jpr and create a new applet named TestListCellRenderer.java using the Applet Wizard.

2. In the UI Designer of TestCellListModel.java, drop a JSplitPanel to the center of the applet. Drop a JScrollPane to the left part of the split pane and a JList to the scroll pane to create jList1. Drop an ImagePanel to the right part of the split pane to create imagePanel1.

3. Switch to the source pane to create images for the flags of several countries, as shown in Listing 8.6. Create an instance of MyListModel named listModel, and set the model property of jList1 to this instance. Create an instance of MyListCellRenderer, and set the cellRenderer property of jList1 to this instance.

4. Generate the ListSelectionEvent handler (valueChanged()) for the list, and implement it to display the selected flag in imagePanel1.

```
package ListDemo;

import java.awt.*;
import java.awt.event.*;
import java.applet.*;
import javax.swing.*;
import com.borland.dbswing.*;
import javax.swing.event.*;

public class TestListCellRenderer extends JApplet
{
  boolean isStandalone = false;
  JSplitPane jSplitPane1 = new JSplitPane();
  JScrollPane jScrollPane1 = new JScrollPane();
  JList jList1 = new JList();
  ImagePanel imagePanel1 = new ImagePanel();

  MyListModel listModel;
```

continues

Listing 8.6 *TestListCellRenderer.java*

```java
        // Create a list cell renderer
        ListCellRenderer myListCellRenderer = new MyListCellRenderer();

        // Construct the applet
        public TestListCellRenderer()
        {
        }

        // Initialize the applet
        public void init()
        {
          try
          {
            jbInit();
          }
          catch(Exception e)
          {
            e.printStackTrace();
          }
        }

        // Component initialization
        private void jbInit() throws Exception
        {
          this.setSize(new Dimension(400, 300));
          jList1.setFixedCellHeight(65);
          jList1.setFixedCellWidth(150);
          jList1.addListSelectionListener(
            new javax.swing.event.ListSelectionListener()
          {
            public void valueChanged(ListSelectionEvent e)
            {
              jList1_valueChanged(e);
            }
          });
          jSplitPane1.setContinuousLayout(true);
          this.getContentPane().add(jSplitPane1, BorderLayout.NORTH);
          jSplitPane1.add(jScrollPane1, JSplitPane.TOP);
          jSplitPane1.add(imagePanel1, JSplitPane.BOTTOM);
          jScrollPane1.getViewport().add(jList1, null);

          // Create images
          Class locator = this.getClass();
          Toolkit toolkit = Toolkit.getDefaultToolkit();

          Image imageUS =
            toolkit.getImage(locator.getResource("images/us.gif"));
          Image imageFrance =
            toolkit.getImage(locator.getResource("images/fr.gif"));
          Image imageUK =
            toolkit.getImage(locator.getResource("images/uk.gif"));
          Image imageGermany =
            toolkit.getImage(locator.getResource("images/germany.gif"));
          Image imageIndia =
            toolkit.getImage(locator.getResource("images/india.gif"));
          Image imageNorway =
            toolkit.getImage(locator.getResource("images/norway.gif"));
          Image imageChina =
```

Listing 8.6 *Continued*

```
            toolkit.getImage(locator.getResource("images/china.gif"));
        Image imageCanada =
            toolkit.getImage(locator.getResource("images/ca.gif"));
        Image imageDenmark =
            toolkit.getImage(locator.getResource("images/denmark.gif"));

        // Create a list model
        listModel = new MyListModel(
            new String[]
            {"United States", "France", "United Kingdom", "Germany",
                "India", "Norway", "China", "Canada", "Denmark"},
            new Image[]
            {imageUS, imageFrance, imageUK, imageGermany, imageIndia,
                imageNorway, imageChina, imageCanada, imageDenmark});

        // Set list model
        jList1.setModel(listModel);

        // Set list cell renderer
        jList1.setCellRenderer(myListCellRenderer);
    }

    // Handler for list selection event
    void jList1_valueChanged(ListSelectionEvent e)
    {
        Image image = listModel.getImage(jList1.getSelectedValue());
        imagePanel1.showImage(image);
    }
}
```

Listing 8.6   *Continued*

Example Review

The example consists of four classes: MyListModel, MyListCellRenderer, ImagePanel, and TestListCellRenderer. The MyListModel class is responsible for storing data that includes image and text for the list. The MyListCellRenderer class is responsible for rendering the cell with image and text. The ImagePanel class simply displays an image in the panel. The TestListCellRenderer class tests the list with the custom list cell renderer.

When you choose a country in the list, the list selection event handler is invoked. This handler obtains the list model for the list, uses the list model to retrieve the country's flag image, and displays the image in the image panel on the right side of the split pane.

The getListCellRendererComponent() method in MyListCellRenderer is passed with parameters list, value, index, isSelected, and isFocused. The list is used to obtain the list model. The value determines the image and name of the country displayed in the cell. If the cell is selected, the background and foreground of the cell are set to the list's selection background and foreground. If the cell is focused, the cell's border is set to the line border; otherwise, it is set to the empty border. The empty border serves as divider between the cells.

continues

331

NOTE

The images may not be displayed immediately, because it takes time to load them. You can use image tracker techniques to ensure that the images are loaded before they are displayed. Tracking loading images is introduced in Chapter 14, "Multimedia," in my *Introduction to Java Programming with JBuilder 3* book.

JComboBox

A *combo box* is a component similar to a list. Both combo box and list are used for selecting items from a list. A combo box allows the user to select one item at a time, while a list permits multiple selections. A combo box displays a drop-down list contained in a popup menu when the combo box is clicked. The selected item can be edited in the cell as if it were a text field.

The constructors of JComboBox are similar to those of JList. An instance of JComboBox can be created using its default constructor or one of the following three constructors:

- `public JComboBox(ComboBoxModel model)`

- `public JComboBox(Object[] objectArray)`

- `public JComboBox(Vector vector)`

The following properties of JComboBox are often useful:

- `actionCommand`: An action command string associated with the JComboBox.

- `editable`: A `boolean` value indicating whether the combo box can be edited. The default value is `false`.

- `itemCount`: The number of items in the combo box. This property is read-only.

- `maximumRowCount`: The maximum number of rows that can be seen without scrolling. The default value is 8.

- `model`: An object that maintains the data for the list. Combo box models must be used explicitly to add or delete items in a combo box.

- `popupVisible`: A `boolean` value indicating whether the popup menu that contains the list is displayed. The default value is false, which means that the user has to click the combo box to display the popup menu.

- `renderer`: An instance of the class that implements the `ListCellRenderer` interface. The renderer is responsible for rendering the cell in the combo box.

- `selectedIndex`: The index of the selected item in the combo box.

- `selectedItem`: The current selected object in the combo box.

Like JList, the JComboBox class delegates the responsibilities of storing and maintaining data to its data model. All combo box models implement the ComboBoxModel interface, which extends the ListModel interface and defines the getSelectedItem() and setSelectedItems() methods for retrieving and setting a selected item. The methods for adding and removing items are defined in the MutableComboBoxModel interface, which extends ComboBoxModel.

When an instance of JComboBox is created without explicitly specifying a model, an instance of DefaultComboBoxModel is used. The DefaultComboBoxModel class extends AbstractListModel and implements MutableComboBoxModel. Recall that the DefaultListModel class also extends AbstractListModel. So DefaultComboBoxModel and DefaultListModel share many common methods.

Unlike JList, the JComboBox class has the methods for adding or removing items from the list. The following methods are useful in operating a JComboBox object:

■ public void addItem(Object item)

  This adds the item of any object into the combo box.

■ public Object getItemAt(int index)

  This gets an item from the combo box at the specified index.

■ public void removeItem(Object anObject)

  Removes an item from the item list.

■ public void removeAllItems()

  Removes all items from the item list.

Combo boxes render cells exactly like lists, because the combo box items are displayed in a list contained in a popup menu.

JComboBox can generate ActionEvent and ItemEvent among many other events. Whenever a new item is selected, JComboBox generates ItemEvent twice, one for deselecting the previously selected item, and the other for selecting the currently selected item. JComboBox generates an ActionEvent after generating ItemEvent.

Example 8.4 Combo Box Demo

This example creates a combo box that contains a list of countries and displays the country flag and the country name in the list cell, as shown in Figure 8.5. When a country is selected in the list, its flag is displayed in a panel below to the combo box.

This example is similar to Example 8.3. A custom data model named MyComboBoxModel is created to store data (flag image and country name), as shown in Listing 8.7. A custom cell renderer, named MyComboBoxRenderer, is created to render the cells, as shown in Listing 8.8. These two classes are almost

continues

Figure 8.5 *The image and the text are displayed in the list cell of a combo box.*

identical to the data model and list renderer in Example 8.3, except for the following differences:

- ▪ MyComboBoxModel extends DefaultComboBoxModel, but MyListModel extends DefaultListModel.

- ▪ The data model obtained from the list parameter in the getListCellRendererComponent() method is casted to MyComboBoxModel, while the data model in MyListCellRenderer is casted to MyListModel.

```
package ComboBoxDemo;

import javax.swing.*;
import java.awt.*;

public class MyComboBoxModel extends DefaultComboBoxModel
{
  public MyComboBoxModel(String[] name, Image[] image)
  {
    for (int i=0; i<name.length; i++)
    {
      addElement(new Object[] {name[i], image[i]});
    }
  }

  public String getName(Object value)
  {
    Object[] array = (Object[])value;
    return (String)array[0];
  }

  public Image getImage(Object value)
  {
```

Listing 8.7 *MyComboBoxModel.java*

```
      Object[] array = (Object[])value;
      return (Image)array[1];
   }
}
```

Listing 8.7 *Continued*

```
package ComboBoxDemo;

import java.awt.*;
import javax.swing.*;
import javax.swing.border.*;
import ListDemo.*;

public class MyComboBoxRenderer implements ListCellRenderer
{
  JPanel listCellPanel = new JPanel();
  ImagePanel imagePanel = new ImagePanel();
  JLabel jlbl = new JLabel(" ", JLabel.LEFT);
  Border lineBorder =
    BorderFactory.createLineBorder(Color.black, 1);
  Border emptyBorder =
    BorderFactory.createEmptyBorder(2, 2, 2, 2);

  public MyComboBoxRenderer()
  {
    imagePanel.setPreferredSize(new Dimension(60, 60));
    listCellPanel.setLayout(new BorderLayout());
    listCellPanel.add(imagePanel, BorderLayout.WEST);
    listCellPanel.add(jlbl, BorderLayout.CENTER);
  }

  public Component getListCellRendererComponent
    (JList list, Object value, int index, boolean isSelected,
     boolean cellHasFocus)
  {
    // TODO: implement this javax.swing.ListCellRenderer method;
    MyComboBoxModel listModel =
      (MyComboBoxModel)list.getModel();
    String country = listModel.getName(value);
    Image image = listModel.getImage(value);
    jlbl.setText(country);
    imagePanel.showImage(image);

    if (isSelected)
    {
      listCellPanel.setForeground(list.getSelectionForeground());
      listCellPanel.setBackground(list.getSelectionBackground());
    }
    else
    {
      listCellPanel.setForeground(list.getForeground());
      listCellPanel.setBackground(list.getBackground());
    }

    if (cellHasFocus)
```

continues

Listing 8.8 *MyComboBoxRenderer.java*

```
                        listCellPanel.setBorder(lineBorder);
                  else
                        listCellPanel.setBorder(emptyBorder);

                  return listCellPanel;
            }
      }
```

Listing 8.1   *Continued*

Let us construct the main program that utilizes the custom combo box model and custom combo box cell renderer in a combo box. Here are the steps to complete the project:

1. Create a new project ComboBoxDemo.jpr, and create a new applet named TestComboBox.java using the Applet Wizard.

2. In the UI Designer of TestComboBox.java, drop an `ImagePanel` to the center of the applet to create `imagePanel1`, and drop a `JComboBox` to create `jcboCountires`.

3. Switch to the source pane to create images for the flags of several countries, as shown in Listing 8.9. Create an instance of `MyComboBoxModel` named `comboBoxModel`, and set the `model` property of `jcboCountries` to this instance. Create an instance of `MyComboBoxRenderer`, and set the `renderer` property of `jcboCountries` to this instance.

4. Generate the `ActionEvent` handler for the combo box, and implement it to display the selected flag in `imagePanel1`.

```
package ComboBoxDemo;

import java.awt.*;
import java.awt.event.*;
import java.applet.*;
import javax.swing.*;
import ListDemo.*;

public class TestComboBox extends JApplet
{
   boolean isStandalone = false;
   ImagePanel imagePanel1 = new ImagePanel();
   JComboBox jcboCountires = new JComboBox();

   MyComboBoxModel comboBoxModel;

   // Create a list cell renderer
   MyComboBoxRenderer myComboBoxRenderer = new MyComboBoxRenderer();

   // Construct the applet
```

Listing 8.9   *TestListCellRenderer.java*

```
public TestComboBox()
{
}

// Initialize the applet
public void init()
{
  try
  {
    jbInit();
  }
  catch(Exception e)
  {
    e.printStackTrace();
  }
}

// Component initialization
private void jbInit() throws Exception
{
  this.setSize(new Dimension(400,300));
  jcboCountires.addActionListener(
    new java.awt.event.ActionListener()
  {

    public void actionPerformed(ActionEvent e)
    {
      jcboCountires_actionPerformed(e);
    }
  });
  this.getContentPane().add(imagePanel1, BorderLayout.CENTER);
  this.getContentPane().add(jcboCountires, BorderLayout.NORTH);

  // Create images
  Class locator = this.getClass();
  Toolkit toolkit = Toolkit.getDefaultToolkit();

  Image imageUS =
    toolkit.getImage(locator.getResource("images/us.gif"));
  Image imageFrance =
    toolkit.getImage(locator.getResource("images/fr.gif"));
  Image imageUK =
    toolkit.getImage(locator.getResource("images/uk.gif"));
  Image imageGermany =
    toolkit.getImage(locator.getResource("images/germany.gif"));
  Image imageIndia =
    toolkit.getImage(locator.getResource("images/india.gif"));
  Image imageNorway =
    toolkit.getImage(locator.getResource("images/norway.gif"));
  Image imageChina =
    toolkit.getImage(locator.getResource("images/china.gif"));
  Image imageCanada =
    toolkit.getImage(locator.getResource("images/ca.gif"));
  Image imageDenmark =
    toolkit.getImage(locator.getResource("images/denmark.gif"));

  // Create a list model
  comboBoxModel = new MyComboBoxModel(
    new String[]
    {"United States", "France",
     "United Kingdom", "Germany",
```

continues

```
                     "India", "Norway", "China", "Canada", "Denmark"},
                  new Image[]
                  {imageUS, imageFrance, imageUK, imageGermany, imageIndia,
                   imageNorway, imageChina, imageCanada, imageDenmark});

         // Set list model
         jcboCountires.setModel(comboBoxModel);

         // Set list cell renderer
         jcboCountires.setRenderer(myComboBoxRenderer);
      }

      // Handler for the combo box selection
      void jcboCountires_actionPerformed(ActionEvent e)
      {
        Image image = comboBoxModel.getImage(
          jcboCountires.getSelectedItem());
        imagePanel1.showImage(image);
      }
    }
```

Listing 8.9   *Continued*

Example Review

If you don't need to provide custom methods in the data model, you can simply use the DefaultComboBoxModel, which is used by all the combo boxes if no data model is explicitly specified. In fact, you don't need the combo box data model as much as you need the list data model for JList, because JComboBox directly supports the methods for adding and removing items in the combo box, but JList does not contain those methods.

Each combo box has a default cell renderer that displays string or icon, but not both at the same time. To display a combination of images, drawings, and text, you need to create a custom renderer.

This example creates a custom data model to hold country names and flag images, and to provide the methods for getting names and images. The methods are used in the custom renderer for displaying images and names in cells in the combo box. The combo box renderer is the same as the list box renderer. They all implement the ListCellRenderer interface. In fact, a combo box cell is displayed in a list contained in a popup menu.

Editing Combo Boxes

Unlike lists, combo boxes can be edited. By default, a combo box is not editable. To make a combo box editable, set its editable property to true. Editing only affects the current item and does not change the contents of the list. Editing changes are lost after another item in the combo box is selected. To make changes permanent, you have to implement the ActionEvent handler to replace the current item with the modified item.

Example 8.5 Editing in a Combo Box

This example creates a simple Web browser to render HTML files. The program lets the user enter a URL in a combo box and save it. When the user presses the Enter key after entering the URL or selects an existing URL from the combo box, the HTML file is displayed in an editor pane, as shown in Figure 8.6.

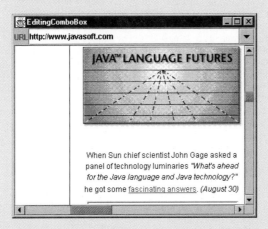

Figure 8.6   *You can enter a URL in the combo box and display the HTML file in an editor pane.*

Here are the steps to complete the project:

1. Reopen the project ComboBoxDemo.jpr, and create a new applet named EditingComboBox.java.

2. In the UI Designer of EditingComboBox.java, drop a JScrollPane to the center of the applet, and drop a JEditorPane to the scroll pane and rename it jep. Drop a JPanel to the north of the applet to create jpURL.

3. Set layout of jpURL to BorderLayout. Drop a JLabel to the west of jpURL, and drop a JComboBox to the center of jpURL to create jcboURL. Set editable of jcboURL to True.

4. Generate an ActionEvent handler for jcboURL, and implement the handler to display the contents at URL in the editor pane, and add the URL to combo box, as shown in Listing 8.10.

5. Generate a hyperlink event handler for the editor pane, and implement it to display the content of the hyperlink in the editor pane, as shown in Listing 8.10.

continues

```
package ComboBoxDemo;

import java.awt.*;
import java.awt.event.*;
import java.applet.*;
import javax.swing.*;
import javax.swing.event.*;
import java.io.IOException;

public class EditingComboBox extends JApplet
{
  boolean isStandalone = false;
  JScrollPane jScrollPane1 = new JScrollPane();
  JEditorPane jep = new JEditorPane();
  JPanel jPanel1 = new JPanel();
  JLabel jLabel1 = new JLabel();
  JComboBox jcboURL = new JComboBox();
  BorderLayout borderLayout1 = new BorderLayout();

  // Construct the applet
  public EditingComboBox()
  {
  }

  // Initialize the applet
  public void init()
  {
    try
    {
      jbInit();
    }
    catch(Exception e)
    {
      e.printStackTrace();
    }
  }

  // Component initialization
  private void jbInit() throws Exception
  {
    this.setSize(new Dimension(400,300));
    jep.setText("jEditorPane1");
    jep.addHyperlinkListener(
      new javax.swing.event.HyperlinkListener()
    {
      public void hyperlinkUpdate(HyperlinkEvent e)
      {
        jep_hyperlinkUpdate(e);
      }
    });
    jLabel1.setText("URL");
    jPanel1.setLayout(borderLayout1);
    jcboURL.setEditable(true);
    jcboURL.addActionListener(new java.awt.event.ActionListener()
    {

      public void actionPerformed(ActionEvent e)
```

Listing 8.10   *EditingComboBox.java*

```
            {
              jcboURL_actionPerformed(e);
            }
      });
      this.getContentPane().add(jScrollPane1, BorderLayout.CENTER);
      this.getContentPane().add(jPanel1, BorderLayout.NORTH);
      jPanel1.add(jLabel1, BorderLayout.WEST);
      jPanel1.add(jcboURL, BorderLayout.CENTER);
      jScrollPane1.getViewport().add(jep, null);
    }

    // Handler for combo box action
    void jcboURL_actionPerformed(ActionEvent e)
    {
      jcboURL.addItem(jcboURL.getSelectedItem());

      try
      {
        // Display the HTML file
        jep.setPage(new URL((String)(jcboURL.getSelectedItem())));
      }
      catch (IOException ex)
      {
        System.out.println(ex);
      }
    }

    // Handler for processing hyperlinks in the HTML file
    void jep_hyperlinkUpdate(HyperlinkEvent e)
    {
      try
      {
        jep.setPage(e.getURL());
      }
      catch (IOException ex)
      {
        System.out.println(ex);
      }
    }
  }
```

Listing 8.10   *Continued*

Example Review

To enable editing, the editable property of the combo box must be true. By default, editable is false.

The user enters a URL of the HTML file in the combo box and presses the Enter key to fire an ActionEvent. The ActionEvent handler stores the URL and displays the URL in the editor pane. You can also select a URL from the combo box.

JTable

JTable is a Swing component that displays data in rows and columns in a two-dimensional grid. Figure 8.7 shows the Swing table in the SwingSet demo.

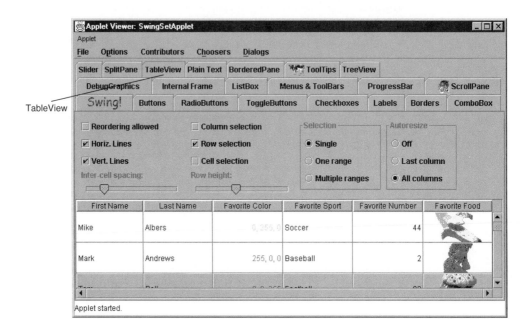

Figure 8.7   *The TableView panel of the SwingSet demo demonstrates the features of* JTable.

JTable doesn't directly support scrolling. To create a scrollable table, you need to create a JScrollPane and add an instance of JTable to the scroll pane. If a table is not placed in a Scroll pane, its column header will not be visible, because the column header is placed in the header of the view port of a scroll pane.

JTable has three different models: a *table model*, a *column model*, and a *list-selection model*. The table model is for storing and processing data. The column model deals with column management. The list-selection model is the same used by JList for selecting rows, columns and cells in a table.

Like JList and JComboBox, JTable has renderers and editors. JTable has many features that make it possible to customize its rendering and editing. JTable also provides many convenient easy-to-use renderers and editors.

There are seven constructors in the JTable class. The builder tool always uses the default constructor to create an instance of JTable. The following constructor constructs a table from a two-dimensional array representing data and an array representing column names:

```
public JTable(Object[][] rowData, Object[] columnNames)
```

For instance, the following statements construct a table as shown in Figure 8.8.

```
// Create table column names
String[] columnNames =
  {"Title", "Author", "Publisher", "In-stock"};

// Create table data
Object[][] data =
{
  {"Introduction to Java Programming", "Y. Daniel Liang",
   "Que Eduction & Training", new Boolean(false)},
  {"Introduction to Java Programming, Second Edition",
   "Y. Daniel Liang", "Que Eduction & Training",
   new Boolean(true)},
  {"Introduction to Java Programming, Thrid Edition",
   "Y. Daniel Liang", "Prentice Hall", new Boolean(true)},
  {"Introduction to Java Programming With Visual J++ 6",
   "Y. Daniel Liang", "Prentice Hall", new Boolean(true)},
  {"Introduction to Java Programming with JBuilder 3",
   "Y. Daniel Liang", "Prentice Hall", new Boolean(true)},
  {"Rapid Java Application Development Using JBuilder 3",
   "Y. Daniel Liang", "Prentice Hall", new Boolean(true)},
};

// Create a table
JTable jTable1 = new JTable(data, columnNames);
```

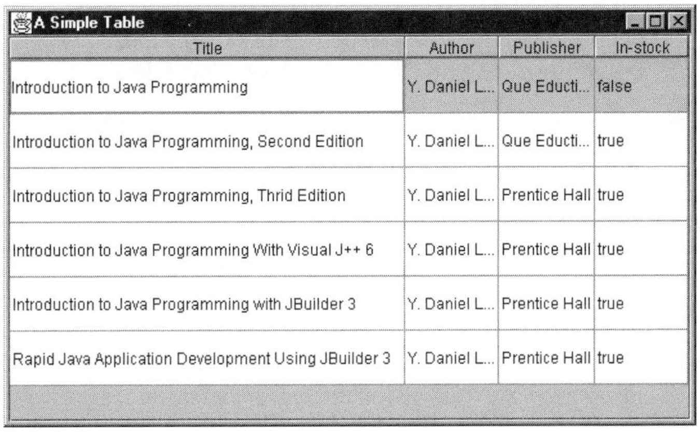

Title	Author	Publisher	In-stock
Introduction to Java Programming	Y. Daniel L...	Que Educti...	false
Introduction to Java Programming, Second Edition	Y. Daniel L...	Que Educti...	true
Introduction to Java Programming, Thrid Edition	Y. Daniel L...	Prentice Hall	true
Introduction to Java Programming With Visual J++ 6	Y. Daniel L...	Prentice Hall	true
Introduction to Java Programming with JBuilder 3	Y. Daniel L...	Prentice Hall	true
Rapid Java Application Development Using JBuilder 3	Y. Daniel L...	Prentice Hall	true

Figure 8.8 *You can construct a simple table using the* `JTable` *constructor.*

Note

`JTable` has many supporting classes. For convenience, all the table classes except `JTable` are grouped in the `javax.swing.table` package.

`JTable` Properties

`JTable` is a powerful control with a variety of properties and methods that provide many ways to customize tables. The following properties are often used:

- **autoCreateColumnsFromModel:** A `boolean` value indicating whether the columns are created in the table. The default value is `true`.

- **autoResizingMode:** You can always resize table columns, but not the rows. This property specifies how columns are resized. Possible values are:

  ```
  JTable.AUTO_RESIZE_OFF
  JTable.AUTO_RESIZE_LAST_COLUMN
  JTable.AUTO_RESIZE_SUBSEQUENT_COLUMNS
  JTable.AUTO_RESIZE_NEXT_COLUMN
  JTable.AUTO_RESIZE_ALL_COLUMNS
  ```

- **cellSelectionEnabled:** A `boolean` value specifying whether individual cells can be selected.

- **columnModel:** An object that maintains the table column data. Table column models are introduced in the section "Table Column Models."

- **columnSelectionAllowed:** A `boolean` value specifying whether column selection is allowed.

- **defaultEditor:** The default editor for table cells. `JTable` provides a set of default editors that can be overridden, if desired. The editors are introduced in the section "Table Renderers and Editors."

- **defaultRenderer:** The default renderer for table cells. `JTable` provides a set of default renderers that can be overridden, if desired. The renderers are introduced in the section "Table Renderers and Editors."

- **editingColumn:** The column of the cell that is currently being edited.

- **editingRow:** The row of the cell that is currently being edited.

- **gridColor:** The color used to draw grid lines.

- **intercellSpacing:** A dimension that represents the horizontal and vertical margins between cells.

- **model:** An object that maintains the table data. Table models are introduced in the section "Table Models."

- **rowHeight:** Row height of the table. The default value is 16 pixels.

- **rowMargin:** The vertical margin between rows.

- **rowCount:** The number of rows in a table.

- **rowSelectionAllowed:** A `boolean` value specifying whether the rows can be selected.

- **selectionBackground:** The background color of selected cells.

- **selectionForeground:** The foreground color of selected cells.

- **selectionMode:** Specifying how table cells can be selected. This property is write-only. The possible values are:

```
ListSelectionModel.SINGLE_SELECTION
ListSelectionModel.SINGLE_INTERVAL_SELECTION
ListSelectionModel.MULTIPLE_INTERVAL_SELECTION
```

■ selectionModel: An object that tracks the selection of table cells. Table selection model is the same as the list selection model.

■ showGrid: A boolean value indicating whether the grid lines are displayed. The default value is true.

■ showHorizontalGrid: A boolean value indicating whether the horizontal grid lines are displayed. The default value is true.

■ showVerticalGrid: A boolean value indicating whether the vertical grid lines are displayed. The default value is true.

■ tableHeader: An instance of JTableHeader that is displayed in the header of the view port in a scroll pane. Table header is usually specified as an array of strings in the table model.

Example 8.6 Testing Table Properties

This example demonstrates the use of several JTable properties. The example creates a table and allows the user to choose an Auto Resize Mode, specify the row height and margin, and indicate whether the grid is shown. A sample run of the program is shown in Figure 8.9.

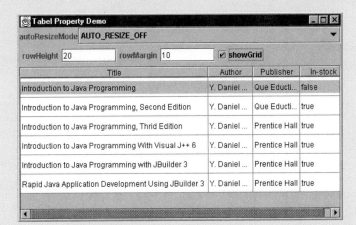

Figure 8.9   *You can specify an auto-resizing mode, row height, and row margin of the table, and specify whether to show grid in the table.*

Here are the steps to complete the project:

1. Create a new project named TableDemo.jpr, and create a new applet named TestTable.java.

continues

345

2. In the UI Designer of TestTable.java, drop a JScrollPane to the center of the applet, and drop a JTable to the scroll pane to create jTable1. Drop a JPanel to north of the applet to create jpProperties.

3. Set layout of jpProperties to BorderLayout. Drop a JPanel to the north of jpProperties to create jpAutoResizeMode. Drop a JPanel to the south of jpProperties to create jpRowGrid.

4. Set layout of jpAutoResizingMode to BorderLayout. Drop a JLabel to he west of jpAutoResizingMode, and drop a JComboBox to the center of jpAutoResizingMode to create jcboAutoResizingMode.

5. Set layout of jpRowGrid to FlowLayout with left alignment. Drop a JLabel, a JTextField, a JLabel, a JTextField, and a JCheckBox to jpRowGrid. Set text of the labels to rowHeight and rowMargin. Rename the text fields to jtfRowHeight and jtfRowMargin. Rename the check box to jchkShowGrid.

6. Initialize the table with table data and column header. Add five auto resizing modes to the combo box.

7. Generate and implement the code for handling combo box selection, for obtaining and using values in the text fields, and for checking and unchecking the showGrid check box, as shown in Listing 8.11.

```java
package TableDemo;

import java.awt.*;
import java.awt.event.*;
import java.applet.*;
import javax.swing.*;
import java.util.*;

public class TestTable extends JApplet
{
  boolean isStandalone = false;
  JScrollPane jScrollPane1 = new JScrollPane();

  // Create table column names
  String[] columnNames =
    {"Title", "Author", "Publisher", "In-stock"};

  // Create table data
  Object[][] data =
  {
    {"Introduction to Java Programming", "Y. Daniel Liang",
     "Que Eduction & Training", new Boolean(false)},
    // omitted for brevity
  };

  // Create a table
  JTable jTable1 = new JTable(data, columnNames);
  JPanel jpProperties = new JPanel();
```

Listing 8.11   *TestTable.java*

```java
    JPanel jpRowGrid = new JPanel();
    JPanel jpAutoResizeMode = new JPanel();
    JLabel jLabel1 = new JLabel();
    JComboBox jcboAutoResizeMode = new JComboBox();
    BorderLayout borderLayout1 = new BorderLayout();
    BorderLayout borderLayout3 = new BorderLayout();
    FlowLayout flowLayout1 = new FlowLayout();
    JLabel jLabel2 = new JLabel();
    JTextField jtfRowHeight = new JTextField();
    JLabel jLabel3 = new JLabel();
    JTextField jtfRowMargin = new JTextField();
    JCheckBox jchkShowGrid = new JCheckBox();

    // Construct the applet
    public TestTable()
    {
    }

    // Initialize the applet
    public void init()
    {
      try
      {
        jbInit();
      }
      catch(Exception e)
      {
        e.printStackTrace();
      }
    }

    // Component initialization
    private void jbInit() throws Exception
    {
      this.setSize(new Dimension(400,300));
      jTable1.setRowHeight(40);
      jLabel1.setText("autoResizeMode");
      jpAutoResizeMode.setLayout(borderLayout3);
      jpRowGrid.setLayout(flowLayout1);
      jpProperties.setLayout(borderLayout1);
      jcboAutoResizeMode.addActionListener(
        new java.awt.event.ActionListener()
      {
        public void actionPerformed(ActionEvent e)
        {
          jcboAutoResizeMode_actionPerformed(e);
        }
      });
      jLabel2.setText("rowHeight");
      jtfRowHeight.setColumns(8);
      jtfRowHeight.addActionListener(
        new java.awt.event.ActionListener()
      {
        public void actionPerformed(ActionEvent e)
        {
          jtfRowHeight_actionPerformed(e);
        }
      });
      jLabel3.setText("rowMargin");
      jtfRowMargin.setCaretPosition(0);
```

continues

```
              jtfRowMargin.setColumns(8);
              jtfRowMargin.addActionListener(
                new java.awt.event.ActionListener()
              {
                public void actionPerformed(ActionEvent e)
                {
                  jtfRowMargin_actionPerformed(e);
                }
              });
              jchkShowGrid.setText("showGrid");
              jchkShowGrid.addActionListener(
                new java.awt.event.ActionListener()
              {
                public void actionPerformed(ActionEvent e)
                {
                  jchkShowGrid_actionPerformed(e);
                }
              });
              flowLayout1.setAlignment(FlowLayout.LEFT);
              this.getContentPane().add(jScrollPane1, BorderLayout.CENTER);
              this.getContentPane().add(jpProperties, BorderLayout.NORTH);
              jpProperties.add(jpAutoResizeMode, BorderLayout.NORTH);
              jpAutoResizeMode.add(jLabel1, BorderLayout.WEST);
              jpAutoResizeMode.add(jcboAutoResizeMode, BorderLayout.CENTER);
              jpProperties.add(jpRowGrid, BorderLayout.SOUTH);
              jpRowGrid.add(jLabel2, null);
              jpRowGrid.add(jtfRowHeight, null);
              jpRowGrid.add(jLabel3, null);
              jpRowGrid.add(jtfRowMargin, null);
              jpRowGrid.add(jchkShowGrid, null);
              jScrollPane1.getViewport().add(jTable1, null);

              // Add auto resize modes to jcboAutoResizeMode
              jcboAutoResizeMode.addItem("AUTO_RESIZE_OFF");
              jcboAutoResizeMode.addItem("AUTO_RESIZE_LAST_COLUMN");
              jcboAutoResizeMode.addItem("AUTO_RESIZE_SUBSEQUENT_COLUMNS");
              jcboAutoResizeMode.addItem("AUTO_RESIZE_NEXT_COLUMN");
              jcboAutoResizeMode.addItem("AUTO_RESIZE_ALL_COLUMNS");
            }

            // Handler for choosing auto resize mode
            void jcboAutoResizeMode_actionPerformed(ActionEvent e)
            {
              String selectedItem =
                (String)jcboAutoResizeMode.getSelectedItem();

              if (selectedItem.equals("AUTO_RESIZE_OFF"))
                jTable1.setAutoResizeMode(JTable.AUTO_RESIZE_OFF);
              else if (selectedItem.equals("AUTO_RESIZE_LAST_COLUMN"))
                jTable1.setAutoResizeMode(JTable.AUTO_RESIZE_LAST_COLUMN);
              else if (selectedItem.equals("AUTO_RESIZE_SUBSEQUENT_COLUMNS"))
                jTable1.setAutoResizeMode(
                  JTable.AUTO_RESIZE_SUBSEQUENT_COLUMNS);
              else if (selectedItem.equals("AUTO_RESIZE_NEXT_COLUMN"))
                jTable1.setAutoResizeMode(JTable.AUTO_RESIZE_NEXT_COLUMN);
              else if (selectedItem.equals("AUTO_RESIZE_ALL_COLUMNS"))
                jTable1.setAutoResizeMode(JTable.AUTO_RESIZE_ALL_COLUMNS);
            }
```

Listing 8.11   *Continued*

```
        // Handler for setting row height
        void jtfRowHeight_actionPerformed(ActionEvent e)
        {
          int rowHeight =
            new Integer(jtfRowHeight.getText().trim()).intValue();
          jTable1.setRowHeight(rowHeight);
        }

        // Handler for setting row margin
        void jtfRowMargin_actionPerformed(ActionEvent e)
        {
          int rowMargin =
            new Integer(jtfRowMargin.getText().trim()).intValue();
          jTable1.setRowMargin(rowMargin);
        }

        // Handler for setting showGrid property
        void jchkShowGrid_actionPerformed(ActionEvent e)
        {
          jTable1.setShowGrid(jchkShowGrid.isSelected());
        }
      }
```

Listing 8.11   *Continued*

Example Review

Initially, each column in the table occupies the same width (75 pixels). You can resize the columns, but not the rows. There are five options for resizing columns: AUTO_RESIZE_OFF, AUTO_RESIZE_LAST_COLUMN, AUTO_RESIZE_SUBSE-QUENT_COLUMNS, AUTO_RESIZE_NEXT_COLUMN, and AUTO_RESIZE_ALL_COLUMNS. With AUTO_RESIZE_OFF, resizing a column does not affect the widths of the other columns. With AUTO_RESIZE_LAST_COLUMN, resizing a column affects the width of the last column. With AUTO_RESIZE_SUBSEQUENT_COLUMNS, resizing a column affects the widths of all the sequent columns. With AUTO_RESIZE_NEXT_COLUMN, resizing a column affects the width of the next columns. With AUTO_RESIZE_ALL_COLUMNS, resizing a column affects the widths of all the columns.

The rowHeight and rowMargin are the properties in the JTable class. To set the width and margin for columns, you need to use the TableColumn class and the table's column model, which are introduced in the sections, " Table Column Models," and "The TableColumn Class."

JTable does not provide methods for manipulating data such as adding or removing rows and columns. Those methods are defined in the table models and table column models.

Table Models

Like `JList` and `JComboBox`, `JTable` delegates data storing and processing to its table data model. A table data model must implement the `TableModel` interface, which defines the methods for registering table model listener, for manipulating cells, and for obtaining row count, column count, column class, and column name.

The `AbstractTableModel` class provides default implementations for most of the methods in `TableModel`. It takes care of the management of listeners and provides some conveniences for generating `TableModelEvents` and dispatching them to the listeners. To create a concrete `TableModel`, you can simply extend `AbstractTableModel` and implement the following three methods at least:

```
public int getRowCount();
public int getColumnCount();
public Object getValueAt(int row, int column);
```

The `DefaultTableModel` class extends `AbstractTableModel` and implements these three methods. Additionally, `DefaultTableModel` provides concrete storage for data. The data are stored as vectors of vectors; i.e., the rows are stored in a vector of objects, and each object in the vector is also a vector of objects, each of which represents an individual cell value.

The following methods in `DefaultTableModel` for accessing and modifying data are often useful:

```
// For processing cells
public Object getValueAt(int row, int column)
public void setValueAt(Object value, int row, int column)
public boolean isCellEditable(int row, int column)

// For processing columns
public void addColumn(Object columnName)
public void addColumn(Object columnName, Object[] columnData)
public void addColumn(Object columnName, Vector columnData)
public int getColumnCount()
public Class getColumnClass(int column)
public String getColumnName()

// For processing rows
public void addRow(Object[] rowData)
public void addRow(Vector rowData)
public int getRowCount()
public void insertRow(int index, Object[] rowData)
public void insertRow(int index, Vector rowData)
public void moveRow(int startIndex, int endIndex, int toIndex)
```

An instance of `DefaultTableModel` can be constructed using the following constructors:

```
public DefaultTableModel()
public DefaultTableModel(int numRows, int numColumns)
public DefaultTableModel(Object[] columnNames, int numRows)
public DefaultTableModel(Object[][] data, object[] columnNames)
public DefaultTableModel(Vector columnNames, int numRows)
public DefaultTableModel(Vector data, Vector columnNames)
```

Table Column Models

Table column models manage columns in a table. You can use column models to select, add, move, and remove table columns. A table column model must implement the TableColumnModel interface, which defines the methods for registering table column model listener, for accessing and manipulating columns.

The DefaultTableColumnModel class is a concrete implementation of TableColumnModel. The DefaultTableColumnModel class stores its columns in a vector and contains an instance of ListSelectionModel for selecting columns.

The following methods in DefaultColumnModel for manipulating and selecting columns are often useful:

```
// For manipulating columns
public void addColumn(TableColumn tableColumn)
public void removeTableColumn(TableColumn tableColumn)
public void moveColumn(int fromIndex, int toIndex)
public int getColumnMargin()
public void setColumnMargin(int newMargin)
public TableColumn getColumn(int columnIndex)
public int getColumnCount()
public int getColumnIndex(Object columnIdentifier)
public Enumeration getColumns()
public int getTotalColumnWidth()

// For selecting columns
public boolean getColumnSelectionAllowed()
public void setColumnSelectionAllowed(boolean flag)
public int getSelectedColumnCount()
public int getSelectedColumns()
public ListSelectionModel getSelectionModel()
public void setSelectionModel(ListSelectionModel newModel)
```

NOTE

Columns can be added or removed from a table column model, but this does not affect the table's data. The columns are not deleted from the table's data.

The **TableColumn** Class

The column model deals with all the columns in a table. The TableColumn class is used to represent an individual column in the table. An instance of TableColumn for a specified column can be obtained using the getColumn(index) method in TableColumnModel, or the getColumn(columnIdentifier) method in JTable.

The following methods in TableColumn are used for manipulating column width and specifying cell renderer, cell editor, and header renderer.

```
// Column width, max width, min width, and preferred width
public int getWidth()
public void setWidth(int width)
public int getMaxWidth()
public void setMaxWidth(int maxWidth)
public int getMinWidth()
public void setMinWidth(int minWidth)
```

```
public int getPreferredWidth()
public void setPreferredWidth(int minWidth)

// Resizes the column to fit the width of its header cell
public void sizeWidthToFit()

// Renderers and editors for the cells in the column
public TableCellEditor getCellEditor()
public void setCellEditor(TableCellEditor anEditor)
public TableCellRenderer getCellRenderer()
public void setCellRenderer(TableCellRenderer aRenderer)
public TableCellRenderer getHeaderRenderer()
public void setHeaderRenderer(TableCellRenderer aRenderer)
```

Example 8.7 Using Table Models

This example demonstrates the use of table models, table column models, list selection models, and the `TableColumn` class. The program allows the user to choose selection mode and selection type, and to add or remove rows and columns, as shown in Figure 8.10.

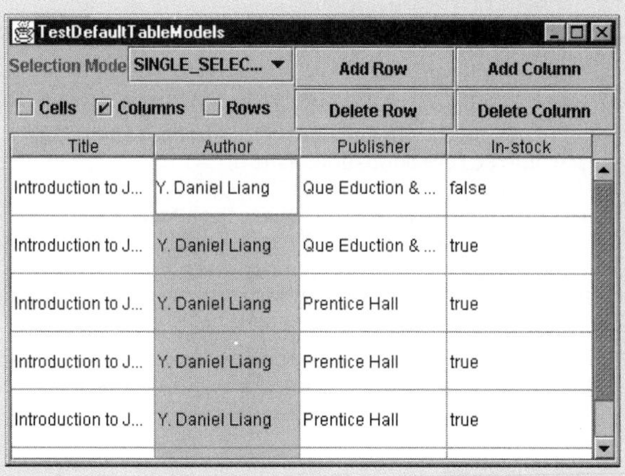

Figure 8.10 *You can add or remove rows and columns in a table.*

Here are the steps to complete the project:

1. Reopen project TableDemo.jpr, and create a new applet named TestDefaultTableModels.java.

2. In the UI Designer of TestDefaultTableModels.java, drop a `JScrollPane` to the center of the applet, and drop a `JTable` to the scroll pane to create `jTable1`. Drop a `JPanel` to the north of the applet to create `jpOperations`.

3. Set `layout` of `jpOperations` to `BorderLayout`. Drop a `JPanel` to the center of `jpOperations` to create `jpSelections`. Drop a `JPanel` to the east of `jpOperations` to create `jpAddRemove`.

4. Set layout of jpSelections to BorderLayout. Drop a JPanel to the north of jpSelections to create jpSelectionMode, and drop a JPanel to the south of jpSelections to create jpSelectionType.

5. Set layout of jpSelectionMode to BorderLayout. Drop a JLabel to the west of jpSelectionMode, and drop a JComboBox to the center of jpSelectionMode.

6. Set layout of jpSelectionType to FlowLayout with left alignment. Drop a JCheckBox three times into jpSelectionType to create jchkCells, jchkColumns, and jchkRows.

7. Set layout of jpAddRemove to GridLayout with two rows and two columns. Drop a JButton four times to create jbtAddRow, jbtAddColumn, jbtDeleteRow, and jbtDeleteColumn.

8. Create an instance, named tableModel, of DefaultTableModel with table data and column, as shown in Listing 8.12, and set the model property of jTable1 to tableModel.

9. Generate the ActionEvent handlers for combo box, check boxes, and buttons, and implement the handlers for choosing a selection mode, choosing selection types, and adding or removing rows and columns, as shown in Listing 8.12.

```
package TableDemo;

import java.awt.*;
import java.awt.event.*;
import java.applet.*;
import javax.swing.*;
import javax.swing.table.*;
import java.util.*;

public class TestDefaultTableModels extends JApplet
{
  boolean isStandalone = false;
  JScrollPane jScrollPane1 = new JScrollPane();
  JTable jTable1 = new JTable();
  JPanel jpOperations = new JPanel();
  JPanel jpSelections = new JPanel();
  JPanel jpSelectionType = new JPanel();
  JPanel jpSelectionMode = new JPanel();
  JLabel jLabel1 = new JLabel();
  JComboBox jcboSelectionMode = new JComboBox();
  BorderLayout borderLayout1 = new BorderLayout();
  BorderLayout borderLayout2 = new BorderLayout();
  BorderLayout borderLayout3 = new BorderLayout();
  JCheckBox jchkCells = new JCheckBox();
  JCheckBox jchkColumns = new JCheckBox();
  JCheckBox jchkRows = new JCheckBox();
  FlowLayout flowLayout1 = new FlowLayout();
```

continues

Listing 8.12   *TestDefaultTableModels.java*

```java
// Create table column names
String[] columnNames =
  {"Title", "Author", "Publisher", "In-stock"};

// Create table data
Object[][] data =
{
  {"Introduction to Java Programming", "Y. Daniel Liang",
    "Que Eduction & Training", new Boolean(false)},
  // omitted for brevity
};

// Create table model
DefaultTableModel tableModel =
  new DefaultTableModel(data, columnNames);
JPanel jpAddRemove = new JPanel();
JButton jbtDeleteColumn = new JButton();
JButton jbtDeleteRow = new JButton();
JButton jbtAddColumn = new JButton();
JButton jbtAddRow = new JButton();
GridLayout gridLayout1 = new GridLayout();

// Construct the applet
public TestDefaultTableModels()
{
}

// Initialize the applet
public void init()
{
  try
  {
    jbInit();
  }
  catch(Exception e)
  {
    e.printStackTrace();
  }
}

// Component initialization
private void jbInit() throws Exception
{
  this.setSize(new Dimension(400,300));
  jTable1.setModel(tableModel);
  jTable1.setRowHeight(40);
  jLabel1.setText("Selection Mode");
  jpSelectionMode.setLayout(borderLayout3);
  jpSelectionType.setLayout(flowLayout1);
  jpSelections.setLayout(borderLayout1);
  jpOperations.setLayout(borderLayout2);
  jcboSelectionMode.addActionListener(
    new java.awt.event.ActionListener()
  {
    public void actionPerformed(ActionEvent e)
    {
      jcboSelectionMode_actionPerformed(e);
    }
  });
```

Listing 8.12 *Continued*

```
        jchkCells.setText("Cells");
        jchkCells.addActionListener(new java.awt.event.ActionListener()
        {
          public void actionPerformed(ActionEvent e)
          {
            jchkCells_actionPerformed(e);
          }
        });
        jchkColumns.setText("Columns");
        jchkColumns.addActionListener(new java.awt.event.ActionListener()
        {
          public void actionPerformed(ActionEvent e)
          {
            jchkColumns_actionPerformed(e);
          }
        });
        jchkRows.setText("Rows");
        jchkRows.addActionListener(new java.awt.event.ActionListener()
        {
          public void actionPerformed(ActionEvent e)
          {
            jchkRows_actionPerformed(e);
          }
        });
        flowLayout1.setAlignment(FlowLayout.LEFT);
        jbtDeleteColumn.setText("Delete Column");
        jbtDeleteColumn.addActionListener(
          new java.awt.event.ActionListener()
        {
          public void actionPerformed(ActionEvent e)
          {
            jbtDeleteColumn_actionPerformed(e);
          }
        });
        jbtDeleteRow.setText("Delete Row");
        jbtDeleteRow.addActionListener(
          new java.awt.event.ActionListener()
        {
          public void actionPerformed(ActionEvent e)
          {
            jbtDeleteRow_actionPerformed(e);
          }
        });
        jbtAddColumn.setText("Add Column");
        jbtAddColumn.addActionListener(
          new java.awt.event.ActionListener()
        {
          public void actionPerformed(ActionEvent e)
          {
            jbtAddColumn_actionPerformed(e);
          }
        });
        jbtAddRow.setText("Add Row");
        jbtAddRow.addActionListener(new java.awt.event.ActionListener()
        {
          public void actionPerformed(ActionEvent e)
          {
            jbtAddRow_actionPerformed(e);
          }
        });
```

continues

355

```java
        jpAddRemove.setLayout(gridLayout1);
        gridLayout1.setColumns(2);
        gridLayout1.setRows(2);
        this.getContentPane().add(jScrollPane1, BorderLayout.CENTER);
        this.getContentPane().add(jpOperations, BorderLayout.NORTH);
        jpOperations.add(jpSelections, BorderLayout.CENTER);
        jpSelections.add(jpSelectionMode, BorderLayout.NORTH);
        jpSelectionMode.add(jLabel1, BorderLayout.WEST);
        jpSelectionMode.add(jcboSelectionMode, BorderLayout.CENTER);
        jpSelections.add(jpSelectionType, BorderLayout.CENTER);
        jpSelectionType.add(jchkCells, null);
        jpSelectionType.add(jchkColumns, null);
        jpSelectionType.add(jchkRows, null);
        jpOperations.add(jpAddRemove, BorderLayout.EAST);
        jpAddRemove.add(jbtAddRow, null);
        jpAddRemove.add(jbtAddColumn, null);
        jpAddRemove.add(jbtDeleteRow, null);
        jpAddRemove.add(jbtDeleteColumn, null);
        jScrollPane1.getViewport().add(jTable1, null);

        // Add selection modes to jcboSelectionMode
        jcboSelectionMode.addItem("SINGLE_SELECTION");
        jcboSelectionMode.addItem("SINGLE_INTERVAL_SELECTION");
        jcboSelectionMode.addItem("MULTIPLE_INTERVAL_SELECTION");
    }

    // Choose a selection mode
    void jcboSelectionMode_actionPerformed(ActionEvent e)
    {
      String selectedItem =
        (String)jcboSelectionMode.getSelectedItem();

      if (selectedItem.equals("SINGLE_SELECTION"))
        jTable1.setSelectionMode(ListSelectionModel.SINGLE_SELECTION);
      else if (selectedItem.equals("SINGLE_INTERVAL_SELECTION"))
        jTable1.setSelectionMode(
          ListSelectionModel.SINGLE_INTERVAL_SELECTION);
      else if (selectedItem.equals("MULTIPLE_INTERVAL_SELECTION"))
        jTable1.setSelectionMode(
          ListSelectionModel.MULTIPLE_INTERVAL_SELECTION);
    }

    // Cell selection enabled
    void jchkCells_actionPerformed(ActionEvent e)
    {
      jTable1.setCellSelectionEnabled(
        jchkCells.isSelected());
    }

    // Column selection enabled
    void jchkColumns_actionPerformed(ActionEvent e)
    {
      jTable1.setColumnSelectionAllowed(
        jchkColumns.isSelected());
    }

    // Row selection enabled
    void jchkRows_actionPerformed(ActionEvent e)
    {
      jTable1.setRowSelectionAllowed(
```

Listing 8.1   *Continued*

```
                    jchkRows.isSelected());
    }

    // Add a new row
    void jbtAddRow_actionPerformed(ActionEvent e)
    {
        tableModel.addRow(new Object[]{" ", " ", " ",
                            new Boolean(false)});
    }

    // Add a new column
    void jbtAddColumn_actionPerformed(ActionEvent e)
    {
        tableModel.addColumn(new String("New Column"),
            new Object[] {"1", "2", "3", "4", "5", "6", "7"});
    }

    // Remove the selected row
    void jbtDeleteRow_actionPerformed(ActionEvent e)
    {
        tableModel.removeRow(jTable1.getSelectedRow());
    }

    // Remove the selected column
    void jbtDeleteColumn_actionPerformed(ActionEvent e)
    {
        DefaultTableColumnModel tableColumnModel =
            (DefaultTableColumnModel)jTable1.getColumnModel();
        int selectedColumn = jTable1.getSelectedColumn();
        tableColumnModel.removeColumn(
            tableColumnModel.getColumn(selectedColumn));
    }
}
```

Listing 8.1   *Continued*

Example Review

The table selection model is the same as the list selection mode. You can choose to select a single object, objects in a single interval, or objects in multiple intervals. The objects can be cells, columns, or rows. The selectable object types can be specified using the following JTable boolean properties:

- cellSelectionAllowed

- columnSelectionAllowed

- rowSelectionAllowed

When you click the Add Row button, a new row is appended to the table. When you click the Add Column button, a new column entitled "New Column" is appended to the table. To delete a row, first select a row, then click the Delete Row button. To delete a column, first select a column, then click the Delete Column button. The program only deletes one row or one column at a

continues

time, you can modify the handlers to enable the deleting of multiple rows and columns.

Some of the methods defined in the column model are also defined in the table model or in the JTable class for convenience. For instance, the addColumn() method defined in the column model is also defined in the table model, and the getColumn() method defined in the column model is also defined in the JTable class.

Table Renderers and Editors

Table cells are painted by cell renderers. By default, a cell object's string representation is displayed and the string can be edited as it was in a text field. JTable maintains a set of predefined renderers and editors, listed in Table 8.1, which can be specified to replace default string renderers and editors.

TABLE 8.1   Predefined Renderers and Editors for Tables

Class	Renderer	Editor
Object	JLabel (left aligned)	JTextField
Date	JLabel (right aligned)	JTextField
Number	JLabel (right aligned)	JTextField
ImageIcon	JLabel (center aligned)	
Boolean	JCheckBox (center aligned)	JCheckBox (center aligned)

The predefined renderers and editors are automatically located and loaded to match the class return from the getColumnClass() method in the table model. To use a predefined renderer or editor for a class, you need to override the getColumnClass() method to return the class of the column as follows:

```
public Class getColumnClass(int column)
{
  return getValueAt(0, column).getClass();
}
```

Example 8.8 Using Predefined Table Renderers and Editors

This example demonstrates using predefined table renderers and editors for boolean values, dates, and image icons, as shown in Figure 8.11.

Here are the steps to complete the project:

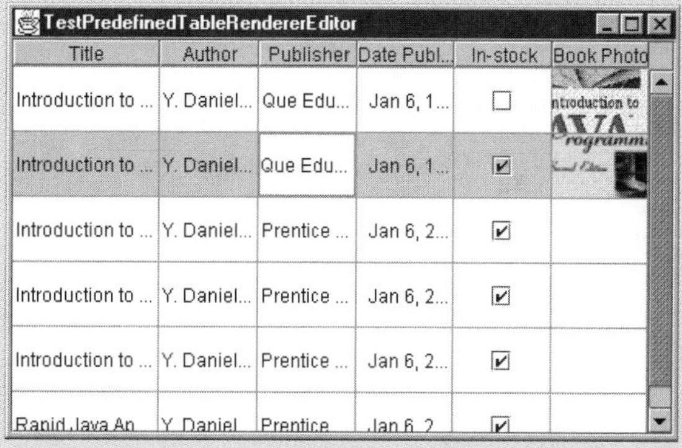

Figure 8.11   JTable *uses predefined renderers and editors for* boolean *values, dates, and image icons.*

1. Reopen project TableDemo.jpr. Create a new class named MyTableModel that extends DefaultTableModel, as shown in Listing 8.13. Create a new applet named TestPredefinedTableRendererEditor.java using the Applet Wizard.

2. In the UI Designer of TestPredefinedTableRendererEditor.java, drop a JScrollPane to the center of the applet and drop a JTable to the scroll pane to create jTable1.

3. Create an instance, named tableModel, of MyTableModel with table data and column, as shown in Listing 8.14 and set the model property of jTable1 to tableModel.

```
package TableDemo;

import javax.swing.*;
import javax.swing.table.*;
import java.util.*;

public class MyTableModel extends DefaultTableModel
{
  public MyTableModel(Object[][] data, Object[] columnNames)
  {
    super(data, columnNames);
  }

  // Override this method to return a class for the column
  public Class getColumnClass(int column)
  {
    return getValueAt(0, column).getClass();
  }
}
```

continues

Listing 8.13   *MyTableModel.java*

```
      // Override this method to determine whether the cell is editable
      public boolean isCellEditable(int row, int column)
      {
        Class columnClass = getColumnClass(column);
        return columnClass != ImageIcon.class &&
          columnClass != Date.class;
      }
    }
```

Listing 8.13   *Continued*

```
    package TableDemo;

    import java.awt.*;
    import java.awt.event.*;
    import java.applet.*;
    import javax.swing.*;
    import java.util.*;

    public class TestPredefinedTableRendererEditor extends JApplet
    {
      boolean isStandalone = false;
      JScrollPane jScrollPane1 = new JScrollPane();
      JTable jTable1 = new JTable();

      // Create table column names
      String[] columnNames =
        {"Title", "Author", "Publisher", "Date Published", "In-stock",
        "Book Photo"};

      // Create table data
      Object[][] data =
      {
        {"Introduction to Java Programming", "Y. Daniel Liang",
        "Que Eduction & Training",
        new GregorianCalendar(1998, 1-1, 6).getTime(),
        new Boolean(false), new ImageIcon("images/intro1e.gif")},
        {"Introduction to Java Programming, Second Edition",
        "Y. Daniel Liang",
        "Que Eduction & Training",
        new GregorianCalendar(1999, 1-1, 6).getTime(),
        new Boolean(true), new ImageIcon("images/intro2e.gif")},
        {"Introduction to Java Programming, Thrid Edition",
        "Y. Daniel Liang", "Prentice Hall",
        new GregorianCalendar(2000, 1-1, 6).getTime(),
        new Boolean(true), new ImageIcon("images/intro3e.gif")},
        {"Introduction to Java Programming With Visual J++ 6",
        "Y. Daniel Liang", "Prentice Hall",
        new GregorianCalendar(2000, 1-1, 6).getTime(),
        new Boolean(true), new ImageIcon("images/intro3e.gif")},
        {"Introduction to Java Programming with JBuilder 3",
        "Y. Daniel Liang", "Prentice Hall",
        new GregorianCalendar(2000, 1-1, 6).getTime(),
        new Boolean(true), new ImageIcon("images/intro3e.gif")},
        {"Rapid Java Application Development Using JBuilder 3",
        "Y. Daniel Liang", "Prentice Hall",
```

Listing 8.14   *TestPredefinedTableRendererEditor.java*

```
                    new GregorianCalendar(2000, 1-1, 6).getTime(),
                    new Boolean(true), new ImageIcon("images/intro3e.gif")},
    };

    // Create table model
    MyTableModel tableModel = new MyTableModel(data, columnNames);

    // Construct the applet
    public TestPredefinedTableRendererEditor()
    {
    }

    // Initialize the applet
    public void init()
    {
      try
      {
        jbInit();
      }
      catch(Exception e)
      {
        e.printStackTrace();
      }
    }

    // Component initialization
    private void jbInit() throws Exception
    {
      this.setSize(new Dimension(400,300));
      jTable1.setModel(tableModel);
      jTable1.setRowHeight(40);
      this.getContentPane().add(jScrollPane1, BorderLayout.CENTER);
      jScrollPane1.getViewport().add(jTable1, null);
    }
  }
```

Listing 8.14 *Continued*

Example Review

The example creates two classes: `MyTableModel` and `TestPredefinedTableRenderer`
`Editor`. `MyTableModel` is an extension of `DefaultTableModel`. The purpose of
`MyTableModel` is to override the default implementation of the `getColumnClass()`
method to return the class of the column, so that an appropriate predefined `JTable`
can be used for the column. By default, `getColumnClass()` returns `Object.class`.

`MyTableModel` also overrides the `isCellEditable()` method. By default,
`isCellEditable()` returns `true`. You can override it to prohibit editing of a cell.
This example does not allow the user to edit image icons and dates. For a cell to
be editable, both `isCellEditable()` in the table model and `isEditing` in `JTable`
class must be true.

The `TestPredefinedTableRendererEditor` class creates a table model using
`MyTableModel`. `JTable` assigns a predefined cell renderer and a predefined editor to
the cell, whose class is specified in the `getColumnClass()` method in `MyTableModel`.

Custom Table Renderers and Editors

Predefined renderers and editors are convenient and easy to use, but their functions are limited. The predefined image icon renderer displays the image icon in a label. The image icon cannot be scaled. If you want the whole image to fit in a cell, you need to create a custom renderer.

A custom renderer can be created by extending the `DefaultTableCellRenderer`, which is a default implementation for the `TableCellRender` interface. The custom renderer must override the `getTableCellRendererComponent()` to return a component for rendering the table cell.

The getTableCellRendererComponent() is defined as follows:

```
public Component getTableCellRendererComponent
  (JTable table, Object value, boolean isSelected,
   boolean isFocused, int row, int column)
```

This method signature is very similar to the `getListCellRendererComponent()` method used to create custom list cell renderers. Their implementations are similar too. The following class `MyImageCellRenderer`, shown in Listing 8.15, creates a renderer for displaying image icons in a panel.

```java
package TableDemo;

import javax.swing.table.*;
import javax.swing.*;
import java.awt.*;
import javax.swing.JTable;
import ListDemo.ImagePanel;

public class MyImageCellRenderer extends DefaultTableCellRenderer
{
  public MyImageCellRenderer()
  {
  }

  public Component getTableCellRendererComponent
    (JTable table, Object value, boolean isSelected,
     boolean isFocused, int row, int column)
  {
    Image image = ((ImageIcon)value).getImage();
    ImagePanel imagePanel = new ImagePanel(image);
    return imagePanel;
  }
}
```

Listing 8.15   *MyImageCellRenderer.java*

You can also create a custom editor. `JTable` provides the `DefaultCellEditor` class, which can be used to edit cell in a text field, a check box, or a combo box. To use it, simply create a text field, a check box, or a combo box, and pass it to `DefaultCellEditor`'s constructor to create an editor.

Example 8.9 Using Custom Table Renderers and Editors

This example demonstrates using custom table renderers to display image icons and using a custom combo editor to edit items. A sample run of the program is shown in Figure 8.12

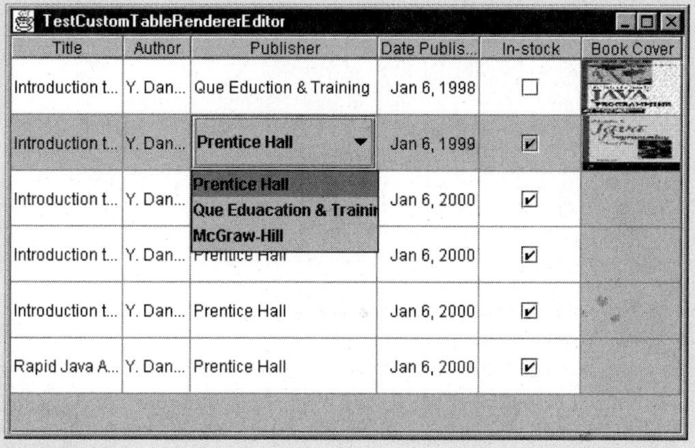

Figure 8.12 *A custom renderer displays a scaled image, and a custom editor edits the Publisher column using a combo box.*

Here are the steps to complete the project:

1. Reopen project TableDemo.jpr. Create a new class named `MyImageCellRenderer` that extends `DefaultTableCellRenderer`, as shown in Listing 8.15. Create a new applet named TestCustomTableRenderer Editor.java using the Applet Wizard.

2. In the UI Designer of TestCustomTableRendererEditor.java, drop a `JScrollPane` to the center of the applet, and drop a `JTable` to the scroll pane to create `jTable1`.

3. Switch to the source pane to create an instance, named `tableModel`, of `MyTableModel` with table data and column names, and set the `model` property of `jTable1` to `tableModel`.

4. Create an instance of `MyImageCellRenderer` and set it as the cell renderer for the Book Cover column.

5. Create an instance of `JComboBox` and add three publisher names, as shown in Listing 8.16. Pass the combo box to the constructor of `DefaultCellEditor` to create a custom editor and set it as the cell editor for the Publisher column.

continues

```
package TableDemo;

import java.awt.*;
import java.awt.event.*;
import java.applet.*;
import javax.swing.*;
import javax.swing.table.*;
import java.util.*;

public class TestCustomTableRendererEditor extends JApplet
{
  boolean isStandalone = false;
  JScrollPane jScrollPane1 = new JScrollPane();
  JTable jTable1 = new JTable();

  // Create table column names
  String[] columnNames =
    {"Title", "Author", "Publisher", "Date Published", "In-stock",
     "Book Cover"};

  // Create table data
  Object[][] data =
  {
    {"Introduction to Java Programming", "Y. Daniel Liang",
     "Que Eduction & Training",
     new GregorianCalendar(1998, 1-1, 6).getTime(),
     new Boolean(false), new ImageIcon("images/intro1e.gif")},
    // omitted for brevity
  };

  // Create table model
  MyTableModel tableModel = new MyTableModel(data, columnNames);

  // Construct the applet
  public TestCustomTableRendererEditor()
  {
  }

  // Initialize the applet
  public void init()
  {
    try
    {
      jbInit();
    }
    catch(Exception e)
    {
      e.printStackTrace();
    }
  }

  // Component initialization
  private void jbInit() throws Exception
  {
    this.setSize(new Dimension(400,300));
    jTable1.setModel(tableModel);
    jTable1.setRowHeight(40);
    this.getContentPane().add(jScrollPane1, BorderLayout.CENTER);
    jScrollPane1.getViewport().add(jTable1, null);
```

Listing 8.16   *TestCustomTableRendererEditor.java*

```
          // Set custom renderer for displaying images
          TableColumn bookCover = jTable1.getColumn("Book Cover");
          bookCover.setCellRenderer(new MyImageCellRenderer());

          // Create a combo box for publishers
          JComboBox jcboPublishers = new JComboBox();
          jcboPublishers.addItem("Prentice Hall");
          jcboPublishers.addItem("Que Eduacation & Training");
          jcboPublishers.addItem("McGraw-Hill");

          // Set combo box as the editor for the publisher column
          TableColumn publisherColumn = jTable1.getColumn("Publisher");
          publisherColumn.setCellEditor(
            new DefaultCellEditor(jcboPublishers));
      }
    }
```

Listing 8.16   *Continued*

Example Review

This example uses the same table model (MyTableModel) that was created in the previous example. By default, image icons are displayed using the predefined image icon renderer. To use MyImageCellRenderer to display the image, you have to explicitly specify the MyImageCellRenderer renderer for the Book Cover column. Likewise, you have to explicitly specify the combo box editor for the Publisher column; otherwise the default editor would be used.

When you edit a cell in the Publisher column, a combo box of three items is displayed. When you select an item from the box, it is displayed in the cell. You did not write the code for handling selections. The selections are handled by the DefaultCellEditor class.

When you resize the Book Cover column, the image is resized to fit into the whole cell. With the predefined image renderer, you can only see part of the image if the cell is smaller than the image.

Table Events

Table events are fired by table models, table column models, and table selection models whenever changes are made to these models. The JTable class does not fire table events. Table models fire TableModelEvent when table data are changed. Table column models fire TableColumnModelEvent when columns are added, removed, or moved, or the column selection changes. Table selection models fire ListSelectionEvent when the selection changes.

To listen for these events, a listener must be registered with an appropriate model and implement the correct listener interface. The following example demonstrates using these events.

Example 8.10 Using Table Events

This example demonstrates handling table events. The program displays messages on a label when a row or a column is selected, when a cell is edited, or when a column is removed. Figure 8.13 is a sample run of the example.

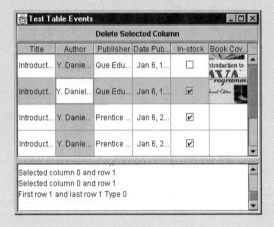

Figure 8.13   *Table event handlers display table events on a text area.*

Here are the steps to complete the project:

1. Reopen project TableDemo.jpr. Create a new applet named Test-TableEvents.java using the Applet Wizard.

2. In the UI Designer of TestTableEvents.java, drop a `JSplitPane` to the center of the applet and set its `orientation` to `VERTICAL`. Drop a `JScrollPane` to the top of the split pane, and drop a `JTable` to the scroll pane to create `jTable1`. Drop a `JScrollPane` to the bottom of the split pane, and drop a `JTextArea` to the scroll pane to create `jtaMessage`. Drop a `JButton` to the north of the applet to create `jbtDeleteColumn`.

3. Switch to the Content pane to create an instance named `tableModel` of `MyTableModel` with table data and column names, and set the `model` property of `jTable1` to `tableModel`. Create an instance named `tableColumm Model` obtained from `jTable1.getColumnModel()`. Create an instance named `selectionModel` obtained from `jTable1.getSelectionModel()`.

4. Switch to the UI Designer. In the Component tree, select `tableModel` in the Other node. In the Events page of the Component inspector for `tableModel`, double-click the value field of `tableChanged` item to generate the handler for table model changed event. Implement the handler to display the changes in the text area, as shown in Listing 8.17.

5. Select `tableModel` in the Other node in the Component tree. In the Events page of the Component inspector for `tableColumnModel`, double-click the value field of `columnRemoved` item to generate the handler for column removed event. Implement the handler to display the remove column index in the text area, as shown in Listing 8.17.

6. Select `selectionModel` in the Other node in the Component tree. In the Events page of the Component inspector for `selectionModel`, double-click the value field of `valueChanged` item to generate the handler for selection event. Implement the handler to display the selected row and column in the text area, as shown in Listing 8.17.

7. Double-click the Delete Selected Column button to generate a handler for button action. Implement the handler to delete the currently selected column, as shown in Listing 8.17.

```
package TableDemo;

import java.awt.*;
import java.awt.event.*;
import java.applet.*;
import javax.swing.*;
import javax.swing.table.*;
import java.util.*;
import javax.swing.event.*;

public class TestTableEvents extends JApplet
{
  boolean isStandalone = false;
  JSplitPane jSplitPane1 = new JSplitPane();
  JScrollPane jScrollPane1 = new JScrollPane();
  JButton jbtDeleteColumn = new JButton();
  JScrollPane jScrollPane2 = new JScrollPane();
  JTextArea jtaMessage = new JTextArea();
  JTable jTable1 = new JTable();

  // Create table column names
  String[] columnNames =
    {"Title", "Author", "Publisher", "Date Published", "In-stock",
     "Book Cover"};

  // Create table data
  Object[][] data =
  {
    {"Introduction to Java Programming", "Y. Daniel Liang",
     "Que Eduction & Training",
     new GregorianCalendar(1998, 1-1, 6).getTime(),
     new Boolean(false), new ImageIcon("images/intro1e.gif")},
     // Omitted for brevity
  };

  // Create table model
  MyTableModel tableModel = new MyTableModel(data, columnNames);
```

continues

Listing 8.17   *TestTableEvents.java*

```
        // Create table column model
        TableColumnModel tableColumnModel = jTable1.getColumnModel();

        // Create selection model
        ListSelectionModel selectionModel = jTable1.getSelectionModel();

        // Construct the applet
        public TestTableEvents()
        {
        }

        // Initialize the applet
        public void init()
        {
          try
          {
            jbInit();
          }
          catch(Exception e)
          {
            e.printStackTrace();
          }
        }

        // Component initialization
        private void jbInit() throws Exception
        {
          this.setSize(new Dimension(400,300));
          jTable1.setColumnSelectionAllowed(true);
          jTable1.setModel(tableModel);
          jTable1.setRowHeight(40);
          selectionModel.addListSelectionListener(
            new javax.swing.event.ListSelectionListener()
          {
            public void valueChanged(ListSelectionEvent e)
            {
              selectionModel_valueChanged(e);
            }
          });
          tableModel.addTableModelListener(
            new javax.swing.event.TableModelListener()
          {
            public void tableChanged(TableModelEvent e)
            {
              tableModel_tableChanged(e);
            }
          });
          jbtDeleteColumn.setText("Delete Selected Column");
          jbtDeleteColumn.addActionListener(
            new java.awt.event.ActionListener()
          {
            public void actionPerformed(ActionEvent e)
            {
              jbtDeleteColumn_actionPerformed(e);
            }
          });
          tableColumnModel.addColumnModelListener(
            new javax.swing.event.TableColumnModelListener()
          {
```

Listing 8.17   *Continued*

```java
      public void columnAdded(TableColumnModelEvent e)
      {
      }

      public void columnMarginChanged(ChangeEvent e)
      {
      }

      public void columnMoved(TableColumnModelEvent e)
      {
      }

      public void columnRemoved(TableColumnModelEvent e)
      {
        tableColumnModel_columnRemoved(e);
      }

      public void columnSelectionChanged(ListSelectionEvent e)
      {
      }
    });
    this.getContentPane().add(jbtDeleteColumn, BorderLayout.NORTH);
    this.getContentPane().add(jSplitPane1, BorderLayout.CENTER);
    jSplitPane1.setOrientation(JSplitPane.VERTICAL_SPLIT);
    jSplitPane1.add(jScrollPane1, JSplitPane.TOP);
    jScrollPane1.getViewport().add(jTable1);
    jSplitPane1.add(jScrollPane2, JSplitPane.BOTTOM);
    jScrollPane2.getViewport().add(jtaMessage);
  }

  // Handler for table change events
  void tableModel_tableChanged(TableModelEvent e)
  {
    jtaMessage.append("First row " + e.getFirstRow() +
      " and last row " + e.getLastRow() + " Type " +
      e.getType() + '\n');
  }

  // Handler for column removed event
  void tableColumnModel_columnRemoved(TableColumnModelEvent e)
  {
    jtaMessage.append("Column " + jTable1.getSelectedColumn() +
      " removed " + '\n');
  }

  // Handler for selection events
  void selectionModel_valueChanged(ListSelectionEvent e)
  {
    jtaMessage.append("Selected column " +
      jTable1.getSelectedColumn() + " and row " +
      jTable1.getSelectedRow() + '\n');
  }

  // Handler for deleting a selected column
  void jbtDeleteColumn_actionPerformed(ActionEvent e)
  {
    int selectedColumn = jTable1.getSelectedColumn();
    tableColumnModel.removeColumn(
      tableColumnModel.getColumn(selectedColumn));
  }
}
```

continues

Example Review

This example creates a table model for the table, and gets the default table column model and default selection model from the table. To make those model instances visible in the Component tree, they are declared as data members of the class. The event handlers for the models are created from the Events page in the Component Inspector.

When a row or a column is selected, a `ListSelectionEvent` is fired by `selectionModel`, which invokes the handler to display the selected row and column in the text area. When the contents or the structure of the table is changed, a `TableModelEvent` is fired by `tableModel`, which invokes the handler to display the last row, last column, and event type in the text area. When a column is deleted by clicking the Delete Selected Column button, a `ColumnModelEvent` is fired by `tableColumnModel`, which invokes the handler to display the index of the deleted column.

JTree

`JTree` is a Swing component that displays data in a treelike hierarchy. Figure 8.14 shows the Swing tree in the SwingSet demo.

All the nodes displayed in the tree are in the form of a hierarchical indexed list. Tree can be used to navigate structured data with hierarchical relationships. The JBuilder Navigation pane, Structure pane, and Component tree are examples of

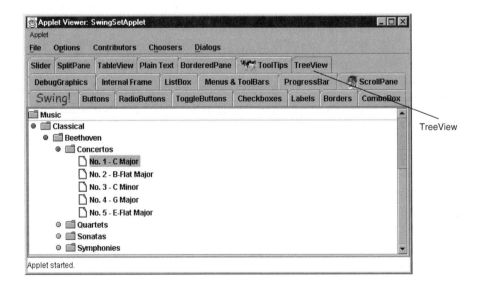

Figure 8.14   *The TreeView panel of the SwingSet demo demonstrates the features of* `JTree`.

displaying items as nodes in a treelike structure. A node can have child nodes. A node is called a *leaf* if it has no children; a node with no parent is called the *root* of its tree; a node with no children is a *leaf*. A tree may consist of many subtrees, each node acting as the root for its own subtree.

A nonleaf node can be expanded or collapsed by double-clicking on the node or on the node's handle in front of the node. The handle usually has a visible sign to indicate whether the node is expanded or collapsed. For example, JBuilder uses the + symbol to indicate that the node is collapsed and the - symbol to indicate that it is expanded.

Like `JTable`, `JTree` is a very complex component with many supporting interfaces and classes. `JTree` is in the `javax.swing` package, but its supporting classes are all included in the `javax.swing.tree` package. These supporting classes are `DefaultMutableTreeNode`, `DefaultTreeModel`, `TreeSelectionModel`, `DefaultTree-CellEditor`, `DefaultTreeCellRenderer`, and `TreePath`.

While `JTree` displays the tree, the data representation of the tree is handled by the `DefaultMutableTreeNode` class, which provides operations for creating nodes, for examining and modifying a node's parent and children, and also for examining the tree to which the node belongs. While the `DefaultMutableTreeNode` represents a node, the `DefaultTreeModel` represents the entire tree. Unlike the `ListModel` or `TableModel`, the tree model does not directly store or manage tree data. Tree data are stored and managed by the `DefaultMutableTreeNode` class. To create a tree model, you first create an instance of `DefaultMutableTreeNode` to represent the root of the tree, and then create an instance of `DefaultTreeModel` fitted with the root.

The `TreeSelectionModel` class handles tree node selection. The `DefaultTreeCell-Renderer` class provides a default tree node renderer that can display a label and/or an icon in a node. The `DefaultTreeCellEditor` can be used to edit the cells in a text field. The `TreePath` class is a support class that represents a set of nodes in a path.

`JTree` has the following useful properties:

- `cellEditor`: An object that is used to edit the cell in a tree node. By default, an instance of `DefaultCellEditor` is used to edit the cells in a text field. Using custom tree cell renderer is introduced in the section, "Tree Node Rendering and Editing."

- `cellRenderer`: An object that is used to render the cells in a tree node. By default, an instance of `DefaultTreeCellRenderer` is used to display nodes in a tree, which can display strings or icons. Using custom tree cell renderer is introduced in the section, "Tree Node Rendering and Editing."

- `editable`: A `boolean` value indicating whether the cell is editable. The default value is `false`.

- `model`: An instance of `TreeModel`.

- `rootVisible`: A `boolean` value indicating whether the root is displayed in the tree. The default value is `true`.

■ rowHeight: The height of the row for the node displayed in the tree. The default height is 16 pixels.

■ selectionModel: An instance of TreeSelectionModel.

Creating Trees

JTree doesn't directly support scrolling. To create a scrollable tree, you need to create a JScrollPane and add an instance of JTree to the scroll pane.

There are several constructors that can be used to create a JTree. You can create a JTree with an array of objects, a vector, or a hash table. The builder tool always uses the default constructor to create an instance of JTree with a default tree model. The default tree is shown in Figure 8.15, because the default tree model is defined in the getDefaultTreeModel() method of the JTree class as follows:

```java
// Excerpted from JTree.java
protected static TreeModel getDefaultTreeModel()
{
  DefaultMutableTreeNode root = new DefaultMutableTreeNode("JTree");
  DefaultMutableTreeNode parent;

  parent = new DefaultMutableTreeNode("colors");
  root.add(parent);
  parent.add(new DefaultMutableTreeNode("blue"));
  parent.add(new DefaultMutableTreeNode("violet"));
  parent.add(new DefaultMutableTreeNode("red"));
  parent.add(new DefaultMutableTreeNode("yellow"));

  parent = new DefaultMutableTreeNode("sports");
  root.add(parent);
  parent.add(new DefaultMutableTreeNode("basketball"));
  parent.add(new DefaultMutableTreeNode("soccer"));

  // Omitted for brevity
  return new DefaultTreeModel(root);
}
```

Figure 8.15   *The default tree constructed with the default constructor of* JTree *displays sample data.*

As demonstrated in the following example, a custom tree model can be created in the same way as the default model.

Example 8.11 Creating Custom Trees

This example creates a tree to display the table of contents of this book, as shown in Figure 8.16.

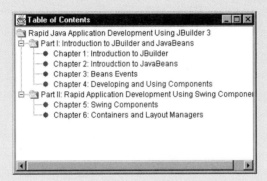

Figure 8.16   *The table of contents of this book is displayed in a tree.*

Here are the steps to complete the example:

1. Create a new project named TreeDemo.jpr and an applet named Test-Tree.java.

2. In the UI Designer of TestTree.java, drop a `JScrollPane` to the center of the applet, and drop a `JTree` to the scroll pane to create jTree1.

3. Create a method named `createTreeModel()` to create a tree model, as shown in Listing 8.18. Declare and create an instance of `TreeModel` named treeModel. Set the `model` property of jTree1 to treeModel.

```java
package TreeDemo;

import java.awt.*;
import java.awt.event.*;
import java.applet.*;
import javax.swing.*;
import javax.swing.tree.*;

public class TestTree extends JApplet
{
  boolean isStandalone = false;
  JScrollPane jScrollPane1 = new JScrollPane();
  JTree jTree1 = new JTree();
  DefaultTreeModel treeModel;
```

continues

Listing 8.18   *TestTree.java*

```java
// Construct the applet
public TestTree()
{
}

// Initialize the applet
public void init()
{
  try
  {
    jbInit();
  }
  catch(Exception e)
  {
    e.printStackTrace();
  }
}

// Component initialization
private void jbInit() throws Exception
{
  // Create a tree model and set the tree model in jTree1
  treeModel = createTreeModel();
  jTree1.setModel(treeModel);

  this.setSize(new Dimension(400,300));
  this.getContentPane().add(jScrollPane1, BorderLayout.CENTER);
  jScrollPane1.getViewport().add(jTree1, null);
}

// Create tree model
private DefaultTreeModel createTreeModel()
{
  DefaultMutableTreeNode root = new DefaultMutableTreeNode
    ("Rapid Java Application Development Using JBuilder 3");

  DefaultMutableTreeNode parent = new DefaultMutableTreeNode
    ("Part I: Introduction to JBuilder and JavaBeans");
  root.add(parent);

  parent.add(new DefaultMutableTreeNode
    ("Chapter 1: Introduction to JBuilder"));
  parent.add(new DefaultMutableTreeNode
    ("Chapter 2: Introudction to JavaBeans"));
  parent.add(new DefaultMutableTreeNode
    ("Chapter 3: Beans Events"));
  parent.add(new DefaultMutableTreeNode
    ("Chapter 4: Developing and Using Components"));

  parent = new DefaultMutableTreeNode
    ("Part II: Rapid Application Development +
     "Using Swing Components");
  root.add(parent);

  parent.add(new DefaultMutableTreeNode
    ("Chapter 5: Swing Components"));
  parent.add(new DefaultMutableTreeNode
    ("Chapter 6: Containers and Layout Managers"));
```

Listing 8.18   *Continued*

374

```
            // Omitted for brevity
            return new DefaultTreeModel(root);
    }
}
```

Listing 8.1   *Continued*

Example Review

The example creates a tree for the table of contents of this book. Each node is created using the DefaultMutableTreeNode class. The createTreeModel() method returns a TreeModel fitted with the root of the tree.

When you drop a JTree to the UI Designer, the default tree model is used. Thus you see the sample data created in the default model. Once you set the model property with the new model, the new data replaces the sample data.

> **NOTE**
> There is a bug to set the model property of an instance of JTree from the Inspector in JBuilder 3.0. Write the code to set this property value programmatically.

Processing Tree Nodes

Swing uses the TreeNode interface to model a single node. The MutableTreeNode interface extends TreeNode. The DefaultMutableTreeNode class is an implementation of MutableTreeNode. The DefaultMutableTreeNode class stores data for a node and provides methods for tree traversal in various orders or for following the path between two nodes. Breadth-first traversal, depth-first traversal, postorder traversal, and preorder traversal are supported. These traversals are often used in algorithm design and are popular topics in data structures course.

The following methods in DefaultMutableTreeNode are often useful:

```
// The useful methods in DefaultMutableTreeNode
public TreeNode getParent() // Return the parent node
public Enumeration children() // Get all children
public boolean isLeaf() // Is the node a leaf
public Enumeration breadthFirstEnumeration()
public Enumeration depthFirstEnumeration()
public Enumeration preorderEnumeration()
public Enumeration postOrderEnumeration()
```

The last four methods create and return an enumeration that traverses the subtree rooted at this node in breadth-first order, depth-first order, preorder, or postorder, respectively. For example, the following code displays the nodes in breadth-first traversal order:

```
Enumeration bf = root.breadthFirstEnumeration();
while (bf.hasMoreElements())
{
  System.out.print(bf.nextElement().toString());
}
```

Swing uses the `TreePath` class to represent a path between an ancestor and a descendant in the tree. Instances of `TreePath` are often instantiated by Swing classes. For instance, the `getLeadSelectionPath()` method in the `TreeSelectionModel` returns the path from the root to the selected node. There are many ways to extract the nodes from a tree path. Often you use the `getLastPathComponent()` method to obtain the last node in the path, and then get all the nodes in the path upward through the link using the `getParent()` method.

The selection of tree nodes is defined in the `TreeSelectionModel` interface. The `DefaultTreeSelectionModel` class is an implementation of the `TreeSelectionModel`, which maintains an array of `TreePath` objects representing the current selection. The last `TreePath` selected, called the *lead path*, can be obtained using the `getLeadSelectionPath()` method. To obtain all the selection path, use the `getSelectionPaths()` method, which returns an array of tree paths.

`TreeSelectionModel` supports three selection modes: *contiguous selection*, *discontiguous selection*, and *single selection*. Single selection allows only one item to be selected. Contiguous selection allows multiple selections, but the selected items must be contiguous. Discontiguous selection is the most flexible; it allows any item to be selected at a given time. The default tree selection mode is discontiguous. To set a selection mode, use the `setSelectionMode()` method in `TreeSelectionModel`. The constants for the three modes are the following:

- `CONTIGUOUS_TREE_SELECTION`

- `DISCONTIGUOUS_TREE_SELECTION`

- `SINGLE_TREE_SELECTION`

The `TreeModel` interface defines operations for inserting or removing tree nodes. The `DefaultTreeModel` class is a concrete implementation of `TreeModel`. To insert or remove a node, use the following methods:

```
public void insertNodeInto(MutableTreeNode newNode,
  MutablTreeNode parent, int index)
public void removeNodeFromParent(MutableTreeNode theNode)
```

Example 8.12 Adding and Removing Nodes

This example uses the classes `DefaultMutableTreeNode`, `TreePath`, `DefaultTreeSelectionModel`, and `DefaultTreeModel`. The example enables the user to add or remove nodes from a tree, as shown in Figure 8.17.

Here are the steps to complete the example:

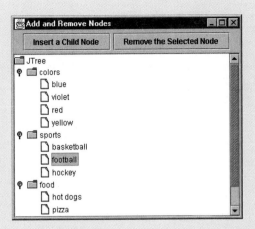

Figure 8.17   *You can add or remove nodes dynamically in a tree.*

1. Reopen the project TreeDemo.jpr and create an applet named ProcessTree.java using the Applet Wizard.

2. In the UI Designer of ProcessTree.java, drop a JScrollPane to the center of the applet, and drop a JTree to the scroll pane to create jTree1. Drop a JPanel to create jpButtons, and add two buttons named jbtAdd and jbtRemove into jpButtons.

3. Declare and obtain the tree model and selection model from jTree1 using the getModel() and getSelectionModel() methods. Set the selection mode to single selection.

4. Generate and implement the code for handling jbtAdd and jtbRemove, as shown in Listing 8.19.

```
package TreeDemo;

import java.awt.*;
import java.awt.event.*;
import java.applet.*;
import javax.swing.*;
import javax.swing.tree.*;

public class ProcessTree extends JApplet
{
  boolean isStandalone = false;
  JScrollPane jScrollPane1 = new JScrollPane();
  JTree jTree1 = new JTree();
  JPanel jpButtons = new JPanel();
  JButton jbtAdd = new JButton();
  JButton jbtRemove = new JButton();
```

continues

Listing 8.19   *ProcessTree.java*

```java
        // Get selection model
        TreeSelectionModel selectionModel = jTree1.getSelectionModel();

        // Get tree model
        DefaultTreeModel treeModel = (DefaultTreeModel)jTree1.getModel();

        // Construct the applet
        public ProcessTree()
        {
        }

        // Initialize the applet
        public void init()
        {
          try
          {
            jbInit();
          }
          catch(Exception e)
          {
            e.printStackTrace();
          }
        }

        // Component initialization
        private void jbInit() throws Exception
        {
          this.setSize(new Dimension(400,300));
          jbtAdd.setText("Insert a Child Node");
          jbtAdd.addActionListener(new java.awt.event.ActionListener()
          {
            public void actionPerformed(ActionEvent e)
            {
              jbtAdd_actionPerformed(e);
            }
          });
          jbtRemove.setText("Remove the Selected Node");
          jbtRemove.addActionListener(new java.awt.event.ActionListener()
          {
            public void actionPerformed(ActionEvent e)
            {
              jbtRemove_actionPerformed(e);
            }
          });
          this.getContentPane().add(jScrollPane1, BorderLayout.CENTER);
          this.getContentPane().add(jpButtons, BorderLayout.NORTH);
          jpButtons.add(jbtAdd, null);
          jpButtons.add(jbtRemove, null);
          jScrollPane1.getViewport().add(jTree1, null);

          // Set single selection
          selectionModel.setSelectionMode(
            TreeSelectionModel.SINGLE_TREE_SELECTION);
        }

        void jbtAdd_actionPerformed(ActionEvent e)
        {
          // Get the selection path
          TreePath path = selectionModel.getLeadSelectionPath();
```

Listing 8.19 *Continued*

```
      // Get the last node in the path
      DefaultMutableTreeNode treeNode =
        (DefaultMutableTreeNode)path.getLastPathComponent();

      // Enter a new node
      String nodeName = JOptionPane.showInputDialog(
        this, "Enter a name for this new node", "Add a Child",
        JOptionPane.QUESTION_MESSAGE);

      // Insert the new node as a child of treeNode
      treeModel.insertNodeInto(new DefaultMutableTreeNode(nodeName),
        treeNode, treeNode.getChildCount());
    }

    void jbtRemove_actionPerformed(ActionEvent e)
    {
      // Get the selection path
      TreePath path = selectionModel.getLeadSelectionPath();

      // Get the last node in the path
      DefaultMutableTreeNode treeNode =
        (DefaultMutableTreeNode)path.getLastPathComponent();

      if (treeNode == treeModel.getRoot())
      {
        JOptionPane.showMessageDialog(this, "Cannot remove the root");
      }
      else
        // Remove the selected node
        treeModel.removeNodeFromParent(treeNode);
    }
  }
```

Listing 8.19   *Continued*

Example Review

The example creates a tree using the default constructor. The getModel()
method returns the tree model, and the getSelectionModel() method obtains
the tree selection model. The methods for inserting and removing nodes
are provided in the tree model, and the tree selection model can be used to
find the selected path using the getLeadSelectionPath() method. The
selected node is the last node in the lead path, which can be found using the
getLastPathComponent() method.

To insert a node, first select a parent in the tree, then click the Insert a Child
Node button, which displays an input dialog box to receive the new node name.
The new node is added as a child of the selected node.

To remove a node, first select the node in the tree, then click the Remove the
Selected Node button. If you attempt to remove the root, a message dialog is
displayed to alert you that the root cannot be removed.

Tree Node Rendering and Editing

Like all the advanced Swing components, JTree delegates node rendering to a renderer. The DefaultTreeCellRenderer interface defines how cells are rendered, which is implemented by the DefaultTreeCellRenderer class. The DefaultTreeCellRenderer class maintains three icon properties named leafIcon, openIcon, and closedIcon for leaf nodes, expanded nodes, and collapsed nodes. It also provides colors for text and background. The following code sets new leaf, open and closed icons, and new background selection color in the tree.

```
DefaultTreeCellRenderer renderer =
    (DefaultTreeCellRenderer)jTree1.getCellRenderer();
renderer.setLeafIcon(leafImageIcon);
renderer.setOpenIcon(openImageIcon);
renderer.setClosedIcon(closedImageIcon);
renderer.setBackgroundSelectionColor(Color.red);
```

> **NOTE**
> The default leaf, open icon, and closed icon are dependent on the look-and-feel.
> For instance, on Windows look-and-feel, the open icon is -, and the closed icon is +.

JTree comes with a default cell editor. If the JTree's editable property is true, the default editor activates a text field for editing when the node is clicked three times. To create a custom editor, you need to extend the DefaultCellEditor class, which is the same class you used in table cell editing. You can use a text field, a check box, or a combo box, and pass it to DefaultCellEditor's constructor to create an editor. The following code uses a combo box for editing colors. The combo box editor is shown in Figure 8.18.

```
// Customize editor
JComboBox jcboColor = new JComboBox();
jcboColor.addItem("red");
jcboColor.addItem("green");
jcboColor.addItem("blue");
jcboColor.addItem("yellow");
jcboColor.addItem("orange");
```

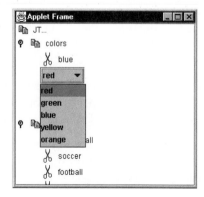

Figure 8.18   *You can supply a custom editor for editing tree nodes.*

```
jTree1.setCellEditor(new DefaultCellEditor(jcboColor));
jTree1.setEditable(true);
```

There are two annoying problems with the editor created in the preceding code. First, the editor is activated with just one mouse click. Second, the editor overlaps the node's icon, as shown in Figure 8.18. The first problem can be fixed by creating a subclass of DefaultCellEditor that overrides the isCellEditable() method, which returns true if the mouse click count is 3. The second problem can be fixed using the DefaultTreeCellEditor as follows. The new editor is shown in Figure 8.19.

```
jTree1.setCellEditor
  (new DefaultTreeCellEditor(jTree1,
   new DefaultTreeCellRenderer(),
   new DefaultCellEditor(jcboColor)));
```

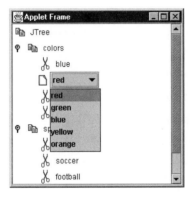

Figure 8.19   *The* DefaultTreeCellEditor *displays an editor that does not overlap a node's icon.*

Tree Events

JTree can fire TreeSelectionEvent and TreeExpansionEvent among many other events. Whenever a new node is selected, JTree fires a TreeSelectionEvent. Whenever a node is expanded or collapsed, JTree fires a TreeExpansionEvent. To handle the tree selection event, a listener must implement the TreeSelectionListener interface, which contains a single handler named valueChanged() method. TreeExpansionListener contains two handlers named treeCollapsed() and treeExpanded() for handling node expansion or node closing.

The following code displays a selected node:

```
void jTree1_valueChanged(TreeSelectionEvent e)
{
  TreePath path = e.getNewLeadSelectionPath();
  TreeNode treeNode = (TreeNode)path.getLastPathComponent();
  System.out.println("The selected node is " + treeNode.toString());
}
```

Chapter Summary

This chapter introduced four advanced Swing components: JList, ComboBox, JTable, and JTree. You learned how to use their data models to store and process data, and how to use selection models to handle data selection, renderer classes to display views, and the editor class to edit cells in these components.

Chapter Review

8.1. Does JList have a method, such as addItem(), for adding an item to a list? How do you add items to a list? Can JList display icons and custom GUI objects in a list? Can a list item be edited? How do you initialize data in a list? How do you specify the maximum number of visible rows in a list without scrolling? How do you specify the height of a list cell? How do you specify the horizontal margin of list cells?

8.2. How do you create a list model? How do you add items to a list model? How do you remove items from a list model?

8.3. What are the three list-selection modes? Can you set the selection modes directly in an instance of JTree? How do you obtain the selected item(s)?

8.4. How do you create a custom list cell renderer?

8.5. What is the handler for handling the ListSelectionEvent?

8.6. Can multiple items be selected from a combo box? Can a combo box item be edited? How do you specify the maximum number of visible rows in a combo box without scrolling? How do you specify the height of a combo box cell? How do you obtain the selected item(s) in a combo box?

8.7. How do you add or remove items from a combo box? Can you add an item using the addItem() method in JComboBox?

8.8. Why is the cell renderer for a combo box the same as the renderer for a list? Can a combo box cell be edited?

8.9. How do you initialize a table? How do you specify the maximum number of visible rows in a table without scrolling? How do you specify the height of a table cell? How do you specify the horizontal margin of combo box cells?

8.10. How do you initialize table contents? What are the properties to show grids, horizontal grids, and vertical grids? What are the properties to specify the table row height, vertical margin, and horizontal margin?

8.11. What is auto resizing of a table column? How many types of auto resizing are available? How do you specify an auto resizing mode?

8.12. How do you add or remove a row? How do you add or remove a column?

8.13. What are the default table renderers and editors? How do you create a custom table cell renderer and editor?

8.14. How do you create a tree? How do you specify the row height of a tree node? How do you obtain the defualt tree model and tree selection model from an instance of JTree?

8.15. How do you initialize data in a tree using `TreeModel`? How do you add a child to an instance of `DefaultMutableTreeNode`?

8.16. How do you add or remove a node from a tree?

8.17. How do you obtain a selected tree node?

8.18. How do you create custom tree cell renderers and editors?

Programming Exercises

8.1. Create a program that shows a list of geometrical shapes along with a label in an instance of `JList`, as shown in Figure 8.20. Display the selected figure in a panel when selecting a figure from the list. The figures are represented in the `FigurePanel` class in Example 7.3, "Using `JTabbedPane`."

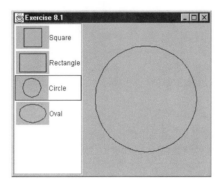

Figure 8.20   *The list displays geometrical shapes and their names.*

8.2. Create a program that shows a list of geometrical shapes along with a label in a combo box, as shown in Figure 8.21. Display the selected figure in a panel when selecting a figure from the list. The figures are represented in the `FigurePanel` class in Example 7.3, "Using `JTabbedPane`."

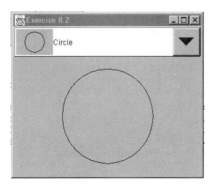

Figure 8.21   *The combo box contains a list of geometrical shapes and the shape names.*

8.3. Create a table for student records. Each record consists of name, birthday, class status, in-state, and a photo, as shown in Figure 8.22. The name is of the `String` type; birthday is of the `Date` type; class status is one of the following four values: Freshman, Sophomore, Junior, Senior, and Graduate; in-state is a `boolean` value indicating whether the student is a resident of the state; and photo is an image icon. The program enables the user to add, remove, or edit a record. Use the default editors for name, birthday, and in-state. Supply a combo box as custom editor for class status.

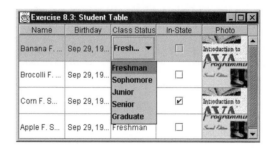

Figure 8.22   *The table displays student records and supports add, remove, and edit operations.*

8.4. Modify Example 8.11 as follows:

- Run it in the look-and-feel of Motif, Metal, or Windows.

- Display the nodes in breadth-first order, depth-first order, preorder, and postorder.

- Set custom icons for leaf, open, and closed nodes, and create custom editors for choosing colors in a combo box.

- Display a paragraph in a text area for each node in the tree, as shown in Figure 8.23.

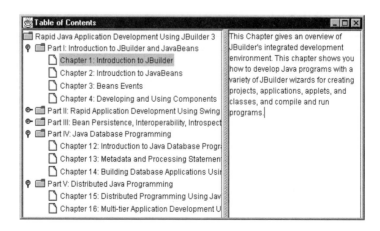

Figure 8.23   *The content of the node is displayed in a text area when a node is clicked.*

PART III

Bean Persistence, Interoperability, Introspection, and Customization

This part of the book introduces JavaBeans API. You will learn how to develop persistent beans, use beans in other tools, implement bound and constraint properties, and create bean property editors.

Chapter 9   Bean Persistence, Versioning, and Using Beans in Other Tools

Chapter 10   Bound and Constraint Properties

Chapter 11   Bean Introspection and Customization

BEAN PERSISTENCE, VERSIONING, AND USING BEANS IN OTHER TOOLS

Objectives

- Understand the concept of bean persistence.
- Know object serialization and use it to store and restore beans persistently.
- Use the `Beans.instantiate()` method to load serialized beans.
- Become familiar with Sun's BeanBox and use it to test bean persistence.
- Customize Object Serialization.
- Use bean versioning to make beans of different versions compatible.
- Explore JavaBeans in Microsoft Visual Basic and Microsoft Word.

Introduction

JBuilder does not store beans during design time. Changes in properties from the Inspector are stored in the source code. The UI Designer reconstructs the user interface by parsing source code. However, other tools, such as Sun's Beanbox, IBM Visual Age for Java, and MS Visual Basic, need to store the beans and then restore them later during design time. Bean persistence ensures that these tools can correctly reconstruct the properties of the bean to the state when it was saved.

This chapter introduces object serialization, which is a Java built-in mechanism to store and restore beans persistently. You will learn Sun's Beanbox, a tool for testing beans, which can be used to verify bean persistence. You will also learn how to customize serialization and use bean versioning to handle different versions of beans. Finally, several examples of the use of JavaBeans in non-Java tools like Visual Basic and Microsoft Word will be demonstrated to give you a broad view of JavaBeans versatility.

Object Serialization and Deserialization

In order to be persistent, a bean has to implement the `java.io.Serializable` interface. The `Serializable` interface is different from many of the interfaces you have used so far. It has no methods, so you don't need to add additional code in your class that implements `Serializable`. Implementing this interface enables the Java serialization mechanism to automate the process of storing the object.

▬ NOTE

There are several other interfaces in the core Java API that do not have methods. One popular example is the `Cloneable` interface. A class implements the `Cloneable` interface to indicate to the `clone()` method in class `Object` that it is legal for that method to make a field-for-field copy of instances of that class.

To appreciate this automation feature and understand how an object is stored, consider what you need to do in order to store an object without using this feature. Suppose you want to store an object of the `MessagePanel` class in Example 2.1 "Writing a Simple Java Bean." To do this you need to store all the current values of the properties in a `MessagePanel` object. The properties defined in `MessagePanel` are `message` (`String`), `centered` (`boolean`), `xCoordinate` (`int`), and `yCoordinate` (`int`). Since `MessagePanel` is a subclass of `JPanel`, the property values of `JPanel` have to be stored as well as the properties of all the `superclasses` of `JPanel`. If a property is of an object type, storing it requires storing all the property values inside this object. As you can see, this is a very tedious process. Fortunately you don't have to go through this process with Java. Since JDK 1.1, Java provides a built-in mechanism to automate the process of writing objects. This process is referred to as *object serialization*. In contrast, the process of reading objects is referred to as *object deserialization*.

To store and restore an object, you need to use the ObjectOutputStream class for storing objects and the ObjectInputStream class for restoring objects. These two classes are built upon several other classes. Figures 9.1 and 9.2 show the hierarchical relationship of these related classes.

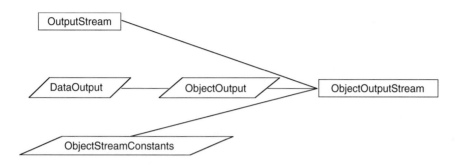

Figure 9.1   ObjectOutputStream *extends* OutputStream *and implements* ObjectOutput *and* ObjectStreamConstants.

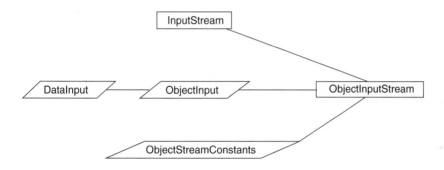

Figure 9.2   ObjectInputStream *extends* InputStream *and implements* ObjectInput *and* ObjectStreamConstants.

ObjectOutputStream implements ObjectOutput, which inherits DataOutput. DataOutput provides methods for writing Java primitive-type values. ObjectOutput extends DataOutput to include output of objects, arrays, and Strings. An ObjectOutputStream writes Java primitive-type values and objects to an OutputStream. Persistent storage can be accomplished using a file for the stream. The format of the output is platform-independent. The OutputStream can also be a network socket stream.

ObjectInputStream is an inverse of ObjectOutputStream. ObjectInputStream implements ObjectInput, which inherits DataInput. DataInput provides methods for reading primitive-type values. ObjectInput extends DataInput to include input of objects, arrays, and Strings. An ObjectInputStream reads the data previously written using an ObjectOutputStream with a file stream and a network socket stream.

Only objects that support the `java.io.Serializable` interface or the `java.io.Externalizable` interface can use `ObjectOutputStream` and `ObjectInputStream`. All the JavaBeans components implement `Serializable`, so they are serializable. The method `writeObject()` is used to write an object to the `ObjectOutputStream`, and `readObject()` is used to read an object from the `ObjectInputStream`. Attempting to store an object that does not support the `Serializable` interface would cause `NotSerializableException`.

When a serializable object is stored, the class of the object is encoded; this includes the class name and the signature of the class, the values of the object's fields and arrays, and the closure of any other objects referenced from the initial object. When a primitive-type value is stored, appropriate methods, such as `writeInt()`, `writeBoolean()` in the `DataOuput` interface, are used. Multiple objects or primitives can be written to the stream. The objects must be read back from the corresponding `ObjectInputstream` with the same types and in the same order as they were written. Java's safe casting should be used to get the desired type. For instance, when reading an object of the `MessagePanel` class, the object should be casted to `MessagePanel`.

Here is an example of creating an `ObjectOutputStream` and storing an object `messagePanel1` of `MessagePanel` and an `int` value to the file named beans.dat.

```
ObjectOutputStream out = new ObjectOutputStream(
  new ObjectOutputStream("beans.dat"));
out.writeObject(messagePanel1);
out.writeInt(5);
```

The corresponding code to restore the object and the `int` value is shown as follows.

```
ObjectInputStream in = new ObjectInputStream(new
ObjectInputStream("beans.dat"));
MessagePanel c = (MessagePanel)in.readObject();
int x = in.readInt();
```

Example 9.1 Testing Object Serialization

This example creates a program to manipulate `MessagePanel`, as shown in Figure 9.3. You will use radio buttons to set the background color, and use two buttons, <= and =>, to move the message to left and right. The Store button is provided to save a `MessagePanel` object, and the Restore button is used to reload the saved `MessagePanel` object.

Follow the steps below to complete the project.

1. Create a new project named SerializationDemo.jpr and create SerializationApplication.java and SerializationFrame.java using the Application Wizard. In Step 1 of 2, check the option "Use only core JDK and Swing classes." In Step 2 of 2 of the Application Wizard, check the options "Generate status bar" and "Center frame on screen," and type "Test Object Serialization" in the Title field.

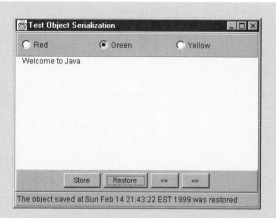

Figure 9.3   *You can use the Store button to save the* MessagePanel *object shown in the middle of the window, and use the Restore button to reload the saved object later.*

2. In the UI Designer of SerializationFrame.java, drop a JPanel to the center of the frame to create jpSerializtion. Set the layout of jpSerializtion to BorderLayout. Drop a JPanel to the north of jpSerializtion to create jpRadioButtons, drop a MessagePanel in the center of jpSerializtion to create messagePanel1, and drop a JPanel to the south of jpSerializtion to create jpButtons.

3. Set the border property of jpRadioButtons and jpButtons to Etched, and messagePanel1 to RaisedBevel.

4. Drop a JRadioButton three times to jpRadioButtons to create jrbRed, jrbGreen, and jrbYellow with text property set to Red, Green, and Yellow. Drop a JButton four times to jpButtons to create jbtStore, jbtRestore, jbtLeft, and jbtRight with text property set to Store, Restore, <=, and =>.

5. Create an instance of ButtoGroup to group the buttons in the jbInit() method.

6. Generate and implement the code for handling the radio buttons and buttons, as shown in Listing 9.1.

```
package SerializationDemo;

import java.awt.*;
import java.awt.event.*;
import javax.swing.*;
import MessagePanelDemo.*;
import java.io.*;
import java.util.*;
```

continues

Listing 9.1   *SerializationFrame.java*

```java
public class SerializationFrame extends JFrame
{
  JLabel statusBar = new JLabel();
  BorderLayout borderLayout1 = new BorderLayout();
  JPanel jpSerialization = new JPanel();
  BorderLayout borderLayout2 = new BorderLayout();
  JPanel jpRadioButtons = new JPanel();
  MessagePanel messagePanel1 = new MessagePanel();
  JPanel jpButtons = new JPanel();
  JRadioButton jrbRed = new JRadioButton();
  JRadioButton jrbGreen = new JRadioButton();
  JRadioButton jrbYellow = new JRadioButton();
  JButton jbtStore = new JButton();
  JButton jbtRestore = new JButton();
  JButton jbtLeft = new JButton();
  JButton jbtRight = new JButton();

  // Construct the frame
  public SerializationFrame()
  {
    enableEvents(AWTEvent.WINDOW_EVENT_MASK);
    try
    {
      jbInit();
    }
    catch(Exception e)
    {
      e.printStackTrace();
    }
  }

  // Component initialization
  private void jbInit() throws Exception
  {
    this.getContentPane().setLayout(borderLayout1);
    this.setSize(new Dimension(400, 300));
    this.setTitle("Test Object Serialization");
    statusBar.setText(" ");
    jpSerialization.setLayout(borderLayout2);
    jrbRed.setText("Red");
    jrbRed.addActionListener(new java.awt.event.ActionListener()
    {
      public void actionPerformed(ActionEvent e)
      {
        jrbRed_actionPerformed(e);
      }
    });
    jrbGreen.setText("Green");
    jrbGreen.addActionListener(new java.awt.event.ActionListener()
    {
      public void actionPerformed(ActionEvent e)
      {
        jrbGreen_actionPerformed(e);
      }
    });
    jrbYellow.setText("Yellow");
    jrbYellow.addActionListener(new java.awt.event.ActionListener()
    {
      public void actionPerformed(ActionEvent e)
      {
```

Listing 9.1   *Continued*

392

```
          jrbYellow_actionPerformed(e);
        }
      });
      jbtStore.setText("Store");
      jbtStore.addActionListener(new java.awt.event.ActionListener()
      {
        public void actionPerformed(ActionEvent e)
        {
          jbtStore_actionPerformed(e);
        }
      });
      jbtRestore.setText("Restore");
      jbtRestore.addActionListener(new java.awt.event.ActionListener()
      {
        public void actionPerformed(ActionEvent e)
        {
          jbtRestore_actionPerformed(e);
        }
      });
      jbtLeft.setText("<=");
      jbtLeft.addActionListener(new java.awt.event.ActionListener()
      {
        public void actionPerformed(ActionEvent e)
        {
          jbtLeft_actionPerformed(e);
        }
      });
      jbtRight.setText("=>");
      jbtRight.addActionListener(new java.awt.event.ActionListener()
      {
        public void actionPerformed(ActionEvent e)
        {
          jbtRight_actionPerformed(e);
        }
      });
      jpRadioButtons.setBorder(BorderFactory.createEtchedBorder());
      jpButtons.setBorder(BorderFactory.createEtchedBorder());
      messagePanel1.setBorder(BorderFactory.createRaisedBevelBorder());
      this.getContentPane().add(statusBar, BorderLayout.SOUTH);
      this.getContentPane().add(jpSerialization, BorderLayout.CENTER);
      jpSerialization.add(jpRadioButtons, BorderLayout.NORTH);
      jpRadioButtons.add(jrbRed, null);
      jpRadioButtons.add(jrbGreen, null);
      jpRadioButtons.add(jrbYellow, null);
      jpSerialization.add(messagePanel1, BorderLayout.CENTER);
      jpSerialization.add(jpButtons, BorderLayout.SOUTH);
      jpButtons.add(jbtStore, null);
      jpButtons.add(jbtRestore, null);
      jpButtons.add(jbtLeft, null);
      jpButtons.add(jbtRight, null);

      // Group radio buttons
      ButtonGroup btg = new ButtonGroup();
      btg.add(jrbRed);
      btg.add(jrbGreen);
      btg.add(jrbYellow);
    }

    // Overridden so we can exit on System Close
    protected void processWindowEvent(WindowEvent e)
    {
```

continues

```
      super.processWindowEvent(e);
      if(e.getID() == WindowEvent.WINDOW_CLOSING)
      {
        System.exit(0);
      }
  }

  // Handler for selecting red background in messagePanel1
  void jrbRed_actionPerformed(ActionEvent e)
  {
    messagePanel1.setBackground(Color.red);
  }

  // Handler for selecting green background in messagePanel1
  void jrbGreen_actionPerformed(ActionEvent e)
  {
    messagePanel1.setBackground(Color.green);
  }

  // Handler for selecting yellow background in messagePanel1
  void jrbYellow_actionPerformed(ActionEvent e)
  {
    messagePanel1.setBackground(Color.yellow);
  }

  // Handler for storing the objects
  void jbtStore_actionPerformed(ActionEvent e)
  {
    try
    {
      ObjectOutputStream out =
        new ObjectOutputStream(new FileOutputStream("beans.dat"));
      out.writeObject(messagePanel1);
      out.writeObject(new Date());
      out.close();
      statusBar.setText("The object is stored in beans.dat");
    }
    catch (IOException ex)
    {
      System.out.println(ex);
    }
  }

  // Handler for restoring the objects
  void jbtRestore_actionPerformed(ActionEvent e)
  {
    try
    {
      ObjectInputStream in =
        new ObjectInputStream(new FileInputStream("beans.dat"));
      MessagePanel c = (MessagePanel)in.readObject();
      Date d = (Date)in.readObject();
      jpSerialization.remove(messagePanel1);
      messagePanel1 = c;
      jpSerialization.add(messagePanel1, BorderLayout.CENTER);
      jpSerialization.repaint();
      in.close();
      statusBar.setText("The object saved at " + d.toString()
        + " is restored");
    }
```

Listing 9.1 *Continued*

```
        catch (IOException ex1)
        {
          System.out.println(ex1);
        }
        catch (ClassNotFoundException ex2)
        {
          System.out.println(ex2);
        }
      }

      // Handler for moving the message left
      void jbtLeft_actionPerformed(ActionEvent e)
      {
        messagePanel1.moveLeft();
      }

      // Handler for moving the message right
      void jbtRight_actionPerformed(ActionEvent e)
      {
        messagePanel1.moveRight();
      }
    }
```

Listing 9.1   *Continued*

Example Review

When you click the Store button, the current state of the messagePanel1 and the current time (new Date()) are saved to file beans.dat using ObjectOutputStream. When you click the Restore button, these objects are read back from the same file. They must be read back in the same order as they were stored. Explicit type casting must be used to ensure that the objects read are of the right type.

In the handler for the Restore button, messagePanel1 was removed from jpSerialization, and then a new messagePanel1 was created and added to jpSerialization. This is necessary to ensure that the newly restored messagePanel1 is used in the windows, not the old copy.

Like many Java classes, java.awt.Component and java.util.Date implement java.io.Serializable, so the objects of these classes or their subclasses can be stored using object streams.

The transient Keyword

By default, all the nonstatic properties of a serialized object are written to the object stream. However, not all the nonstatic properties can be serialized. For example, since the java.awt.Thread class does not implement Serializable, a Thread object cannot be serialized. The transient keyword should be used to mark a non-serializable property, as shown in Example 4.1, "Creating a Clock Component," so that it is not stored during serialization of the object that contains the property.

The transient keyword can also be used to mark a property not to be stored for security reasons. Since the state of the object is stored into a stream of bytes using a file stream or a network socket stream, the stream could be modified to result in a change in the actual value of the property. To see how easy it would be to tamper with the data, just modify beans.dat using a Hex editor like Hex Workshop, which is a shareware product available from Break Point Software at **www.bpsoft.com**. Suppose you change the word Java to C++ in beans.dat, as shown in Figure 9.4. Welcome to C++ is displayed on the panel when the Restore button is clicked, as shown in Figure 9.5.

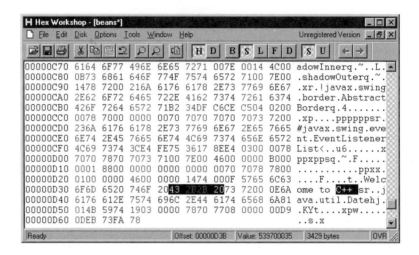

Figure 9.4   *You can use Hex Workshop to modify the beans.dat file.*

Figure 9.5   *The contents of beans.dat are restored. The modified message* Welcome to C++ *is displayed.*

Instantiating Serialized Beans

A serialized bean can be directly loaded to the program without using the new operator. This is an important advance in component-based software deployment, because it allows different users to use different versions of the bean without changing the application. Suppose your application requires a Clock bean; you can ship the application along with a serialized Clock bean tailored for users in London, and ship the same application with a serialized Clock bean tailored for users in Paris.

The static method `instantiate()` in the `java.beans.Beans` class is designed to dynamically load the serialized bean.

```
public static Object instantiate(ClassLoader cls, String beanName)
    throws IOException, ClassNotFoundException
```

The first argument is a class loader. If it is `null`, the system class loader is used. The second argument is the name of bean. This method searches for the bean with the specified name and a .ser file extension. If not found, an attempt is made to find a class file with the specified name. If this attempt fails, a `ClassNotFoundException` is thrown. The `instantiate()` method may also throw `IOException` if the serialized bean file is corrupted.

You can customize JBuilder so that the code it generates uses `Beans.instantiate()` instead of the `new` operator by checking the "Use Beans.instantiate" option in the Code Style page of the Project Properties dialog box.

It is not difficult to write a program to store a bean, but the simplest way to serialize a bean is to use the UI Designer. Here are the steps to serialize a `MessagePanel` bean in Example 9.1.

1. Select `messagePanel1` in the UI Designer in Example 9.1.

2. Customize `messagePanel1` to set the `message` property to Welcome to HTML, `xCoordinate` to 40, and `yCoordinate` to 40.

3. Right-click the mouse to display a popup menu, as shown in Figure 9.6.

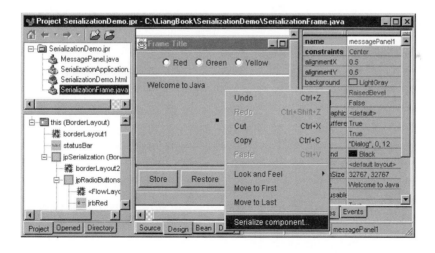

Figure 9.6 *You can customize a bean and save it in a file by choosing Serialize component in the UI Designer.*

4. Choose Serialize component on the menu to bring up a dialog box, as shown in Figure 9.7. Click OK to save the bean in a file named after the class with a .ser extension.

Figure 9.7   *The bean is saved to a file named after the class of the bean with a .ser extension.*

Example 9.2 Instantiating Beans

This example demonstrates generating code using the `Beans.instantiate()` method in JBuilder. You will create a program similar to Example 2.2, "Moving Message on a Panel." A sample run of the program is shown in Figure 9.8.

Figure 9.8   *You can move the message to left and right using the buttons.*

Follow the steps below to complete the project.

1. Create a new project named BeanInstantiationDemo.jpr, and check the option "Use Beans.instantiate" in the Code Style page of the Project Properties dialog box. Create BeanInstantiationApplet.java using the Applet Wizard.

2. In the UI Designer of BeanInstantiationApplet.java, drop a `MessagePanel` to the center of the applet to create `messagePanel1`, and drop a `JPanel` to the south to create `jPanel1`.

3. Drop a `JButton` twice to `jPanel1` to create `jButton1` and `jButton2`. Rename them `jbtLeft` and `jbtRight`.

4. Double-click `jbtLeft` in the UI Designer to generate the code for moving the message to the left. Implement `jbtLeft_actionPerformed()` as shown in Listing 9.2. You can generate and implement `jbtRight_action Performed()` similarly.

```java
package BeanInstantiationDemo;

import java.awt.*;
import java.awt.event.*;
import java.applet.*;
import javax.swing.*;
import MessagePanelDemo.*;
import java.beans.*;

public class BeanInstantiationApplet extends JApplet
{
  boolean isStandalone = false;
  MessagePanel messagePanel1;
  JPanel jPanel1;
  JButton jbtLeft;
  JButton jbtRight;

  // Construct the applet
  public BeanInstantiationApplet()
  {
  }

  // Initialize the applet
  public void init()
  {
    try
    {
      jbInit();
    }
    catch(Exception e)
    {
      e.printStackTrace();
    }
  }

  // Component initialization
  private void jbInit() throws Exception
  {
    messagePanel1 = (MessagePanel)Beans.instantiate(
      getClass().getClassLoader(), MessagePanel.class.getName());
    jPanel1 = (JPanel)Beans.instantiate(getClass().getClassLoader(),
      JPanel.class.getName());
    jbtLeft = (JButton)Beans.instantiate(
      getClass().getClassLoader(),
      JButton.class.getName());
    jbtRight = (JButton)Beans.instantiate(
      getClass().getClassLoader(),
      JButton.class.getName());
    this.setSize(new Dimension(400,300));
    jbtLeft.setText("<=");
    jbtLeft.addActionListener(new java.awt.event.ActionListener()
    {
      public void actionPerformed(ActionEvent e)
      {
        jbtLeft_actionPerformed(e);
      }
    });
    jbtRight.setText("=>");
```

continues

Listing 9.2   *BeanInstantiationApplet.java*

```
      jbtRight.addActionListener(new java.awt.event.ActionListener()
      {
        public void actionPerformed(ActionEvent e)
        {
          jbtRight_actionPerformed(e);
        }
      });
      jPanel1.setBorder(BorderFactory.createEtchedBorder());
      this.getContentPane().add(messagePanel1, BorderLayout.CENTER);
      this.getContentPane().add(jPanel1, BorderLayout.SOUTH);
      jPanel1.add(jbtLeft, null);
      jPanel1.add(jbtRight, null);
    }

    void jbtLeft_actionPerformed(ActionEvent e)
    {
      messagePanel1.moveLeft();
    }

    void jbtRight_actionPerformed(ActionEvent e)
    {
      messagePanel1.moveRight();
    }
  }
```

Listing 9.2 *Continued*

Example Review

Since you have set the option "Use Beans.instantiate" for the project, JBuilder uses the Beans.instantiate() method to instantiate a bean whenever the bean is dropped on the UI Designer. The getClass() method defined in the Object class returns the runtime class of the object. The getClassLoader() method determines the class loader for the class.

MessagePanelDemo.MessagePanel.class is an instance of the Class class, which is generated when the Java Virtual Machine loads the MessagePanel class. MessagePanel.class, referred to as a companion class for MessagePanel, provides useful information about the MessagePanel, such as, for example, its name and the names of variables and methods in the MessagePanel. MessagePanelDemo.MessagePanel.class.getName() returns the name of the class, which is MessagePanel.

You may wonder why JBuilder does not generate "MessagePanelDemo.MessagePanel" to replace MessagePanelDemo.MessagePanel.class.getName(). If so, it would work fine locally on the machine that you use to develop this program, but it would fail on a network, because the applets are prohibited from accessing local files.

The BeanBox

You have developed beans and wanted to know whether they can be used in a variety of tools. JavaSoft provides a BeanBox for testing bean properties, events, and persistence, and for demonstrating the use of beans. The BeanBox utility is compressed in a file named bdk1_1-win.exe, which can be obtained from **http://www.javasoft.com/beans/software/bdk_download.html.**

TIP

Double-click bdk1_1-win.exe in the windows to install the BeanBox. In the Choose Install Folder dialog of the BDK installation, choose c:\BDK1.1 instead of c:\Programs Files\BDK1.1, as shown in Figure 9.9. Installing into a directory path that contains spaces may cause problems for environment variables used by the various tools that come with JDK.

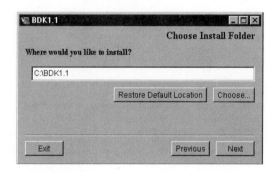

Figure 9.9   *You should install BDK in a directory path without spaces.*

After a successful installation, you can start to run BeanBox from the DOS prompt by the **run** command at the BeanBox directory. The BeanBox directory is under the BDK1.1 directory. When the BeanBox starts, you first see a message box indicating that the BeanBox is analyzing the packages and loading the beans. The beans are packaged in the .jar archive files stored in the jars directory. Several .jar files are installed by default in this directory, and the beans in these .jar files are analyzed and loaded during start-up. If you want your beans to be loaded when the BeanBox starts, place their .jar files in this directory.

NOTE

Running the BeanBox requires that the JDK 1.2 bin directory in the DOS environment path. To set the path, type the following command: set path=%path%;c:\jbuilder3\java\bin.

After the BeanBox is started, you will see four separate windows entitled ToolBox, BeanBox, Properties, and Method Tracer, as shown in Figure 9.10. The ToolBox consists of all the beans available for use by the BeanBox. The BeanBox window is where you test and manipulate beans installed in the ToolBox window. The Property window enables you to set or modify bean properties. The Method Tracer traces the methods in the bean.

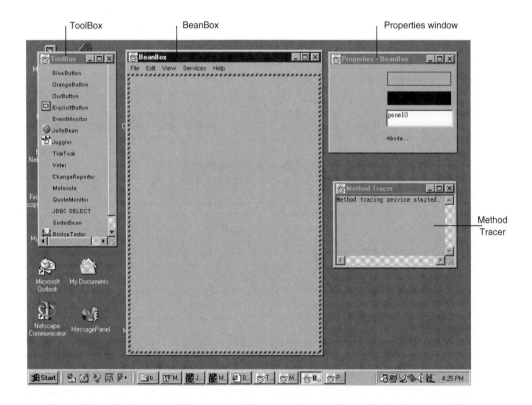

Figure 9.10   *The BeanBox consists of four independent windows entitled ToolBox, BeanBox, Properties, and Method Tracer.*

By default, the ToolBox contains 16 beans. Some beans have associated icons appearing on the left of the bean name. You will learn how to specify bean icons in Chapter 11, "Bean Introspection and Customization." A new bean can be added to the ToolBox by placing its .jar file in the jars directory or by using File, LoadJar from the menu. The BeanBox can be used to test bean properties, events, and persistence, and it can also be used to create applets from the beans. Here is an example of using the BeanBox to create an applet for controlling clocks.

Example 9.3 Using BeanBox

This example installs a `Clock` component to ToolBox and uses the BeanBox to assemble an applet with a Start button and a Stop button to control the clock in the BeanBox. Recall that the `Clock` bean was created in Example 4.1. Here are the steps to complete the project.

1. The BeanBox requires the beans to be packaged in a .jar file before it can be loaded to the ToolBox. The simplest way to package a bean and its supporting classes is to use the Deployment Wizard. Open project Clock-Demo. Choose Wizards, Deployment Wizard to launch the Deployment Wizard. Check only Clock.java. Type C:\LiangBook\Clock.jar in the Output file field, as shown in Figure 9.11, and click Next to display the dialog box, as shown in Figure 9.12. Uncheck javax and click Finish to package the bean without including the Swing components.

Figure 9.11 *The Deployment Wizard is used to package and its dependant files Clock.class into Clock.jar.*

continues

Figure 9.12   *The Deployment Wizard searches for the dependent files, and you can decide whether to include them in the package.*

2. Start BeanBox. Choose File, LoadJar to load the Clock bean into the ToolBox from C:\LiangBook\Clock.jar.

3. Select the Clock bean in the ToolBox. The cursor becomes a crosshair upon selected. Drop it in the BeanBox, as shown in Figure 9.13. With the bean selected in the BeanBox (a hatched border indicates that the bean

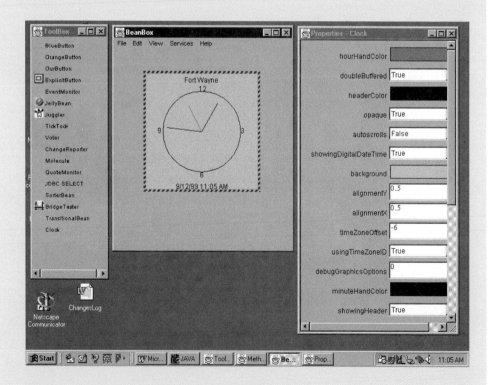

Figure 9.13   *A* Clock *bean is created in the BeanBox with its* hourHandColor *set to red, and* showingHeader *and* showingDigitalDateTime *set to True.*

has been selected), you can move it to desired location or resize it to the preferred size. With the `Clock` bean selected in the BeanBox, set `showingHeader` and `showingDigitalClock` to True and `hourHandColor` to red in the Properties window.

TIP

If you accidentally selected a bean other than the `Clock` bean in the ToolBox, you have to remove it in the BeanBox by choosing Edit, Cut to delete it.

NOTE

A property will not be shown in the Property window if it has no default value explicitly specified in the bean component. For example, if the default header "Fort Wayne" was not given the `clock` class, the property `header` would not be shown in the property window.

---

4. Select `OurButton` from the ToolBox, drop it to the BeanBox, and set its label to Start in the Properties window. Repeat the same operation to create another button labeled Stop.

5. Now you are ready to hook up the Start button to the `start()` method, and the Stop button to the `stop()` method, in the `Clock` bean. With the Start button selected, choose Edit, Events, mouse, mouseClicked, as shown in Figure 9.14. You will see a red line originating from the Start button, as shown in Figure 9.15. Click on the `Clock` bean to hook up the button with the bean. You will see a list of methods in Figure 9.16. Select start and press OK to let BeanBox generate adapters and other needed code to carry out the button-click action. Similarly you can hook the Stop button to the `stop()` method in the `Clock` bean.

6. By now you have created two buttons and associated the button-press action to the `start()` and `stop()` methods in the `Clock` bean. To put all the beans in the BeanBox in a new applet, choose File, Make Applet. A dialog box pops up to let you specify a JAR file name and an applet class name, as shown in Figure 9.17. Simply accept the default names and press OK to let the BeanBox generate the JAR file and the myApplet.html for running the applet.

The BeanBox generates an applet corresponding to a BeanBox layout. The data and classes needed for this applet are packaged into a JAR file. Run myApplet.html from appletviewer or from a Java Plug-in in a Web browser to test the applet. Figure 9.18 shows a sample run of the applet in appletviewer.

continues

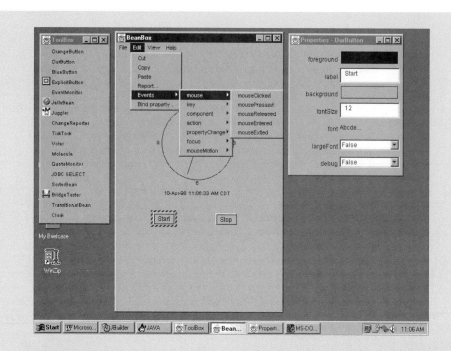

Figure 9.14   *With the Start button selected, you can implement mouse-click events on the button.*

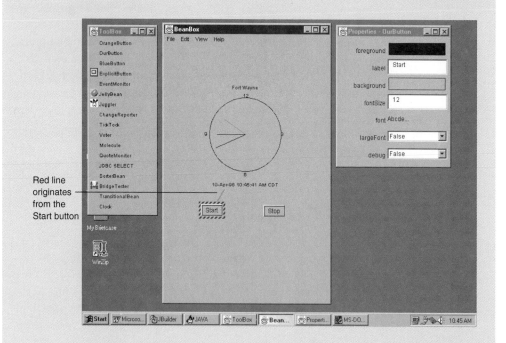

Figure 9.15   *The red line originating from the Start button indicates that the Start button is the source of the event.*

Figure 9.16   *The EventTargetDialog allows you to choose a method on the target for handling the source object event.*

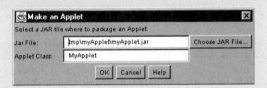

Figure 9.17   *The BeanBox generates files for running the applet when you click OK in the Make an Applet dialog box.*

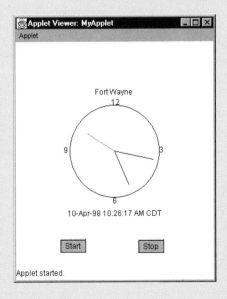

Figure 9.18   *The clock starts when the Start button is pressed, and stops when the Stop button is pressed.*

continues

Example Review

Although BeanBox is not a full-fledged Java builder tool, it demonstrates an interesting way to create applications. Unlike JBuilder, the BeanBox does not generate source code for the project. The applet was generated in the form of stored objects using serialization. Figure 9.19 shows the contents of the generated JAR file in WinZip. The data file contains the beans in the applet. These beans are loaded when the applet starts.

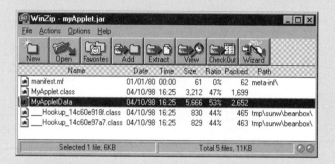

Figure 9.19   *The generated JAR file contains MyApplet.class, two adapter classes, and serialized data file for the* Clock *bean, and two button beans.*

Creating applets is not the only thing you do with the BeanBox. You can use it to test bean persistence. JBuilder does not have a utility for testing persistence. In fact, the beans you have developed with JBuilder may not be persistent. A bean that can be saved in BeanBox with the Save command from the File menu is serializable. If the bean restores all the previous behaviors after it is loaded back from its saved file using the Load command from the File menu, then the bean is persistent.

You can test the bean in the BeanBox by selecting `Disable Design Mode`. The ToolBox and Properties windows disappear when the BeanBox is in runtime mode. To switch back to design mode, select `Enable Design Mode` from the View menu.

It is interesting to see how a button is hooked with the clock in the BeanBox by originating a line from a button (Source) to the clock (target). This approach, referred to as *visual event design,* is also used in IBM Visual Age for Java and Symantec Visual Café.

Customizing Serialization

A serialized bean is not guaranteed to be persistent. If you save a clock bean in the BeanBox and then reload it, you would notice that the clock is not ticking. Obviously the clock is not restored to the correct running state. This is because the thread that controls the clock is not restarted after being restored. To make the `Clock` bean persistent, you need to recreate the thread and start it after the bean is loaded. The bean is saved using the `writeObject()` method and loaded to the BeanBox using the `readObject()` method by Java's built-in serialization system. You can implement these methods to add customized operations to preserve bean persistence. In the case of the `Clock` bean, you can add code to stop the clock before saving bean properties and add code to create and start the thread after the properties are restored.

The `writeObject()` and `readObject()` methods you will implement must have the following exact signatures.

```
private void writeObject(java.io.ObjectOutputStream out)
   throws IOException

private void readObject(java.io.ObjectInputStream in)
   throws IOException, ClassNotFoundException
```

The `writeObject()` method is responsible for saving the state of the object. The default mechanism for saving the Object's fields can be invoked by calling `out.defaultWriteObject()`. The `readObject()` method is responsible for restoring the state of the object by reading the data stored by the `writeObject()` method. The default mechanism for restoring the object can be invoked by calling `in.defaultReadObject()`, which restores the fields that were written using the `out.defaultWriteObject()` method.

Example 9.4 Making the `Clock` Component Persistent

This example implements the `writeObject()` and `readObject()` methods to add additional operations to make the `Clock` bean persistent. The new Clock component named `PersistentClock` is presented in Listing 9.3.

```
package PersistentClockDemo;

import java.io.*;
import ClockDemo.Clock;

public class PersistentClock extends Clock
{
  // Restore clock to the persistent state
  private void readObject(ObjectInputStream in)
    throws IOException, ClassNotFoundException
  {
```

continues

Listing 9.3   *PersistentClock.java*

```
        in.defaultReadObject();
        thread = new Thread(this);
        thread.start();
    }

    // Store clock
    private void writeObject(ObjectOutputStream out)
      throws IOException
    {
      thread = null;
      out.defaultWriteObject();
    }
}
```

Listing 9.3 *Continued*

Example Review

You have to use the exact signatures for readObject() and writeObject() methods. The common misperception is that these two methods are defined in the Serializable interface. They are, however, two unique methods in the Java serialization mechanism, which are invoked when an object of the class is serialized or deserialized.

Often the default readObject() and writeObject() methods are sufficient to maintain bean persistence. Customizing serialization is needed when the bean contains nonserializable data, such as a thread, that needs to be restored, as in the case of the Clock bean.

The Serializable interface provides a valuable mechanism to automate the process of storing and restoring the state of a bean. You can define your own mechanism to store and restore object data by implementing the Externalizable interface. This interface is a subclass of Serializable and has two public methods, writeExternal() and readExternal(), with the following signatures.

```
public void writeExternal(ObjectOutput out) throws IOException

public void readExternal(ObjectInput in)
    throws IOException, ClassNotFoundException
```

Example 9.5 Using the Externalizable Interface

This example uses the Externalizable interface to store and restore a Clock bean. The new Clock component named ExternalizedClock is presented in Listing 9.4.

```java
package ExternalizedClockDemo;

import java.awt.*;
import java.io.*;
import PersistentClockDemo.PersistentClock;

public class ExternalizedClock extends PersistentClock
  implements Externalizable
{
  // Restore clock
  public void readExternal(ObjectInput in)
    throws IOException, ClassNotFoundException
  {
    setShowingDigitalDateTime(in.readBoolean());
    setTimeZoneID(in.readUTF());
    setSecondHandColor((Color)in.readObject());
    setMinuteHandColor((Color)in.readObject());
    setHourHandColor((Color)in.readObject());
    setDigitalDateTimeColor((Color)in.readObject());
    setRunning(in.readBoolean());
    thread = new Thread(this);
    thread.start();
  }

  // Store clock
  public void writeExternal(ObjectOutput out) throws IOException
  {
    thread = null;
    out.writeBoolean(isShowingDigitalDateTime());
    out.writeUTF(getTimeZoneID());
    out.writeObject(getSecondHandColor());
    out.writeObject(getMinuteHandColor());
    out.writeObject(getHourHandColor());
    out.writeObject(getDigitalDateTimeColor());
    out.writeBoolean(isRunning());
  }
}
```

Listing 9.4 *ExternalizedClock.java*

Example Review

When a bean of the component that implements Externalizable is stored in a builder tool like BeanBox, the builder tool invokes the bean's writeExternal() method. The builder tool invokes the readExternal() method to restore the bean. These methods are fully responsible for storing and restoring object data. You have total control over what data are stored (including the data defined in the superclass).

■ NOTE

The readObject() and writeObject() methods are private and use Input ObjectStream and OutputObjectStream, but the readExternal() and writeExternal() methods are public, and read and write data using InputObject and OutputObject.

Bean Versioning

The bean components you have developed are subject to upgrade and modification. For example, you may add a new property named `showing` in `MessagePanelDemo.MessagePanel` to control whether the message is shown. If you have stored a `MessagePanel` bean in the beans.dat file using `SerializationDemo.SerializationApplication` with the old version of `MessagePanel`, you cannot restore the bean from the file using the new `MessagePanel`, as shown in Figure 9.20. The error message shown in Figure 9.21 would appear in the DOS window when you attempt to read the old file using `SerializationDemo.SerializationApplication` with the new bean.

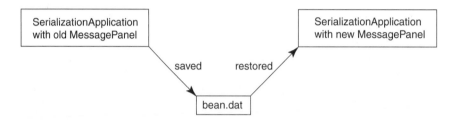

Figure 9.20   *The beans saved in beans.dat cannot be restored with the new* `MessagePanel` *unless you use bean versioning.*

Figure 9.21   *The* `InvalidClassException` *indicates that a different version of class is used.*

The bean was stored in the old version, but the program that reads the bean uses a new version. This difference is detected by the Java runtime system. Java assigns every class a unique ID, known as the *serialVersionUID*, which is determined by the structure of the class, including package name, class name, interface name, data fields, and methods defined in the class. When a bean is saved, its ID is saved.

When the bean is restored, its ID is compared with the current bean ID. The Java runtime system refuses to restore the saved bean if its ID differs from the current bean ID. However, a class can indicate that it is compatible with an old version of itself by specifying the ID of the old version in the new class, which forces the Java runtime system to assign the new bean the specified ID. For this to occur, you must first find the ID of the old class. JDK contains a command line utility serialver to let you find the ID of a class. For example, the command

```
serialver MessagePanelDemo.MessagePanel
```

gets the ID of the class, as shown in Figure 9.22. If you type the command **serialver** with option **-show**, a graphic dialog box is displayed, as shown in Figure 9.23.

Figure 9.22   *The serialver command finds the ID of the class.*

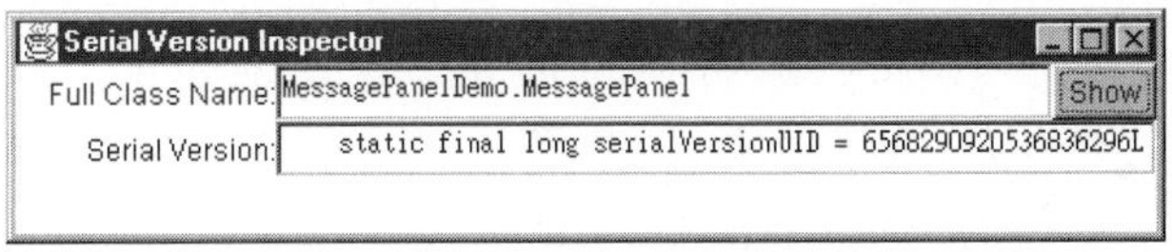

Figure 9.23   *The graphic version of the serialver command finds the ID of the class.*

To specify that the new class is compatible with its old version, add the old class's ID as a static final long constant named serialVersionUID in the new class, so that the new class uses the same ID as its old version. For example, to make the new MessagePanel compatible with its old version, add the following statement in the new MessagePanel:

```
static final long serialVersionUID = 6096437624398179359L;
```

With this declaration, the new program can read beans saved with the old version, and the old program can read beans saved with the new version, because the beans of both versions have the same ID. If the two beans differ only on the methods, then reading the objects poses no problem. However, if the two beans differ on data fields, special handling is needed to convert the stream object to the current version. Consider the following cases.

413

■ If two fields have the same name but different types, the `InvalidClassException` is thrown with the message, indicating that the two data types are incompatible.

■ If the object in the stream has a data field that is not present in the current version, these data are ignored.

■ If the current version has data that are not in the object in the stream, they are set to their default value when restored. For example, the data are null for objects, false for `boolean` type, and zero for numbers.

Example 9.6 Testing Bean Versioning

This example uses bean versioning to restore old files using new classes. You will add a new field `showing` to `MessagePanel` to control whether the message is shown. Here are the steps to complete the project:

1. Run `SerializationDemo.SerializationApplication`, select yellow color, and press the Store button to store the current `MessagePanel` in beans.dat file.

2. Record the ID of the `MessagePanel` class using the serialver utility, and create a new `MessagePanel` class in the SerializationDemo project, as shown in Listing 9.5 with the same ID as the old version's. This new class replaces the old `MessagePanel` in the same directory.

3. Compile the new class and restart `SerializationDemo.Serialization Application`. Press the Restore button in the frame. You will see a yellow background message panel with no message shown. This is because the `showing` property is not defined in the old version and becomes `false` when the object is loaded from the stream.

```
package SerializationDemo;

import javax.swing.*;
import java.awt.*;

public class MessagePanel extends JPanel
{
  // Specify the bean ID using the ID of the previous version
  static final long serialVersionUID = 6568290920536836296L;

  // Add a new property
  private boolean showing = true;

  private String message = "Welcome to Java"; // Message to display

  // (x, y) coordinates where the message is displayed
  private int xCoordinate = 20;
  private int yCoordinate = 20;
```

Listing 9.5   *The new MessagePanel.java*

```java
// Indicating whether the message is displayed in the center
private boolean centered;

// Default constructor
public MessagePanel()
{
  repaint();
}

// Contructor with a message parameter
public MessagePanel(String message)
{
  this.message = message;
  repaint();
}

public String getMessage()
{
  return message;
}

public void setMessage(String message)
{
  this.message = message;
}

public int getXCoordinate()
{
  return xCoordinate;
}

public void setXCoordinate(int x)
{
  this.xCoordinate = x;
}

public int getYCoordinate()
{
  return yCoordinate;
}

public void setYCoordinate(int y)
{
  this.yCoordinate = y;
}

public boolean isCentered()
{
  return centered;
}

public void setCentered(boolean centered)
{
  this.centered = centered;
}

// Display the message at specified location
public void paintComponent(Graphics g)
{
  super.paintComponent(g);
```

continues

415

```
      if (centered)
      {
        // Get font metrics for the font
        FontMetrics fm = g.getFontMetrics(getFont());

        // Find the center location to display
        int w = fm.stringWidth(message);  // Get the string width
        int h = fm.getAscent(); // Get the string height
        xCoordinate = (getSize().width-w)/2;
        yCoordinate = (getSize().height+h)/2;
      }

      g.drawString(message, xCoordinate, yCoordinate);
    }

    public Dimension getPreferredSize()
    {
      return new Dimension(200, 100);
    }

    public Dimension getMinimumSize()
    {
      return new Dimension(200, 100);
    }

    // Move the message in the pane to the left
    public void moveLeft()
    {
      if (getXCoordinate() > 10)
      {
        // Shift the message to the left
        setXCoordinate(getXCoordinate()-10);
        repaint();
      }
    }

    // Move the message in the panel to the right
    public void moveRight()
    {
      if (getXCoordinate() < getSize().width - 20)
      {
        // Shift the message to the right
        setXCoordinate(getXCoordinate()+10);
        repaint();
      }
    }

    // The getter method for the showing property
    public boolean getShowing()
    {
      return showing;
    }

    // The setter method for the showing property
    public void setShowing(boolean showing)
    {
      this.showing = showing;
      repaint();
    }
  }
```

Listing 9.5 *Continued*

Example Review

There are two MessagePanel.java files. One is in the project MessagePanel Demo, which was created in Example 2.1. The other is the new one created in this example, which is stored in the project SerializationDemo. After this new file is created, the new `MessagePanel` class is used when running `Serialization-Demo.SerializationApplication`. The new `MessagePanel` is assigned the same ID as its previous version, so you can restore the `MessagePanel` beans that were saved with the previous version of `MessagePanel`.

Assigning the new class the same ID as its old version does not guarantee compatibility. To ensure that the new class is backward-compatible with the old version, do not delete a data field, change its declaration to `transient` or `static`, or change it to a different type.

JavaBeans Bridge for ActiveX

You have developed software components using JavaBeans. The JavaBeans are tied to the Java language. Naturally you might assume that their use is limited to Java tools and applications. You would have been right when JavaBeans was first introduced in 1997, but today there are tools available to convert JavaBeans to ActiveX components, which are supported by many Windows-based tools and applications.

ActiveX is a subset of Microsoft Component Object Model, known as COM, which is a language-independent specification of component architecture. Other competing component architectures are OpenDoc introduced by IBM, and CORBA, proposed and widely supported by a consortium of all the leading technology companies except Microsoft. IBM, NetScape, ORACLE, SUN, and several other companies have sponsored a proposal to the consortium to include JavaBeans in CORBA. A merger between JavaBeans and CORBA is on the horizon. It is likely that JavaBeans will be included in CORBA 3.0.

This section demonstrates the conversion of JavaBeans components to ActiveX components, and uses these components as ActiveX controls in MS Visual Basic and MS Word.

The software for converting a component from JavaBeans to ActiveX is called *JavaBeans Bridge to ActiveX Packager*. This conversion utility was a separate product before JDK 1.2. In JDK 1.2, it is integrated in the JDK's **java** command.

Converting JavaBeans Components to ActiveX Components

Follow the steps below to convert the `PersistentClock` bean into an ActiveX component.

1. Start the Packager.

   Run the following command from the c:\jbuilder3\java\jre directory:

   ```
   bin\java.exe -cp lib\rt.jar;lib\jaws.jar sun.beans.ole.
   Packager
   ```

   The Packager tool's opening screen appears as shown in Figure 9.24.

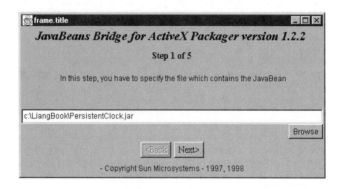

Figure 9.24 *Specify an archive file that contains the bean in Step 1 of 5 of the ActiveX Packager for Beans tool.*

2. Specify the JAR file.

   Since the Packager tool requires beans to be included in the archive file, you need to use JBuilder's Deployment Wizard to create an archive file for `PersistentClock`. Suppose the archive file is created in c:\Liang-Book\PersistentClock.jar. Type this file with the entire path in the text field in Figure 9.24 or browse for the file by clicking the Browse button. Click the Next button after you have added the file in the text field. The Packager tool's Step 2 of 5 appears as shown in Figure 9.25.

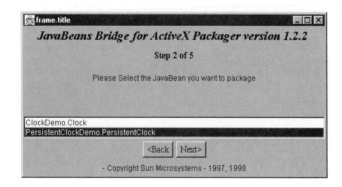

Figure 9.25 *Select a bean for conversion to an ActiveX component from the archive in Step 2 of 5.*

3. Select the JavaBeans Component.

> Packager tool Step 2 of 5 displays all the beans contained in the archive file. In this case you see Clock and PersistentClock, because Clock is in PersistentClock.jar. Select PersistentClock and click the Next button. The Packager tool's Step 3 of 5 appears as shown in Figure 9.26.

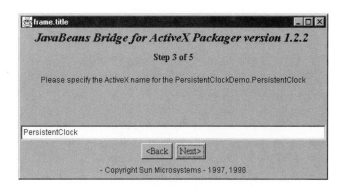

Figure 9.26 *Step 3 of 5 lets you specify an ActiveX control name for the bean to be packaged.*

4. Specify an ActiveX name.

> Packager tool Step 3 of 5 lets you specify an ActiveX control name for the bean to be packaged. By default the bean's name is used. Note that Bean Control is appended to this name as the complete ActiveX control name recognized by the Windows system. If the control name used is PersistentClock, then the full name is PersistentClock Bean Control. Type PersistentClock in the text field, and click the Next button to continue. Step 4 of 5 of the Packager tool appears as shown in Figure 9.27.

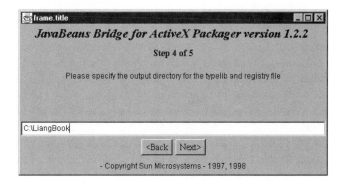

Figure 9.27 *Step 4 of 5 lets you specify the output directory for the TypeLib and Registry file.*

5. Specify an Output Directory.

Packager tool will generate the TypeLib file and Registry file to contain ActiveX control information for the bean. By default, C:\bdk1.1\ bridge\classes is used. Type C:\LiangBook and click the Next button to continue. Step 5 of 5 of the Package tool appears as shown in Figure 9.28.

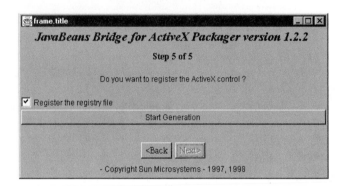

Figure 9.28   *Step 5 of 5 lets you specify the output directory for the TypeLib and Registry file.*

6. Generate and Register ActiveX Control.

Click the Start Generation button to generate an ActiveX control. The packager tool generates PersistentClock.reg and PersistentClock.tlb in C:\LiangBook and displays the generation status as shown in Figure 9.29. Click OK to close the Packaging tool.

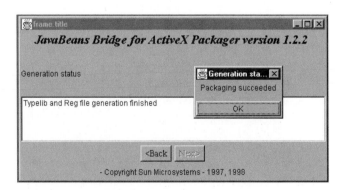

Figure 9.29   *The Packager tool generates Windows TypeLib and Reg files.*

You are ready to use the bean as an ActiveX component in Windows tools. You will see examples of using it in MS Visual Basic and MS Word.

Example 9.7 Using JavaBeans in Visual Basic

This example creates a project with a Start button and a Stop button to control a `PersistentClock` bean using MS Visual Basic. Here are the steps to use the bean in Visual Basic 5.

1. Start Visual Basic with a new project, as shown in Figure 9.30. Choose Project, Components to reveal a list of components, as shown in Figure 9.31. Check `PersistentClock Bean Control` and click OK. The PersistentClock Bean Control is added to the toolbox, as shown in Figure 9.32.

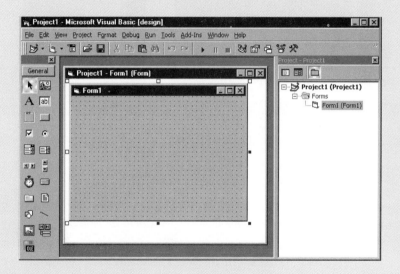

Figure 9.30 *Visual Basic 5 is launched with a new project.*

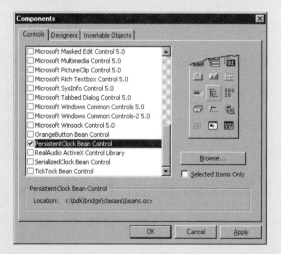

Figure 9.31 *The Component dialog box lets you choose a component to install in the Toolbox.*

continues

421

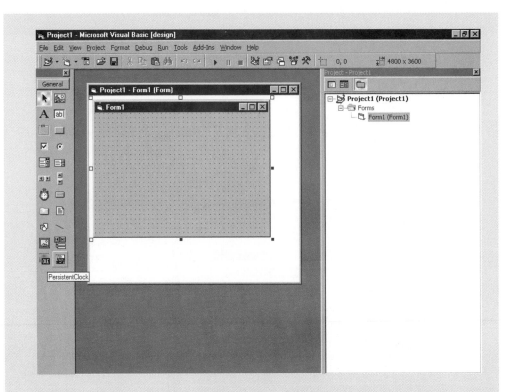

Figure 9.32   *The PersistentClock Bean Control is installed in the Toolbox.*

2. Click the PersistentClock Bean Control in the Toolbox, and click-and-drop it on the frame. An instance `PersistentClock1` of `PersistentClock` is created. Choose View, Property Windows to reveal the property editor, as shown in Figure 9.33. All the `PersistentClock` bean properties can now be manipulated from the Properties Window for `PersistentClock1`.

3. Add two buttons and change their captions to "Start" and "Stop." Implement the button-click procedure for the Start button with `persistentClock1.start`, and the button-click procedure for the Stop button with `persistentClock1.stop`. A sample run of the program is shown in Figure 9.34.

Example Review

The bean is registered with the Windows registry after a successful conversion from a JavaBeans component to an ActiveX component using the JavaBeans Bridge for ActiveX Packager. The bean is registered as an ActiveX component that can be used in Visual Basic.

The beans used in Visual Basic must be serializable, because they need to be stored during design time. If a bean is not serializable, you would get an error message indicating that it cannot be stored when you close a form during design time.

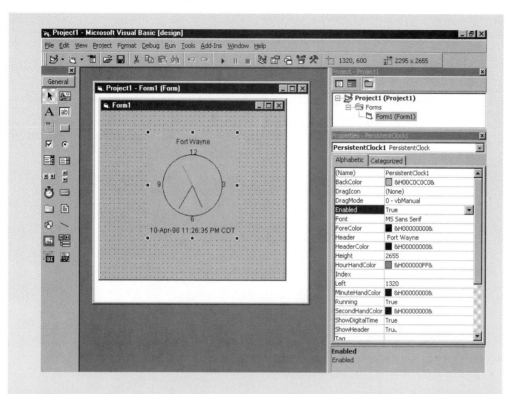

Figure 9.33 *The* PersistentClock1 *control's properties can be changed from the Properties window.*

Figure 9.34 *The* PersistentClock *is controlled by the Start and Stop buttons.*

Example 9.8 Using JavaBeans in Word

In this example, you will insert a `PersistentClock` bean in a Word document. Follow the steps below to complete the project.

1. Start Microsoft Word to create a new document. Choose Object from the Insert menu to bring up the Object dialog box, as shown in Figure 9.35. Select `PersistentClock Bean Control` from the list of components in the Object dialog box.

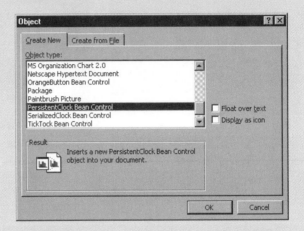

Figure 9.35   *You can insert a JavaBean component from the Object dialog box.*

2. Select `PersistentClock` Bean Control and press OK to insert a bean in the document, as shown in Figure 9.36.

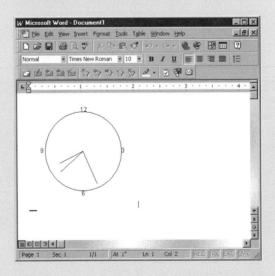

Figure 9.36   *A PersistentClock bean is inserted in a Microsoft Word document.*

Chapter Summary

This chapter addressed the issues of bean interoperability and compatibility. Bean persistence ensures that a bean can be restored to its state when it was saved. This feature makes beans useful in the Java and non-Java builder tools that require beans to be stored during design time. Bean versioning makes different versions of the beans compatible. You also learned to use the BeanBox to test bean components and use the beans in non-Java builder tools like MS Visual Basic and MS Word.

Chapter Review

9.1. How do you declare a class so that its objects will be serializable?

9.2. How does the `writeObject()` method serialize an object, and how does the `readObject()` method deserialize an object?

9.3. How do you serialize a component in the UI Designer?

9.4. What is the `transient` modifier for?

9.5. How do you load a bean directly without using the `new` operator?

9.6. How do you set the JBuilder project to generate the code using the `Beans.instantiate()` method to instantiate beans?

9.7. How do you install a bean into the ToolBox window in the BeanBox? How do you associate a source bean with a target bean in the BeanBox?

9.8. How do you customize serialization by implementing the `readObject()` and `writeObject()` methods? How do you customize serialization using the `Externalizable` interface? Is `Externalizable` a subclass of `Serializable`?

9.9. How do you enable the new class to deserialize a bean that was serialized with the old version of the class? How do you create the *serialVersionUID*?

9.10. What is the purpose of the JavaBeans Bridge for ActiveX Packager?

Programming Exercises

9.1. Create an application to register students, as shown in Figure 9.37. Student information is defined in a serializable class as follows:

Figure 9.37 *The program gathers the name and address, and stores it in a file.*

425

```java
// Student.java: Student class encapsulates student information
import java.io.*;

public class Student implements Serializable
{
  private String name;
  private String street;
  private String city;
  private String state;
  private String zip;

  // Default constructor
  public Student()
  {
  }

  // Construct a Student with specified name, street, city, state,
  // and zip
  public Student(String name, String street, String city,
    String state, String zip)
  {
    this.name = name;
    this.street = street;
    this.city = city;
    this.state = state;
    this.zip = zip;
  }

  public String getName()
  {
    return name;
  }

  public String getStreet()
  {
    return street;
  }

  public String getCity()
  {
    return city;
  }

  public String getState()
  {
    return state;
  }

  public String getZip()
  {
    return zip;
  }
}
```

Your program stores student objects in a data file.

9.2. In the UI Designer of JBuilder, create an instance of Clock, customize it for London, and serialize it as London.ser. Customize it for New York, and serialize it as NewYork.ser. Create an applet that contains these two clocks using the `Beans.instantiate()` method.

CHAPTER 10

BOUND AND CONSTRAINT PROPERTIES

Objectives

- Understand the concept of bound and constraint properties.
- Know the role of bound properties in implementing builder tool's property editors.
- Learn to implement bound and constraint properties.
- Create bound and constraint properties using the Bean Designer.
- Use bound properties to simplify the implementation of model-view components.

Introduction

A *bound property* of a component is one for which a property notification service is provided when the property changes. Bound properties are very useful in the implementation of property editors for beans, and they are used to notify the beans of changes of property values in the editor. Constraint properties allow the listener component to verify the property change to determine whether to accept or reject it.

Implementing Bound Properties

The implementation of bound properties is based on the JavaBeans event model. The event set `java.beans.PropertyChangeEvent` and `java.beans.PropertyChangeListener` is provided to facilitate bean communications through bound properties. When a change is detected, the source bean creates a `PropertyChangeEvent` and invokes the listener's `propertyChange()` method defined in `PropertyChangeListener`.

The `PropertyChangeListener` interface is used to notify changes to bound properties. In order to support bound properties, the source component must declare a variable of `PropertyChangeListener` and implement a pair of `PropertyChangeListener` registration methods. When a change of the bound property occurs in the source bean, a `PropertyChangeEvent` is constructed and passed to the `propertyChange()` method implemented in the listener bean.

To construct a `PropertyChangeEvent`, use the constructor

```
PropertyChangeEvent(source, propertyName, oldValue, newValue)
```

In the listener handler, you can get the property name using the `getPropertyName()` method, and the old and new values of the bound property using the `getOldValue()` and `getNewValue()` methods from an instance of `PropertyChangeEvent`.

Example 10.1 Beans Communications Through Bound Properties

This example creates a property editor for the `Clock` component in Example 4.1, "Creating a `Clock` Component." This property editor can be used during runtime to change the properties of `Clock`. The property editor window is popped up, as shown in Figure 10.1, when the user presses on the clock using the right mouse button. The change of a property in the editor is passed to the `Clock` bean through its bound property.

For simplicity, the property editor will contain only five representative properties from the `Clock` component: `hourHandColor`, `showingDigitalTime`, `timeZone`, `timeZoneOffset`, and `usingTimeZoneID`. Here are the steps to create the editor:

1. Create a new project named ClockEditorDemo.jpr. Choose File, New and click the Frame icon to create ClockEditor.java, which extends `JFrame` using the Frame Wizard. Switch to the UI Designer of ClockEditor.java.

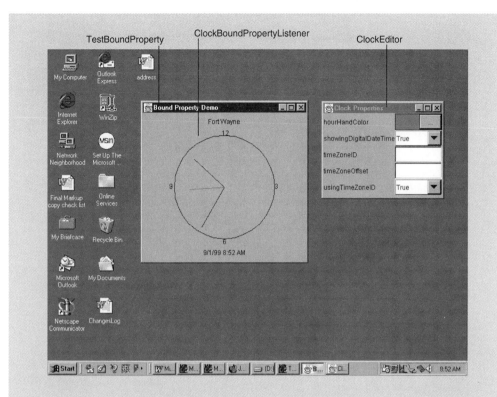

Figure 10.1   *You can set the property values in* Clock *from the property editor.*

2. Drop a JPanel to the west of the frame to create jpLabels, and drop a JPanel to the center of the frame to create jpProperties.

3. Set the layout property of jpLabels to GridLayout with five rows. Drop a JLabel to jpLabels five times, and set the text property of the labels to hourHandColor, showingDigitalDateTime, timeZoneID, timeZoneOffset, and usingTimeZoneID.

4. Set the layout property of jpProerties to GridLayout with five rows. Drop a JPanel to jpProperties to create jpColor. Set its layout to BorderLayout and its border to Line. Drop a JLabel to the center of jpColor to create jlblColor, and drop a JButton to jpColor to create jbtColor. Set the opaque property of jlblColor to True. Set the text property of jbtColor to ellipsis symbol (. . .).

5. Drop a JComboBox to jpProperties to create jcboShowingDigitalDateTime. Drop a JTextField twice into jpProperties to create jtfTimeZoneID and jtfTimeZoneOffset. Drop a JComboBox to jpProperties to create jcboUsingTimeZoneID.

6. Select the UI Designer in the Component tree, drop a JColorChooser from the Swing Containers page to the UI to create jColorChooser1.

continues

7. Now that you have created the UI for the property editor, you are ready to write the code to send the bound properties to the listener. Import `java.beans.*` and declare a listener to be `PropertyChangeListener` and implement registration methods `addPropertyChangeListener()` and `removePropertyChangeListener()`, as shown in Listing 10.1.

8. Double-click on `jbtColor` to generate the adapter and handler `jbtColor_actionPerformed(ActionEvent e)` for the button. Implement the handler and the `fire()` method, as shown in Listing 10.1.

9. Add items "True" and "False" into `jcboShowingDigitalDateTime` and `jcboUsingTimeZoneID` in the `jbInit()` method as follows:

```
jcboShowingDigitalDateTime.addItem("True");
jcboShowingDigitalDateTime.addItem("False");
jcboUsingTimeZoneID.addItem("True");
jcboUsingTimeZoneID.addItem("False");
```

10. Double-click `jcboShowingDigitalDateTime` to generate the adapter and handler for handling selection of True and False from the combo box. Implement the handler as shown in Listing 10.1. Similarly, generate the code for handling the selection of item in `jcboUsingTimeZone`.

11. Double-click `jtfTimeZoneID` to generate the adapter and handler for changing the time zone value, and implement as shown in Listing 10.1. You can similarly generate and implement the handler for `jtfTimeZoneOffset`.

```java
package ClockEditorDemo;

import java.awt.*;
import javax.swing.*;
import java.beans.*;
import java.awt.event.*;

public class ClockEditor extends JFrame
{
  JPanel jpLabels = new JPanel();
  JLabel jLabel1 = new JLabel();
  JLabel jLabel2 = new JLabel();
  GridLayout gridLayout1 = new GridLayout();
  JLabel jLabel3 = new JLabel();
  JLabel jLabel4 = new JLabel();
  JLabel jLabel5 = new JLabel();
  JPanel jpProperties = new JPanel();
  GridLayout gridLayout2 = new GridLayout();
  JPanel jpColor = new JPanel();
  JComboBox jcboShowingDigitalDateTime = new JComboBox();
  JTextField jtfTimeZoneID = new JTextField();
  JTextField jtfTimeZoneOffset = new JTextField();
  JComboBox jcboUsingTimeZoneID = new JComboBox();
  BorderLayout borderLayout1 = new BorderLayout();
  JLabel jlblColor = new JLabel();
  JButton jbtColor = new JButton();
  JColorChooser jColorChooser1 = new JColorChooser();
```

Listing 10.1   *ClockEditor.java*

```java
    // The ClockEditor component is the source of PropertyChangeEvent
    private PropertyChangeListener listener;

    // Track the previous property values
    private String oldShowingDigitalDateTime = new String();
    private String oldUsingTimeZoneID = new String();
    private String oldTimeZoneID = new String();
    private int oldTimeZoneOffset = 0;

    // Default constructor
    public ClockEditor()
    {
      try
      {
        jbInit();
      }
      catch(Exception e)
      {
        e.printStackTrace();
      }
    }

    private void jbInit() throws Exception
    {
      jLabel1.setText("hourHandColor");
      jLabel2.setText("showingDigitalDateTime");
      jpLabels.setLayout(gridLayout1);
      gridLayout1.setRows(5);
      jLabel3.setText("timeZoneID");
      jLabel4.setText("timeZoneOffset");
      jLabel5.setText("usingTimeZoneID");
      jpProperties.setLayout(gridLayout2);
      gridLayout2.setRows(5);
      jpColor.setLayout(borderLayout1);
      jbtColor.setText("...");
      jbtColor.addActionListener(new java.awt.event.ActionListener()
      {
        public void actionPerformed(ActionEvent e)
        {
          jbtColor_actionPerformed(e);
        }
      });
      this.setTitle("Clock Properties");
      jColorChooser1.setName("");
      jpColor.setBorder(BorderFactory.createLineBorder(Color.black));
      jcboShowingDigitalDateTime.addActionListener(
        new java.awt.event.ActionListener()
      {
        public void actionPerformed(ActionEvent e)
        {
          jcboShowingDigitalDateTime_actionPerformed(e);
        }
      });
      jtfTimeZoneID.addActionListener(
        new java.awt.event.ActionListener()
      {
        public void actionPerformed(ActionEvent e)
        {
          jtfTimeZoneID_actionPerformed(e);
        }
```

continues

431

```
      });
      jtfTimeZoneOffset.addActionListener(
        new java.awt.event.ActionListener()
      {
        public void actionPerformed(ActionEvent e)
        {
          jtfTimeZoneOffset_actionPerformed(e);
        }
      });
      jcboUsingTimeZoneID.addActionListener(
        new java.awt.event.ActionListener()
      {
        public void actionPerformed(ActionEvent e)
        {
          jcboUsingTimeZoneID_actionPerformed(e);
        }
      });
      jlblColor.setOpaque(true);
      this.getContentPane().add(jpLabels, BorderLayout.WEST);
      jpLabels.add(jLabel1, null);
      jpLabels.add(jLabel2, null);
      jpLabels.add(jLabel3, null);
      jpLabels.add(jLabel4, null);
      jpLabels.add(jLabel5, null);
      this.getContentPane().add(jpProperties, BorderLayout.CENTER);
      jpProperties.add(jpColor, null);
      jpColor.add(jlblColor, BorderLayout.CENTER);
      jpColor.add(jbtColor, BorderLayout.EAST);
      jpProperties.add(jcboShowingDigitalDateTime, null);
      jpProperties.add(jtfTimeZoneID, null);
      jpProperties.add(jtfTimeZoneOffset, null);
      jpProperties.add(jcboUsingTimeZoneID, null);

      // Initialize combo boxes
      jcboShowingDigitalDateTime.addItem("True");
      jcboShowingDigitalDateTime.addItem("False");
      jcboUsingTimeZoneID.addItem("True");
      jcboUsingTimeZoneID.addItem("False");
    }

    // Add property change listener
    public void addPropertyChangeListener(PropertyChangeListener l)
    {
      listener = l;
    }

    // Remove property change listener
    public void removePropertyChangeListener(PropertyChangeListener l)
    {
      listener = null;
    }

    // Choose hour hand color
    void jbtColor_actionPerformed(ActionEvent e)
    {
      Color oldColor = jlblColor.getBackground();
      jColorChooser1.setColor(oldColor);
```

Listing 10.1   *Continued*

```
      Color selectedColor =
        JColorChooser.showDialog(this, "Choose Color",
          jlblColor.getBackground());

      if ((selectedColor != null) && !(oldColor.equals(selectedColor)))
      {
        jlblColor.setBackground(selectedColor);
        fire("hourHandColor", selectedColor);
        oldColor = jlblColor.getBackground();
      }

      if (selectedColor != null)
        jlblColor.setBackground(selectedColor);
    }

    // Fire property change event
    private void fire(String propertyName, Object newValue)
    {
      if (listener != null)
        listener.propertyChange(
          new PropertyChangeEvent(this, propertyName, null, newValue));
    }

    // Change showingDigitalDateTime property
    void jcboShowingDigitalDateTime_actionPerformed(ActionEvent e)
    {
      if (!(oldShowingDigitalDateTime.equals
        (jcboShowingDigitalDateTime.getSelectedItem())))
      {
        if
          (jcboShowingDigitalDateTime.getSelectedItem().equals("True"))
          fire("showingDigitalDateTime", new Boolean(true));
        else
          fire("showingDigitalDateTime", new Boolean(false));

        oldShowingDigitalDateTime =
          (String)jcboShowingDigitalDateTime.getSelectedItem();
      }
    }

    // Change timeZoneID property
    void jtfTimeZoneID_actionPerformed(ActionEvent e)
    {
      if (!(oldTimeZoneID.equals(jtfTimeZoneID.getText().trim())))
      {
        fire("timeZoneID", jtfTimeZoneID.getText().trim());
        oldTimeZoneID = jtfTimeZoneID.getText().trim();
      }
    }

    // Change timeZoneOffset property
    void jtfTimeZoneOffset_actionPerformed(ActionEvent e)
    {
      int newTimeZoneOffset =
        new Integer(jtfTimeZoneOffset.getText().trim()).intValue();
      if (!(oldTimeZoneOffset == newTimeZoneOffset))
      {
        fire("timeZoneOffset", new Integer(newTimeZoneOffset));
        oldTimeZoneOffset = newTimeZoneOffset;
      }
    }
```

continues

433

```
                   // Change usingTimeZoneID property
                   void jcboUsingTimeZoneID_actionPerformed(ActionEvent e)
                   {
                     if (!(oldUsingTimeZoneID.equals
                       (jcboUsingTimeZoneID.getSelectedItem()))))
                     {
                       if (jcboUsingTimeZoneID.getSelectedItem().equals("True"))
                         fire("usingTimeZoneID", new Boolean(true));
                       else
                         fire("usingTimeZoneID", new Boolean(false));
                       oldUsingTimeZoneID =
                         (String)jcboUsingTimeZoneID.getSelectedItem();
                     }
                   }
                 }
```

Listing 10.1   *Continued*

Any beans that implement the `PropertyChangeListener` can be the listeners for the `ClockEditor` component. The following component `ClockBoundPropertyListener` shown in Listing 10.2, derived from `Clock`, listens for changes in the bound properties `handHourColor`, `showingDigitalDateTime`, `TimeZoneID`, and `TimeZoneOffset`.

```
package ClockEditorDemo;

import ClockDemo.Clock;
import java.awt.*;
import java.beans.*;

public class ClockBoundPropertyListener
  extends Clock implements PropertyChangeListener
{
  public ClockBoundPropertyListener()
  { }

  public void propertyChange(PropertyChangeEvent e)
  {
    if (e.getPropertyName() == "hourHandColor")
      setHourHandColor((Color)e.getNewValue());

    if (e.getPropertyName() == "showingDigitalDateTime")
      setShowingDigitalDateTime(
        ((Boolean)e.getNewValue()).booleanValue());

    if (e.getPropertyName() == "timeZoneID")
      setTimeZoneID((String)e.getNewValue());

    if (e.getPropertyName() == "timeZoneOffset")
      setTimeZoneOffset(
        ((Integer)e.getNewValue()).intValue());

    if (e.getPropertyName() == "usingTimeZoneID")
      setUsingTimeZoneID(((Boolean)e.getNewValue()).booleanValue());
  }
}
```

Listing 10.2   *ClockBoundPropertyListener.java*

Follow the steps below to create a test program to hook the listener bean with the source bean and to see how they interact.

1. Create an applet named TestBoundProperty.java using the Applet Wizard. In the UI Designer of TestBoundProperty.java, drop a `ClockBound-PropertyListener` from the Component palette to the center of the applet to create an instance renamed `clock`. Select UI from the Component tree and drop a `ClockEditor` from the Component palette to the applet to create an instance renamed `editor`.

2. In the Inspector of `editor`, double-click the value field of `propertyChange` in the Events page to generate the adapter and handler for bound property change. Implement the `editor_propertyChange()` method, as shown in Listing 10.3, to notify bound property changes to `clock`. The `clock` object becomes a listener for `editor`.

3. In the Events page of `clock`, double-click the value field of `mousePressed` to generate the adapter and handler. Implement `clock_mousePressed()` method, as shown in Listing 10.3, to handle mouse press actions.

4. Run `TestBoundProperty` to test the project. Point the mouse to the clock and click the right mouse button to bring up the property editor, as shown in Figure 10.1. Click the ellipsis button to bring up the dialog box for choosing color. Choose True in the value field of `showingDigitalDateTime` to display date and time. Type a time zone ID (i.e., CST) and press return to set the time zone for the clock. Type a numeric value (i.e., -6) for setting a new time with the specified offset to GMT with `usingTimeZoneID` set to False.

```java
package ClockEditorDemo;

import java.awt.*;
import java.awt.event.*;
import java.applet.*;
import javax.swing.*;
import java.beans.*;

public class TestBoundProperty extends JApplet
{
  boolean isStandalone = false;
  ClockBoundPropertyListener clock = new ClockBoundPropertyListener();
  ClockEditor editor = new ClockEditor();

  // Construct the applet
  public TestBoundProperty()
  {
  }

  // Initialize the applet
  public void init()
  {
```

Listing 10.3   *TestBoundProperty.java*

```
                    try
                    {
                      jbInit();
                    }
                    catch(Exception e)
                    {
                      e.printStackTrace();
                    }
                  }

                  // Component initialization
                  private void jbInit() throws Exception
                  {
                    this.setSize(new Dimension(400,300));
                    editor.addPropertyChangeListener(
                      new java.beans.PropertyChangeListener()
                      {
                        public void propertyChange(PropertyChangeEvent e)
                        {
                          editor_propertyChange(e);
                        }
                      });
                    clock.addMouseListener(new java.awt.event.MouseAdapter()
                      {
                        public void mousePressed(MouseEvent e)
                        {
                          clock_mousePressed(e);
                        }
                      });
                    this.getContentPane().add(clock, BorderLayout.CENTER);
                  }

                  // Change property values in clock
                  void editor_propertyChange(PropertyChangeEvent e)
                  {
                    clock.propertyChange(e);
                  }

                  // Activate the property editor
                  void clock_mousePressed(MouseEvent e)
                  {
                    if (e.isMetaDown()) // Detect right button pressed
                    {
                      editor.pack();
                      editor.setVisible(true);
                    }
                  }
                }
              }
```

Listing 10.3   *Continued*

Example Review

The implementation of this project and the relationship of the classes in the project are shown in Figure 10.2.

The use of PropertyChangeEvent is usually associated with a bound property of the bean. Theoretically, however, it could be used with no relation to any property of the bean.

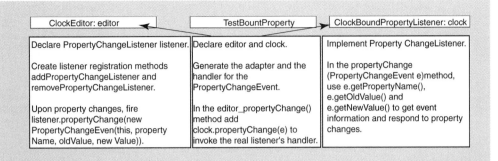

ClockEditor: editor	TestBountProperty	ClockBoundPropertyListener: clock
Declare PropertyChangeListener listener. Create listener registration methods addPropertyChangeListener and removePropertyChangeListener. Upon property changes, fire listener.propertyChange(new PropertyChangeEven(this, property Name, oldValue, new Value)).	Declare editor and clock. Generate the adapter and the handler for the PropertyChangeEvent. In the editor_propertyChange() method add clock.propertyChange(e) to invoke the real listener's handler.	Implement Property ChangeListener. In the propertyChange (PropertyChangeEvent e)method, use e.getPropertyName(), e.getOldValue() and e.getNewValue() to get event information and respond to property changes.

Figure 10.2 *Changes in bound properties in* editor *are notified to* clock *through the adapter created in* TestBoundProperty.

A PropertyChangeEvent is fired in editor when changes in the bound property occur. The bean fires the PropertyChangeEvent only when the new value of the property is different from its old value.

The ClockEditor class uses unicasting for simplicity. It can be modified to enable multicasting. When using adapters in tools like JBuilder, the effect of multicasting can be easily achieved for unicasting source components. For example, if you have two clocks (say clock1 and clock2) in the applet, you could simply write the code in the editor_propertyChange() method like this to invoke the handlers from clock1 and clock2:

```
void editor_propertyChange(PropertyChangeEvent e)
{
  clock1.propertyChange(e);
  clock2.propertyChange(e);
}
```

However, this approach is not equivalent to multicasting. For instance, if an exception is raised in the course of executing clock1.propertyChange(e), clock2 will not have a chance to respond to the PropertyChangeEvent.

TIP

The constructor of PropertyChangeEvent is

```
PropertyChangeEvent(Object source, string propertyName, Object
  oldValue, Object newValue);
```

If the property is of the primitive data type, its value has to be wrapped using the wrapper class in order to pass it the PropertyChangeEvent.

The PropertyChangeSupport Class

Java also provides a utility class java.beans.PropertyChangeSupport that can be used to simplify creating source components with bound properties. You can either inherit from this class or use an instance of this class as a member field of your bean and delegate various works to it. To use it for supporting bound properties in the ClockEditor class, follow the steps below.

1. Declare an instance of PropertyChangeSupport, or its subclass. For example,

```
private PropertyChangeSupport changes =
  new PropertyChangeSupport(this);
```

2. To report a bound property update to any registered listeners, invoke the firePropertyChange() method as follows:

```
changes.firePropertyChange("color", null, jColorChooser1.getColor());
```

3. The firePropertyChange() method automatically checks whether the new value is the same as the old value and fires the event only when they are different.

4. Implement the registration methods as follows:

```
public void addPropertyChangeListener(PropertyChangeListener l)
{
  changes.addPropertyChangeListener(l);
}

public void removePropertyChangeListener(PropertyChangeListener l)
{
  changes.removePropertyChangeListener(l);
}
```

■■■ **NOTE**

Contrary to many support classes in Java, PropertyChangeSupport is not a subclass of PropertyChangeListener. You create an instance of PropertyChangeSupport for the source bean using the PropertyChangeSupport's constructor PropertyChangeSupport(sourceBean), and this instance handles property changes in the source bean.

You will see examples of using PropertyChangeSupport in the following section.

Using the Bean Designer to Create Bound Properties

You can use the Bean Designer to create a bound property and generate the necessary code for handling it. The Bean Designer uses the PropertyChangeSupport class to support bound properties. The following example demonstrates the use of the Bean Designer to create bound properties.

Example 10.2 Using the Bean Designer to Create Bound Properties

This example rewrites ClockEditor.java, as presented in Example 10.1, using the Bean Designer.

Here are the steps to complete the project.

1. Reopen project ClockEditorDemo. Create a new frame named ClockEditorUsingSupportClass.java using the Frame Wizard.

2. Repeat Steps 2, 3, 4, 5, and 6 in the example for creating `ClockEditor` to create the same UI for `ClockEditorUsingSupportClass`.

3. With ClockEditorUsingSupportClass.java selected in the Navigation pane, choose the Bean tab in the Content pane to start the Bean Designer. In the Properties page of the Bean Designer, click "Add Properties" to bring up the New Property dialog box, as shown in Figure 10.3.

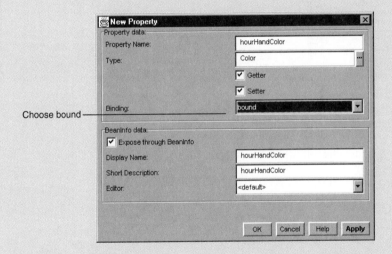

Figure 10.3   *You need to choose bound in the Binding field of the New Property dialog box to create a bound property.*

4. Type hourHandColor in the Name field, type Color in the Type field, choose bound in Binding, as shown in Figure 10.3. Click Apply to create the bound property `hourHandColor`. JBuilder automatically generated the code for this bound property, and the property change listener.

5. Similarly, create bound properties `showingDigitalDateTime`, `timeZoneID`, `timeZoneOffset`, and `usingTimeZoneID`, as shown in Figure 10.4.

6. With ClockEditorUsingSupportClass.java selected in the Navigation pane, click the Design tab to switch to the UI Designer. Generate the event handlers for `jbtColor`, `jcboShowingDigitalDateTime`, `jtfTimeZoneID`, `jtfTimeZoneOffset`, and `jcboUsingTimeZoneID`. Implement these handlers as shown in Listing 10.4.

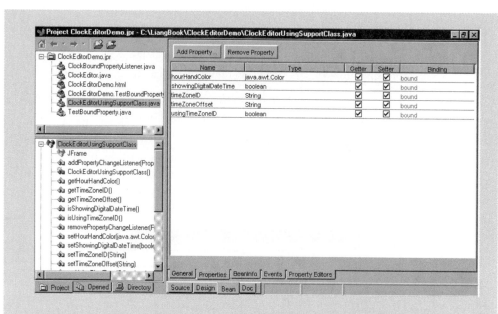

Figure 10.4 `ClockEditorUsingSupportClass` *contains five bound properties.*

7. Change the following statement

```
ClockEditor editor = new ClockEditor();
```

in TestBoundProperty.java to

```
ClockEditorUsingSupportClass editor =
  new ClockEditorUsingSupportClass();
```

8. Run the program. It should work the same as Example 10.1.

```
package ClockEditorDemo;

import java.awt.*;
import javax.swing.*;
import java.beans.*;
import java.awt.event.*;

public class ClockEditorUsingSupportClass extends JFrame
{
  private java.awt.Color hourHandColor;
  private transient PropertyChangeSupport propertyChangeListeners
    = new PropertyChangeSupport(this);
  private boolean showingDigitalDateTime;
  private String timeZoneID;
  private boolean usingTimeZoneID;

  JPanel jpLabels = new JPanel();
  JLabel jLabel1 = new JLabel();
  JLabel jLabel2 = new JLabel();
```

Listing 10.4 *ClockEditorUsingSupportClass.java*

```
GridLayout gridLayout1 = new GridLayout();
JLabel jLabel3 = new JLabel();
JLabel jLabel4 = new JLabel();
JLabel jLabel5 = new JLabel();
JPanel jpProperties = new JPanel();
GridLayout gridLayout2 = new GridLayout();
JPanel jpColor = new JPanel();
JComboBox jcboShowingDigitalDateTime = new JComboBox();
JTextField jtfTimeZoneID = new JTextField();
JTextField jtfTimeZoneOffset = new JTextField();
JComboBox jcboUsingTimeZoneID = new JComboBox();
BorderLayout borderLayout1 = new BorderLayout();
JLabel jlblColor = new JLabel();
JButton jbtColor = new JButton();
JColorChooser jColorChooser1 = new JColorChooser();
private int timeZoneOffset;

public ClockEditorUsingSupportClass()
{
  try
  {
    jbInit();
  }
  catch(Exception e)
  {
    e.printStackTrace();
  }
}

public java.awt.Color getHourHandColor()
{
  return hourHandColor;
}

public void setHourHandColor(java.awt.Color newHourHandColor)
{
  java.awt.Color  oldHourHandColor = hourHandColor;
  hourHandColor = newHourHandColor;
  propertyChangeListeners.firePropertyChange
    ("hourHandColor", oldHourHandColor, newHourHandColor);
}

public synchronized void removePropertyChangeListener
  (PropertyChangeListener l)
{
  super.removePropertyChangeListener(l);
  propertyChangeListeners.removePropertyChangeListener(l);
}

public synchronized void addPropertyChangeListener
  (PropertyChangeListener l)
{
  super.addPropertyChangeListener(l);
  propertyChangeListeners.addPropertyChangeListener(l);
}

public void setShowingDigitalDateTime
  (boolean newShowingDigitalDateTime)
{
```

continues

441

```
      boolean  oldShowingDigitalDateTime = showingDigitalDateTime;
      showingDigitalDateTime = newShowingDigitalDateTime;
      propertyChangeListeners.firePropertyChange(
        "showingDigitalDateTime",
        new Boolean(oldShowingDigitalDateTime),
        new Boolean(newShowingDigitalDateTime));
    }

    public boolean isShowingDigitalDateTime()
    {
      return showingDigitalDateTime;
    }

    public void setTimeZoneID(String newTimeZoneID)
    {
      String  oldTimeZoneID = timeZoneID;
      timeZoneID = newTimeZoneID;
      propertyChangeListeners.firePropertyChange("timeZoneID",
        oldTimeZoneID, newTimeZoneID);
    }

    public String getTimeZoneID()
    {
      return timeZoneID;
    }

    public void setTimeZoneOffset(int newTimeZoneOffset)
    {
      int  oldTimeZoneOffset = timeZoneOffset;
      timeZoneOffset = newTimeZoneOffset;
      propertyChangeListeners.firePropertyChange("timeZoneOffset",
        new Integer(oldTimeZoneOffset),
        new Integer(newTimeZoneOffset));
    }

    public int getTimeZoneOffset()
    {
      return timeZoneOffset;
    }

    public void setUsingTimeZoneID(boolean newUsingTimeZoneID)
    {
      boolean  oldUsingTimeZoneID = usingTimeZoneID;
      usingTimeZoneID = newUsingTimeZoneID;
      propertyChangeListeners.firePropertyChange("usingTimeZoneID",
        new Boolean(oldUsingTimeZoneID),
        new Boolean(newUsingTimeZoneID));
    }

    public boolean isUsingTimeZoneID()
    {
      return usingTimeZoneID;
    }

    private void jbInit() throws Exception
    {
      jLabel1.setText("hourHandColor");
      jLabel2.setText("showingDigitalDateTime");
```

Listing 10.4   *Continued*

442

```
jpLabels.setLayout(gridLayout1);
gridLayout1.setRows(5);
jLabel3.setText("timeZoneID");
jLabel4.setText("timeZoneOffset");
jLabel5.setText("usingTimeZoneID");
jpProperties.setLayout(gridLayout2);
gridLayout2.setRows(5);
jpColor.setLayout(borderLayout1);
jbtColor.setText("...");
jbtColor.addActionListener(new java.awt.event.ActionListener()
{
  public void actionPerformed(ActionEvent e)
  {
    jbtColor_actionPerformed(e);
  }
});
this.setTitle("Clock Properties");
jColorChooser1.setName("");
jpColor.setBorder(BorderFactory.createLineBorder(Color.black));
jcboShowingDigitalDateTime.addActionListener(
  new java.awt.event.ActionListener()
{
  public void actionPerformed(ActionEvent e)
  {
    jcboShowingDigitalDateTime_actionPerformed(e);
  }
});
jtfTimeZoneID.addActionListener(
  new java.awt.event.ActionListener()
{
  public void actionPerformed(ActionEvent e)
  {
    jtfTimeZoneID_actionPerformed(e);
  }
});
jtfTimeZoneOffset.addActionListener(
  new java.awt.event.ActionListener()
{
  public void actionPerformed(ActionEvent e)
  {
    jtfTimeZoneOffset_actionPerformed(e);
  }
});
jcboUsingTimeZoneID.addActionListener(
  new java.awt.event.ActionListener()
{
  public void actionPerformed(ActionEvent e)
  {
    jcboUsingTimeZoneID_actionPerformed(e);
  }
});
jlblColor.setOpaque(true);
this.getContentPane().add(jpLabels, BorderLayout.WEST);
jpLabels.add(jLabel1, null);
jpLabels.add(jLabel2, null);
jpLabels.add(jLabel3, null);
jpLabels.add(jLabel4, null);
jpLabels.add(jLabel5, null);
this.getContentPane().add(jpProperties, BorderLayout.CENTER);
jpProperties.add(jpColor, null);
jpColor.add(jlblColor, BorderLayout.CENTER);
```

continues

```java
        jpColor.add(jbtColor, BorderLayout.EAST);
        jpProperties.add(jcboShowingDigitalDateTime, null);
        jpProperties.add(jtfTimeZoneID, null);
        jpProperties.add(jtfTimeZoneOffset, null);
        jpProperties.add(jcboUsingTimeZoneID, null);

        // Initialize combo boxes
        jcboShowingDigitalDateTime.addItem("True");
        jcboShowingDigitalDateTime.addItem("False");
        jcboUsingTimeZoneID.addItem("True");
        jcboUsingTimeZoneID.addItem("False");
    }

    // Choose hour hand color
    void jbtColor_actionPerformed(ActionEvent e)
    {
        jColorChooser1.setColor(jlblColor.getBackground());

        Color selectedColor =
            JColorChooser.showDialog(this, "Choose Color",
                jlblColor.getBackground());

        if (selectedColor != null)
        {
            setHourHandColor(selectedColor);
            jlblColor.setBackground(selectedColor);
        }
    }

    // Change showingDigitalDateTime property
    void jcboShowingDigitalDateTime_actionPerformed(ActionEvent e)
    {
        if (jcboShowingDigitalDateTime.getSelectedItem().equals("True"))
            setShowingDigitalDateTime(true);
        else
            setShowingDigitalDateTime(false);
    }

    // Change timeZoneID property
    void jtfTimeZoneID_actionPerformed(ActionEvent e)
    {
        setTimeZoneID(jtfTimeZoneID.getText().trim());
    }

    // Change timeZoneOffset property
    void jtfTimeZoneOffset_actionPerformed(ActionEvent e)
    {
        setTimeZoneOffset(
            new Integer(jtfTimeZoneOffset.getText().trim()).intValue());
    }

    // Change usingTimeZoneID property
    void jcboUsingTimeZoneID_actionPerformed(ActionEvent e)
    {
        if (jcboUsingTimeZoneID.getSelectedItem().equals("True"))
            setUsingTimeZoneID(true);
        else
            setUsingTimeZoneID(false);
    }
}
```

Listing 10.4 *Continued*

Implementing Constraint Properties

When a constraint property changes, the source bean creates an instance of PropertyChangeEvent and invokes the vetoableChange() method. If the listener rejects the change, it throws a PropertyVetoException. The source bean then catches this exception and reverts to the old value.

Often the bound property and the constraint property are used together to verify and update the property in a so-called *two-phase approach*. The constraint property is used first to check whether the change is valid; if it is, the bound property is used to actually commit the change; if it is invalid, no change is made.

As in the case of the PropertyChangeSupport class, JavaBeans provides java.beans. VetoableChangeSupport to simplify the implementation of the constraint properties. The use of VetoableChangeSupport is similar to the PropertyChangeSupport class.

Example 10.3 Using Constraint Properties

This example modifies Example 10.2 to allow the listener (clock) to reject any values of timeZoneOffset not in the range between -12 and 12. The example creates a new editor bean component EditorClassSupportConstraint that generates constraint property changes, and a new clock component ClockConstraintPropertyListener to listen for constraint property changes. Since EditorClassSupportConstraint extends EditorClass, and ClockConstraintPropertyListener extends ClockBoundPropertyListener, these two new classes need to reference superclass data members and override some handlers. For convenience, this example will be created in the project ClockEditorDemo.

Follow the steps below to complete the project.

1. Reopen project ClockEditorDemo.jpr and create ClockEditorSupportConstraint, which extends EditorClass with capabilities of firing constraint property on timeZoneOffset, as shown in Listing 10.5. Compile and install it in the Component palette.

2. Create ClockConstraintPropertyListener, which extends ClockBoundPropertyListener and implements VetoableChangeListener with capabilities of handling constraint property changes, as shown in Listing 10.6. Compile and install it in the Component palette.

3. Create a new applet named TestConstraintProperty.java using the Applet Wizard. In the UI Designer of TestConstraintProperty.java, drop a ClockConstraintPropertyListener to the center of the applet, and a ClockEditorSupportConstraint to the applet, and change their names to clock and editor, respectively.

4. In the Events page of editor, double-click on the value field of propertyChange to generate the adapter and the handler for bound property change. Double-click on the value field of vetoableChange to

generate the adapter and the handler for constraint property change. Implement these two handlers as shown in Listing 10.7.

5. In the Events page of clock, double-click on the value field of mousePressed to generate the adapter and the handler for mouse-pressed action on clock. Implement the handler, as shown in Listing 10.7, to display the editor upon a right-click of the mouse.

6. Run "TestConstraintProperty" to test the project. Point the mouse to the clock and click the right mouse button to display the property editor. Select False in usingTimeZoneID field, type 10 in the timeZoneOffset field, and press the ENTER key. You will see that the hour hand was moved. Enter 13 in the timeZoneOffset field and press the ENTER key. You will see that nothing happens, because this value is rejected by the listener.

```java
package ClockEditorDemo;

import java.awt.*;
import java.beans.*;
import java.awt.event.*;

public class ClockEditorSupportConstraint
  extends ClockEditorUsingSupportClass
{
  // Declare an instance of VetoableChangeSupport for verifying
  // property change
  private VetoableChangeSupport vetoes =
    new VetoableChangeSupport(this);

  public ClockEditorSupportConstraint()
  { }

  // Add listener for vetoable change
  public void addVetoableChangeListener(VetoableChangeListener l)
  {
    vetoes.addVetoableChangeListener(l);
  }

  // Remove listener for vetoable change
  public void removeVetoableChangeListener(VetoableChangeListener l)
  {
    vetoes.removeVetoableChangeListener(l);
  }

  // Override this method defined in the super class
  void jtfTimeZoneOffset_actionPerformed(ActionEvent e)
  {
    try
    {
      vetoes.fireVetoableChange("timeZoneOffset",
        new Integer(getTimeZoneOffset()),
        new Integer(jtfTimeZoneOffset.getText().trim()));
      super.jtfTimeZoneOffset_actionPerformed(e);
    }
```

Listing 10.5 *ClockEditorSupportConstraint.java*

```
          catch (PropertyVetoException ex)
          {
            jtfTimeZoneOffset.setText(
              new Integer(getTimeZoneOffset()).toString());
          }
        }
      }
```

Listing 10.5   *Continued*

```
      package ClockEditorDemo;

      import java.awt.*;
      import java.beans.*;

      public class ClockConstraintPropertyListener
      extends ClockBoundPropertyListener
        implements VetoableChangeListener
      {
        public ClockConstraintPropertyListener()
        { }

        public void vetoableChange(PropertyChangeEvent e)
          throws PropertyVetoException
        {
          if (e.getPropertyName() == "timeZoneOffset")
          {
            int timeZoneOffset = ((Integer)e.getNewValue()).intValue();
            if (timeZoneOffset > 12 || timeZoneOffset < -12)
              throw new PropertyVetoException("Invalid timeZoneOffset", e);
          }
        }
      }
```

Listing 10.6   *ClockConstraintPropertyListener.java*

```
      package ClockEditorDemo;

      import java.awt.*;
      import java.awt.event.*;
      import java.applet.*;
      import javax.swing.*;
      import java.beans.*;

      public class TestConstraintProperty extends JApplet
      {
        boolean isStandalone = false;
        ClockConstraintPropertyListener clock =
          new ClockConstraintPropertyListener();
        ClockEditorSupportConstraint editor =
          new ClockEditorSupportConstraint();

        // Construct the applet
        public TestConstraintProperty()
        {
        }
```

continues

Listing 10.7   *TestConstraintProperty.java.java*

```java
          // Initialize the applet
          public void init()
          {
            try
            {
              jbInit();
            }
            catch(Exception e)
            {
              e.printStackTrace();
            }
          }

          // Component initialization
          private void jbInit() throws Exception
          {
            this.setSize(new Dimension(400,300));
            editor.addPropertyChangeListener(
              new java.beans.PropertyChangeListener()
            {
              public void propertyChange(PropertyChangeEvent e)
              {
                editor_propertyChange(e);
              }
            });
            clock.addMouseListener(new java.awt.event.MouseAdapter()
            {
              public void mousePressed(MouseEvent e)
              {
                clock_mousePressed(e);
              }
            });
            editor.addVetoableChangeListener(
              new java.beans.VetoableChangeListener()
            {
              public void vetoableChange(PropertyChangeEvent e)
                throws PropertyVetoException
              {
                editor_vetoableChange(e);
              }
            });
            this.getContentPane().add(clock, BorderLayout.CENTER);
          }

          // Change property values in clock
          void editor_propertyChange(PropertyChangeEvent e)
          {
            clock.propertyChange(e);
          }

          // Activate the property editor
          void clock_mousePressed(MouseEvent e)
          {
            if (e.isMetaDown()) // Detect right button pressed
            {
              editor.pack();
              editor.setVisible(true);
            }
          }
```

Listing 10.7   *Continued*

```
            // Veto property values in clock if necessary
            void editor_vetoableChange(PropertyChangeEvent e)
              throws PropertyVetoException
            {
              clock.vetoableChange(e);
            }
         }
```

Listing 10.7   *Continued*

Example Review

The implementation of the project and the relationship of the classes in the project are shown in Figure 10.5.

Figure 10.5   *Changes of constraint properties in* editor *are notified to* clock *through the adapter created in* TestConstraintProperty.

It is worth noting that Java does not have a class named VetoableChangeEvent. Both VetoChangeListener and PropertyChangeListener listen for PropertyChangeEvent.

When invoking firePropertyChange(), all three parameters (propertyName, oldValue, and newValue) must be given, and they must be nonnull. Similar to firePropertyChange(), the fireVetoableChange() method does not fire PropertyChangeEvent if the new value is the same as the old value, which reduces the danger of infinite loops when methods are cross-connected in cases.

When firePropertyChange(), invoked from the jtfTimeZoneOffset_action-Performed() method in the ClockEditorSupportConstraint class, throws a PropertyVetoException, the other statements in this method are skipped. In consequence, the property is not changed in the clock. Furthermore, timeZoneOffset is reset to the previous value in the catch clause.

You can use the Bean Designer to create constraint properties and generate the needed code to carry out the task for handling constraint properties in the same way as you created bound properties using the Bean Designer.

Implementing Model-View Components Using Bound and Constraint Properties

Bound properties are ideal for implementing the model-view components. In Example 4.3, "Developing Model-View Components," you created a model, named `CircleModel`, which notifies the listeners of its property changes through an `ActionEvent`. The notification is implemented in the property's setter method using the `fireActionPerformed()` method. Instead of firing an `ActionEvent` with every property change, you can simply make it a bound or a constraint property. Using bound and constraint properties simplifies the task of creating the model and the views.

The following example demonstrates creating model-view components using bound properties.

Example 10.4 Implementing Model-View Components Using Bound Properties

This example rewrites Example 4.3 to create a new circle model, circle editor, and circle view, named `CircleModelUsingBoundProperties`, `CircleEditorUsingBoundProperties`, and `CircleViewUsingBoundProperties`, respectively. The `CircleEditorUsingBoundProperties` class is like a property editor that enables you to change the properties of the circle. The `CircleViewBoundProperties` class displays the circle visually and enables you to increase or decrease the radius with a mouse click on the left or right button. Both `CircleEditorUsing-BoundProperties` and `CircleViewUsingBoundProperties` are views that use the data stored in `CircleModelUsingBoundProperties`. A sample run of the test program that uses these three components is shown in Figure 10.6.

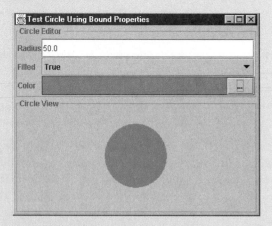

Figure 10.6   *You can change the circle property from the circle editor and increase or decrease the circle radius by clicking the left or right button.*

The following are the steps to create CircleModelUsingBoundProperties.

1. Create a new project named ModelViewUsingBoundPropertiesDemo.jpr, and create `CircleModelUsingBoundProperties` using the JavaBeans Wizard.

2. With CircleModelUsingBoundProperties.java selected in the Navigation pane, choose the Bean tab in the Content pane to start the Bean Designer. Choose the Properties tab, and click the Add Properties button to bring up the New Property dialog box. Add three bound properties `color`, `filled`, and `radius` with type `java.awt.Color`, `boolean`, and `double`, respectively. For each property, choose bound in the binding field. `CircleModelUsingBoundProperties` is generated, as shown in Listing 10.8.

```
package ModelViewUsingBoundPropertiesDemo;

import java.beans.*;

public class CircleModelUsingBoundProperties
{
  private double radius;
  private transient PropertyChangeSupport propertyChangeListeners
    = new PropertyChangeSupport(this);
  private boolean filled = true;
  private java.awt.Color color;

  public CircleModelUsingBoundProperties()
  {
  }

  public double getRadius()
  {
    return radius;
  }

  public void setRadius(double newRadius)
  {
    double  oldRadius = radius;
    radius = newRadius;
    propertyChangeListeners.firePropertyChange(
      "radius", new Double(oldRadius), new Double(newRadius));
  }

  public synchronized void removePropertyChangeListener
    (PropertyChangeListener l)
  {
    propertyChangeListeners.removePropertyChangeListener(l);
  }

  public synchronized void addPropertyChangeListener
    (PropertyChangeListener l)
  {
    propertyChangeListeners.addPropertyChangeListener(l);
  }
```

continues

Listing 10.8 *CircleModelUsingBoundProperties.java*

```
        public void setFilled(boolean newFilled)
        {
          boolean  oldFilled = filled;
          filled = newFilled;
          propertyChangeListeners.firePropertyChange(
            "filled", new Boolean(oldFilled), new Boolean(newFilled));
        }

        public boolean isFilled()
        {
          return filled;
        }

        public void setColor(java.awt.Color newColor)
        {
          java.awt.Color  oldColor = color;
          color = newColor;
          propertyChangeListeners.firePropertyChange
            ("color", oldColor, newColor);
        }

        public java.awt.Color getColor()
        {
          return color;
        }
      }
```

Listing 10.8 *Continued*

The following are the steps to create `CircleEditorUsingBoundProperties`.

1. Create `CircleEditorUsingBoundProperties` that extends `JPanel` using the JavaBean Wizard.

2. In the UI Designer of CircleEditorUsingBoundProperties.java, drop a `JPanel` to the west of the panel to create jpLabels, and drop a `JPanel` to the center of the applet to create jpProperties.

3. Set the `layout` of jpLabels to `GridLayout` with three rows. Drop a `JLabel` three times to jpLabels to create labels "Radius," "Filled," and "Color." Set the `layout` of jpProperties to `GridLayout` with three rows. Drop a `JTextField`, a `JComboBox`, and a `JPanel` into jpProperties to create jtfRadius, jcbFilled, and jpColor. Set the `layout` of jpColor to `BorderLayout`. Drop a `JLabel` and `JButton` into the center and each of jpColor to create jlblColor and jbtColor.

4. Select UI in the Component tree, and drop a `JColorChooser` to create jColorChooser1.

5. Choose the Bean tab in Content pane to switch to the Bean Designer. Add a property named `model` with type `CircleModelUsingBoundProperties`. Modify the `setModel()` method to register model and initialize value in the editor.

6. Choose the Design tab to switch back to the UI Designer. Double-click jtfRadius to generate the code for handling text input. Double-click jcbFilled to generate the code for handling the selection of combo box values. Double-click jbtColor to generate the code for handling the button action. Implement these event handlers as shown in Listing 10.9.

7. Add items True and False in the jcbFilled combo box.

8. Use the Implement Interface Wizard to implement the PropertyChange-Listener, and implement the handler propertyChange() to update the values in the editor.

```java
package ModelViewUsingBoundPropertiesDemo;

import java.awt.*;
import javax.swing.*;
import java.awt.event.*;
import java.beans.PropertyChangeEvent;
import java.beans.PropertyChangeListener;

public class CircleEditorUsingBoundProperties
  extends JPanel implements PropertyChangeListener
{
  JPanel jpLabels = new JPanel();
  JPanel jpProperties = new JPanel();
  JLabel jLabel1 = new JLabel();
  JLabel jLabel2 = new JLabel();
  JLabel jLabel3 = new JLabel();
  JTextField jtfRadius = new JTextField();
  JComboBox jcboFilled = new JComboBox();
  JPanel jpColor = new JPanel();
  JLabel jlblColor = new JLabel();
  JButton jbtColor = new JButton();
  BorderLayout borderLayout2 = new BorderLayout();
  BorderLayout borderLayout1 = new BorderLayout();
  GridLayout gridLayout1 = new GridLayout();
  GridLayout gridLayout2 = new GridLayout();

  private CircleModelUsingBoundProperties model;

  public CircleEditorUsingBoundProperties()
  {
    try
    {
      jbInit();
    }
    catch (Exception ex)
    {
      ex.printStackTrace();
    }
  }

  private void jbInit() throws Exception
  {
```

continues

Listing 10.9   *CircleEditorUsingBoundProperties.java*

```
            jLabel1.setText("Radius");
            jLabel2.setText("Filled");
            jLabel3.setText("Color");
            jlblColor.setBackground(Color.black);
            jlblColor.setOpaque(true);
            jpColor.setLayout(borderLayout2);
            jbtColor.setText("jButton1");
            jbtColor.setText("...");
            jbtColor.addActionListener(new java.awt.event.ActionListener()
            {
              public void actionPerformed(ActionEvent e)
              {
                jbtColor_actionPerformed(e);
              }
            });
            jtfRadius.addActionListener(new java.awt.event.ActionListener()
            {
              public void actionPerformed(ActionEvent e)
              {
                jtfRadius_actionPerformed(e);
              }
            });
            this.setLayout(borderLayout1);
            jpLabels.setLayout(gridLayout1);
            gridLayout1.setRows(3);
            jpProperties.setLayout(gridLayout2);
            gridLayout2.setRows(3);
            jcboFilled.addActionListener(new java.awt.event.ActionListener()
            {
              public void actionPerformed(ActionEvent e)
              {
                jcboFilled_actionPerformed(e);
              }
            });
            jpColor.setBorder(BorderFactory.createLineBorder(Color.black));
            this.add(jpLabels, BorderLayout.WEST);
            jpLabels.add(jLabel1, null);
            jpLabels.add(jLabel2, null);
            jpLabels.add(jLabel3, null);
            this.add(jpProperties, BorderLayout.CENTER);
            jpProperties.add(jtfRadius, null);
            jpProperties.add(jcboFilled, null);
            jpProperties.add(jpColor, null);
            jpColor.add(jlblColor, BorderLayout.CENTER);
            jpColor.add(jbtColor, BorderLayout.EAST);

            // Add items True and False in the combo box
            jcboFilled.addItem("True");
            jcboFilled.addItem("False");
          }

          void jtfRadius_actionPerformed(ActionEvent e)
          {
            model.setRadius(
              new Double(jtfRadius.getText()).doubleValue());
          }

          public void setModel(CircleModelUsingBoundProperties newModel)
```

Listing 10.9   *Continued*

454

```
{
  model = newModel;

  // Register listener
  if (model != null)
  {
    model.addPropertyChangeListener(this);
    updateEditor();
  }
  else
  {
    model.removePropertyChangeListener(this);
  }
}

public CircleModelUsingBoundProperties getModel()
{
  return model;
}

public void propertyChange(PropertyChangeEvent evt)
{
  // TODO: implement this java.beans.PropertyChangeListener method;
  updateEditor();
}

// Update property values in the editor
private void updateEditor()
{
  // Update radius
  jtfRadius.setText(new Double(model.getRadius()).toString());

  // Update filled
  if (model.isFilled())
  {
    jcboFilled.setSelectedIndex(0);
  }
  else
  {
    jcboFilled.setSelectedIndex(1);
  }

  // Update color
  jlblColor.setBackground(model.getColor());
}

void jcboFilled_actionPerformed(ActionEvent e)
{
  if (((String)jcboFilled.getSelectedItem()).equals("True"))
  {
    if (model != null) model.setFilled(true);
  }
  else
  {
    if (model != null) model.setFilled(false);
  }
}

void jbtColor_actionPerformed(ActionEvent e)
{
```

continues

455

```
      Color selectedColor =
        JColorChooser.showDialog(this, "Choose Color",
          jlblColor.getBackground());

      if (selectedColor != null)
      {
        model.setColor(selectedColor);
        jlblColor.setBackground(selectedColor);
      }
    }
  }
}
```

Listing 10.9 *Continued*

The following are the steps to create `CircleViewBoundProperties`.

1. Create `CircleViewUsingBoundProperties` to extend `JPanel` using the Java-Beans Wizard.

2. Choose the Bean tab in Content pane to switch to the Bean Designer. Add a property named `model` with type `CircleModelUsingBoundProper-ties`. Modify the `setModel()` method to register model and initialize value in the view.

3. Use the Implement Interface Wizard to implement the `PropertyChange-Listener`, and implement the handler `propertyChange()` to repaint the circle in the view.

4. Override the `paintComponent()` method to draw the circle on the panel, as shown in Listing 10.10.

```
package ModelViewUsingBoundPropertiesDemo;

import java.awt.*;
import javax.swing.*;
import java.beans.PropertyChangeEvent;
import java.beans.PropertyChangeListener;
import java.awt.event.*;

public class CircleViewUsingBoundProperties
  extends JPanel implements PropertyChangeListener
{
  BorderLayout borderLayout1 = new BorderLayout();
  private CircleModelUsingBoundProperties model;

  public CircleViewUsingBoundProperties()
  {
    try
    {
      jbInit();
    }
```

Listing 10.10 *CircleViewUsingBoundProperties.java*

```
      catch (Exception ex)
      {
        ex.printStackTrace();
      }
    }

    private void jbInit() throws Exception
    {
      this.setOpaque(false);
      this.addMouseListener(new java.awt.event.MouseAdapter()
      {
        public void mouseClicked(MouseEvent e)
        {
          this_mouseClicked(e);
        }
      });
      this.setLayout(borderLayout1);
    }

    public void propertyChange(PropertyChangeEvent evt)
    {
      // TODO: implement this java.beans.PropertyChangeListener method;
      repaint();
    }

    public void setModel(CircleModelUsingBoundProperties newModel)
    {
      model = newModel;

      // Register listener
      if (model != null)
      {
        model.addPropertyChangeListener(this);
      }
      else
      {
        model.removePropertyChangeListener(this);
      }
    }

    public CircleModelUsingBoundProperties getModel()
    {
      return model;
    }

    // Paint the circle
    public void paintComponent(Graphics g)
    {
      super.paintComponent(g);

      if (model == null) return;

      g.setColor(model.getColor());

      int xCenter = getSize().width/2;
      int yCenter = getSize().height/2;
      int radius = (int)model.getRadius();

      if (model.isFilled())
      {
```

continues

457

```
        g.fillOval(xCenter - radius, yCenter - radius,
          2*radius, 2*radius);
    }
    else
    {
        g.drawOval(xCenter - radius, yCenter - radius,
          2*radius, 2*radius);
    }
  }

  void this_mouseClicked(MouseEvent e)
  {
    if (model == null) return;

    if (e.isMetaDown())
      model.setRadius(model.getRadius()-5);
    else
      model.setRadius(model.getRadius()+5);
  }
}
```

Listing 10.10   *Continued*

Finally, let us put the model and views together to create a test program as follows:

1. Create an applet named TestCircleUsingBoundProperties using the Applet Wizard.

2. Drop a `CircleEditorUsingBoundProperties` to the north of the applet to create editor. Drop a `CircleViewUsingBoundProperties` to the center of the applet to create view. Set the border of editor to Circle Editor, and the border of view to Circle View.

3. Drop a `CircleModelUsingBoundProperties` to the UI Designer to create circleModel. Set the model property of editor and view to circleModel.

The generated code for `TestCircleUsingBoundProperties` is shown in Listing 10.11.

```
package ModelViewUsingBoundPropertiesDemo;

import java.awt.*;
import java.awt.event.*;
import java.applet.*;
import javax.swing.*;
import javax.swing.border.*;

public class TestCircleUsingBoundProperties extends JApplet
{
  boolean isStandalone = false;
  CircleEditorUsingBoundProperties editor
    = new CircleEditorUsingBoundProperties();
```

Listing 10.11   *CircleViewUsingBoundProperties.java*

```
            CircleViewUsingBoundProperties view
              = new CircleViewUsingBoundProperties();
            CircleModelUsingBoundProperties circleModel
              = new CircleModelUsingBoundProperties();
            BorderLayout borderLayout1 = new BorderLayout();
            TitledBorder titledBorder1;
            TitledBorder titledBorder2;

            // Construct the applet
            public TestCircleUsingBoundProperties()
            {
            }

            // Initialize the applet
            public void init()
            {
              try
              {
              jbInit();
              }
              catch (Exception e)
              {
              e.printStackTrace();
              }
            }

            // Component initialization
            private void jbInit() throws Exception
            {
              titledBorder1 = new TitledBorder("");
              titledBorder2 = new TitledBorder("");
              this.setSize(400,300);
              this.getContentPane().setLayout(borderLayout1);
              editor.setBorder(titledBorder1);
              editor.setModel(circleModel);
              view.setBorder(titledBorder2);
              view.setModel(circleModel);
              circleModel.setRadius(20.0);
              titledBorder1.setTitle("Circle Editor");
              titledBorder2.setTitle("Circle View");
              this.getContentPane().add(editor, BorderLayout.NORTH);
              this.getContentPane().add(view, BorderLayout.CENTER);
            }
          }
```

Listing 10.11 *Continued*

Example Review

Through the circleModel property, the objects editor, view, and circleModel are glued together. The property values of these objects are synchronized. A change in a property value in one object is immediately changed in the other objects.

The properties radius, filled, and color are defined as bound properties in the CircleModelUsingBoundProperties model. The editor and view are the listeners of these properties. Whenever there is a change in one of these properties, the listeners of the model are notified to update the property values through `circleModel`.

`CircleEditorUsingBoundProperties` and `CircleViewUsingBoundProperties` are both views for the data model `CircleModelUsingBoundProperties`.

`CircleEditorUsingBoundProperties` allows you to edit circle properties `radius`, `filled`, and `color`. `CircleViewUsingBoundProperties` allows you to increase the radius with a right mouse click and decrease the radius with a left mouse click.

Chapter Summary

Bound and constraint properties provide a mechanism that notifies the listener beans of changes to the properties of one bean. Constraint properties allow the listener beans to veto the change. Bound and constraint properties are useful in developing beans that are related through mutual properties.

Chapter Review

10.1. Does a bound property or a constraint property use a special data type for declaration? How do you declare a bound property? How do you declare a constraint property?

10.2. Is `PropertyChangeSupport` a subclass of `PropertyChangeListener`? What are the differences between using `PropertyChangeSupport` and `PropertyChange-Listener`?

Programming Exercises

10.1. Rewrite Exercise 4.4 using bound properties.

10.2. Rewrite Exercise 4.5 using bound properties.

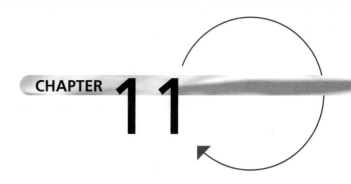

BEAN INTROSPECTION AND CUSTOMIZATION

Objectives

@ Use a bean information class to control the properties and events of the component to be exposed in builder tools.

@ Analyze beans using the `java.beans.Introspector` class.

@ Become familiar with the BeanInsight Wizard.

@ Develop and deploy custom property editors.

@ Create custom property editors and generate `BeanInfo` classes using the Bean Designer.

@ Create GUI custom property editors.

@ Create customizers for editing a group of related properties.

Introduction

If your component follows the standard design patterns, the builder tool can automatically recognize the properties and events it supports through introspection of a bean during design time. You can then use the property editors from the Component Inspector to view and modify the bean's properties. You can also inspect the events and let the builder tool generate event listener adapters for them. The design patterns provide a simple framework that allows you to develop components that support introspection. You are not limited to using the standard patterns, however. You can choose to provide your own bean information class to describe the properties and events to be exposed, and it would supersede the standard design patterns for the properties and events.

In this chapter, you will learn how to use `BeanInfo` classes to describe beans to a builder tool, create customer editors for editing individual properties, and use customizers for editing a group of related properties.

Creating `BeanInfo` Classes

To specify component information, you need to create a class that describes your component, thereby allowing you to hide or expose properties and events, give them aliases for design purposes, and give them brief descriptions that will be visible in design tools. This class is referred to as the *bean information* class (or `BeanInfo`) for the component. The bean information class causes specified properties and events of a component to appear in the Component Inspector.

The bean information class can be outlined as follows:

```
public class MyClassBeanInfo implements BeanInfo
{
  public BeanDescriptor getBeanDescriptor()
  {
    // TODO: implement this java.beans.BeanInfo method;
  }

  public EventSetDescriptor[] getEventSetDescriptors()
  {
    // TODO: implement this java.beans.BeanInfo method;
  }

  public int getDefaultEventIndex()
  {
    // TODO: implement this java.beans.BeanInfo method;
  }

  public PropertyDescriptor[] getPropertyDescriptors()
  {
    // TODO: implement this java.beans.BeanInfo method;
  }

  public int getDefaultPropertyIndex()
  {
    // TODO: implement this java.beans.BeanInfo method;
  }
```

```
   public MethodDescriptor[] getMethodDescriptors()
   {
     // TODO: implement this java.beans.BeanInfo method;
   }

   public BeanInfo[] getAdditionalBeanInfo()
   {
     // TODO: implement this java.beans.BeanInfo method;
   }

   public Image getIcon(int iconKind)
   {
     // TODO: implement this java.beans.BeanInfo method;
   }
 }
```

Place the bean information class in the same package with the component. By default, the bean information class should be named <Component>BeanInfo, which directly implements the java.beans.BeanInfo interface or extends the java.beans.SimpleBeanInfo class. The BeanInfo interface provides methods for learning about properties and events, and for specifying bean image icons. You can create a customer bean information class by directly implementing the BeanInfo interface, but it is easier to extend the SimpleBeanInfo class. SimpleBeanInfo is a support class that itself implements BeanInfo interface. All the methods return null. You can override these methods to provide explicit information on the properties, events, and methods of the beans.

You need to provide your own BeanInfo classes if

- You have existing classes that don't follow the naming patterns for properties or events. These classes were developed before the JavaBeans API was introduced.

- You don't want to give the user of your bean access to every public property at design time.

- You wish to use a particular custom editor with some property that might otherwise be assigned a default editor.

A BeanInfo class contains the following methods to describe bean properties, events, and other useful information to the builder tool.

- The getPropertyDescriptors() method describes properties and returns an array of objects of the PropertyDescriptor class.

- The getEventSetDescriptors() method describes event sets and returns an array of objects of the EventSetDescriptor class.

- The getIcon() method describes an icon that can be used to represent the bean in the builder tool.

- The getBeanDescriptor() method describes the customizer for the bean. The customizer is introduced in the section "Creating Component Customizers."

To provide property information, you need to override `getPropertyDescriptors()` with the code to instantiate an array of `PropertyDescriptor` objects containing information on each property of the component you want the builder tool to access.

To provide event information, you need to override `getEventSetDescriptors()` with the code to instantiate an array of `EventSetDescriptor` objects containing information on each event set your bean may generate.

The `PropertyDescriptor` Class

A `PropertyDescriptor` object describes a property, its accessor methods, and the custom editor for the property to the builder tool. Suppose you developed the `Circle` class before the JavaBeans standards were introduced. The property `radius` of `Circle` is read and written using the methods `getRad()` and `setRad()`, rather than the standard names `getRadius()` and `setRadius()`. To describe `radius` as a bean property to the builder tool, construct a `PropertyDescriptor` object as follows:

```
new PropertyDescriptor("radius", Circle.class, "getRad", "setRad");
```

This object describes the `radius` property in the `Circle` class with getter and setter methods `getRad()` and `setRad()`. If the accessor methods conform to the design patterns with the names `getRadius()` and `setRadius()`, you could simply construct a property descriptor using the following constructor:

```
new PropertyDescriptor("radius", Circle.class);
```

The following instance methods of the `PropertyDescriptor` objects are useful to get property information and set custom property editors.

- **`public Class getPropertyType()`**

This returns the data type of the property. The `java.lang.Class` class encapsulates the class information, including the class name, data members, methods, and superclass.

- **`public Method getReadMethod()`**

This returns the method that is used to read the property if the method is defined in the component; otherwise, it returns `null`. The `java.lang.reflect.Method` class encapsulates the method information, including the method name, return type, and parameter profile.

- **`public Class getPropertyEditorClass()`**

This returns a custom editor class that has been registered for this property. The custom editor class is registered using the `setPropertyEditorClass()` method as follows:

- **`public void setPropertyEditorClass(Class propertyEditorClass)`**

Usually a default property editor is used. However, if for some reason you want to associate a particular property editor with a given property, you can do it with this method. You will learn how to customize editors in the section "Customizing Property Editors."

The `EventSetDescriptor` Class

An `EventSetDescriptor` describes a group of events fired by a given Java bean. The given group of events are all delivered as method calls on a single event listener interface, and an event listener object can be registered via a call on a registration method supplied by the event source.

Suppose your `Circle` component fires `SmallRadiusEvent` when radius is less than 10. The listener interface of the event is `SRListener`, and two methods, `radiusChanging()` and `radiusChanged()`, are defined in the interface. You may create an `EventSetDescriptor` object to describe the event set to the builder tool as follows:

```
new EventSetDesriptor(Circle.class, "SmallRadiusEvent", "SRListener",
  {"radiusChanging", "radiusChanged"}, "addRadiusListener",
    "removeRadiusListener");
```

The `EventSetDescriptor` provides instance methods to get the event set information, such as the listener type (`getListenerType()`), and listener registration methods (`getListenerMethods()`).

The `MethodDescriptor` Class

A `MethodDescriptor` describes a particular method of external access from other components that is supported by a Java bean. The `MethodDescriptor` class provides the `getMethod()` method for getting the method that this `MethodDescriptor` encapsulates, and the `getParameterDescriptor()` method for getting the `Parameter-Descriptor` for each of this `MethodDescriptor`'s method's parameters.

Specifying Image Icons

You can specify an image icon to graphically represent a bean in the Component palette of the builder tool. In JBuilder, this can be done in two ways. One way is to set the icon from the Palette Properties dialog window when installing and configuring the bean, as shown in Figure 2.7. The other is to specify it in the `BeanInfo` class by overriding the `getIcon()` method, whose signature is shown below.

```
public Image getIcon(int iconKind)
```

There are four types of icons represented in the following constants:

- `ICON_COLOR_16x16`—A 16 × 16-pixel color icon.
- `ICON_MONO_16x16`—A 16 × 16-pixel monochrome icon.
- `ICON_COLOR_32x32`—A 32 × 32-pixel color icon.
- `ICON_MONO_32x32`—A 32 × 32-pixel monochrome icon.

The `iconKind` parameter is determined by the builder tool that displays the bean icon. You override `getIcon()` with the code that loads the image based on `iconKind`. To load, use the `loadImage()` method provided in the `SimpleBeanInfo` class. This method returns `null` if loading fails.

■■■ NOTE
Some builder tools (not JBuilder) allow you to inspect all the public methods; you can provide custom information on the methods by overriding the `getMethodDescriptors()` method with the code to instantiate an array of `MethodDescriptor` objects containing information on the public methods in the component.

Example 11.1 Using the `BeanInfo` Class

This example demonstrates how to develop and use the `BeanInfo` class for a bean component. First, a new component named `Circle` will be created with a property field `radius`, whose accessor methods are deliberately named `readRadius` and `writeRadius`, which do not follow the standard design patterns. Another property named filled, with standard accessor methods, `isFilled()` and `setFilled()`. Second, you will create the `CircleBeanInfo` class to describe the properties and events.

Follow the steps below to complete the project.

1. Create a new project named BeanInfoDemo.jpr, and create a new class named `Circle` using the New Java File Wizard, as shown in Listing 11.1.

```
package BeanInfoDemo;

import javax.swing.*;
import java.awt.*;

public class Circle extends JPanel
{
  private int radius = 30;
  private boolean filled;

  public Circle()
  {
  }

  public int readRadius()
  {
    return radius;
  }

  public void writeRadius(int radius)
  {
    this.radius = radius;
  }

  public boolean isFilled()
  {
    return filled;
  }
}
```

Listing 11.1 *Circle.java*

```
        public void setFilled(boolean filled)
        {
          this.filled = filled;
        }

        public void paintComponent(Graphics g)
        {
          super.paintComponent(g);

          int xCenter = getSize().width/2;
          int yCenter = getSize().height/2;

          if (filled)
            g.fillOval(xCenter - radius, yCenter - radius,
              2*radius, 2*radius);
          else
            g.drawOval(xCenter - radius, yCenter - radius,
              2*radius, 2*radius);
        }
      }
```

Listing 11.1 *Continued*

2. Suppose you want the properties radius and filled, and the mouse event to be exposed to the builder tool, and you also want to provide two color icons (test16.gif and test32.gif) for the builder tool to use. Create the CircleBeanInfo, as shown in Listing 11.2.

```
package BeanInfoDemo;

import java.beans.*;
import java.awt.event.MouseListener;
import java.awt.Image;

public class CircleBeanInfo extends SimpleBeanInfo
{
  public PropertyDescriptor[] getPropertyDescriptors()
  {
    try
    {
      PropertyDescriptor pdsRadius = new PropertyDescriptor
        ("radius", Circle.class, "readRadius", "writeRadius");
      PropertyDescriptor pdsFilled = new PropertyDescriptor
        ("filled", Circle.class);
      PropertyDescriptor[] pds = {pdsRadius, pdsFilled};
      return pds;
    }
    catch (IntrospectionException e)
    {
      return null;
    }
  }

  public EventSetDescriptor[] getEventSetDescriptors()
```

continues

Listing 11.2 *CircleBeanInfo.java*

```
    {
      try
      {
        String[] methodNames = {"mouseClicked", "mouseEntered",
          "mouseExited", "mousePressed", "mouseReleased"};
        EventSetDescriptor esMouseEvent = new EventSetDescriptor
          (Circle.class, "MouseEvent", MouseListener.class,
            methodNames, "addMouseListener", "removeMouseListener");
        EventSetDescriptor[] es = {esMouseEvent};
        return es;
      }
      catch (IntrospectionException e)
      {
        return null;
      }
    }

    public Image getIcon(int iconKind)
    {
      if (iconKind == BeanInfo.ICON_COLOR_16x16)
        return loadImage("test16.gif");
      else if (iconKind == BeanInfo.ICON_COLOR_32x32)
        return loadImage("test32.gif");
      return null;
    }
  }
```

Listing 11.2 *Continued*

3. Install `Circle` in the Component palette. Create Test.java using the Applet Wizard.

4. In the UI designer of Test.java, drop a `Circle` bean to the frame. You will see properties `radius` and `filled` in the Inspector shown in Figure 11.1, and the `MouseEvent` handlers on the Event page of the Inspector shown in Figure 11.2.

TIP

When the UI Designer first inspects the component, it creates a text file containing the properties, methods, and events of the bean component in the PME directory of the JBuilder installation folder. If the component or the `BeanInfo` class is modified, you need to exit JBuilder, delete the PME file for the component, and restart JBuilder.

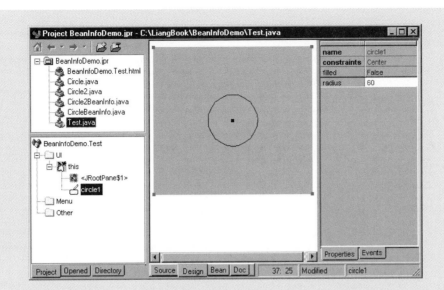

Figure 11.1 *The properties described in the* CircleBeanInfo *class are shown on the Properties page of the Inspector.*

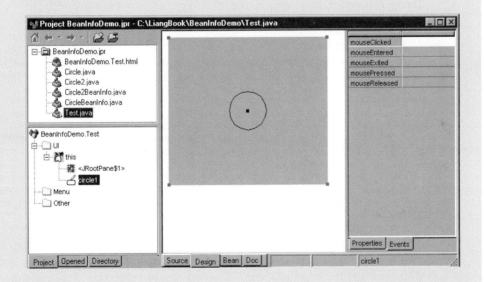

Figure 11.2 *The event listener methods described in the* CircleBeanInfo *classes are shown on the Events page of the Inspector.*

Example Review

The `PropertyDescriptor` object `pdsRadius`, shown below, describes property radius and its accessor methods `readRadius()` and `writeRadius()`.

```
PropertyDescriptor pdsRadius = new PropertyDescriptor
  ("radius", Circle.class, "readRadius", "writeRadius");
```

The `PropertyDescriptor` object `pdsFilled`, shown below, describes that the property `filled` uses its default accessor methods.

```
PropertyDescriptor pdsFilled =
  new PropertyDescriptor("filled", Circle.class);
```

The `EventSetDescriptor` object `esMouseEvent`, shown below, describes the mouse event source, mouse event name, mouse event listener, mouse event handlers, and mouse event registration methods, where `methodNames` is an array of strings containing all the handlers.

```
EventSetDescriptor esMouseEvent = new EventSetDescriptor
  (Circle.class, "MouseEvent", MouseListener.class,
   methodNames, "addMouseListener", "removeMouseListener");
```

Since the constructors for `PropertyDescriptor` and `EventSetDescriptor` may throw `IntrospectionException`, the try/catch block is necessary to wrap the code that invokes the constructors.

If you don't override `getPropertyDescriptors()`, the builder tool will obtain the bean properties through automatic analysis based on the design patterns. If `getPropertyDescriptors()` is overridden, only the properties described in the method are accessible in the Inspector. The same principle applies to the `getEventSetDescriptors()` method.

The `CircleBeanInfo` provides two color icons for the bean. If the builder tool does not support color icons, a builder tool default icon will be used.

Inspecting Bean Components

To programmatically discover which properties and events are exposed during *runtime* in a bean, you can use the `java.beans.Introspector` class to analyze the bean. This class uses the Java Reflection API to expose the properties, events, and methods that the bean supports. The Reflection API comprises the `Class` class in the `java.lang` package and the `Constructor`, `Field`, `Member`, `Method`, and `Modifier` classes in the `java.lang.reflect` package.

All the builder tools use the `java.beans.Introspector` class to analyze beans and present the analysis to the user in the Inspector. The `Introspector` class provides a standard way for tools to learn about the properties, events, and methods supported by a target Java bean.

For each of these three kinds of information, the Introspector will separately analyze the bean's class and superclasses, looking for explicit or implicit information, and will use that information to build a BeanInfo object that comprehensively describes the target bean.

If the component's BeanInfo class exists, the non-null return values of the getPropertyDescriptors(), getEventSetDescriptors(), and getMethodDescriptors() provide the information of the properties, event sets, and methods. If the return value is null or the component's BeanInfo class does not exist, the Introspector uses standard design patterns to analyze the bean.

To use the Introspector class programmatically, simply use the static method get-BeanInfo(beanClass) in the Introspector class to create an object of the BeanInfo interface. You can then use the BeanInfo object's getPropertyDescriptors(), getEventSetDescriptors(), and getMethodDescriptors() methods to get properties, event sets, and methods.

Example 11.2 Analyzing Components

This example uses the Introspector class to create a program to discover the properties, event sets, and methods of the components. The program enables you to enter a fully qualified class name and select the type of information (properties, events, and methods). The information is displayed in a text area, as shown in Figure 11.3.

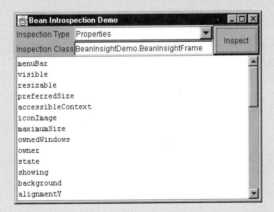

Figure 11.3   *The program lets you specify a class and choose the type of information for introspection.*

Follow the steps below to build the project.

1. Create a new project named BeanInsightDemo.jpr, and create Bean-InsightApplication.java and BeanInsightFrame.java using the Application Wizard.

2. With BeanInsightFrame.java selected in the Navigation pane, switch to the UI Designer. Drop a `JPanel` into the north of the frame to create `jpInspect`. Drop a `JScrollPane` to the center of the frame, and drop a `JTextArea` into the scroll pane to create `jta`.

3. Set the `layout` of `jpInspect` to `BorderLayout`. Drop a `JPanel` to the west of `jpInspect` to create `jpLabels`, drop a `JPanel` to the center of the `jpInspect` to create `jpSelections`, and drop a `JButton` to the east of `jpInspect` to create `jbtInspect`.

4. Set the `layout` of `jpLabels` to `GridLayout` with two rows, and drop a `JLabel` twice into `jpLabels` to create the labels with `text` "Inspection Type" and "Inspection Class."

5. Set the `layout` of `jpSelections` to `GridLayout` with two rows. Drop a `JComboBox` into it to create `jcboTypes`, and drop a `JTextField` into it to create `jtfClass`.

6. Insert the code in the `jbInit()` method to add the items into the combo box as follows:

```
jcoboTypes.addItem("Properties");
jcoboTypes.addItem("Events");
jcoboTypes.addItem("Methods");
```

7. Double-click `jcoboTypes` to generate the code for handling selection of inspection types. Implement the handler as shown in Listing 11.3.

8. Double-click `jbtInspect` to generate the code for inspecting the bean. Implement the handler as shown in Listing 11.3.

9. Hand-code the `introspectBean()` method to introspect the selected information from the component. The complete code for BeanInsightFrame.java is listed below. Run BeanInsightApplication.java to test the program.

```
package BeanInsightDemo;

import java.awt.*;
import java.awt.event.*;
import javax.swing.*;
import java.beans.*;

public class BeanInsightFrame extends JFrame
{
  BorderLayout borderLayout1 = new BorderLayout();
  JPanel jpInspect = new JPanel();
  JScrollPane jScrollPane1 = new JScrollPane();
  JTextArea jta = new JTextArea();
  JPanel jpLabels = new JPanel();
```

Listing 11.3   *BeanInsightFrame.java*

```
    JLabel jLabel1 = new JLabel();
    JLabel jLabel2 = new JLabel();
    BorderLayout borderLayout2 = new BorderLayout();
    GridLayout gridLayout1 = new GridLayout();
    JPanel jpSelections = new JPanel();
    GridLayout gridLayout2 = new GridLayout();
    JComboBox jcboTypes = new JComboBox();
    JTextField jtfClass = new JTextField();
    JButton jbtInspect = new JButton();

    // Declare introspection type
    private String introspectionType = "Properties";

    // Construct the frame
    public BeanInsightFrame()
    {
      enableEvents(AWTEvent.WINDOW_EVENT_MASK);
      try
      {
        jbInit();
      }
      catch(Exception e)
      {
        e.printStackTrace();
      }
    }

    // Component initialization
    private void jbInit() throws Exception
    {
      this.getContentPane().setLayout(borderLayout1);
      this.setSize(new Dimension(400, 300));
      this.setTitle("Bean Introspection Demo");
      jLabel1.setText("Inspection Type");
      jLabel2.setText("Inspection Class");
      jpInspect.setLayout(borderLayout2);
      jpLabels.setLayout(gridLayout1);
      gridLayout1.setRows(2);
      jpSelections.setLayout(gridLayout2);
      gridLayout2.setRows(2);
      jbtInspect.setText("Inspect");
      jbtInspect.addActionListener(new java.awt.event.ActionListener()
      {
        public void actionPerformed(ActionEvent e)
        {
          jbtInspect_actionPerformed(e);
        }
      });
      jcboTypes.addActionListener(new java.awt.event.ActionListener()
      {
        public void actionPerformed(ActionEvent e)
        {
          jcboTypes_actionPerformed(e);
        }
      });
      this.getContentPane().add(jpInspect, BorderLayout.NORTH);
      jpInspect.add(jpLabels, BorderLayout.WEST);
      jpLabels.add(jLabel1, null);
      jpLabels.add(jLabel2, null);
      jpInspect.add(jpSelections, BorderLayout.CENTER);
```

continues

473

```
      jpSelections.add(jcboTypes, null);
      jpSelections.add(jtfClass, null);
      jpInspect.add(jbtInspect, BorderLayout.EAST);
      this.getContentPane().add(jScrollPane1, BorderLayout.CENTER);
      jScrollPane1.getViewport().add(jta, null);

      // Initialize combo box
      jcboTypes.addItem("Properties");
      jcboTypes.addItem("Events");
      jcboTypes.addItem("Methods");
    }

    // Overridden  so we can exit on System Close
    protected void processWindowEvent(WindowEvent e)
    {
      super.processWindowEvent(e);
      if(e.getID() == WindowEvent.WINDOW_CLOSING)
      {
        System.exit(0);
      }
    }

    // Handler for selecting inspection types
    void jcboTypes_actionPerformed(ActionEvent e)
    {
      introspectionType = (String)jcboTypes.getSelectedItem();
    }

    // Handler for the Inspect button
    void jbtInspect_actionPerformed(ActionEvent e)
    {
      try
      {
        introspectBean(Class.forName(jtfClass.getText()));
      }
      catch (ClassNotFoundException ex)
      {
        System.out.println("class not found");
      }
    }

    // Invoked from the button action to introspect a bean
    public void introspectBean(Class beanClass)
    {
      try
      {
        BeanInfo bi = Introspector.getBeanInfo(beanClass);
        if (introspectionType.equals("Properties"))
        {
          PropertyDescriptor[] pd = bi.getPropertyDescriptors();
          for (int i=0; i<pd.length; i++)
            jta.append(pd[i].getName() + "\n");
        }
        else if (introspectionType.equals("Events"))
        {
          EventSetDescriptor[] ed = bi.getEventSetDescriptors();
```

Listing 11.3   *Continued*

```
            for (int i=0; i<ed.length; i++)
              jta.append(ed[i].getName() + "\n");
          }
          else if (introspectionType.equals("Methods"))
          {
            MethodDescriptor[] md = bi.getMethodDescriptors();
            for (int i=0; i<md.length; i++)
              jta.append(md[i].getName() + "\n");
          }
        }
        catch (IntrospectionException ex)
        {
          System.out.println("Error during introspection");
        }
      }
    }
```

Listing 11.3   *Continued*

Example Review

The `getBeanInfo(beanClass)` method is static and may throw `Introspection-Exception`. The `Introspector` class also provides another overloaded method, `getBeanInfo(beanClass, stopClass)`, to let you introspect a Java bean and learn all about its properties, events, and methods in the class/superclass chain up to the `stopClass`.

You need to provide a fully qualified class name in the text field for introspection. For example, enter `BeanInsightDemo.BeanInsightFrame` for introspection of `BeanInsightFrame.class`.

Using the BeanInsight Wizard

JBuilder provides a convenient wizard called *BeanInsight* to let you inspect the bean and view its detailed information on BeanInfo, properties, event set, property editors, etc. You can start BeanInsight from the Wizard menu to display the BeanInsight dialog box, as shown in Figure 11.4. To examine a bean, click the Select Bean button to select a bean, or type a bean in the text field to examine it, then click the Examine button to see the results. To view details, click View Details to display the View Details dialog box, as shown in Figure 11.5.

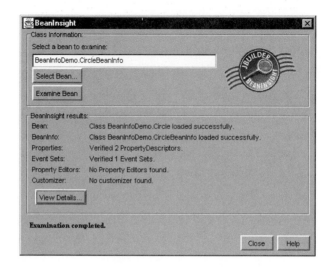

Figure 11.4   *The BeanInsight wizard lets you inspect a bean and reveal its details.*

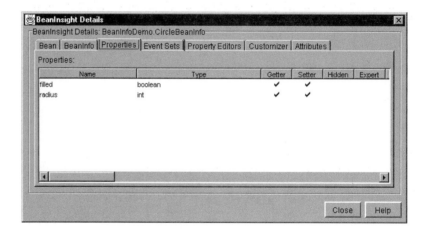

Figure 11.5   *The BeanInsight Details dialog box lets you inspect the details of a bean.*

Customizing Property Editors

JBuilder provides standard editors for the properties of primitive data types, arrays of strings, and several commonly used object types, such as Color and Font. You can, however, create your own property editors to complement or customize property editing.

To create your own property editor and enable the Inspector to use it to edit the property, you must

■   Create a property editor class that directly implements the java.beans.Property-Editor interface, or extends the java.beans.PropertyEditorSupport class.

■   Specify that the custom editor for the property in the `BeanInfo` class is to supersede the standard editor for the property.

The `PropertyEditor` interface provides several ways to update and display property values. How property values are displayed and edited depends on which methods of the `PropertyEditor` interface you implement.

Displaying Property Values

The builder tool invokes one of the following three methods in the `PropertyEditor` to display a property value:

■   `public String getAsText()`

This method returns the property value as a string to be displayed in the Component Inspector.

■   `public String[] getTags()`

This method returns a list of allowed property values to be displayed as a dropdown menu in the Component Inspector.

■   `public void paintValue()`

This method paints a representation of the value into the value field of the property in the Component Inspector. You need to return `true` in the `isPaintable()` method to enable the `paintValue()` method. An example of using the `paintValue()` method is the `Color` property value, in which a small rectangle for color is displayed along with a description of the color.

Editing Property Values

The builder tool invokes one of the following two methods in the `PropertyEditor` to edit a property value:

■   `public void setAsText(String text) throws IllegalArgumentException`

This method can be used to retrieve the value as text from the Component Inspector, parse the text to an appropriate value, and then invoke the `setValue()` method to set the value in `PropertyEditor`. This method may raise `java.lang.IllegalArgumentException` if the `text` is badly formatted or if this kind of property cannot be expressed as text.

■   `public Component getCustomEditor()`

This method returns a GUI component that serves as a custom editor for the property. Examples of such editors are the color editor and font editor in JBuilder.

Creating Property Editors

Each property editor must implement the `getJavaInitializationString()` method, which returns a string representation of the property value for use by the builder tool to generate the code for the property change. For example, if you change the message property for a MessagePanel bean in the Component Inspector to "Welcome to HTML," JBuilder generates the code setMessage("Welcome to HTML") in the jbInit() method. The "Welcome to HTML" is returned from invoking the getJavaInitializationString() method.

Each property editor must maintain a list of event listeners that are interested in changes to the property value. When the user changes the value in the Component Inspector through setAsText() or through a GUI editor, it must send a PropertyChangeEvent to all registered listeners. The PropertyEditor class defines the standard event registration and removal methods addPropertyChangeListener() and removePropertyChangeListener().

The PropertyEditorSupport class is often used to create custom editors. This support class implements all of the methods in the PropertyEditor interface. For example, the getAsText() and setAsText() are implemented as follows:

```
public String getAsText()
{
  return ("" + value); // Return a string
}

public void setAsText(String text)
  throws java.lang.IllegalArgumentException
{
  if (value instanceof String)
  {
    setValue(text);
    return;
  }
  throw new java.lang.IllegalArgumentException(text);
}
```

The PropertyEditorSupport also notifies the property changes in the setValue() method. The setValue() method is implemented as follows:

```
public void setValue(Object value)
{
  this.value = value;
  firePropertyChange();
}
```

The variable value is defined in the PropertyEditorSupport class to hold the property. The setValue() method fires the PropertyChangeEvent to the builder tool so it can respond to the property change and display the new property in the Component Inspector by invoking the getAsText() method.

Your property editor must have a default constructor if it directly implements the PropertyEditor interface, so that it can be instantiated by a builder tool. If your property editor extends the PropertyEditorSupport class, you do not have to provide constructors, since PropertyEditorSupport has a default constructor.

Example 11.3 Providing Custom Property Editors

This example creates a class named Student that describes student information, containing student full name, age, and gender. The full name, consisting of the first name, the middle name, and the last name, is edited using JBuilder's standard string editor. The example creates an editor for the age property to restrict the age to the range between 0 and 150, inclusively. For the gender property, the example provides an editor that lets the user choose Male and Female from a combo box.

The Student class with properties fullName, age, and gender is created using the JavaBean Wizard, and its source code is given in Listing 11.4. The properties are displayed in the text fields in a panel.

```java
package SimplePropertyEditorDemo;

import java.awt.*;
import javax.swing.*;
import java.util.*;

public class Student extends JPanel
{
  BorderLayout borderLayout1 = new BorderLayout();
  JPanel jPanel1 = new JPanel();
  JLabel jLabel1 = new JLabel();
  JLabel jLabel2 = new JLabel();
  JLabel jLabel3 = new JLabel();
  GridLayout gridLayout1 = new GridLayout();
  JPanel jPanel2 = new JPanel();
  JTextField jtfName = new JTextField();
  JTextField jtfAge = new JTextField();
  JTextField jtfGender = new JTextField();
  GridLayout gridLayout2 = new GridLayout();

  // Student properties
  private String firstName = "Yong";
  private String middleName = "Daniel";
  private String lastName = "Liang";
  private int age = 19;
  private String gender = "male";

  public Student()
  {
    try
    {
      jbInit();
    }
    catch(Exception ex)
    {
      ex.printStackTrace();
    }
  }
```

continues

Listing 11.4   *Student.java*

```java
private void jbInit() throws Exception
{
  this.setLayout(borderLayout1);
  jLabel1.setText("Name");
  jLabel2.setText("Age");
  jLabel3.setText("Gender");
  jPanel1.setLayout(gridLayout1);
  gridLayout1.setRows(3);
  jPanel2.setLayout(gridLayout2);
  gridLayout2.setRows(3);
  this.add(jPanel1, BorderLayout.WEST);
  jPanel1.add(jLabel1, null);
  jPanel1.add(jLabel2, null);
  jPanel1.add(jLabel3, null);
  this.add(jPanel2, BorderLayout.CENTER);
  jPanel2.add(jtfName, null);
  jPanel2.add(jtfAge, null);
  jPanel2.add(jtfGender, null);
}

public String getFullName()
{
  return firstName + "," + middleName + "," + lastName;
}

public void setFullName(String fullname)
{
  StringTokenizer st = new StringTokenizer(fullname, ",");
  try
  {
    firstName = st.nextToken();
    middleName = st.nextToken();
    lastName = st.nextToken();
  }
  catch (Exception e)
  {
    System.out.println("Names are not formed right");
  }

  jtfName.setText(firstName + " " + middleName + " " + lastName);
}

public int getAge()
{
  return age;
}

public void setAge(int age)
{
  this.age = age;
  jtfAge.setText(new Integer(age).toString());
}

public String getGender()
{
  return gender;
}
```

Listing 11.4   *Continued*

```
      public void setGender(String gender)
      {
        this.gender = gender;
        jtfGender.setText(gender);
      }
    }
```

The editor AgeEditor for editing the age property shown in Listing 11.5 restricts the user to enter an integer between 0 and 150 for age.

Listing 11.4   *Continued*

```
    package SimplePropertyEditorDemo;
      import java.beans.PropertyEditorSupport;

    public class AgeEditor extends PropertyEditorSupport
    {
      public String getAsText()
      {
        return getValue().toString();
      }

      public void setAsText(String text) throws IllegalArgumentException
      {
        Integer val = new Integer(text);
        if (val.intValue()<= 0)
          throw new IllegalArgumentException("Age may not be negative");
        else if (val.intValue() >= 150)
          throw new IllegalArgumentException(
            "Age may not be greater than 150");
        setValue(val);
      }

      public String getJavaInitializationString()
      {
        return getAsText();
      }
    }
```

Listing 11.5   *AgeEditor.java*

The editor GenderEditor (see Listing 11.6) for editing the gender property shown below lets the user choose the value "Male" or "Female" from a choice list.

```
    package SimplePropertyEditorDemo;

    import java.beans.PropertyEditorSupport;

    public class GenderEditor extends PropertyEditorSupport
    {
      public String[] getTags()
      {
```

continues

Listing 11.6   *GenderEditor.java*

```
      String[] choices = {"Male", "Female"};
      return choices;
    }

    public String getJavaInitializationString()
    {
      return "\"" + getValue().toString() + "\"";
    }
  }
```

You need to provide a BeanInfo class StudentBeanInfo (see Listing 11.7) to describe the custom editor to the builder tool, as follows:

Listing 11.6 *Continued*

```
package SimplePropertyEditorDemo;

import java.beans.*;

public class StudentBeanInfo extends SimpleBeanInfo
{
  public PropertyDescriptor[] getPropertyDescriptors()
  {
    try
    {
      PropertyDescriptor pdsFullName = new PropertyDescriptor
        ("fullName", Student.class);
      PropertyDescriptor pdsAge = new PropertyDescriptor
        ("age", Student.class);
      pdsAge.setPropertyEditorClass(AgeEditor.class);
      PropertyDescriptor pdsGender = new PropertyDescriptor
        ("gender", Student.class);
      pdsGender.setPropertyEditorClass(GenderEditor.class);
      PropertyDescriptor[] pds = {pdsFullName, pdsAge, pdsGender};
      return pds;
    }
    catch (IntrospectionException e)
    {
      return null;
    }
  }
}
```

Listing 11.7 *StudentBeanInfo.java*

Follow the steps below to complete the example.

1. Create a project named SimplePropertyEditorDemo.jpr, and create an applet TestSimplePropertyEditor.java using the Applet Wizard.

2. Create and compile Student, AgeEditor, GenderEditor, and StudentBeanInfo, and install Student in the Component palette.

3. With TestSimplePropertyEditor.java selected in the Navigation pane, switch to the UI Designer and drop a Student bean to the center of the applet to create student1.

4. With student1 selected, test editing the age property by entering integers in and out of the permissible age range, and test editing the property by choosing Male or Female from a choice menu, as shown in Figure 11.6.

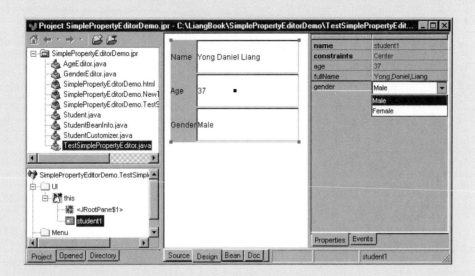

Figure 11.6   *The built-in property is used for editing* fullName, *and the custom property editors* AgeEditor *and* GenderEditor *are used for editing* age *and* gender.

Example Review

The fullName property is a string consisting of firstName, middleName, and lastName separated by commas, such as "Yong,Daniel,Liang." Adhere to this pattern when modifying the property. The property editor does not validate the change. For example, if you change the value of fullName to "Yong Daniel Liang," JBuilder would generate the following incorrect code in the jbInit() method:

```
student1.setFullName("Yong Daniel Liang");
```

The AgeEditor can validate changes in the value of the age property. If you enter a value that is not within the permissible range, the property editor rejects it and generates no code. To understand how this editor works, let us examine it at the Component Inspector. When the user presses the RETURN key with the mouse pointed at the value column of the age property, the builder tool invokes the property editor's setAsText() method, which reads the value as text from the Component Inspector and validates the value. If the value is valid, the setValue() method sets the value as an Integer object; otherwise, an IllegalArgumentException is raised and the change is aborted. In the case of a valid change, the builder tool invokes the getAsText() method to get the Integer object and converts it into text for display on the Component

Inspector. Finally, a builder tool generates the following code to reflect the change by invoking the `getJavaInitializationString()` method:

```
student1.setAge(ageEditor.getJavaInitializationString());
```

Here, `ageEditor` is an instance of `AgeEditor`.

The `GenderEditor` is an enumeration-type editor that allows the user to choose a value from a drop-down choice list, hence eliminating the necessity of data validation. When the user double-clicks the value column of the `gender` property, the Component Inspector displays a list of values by invoking the property editor's `getTags()` method, which predefines a list of values for the user to choose. Upon choosing a value from the choice menu, a builder tool invokes `getAsText()` to get the value and present it to the Component Inspector. Finally, the builder tool generates the code for setting `gender` property programmatically in the source code by invoking the `getJavaInitializationString()` method, which returns the text of the selected value enclosed by double-quote symbols.

The builder tool does not recognize the custom editors unless they are described in the `BeanInfo` class. The customer editor should be stored in the same directory with the `BeanInfo` class. The `setPropertyEditor(editorClassName)` of a `PropertyDescriptor` object sets the editor for the property. The following statements set the property editors for the properties `age` and `gender`:

```
pdsAge.setPropertyEditorClass(AgeEditor.class);
pdsGender.setPropertyEditorClass(GenderEditor.class);
```

The `FeatureDescriptor` Class

The `FeatureDescriptor` class is the common base class for the bean descriptor classes, such as `PropertyDescriptor`, `EventSetDescriptor`, and `MethodDescriptor`. The following methods of the `FeatureDescriptor` class are often used to set and retrieve common information for any of the introspection descriptors in the `BeanInfo` class.

■   `public void setHidden(boolean hidden)`

This method specifies whether the property is hidden. By default it is not hidden. A hidden property is not displayed in the builder tool. In JBuilder, you can right-click the Inspector and set Property Exposure Level hidden to reveal hidden properties of the component.

■   `public void setDisplayName(String displayName)`

This method sets a display name for this feature. For example, you can use it to set a display name for a property descriptor. This name is displayed as a tool tip in the Inspector.

■   `public void setValue(String attributeName, Object value)`

Associate a named attribute with this feature. You can use it to associate string values to an enumeration property.

Using the Bean Designer to Create Property Editors and Generate BeanInfo Classes

You can use the Bean Designer to create property editor templates and generate the BeanInfo class automatically, as demonstrated in the following example. You can then modify the BeanInfo class if necessary to insert additionally features.

Example 11.4 Creating the TimeZoneIDEditor **and the** BeanInfo **Class for the** Clock **Component**

The Clock component in Example 4.1, "Creating a Clock Component," contains a timeZoneID property. In this example, you will create a drop-down menu for the timeZoneID property so that the user can select a timeZoneID from a list of available IDs.

Here are the steps in creating a property editor named TimeZoneIDEditor.

1. Open Project ClockDemo.jpr. With Clock.java selected in the Navigation pane, choose the Bean tab in the Content pane to switch to the Bean Designer.

2. In the Bean Designer, choose the Property Editor tab to create or import property editors. Click "Create Custom Property Editor" to bring up the New Property Editor dialog box, as shown in Figure 11.7.

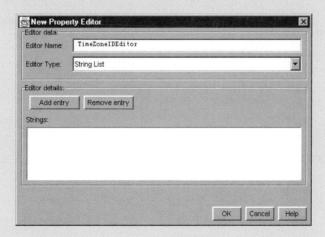

Figure 11.7 *You can use the New Property Editor dialog box to create templates for property editors.*

continues

---

3. Type TimeZoneIDEditor in the Editor Name field, and choose String List in the Editor Type. Click OK to generate TimeZoneIDEditor.java, as shown in Figure 11.8.

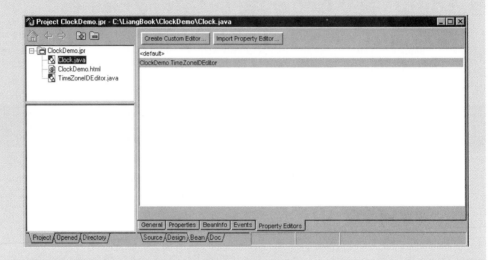

Figure 11.8   *The* TimeZoneIDEditor *was created by the Bean Designer.*

4. Select TimeZoneIDEditor.java in the Navigation pane, and modify the getTags() method to return a list of available time zone IDs, as shown in Listing 11.8.

5. With Clock.java selected in the Navigation pane, choose the BeanInfo tab in the Bean Designer to generate the BeanInfo class. Check the option "Expose superclass BeanInfo" to expose all the properties and events in the superclass of Clock, as shown in Figure 11.9. In the Editor column, choose TimeZoneIDEditor for the timeZoneID property. In the Display Name column for the property running, type "Enable the clock to run." The Display Name is a ToolTip for the property in the Component Inspector. In the Icons section, choose clock16.gif and clock32.gif for the respective color icons.

6. Click the button "Generate Bean Info" to generate ClockBeanInfo.

7. Modify the generated ClockBeanInfo class to add the feature for displaying enumeration values for the properties dateStyle and timeStyle using the setValue() method in the FeatureDescriptor class, as shown in Listing 11.9.

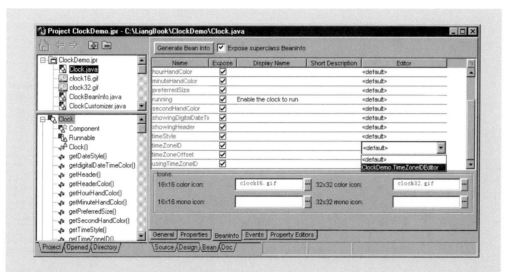

Figure 11.9   *The Bean Designer can automatically generate the* BeanInfo *class.*

```
package ClockDemo;

import java.beans.*;
import java.util.TimeZone;

public class TimeZoneIDEditor extends PropertyEditorSupport
{
  public TimeZoneIDEditor()
  {
  }

  public String[] getTags()
  {
    return TimeZone.getAvailableIDs();
  }

  public String getJavaInitializationString()
  {
    return "\"" + getAsText() + "\"";
  }

  public void setAsText(String text) throws IllegalArgumentException
  {
    setValue(text);
  }
}
```

continues

Listing 11.8   *TimeZoneIDEditor.java*

```
package ClockDemo;

import java.beans.*;

public class ClockBeanInfo extends SimpleBeanInfo
{
  Class beanClass = Clock.class;
  String iconColor16x16Filename = "clock16.gif";
  String iconColor32x32Filename = "clock32.gif";
  String iconMono16x16Filename;
  String iconMono32x32Filename;

  public ClockBeanInfo()
  {
  }

  // Specify the customizer, which will be introduced in Example 11.6
  public BeanDescriptor getBeanDescriptor()
  {
    return new BeanDescriptor(Clock.class, ClockCustomizer.class);
  }


  public PropertyDescriptor[] getPropertyDescriptors()
  {
    try
    {
      PropertyDescriptor _dateStyle = new PropertyDescriptor
        ("dateStyle", beanClass, "getDateStyle", "setDateStyle");
      PropertyDescriptor _digitalDateTimeColor =
        new PropertyDescriptor("digitalDateTimeColor", beanClass,
          "getDigitalDateTimeColor", "setDigitalDateTimeColor");
      PropertyDescriptor _header = new PropertyDescriptor
        ("header", beanClass, "getHeader", "setHeader");
      PropertyDescriptor _headerColor = new PropertyDescriptor
        ("headerColor", beanClass, "getHeaderColor",
         "setHeaderColor");
      PropertyDescriptor _hourHandColor = new PropertyDescriptor
        ("hourHandColor", beanClass,
         "getHourHandColor", "setHourHandColor");
      PropertyDescriptor _minuteHandColor = new PropertyDescriptor
        ("minuteHandColor", beanClass,
         "getMinuteHandColor", "setMinuteHandColor");
      PropertyDescriptor _preferredSize = new PropertyDescriptor
        ("preferredSize", beanClass, "getPreferredSize", null);
      PropertyDescriptor _running = new PropertyDescriptor
        ("running", beanClass, "isRunning", "setRunning");
      running.setDisplayName("Enable the clock to run");
      PropertyDescriptor _secondHandColor = new PropertyDescriptor
        ("secondHandColor", beanClass,
         "getSecondHandColor", "setSecondHandColor");
      PropertyDescriptor _showingDigitalDateTime =
        new PropertyDescriptor
        ("showingDigitalDateTime", beanClass,
         "isShowingDigitalDateTime", "setShowingDigitalDateTime");
      PropertyDescriptor _showingHeader = new PropertyDescriptor
        ("showingHeader", beanClass,
         "isShowingHeader", "setShowingHeader");
      PropertyDescriptor _timeStyle =
        new PropertyDescriptor("timeStyle",
        beanClass, "getTimeStyle", "setTimeStyle");
```

Listing 11.9   *ClockBeanInfo.java*

```
          PropertyDescriptor _timeZoneID = new PropertyDescriptor
            ("timeZoneID", beanClass, "getTimeZoneID", "setTimeZoneID");
          timeZoneID.setPropertyEditorClass
            (ClockDemo.TimeZoneIDEditor.class);
          PropertyDescriptor _timeZoneOffset = new PropertyDescriptor
            ("timeZoneOffset", beanClass,
              "getTimeZoneOffset", "setTimeZoneOffset");
          PropertyDescriptor _usingTimeZoneID = new PropertyDescriptor
            ("usingTimeZoneID", beanClass,
              "isUsingTimeZoneID", "setUsingTimeZoneID");

          // Set the enumeration values in the timeStyle property
          timeStyle.setValue("enumerationValues", new Object[] {
            "FULL - 0", new Integer(0), "0",
            "LONG - 1", new Integer(1), "1",
            "MEDIUM - 2", new Integer(2), "2",
            "SHORT - 3", new Integer(3), "3",
          });

          // Set the enumeration values in the dateStyle property
          dateStyle.setValue("enumerationValues", new Object[] {
            "FULL - 0", new Integer(0), "0",
            "LONG - 1", new Integer(1), "1",
            "MEDIUM - 2", new Integer(2), "2",
            "SHORT - 3", new Integer(3), "3",
          });

          PropertyDescriptor[] pds = new PropertyDescriptor[] {
            dateStyle,
            digitalDateTimeColor,
            header,
            headerColor,
            hourHandColor,
            minuteHandColor,
            preferredSize,
            running,
            secondHandColor,
            showingDigitalDateTime,
            showingHeader,
            timeStyle,
            timeZoneID,
            timeZoneOffset,
            usingTimeZoneID,};
          return pds;
        }
        catch(IntrospectionException ex)
        {
          ex.printStackTrace();
          return null;
        }
      }

      // Expose PME( Properties, Methods, and Events) in the superclass
      public BeanInfo[] getAdditionalBeanInfo()
      {
        Class superclass = beanClass.getSuperclass();
        try
        {
          BeanInfo superBeanInfo = Introspector.getBeanInfo(superclass);
```

continues

Listing 11.9   *Continued*

```
          return new BeanInfo[] { superBeanInfo };
        }
        catch(IntrospectionException ex)
        {
          ex.printStackTrace();
          return null;
        }
    }
  }
```

Listing 11.9   *Continued*

Example Review

Since you chose the String List as the Editor Type for the property editor in the New Property Editor dialog box in Figure 11.7, the Bean Designer generates the TimeZoneIDEditor.java with a default getTags() method for displaying the timeZoneID property in a drop-down choice menu. The getTags() method returns a list of available time zone IDs, which can be obtained using the TimeZone.getAvailableIDs() method.

The ClockBeanInfo class was completely generated with no coding. The getAdditionalBeanInfo() method in the BeanInfo interface allows a BeanInfo object to return an arbitrary collection of other BeanInfo objects that provide additional information on the current bean. In this example, it returns the BeanInfo object of its superclass. If there are conflicts or overlaps between the information provided by different BeanInfo objects, then the current BeanInfo takes precedence over the getAdditionalBeanInfo objects, and later elements in the array take precedence over earlier ones.

The setDisplayName() method of a PropertyDescriptor object sets a ToolTip for property. You can see the ToolTip in the Component Inspector, as shown in Figure 11.10.

The setDisplayName() is actually defined in the FeatureDescriptor class, which is a base class for PropertyDescriptor, EventSetDescriptor, and MethodDescriptor. It supports some common information that can be set and retrieved for any of the introspection descriptors. In addition to setting a ToolTip using the setDisplayName() method, you can use the setValue() method in the FeatureDescriptor class to associate a property value with a string representing the value in the Component Inspector. For example, you can associate the dateStyle property values with strings using the following statement:

```
dateStyle.setValue("enumerationValues",
  new Object[]
  {
    "FULL - 0", new Integer(0), "0",
    "LONG - 1", new Integer(1), "1",
    "MEDIUM - 2", new Integer(2), "2",
    "SHORT - 3", new Integer(3), "3",
  });
```

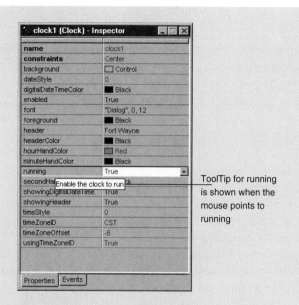

ToolTip for running
is shown when the
mouse points to
running

Figure 11.10 *The Display Name "Enable the clock to run" for the* running *property is shown as a ToolTip in the Component Inspector.*

You will see strings "FULL - 0," "LONG - 1," "MEDIUM - 2," and "SHORT - 3" in the value field of dateStyle as a drop-down choice menu, as shown in Figure 11.11.

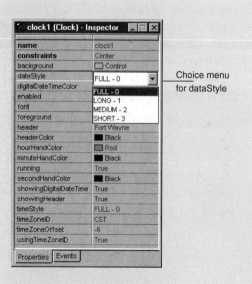

Choice menu
for dataStyle

Figure 11.11 *The* dateStyle *property values (0, 1, 2, 3) are represented by strings in a drop-down choice menu.*

> **NOTE**
> JBuilder's Bean Designer does not work with properties and events that vio-
> late the standard naming conventions. You cannot use the Bean Designer to
> generate a `BeanInfo` class that contains nonstandard properties or events.

Creating GUI Custom Editors

While standard editors, customized simple editors, or enumeration-type editors
will meet most of your needs, there are situations in which you might want to use
more specialized and elaborated editors. For example, the `Color` editor allows you
to choose colors visually for a property of the `Color` type. The property with advanced editors appears in the Component Inspector with an ellipsis at the right of
the value column when the property is selected. The editor pops up a GUI component when the user clicks the ellipsis. Therefore, the advanced editor is also referred to as a *popup property editor*, or GUI property editor.

To create a GUI property editor like the `Color` editor, override the methods
`supportsCustomEditor()` and `getCustomEditor()` in addition to other methods in
the `PropertyEditorSupport` class that you may need to use.

By default, `supportsCustomEditor()` returns `false`. To use a GUI editor, this
method must return `true` to enable a builder tool to invoke the `getCustomEditor()`
method to start the GUI editor.

By default, `getCustomEditor()` returns `null`. You need to implement
`getCustomEditor()` to return a `Component` as the GUI editor. You need to create
a class that extends `Component` or a subclass of `Component` so that you can create
an object of this class and have it returned from the `getCustomEditor()` method.
JBuilder automatically creates a standard dialog box to hold the object, as in the
Color editor shown in Figure 11.12.

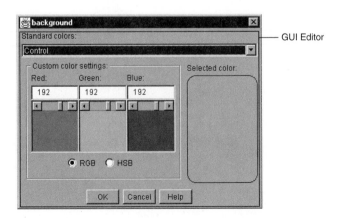

Figure 11.12   *The editor is placed in the dialog box created by JBuilder.*

The dialog window has three buttons: "OK," "Cancel," and "Help." "OK" signifies acceptance of the selected value, "Cancel" voids the selected value, and "Help" brings up the JBuilder Help Viewer.

Example 11.5 Creating GUI Property Editors

This example creates an editor for selecting an image file. The editor enables the user to browse a set of images and select one from the set. Suppose four images are available in the set. A sample run of the property editor is shown in Figure 11.13.

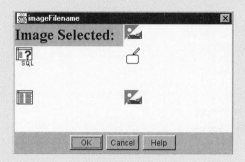

Figure 11.13   *The user selects an image by pointing the mouse, double-clicking on the image, and pressing OK.*

The example involves the following classes:

ImageViewer—the component for displaying an image. This component extends java.awt.Component and contains two properties, imageFilename and stretched. The imageFilename property specifies the filename for the image to be displayed. The stretched property indicates whether the image is stretched to fill in the entire viewing area. The complete code of this class is shown in Listing 11.9.

ImageFilenameEditor—the property editor for imageFilename. This class extends PropertyEditorSupport and contains an object of ImageFilenameGUIEditor as the GUI editor. The complete code of this class is shown in List-ing 11.10.

ImageFilenameGUIEditor—the GUI component for choosing imageFilename. This class extends JPanel and implements MouseListener. It displays four images for selection using the mouse. An instance of this class is returned from the getCustomEditor() method. A builder tool invokes getCustomEditor() to get the GUI editor and display it from the Component Inspector. The complete code of this class is shown in Listing 11.11.

continues

ImageViewerBeanInfo—the BeanInfo class for ImageViewer. This class describes all the properties of the ImageViewer class and the GUI property editor for imageFilename to the builder tool. This class can be generated using the Bean Designer. The complete code of this class is shown in Listing 11.12.

TestImageViewer—for testing the ImageViewer class and its supporting classes: ImageFilenameEditor, ImageFilenameGUIEditor, and ImageViewerBeanInfo.

```java
package GUIPropertyEditorDemo;

import java.awt.*;
import java.net.URL;
import java.awt.image.ImageProducer;

public class ImageViewer extends Component
{
  private Image currentImage = null;
  private String imageFilename = "";
  private boolean strectched;

  public void setImageFilename(String imageFilename)
  {
    this.imageFilename = imageFilename;
    Class myClass = getClass();
    try
    {
      URL url = myClass.getResource(imageFilename);
      currentImage = createImage((ImageProducer)url.getContent());
    }
    catch (Exception ex)
    { }
    repaint();
  }

  public String getImageFilename()
  {
    return imageFilename;
  }

  public void paint(Graphics g)
  {
    if (currentImage != null)
      if (isStrectched())
        g.drawImage(currentImage, 0, 0,
          getSize().width, getSize().height, this);
      else
        g.drawImage(currentImage, 0, 0, this);
  }

  public void setStrectched(boolean newStrectched)
  {
    strectched = newStrectched;
  }
```

Listing 11.9   *ImageViewer.java*

```
      public boolean isStrectched()
      {
        return strectched;
      }
    }
```

Listing 11.9   *Continued*

```
    package GUIPropertyEditorDemo;

    import java.awt.*;
    import java.beans.*;

    public class ImageFilenameEditor extends PropertyEditorSupport
    {
      private String imageFilename = "";
      private ImageFilenameGUIEditor guiEditor;

      public void setAsText(String text)
      {
        setValue(text);
      }

      public void setValue(Object o)
      {
        imageFilename = (String)o;
        if (guiEditor != null)
          guiEditor.imageFilename = imageFilename;

        firePropertyChange();
      }

      public Object getValue()
      {
        if (guiEditor != null)
          this.imageFilename = guiEditor.imageFilename;

        return imageFilename;
      }

      public String getAsText()
      {
        return imageFilename;
      }

      public boolean supportsCustomEditor()
      {
        return true;
      }

      public Component getCustomEditor()
      {
        if (guiEditor == null)
          guiEditor =  new ImageFilenameGUIEditor(imageFilename);
        return guiEditor;
      }
```

Listing 11.10   *ImageFilenameEditor.java*

```java
      public String getJavaInitializationString()
      {
        return "\"" + getAsText() + "\"";
      }
    }
```

Listing 11.10   *Continued*

```java
    package GUIPropertyEditorDemo;

    import java.awt.*;
    import java.awt.event.*;
    import javax.swing.*;
    import javax.swing.border.*;

    public class ImageFilenameGUIEditor extends JPanel
      implements MouseListener
    {
      private ImageViewer selectedImageViewer = new ImageViewer();
      String imageFilename = "";

      public ImageFilenameGUIEditor(String imageFilename)
      {
        // Create panel p for holding images for selection
        JPanel p = new JPanel();
        p.setLayout(new GridLayout(2, 2, 0, 0));
        p.setBorder(new TitledBorder("Choose an Image"));

        // Place images in the panel p
        ImageViewer[] ImageViewer = new ImageViewer[4];
        for (int i=0; i<4; i++)
        {
          ImageViewer[i] = new ImageViewer();
          ImageViewer[i].addMouseListener(this);
          p.add(ImageViewer[i]);
        }

        ImageViewer[0].setImageFilename("query.gif");
        ImageViewer[1].setImageFilename("shape.gif");
        ImageViewer[2].setImageFilename("table.gif");
        ImageViewer[3].setImageFilename("trimage.gif");

        // Panel p1 for organizing the selected image
        JPanel p1 = new JPanel();
        p1.setLayout(new GridLayout(1, 2, 0, 0));

        // Create a label
        JLabel jlbl;
        p1.add(jlbl = new JLabel("Image Selected:"));
        jlbl.setFont(new Font("TimesRoman", Font.BOLD, 24));

        // Create selectedImageViewer
        selectedImageViewer.setBackground(Color.yellow);
        selectedImageViewer.setImageFilename(imageFilename);
        p1.add(selectedImageViewer);

        // Place p and p1 in the main panel
        this.setLayout(new BorderLayout());
        this.add("North", p1);
```

Listing 11.11   *ImageFilenameGUIEditor.java*

496

```
            this.add("Center", p);
          }
          public Dimension getPreferredSize()
          {
            return new Dimension(350, 150);
          }

          public void mouseClicked(MouseEvent e)
          {
            ImageViewer imageViewer = (ImageViewer)e.getComponent();
            imageFilename = imageViewer.getImageFilename();
            selectedImageViewer.setImageFilename(imageFilename);
          }

          public void mousePressed(MouseEvent e)
          {  }

          public void mouseReleased(MouseEvent e)
          {  }

          public void mouseEntered(MouseEvent e)
          {  }

          public void mouseExited(MouseEvent e)
          {  }
        }
```

Listing 11.11 *Continued*

```
        package GUIPropertyEditorDemo;

        import java.beans.*;

        public class ImageViewerBeanInfo extends SimpleBeanInfo
        {
          Class beanClass = ImageViewer.class;
          String iconColor16x16Filename;
          String iconColor32x32Filename;
          String iconMono16x16Filename;
          String iconMono32x32Filename;


          public ImageViewerBeanInfo()
          {
          }

          public PropertyDescriptor[] getPropertyDescriptors()
          {
            try
            {
              PropertyDescriptor _imageFilename = new PropertyDescriptor
                ("imageFilename", beanClass, "getImageFilename",
                 "setImageFilename");
              imageFilename.setPropertyEditorClass
                (GUIPropertyEditorDemo.ImageFilenameEditor.class);

              PropertyDescriptor _strectched = new PropertyDescriptor
                ("strectched", beanClass, "isStrectched", "setStrectched");
```

continues

Listing 11.12 *ImageViewerBeanInfo.java*

```
            strectched.setDisplayName("strectched");
            strectched.setShortDescription("strectched");

            PropertyDescriptor[] pds = new PropertyDescriptor[] {
              imageFilename,
              strectched,
            };
            return pds;
          }
          catch (IntrospectionException ex)
          {
            ex.printStackTrace();
            return null;
          }
        }

        public BeanInfo[] getAdditionalBeanInfo()
        {
          Class superclass = beanClass.getSuperclass();
          try
          {
            BeanInfo superBeanInfo = Introspector.getBeanInfo(superclass);
            return new BeanInfo[] { superBeanInfo };
          }
          catch (IntrospectionException ex)
          {
            ex.printStackTrace();
            return null;
          }
        }
      }
```

Listing 11.12 *Continued*

Follow the steps below to complete the example.

1. Create a new project named GUIPropertyEditorDemo.jpr.

2. Create and compile `ImageViewer`, `ImageFilenameEditor`, `ImageFilenameGUIEditor`, and `ImageViewerBeanInfo`, and install `ImageViewer` in the Component palette.

3. Create TestImageViewer.java using the Applet Wizard. With TestImageViewer.java selected in the Navigation pane, switch to the UI Designer. Drop a `JTabbedPane` from the Swing Containers page to the applet to create jTabbedPane1.

4. With jTabbedPane1 selected, drop an `ImageViewer` from the Component palette four times to create imageViewer1, imageViewer2, imageViewer3, and imageViewer4.

5. In the Inspector of imageViewer1, double-click the ellipsis button in the value field of the imageFilename property to display the editor for imageFilename, as shown in Figure 11.13. Double-click the first image icon and then press OK; you will see the new image displayed in

imageViewer1 and imageViewer1.setImageFilename("query.gif") inserted in the jbInit() method. Set the stretched property to true so that the image is stretched to cover the entire viewing area, as shown in Figure 11.14.

6. Repeat Step 5 for imageViewer2, imageViewer3, and imageViewer4, choose an image from the editor, and set the stretched property to true.

Figure 11.14   *The* imageFilename *is selected from a GUI property editor, which is shown in Figure 11.13.*

7. Run the program. Select four tabs in the tab set panel to see the images. The complete code for TestImageViewer.java is shown in Listing 11.13.

```java
package GUIPropertyEditorDemo;

import java.awt.*;
import java.awt.event.*;
import java.applet.*;
import javax.swing.*;

public class TestImageViewer extends JApplet
{
  boolean isStandalone = false;
  JTabbedPane jTabbedPane1 = new JTabbedPane();
  ImageViewer imageViewer1 = new ImageViewer();
  ImageViewer imageViewer2 = new ImageViewer();
  ImageViewer imageViewer3 = new ImageViewer();
  ImageViewer imageViewer4 = new ImageViewer();

  // Construct the applet
  public TestImageViewer()
  {
  }
```

continues

Listing 11.13   *TestImageViewer.java*

```
      // Initialize the applet
      public void init()
      {
        try
        {
        jbInit();
        }
        catch (Exception e)
        {
        e.printStackTrace();
        }
      }

      // Component initialization
      private void jbInit() throws Exception
      {
        this.setSize(400,300);
        imageViewer1.setStrectched(true);
        imageViewer2.setStrectched(true);
        imageViewer3.setStrectched(true);
        imageViewer4.setStrectched(true);
        imageViewer4.setImageFilename("trimage.gif");
        imageViewer3.setImageFilename("table.gif");
        imageViewer2.setImageFilename("shape.gif");
        imageViewer1.setImageFilename("query.gif");
        this.getContentPane().add(jTabbedPane1, BorderLayout.CENTER);
        jTabbedPane1.addTab("imageViewer1", imageViewer1);
        jTabbedPane1.addTab("imageViewer2", imageViewer2);
        jTabbedPane1.addTab("imageViewer3", imageViewer3);
        jTabbedPane1.addTab("imageViewer4", imageViewer4);
      }
    }
```

Listing 11.13 *Continued*

Example Review

The `ImageViewer` component displays an image stored in the file named `imageFilename`. The code reproduced below creates the image.

```
Class myClass = getClass();
try
{
  URL url = myClass.getResource(imageFilename);
  currentImage = createImage((ImageProducer)url.getContent());
}
catch (Exception ex) {}
```

The `Class` class's `getResource()` method gets the address of the image. The `ImageProducer` produces image data, and the `createImage()` method creates an image from the specified image producer.

Since `ImageViewer` extends `Component`, it can be used with AWT components as well as Swing components.

The `ImageFilenameEditor` class, extending `PropertyEditorSupport`, facilitates intercommunication between the GUI property editor and the builder tool, as shown in Figure 11.15.

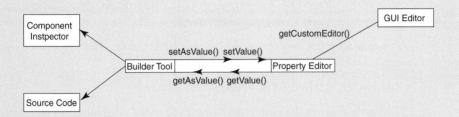

Figure 11.15   *The user selects an image from the GUI editor; the builder tool displays the image file name on the Component Inspector and updates the source code for setting the image in* `jbInit()`.

Since `supportsCustomEditor()` returns `true`, the GUI property editor `guiEditor` (an instance of `ImageFilenameGUIEditor`) is used for editing `guiEditor.image-Filename`, which lets the user choose an image graphically and sets the corresponding file name for the image in `guiEditor.imageFilename`.

The `getValue()` method returns the `imageFilename` value chosen from the `guiEditor` instance, and `getAsText()` returns `imageFilename` as a string. The `setAsText()` method invokes `setValue()` to set `imageFilename` from the Component Inspector to `guiEditor.imageFilename`.

The `ImageViewerBeanInfo` class describes the `imageFilename` property of the `ImageViewer` class and specifies its custom editor `ImageFilenameEditor`.

`TestImageViewer` uses a `JTabbedPane` to hold four instances of `ImageViewer`. `ImageFilenameEditor`, `ImageFilenameGUIEditor`, and `ImageViewerBeanInfo` classes are used only during design time and are not needed at runtime.

Creating Component Customizers

Bean properties can be edited with default property editors, custom property editors, or GUI property editors. Property editors enable you to edit single property values in the Component Inspector, so that all the properties are edited independently. Some properties, however, are related. The value of one property may affect the selection of the values of other properties. For example, the `Clock` component contains properties `showingDigitalDateTime`, `dateStyle`, and `timeStyle`. These three properties are related. You do not have to set `dateStyle` and `timeStyle` if `showingDigitalDateTime` is false. It would be nice to disable the selection of `dateStyle` and `timeStyle` when `showingDigitalDateTime` is false. This feature cannot be implemented by property editors, but it can be done with customizers.

A customizer is a GUI component that makes it possible to edit a group of properties at once. You can implement the rules of editing in a customizer to edit the properties interactively. A customizer is usually a panel displayed in a dialog box created by the builder tool. The dialog box in JBuilder is similar to the one used by the GUI property editor. A customizer is not limited to just one window. You can create many wizard-like dialog boxes to collect information from the user and edit the properties based on the user's responses.

A customizer must implement the `Customizer` interface. The `Customizer` interface contains the following three methods:

- `public abstract void setObject(Object bean)`

This method passes the bean to be customized to the customizer, so that it can find the state of the bean, update the bean, and interact with the bean. The builder tool starts a customizer by invoking this method.

- `public abstract void addPropertyChangeListener(PropertyChangeListener listener)`

This method registers a listener for the `PropertyChange` event. When a build tool starts a customizer, it creates an instance of the customizer and registers a listener to listen for property changes by invoking this method. Whenever a property is changed, the customizer should fire a `PropertyChange` event to notify the builder tool so that it can update the bean accordingly.

- `public abstract void removePropertyChangeListener(PropertyChangeListener listener)`

This method removes a listener for the `PropertyChange` event.

By convention, the name of a customizer should be the same as the name of the component it customizes with "Customizer" appended to it. For example, if your component is named `Clock`, the customizer should be named `ClockCustomizer`. Following this naming convention, a customizer can be automatically recognized by builder tools without the need to create a `BeanInfo` class. If a `BeanInfo` class is used to describe a component, you have to specify the name of the customizer in the `getBeanDescriptor()` method. For example, since you created `ClockBeanInfo` for the `Clock` class, you must implement the `getBeanDescriptor()` method in the `ClockBeanInfo` class, as follows:

```
public BeanDescriptor getBeanDescriptor()
{
  return new BeanDescriptor(Clock.class, ClockCustomizer.class);
}
```

Finally, how does a user start a customizer? It depends on the builder tool. In JBuilder, you can start the customizer in the following steps:

1. Select the bean in the UI Designer.

2. Right-click the mouse button to display a popup menu.

3. Choose the Customizer item from the popup menu. (If the bean does not have a customizer, this item will not be shown in the menu.)

Example 11.6 Creating a Customizer for the Clock Component

In this example, a customizer is created to set values for properties showingDigitalDateTime, dateStyle, and timeStyle in the Clock component, as shown in Figure 11.16.

Figure 11.16 *This customizer enables you to set values for properties that specify whether and how to display a digital date and time in a clock.*

Follow the steps below to complete the example.

1. Reopen the ClockDemo project, and create ClockCustomizer that extends JPanel using the JavaBean Wizard.

2. In the UI Designer for ClockCustomizer, set the layout of the panel (this) to BorderLayout. Drop a JCheckBox to the south of the panel to create jCheckBox1.

3. Drop a JPanel to the center of the panel to create jPanel1 with GridLayout. Drop a JPanel twice into jPanel1 to create jPanel2 and jPanel3. Rename jPanel2 to jpDateStyle, jPanel3 to jpTimeStyle. In the Inspector for jpDateStyle, select titled from the drop-down choice menu for the border property to create titleBorder1. titleBorder1 is an instance of TitleBorder and appears under the Other node in the Component tree. In the Inspector for titleBorder1, change the title to "Date Style." Similarly, create a border titled "Time Style" for jpTimeStyle.

4. With jpDateStyle selected in the Component tree, set its layout to GridLayout with four rows. Drop a JRadioButton four times to jpDateStyle to create jRadioButton1, jRadioButton2, jRadioButton3, and jRadioButton4. Set the text property of the buttons to Full, LONG, MEDIUM, and SHORT, respectively. Similarly, you can add four JRadioButton named jRadioButton5, jRadioButton6, jRadioButton7, and jRadioButton8 with text FULL, LONG, MEDIUM, and SHORT into the jpTimeStyle panel.

5. Declare and create two instances of ButtonGroup, named buttonGroup1 and buttonGroup2. Group the date style radio buttons in buttonGroup1

continues

and group the time style radio buttons in groupButton2 using the add() method, as shown in Listing 11.14.

6. Implement the java.beans.Customizer interface using the Implement Interface Wizard to generate methods setObject(), addPropertyChangeListener(), and removePropertyChangeListener(). Declare and create an instance of PropertyChangeSupport, and complete these methods as shown in Listing 11.14.

7. Implement the ItemListener interface using the Implement Interface Wizard. Register the customizer (this) as the listener for all the radio buttons and the check box. Implement the itemStateChanged() handler to process the change of the state of the check box and eight radio buttons, as shown in Listing 11.14.

```java
package ClockDemo;

import java.awt.*;
import javax.swing.*;
import javax.swing.border.*;
import java.awt.event.*;
import java.text.DateFormat;
import java.beans.*;

public class ClockCustomizer extends JPanel
  implements Customizer, ItemListener
{
  // **variables declared manually
  // Declare a variable for notifying property change
  PropertyChangeSupport pcs = null;
  // Declare buttonGroup1 to group date style radio buttons
  ButtonGroup buttonGroup1 = new ButtonGroup();
  // Declare buttonGroup2 to group time style radio buttons
  ButtonGroup buttonGroup2= new ButtonGroup();
  // Declare a variable for Clock
  Clock clock = null;

  // —Variables created automatically
  BorderLayout borderLayout1 = new BorderLayout();
  JCheckBox jCheckBox1 = new JCheckBox();
  JPanel jPanel1 = new JPanel();
  GridLayout gridLayout1 = new GridLayout();
  JPanel jpDateStyle = new JPanel();
  JPanel jpTimeStyle = new JPanel();
  TitledBorder titledBorder1;
  TitledBorder titledBorder2;
  JRadioButton jRadioButton1 = new JRadioButton();
  JRadioButton jRadioButton2 = new JRadioButton();
  JRadioButton jRadioButton3 = new JRadioButton();
  JRadioButton jRadioButton4 = new JRadioButton();
  JRadioButton jRadioButton5 = new JRadioButton();
  JRadioButton jRadioButton6 = new JRadioButton();
  JRadioButton jRadioButton7 = new JRadioButton();
  JRadioButton jRadioButton8 = new JRadioButton();
```

Listing 11.14 *ClockCustomizer.java*

```
GridLayout gridLayout2 = new GridLayout();
GridLayout gridLayout3 = new GridLayout();

public ClockCustomizer()
{ // Delete the code for invoking jbInit() here.
  // jbInit() should be invoked from setObject(),
  // because setObject() before invoking jbInit().
}

private void jbInit() throws Exception
{
  titledBorder1 = new TitledBorder("Date Style");
  titledBorder2 = new TitledBorder("Time Style");
  jpTimeStyle.setLayout(gridLayout3);
  jpTimeStyle.setBorder(titledBorder2);
  jRadioButton1.setText("FULL");
  jRadioButton2.setText("LONG");
  jRadioButton3.setText("MEDIUM");
  jRadioButton3.setName("");
  jRadioButton4.setText("SHORT");
  jRadioButton5.setText("FULL");
  jRadioButton6.setText("LONG");
  jRadioButton7.setText("MEDIUM");
  jRadioButton8.setText("SHORT");
  jpDateStyle.setBorder(titledBorder1);
  jpDateStyle.setLayout(gridLayout2);
  jCheckBox1.setText("Show Digital Time");
  jCheckBox1.setHorizontalAlignment(0);
  gridLayout1.setHgap(5);
  jPanel1.setLayout(gridLayout1);
  this.setLayout(borderLayout1);
  gridLayout2.setRows(4);
  gridLayout3.setRows(4);
  this.add(jCheckBox1, BorderLayout.SOUTH);
  this.add(jPanel1, BorderLayout.CENTER);
  jPanel1.add(jpDateStyle, null);
  jpDateStyle.add(jRadioButton1, null);
  jpDateStyle.add(jRadioButton2, null);
  jpDateStyle.add(jRadioButton3, null);
  jpDateStyle.add(jRadioButton4, null);
  jPanel1.add(jpTimeStyle, null);
  jpTimeStyle.add(jRadioButton5, null);
  jpTimeStyle.add(jRadioButton6, null);
  jpTimeStyle.add(jRadioButton7, null);
  jpTimeStyle.add(jRadioButton8, null);

  // Group date style radio buttons
  buttonGroup1.add(jRadioButton1);
  buttonGroup1.add(jRadioButton2);
  buttonGroup1.add(jRadioButton3);
  buttonGroup1.add(jRadioButton4);

  // Group date style radio buttons
  buttonGroup2.add(jRadioButton5);
  buttonGroup2.add(jRadioButton6);
  buttonGroup2.add(jRadioButton7);
  buttonGroup2.add(jRadioButton8);

  // Register listeners
  jRadioButton1.addItemListener(this);
```

continues

```
        jRadioButton2.addItemListener(this);
        jRadioButton3.addItemListener(this);
        jRadioButton4.addItemListener(this);
        jRadioButton5.addItemListener(this);
        jRadioButton6.addItemListener(this);
        jRadioButton7.addItemListener(this);
        jRadioButton8.addItemListener(this);
        jCheckBox1.addItemListener(this);
    }

    public void setObject(Object bean)
    {
        //TODO: implement this java.beans.Customizer method;
        //jbInit() is fired from here instead of the constructor because
        //it is assumed in the Beans Spec that setObject() is called
          first.
        try { jbInit(); } catch (Exception e) { e.printStackTrace(); }

        if(bean instanceof Clock)
        {
            clock = (Clock)bean;

            jCheckBox1.setSelected(clock.isShowingDigitalDateTime());

            switch (clock.getDateStyle())
            {
                case 0: jRadioButton1.setSelected(true); break;
                case 1: jRadioButton2.setSelected(true); break;
                case 2: jRadioButton3.setSelected(true); break;
                case 3: jRadioButton4.setSelected(true); break;
            }

            switch (clock.getTimeStyle())
            {
                case 0: jRadioButton5.setSelected(true); break;
                case 1: jRadioButton6.setSelected(true); break;
                case 2: jRadioButton7.setSelected(true); break;
                case 3: jRadioButton8.setSelected(true); break;
            }
        }
    }

    // Required by implementation of Customizer Interface
    public void addPropertyChangeListener(PropertyChangeListener parm1)
    {
        if (pcs == null)
            pcs = new PropertyChangeSupport(this);
        pcs.addPropertyChangeListener(parm1);
    }

    // Required by implementation of Customizer Interface
    public void removePropertyChangeListener
        (PropertyChangeListener parm1)
    {
        if (pcs != null)
            pcs.removePropertyChangeListener(parm1);
    }
```

Listing 11.14 *Continued*

```
public void itemStateChanged(ItemEvent e)
{
  if (e.getSource() instanceof JCheckBox)
  {
    if (clock != null)
      clock.setShowingDigitalDateTime(jCheckBox1.isSelected());
    if (pcs != null)
      pcs.firePropertyChange("showingDigitalDateTime",
        new Boolean(!jCheckBox1.isSelected()),
        new Boolean(jCheckBox1.isSelected()));

    // Enable radio buttons for date style and time style
    // if showingDigitalDateTime is checked
    if (jCheckBox1.isSelected())
    {
      jRadioButton1.setEnabled(true);
      jRadioButton2.setEnabled(true);
      jRadioButton3.setEnabled(true);
      jRadioButton4.setEnabled(true);
      jRadioButton5.setEnabled(true);
      jRadioButton6.setEnabled(true);
      jRadioButton7.setEnabled(true);
      jRadioButton8.setEnabled(true);
    }
    else
    {
      jRadioButton1.setEnabled(false);
      jRadioButton2.setEnabled(false);
      jRadioButton3.setEnabled(false);
      jRadioButton4.setEnabled(false);
      jRadioButton5.setEnabled(false);
      jRadioButton6.setEnabled(false);
      jRadioButton7.setEnabled(false);
      jRadioButton8.setEnabled(false);
    }
  }
  else // A radio button is changed
  {
    int currentDateStyle = clock.getDateStyle();
    int newDateStyle = currentDateStyle;

    if (jRadioButton1.isSelected())
      newDateStyle = 0;
    else if (jRadioButton2.isSelected())
      newDateStyle = 1;
    else if (jRadioButton3.isSelected())
      newDateStyle = 2;
    else if (jRadioButton4.isSelected())
      newDateStyle = 3;

    clock.setDateStyle(newDateStyle);
    if (pcs != null)
      pcs.firePropertyChange("dateStyle",
        new Integer(currentDateStyle), new Integer(newDateStyle));

    int currentTimeStyle = clock.getTimeStyle();
    int newTimeStyle = currentTimeStyle;

    if (jRadioButton5.isSelected())
      newTimeStyle = 0;
```

continues

```
              else if (jRadioButton6.isSelected())
                newTimeStyle = 1;
              else if (jRadioButton7.isSelected())
                newTimeStyle = 2;
              else if (jRadioButton8.isSelected())
                newTimeStyle = 3;

              clock.setTimeStyle(newTimeStyle);
              if (pcs != null)
                pcs.firePropertyChange("timeStyle",
                  new Integer(currentTimeStyle), new Integer(newTimeStyle));
          }
        }
      }
```

Listing 11.14   *Continued*

Example Review

ClockCustomizer implements the Customizer interface. The setObject() method is invoked first by the builder tool when the customizer starts. For this reason, the statement for invoking the jbInit() statement is moved from the constructor to the setObject() method, so that you can initialize the customizer to display the current state of the clock passed from the builder tool. The implementation of addPropertyChangeListener() and removePropertyChange-Listener() involves registering and unregistering the listener with an instance of PropertyChangeSupport named pcs.

You could use the UI Designer to generate nine ItemEvent adapters for the check box and eight radio buttons. However, a more efficient way in this example is to use a single centralized adapter to handle all the item events from the check box and the radio buttons.

When a check box is unchecked, all the radio buttons are disabled, since there is no need to set date style or time style when the date and time are not displayed. Whenever a property is changed, the builder tool is notified by invoking pcs.firePropertyChange("propertyName", oldValue, newValue). The builder tool updates the bean property by generating a statement in the jbInit() method code using the property's setter method. To ensure that a change takes effect during design, you need to invoke the property's setter method in the customizer. For instance, the following code

```
    clock.setShowingDigitalDateTime(jCheckBox1.isSelected());
```

updates clock's showingDigitalDateTime property in the UI Designer.

The customizer is contained in a dialog box created by JBuilder. The dialog box contains an OK button and a Cancel button. You can close the customizer by clicking either of them. The functions of these two buttons are identical in the customizers, since the builder tool has already been notified of the property changes through the property change listener pcs. Recall that the OK and Cancel buttons in the dialog box for a GUI property editor are different. Clicking OK saves the editing change, whereas clicking Cancel does not.

Chapter Summary

This chapter introduced the JavaBeans API that a builder tool can use to discover the properties, methods, and events of a bean so that it can be manipulated visually during design time. You learned how to create custom property editors, GUI property editors, and customizers for editing bean properties. You also learned how to use the BeanInsight Wizard to inspect beans and the Bean Designer to create BeanInfo classes.

Chapter Review

11.1. Are the BeanInfo class, the property editor class, and the customizer class necessary at runtime?

11.2. How do you expose properties whose getter and setter methods do not follow standard naming patterns?

11.3. How do you expose events whose registration and removal methods do not follow standard naming patterns?

11.4. How do you programmatically inspect bean properties and events at runtime?

11.5. Describe the methods getAsText(), setAsText(), getValue(), setValue(), and getTags() in the PropertyEditor interface.

11.6. Describe the implementation of the PropertyEditorSupport class. How are the methods getAsText(), setAsText(), getValue(), setValue(), and getTags() implemented in the PropertyEditorSupport class?

11.7. How do you create a custom property editor to display property values in a choice menu in the Component Inspector?

11.8. How do you specify a custom property editor in the BeanInfo class?

11.9. Describe the role of the methods setDisplayName() and setValue() in the FeatureDescriptor class.

11.10. How do you create a property editor using the Bean Designer? How do you generate a BeanInfo class using the Bean Designer?

11.11. How should the methods getCustomEditor() and supportsCustomEditor() be implemented to create a GUI property editor? How do you start a GUI property editor in the Component Inspector? How is a GUI property displayed?

11.12. Describe the methods `setObject()`, `addPropertyChangeListener()`, and `removePropertyChangeListener()` in the `Customizer` interface. How do you start a customizer? How is a customizer displayed? How do you specify a customizer in the `BeanInfo` class?

Programming Exercises

11.1. The `CalendarControlBean` in the sixth exercise in Chapter 4, "Developing and Using Components," contains the `month` property and the `year` property. Both properties are `int` values. Create a property editor for the property `month` to display locale-sensitive month names in a choice menu, as shown in Figure 11.17, and create a property editor for the property `year` to display and validate `year` to ensure that `year` is nonnegative.

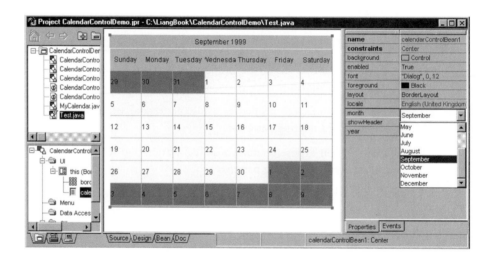

Figure 11.17   *The* month *property is displayed in a choice menu of month names.*

11.2. Create a GUI property editor for selecting colors just like the one used in JBuilder.

11.3. The Student class in Example 11.3 contains a property named `fullName`, which consists of first name, middle name, and last name. The entire full name must be edited once in the Component Inspector. Create a customizer for the Student class to enable the user to edit first name, middle name, and last name separately. The customizer is shown in Figure 11.18. The name labels are placed in a `JPanel` named `labelPanel` of GridLayout, and the text fields are placed in a `JPanel` named `textPanel` of GridLayout. `labelPanel` and textPanel are placed in a JPanel of BorderLayout, with labelPanel on the east and textPanel in the center. The Apply button applies the change to the bean, and the Revert button restores the original names in the bean.

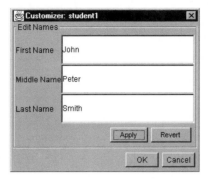

Figure 11.18   *The StudentCustomizer enables you to edit first name, middle name, and last name separately.*

PART IV

JAVA DATABASE PROGRAMMING

This part of the book discusses how to use Java to develop database projects. You will learn the Java database programming interface, create and process SQL statements, and use JBuilder database beans to rapidly develop Java database applications.

CHAPTER 12   INTRODUCTION TO JAVA DATABASE PROGRAMMING

CHAPTER 13   METADATA AND PROCESSING STATEMENTS

CHAPTER 14   APPLICATIONS USING JBUILDER DATAEXPRESS
AND DATA-AWARE COMPONENTS

INTRODUCTION TO JAVA DATABASE PROGRAMMING

Objectives

- ◉ Understand the architecture of JDBC.
- ◉ Know the four types of JDBC drivers.
- ◉ Become familiar with representative JDBC drivers.
- ◉ Be able to write simple JDBC programs.

Introduction

JDBC is a Java API that provides Java programmers with a uniform interface for accessing and manipulating a wide range of relational databases. Before JDBC, database clients were typically developed using Microsoft Visual Basic, Borland Delphi, and other development tools provided by database vendors, such as Power-Builder by Sybase and Oracle Developer 2000 by Oracle. These are excellent Rapid Application Development tools, but the programs developed with them can only run on certain platforms. With JDBC, you can write database programs that run on any platform that has a Java virtual machine with an appropriate JDBC driver.

The relationship among Java programs, JDBC API, JDBC drivers, and relational databases is shown in Figure 12.1. The JDBC API is a set of Java interfaces and classes used to write Java programs for accessing and manipulating relational data-bases. Since a JDBC driver serves as the interface to facilitate communications between JDBC and a proprietary database, JDBC drivers are database-specific. You need Oracle JDBC drivers to access Oracle database, and Sybase JDBC drivers to access Sybase database. Even for the same vendor, the drivers may be different for different versions of a database. For instance, the JDBC driver for Oracle 8 is different from the one for Oracle 7. A JDBC-ODBC bridge driver is included in JDK 1.2 to support Java programs that access databases through ODBC drivers.

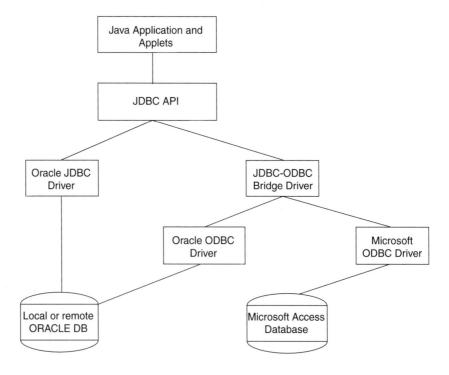

Figure 12.1   *Java programs access and manipulate databases through JDBC API and JDBC drivers.*

Overview of the JDBC API

The JDBC API is a Java application programming interface to generic SQL databases that enables Java developers to develop DBMS-independent Java applications using a uniform interface.

The JDBC API consists of classes and interfaces for establishing connections with databases, sending SQL statements to databases, and processing the results of the SQL statements. The JDBC interfaces and classes can be classified into types of driver, connection, statement, result set, and processing support, as shown in Table 12.1.

NOTE

JDBC is the trademarked name of a Java API that supports Java programs to access relational databases. JDBC is not an acronym, but it is often thought to stand for Java Database Connectivity.

TABLE 12.1   JDBC Classes

Type	*Class/Interface*
Driver management	java.sql.Driver (Interface)
	java.sql.DriverPropertyInfo
	java.sql.DriverManager
Establishing connections	java.sql.Connection (Interface)
Processing statements	java.sql.Statement (Interface)
	java.sql.PreparedStatement (Interface)
	java.sql.CallableStatement (Interface)
Handling result sets	java.sql.ResultSet (Interface)
Exceptions	java.sql.SQLException
	java.sql.SQLWarning
	java.sql.SQLTruncation
Support classes	java.sql.Date
	java.sql.Time
	java.sql.TimeStamp
	java.sql.Types

The interfaces define a framework for generic SQL database access. The JDBC driver vendors provide implementation for these interfaces. The relationship of these interfaces and classes is shown in Figure 12.2. A JDBC application loads an appropriate driver using the Driver interface, connects to the database using the Connection interface, creates and executes SQL statements using the Statement interface, and processes the result using the ResultSet interface.

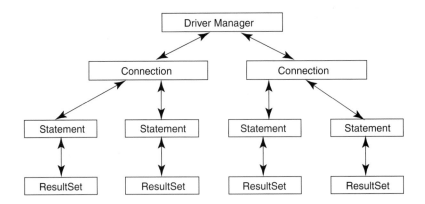

Figure 12.2 *JDBC classes enable Java programs to connect to the database, send SQL statements, and process results.*

Developing JDBC Applications

The JDBC interfaces and classes are the building blocks in the development of Java database programs. A typical Java program takes the following steps to access the database, as shown in Figure 12.2.

1. Loading drivers.

   JDBC allows multiple drivers to be loaded in one program. A program can load a JDBC driver at any time. For example, `MyDriver` is loaded with the following statement:

   ```
   Class.forName("MyDriver");
   ```

   The statement loads the driver. The driver is automatically registered with the driver manager. You may use `DriverManager.registerDrier()` to explicitly register a driver with the driver manager. For example, the following statement registers `MyDriver`.

   ```
   DriverManager.registerDriver(new MyDriver());
   ```

2. Establishing connections.

   Once the driver is loaded and registered with the driver manager, the `DriveManager` is capable of choosing an appropriate one from a list of registered drivers to fulfill the connection to the database. You simply invoke `DriverManager.getConnection()` to establish a session with the database. In the rare case that more than one driver is suitable to connect to a database and you want a particular driver to be chosen, the `connect()` method in a `Driver` object can be invoked directly to use the driver to connect to a given database.

3. Creating and executing statements.

   You can create SQL statements in three types: `Statement`, `PrepareStatement`, or `CallableStatement`. These can be executed using `executeQuery()`, `executeUpdate()`, or `execute()`. The result of the query is returned in `ResultSet`.

4. Processing `ResultSet`.

The `ResultSet` is a table whose rows are retrieved in sequence. You can use various get methods to retrieve values from a current row. The initial row is `null`, the `next()` method sets the current row to the first row in the table, and subsequent invocation of the `next()` method sets the current row to the second, third, and so on, to the last row.

Here is a simple example (see Listing 12.1) of connecting to a database, executing a simple query, and processing the query result.

```java
package SimpleJDBCDemo;

import java.sql.*;

public class SimpleJdbc
{
  public static void main(String args [])
    throws SQLException, ClassNotFoundException
  {
    // Load the JDBC driver
    Class.forName("sun.jdbc.odbc.JdbcOdbcDriver");
    System.out.println("Driver loaded");

    // Establish a connection
    Connection conn = DriverManager.getConnection
      ("jdbc:odbc:LiangBookDB_MDB", "", "" );
    System.out.println("Database connected");

    // Create a statement
    Statement stmt = conn.createStatement();

    // Select the columns from the STUDENT table
    ResultSet rset = stmt.executeQuery
      ("select FIRSTNAME, MI, LASTNAME from STUDENT");

    // Iterate through the result and print the student names
    while (rset.next())
      System.out.println(rset.getString(1)+" "+rset.getString(2)
        +". "+rset.getString(3));
  }
}
```

Listing 12.1   *SimpleJDBC.java*

The statement

```java
Class.forName("sun.jdbc.odbc.JdbcOdbcDriver")
```

loads the JdbcOdbcDriver for connecting to an ODBC data source, such as Microsoft Access Database. In Example 12.2, you will learn how to set up the ODBC data source to test this program.

The statement

```java
Connection conn = DriverManager.getConnection
  ("jdbc:odbc:LiangBookDB_MDB", "", "");
```

creates a `Connection` object `conn`, which represents a logical session for sending SQL statements and getting query results back from the database. You can create an instance of `Statement` for executing static queries as used in the example, create `PreparedStatement` for precompiled SQL statements, or create `CallableStatement` for executing stored procedures. Their applications are discussed in Chapter 13, "Metadata and Statements."

The statement

```
ResultSet rset = stmt.executeQuery
    ("select FIRSTNAME, MI, LASTNAME from STUDENT");
```

executes the query and returns the result in a `ResultSet` object, which can be perceived as a table of three columns consisting of FIRSTNAME, MI, and LAST-NAME. The `getString(1)`, `getString(2)`, and `getString(3)` methods retrieve the column values for FIRSTNAME, MI, and LASTNAME, respectively. Alternatively, you can use `getString("FIRSTNAME")`, `getString("MI")`, and `getString("LASTNAME")` to retrieve the same three column values.

The `Driver` Interface

The `Driver` interface is database-specific. The JDBC vendor should implement this interface and provide proprietary database information to enable Java programs to communicate with the database.

An appropriate driver must be loaded before your application can attempt to connect to a database. The driver can be loaded using the following statement.

```
Class.forName("TheDriverName")
```

This statement attempts to locate, load, and link the driver class. If it succeeds, it returns an anonymous `Class` object representing the driver class. You don't need to return an explicit driver reference, because each newly loaded driver is capable of registering itself with the `DriverManager`.

The driver is anonymous; you don't need to reference it explicitly to make a database connection. After the driver is registered, the `DriverManager` can use it to make database connections. If the driver is not found, the method throws a `Class-NotFoundException`.

The `DriverManager` Class

The `DriverManager` class, a layer of JDBC working between the driver and the user, is responsible for registering and managing the drivers. It serves as a ringmaster to keep track of all the registered drivers, establishing a connection between the database and an appropriate driver.

All the methods in `DriverManager` are static. A programmer can use its `getConnection()` method to get a connection to the database, which returns an object of Connection. For example, the following statement connects the database at specified url with username and password.

```
Connection con = DriverManager.getConnection(url, username, password);
```

The DriverPropertyInfo Class

The DriverPropertyInfo class is used by advanced programmers to manage specific properties of a Driver instance. It should be used only by developers who need to interact with a driver to discover and supply properties for connections.

The Connection Interface

A Connection instance represents a session with a specific database. In the context of a Connection instance, SQL statements are sent to the database for execution, and the results of the execution, if any, are returned. Think of a connection as a pipeline through which database transactions travel back and forth between your program and the database.

A Connection instance can be used to create various Statement objects for executing SQL statements and stored procedures using the createStatement() method. You can also use it to set transaction properties for the connection. By default the Connection instance automatically commits changes after executing each statement. If auto commit has been disabled, an explicit commit must be done or database changes will not be saved.

You can use the getMetaData() method to get an object of DataBaseMetaData that describes the connected database information on the tables, views, supported SQL grammar, stored procedures, and capabilities of this connection, etc. Chapter 13, "Database Metadata and Statements," gives an in-depth look on retrieving metadata.

The Statement, PreparedStatement, and CallableStatement Interfaces

The Statement, PreparedStatement, and CallableStatement interfaces are related in a hierarchical relationship. CallableStatement inherits PreparedStatement, which inherits Statement. These interfaces are used for sending SQL statements to the database for execution on a given connection. A Statement object is used to execute a static SQL statement; a PreparedStatement object is used to execute a precompiled SQL statement with or without IN parameters; and a callablestatement object is used to execute a call to a stored procedure in the database.

The executeQuery() method of the object is used if the statement is a SQL SELECT query, and the executeUpdate() method is used if the statement is a SQL INSERT, UPDATE, or DELETE and also a SQL DDL (Data Definition Language) statement like CREATE TABLE, CREATE VIEW, DROP TABLE, DROP VIEW.

The executeQuery() method returns the query result in a ResultSet object. Only one ResultSet per Statement can be open at any point in time. Therefore, if the reading of one ResultSet is interleaved with the reading of another, each must have been generated by different statements. All statement-execute methods implicitly close a statement's current ResultSet if an open one exists.

When executing a stored procedure, the execution may return multiple result sets. The execute() method should be used to execute the SQL statement in this case. You can then use getResultSet() or getUpdateCount() to retrieve the result, and getMoreResults() to move to the next result set.

The ResultSet Interface

A ResultSet provides access to a table of data generated by executing a statement. The table rows are retrieved in sequence. The column values within a row can be accessed in any order.

A ResultSet maintains a cursor pointing to its current row of data. Initially the cursor is positioned before the first row. The next() method moves the cursor to the next row. The first call to next() makes the first row the current row, the second call makes the second row the current row, etc.

Various get methods are provided to retrieve column values for the current row. You can retrieve values either by using the index number of the column or by using the name of the column. For example, to retrieve a column of the String type, you may use rs.getString("ColumnName"), where rs is an object of ResultSet.

The SQL Exception Classes

The JDBC methods may raise the SQLException, SQLWarning, and DataTrucation exceptions.

Almost all the methods in JDBC throw SQLException. The SQLException class provides information on a database access error. The SQLWarning exception, a subclass of SQLException, provides information on a database access warnings. Warnings are silently chained to the object whose method caused it to be reported. A SQLWarning exception may be ignored in order to allow the normal course of the execution to proceed. The DataTrucation exception is raised when JDBC unexpectedly truncates a data value.

The DatabaseMetaData Interface

The DatabaseMetaData interface enables you to obtain information about the database, such as tables, views, columns, primary keys, and foreign keys.

Many of these methods return the information in ResultSet. You can use the normal ResultSet methods, such as getString() and getInt(), to retrieve the data from these ResultSets. If a given form of metadata is not available, these methods should throw a SQLException. For example, to find all the catalogs in the database, you can use the getCatalogs() method to return a list of catalogs in an object of ResultSet, then retrieve all the catalogs from the result set.

The `ResultSetMetaData` Interface

The `ResultSetMetaData` interface provides various methods for getting information about a `ResultSet` object. You can use a `ResultSetMetaData` object to get the number of columns and find out about the types and properties of the columns in a `ResultSet`.

The JDBC Support Classes

JDBC provides support classes `Date`, `Time`, and `TimeStamp` for accepting and processing SQL DATE, TIME, and TIMESTAMP values. All these classes extend the `java.util.Date` class.

JDBC also provides a support class `Types` that contains a list of predefined constants for identifying SQL types that can be used in JDBC. No methods are defined in this class.

JDBC Drivers

A JDBC driver is a software component that works between JDBC and the database. The driver is responsible for accepting SQL statements, sending them to the database system, and returning the execution results to JDBC. The driver is specific to each database. For instance, to enable JDBC to connect to the Oracle database, you need a JDBC driver that works specifically for Oracle. Even among Oracle databases, the drivers are different for various versions of Oracle DBMS.

There are many JDBC drivers now available on the market. They can be classified into the four types listed in Table 12.2.

TABLE 12.2   JDBC Driver Types

Types of Drivers	Description
Type 1: JDBC-ODBC Bridge	Provides access through ODBC drivers
Type 2: Native-API	Provides access through native database API
Type 3: Middle-tier	Provides access through a middle-tier server
Type 4: Native-protocol	Provides access through a network protocol used by DBMS

■■■ NOTE

The JDBC API was initially designed based on JDK 1.02, known as *JDBC 1*. When JDBC 1 was released, many important Java technologies, such as JavaBeans and Java Internationalization, had not yet been developed. With the release of JDK 1.2, JavaSoft added new features and made some enhancements to JDBC 1. The new JDBC product is known as *JDBC 2*. JDBC 1 is compatible with JDK 1.2. Any applications developed with JDBC 1 will continue to work under JDK 1.2. However, you will need JDBC 2 drivers to use the new features in JDBC 2.

Type 1: JDBC-ODBC Bridge Driver

ODBC (Open DataBase Connectivity) is an API for accessing relational databases. It was originally designed to enable database clients on PCs to access databases on a server by Microsoft. It became a popular industry standard API for connecting to the relational databases for the client on all types of platforms. Since ODBC is widely available, it makes sense to provide a driver that accesses the database through ODBC drivers. Such a driver is referred to as a *JDBC-ODBC bridge driver.*

A JDBC-ODBC driver is bundled with JDK 1.1 and JDK 1.2, which is a joint product by Sun and Intersolv. This driver bridges JDBC with ODBC by mapping the JDBC calls into ODBC calls, and the ODBC calls interact with the database, as shown in Figure 12.3.

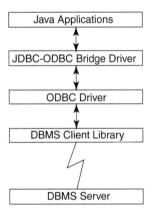

Figure 12.3   *The JDBC-ODBC bridge driver maps JDBC calls to ODBC calls.*

The JDBC-ODBC bridge driver provides convenient access to all the existing systems, since most of the database systems already have ODBC drivers. However, the driver is slow and is not suitable for applets. The ODBC drivers are specific to the database. For example, you need an Oracle ODBC driver to access Oracle databases. The JDBC application using the JDBC-ODBC bridge driver requires that the ODBC driver and the client database library must be loaded on the client machine. This approach is obviously not efficient, since it requires the JDBC driver to talk to the database via an ODBC driver. Since the ODBC drivers is written in C, the driver cannot be downloaded and used by applets.

Type 2: Native-API Driver

This kind of driver converts JDBC calls into native database calls and communicates directly with the database server, as shown in Figure 12.4.

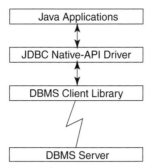

Figure 12.4   *The JDBC Native-API driver maps JDBC calls to Native API calls.*

Native-API drivers are usually provided by database vendors. For example, Oracle provides a native-API driver that maps JDBC with the Oracle Call Interface. Like the bridge driver, this driver requires some binary code for the native database API to be loaded on the client machine. But it is more efficient than the JDBC-ODBC bridge approach, since it allows you to talk to the database directly.

Type 3: Middle-Tier Driver

This kind of driver converts JDBC calls into a DBMS-independent network protocol and sends them to a middle-tier server. The server then translates the calls to a DBMS-specific protocol for Oracle, Sybase, Informix, InterBase, or other DBMS, as shown in Figure 12.5.

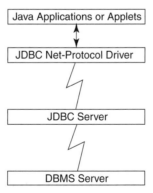

Figure 12.5   *The middle-tier driver maps JDBC calls to a DBMS-independent middle-tier server that communicates with proprietary DBMS.*

The middle-tier JDBC server connects to Java applications or applets with a database server. Inprise's InterClient and Symantec's dbAnyWhere are middle-tier servers based on this kind of architecture. The middle-tier server can reside on a machine different from the client and the DBMS server.

525

The middle-tier driver is a pure Java JDBC driver that enables platform-independent, client/server development for the Internet. The advantage of a pure Java driver versus a native-code driver is that you can deploy applets without having to manually load platform-specific JDBC drivers on each client system. Since the Web servers automatically download the drive classes along with the applets, there is no need to manage local native database libraries, and this simplifies administration and maintenance of customer applications. As part of a Java applet, the driver can be dynamically updated, further reducing the cost of application deployment and maintenance.

Type 4: Native-Protocol Driver

The native-protocol driver converts JDBC calls into network protocol used by a DBMS and communicates with the DBMS directly, as shown in Figure 12.6.

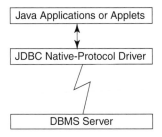

Figure 12.6   *The native-protocol driver facilitates communications between Java applications and applets with a DBMS server.*

Like the middle-tier driver, this kind of driver does not require any database specific binary code to be loaded on the client. The native-protocol driver, however, is more flexible than the middle-tier driver, because it eliminates the middle-tier JDBC server.

NOTE
The JDBC-ODBC driver and the native-API driver use native methods, which makes them platform-specific. They are not suitable for Java applets intended to be downloaded into browsers running on universal platforms. Middle-tier drivers are preferred for use with multi-tier architecture where connectors are used to link clients with database servers. Native-protocol drivers are ideal for direct access to the database. Both middle-tier and native-protocol drivers are written in 100% pure Java; thus they are suitable for Java applets.

Connecting to Databases Using JDBC Drivers

A number of JDBC drivers have already been developed. Many of them can be downloaded from vendors for 30 or more days of evaluation. Information for locating the drivers can be obtained from the following URL.

`www.javasoft.com/products/jdbc/drivers.html`

This section provides examples of the four types of JDBC drivers. Specifically, you will use the Sun JDBC-ODBC driver, the Oracle JDBC OCI driver (native-API), the Inprise InterClient driver (middle-tier), and the Oracle thin-client driver (native-protocol).

NOTE

A driver is not just of a single class. In fact a JDBC driver is a set of classes that provide mappings between JDBC and a specific database. The driver must include classes that implement the eight interfaces in the `java.sql` package: `Driver`, `Connection`, `Statement`, `PreparedStatement`, `CallableStatement`, `ResultSet`, `DatabaseMetaData`, and `ResultSetMetaData`. For example, the `sun.jdbc.odbc.JdbcOdbcStatement` class implements `java.sql.Statement`. Figure 12.7 lists all the classes in the Sun JDBC-ODBC driver bundled in the JDK 1.1 classes.zip file using the WinZip utility. These classes are used by JDBC, not directly by JDBC programmers.

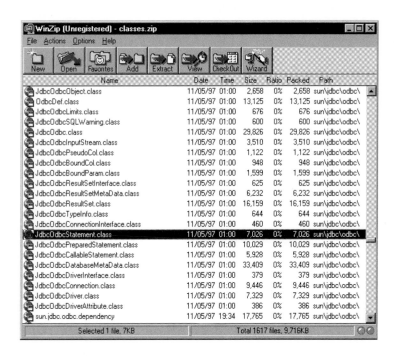

Figure 12.7 *The Sun JDBC-ODBC driver contains classes that enable JDBC to interact with the ODBC drivers.*

JDBC URL Naming Conventions

How does a Java program find its database? It finds the database by using its JDBC URL. A JDBC URL provides a way for the appropriate driver to identify the database. The standard syntax of a URL is:

```
jdbc:<subprotocol>:<datasource>
```

The first part of the syntax is always jdbc. The second part is the subprotocol specified by the driver vendor. For example, the subprotocol for Oracle drivers is always oracle. The datasource consists of the database name and the host machine where the database resides. Information needed to access the data source, such as the user's login name and password, may be included in datasource, or may be supplied separately.

The subprotocol is used by the DriverManager class to associate an appropriate driver with the database. When the DriverManager class presents the subprotocol of the URL to its list of registered drivers, the driver that matches the protocol is used to establish a connection to the database specified in the data source. The subprotocol name is defined by the vendor, but it must be registered with JavaSoft to avoid naming conflicts. JavaSoft acts as an informal registry for JDBC subprotocol names.

The subprotocol odbc is reserved for JDBC-ODBC bridge drivers. For example, the URL to access an ODBC data source "MyDataSource" through a JDBC-ODBC driver is

```
jdbc:odbc:MyDataSource
```

In this example, the subprotocol is odbc, and the hostname is the ODBC data source "MyDataSource."

The subprotocol may consist of several words. For example, the subprotocol oracle:oci7 is reserved for accessing Oracle 7 database through native Oracle OCI (Oracle Call Interface), and oracle:thin is reserved for accessing Oracle 7 without using native Oracle OCI.

The JDBC URL provides an indirection in the data source. You may use a logical host or database name that is dynamically translated to an actual name by a network naming system. For example, the URL to access a remote Oracle 7 database using the Oracle JDBC OCI7 driver may look like:

```
jdbc:oracle:oci7:@sun
```

In this example, sun is an Oracle TNS (Transparent Network System) logical name defined by the Oracle user on the client side. TNS is a protocol used for networking Oracle database. The logical name sun contains information about the database name, the host name, and the port number of the database process on the server.

Using the JDBC-ODBC Driver

To use the JDBC-ODBC driver to access databases in Java, two drivers must be installed on the client machine: a universal JDBC-ODBC bridge driver and a vendor-specific ODBC driver. The JDBC-ODBC driver comes with JDK 1.1 or higher, or any Java development tool that supports JDK 1.1. The ODBC driver is not included in JDK 1.1 and is usually provided by database vendors. The example chosen to demonstrate the JDBC-ODBC approach in this section is the Microsoft ODBC driver for the MS-Access database on Windows 95, since it is bundled with Microsoft Office Suite and widely available to many readers.

■ **NOTE**

Using the JDBC-ODBC approach, the database is not necessarily on the same machine with the client. For example, you may use an Oracle ODBC driver to access a remote Oracle database.

Example 12.1 Testing the JDBC-ODBC Bridge Driver

This example develops a Java program that creates a table named STUDENT in an MS Access database. Each record consists of student FIRSTNAME, MI, and LASTNAME. Your program inserts two records into STUDENT and then displays all the records on the console.

Follow the steps below to complete the project.

1. Install an MS ODBC driver for MS Access if necessary.

   The "typical installation" option of MS Access does not include the ODBC driver. If necessary, reinstall MS Access to get the proper ODBC driver on your system. Upon successful installation, you have the file odbcjt32.DLL in \windows\system directory and should also see a "32-bit ODBC" icon appearing on the control panel.

2. Set up a Data Source as the database for storing the STUDENT table.

   2.1. From the Windows Start button, choose Setting, Control Panel to bring up the Control Panel dialog box.

   2.2. Double-click the "32bit ODBC" icon to bring up the "ODBC Data Source Administrator," as shown in Figure 12.8.

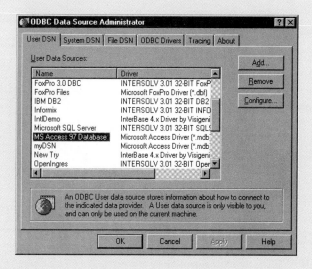

Figure 12.8 *The ODBC Data Source Administrator is the main dialog box to manage the data source and the drivers.*

2.3. Click Add to bring up the "Create New Data Source" dialog box, as shown in Figure 12.9.

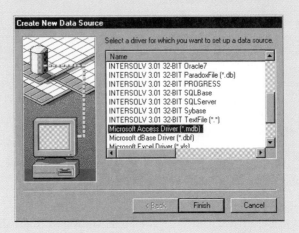

Figure 12.9 *Select a proper driver for the Data Source in the "Create New Data Source" window.*

2.4. Select Microsoft Access Driver and Press "Finish" to bring the "ODBC Microsoft Access 97 Setup" dialog window, as shown in Figure 12.10. Type "LiangBookDB_MDB" in the Data Source Name field, and type "Test JDBC-ODBC bridge driver" in the Description filed. Press Create to bring up the "New Database" dialog window, as shown in Figure 12.11.

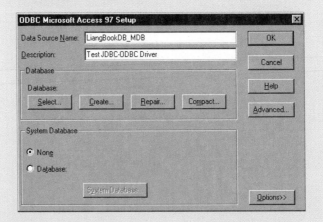

Figure 12.10 *Specify the Data Source Name to associate it with a database in the "ODBC Microsoft Access 97 Setup" window.*

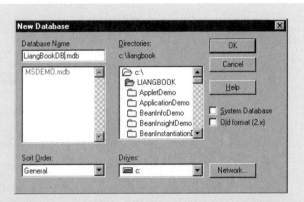

Figure 12.11 *Specify the physical database file name that corresponds to the data source name in the "New Database" window.*

2.5. Type C:\LiangBook\LiangBookDB.mdb in the database name field, and select a directory where you want the database to be placed, as shown in Figure 12.11. Press OK, and you should see a message on a message box notifying that the database was successfully created.

3. Create a new project JdbcOdbcDemo.jpr, and create the program named TestJdbcOdbc (see Listing 12.2) to create a STUDENT table, insert two records, and retrieve the records from the database.

```java
package JdbcOdbcDemo;

import java.sql.*;

public class TestJdbcOdbc
{
  public static void main(String[] args)
    throws SQLException, ClassNotFoundException
  {
    // Load the JDBC-ODBC bridge driver
    Class.forName("sun.jdbc.odbc.JdbcOdbcDriver");
    System.out.println("Driver loaded");

    // Establish connection
    Connection conn = DriverManager.getConnection
      ("jdbc:odbc:LiangBookDB_MDB", "", "");
    System.out.println("Database connected");

    // Create a statement
    Statement stmt = conn.createStatement();

    try
    {
      // Create the STUDENT TABLE
      stmt.executeUpdate(
```

continues

Listing 12.2 *TestJdbcOdbcDemo.java*

531

```
              "create table STUDENT(FIRSTNAME CHAR(20), " +
              + "MI CHAR(1), LASTNAME CHAR(20))");
          }
          catch (SQLException ex)
          {
            System.out.println("Table STUDENT already exists");
          }

          // Insert two records into the STUDENT TABLE
          stmt.executeUpdate(
            "insert into STUDENT values ('John', 'F', 'Smith')");
          stmt.executeUpdate(
            "insert into STUDENT values ('Wade', 'E', 'Bush')");

          // Select the column student from the STUDENT table
          ResultSet rset = stmt.executeQuery
            ("select FIRSTNAME, MI, LASTNAME from STUDENT");

          // Iterate through the result and print the student names
          while (rset.next())
            System.out.println(rset.getString(1).trim() + " " +
              rset.getString(2) + ". " + rset.getString(3).trim());
        }
      }
```

Listing 12.2 *Continued*

4. Compile and test the program. A sample run of the program is shown in Figure 12.12.

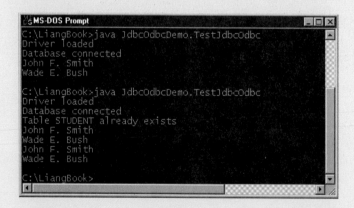

Figure 12.12   *The Java program accesses an MS Access data source through the JDBC-ODBC bridge driver.*

Example Review

Java does not run on 16-bit platforms. You must use a 32-bit ODBC driver, not a 16-bit ODBC driver. The program was tested using MS Access 97. It should also work with MS Access 95.

The URL of a data source for a JDBC-ODBC connection is jdbc:odbc:ODBC-Source-Name. So jdbc:odbc:LiangBookDB_MDB is the URL used in the statement

```
Connection conn = DriverManager.getConnection
  ("jdbc:odbc: LiangBookDB_MDB", "", "" );
```

to establish a connection to the data source Sample.

The program creates the STUDENT table, inserts two records, and displays the records in the table. The SQL statements are passed as string arguments.

 TIP

When executing this example, close MS Access, because only one active session is allowed.

Using the Native-API Driver

A native-API driver translates JDBC calls directly into calls on the DBMS-specific client API. Thus, you must install the JDBC driver as well as the DBMS client-side library. Major enterprise database vendors like Oracle, Sybase, and Informix already provide native support of database connectivity for the development tools, such as Visual Basic and Borland Delphi, among many others, through their proprietary client API. The support extended by these companies enables JDBC to talk directly to the client API through the native-API driver.

Oracle, the most popular database, is used by many large corporations. In this section, you will learn how to use the Oracle JDBC OCI driver to develop a Java application that accesses a remote Oracle database. Oracle's JDBC OCI driver is a native-API driver that provides an implementation of the JDBC interfaces on top of the OCI (Oracle Call Interface) to interact with an Oracle database. This driver can access local or remote Oracle 7.3.2 or higher from a client on Solaris, Windows 95/98, or Windows NT.

Example 12.2 Using the Oracle JDBC OCI Driver

This example develops a Java program that simply gets the system time from a remote database. The server is accessible on the Internet with the host name sesrv00.ipfw.edu (IP address 149.164.30.143). An Oracle 7.3.2 database is running on the server. You can access the database using username **scott** and password **tiger**.

Follow the steps below to set up the client on Windows 95.

1. Install Oracle 7.3.4 client if necessary. Oracle 7.3.4 client includes SQL*Net and all other dependent files required to support JDBC OCI driver to connect to the Oracle server. SQL*NET is an Oracle proprietary product that supports network service to the server from the client. (You can download Oracle 7.3.4 client for 60 days of evaluation from **http://www.oracle.com/products/trial/html/trial.html.**)

2. Download the Oracle JDBC OCI driver for Windows 95 from http://www.oracle.com/products/free_software/index.html and unzip the files into c:\orawin95\jdbcoci7.

3. Add the Oracle TNS alias name for the sample database in the \ORAWIN95\NETOWRK\ADMIN\TNSNAMES.ORA file as follows, so that this program can access my Oracle test database.

```
sun =
  (DESCRIPTION =
    (ADDRESS_LIST =
      (ADDRESS =
        (PROTOCOL = TCP)
        (HOST = 149.164.30.143)
        (PORT = 1521)
      )
    )
    (CONNECT_DATA =
      (SID = test)
    )
  )
```

4. Create a new project named OraJdbcOci7Demo.jpr, and create a new class that connects to the test database on sesrv00.ipfw.edu and obtains current system time. The program is given in Listing 12.3.

5. To run the program from JBuilder, you need to add c:\orawin95\jdbcoci7\lib\classes111.zip in the Java libraries in the Project Properties. To run the program from a DOS prompt, add c:\orawin95\jdbcoci\lib\classes111.zip to your CLASSPATH and add c:\orawin95\jdbcoci7\lib to your PATH in the autoexec.bat file.

```
package OraJdbcOci7Demo;

import java.sql.*;

public class TestOraJdbcOci7
{
  public static void main(String[] args)
    throws SQLException, ClassNotFoundException
  {
    // Load the Oracle JDBC driver
    Class.forName ("oracle.jdbc.driver.OracleDriver");
    System.out.println("Driver loaded");

    // Connect to the sample database
    Connection conn = DriverManager.getConnection
      ("jdbc:oracle:oci7:@sun", "scott", "tiger");
    System.out.println("Database connected");

    // Create a Statement
    Statement stmt = conn.createStatement();

    // Select the date and time from the server
    ResultSet rset = stmt.executeQuery("SELECT sysdate FROM Dual");

    // Show the system date and time
    while (rset.next())
      System.out.println(rset.getString(1));
  }
}
```

Listing 12.3   *TestOraJdbcOci7.java*

6. Compile and run the program. A sample run of the program is shown in Figure 12.13.

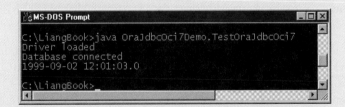

Figure 12.13   *Using an Oracle 7 JDBC OCI driver, the Java program accesses a remote data-base and obtains the time from the server.*

Example Review

The Oracle7 JDBC OCI connection url is jdbc:oracle:oci7@tnsname. So the following statement

continues

535

```
Connection conn = DriverManager.getConnection
  ("jdbc:oracle:oci7:@sun", "scott", "tiger");
```

establishes a connection to the remote database using username **scott** and password **tiger**.

The SQL statement "SELECT sysdate FROM Dual" is specific to Oracle, which returns the current system date and time on the database server.

The success of this example depends on a sequence of steps, each of which must be done exactly right to avoid frustrating errors. Here is a list of things to check:

- Check whether the server is alive using ping sesrv00.ipfw.edu.

- Check whether you can log on to the database using **sqlplus scott/ tiger@sun**. If failed, check whether you have created a right alias in the TNSNAME.ORA file for the database server.

- If you get a `ClassNotFoundException`, it is likely that you did not set c:\orawin95\jdbcoci7\lib\classes111.zip in the classpath.

- if you get an error indicating that oci73jdbc.dll file is not found, it is because you did not add c:\orawin95\jdbcoci7\lib in the path.

Using the Native-Protocol Driver

A native-protocol driver translates JDBC calls into network protocol used by a DBMS and communicates with the DBMS directly. Since some part of the network protocol for facilitating database communications is vendor-specific, a driver of this kind is usually provided by the vendor. The driver is written in 100% pure Java to implement high-level network communication to the server. Since the native-protocol driver, unlike the native-API driver, does not require that any database specific binary code be loaded on the client, it is suitable for deploying Java applets.

In this section, you will learn how to use the Oracle JDBC thin driver to develop Java applets for accessing remote Oracle databases. Oracle's JDBC thin driver is a native-protocol driver that provides an implementation of the Oracle high-level communications protocol known as *TNS* (*Transparent Network Substrate*). This driver can access local and remote servers of Oracle 7.3.2 or higher from a client on any platform.

Example 12.3 Using the Oracle JDBC Thin Driver

This example develops a Java applet that connects to a remote Oracle 7.3.2 server using an Oracle JDBC Thin driver. After the connection is established, the program obtains the system time from the server and displays it on the applet.

Follow the steps below to complete the project.

1. Download the Oracle Thin driver for Windows 95 from http://www. oracle.com/products/free_software/index.html and unzip the files into c:\orawin95\jdbcthin.

2. Create a new project named OraJdbcThinDemo.jpr, and create an applet named `TestOraJDBCThin` that connects to the test database on sesrv00. ipfw.edu, obtains current system time from the server, and displays it on the applet. The program is given in Listing 12.4.

3. Add c:\orawin95\jdbcthin\lib\classes111.zip in the libraries in the Project Properties. Compile TestOraJdbcThin.java and run the program. A sample run of the program is shown in Figure 12.14.

```java
package OraJdbcThinDemo;

import java.awt.*;
import java.awt.event.*;
import java.applet.*;
import javax.swing.*;
import java.sql.*;

public class TestOraJdbcThin extends JApplet
{
  // SQL Statement
  Statement stmt;

  boolean isStandalone = false;
  JPanel jPanel1 = new JPanel();
  JTextArea jtaOutput = new JTextArea();
  BorderLayout borderLayout1 = new BorderLayout();
  JLabel jLabel1 = new JLabel();
  JTextField jtfTime = new JTextField();
  JButton jbtGetTime = new JButton();

  // Construct the applet
  public TestOraJdbcThin()
  {
  }

  // Initialize the applet
  public void init()
  {
    try
    {
      jbInit();
    }
    catch(Exception e)
    {
      e.printStackTrace();
    }
  }

  // Component initialization
  private void jbInit() throws Exception
```

continues

Listing 12.4   *TestOraJdbcThin.java*

```
{
  this.setSize(new Dimension(400,300));
  jPanel1.setLayout(borderLayout1);
  jLabel1.setText("Server Time");
  jbtGetTime.setText("Get Server Time");
  jbtGetTime.addActionListener(new java.awt.event.ActionListener()
  {
    public void actionPerformed(ActionEvent e)
    {
      jbtGetTime_actionPerformed(e);
    }
  });
  this.getContentPane().add(jPanel1, BorderLayout.NORTH);
  jPanel1.add(jLabel1, BorderLayout.WEST);
  jPanel1.add(jtfTime, BorderLayout.CENTER);
  jPanel1.add(jbtGetTime, BorderLayout.EAST);
  this.getContentPane().add(jtaOutput, BorderLayout.CENTER);

  // Initialized JDBC
  initializeJDBC();
}

private void initializeJDBC()
{
  try
  {
    // Declare driver and connection string
    String driver = "oracle.jdbc.driver.OracleDriver";

    // Load the Oracle JDBC Thin driver
    Class.forName("oracle.jdbc.driver.OracleDriver");
    jtaOutput.append("Driver oracle.jdbc.driver.OracleDriver" +
      " loaded"+'\n');

    // Connect to the sample database
    Connection conn = DriverManager.getConnection
      ("jdbc:oracle:thin:@sesrv00.ipfw.edu:1521:test",
        "scott", "tiger");
    jtaOutput.append("Database jdbc:oracle:thin:scott/tiger" +
      "@sesrv00.ipfw.edu:1521:test connected"+'\n');

    // Create a Statement
    stmt = conn.createStatement();
  }
  catch (Exception ex)
  {
    jtaOutput.append(ex.getMessage() + '\n');
  }
}

// Main method
public static void main(String[] args)
{
  TestOraJdbcThin applet = new TestOraJdbcThin();
  applet.isStandalone = true;
  JFrame frame = new JFrame();
  frame.setTitle("Applet Frame");
  frame.getContentPane().add(applet, BorderLayout.CENTER);
```

Listing 12.4   *Continued*

```
            applet.init();
            applet.start();
            frame.setSize(400,320);
            Dimension d = Toolkit.getDefaultToolkit().getScreenSize();
            frame.setLocation((d.width - frame.getSize().width) / 2,
              (d.height - frame.getSize().height) / 2);
            frame.setVisible(true);
          }

          void jbtGetTime_actionPerformed(ActionEvent e)
          {
            String query = "SELECT sysdate FROM Dual";
            if (e.getSource() instanceof JButton)
            {
              try
              {
                // Execute the query
                jtaOutput.append("Executing query " + query + "\n");
                ResultSet rset = stmt.executeQuery(query);

                // Display the time
                while (rset.next())
                  jtfTime.setText(rset.getString(1));
              }
              catch (Exception ex)
              {
                jtaOutput.append(ex.getMessage() + '\n');
              }
            }
          }
        }
```

Listing 12.4   *Continued*

Figure 12.14   *Using the Oracle JDBC Thin driver, the Java applet accesses a remote database and obtains the time from the server.*

continues

539

Example Review

The Oracle JDBC Thin connection URL is `jdbc:oracle:thin:@hostname:port:sid`. So the following statement

```
Connection conn = DriverManager.getConnection
  ("jdbc:oracle:thin:@sesrv00.ipfw.edu:1521:test",
   "scott", "tiger");
```

establishes a connection to the remote database on sesrv00.ipfw.edu using username **scott** and password **tiger** to the database with a system id test whose listener is at port 1521.

You can test the applet using the appletviewer utility, as shown in Figure 12.14. This applet can be deployed on the server where the database is located so that any client on the Internet can run it from a Web browser. Since the client may not have the Oracle Thin driver, you should make the driver available along with the applet in one archive file. This archive file can be created as follows:

1. Copy c:\Drawings\jdbcthin\lib\classes111.zip to TestOraJdbcThin.zip.

2. Add TestOraJdbcThin.class into TestOraJdbcThin.zip using the WinZip utility.

3. Add TestOraJdbcThin$1.class into TestOraJdbcThin.zip using the WinZip utility. TestOraJdbcThin$1.class is for the anonymous inner class for listening to the button action.

You need to deploy TestOraJdbcThin.zip and TestOraJdbcThin.html on the server. TestOraJdbcThin.html should use the applet tag with a reference to the Zip file as follows:

```
<applet
  code="TestOraJdbcThin"
  archive="TestOraJdbcThin.zip"
  width=500
  height=200
  >
</applet>
```

■■■ NOTE

To access the database from an applet, it is necessary, because of security restrictions, for the applet to be downloaded from the server where the Oracle database is located. Hence, you have to deploy the applet on the server.

Using the Middle-Tier Driver

A middle-tier driver communicates with a DBMS database through a JDBC server. InterClient is a middle-tier JDBC driver used to connect Java applications or applets with an InterBase server. Borland's InterBase is a small-footprint, embedded database. It is simple, robust, portable, and flexible. It is ideal for use in embedded systems.

The InterClient product consists of two essential components: InterClient and InterServer.

■ InterClient: The driver that enables Java clients to connect to the InterServer server. It can be installed on the Java application machine. If you run a Java applet, the driver must either reside on the browser machine or be downloadable from the server where the applet is stored. The client can be any machine that supports Java.

■ InterServer: Manages the transfer of information and calls between the Client and the InterBase Server. InterServer can run on Windows 95/98, Windows NT 4.0, Solaris 2.5.x, HP-UX 10.x, and Linux.

The InterClient driver and InterBase server are bundled with JBuilder 3 Enterprise Edition. You can use them to develop and test Java database applications in JBuilder 3, but you are not licensed to deploy the applications. In this section, you will learn how to use the InterClient driver to develop and deploy Java applets to access an InterBase database.

Example 12.4 Using the Borland InterClient Driver Accessing InterBase Servers

This example develops a Java applet to view, insert, or update staff information stored in an InterBase database. A sample run of the program is shown in Figure 12.15.

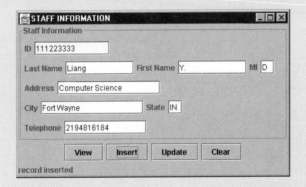

Figure 12.15 *The* TestInterClient *applet, which accesses an InterBase local server, lets you view, insert, and update staff records.*

continues

Follow the steps below to complete the project.

1. Prepare the database.

   1.1. From the Windows Start button, choose Programs, InterBase, Inter-Base Windows ISQL, to start InterBase Interactive SQL utility, as shown in Figure 12.16.

Figure 12.16   *The Interactive SQL utility allows you to manage the database and execute SQL against a database interactively.*

   1.2. In the Interactive SQL window, choose File, Create Database to bring up the "Create Database" dialog window, as shown in Figure 12.17. Enter C:\LiangBook\LiangBookDB.gdb in the Database field, enter SYSDBA in the Username field, and enter masterkey in the Password field. Click OK to close the window.

NOTE

The SYSDAB account was automatically created when a new InterBase database was installed. To use a user name other than SYSDBA, you have to create a new user account.

   1.3. In the Interactive SQL window, as shown in Figure 12.16, choose File, Connect to Database to bring up the "Database Connect" dialog window, as shown in Figure 12.18. Select C:\LiangBook\Liang-BookDB.gdb in the Database field, and enter SYSDBA in the

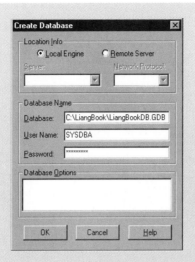

Figure 12.17   *The "Create Database" window enables you to create a new local database in a specified database file.*

Figure 12.18   *The "Database Connected" dialog window lets you connect to a specified database.*

Username field and masterkey in the Password field. Click OK to close the dialog window.

1.4. Type the following SQL statement in the SQL Statement window to create a table STAFF. Click Run to execute it. Close the Interactive SQL window.

```
CREATE TABLE STAFF
(
  ID CHAR(9) NOT NULL,
  LASTNAME VARCHAR(15),
```

continues

```
                    FIRSTNAME VARCHAR(15),
                    MI CHAR(1),
                    ADDRESS VARCHAR(20),
                    CITY VARCHAR(20),
                    STATE CHAR(2),
                    TELEPHONE CHAR(10),
                    PRIMARY KEY (ID)
                  );
```

2. Design UI and write the code.

   2.1. Create a new project named InterClientDemo.jpr, and create an applet TestInterClient.java using the Applet Wizard.

   2.2. In the UI Designer for TestInterClient.java, drop a JPanel to the center of the applet to create jPanel1, and drop a JLable to the north to create jLabel1. Rename them jpDisplay and jlblStatus.

   2.3. Set the layout of jpDisplay to BorderLayout. Drop a JPanel twice into jpDisplay, one is to the center of jpDisplay and the other to the south, and rename them jpStaff and jpButton.

   2.4. In the border property of jpStaff, choose titled to create an instance of titledBorder1. Select titledBorder1 in the Other node in the Component tree and set its title to "Staff Information."

   2.5. Set the layout of jpStaff to GridLayout with the row property set to 5 and the column property set to 1. Drop a JPanel into jpStaff five time to create jPanel1, jPanel2, jPanel3, jPanel4, and jPanel5. Create a label and a text field for ID in jPanel1. Create labels and text fields for Last Name, First Name, and MI in jPanel2. Create a label and a text field for Address in jPanel3. Create labels and text fields for City and State in jPanel4. Create a label and a text field for Telephone in jPanel5. Rename the text fields to jtfID, jtfLastName, jtfFirstName, jtfMI, jtfAddress, jtfCity, jtfState, and jtfTelephone.

   2.6. Add four buttons labeled "View," "Insert," "Update," and "Clear" to jpButtons, and rename the buttons jbtView, jbtInsert, jbtUpdate, and jbtClear. Generate the handlers for these buttons.

   2.7. Create a method named initializeDB to initialize the JDBC connection to a local InterBase database. Invoke this method from the jbInit method. Create the code for implementing the button handlers, as shown in Listing 12.5.

3. Test TestTestClient.

   3.1. Start InterBase server if it is not running. From the Windows Start button, choose Programs, InterBase, InterBase Server.

   3.2. Start InterClient JDBC server. From the Windows Start button, choose Programs, InterBase InterClient, InterServer.

3.3. Add the InterClient driver in the project library from the Project Properties window.

3.4. You can run TestClient as an application or as an applet. A sample run of the program is shown in Figure 12.15.

```
package InterClientDemo;

import java.awt.*;
import java.awt.event.*;
import java.applet.*;
import javax.swing.*;
import java.sql.*;
import javax.swing.border.*;

public class TestInterClient extends JApplet
{
  boolean isStandalone = false;
  JPanel jpDisplay = new JPanel();
  JLabel jlblStatus = new JLabel();
  JPanel jpButtons = new JPanel();
  BorderLayout borderLayout1 = new BorderLayout();
  JPanel jpStaff = new JPanel();
  JButton jbtView = new JButton();
  JButton jbtInsert = new JButton();
  JButton jbtUpdate = new JButton();
  JButton jbtClear = new JButton();
  JPanel jPanel1 = new JPanel();
  JPanel jPanel2 = new JPanel();
  JPanel jPanel3 = new JPanel();
  JPanel jPanel4 = new JPanel();
  JPanel jPanel5 = new JPanel();
  JLabel jLabel2 = new JLabel();
  JLabel jLabel3 = new JLabel();
  JLabel jLabel4 = new JLabel();
  FlowLayout flowLayout1 = new FlowLayout();
  FlowLayout flowLayout2 = new FlowLayout();
  FlowLayout flowLayout3 = new FlowLayout();
  JTextField jtfID = new JTextField();
  JTextField jtfLastName = new JTextField();
  JLabel jLabel5 = new JLabel();
  JTextField jtfFirstName = new JTextField();
  JLabel jLabel6 = new JLabel();
  JTextField jtfMI = new JTextField();
  JTextField jtfAddress = new JTextField();
  JLabel jLabel7 = new JLabel();
  JTextField jtfCity = new JTextField();
  JLabel jLabel8 = new JLabel();
  JTextField jtfState = new JTextField();
  FlowLayout flowLayout4 = new FlowLayout();
  JLabel jLabel9 = new JLabel();
  JTextField jtfTelephone = new JTextField();
  FlowLayout flowLayout5 = new FlowLayout();

  // The Statement for processing queries
  Statement stmt;
```

continues

Listing 12.5   *TestInterClient.java*

```
        TitledBorder titledBorder1;
        GridLayout gridLayout1 = new GridLayout();

        // Construct the applet
        public TestInterClient()
        {
        }

        // Initialize the applet
        public void init()
        {
          try
          {
          jbInit();
          }
          catch (Exception e)
          {
          e.printStackTrace();
          }
        }

        private void jbInit() throws Exception
        {
          titledBorder1 = new TitledBorder("");
          this.setSize(400,300);
          jpDisplay.setLayout(borderLayout1);
          jpStaff.setLayout(gridLayout1);
          jbtView.setText("View");
          jbtView.addActionListener(new java.awt.event.ActionListener()
          {
            public void actionPerformed(ActionEvent e)
            {
              jbtView_actionPerformed(e);
            }
          });
          jbtInsert.setText("Insert");
          jbtInsert.addActionListener(new java.awt.event.ActionListener()
          {
            public void actionPerformed(ActionEvent e)
            {
              jbtInsert_actionPerformed(e);
            }
          });
          jbtUpdate.setText("Update");
          jbtUpdate.addActionListener(new java.awt.event.ActionListener()
          {
            public void actionPerformed(ActionEvent e)
            {
              jbtUpdate_actionPerformed(e);
            }
          });
          jbtClear.setText("Clear");
          jbtClear.addActionListener(new java.awt.event.ActionListener()
          {
            public void actionPerformed(ActionEvent e)
            {
              jbtClear_actionPerformed(e);
            }
          });
```

Listing 12.5 *Continued*

```
jPanel5.setLayout(flowLayout5);
jPanel4.setLayout(flowLayout4);
jPanel3.setLayout(flowLayout3);
jPanel2.setLayout(flowLayout2);
jPanel1.setLayout(flowLayout1);
jLabel2.setText("ID");
jLabel3.setText("Last Name");
jLabel4.setText("Address");
flowLayout1.setAlignment(0);
flowLayout2.setAlignment(0);
flowLayout3.setAlignment(0);
jtfID.setColumns(11);
jtfID.setBackground(Color.yellow);
jtfLastName.setColumns(10);
jLabel5.setText("First Name");
jtfFirstName.setColumns(10);
jLabel6.setText("MI");
jtfMI.setColumns(2);
jtfAddress.setColumns(15);
jLabel7.setText("City");
jtfCity.setColumns(15);
jLabel8.setText("State");
jtfState.setColumns(2);
flowLayout4.setAlignment(0);
jLabel9.setText("Telephone");
jtfTelephone.setColumns(12);
flowLayout5.setAlignment(0);
jlblStatus.setBackground(Color.pink);
jlblStatus.setText("Connecting ...");
jpStaff.setBorder(titledBorder1);
titledBorder1.setTitle("Staff Information");
gridLayout1.setColumns(1);
gridLayout1.setRows(5);
this.getContentPane().add(jpDisplay, BorderLayout.CENTER);
jpDisplay.add(jpButtons, BorderLayout.SOUTH);
jpButtons.add(jbtView, null);
jpButtons.add(jbtInsert, null);
jpButtons.add(jbtUpdate, null);
jpButtons.add(jbtClear, null);
jpDisplay.add(jpStaff, BorderLayout.CENTER);
jpStaff.add(jPanel1, null);
jPanel1.add(jLabel2, null);
jPanel1.add(jtfID, null);
jpStaff.add(jPanel2, null);
jPanel2.add(jLabel3, null);
jPanel2.add(jtfLastName, null);
jPanel2.add(jLabel5, null);
jPanel2.add(jtfFirstName, null);
jPanel2.add(jLabel6, null);
jPanel2.add(jtfMI, null);
jpStaff.add(jPanel3, null);
jpStaff.add(jPanel4, null);
jPanel4.add(jLabel7, null);
jPanel4.add(jtfCity, null);
jPanel4.add(jLabel8, null);
jPanel4.add(jtfState, null);
jpStaff.add(jPanel5, null);
jPanel5.add(jLabel9, null);
jPanel5.add(jtfTelephone, null);
jPanel3.add(jLabel4, null);
```

continues

```
      jPanel3.add(jtfAddress, null);
      this.getContentPane().add(jlblStatus, BorderLayout.SOUTH);

      // Connect to the database
      initializeDB();
    }

    private void initializeDB()
    {
      try
      {
        // Load the driver
        Class.forName("interbase.interclient.Driver");
        System.out.println("Driver loaded\n");

        // Connect to the local InterBase database
        Connection conn = DriverManager.getConnection(
          "jdbc:interbase://localhost/C:/LiangBook/LiangBookDB.gdb",
          "SYSDBA", "masterkey");
        jlblStatus.setText("Database connected\n");

        // Create a statement
        stmt = conn.createStatement();
      }
      catch (Exception ex)
      {
        jlblStatus.setText("Connection failed: " + ex);
      }
    }

    void jbtInsert_actionPerformed(ActionEvent e)
    {
      insert();
    }

    void jbtView_actionPerformed(ActionEvent e)
    {
      view();
    }

    void jbtUpdate_actionPerformed(ActionEvent e)
    {
      update();
    }

    void jbtClear_actionPerformed(ActionEvent e)
    {
      clear();
    }

    // View record by ID
    private void view()
    {
      // Build a SQL SELECT statement
      String query = "SELECT * FROM STAFF WHERE ID = "
        + "'" + jtfID.getText().trim() + "'";

      try
      {
```

Listing 12.5 *Continued*

```java
      // Execute query
      ResultSet rs = stmt.executeQuery(query);
      loadToTextField(rs);
    }
    catch(SQLException ex)
    {
      jlblStatus.setText("Select failed: " + ex);
    }
  }

  // Load the record into text fields
  private void loadToTextField(ResultSet rs) throws SQLException
  {
    if (rs.next())
    {
      jtfLastName.setText(rs.getString(2));
      jtfFirstName.setText(rs.getString(3));
      jtfMI.setText(rs.getString(4));
      jtfAddress.setText(rs.getString(5));
      jtfCity.setText(rs.getString(6));
      jtfState.setText(rs.getString(7));
      jtfTelephone.setText(rs.getString(8));
    }
    else
      jlblStatus.setText("Record not found");
  }

  // Insert a new record
  private void insert()
  {
    // Build a SQL INSERT statement
    String insertStmt =
      "INSERT INTO STAFF(ID, LastName, FirstName, MI, Address, " +
      " City, State, Telephone) VALUES('" +
      jtfID.getText().trim() + "','" +
      jtfLastName.getText().trim() + "','" +
      jtfFirstName.getText().trim() + "','" +
      jtfMI.getText().trim() + "','" +
      jtfAddress.getText().trim() + "','" +
      jtfCity.getText().trim() + "','" +
      jtfState.getText().trim() + "','" +
      jtfTelephone.getText().trim() + "');";

    try
    {
      stmt.executeUpdate(insertStmt);
    }
    catch (SQLException ex)
    {
      jlblStatus.setText("Insertion failed: " + ex);
    }

    jlblStatus.setText("record inserted");
  }

  // Update a record
  private void update()
  {
    // Build a SQL UPDATE statement
    String updateStmt = "UPDATE STAFF " +
```

continues

549

```
            "SET LastName = '" + jtfLastName.getText().trim() + "'," +
            "FirstName = '" + jtfFirstName.getText().trim() + "'," +
            "MI = '" + jtfMI.getText().trim() + "'," +
            "Address = '" + jtfAddress.getText().trim() + "'," +
            "City = '" + jtfCity.getText().trim() + "'," +
            "State = '" + jtfState.getText().trim() + "'," +
            "Telephone = '" + jtfTelephone.getText().trim() + "' " +
            "WHERE ID = '" + jtfID.getText().trim() + "'";

      try
      {
        stmt.executeUpdate(updateStmt);
        jlblStatus.setText("Record updated");
      }
      catch(SQLException ex)
      {
        jlblStatus.setText("Update failed: " + ex);
      }
    }

    // Clear text fields
    private void clear()
    {
      jtfID.setText(null);
      jtfLastName.setText(null);
      jtfFirstName.setText(null);
      jtfMI.setText(null);
      jtfAddress.setText(null);
      jtfCity.setText(null);
      jtfState.setText(null);
      jtfTelephone.setText(null);
    }
  }
```

Listing 12.1   *Continued*

Example Review

To run the program from JBuilder, you must add the InterClient driver to the project library from the Project Properties window. To run the program from a DOS prompt, add C:\"Program Files"\"InterBase Corp"\InterClient\interclient.jar to the classpath environment variable.

Like all JDBC driver classes, the `interbase.interclient.Driver` implements the `java.sql.Driver` interface. To access an InterBase database, the InterClient driver communicates via a TCP/IP connection with an InterServer process that forwards InterClient requests to the InterBase server. InterBase processes the SQL statements and passes the results back to the InterServer, which then passes them to the InterClient driver.

InterClient URLs have the following format:

```
jdbc:interbase://server/full_db_path
```

where *server* is the hostname of the InterBase server, and *full_db_path* is the full pathname of a database file, including the server's root (/) directory. If the InterBase server runs locally, the *server* should be localhost. In this example, the following statement is used to connect to a local InterBase in C:\LiangBook\ LiangBookDB.gdb.

```
Connection conn = DriverManager.getConnection(
  "jdbc:interbase://localhost/C:/LiangBook/LiangBookDB.gdb",
  "SYSDBA", "masterkey");
```

A static SQL statement is constructed for each SQL operation. A more efficient approach is to use a prepared statement. Prepared statements will be introduced in the next chapter.

NOTE
The InterBase bundled with the JBuilder Enterprise edition is a local server licensed for only one concurrent connection. Please close any active sessions of InterBase server before testing the program.

Chapter Summary

This chapter introduced JDBC, which is the Java API for accessing relational databases. You learned how to write a simple JDBC program by loading the driver, connecting to the database, creating statements, executing the statements, and processing statements. This chapter also provided step-by-step instructions for working with four types of representative JDBC drivers.

Chapter Review

12.1. Describe the following JDBC interfaces: `Driver`, `Connection`, `Statement`, and `ResultSet`.

12.2. How do you instantiate a JDBC driver?

12.3. How do you create a JDBC connection? What is the syntax for a JDBC URL?

12.4. How do you create an instance of `Statement`? How do you execute a statement? Does every execution of the statement return a `ResultSet`?

12.5. How do you retrieve values in a `ResultSet`?

12.6. What are the four types of JDBC drivers? Which types of drivers require the DBMS client library? Which types of drivers can be downloaded and maintained on the server side?

Programming Exercises

12.1. Write an applet to show the number of visits made to a Web page. The count should be stored on the server side in a database table. Every time the page is visited or reloaded, the applet should send a request to the server, and the server should increase the count and send it to the applet. The applet should then display the count in a message, such as You are visitor number: 1000.

12.2. Write an applet to get stock quotes. The stock information is stored in a table consisting of six fields: stock symbol, stock share value, the high of the day, the low of the day, the highest value and lowest value in the last 52 weeks. To get a stock quote, the user enters the stock symbol and presses ENTER in the text field for the stock symbol to display the stock information.

12.3. Modify Example 12.4 to add a new button named "Delete" that enables the user to delete a record with the specified ID in the Staff table.

13

METADATA AND STATEMENTS

Objectives

- Explore database metadata using the `DatabaseMetaData` and `ResultSetMetaData` interface.

- Create and execute statements using the `Statement`, `PreparedStatement`, and `CallableStatement` interfaces.

Introduction

Chapter 12, "Introduction to Java Database Programming," presented an overview of the JDBC concept and examples of using various drivers to connect to databases. JDBC is a comprehensive approach to the development of platform-independent Java database applications. This chapter gives an in-depth look at metadata and statements.

Getting Database MetaData

Database *metadata* is the information that describes database itself. JDBC provides the DatabaseMetaData interface for obtaining database-wide information and the ResultSetMetaData interface for obtaining the information on the specific ResultSet.

The DatabaseMetaData interface provides more than 100 methods for getting database metadata concerning the database as a whole. These methods can be divided into three groups: for retrieving general information, for finding database capabilities, and for getting object descriptions. The general information includes the URL, username, product name, product version, driver name, driver version, available functions, available data types, and so on. Information on database capabilities includes such matters as whether the database supports the GROUP BY operator, the ALTER TABLE command with add column option, and entry-level or full ANSI92 SQL grammar. Examples of database objects are tables, views, and procedures.

The methods for general information usually return a string, an integer, or a boolean value that describe the database information, except that the method for retrieving available data types returns a ResultSet. Most methods of this type don't have parameters. Table 13.1 gives some of these methods for retrieving database information.

The methods for finding database capabilities return a boolean value indicating whether the database possesses a certain capability. Most of methods of this type don't have parameters and are named with prefix *supports*. Table 13.2 gives some of these methods for finding database capabilities.

The methods for getting database objects return lists of information in ResultSets. You can use the normal ResultSet methods, such as getString() and getInt(), to retrieve data from these ResultSets. If a given form of metadata is not available, these methods should throw a SQLException.

Many of these methods take arguments that are string patterns. Within a pattern string, "%" means a match with any substring of 0 or more characters, and "_" means a match with any one character. Only metadata entries matching the search pattern are returned. If a search pattern argument is set to a null reference, it means that the argument's criteria should be dropped from the search.

A SQLException will be thrown if a driver does not support a metadata method. In the case of methods that return a ResultSet, either a ResultSet (which may be empty) is returned or a SQLException is thrown.

TABLE 13.1   Some Methods for Retrieving General Information
in the DatabaseMetaData Interface

Method name	Description
allProcduresAreCallable	Returns true if all the procedures returned by getProcedures() can be called by the current user
allTablesAreSelectable	Returns true if all the tables returned by getTable can be selected by the current user
getURL	Gets the URL of the database
getUserName	Gets the username of the currently connected user
getDataBaseProductName	Gets the name of the database product
getDataBaseProductVersion	Gets the version of the database product
getDriverName	Gets the JDBC driver name for connecting to the database
getDriverVersion	Gets the JDBC driver version
getNumericFunctions	Gets a list of comma-separated numeric functions
getStringFunctions	Gets a list of comma-separated string functions
getSystemFunctions	Gets a list of comma-separated system function
getTimeDateFunctions	Gets a list of comma-separated time and date function
getMaxConnections	Gets the maximum number of active connections to the database
getMaxCursorNameLength	Gets the maximum cursor name length
getMaxSchemaNameLength	Gets the maximum schema name length
getMaxRowLength	Gets the maximum length of a single row
getMaxStatementLength	Gets the maximum length of a SQL statement
getMaxTableNameLength	Gets the maximum length of a table name
isReadOnly()	Returns true if the database is in read-only mode
storesLowerCaseIdentifiers	Returns true if the database treats mixed-case unquoted SQL identifiers as case insensitive and stores them in lower case
storesLowerCaseQuotedIdentifiers	Returns true if the database treats mixed-case quoted SQL identifiers as case insensitive and stores them in lower case
storesMixedCaseIdentifiers	If the database treats mixed-case unquoted SQL identifiers as case insensitive and stores them in mixed case
useLocalFiles	Returns true if the database stores tables in a local file
useLocalFilesPerTable	Returns true if the database uses a file for each table
getTypeInfo	Returns a ResultSet of all the SQL types supported by this database

TABLE 13.2   Some Methods for Finding Database Capabilities
in the DatabaseMetaData Interface

Method name	Description
supportsAlterTableWithAddColumn	Is "ALTER TABLE" with add column supported?
supportsAlterTableWithDropColumn	Is "ALTER TABLE" with drop column supported?
supportsANSI92EntryLevelSQL	Is the ANSI92 entry-level SQL grammar supported? All JDBC-Compliant drivers must return true.
supportsANSI92FullSQL	Is the ANSI full-SQL grammar supported?
supportsANSI92IntermediateSQL	Is the ANSI92 intermediate-SQL grammar supported?
supportsFullOuterJoins	Are full-nested outer joins supported?
supportsGroupBy	Is some form of "GROUP BY" clause supported?
supportsGroupByBeyondSelect	Can a "GROUP BY" clause add columns not in the SELECT provided it specifies all the columns in the SELECT?
supportsIntegrityEnhancementFacility	Is the SQL Integrity Enhancement Facility supported?
supportsMultipleTransactions	Are multiple transactions allowed?
supportsOrderUnrelated	Can an "ORDER BY" clause use columns not in the SELECT?
supportsOuterJoin	Is some form of outer join supported?
supportsPositionDelete	Is positioned DELETE supported?
supportsPositionUpdate	Is positioned UPDATE supported?
supportsSelectForUpdate	Is SELECT for UPDATE supported?
supportsUnion	Is SQL UNION supported?
supportsUnionALL	Is SQL UNION ALL supported?

Table 13.3 lists some of the methods for getting database object information.

The ResultSetMetaData interface describes information pertaining to the result set. A ResultSetMetaData object can be used to find out about the types and properties of the columns in a ResultSet. The methods in ResultSetMetaData have a single int parameter representing the column except that the getColumnCount() method has no parameters. All these methods return int, boolean, or String. The ResultSetMetaData interface has fewer methods than the DatabaseMetaData interface. Table 13.4 lists all the methods defined in ResultSetMetaData.

TABLE 13.3   Some Methods for Getting Database Objects
in the DatabaseMetaData Interface

Method Name	Parameter	Description
getCatalogs	()	Gets catalog names in this database
getColumns	(String catalog, String schemaPattern, String tableNamePattern, String columnNamePattern)	Gets a description of columns
getColumnPrivileges	(String catalog, String schemaPattern, String tableNamePattern, String columnNamePattern)	Gets a description of the access rights of a table's columns
getExportedKeys	(String catalog, String schema, String table)	Gets a description of the primary key columns that are referenced by a table's foreign key columns
getImportedKeys	(String catalog, String schema, String table)	Gets a description of the primary key columns referenced by a table's foreign key columns
getIndexInfo	(String catalog, String schema, String table, boolean unique, boolean approximate)	Gets a description of a table's indices and statistics
getPrimaryKeys	(String catalog, String schema, String table)	Gets the primary key in a table
getProcedures	(String catalog, String schemaPattern, String procedureNamePattern)	Gets a description of stored procedures
getProceduresColumns	(String catalog, String schemaPattern, String procedureNamePattern, String columnNamePattern)	Gets a description of a catalog's stored procedure peramaters and result columns
getTables	(String catalog, String schemaPattern, String tableNamePattern, String[] types)	Gets a description of tables
getTablePrivileges	(String catalog, String schemaPattern, String tableNamePattern)	Gets a description of the access rights for each table available in a catalog
getSchemas	()	Gets all the schemas in this database

TABLE 13.4   Methods in the ResultSetMetaData Interface

Method Name	Description
getCatalogName	Gets the catalog name of the table of the column
getColumnCount	Gets the number of columns in the ResultSet
getColumnDisplaySize	Gets the column's maximum width in characters
GetColumnLabel	Gets the column's title for use in printouts and displays
getColumnName	Gets the column's name
getColumnType	Gets the column's type in int, listed in java.sql.Types
getColumnTypeName	Gets the column's type in String
getPrecision	Gets the column's decimal precision
getScale	Gets the column's number of digits to right of the decimal point
getSchemaName	Gets the schema name of the table of the column
getTableName	Gets the table name of the column
isAutoIncrement	Is the column automatically numbered, thus read-only?
isCaseSensitive	Is the column case-sensitive?
isCashValue	Is the column a monetary value?
IsDefinitelyWritable	Will a write on the column definitely succeed?
isNullable	Does the column accept null?
isReadOnly	Is the column read-only?
isSearchable	Can the column be used in a where clause?
isSigned	Is the column a signed number?
isWritable	Is it possible for a write on the column to succeed?

For more detailed information about the methods defined in the DatabaseMetaData and ResultSetMetaData interfaces, please consult the JDBC API documentation.

Example 13.1   Discovering Databases

In this example, you will develop a useful utility to discover database information. A sample run of the utility is shown in Figure 13.1. The utility contains three menus: File, MetaData, and Extract. The File menu contains three commands: Connect to Database, Disconnect, and Exit. The Connect to Database command displays a dialog box, as shown in Figure 13.2, which lets you specify a database to connect. The Disconnect command disconnects an active database session. The Exit command terminates the program. The Metadata menu contains four commands: General Information, Functions, Data Types, and Table

Types. The Extract menu contains just one command named Tables to display a dialog box, as shown in Figure 13.3, that lets you choose a table name and show its primary key, its column definition, and its contents.

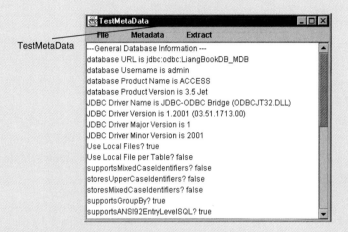

TestMetaData

Figure 13.1   *The TestMetaData utility explores database information.*

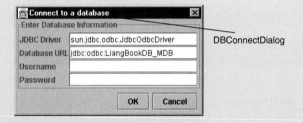

DBConnectDialog

Figure 13.2   *You can specify a database to connect in the Database Connect dialog box.*

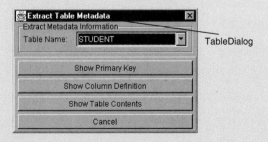

TableDialog

Figure 13.3   *You can choose a table name and show its primary key, its column definition, and its contents in the Extract Table Metadata dialog box.*

continues

The utility consists of three classes: TestMetaData (see Listing 13.1), DBConnect-Dialog (see Listing 13.2), and TableDialog (see Listing 13.3). TestMetaData displays the main interface with the menus and a text area inside a scroll pane. The text area is used to display the output from the menu commands. DBConnect-Dialog is a subclass of JDialog for gathering the connection information of the database and establishing connections. TableDialog is a subclass of JDialog that lets you choose a table name. The dialog box contains four buttons: Show Primary Key, Show Table Definition, Show Table Contents, and Cancel.

TestMetaData also contains the following methods for obtaining a particular type of database information:

- showGeneralDBInfo(): shows general information about the database, such as the database URL, current user name, the JDBC driver name, whether the database supports ANSI92, etc., as shown in Figure 13.1.

- showFunctions(): shows the standard functions supported by the database, as shown in Figure 13.4.

- showDataTypes(): shows the data types supported by the database, as shown in Figure 13.5.

- showTableTypes(): shows the table types supported by the database, as shown in Figure 13.6.

- showPrimaryKeyInfo(String tableName): shows the primary key of the table, as shown in Figure 13.7. This method is invoked in TableDialog.

- showColumns(String tableName): shows the columns of the table, as shown in Figure 13.8. This method is invoked in TableDialog.

- showTableContents(String tableName): shows the contents of the table, as shown in Figure 13.9. This method is invoked in TableDialog.

Figure 13.4   *The Functions menu command displays the functions supported in the database.*

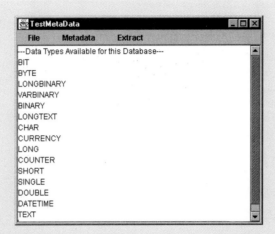

Figure 13.5 *The Data Types menu command displays the data types supported in the database.*

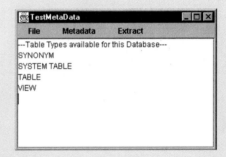

Figure 13.6 *The Table Types menu command displays the table types supported in the database.*

Figure 13.7 *The Show Primary Key button in* `TableDialog` *displays the primary key for the specified table.*

continues

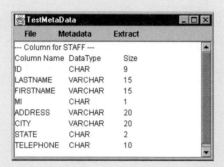

Figure 13.8   *The Show Column Definition button in* TableDialog *displays column name, type, and size for the specified table.*

Figure 13.9   *The Show Table Contents button in* TableDialog *displays the contents of the specified table.*

Here are the steps to complete the project.

1. Create a new project named MetaDataDemo.jpr, and create an applet named TestMetaData using the Applet Wizard. Create a dialog named DBConnectDialog that extends JDialog using the Dialog Wizard. The Dialog Wizard can be accessed from the Object Gallery. Create another dialog named TableDialog that extends JDialog.

2. Build DBConnectDialog as follows:

   2.1. With DBConnectDialog.java selected in the Navigation pane, select the Design tab in the Content pane to switch to UI Designer. By default, an instance of JPanel, named panel1, was automatically created when you created DBConnectDialog using the Dialog Wizard. Set the layout of panel1 to BorderLayout.

   2.2. Drop a JPanel to the center of panel1 to create jPanel1, and drop a JPanel to the south in panel1 to create jPanel2. Set the layout of jPanel1 to BorderLayout. Choose titled in the border property to create titledBorder1. Set the title property to "Enter Database Information" in the property editor for titledBorder1.

2.3. Drop a JPanel to the west of jPanel1 to create jPanel3, and drop a JPanel to the center of jPanel1 to create jPanel4. Set the layout of both jPanel3 and jPanel4 to GirdLayout, with the row property set to 4 and the column property set to 1.

2.4. Drop a JLabel four times to jPanel3, and set the text of the labels to "JDBC Driver," "Database URL," "Username," and "Password." Drop a JTextField three times to jPanel4, and rename the text fields jtfDriver, jtfURL, and jtfUsername. Drop a JPasswordField to jPanel4 and rename the object jpfPassword.

2.5. Set the layout of jPanel2 to FlowLayout with right alignment. Drop a JButton twice to create buttons OK and Cancel, and rename the buttons jbtOK and jbkCancel.

2.6. Declare a public data field named connection of the Connection type in DBConnectionDialog. This field stores the connection to the database once a connected session is established. Generate and implement the handlers for the OK and Cancel buttons, as shown in Listing 13.2.

3. Build TestMetaData as follows:

3.1. With TestMetaData.java selected in the Navigation pane, switch the UI Designer. Drop a JScrollPane from the Swing Containers page to the center of the applet (this) to create jScrollPane1. Drop a JTextArea into jScrollPane1 and rename the object to jtaOutput.

3.2. Drop a JMenuBar from the Swing Containers page to the UI to create jMenuBar1. Double-click jMenuBar1 to switch to the Menu Designer. Add a menu labeled File with three menu items "Connect to Database," "Disconnect," and "Exit," and add a separator between Disconnect and Exit. Add a menu named MetaData with four menu items "General Information," "Functions," "Data Types," and "Table Types." Add a menu named Extract with a menu item "Tables." Rename the menu item components jmiConnect, jmiDisconnect, jmiExit, jmiGeneralInfo, jmiFunction, jmiDataTypes, jmiTableTypes, and jmiTables.

3.3. Set the JMenuBar property of the applet to jMenuBar1.

3.4. Install DBConnectDialog in the Component palette, and drop a DBConnectDialog to the applet to create dBConnectDialog1. Set its modal property to True.

continues

3.5. Generate and implement the code for handling the action events for menu items, as shown in Listing 13.1.

4. Build `TableDialog` as follows:

4.1. With TableDialog.java selected in the Navigation pane, switch to UI Designer. By default, an instance of `JPanel`, named `panel1`, was automatically created when you created `TableDialog` using the Dialog Wizard. Set the `layout` of `panel1` to `BorderLayout`.

4.2. Drop a `JPanel` to the north of `panel1` to create `jPanel1`, and drop a `JPanel` to the center of `panel1` to create `jPanel2`. Set the `layout` of `jPanel1` to `BorderLayout`, and select the `border` property to titled. Set the `title` to "Select a table" in the property editor for `titledBorder1`.

4.3. Drop a `JLabel` to the west of `jPanel1`, and set its text to "Table Name." Drop a `JComboBox` to the center of `jPanel1`, and rename it `jcboTableNames`.

4.4. Set the `layout` of `jPanel2` to `GridLayout` with the row property set to 4 and the column property set to 1. Drop a `JButton` four times to `jPanel2` with their text properties set to "Show Primary Key," "Show Column Definition," "Show Table Contents," and "Cancel." Rename the buttons `jbtPrimaryKey`, `jbtColumn`, `jbtTableContents`, and `jbtCancel`.

4.5. Generate and implement the code for handling action events for the buttons, and for filling table names in the combo box, as shown in Listing 13.3.

4.6. Create a property named `testMetaData` (an instance of `TestMetaData`) so that `TableDialog` can access data members in the `TestMetaData` class. In the setter method of this property, invoke the method for filling in the table names in the combo box.

```java
package MetaDataDemo;

import java.sql.*;
import java.awt.*;
import java.awt.event.*;
import javax.swing.*;
import java.util.StringTokenizer;

public class TestMetaData extends JApplet
{
  // dbMetaData is for viewing database Metadata
  DatabaseMetaData dbMetaData;
```

Listing 13.1   *TestMetaData.java*

```
boolean isStandalone = false;
JMenuBar jMenuBar1 = new JMenuBar();
JMenu jMenu1 = new JMenu();
JMenuItem jmiConnect = new JMenuItem();
JMenuItem jmiDisconnect = new JMenuItem();
JMenuItem jmiExit = new JMenuItem();
JMenu jMenu2 = new JMenu();
JMenuItem jmiGeneralInfo = new JMenuItem();
JMenuItem jmiFunctions = new JMenuItem();
JMenuItem jmiDataTypes = new JMenuItem();
JMenu jMenu3 = new JMenu();
JMenuItem jmiTables = new JMenuItem();
DBConnectDialog dBConnectDialog1 = new DBConnectDialog();
TableDialog tableDialog1 = new TableDialog();
JScrollPane jScrollPane1 = new JScrollPane();
JTextArea jtaOutput = new JTextArea();
JMenuItem jmiTableTypes = new JMenuItem();

// Construct the applet
public TestMetaData()
{
}

// Initialize the applet
public void init()
{
  try
  {
    jbInit();
  }
  catch(Exception e)
  {
    e.printStackTrace();
  }
}

// Component initialization
private void jbInit() throws Exception
{
  this.setJMenuBar(jMenuBar1);
  this.setSize(new Dimension(400,300));
  jmiConnect.setText("Connect to Database");
  jmiConnect.addActionListener(new java.awt.event.ActionListener()
  {
    public void actionPerformed(ActionEvent e)
    {
      jmiConnect_actionPerformed(e);
    }
  });
  jmiDisconnect.setText("Disconnect");
  jmiDisconnect.addActionListener(
    new java.awt.event.ActionListener()
  {
    public void actionPerformed(ActionEvent e)
    {
      jmiDisconnect_actionPerformed(e);
    }
  });
  jmiExit.setText("Exit");
```

continues

565

```
        jmiExit.addActionListener(new java.awt.event.ActionListener()
        {
          public void actionPerformed(ActionEvent e)
          {
            jmiExit_actionPerformed(e);
          }
        });
        jMenu2.setText("Metadata");
        jmiGeneralInfo.setText("General Information");
        jmiGeneralInfo.addActionListener(
          new java.awt.event.ActionListener()
        {
          public void actionPerformed(ActionEvent e)
          {
            jmiGeneralInfo_actionPerformed(e);
          }
        });
        jmiFunctions.setText("Functions");
        jmiFunctions.addActionListener(
          new java.awt.event.ActionListener()
        {
          public void actionPerformed(ActionEvent e)
          {
            jmiFunctions_actionPerformed(e);
          }
        });
        jmiDataTypes.setText("Data Types");
        jmiDataTypes.addActionListener(
          new java.awt.event.ActionListener()
        {
          public void actionPerformed(ActionEvent e)
          {
            jmiDataTypes_actionPerformed(e);
          }
        });
        jMenu3.setText("Extract");
        jmiTables.setText("Tables");
        jmiTables.addActionListener(new java.awt.event.ActionListener()
        {
          public void actionPerformed(ActionEvent e)
          {
            jmiTables_actionPerformed(e);
          }
        });
        jMenu1.setText("File");
        dBConnectDialog1.setModal(true);
        jmiTableTypes.setText("Table Types");
        jmiTableTypes.addActionListener(
          new java.awt.event.ActionListener()
        {
          public void actionPerformed(ActionEvent e)
          {
            jmiTableTypes_actionPerformed(e);
          }
        });
        jMenuBar1.add(jMenu1);
        jMenuBar1.add(jMenu2);
        jMenuBar1.add(jMenu3);
```

Listing 13.1   *Continued*

```
      jMenu1.add(jmiConnect);
      jMenu1.add(jmiDisconnect);
      jMenu1.addSeparator();
      jMenu1.add(jmiExit);
      jMenu2.add(jmiGeneralInfo);
      jMenu2.add(jmiFunctions);
      jMenu2.add(jmiDataTypes);
      jMenu2.add(jmiTableTypes);
      jMenu3.add(jmiTables);

      this.getContentPane().add(jScrollPane1, BorderLayout.CENTER);
      jScrollPane1.getViewport().add(jtaOutput, null);
    }

    void jmiConnect_actionPerformed(ActionEvent e)
    {
      dBConnectDialog1.setVisible(true);

      try
      {
        if (dBConnectDialog1.connection != null)
          dbMetaData = dBConnectDialog1.connection.getMetaData();
      }
      catch (SQLException ex)
      {
        jtaOutput.setText(ex.getMessage());
      }
    }

    void jmiDisconnect_actionPerformed(ActionEvent e)
    {
      dBConnectDialog1.connection = null;
      dbMetaData = null;
    }

    void jmiExit_actionPerformed(ActionEvent e)
    {
      System.exit(0);
    }

    void jmiGeneralInfo_actionPerformed(ActionEvent e)
    {
      try
      {
        showGeneralDBInfo();
      }
      catch (SQLException ex)
      {
        jtaOutput.setText(ex.getMessage());
      }
    }

    void jmiFunctions_actionPerformed(ActionEvent e)
    {
      try
      {
        showFunctions();
      }
      catch (SQLException ex)
      {
```

continues

```
          jtaOutput.setText(ex.getMessage());
      }
   }

   void jmiDataTypes_actionPerformed(ActionEvent e)
   {
     try
     {
       showDataTypes();
     }
     catch (SQLException ex)
     {
       jtaOutput.setText(ex.getMessage());
     }
   }

   void jmiTableTypes_actionPerformed(ActionEvent e)
   {
     try
     {
       showTableTypes();
     }
     catch (SQLException ex)
     {
       jtaOutput.setText(ex.getMessage());
     }
   }

   void jmiTables_actionPerformed(ActionEvent e)
   {
     tableDialog1.setVisible(true);
     tableDialog1.setTestMetaData(this);
   }

   // Show information about the database
   public void showGeneralDBInfo() throws SQLException
   {
     jtaOutput.setText(null);
     jtaOutput.append("—-General Database Information —-\n");
     jtaOutput.append("database URL is " + dbMetaData.getURL()+'\n');
     jtaOutput.append("database Username is " +
       dbMetaData.getUserName()+'\n');
     jtaOutput.append("database Product Name is " +
       dbMetaData.getDatabaseProductName()+'\n');
     jtaOutput.append("database Product Version is " +
       dbMetaData.getDatabaseProductVersion()+'\n');
     jtaOutput.append("JDBC Driver Name is " +
       dbMetaData.getDriverName()+'\n');
     jtaOutput.append("JDBC Driver Version is " +
       dbMetaData.getDriverVersion()+'\n');
     jtaOutput.append("JDBC Driver Major Version is " +
       dbMetaData.getDriverMajorVersion()+'\n');
     jtaOutput.append("JDBC Driver Minor Version is " +
       dbMetaData.getDriverMinorVersion()+'\n');
     jtaOutput.append("Use Local Files? " +
       dbMetaData.usesLocalFiles()+'\n');
     jtaOutput.append("Use Local File per Table? " +
       dbMetaData.usesLocalFilePerTable()+'\n');
     jtaOutput.append("supportsMixedCaseIdentifiers? " +
```

Listing 13.1   *Continued*

```
        dbMetaData.supportsMixedCaseIdentifiers()+'\n');
      jtaOutput.append("storesUpperCaseIdentifiers? " +
        dbMetaData.storesUpperCaseIdentifiers()+'\n');
      jtaOutput.append("storesMixedCaseIdentifiers? " +
        dbMetaData.storesMixedCaseIdentifiers()+'\n');
      jtaOutput.append("supportsGroupBy? " +
        dbMetaData.supportsGroupBy()+'\n');
      jtaOutput.append("supportsANSI92EntryLevelSQL? " +
        dbMetaData.supportsANSI92EntryLevelSQL()+'\n');
      jtaOutput.append("supportsOuterJoins? " +
        dbMetaData.supportsOuterJoins()+'\n');
      jtaOutput.append("supportsAlterTableWithAddColumn? " +
        dbMetaData.supportsAlterTableWithAddColumn()+'\n');
      jtaOutput.append("supportsAlterTableWithDropColumn? " +
        dbMetaData.supportsAlterTableWithDropColumn()+'\n');
      jtaOutput.append("MaxTableNameLentgh is " +
        dbMetaData.getMaxTableNameLength()+'\n');
      jtaOutput.append("MaxColumnsInTable is " +
        dbMetaData.getMaxColumnsInTable()+'\n');
      jtaOutput.append("MaxStatements is " +
        dbMetaData.getMaxStatements()+'\n');
      jtaOutput.append("MaxColumnsInSelect is " +
        dbMetaData.getMaxColumnsInSelect()+'\n');
      jtaOutput.append("isCatalogAtStart? " +
        dbMetaData.isCatalogAtStart()+'\n');
      jtaOutput.append("supportsSelectForUpdate? " +
        dbMetaData.supportsSelectForUpdate()+'\n');
      jtaOutput.append("supportsStoredProcedures? " +
        dbMetaData.supportsStoredProcedures()+'\n');
      jtaOutput.append("supportsUnion? " +
        dbMetaData.supportsUnion()+'\n');
      jtaOutput.append("Max number of connections is " +
        dbMetaData.getMaxConnections()+'\n');
      jtaOutput.append("supportsTransactions? " +
        dbMetaData.supportsTransactions()+'\n');
      jtaOutput.append(
        "supportsDataDefinitionAndDataManipulationTransactions? " +
        dbMetaData.
          supportsDataDefinitionAndDataManipulationTransactions()+'\n');
      jtaOutput.append("getSchemaTerm is " +
        dbMetaData.getSchemaTerm()+'\n');
      jtaOutput.append("getProcedureTerm is " +
        dbMetaData.getProcedureTerm()+'\n');
      jtaOutput.append("getCatalogTerm is " +
        dbMetaData.getCatalogTerm()+'\n');
  }

  // Show available database functions
  public void showFunctions() throws SQLException
  {
    jtaOutput.setText(null);
    jtaOutput.append("--- Numerical Functions ---\n");
    showFunctions(dbMetaData.getNumericFunctions());
    jtaOutput.append("--- String Functions ---\n");
    showFunctions(dbMetaData.getStringFunctions());
    jtaOutput.append("--- System Functions ---\n");
    showFunctions(dbMetaData.getSystemFunctions());
    jtaOutput.append("--- Date and Time Functions ---\n");
    showFunctions(dbMetaData.getTimeDateFunctions());
  }
```

continues

```java
        public void showFunctions(String s)
        {
          StringTokenizer st = new StringTokenizer(s, ",");
          while (st.hasMoreTokens())
            jtaOutput.append(st.nextToken()+'\n');
        }

        // Show available data types
        public void showDataTypes() throws SQLException
        {
          jtaOutput.setText(null);
          jtaOutput.append("---Data Types Available for this Database---\n"
        );
          ResultSet rs = dbMetaData.getTypeInfo();
          while (rs.next())
            jtaOutput.append(rs.getString(1)+'\n');
        }

        // Show available table types
        public void showTableTypes() throws SQLException
        {
          jtaOutput.setText(null);
          jtaOutput.append(
            "---Table Types available for this Database---\n" );
          ResultSet rs = dbMetaData.getTableTypes();

          while (rs.next())
            jtaOutput.append(rs.getString(1)+'\n');
        }
      }
```

Listing 13.1   *Continued*

```java
      package MetaDataDemo;

      import java.awt.*;
      import javax.swing.*;
      import javax.swing.border.*;
      import java.awt.event.*;
      import java.sql.*;

      public class DBConnectDialog extends JDialog
      {
        // Connection to the database
        public Connection connection = null;

        JPanel panel1 = new JPanel();
        BorderLayout borderLayout1 = new BorderLayout();
        JPanel jPanel1 = new JPanel();
        JPanel jPanel2 = new JPanel();
        FlowLayout flowLayout1 = new FlowLayout();
        JButton jbtOK = new JButton();
        JButton jbtCancel = new JButton();
        TitledBorder titledBorder1;
        BorderLayout borderLayout2 = new BorderLayout();
        JPanel jPanel3 = new JPanel();
        JPanel jPanel4 = new JPanel();
```

Listing 13.2   *DBConnectDialog.java*

```
      GridLayout gridLayout1 = new GridLayout();
      JLabel jLabel1 = new JLabel();
      JLabel jLabel2 = new JLabel();
      JLabel jLabel3 = new JLabel();
      JLabel jLabel4 = new JLabel();
      GridLayout gridLayout2 = new GridLayout();
      JTextField jtfDriver = new JTextField();
      JTextField jtfURL = new JTextField();
      JTextField jtfUsername = new JTextField();
      JPasswordField jpfPassword = new JPasswordField();

      // Constructor
      public DBConnectDialog(Frame frame, String title, boolean modal)
      {
        super(frame, title, modal);
        try
        {
          jbInit();
          pack();
        }
        catch (Exception ex)
        {
          ex.printStackTrace();
        }
      }

      // Default constructor
      public DBConnectDialog()
      {
        this(null, "", false);
      }

      void jbInit() throws Exception
      {
        titledBorder1 = new TitledBorder("");
        panel1.setLayout(borderLayout1);
        jPanel2.setLayout(flowLayout1);
        flowLayout1.setAlignment(2);
        jbtOK.setText("OK");
        jbtOK.addActionListener(new java.awt.event.ActionListener()
        {
          public void actionPerformed(ActionEvent e)
          {
            jbtOK_actionPerformed(e);
          }
        });
        jbtCancel.setText("Cancel");
        jbtCancel.addActionListener(new java.awt.event.ActionListener()
        {
          public void actionPerformed(ActionEvent e)
          {
            jbtCancel_actionPerformed(e);
          }
        });
        jPanel1.setBorder(titledBorder1);
        jPanel1.setLayout(borderLayout2);
        titledBorder1.setTitle("Enter Database Information");
        jPanel3.setLayout(gridLayout1);
        jLabel1.setText("JDBC Driver");
        jLabel2.setText("Database URL");
```

continues

571

```
            jLabel3.setText("Username");
            jLabel4.setText("Password");
            gridLayout1.setColumns(1);
            gridLayout1.setRows(4);
            jPanel4.setLayout(gridLayout2);
            gridLayout2.setColumns(1);
            gridLayout2.setHgap(10);
            gridLayout2.setRows(4);

            // for JDBC-ODBC
            jtfDriver.setText("sun.jdbc.odbc.JdbcOdbcDriver");
            jtfURL.setText("jdbc:odbc:LiangBookDB_MDB");

            /* for InterClient
            jtfDriver.setText("interbase.interclient.Driver");
            jtfURL.setText(
              "jdbc:interbase://localhost/C:/LiangBook/LiangBookDB.gdb");
            jtfUsername.setText("SYSDBA");
            jpfPassword.setText("masterkey");
            */

            /* for Oracle Type 4 driver
            jtfDriver.setText("oracle.jdbc.driver.OracleDriver");
            jtfURL.setText("jdbc:oracle:thin:@sesrv00.ipfw.edu:1521:test");
            jtfUsername.setText("scott");
            jpfPassword.setText("tiger");
            */

            this.setTitle("Connect to a database");
            getContentPane().add(panel1);
            panel1.add(jPanel1, BorderLayout.CENTER);
            jPanel1.add(jPanel3, BorderLayout.WEST);
            jPanel3.add(jLabel1, null);
            jPanel3.add(jLabel2, null);
            jPanel3.add(jLabel3, null);
            jPanel3.add(jLabel4, null);
            jPanel1.add(jPanel4, BorderLayout.CENTER);
            jPanel4.add(jtfDriver, null);
            jPanel4.add(jtfURL, null);
            jPanel4.add(jtfUsername, null);
            jPanel4.add(jpfPassword, null);
            panel1.add(jPanel2, BorderLayout.SOUTH);
            jPanel2.add(jbtOK, null);
            jPanel2.add(jbtCancel, null);
          }

          void jbtOK_actionPerformed(ActionEvent e)
          {
            // Get database information from the user input
            String driver = jtfDriver.getText().trim();
            String url = jtfURL.getText().trim();
            String username = jtfUsername.getText().trim();
            String password = new String(jpfPassword.getPassword());

            // Connection to the database
            try
            {
              Class.forName(driver);
```

Listing 13.2   *Continued*

```
          System.out.println("Driver " + driver + "loaded\n");
          connection = DriverManager.getConnection(
            url, username, password);
          System.out.println("Connected to " + url + '\n');
          setVisible(false);
        }
        catch (java.lang.Exception ex)
        {
          ex.printStackTrace();
        }
      }

      void jbtCancel_actionPerformed(ActionEvent e)
      {
        // Close the dialog box
        setVisible(false);
      }
    }
```

Listing 13.2 *Continued*

```
    package MetaDataDemo;

    import java.awt.*;
    import javax.swing.*;
    import javax.swing.border.*;
    import java.awt.event.*;
    import java.sql.*;

    public class TableDialog extends JDialog
    {
      // dbMetaData is passed from TestMetaData.dbMetaData
      DatabaseMetaData dbMetaData;

      // jtaOutput is passed from TestMetaData.jtaOutput
      JTextArea jtaOutput;

      JPanel panel1 = new JPanel();
      BorderLayout borderLayout1 = new BorderLayout();
      JPanel jPanel1 = new JPanel();
      JPanel jPanel2 = new JPanel();
      BorderLayout borderLayout2 = new BorderLayout();
      JLabel jLabel1 = new JLabel();
      JComboBox jcboTableNames = new JComboBox();
      TitledBorder titledBorder1;
      JButton jbtPrimaryKey = new JButton();
      JButton jbtColumn = new JButton();
      JButton jbtTableContents = new JButton();
      JButton jbtCancel = new JButton();
      GridLayout gridLayout1 = new GridLayout();
      private MetaDataDemo.TestMetaData testMetaData;

      // Constructor
      public TableDialog(Frame frame, String title, boolean modal)
      {
        super(frame, title, modal);
        try
```

continues

Listing 13.3 *TableDialog.java*

```
      {
        jbInit();
        pack();
      }
      catch(Exception ex)
      {
        ex.printStackTrace();
      }
    }

    // Default constructor
    public TableDialog()
    {
      this(null, "", false);
    }

    void jbInit() throws Exception
    {
      titledBorder1 = new TitledBorder("");
      panel1.setLayout(borderLayout1);
      jPanel1.setLayout(borderLayout2);
      jLabel1.setText("Table Name");
      jPanel1.setBorder(titledBorder1);
      titledBorder1.setTitle("Select a table");
      jPanel2.setLayout(gridLayout1);
      jbtPrimaryKey.setText("Show Primary Key");
      jbtPrimaryKey.addActionListener(
        new java.awt.event.ActionListener()
      {
        public void actionPerformed(ActionEvent e)
        {
          jbtPrimaryKey_actionPerformed(e);
        }
      });
      jbtColumn.setText("Show Column Definition");
      jbtColumn.addActionListener(new java.awt.event.ActionListener()
      {
        public void actionPerformed(ActionEvent e)
        {
          jbtColumn_actionPerformed(e);
        }
      });
      jbtTableContents.setText("Show Table Contents");
      jbtTableContents.addActionListener(
        new java.awt.event.ActionListener()
      {
        public void actionPerformed(ActionEvent e)
        {
          jbtTableContents_actionPerformed(e);
        }
      });
      jbtCancel.setText("Cancel");
      jbtCancel.addActionListener(new java.awt.event.ActionListener()
      {
        public void actionPerformed(ActionEvent e)
        {
          jbtCancel_actionPerformed(e);
        }
```

Listing 13.3 *Continued*

```java
      });
      gridLayout1.setColumns(1);
      gridLayout1.setRows(4);
      this.setTitle("Extract table information");
      getContentPane().add(panel1);
      panel1.add(jPanel1, BorderLayout.NORTH);
      jPanel1.add(jLabel1, BorderLayout.WEST);
      jPanel1.add(jcboTableNames, BorderLayout.CENTER);
      panel1.add(jPanel2, BorderLayout.CENTER);
      jPanel2.add(jbtPrimaryKey, null);
      jPanel2.add(jbtColumn, null);
      jPanel2.add(jbtTableContents, null);
      jPanel2.add(jbtCancel, null);
    }

    void jbtPrimaryKey_actionPerformed(ActionEvent e)
    {
      try
      {
        showPrimaryKeyInfo((String)jcboTableNames.getSelectedItem());
      }
      catch (SQLException ex)
      {
        jtaOutput.setText(ex.getMessage());
      }
    }

    void jbtColumn_actionPerformed(ActionEvent e)
    {
      try
      {
        showColumns((String)jcboTableNames.getSelectedItem());
      }
      catch (SQLException ex)
      {
        jtaOutput.setText(ex.getMessage());
      }
    }

    void jbtTableContents_actionPerformed(ActionEvent e)
    {
      try
      {
        showTableContents((String)jcboTableNames.getSelectedItem());
      }
      catch (SQLException ex)
      {
        jtaOutput.setText(ex.getMessage());
      }
    }

    void jbtCancel_actionPerformed(ActionEvent e)
    {
      // Close the dialog box
      setVisible(false);
    }

    // Fill in the table names in the combo box
    private void fillTableNames()
    {
```

continues

575

```java
      try
      {
        //Retrieve a list of all available tables.
        ResultSet rs = dbMetaData.getTables("", "", "%", null );

        if (rs == null)
        {
          //No tables were found.
          jcboTableNames.addItem("<none>");
        }
        else
        {
          while (rs.next())
            jcboTableNames.addItem(rs.getString(3));
        }
      }
      catch (java.sql.SQLException ex)
      {
        jtaOutput.setText(ex.getMessage());
      }
    }

    // Show primary key information
    public void showPrimaryKeyInfo(String tableName)
      throws SQLException
    {
      jtaOutput.setText(null);
      jtaOutput.append("Primary Key for Table " + tableName + " is ");
      ResultSet rs = dbMetaData.getPrimaryKeys("", "", tableName);
      while (rs.next())
        jtaOutput.append(rs.getString(4));
    }

    //Show column information
    public void showColumns(String tableName) throws SQLException
    {
      jtaOutput.setText(null);
      jtaOutput.append("--- Column for " + tableName + " ---\n");
      ResultSet rs = dbMetaData.getColumns("", "", tableName, null);
      jtaOutput.append("Column Name\tDataType\tSize\n");

      while (rs.next())
        jtaOutput.append(rs.getString(4)+'\t'+rs.getString(6)+'\t'+
          rs.getString(7)+'\n');
    }

    // Show table contents
    public void showTableContents(String tableName) throws SQLException
    {
      Statement stmt =
        testMetaData.dBConnectDialog1.connection.createStatement();
      ResultSet rs = stmt.executeQuery("SELECT * FROM " + tableName);
      ResultSetMetaData rsMetaData = rs.getMetaData();
      int colCount = rsMetaData.getColumnCount();

      StringBuffer strBuf = new StringBuffer();
      jtaOutput.setText(null);
```

Listing 13.3 *Continued*

```
            strBuf.append("--- Contents for " + tableName + " Table ---\n");
            for (int i=1; i<colCount; i++)
              strBuf.append(rsMetaData.getColumnName(i)+"\t");
            strBuf.append(
              "\n— — — — — — — — — — — — — — — — — — — — —\n");

            while (rs.next())
            {
              for (int i=1; i<colCount; i++)
                strBuf.append(rs.getString(i)+'\t');
              strBuf.append("\n");
            }

            jtaOutput.setText(strBuf.toString());
          }

          public void setTestMetaData(
            MetaDataDemo.TestMetaData newTestMetaData)
          {
            testMetaData = newTestMetaData;
            dbMetaData = testMetaData.dbMetaData;
            jtaOutput = testMetaData.jtaOutput;
            fillTableNames();
          }

          public MetaDataDemo.TestMetaData getTestMetaData()
          {
            return testMetaData;
          }
        }
```

Listing 13.3   *Continued*

Example Review

The variable connection encapsulates all the work in the DBConnectDialog class. An instance of DBConnectDialog was created in TestMetaData, and the dialog box is displayed when the Connect to Database menu command is issued. The program attempts to establish a connection when the OK button is clicked in the dialog box. This variable is non-null if a connection to the database is established. The classes DBConnectDialog, TestMetaData, and TableDialog are related through the connection variable.

Once connected, dbMetaData (an instance of DatabaseMetaData) is created in the TestMetaData class. You can then obtain general information, available functions, data types, and table types through dbMetaData in TestMetaData.

The TableDialog class exposes the information on a specific table. The instance of TestMetaData is passed to TableDialog using the setTestMetaData() method in the TableDialog class. TableDialog can access dbMetaData and jtaOutput in TestMetaData, and can reference the connection variable in the DBConnectDialog through TestMetaData.

The UI of `TestMetaData` consists of the menus and a text field inside a scroll pane. The `modal` property in `dBConnectDialog1` must be set to true, for otherwise the try/catch block after the statement

```
dBConnectDialog1.setVisible(true);
```

would be executed immediately and no connection has been established.

■ NOTE

Not all the JDBC drivers implement all the features proposed in the `DatabaseMetaData` interface. For instance, the JDBC-ODBC driver does not support extract table information, and the InterClient driver does fully support the general database information retrieval.

■ TIP

You can use the JDBC Explorer to view database metadata. The JDBC Explorer can be accessed from the Tools menu. This is a pure-Java utility that enables you to browse a set of databases, its associated tables, views, and stored procedures in addition to database metadata. For more information, please refer to "JDBC Explorer User Guide" in JBuilder Help. JDBC Explorer is not available in JBuilder 3 Standard Edition.

Statement

Once a connection to a particular database is established, it can be used to send SQL statements from your program to the database. JDBC provides `Statement`, `PreparedStatement`, and `CallableStatement` interfaces to facilitate sending statements to a database for execution and receiving execution results from the database, as shown in Figure 13.10.

The `Statement` interface is used to execute static SQL statements that contain no parameters. The `PreparedStatement`, extending `Statement`, is used to execute a precompiled SQL statement with or without IN parameters. The `CallableStatement`, extending `PreparedStatement`, is used to execute a call to a database-stored procedure.

If a `Connection` object is perceived as a cable linking your program to a database, an object of `Statement` or its subclass can be viewed as a cart that takes the SQL statements for execution by the database and brings the result back to the program. A `Statement` object is created using the `createStatement()` method in the `Connection` interface. For example, the following code in Example 13.1 creates a `Statement` stmt on a particular `Connection` conn.

```
Connection conn = DriverManager.getConnection
  ("jdbc:odbc:LiangBookDB_MDB", "", "" );
Statement stmt = conn.createStatement();
```

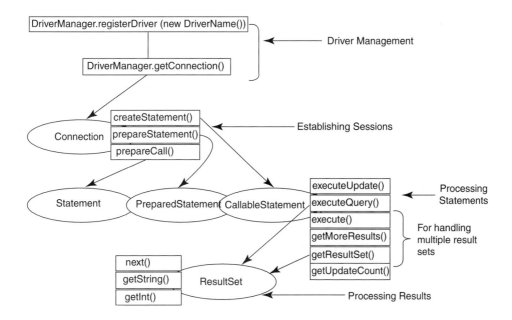

Figure 13.10   *JDBC classes enable Java programs to connect to the database, send SQL statements, and process results.*

The Statement interface provides many methods listed in Table 13.5 for executing various types of SQL statements, getting execution results and information, and controlling the executions.

The execute(), executeQuery(), and executeUpdate() Methods

The methods for executing SQL statements are execute(), executeQuery(), and executeUpdate(), each of which accepts a string containing a SQL statement as an argument. This string is passed to the database for execution. The execute() method should be used if the execution produces multiple result sets, multiple update counts, or a combination of result sets and update counts. The executeQuery() method should be used if the execution produces a single result set, such as the SQL SELECT statement. The executeUpdate() method should be used if the statement results in a single or none update count, such as the SQL INSERT, DELETE, UPDATE, or a SQL DDL statement.

The executeQuery() method returns a ResultSet object. The executeUpdate() returns an update count, i.e., an int value for the number of rows affected by the SQL statements. This value is the number of rows inserted, deleted, or updated for successful execution of a SQL INSERT, DELETE, or UPDATE statement. This value is 0 for a SQL DDL statement.

TABLE 13.5   Statement **Methods**

Method Name	Description
cancel	Called by one thread to cancel a statement being executed by another thread
clearWarning	Clears the warnings for the current SQL statement
close	Closes the statement for immediately releasing the associated resource
execute	Executes a SQL statement that may return multiple result sets
executeQuery	Execute a SQL statement that returns a single result set
executeUpdate	Executes a SQL INSERT, UPDATE, DELETE, or SQL DDL statement
getMaxFieldSize	Gets a maximum size for all the columns a result set can have
getMaxRows	Gets the maximum numbers of rows a result set can contain
getMoreResults	Moves to the next result set. Used for SQL statements that return multiple results
getQueryTimeout	Gets the number of seconds the driver will wait for a statement to execute
getResultSet	Returns a ResultSet for the current result
getUpdateCount	Returns current result as an update count. Used for SQL INSERT, UPDATE, and DELETE statements
getWarnings	Returns a SQLWarning for the current statement
setCursorName	Sets the cursor name for subsequent use in SQL positioned update/delete statements
setEscapeProcessing	Sets true or false on escape processing for the statement
setMaxFieldSize	Sets the maximum size for a column in a result set
setMaxRows	Sets the maximum number of rows in a result set
setQueryTimeout	Sets the maximum time for a driver to wait for a statement to execute

The execute() method returns a boolean value. The value is true if the first result is a ResultSet; false if it returns an update count or there are no more results. The getResultSet() and getUpdateCount() are called to process the result produced by the execute() method. The getResultSet() method is used to get the current result set. If the current result is an update count, or there are no more results, getResultSet() returns null. The getUpdateCount() method returns the current result as an update count; if the result is a ResultSet or there are no more results, -1 is returned. When getUpdateCount() returns -1, this means that the result is a ResultSet or that there are no more results. To determine what -1 really means, you can call getResultSet(). If both getResultSet() return null and getUpdateCount() returns -1, there are no more results.

After the current result, whether a ResultSet or an update count, you need to call getMoreResults() to move to a statement's next result. This method returns a boolean value, which returns true if the result is a ResultSet; false if it is an update count or there are no more results. If getMoreResults() returns false and getUpdateCount() returns -1, there are no more results.

Example 13.2 Using Statement to Execute Static SQL Statements

In this example, you will write a program to create an address book for viewing addresses and inserting new addresses. The addresses are stored in an Address table consisting of the following fields: FIRSTNAME, MI, LASTNAME, STREET, CITY, STATE, ZIP, TELEPHONE, and EMAIL, defined in the following statement:

```
CREATE TABLE ADDRESSBOOK
(
  FIRSTNAME VARCHAR(15),
  MI CHAR(1),
  LASTNAME VARCHAR(15),
  ADDRESS VARCHAR(40),
  CITY VARCHAR(20),
  STATE CHAR(2),
  ZIP CHAR(5),
  TELEPHONE CHAR(10),
  EMAIL CHAR(30)
);
```

The program contains two menus: File and Operation. The File menu contains menu items "Connect to Database" and "Exit," as shown in Figure 13.11. The Operation menu contains a single menu item, "Using Static SQL Statements." Choosing "Connect to Database" brings up a dialog box, as shown in Figure 13.2, to let you connect to a database. After your program is connected to the database, you may choose "Using Static SQL Statements" to view and insert an address, as shown in Figure 13.12. To view an address, enter the first name and the last name, then click the Search button. The Insert button inserts a new address in the database. The Clear button clears all the fields.

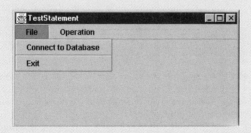

Figure 13.11   *You may connect to a JDBC compliant database and test static SQL statements in this program.*

continues

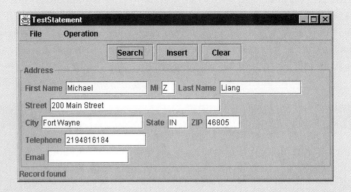

Figure 13.12   *Static SQL statements are used in this program to retrieve and modify database information.*

The project can be divided into two steps: creating the applet with menus, and creating the panel for processing the address. The panel is placed to the applet when the "Using Static SQL Statements" menu is selected after connecting to a particular database.

1. Creating the frame with menus

   1.1. Create a new project named StatementDemo.jpr, and create an applet named TestStatement using the Applet Wizard.

   1.2. With TestStatement.java selected in the Navigation pane, switch to the UI Designer in the Content pane. Drop a `JMenuBar` to the Content pane to create `jMenuBar1`. Double-click `jMenuBar1` in the Component tree to bring up the Menu Designer.

   1.3. Create the File menu and add menu items "Connect to Database," a separator, and "Exit" in the File menu. Create the Operation menu and add a menu item "Using Static SQL Statements" in the Operation menu. Change the menu item names to `jmiConnect`, `jmiExit`, and `jmiStaticSQL`.

   1.4. Drop a `DBConnectDialog` from the Component palette to create `dBConnectDialog1`. Set its `modal` property to True. `DBConnecDialog` was created in Example 13.1.

   1.5. Set the `JMenuBar` property of the applet to `jMenuBar1`.

   1.6. Generate and implement the code for handling the menu commands "Connect to Database," "Exit," and "Using Static SQL Statements," as shown in Listing 13.4.

```
package StatementDemo;

import java.awt.*;
import java.awt.event.*;
import java.applet.*;
import javax.swing.*;
import MetaDataDemo.*;

public class TestStatement extends JApplet
{
  boolean isStandalone = false;
  JMenuBar jMenuBar1 = new JMenuBar();
  JMenu jMenu1 = new JMenu();
  JMenuItem jmiConnect = new JMenuItem();
  JMenu jMenu2 = new JMenu();
  JMenuItem jmiStaticSQL = new JMenuItem();
  JMenuItem jmiExit = new JMenuItem();
  DBConnectDialog dBConnectDialog1 = new DBConnectDialog();

  // Construct the applet
  public TestStatement()
  {
  }

  // Initialize the applet
  public void init()
  {
    try
    {
      jbInit();
    }
    catch(Exception e)
    {
      e.printStackTrace();
    }
  }

  // Component initialization
  private void jbInit() throws Exception
  {
    this.setJMenuBar(jMenuBar1);
    this.setSize(new Dimension(400,300));
    jMenu1.setText("File");
    jmiConnect.setText("Connect to Database");
    jmiConnect.addActionListener(new java.awt.event.ActionListener()
    {
      public void actionPerformed(ActionEvent e)
      {
        jmiConnect_actionPerformed(e);
      }
    });
    jMenu2.setText("Operation");
    jmiStaticSQL.setText("Using Static SQL Statements");
    jmiStaticSQL.addActionListener(
      new java.awt.event.ActionListener()
    {
      public void actionPerformed(ActionEvent e)
      {
```

continues

Listing 13.4   *TestStatement.java*

```
              jmiStaticSQL_actionPerformed(e);
          }
        });
        jmiExit.setText("Exit");
        jmiExit.addActionListener(new java.awt.event.ActionListener()
        {
          public void actionPerformed(ActionEvent e)
          {
            jmiExit_actionPerformed(e);
          }
        });
        dBConnectDialog1.setModal(true);
        jMenuBar1.add(jMenu1);
        jMenuBar1.add(jMenu2);
        jMenu1.add(jmiConnect);
        jMenu1.addSeparator();
        jMenu1.add(jmiExit);
        jMenu2.add(jmiStaticSQL);
      }

      // Handler for Connect menu command
      void jmiConnect_actionPerformed(ActionEvent e)
      {
        dBConnectDialog1.setVisible(true);
      }

      // Handler for static SQL demo
      void jmiStaticSQL_actionPerformed(ActionEvent e)
      {
        if (dBConnectDialog1.connection != null)
        {
          // Add AddressBook panel to the applet
          this.getContentPane().add(
            new AddressBook(dBConnectDialog1.connection),
            BorderLayout.CENTER);

          this.validate();
        }
        else
          System.out.println("Database not connected");
      }

      void jmiExit_actionPerformed(ActionEvent e)
      {
        System.exit(0);
      }
    }
```

Listing 13.4 *Continued*

2. Creating the AddressBook panel

    2.1. Create AddressBook that inherits JPanel using the JavaBean Wizard from the Object Gallery.

    2.2. Use the UI Designer to lay out the UI components in the panel.

2.3. Drop a `JPanel` to the center of `AddressBook` to create `jpAddress`. Set its `layout` to `GridLayout`, with row set to 5 and column set to 1. Drop a `JPanel` five times to `jpAddress`, and drop appropriate labels and text fields for displaying address into these panels. Set the `text` property of the labels to "First Name," "MI," "Last Name," "Street," "City," "State," "Zip," "Telephone," and "Email." Rename the text fields `jtfFirstName`, `jtfMI`, `jtfLastName`, `jtfStreet`, `jtfCity`, `jtfState`, `jtfZip`, `jtfTelephone`, and `jtfEmail`. Set an appropriate value in the `column` property of each text field.

2.4. Drop a `JPanel` to the north of `AddressBook` to create `jpButton`. Drop a `JButton` three times into `jpButton` to create the Search, Insert, and Clear buttons. Rename them `jbtSearch`, `jbtInsert`, and `jbtClear`.

2.5. Drop a `JLabel` to the south of `AddressBook` to create `jlblStatus`.

2.6. Create a variable connection of the `java.sql.Connection` type in `AddressBook`, and create a new constructor with a parameter of the `Connection` type, as shown in Listing 13.5.

2.7. Generate and implement the code for handling the three buttons, as shown in Listing 13.5.

```
package StatementDemo;

import java.awt.*;
import javax.swing.*;
import javax.swing.border.*;
import java.awt.event.*;
import java.sql.*;

public class AddressBook extends JPanel
{
  BorderLayout borderLayout1 = new BorderLayout();
  JPanel jpAddress = new JPanel();
  JPanel jpButtons = new JPanel();
  GridLayout gridLayout1 = new GridLayout();
  JPanel jPanel3 = new JPanel();
  JPanel jPanel4 = new JPanel();
  JPanel jPanel5 = new JPanel();
  JPanel jPanel6 = new JPanel();
  JPanel jPanel7 = new JPanel();
  JLabel jLabel1 = new JLabel();
  protected JTextField jtfFirstName = new JTextField();
  JLabel jLabel2 = new JLabel();
  protected JTextField jtfMI = new JTextField();
  JLabel jLabel3 = new JLabel();
  protected JTextField jtfLastName = new JTextField();
  FlowLayout flowLayout1 = new FlowLayout();
  TitledBorder titledBorder1;
```

continues

Listing 13.5   *AddressBook.java*

```
            JLabel jLabel4 = new JLabel();
            protected JTextField jtfStreet = new JTextField();
            FlowLayout flowLayout2 = new FlowLayout();
            JLabel jLabel5 = new JLabel();
            protected JTextField jtfCity = new JTextField();
            JLabel jLabel6 = new JLabel();
            protected JTextField jtfState = new JTextField();
            JLabel jLabel7 = new JLabel();
            protected JTextField jtfZip = new JTextField();
            FlowLayout flowLayout3 = new FlowLayout();
            JLabel jLabel8 = new JLabel();
            protected JTextField jtfTelephone = new JTextField();
            FlowLayout flowLayout4 = new FlowLayout();
            FlowLayout flowLayout5 = new FlowLayout();
            JLabel jLabel9 = new JLabel();
            protected JTextField jtfEmail = new JTextField();
            JButton jbtSearch = new JButton();
            JButton jbtInset = new JButton();
            JButton jbtClear = new JButton();
            protected JLabel jlblStatus = new JLabel();

            // Database connection passed from DBConnectDialog
            Connection connection;

            // Default constructor
            public AddressBook()
            {
              try
              {
                jbInit();
              }
              catch(Exception ex)
              {
                ex.printStackTrace();
              }
            }

            // New constructor
            public AddressBook(Connection connection)
            {
              this();
              this.connection = connection;
              jlblStatus.setText("Using static SQL statements");
            }

            private void jbInit() throws Exception
            {
              titledBorder1 = new TitledBorder("");
              this.setLayout(borderLayout1);
              jpAddress.setLayout(gridLayout1);
              gridLayout1.setRows(5);
              jLabel1.setText("First Name");
              jtfFirstName.setBackground(Color.yellow);
              jtfFirstName.setColumns(12);
              jLabel2.setText("MI");
              jtfMI.setColumns(2);
              jLabel3.setText("Last Name");
              jtfLastName.setBackground(Color.yellow);
```

Listing 13.5   *Continued*

```
jtfLastName.setColumns(12);
jPanel3.setLayout(flowLayout1);
flowLayout1.setAlignment(FlowLayout.LEFT);
jLabel4.setText("Street");
jtfStreet.setColumns(25);
jPanel4.setLayout(flowLayout2);
flowLayout2.setAlignment(FlowLayout.LEFT);
jLabel5.setText("City");
jtfCity.setColumns(15);
jLabel6.setText("State");
jtfState.setColumns(3);
jLabel7.setText("ZIP");
jtfZip.setColumns(5);
jPanel5.setLayout(flowLayout3);
flowLayout3.setAlignment(FlowLayout.LEFT);
jLabel8.setText("Telephone");
jtfTelephone.setColumns(12);
jPanel6.setLayout(flowLayout4);
flowLayout4.setAlignment(FlowLayout.LEFT);
jPanel7.setLayout(flowLayout5);
flowLayout5.setAlignment(FlowLayout.LEFT);
jLabel9.setText("Email");
jtfEmail.setColumns(12);
jbtSearch.setText("Search");
jbtSearch.addActionListener(new java.awt.event.ActionListener()
{
  public void actionPerformed(ActionEvent e)
  {
    jbtSearch_actionPerformed(e);
  }
});
jbtInset.setText("Insert");
jbtInset.addActionListener(new java.awt.event.ActionListener()
{
  public void actionPerformed(ActionEvent e)
  {
    jbtInset_actionPerformed(e);
  }
});
jbtClear.setText("Clear");
jbtClear.addActionListener(new java.awt.event.ActionListener()
{
  public void actionPerformed(ActionEvent e)
  {
    jbtClear_actionPerformed(e);
  }
});
titledBorder1.setTitle("Address");
jpAddress.setBorder(titledBorder1);
jlblStatus.setText("jLabel10");
this.add(jpAddress, BorderLayout.CENTER);
jpAddress.add(jPanel3, null);
jPanel3.add(jLabel1, null);
jPanel3.add(jtfFirstName, null);
jPanel3.add(jLabel2, null);
jPanel3.add(jtfMI, null);
jPanel3.add(jLabel3, null);
jPanel3.add(jtfLastName, null);
jpAddress.add(jPanel4, null);
jPanel4.add(jLabel4, null);
```

continues

587

```
            jPanel4.add(jtfStreet, null);
            jpAddress.add(jPanel5, null);
            jPanel5.add(jLabel5, null);
            jPanel5.add(jtfCity, null);
            jPanel5.add(jLabel6, null);
            jPanel5.add(jtfState, null);
            jPanel5.add(jLabel7, null);
            jPanel5.add(jtfZip, null);
            jpAddress.add(jPanel6, null);
            jPanel6.add(jLabel8, null);
            jPanel6.add(jtfTelephone, null);
            jpAddress.add(jPanel7, null);
            jPanel7.add(jLabel9, null);
            jPanel7.add(jtfEmail, null);
            this.add(jpButtons, BorderLayout.NORTH);
            jpButtons.add(jbtSearch, null);
            jpButtons.add(jbtInset, null);
            jpButtons.add(jbtClear, null);
            this.add(jlblStatus, BorderLayout.SOUTH);
          }

          public void setConnection(java.sql.Connection newConnection)
          {
            connection = newConnection;
          }

          void jbtSearch_actionPerformed(ActionEvent e)
          {
            select();
          }

          void jbtInset_actionPerformed(ActionEvent e)
          {
            insert();
          }

          void jbtClear_actionPerformed(ActionEvent e)
          {
            clear();
          }

          protected void select()
          {
            String query = "SELECT * FROM ADDRESSBOOK WHERE " +
              "FIRSTNAME = " +
              "'" + jtfFirstName.getText().trim() + "'" +
              " AND LASTNAME = " +
              "'" + jtfLastName.getText().trim()+"'";

            try
            {
              Statement stmt = connection.createStatement();
              ResultSet rs = stmt.executeQuery(query);

              if (rs.next())
              {
                jtfMI.setText(rs.getString(2));
                jtfStreet.setText(rs.getString(4));
```

Listing 13.5   *Continued*

```
                jtfCity.setText(rs.getString(5));
                jtfState.setText(rs.getString(6));
                jtfZip.setText(rs.getString(7));
                jtfTelephone.setText(rs.getString(8));
                jtfEmail.setText(rs.getString(9));

                jlblStatus.setText("Record found");
            }
            else
            {
                jlblStatus.setText("Record not found");
            }
        }
        catch (SQLException ex)
        {
            jlblStatus.setText(ex.getMessage());
        }
    }

    protected void insert()
    {
        String sqlInsert = "INSERT INTO ADDRESSBOOK VALUES (" +
            "'" + jtfFirstName.getText().trim() + "'" + "," +
            "'" + jtfMI.getText().trim() + "'" + "," +
            "'" + jtfLastName.getText().trim() + "'" + "," +
            "'" + jtfStreet.getText().trim() + "'" + "," +
            "'" + jtfCity.getText().trim() + "'" + "," +
            "'" + jtfState.getText().trim() + "'" + "," +
            "'" + jtfZip.getText().trim() + "'" + "," +
            "'" + jtfTelephone.getText().trim() + "'" + "," +
            "'" + jtfEmail.getText().trim()+ "'" + ")";

        try
        {
            Statement stmt = connection.createStatement();
            int t = stmt.executeUpdate(sqlInsert);
            jlblStatus.setText("Insertion succeeded");
        }
        catch (SQLException ex)
        {
            jlblStatus.setText(ex.getMessage());
        }
    }

    protected void clear()
    {
        jtfFirstName.setText(null);
        jtfMI.setText(null);
        jtfLastName.setText(null);
        jtfStreet.setText(null);
        jtfCity.setText(null);
        jtfState.setText(null);
        jtfZip.setText(null);
        jtfTelephone.setText(null);
        jtfEmail.setText(null);
    }
}
```

continues

Listing 13.5   *Continued*

Example Review

You click the Connect to Database menu command to create an instance of DBConnectDialog and display the dialog box for establishing a database connection. After a connection to a particular database is established, you can click the Using Static SQL Statements menu command to display the AddressBook panel. The constructor of AddressBook has a parameter of the Connection type. The dBconnectDialog1.connection is passed to the constructor of AddressBook to create an instance of AddressBook.

Static SQL statements are constructed to perform SQL SELECT and SQL INSERT operations. A SQL Statement instance stmt is created to execute the static SQL statements. stmt.executeQuery(sqlSelect) executes a SQL SELECT statement in the string sqlSelect, which returns a ResultSet; stmt.executeUpdate(sqlInsert) executes a SQL INSERT statement. In the example, only the first record in the ResultSet is displayed on the AddressBook panel.

The AddressBook class will be used as a superclass in Example 13.3, "Using PreparedStatement for Executing Dynamic SQL Statements." This example, stored in a different package, needs to reference the text fields, such as jtfFirstName and the status label jtfStatus. To make these objects accessible to Example 13.3, the modifier protected was added on each of the text fields and jlblStatus in AddressBook.

PreparedStatement

The PreparedStatement interface is designed to execute dynamic SQL statements and SQL-stored procedures with IN parameters. These SQL statements and stored procedures are precompiled for efficient use when executing repeatedly.

A PreparedStatement object is created using the preparedStatement() method in the Connection interface. For example, the following code creates a PreparedStatement pstmt on a particular Connection connection for a SQL INSERT statement.

```
Statement stmt = connection.prepareStatement
    ("INSERT INTO ADDRESSBOOK (FIRSTNAME, MI, LASTNAME)
    VALUES (?, ?, ?)");
```

This INSERT statement has three question marks as placeholders for parameters representing values for FIRSTNAME, MI, and LASTNAME in a record of the ADDRESSBOOK table.

As a subclass of Statement, the PreparedStatement interface inherits all the methods defined in Statement. Additionally, it provides the methods for setting parameters in the object of PreparedStatement. These methods are used to set the values for the parameters before executing statements or procedures. In general, the set methods have the following name and signature:

```
setX(int parameterIndex, X value);
```

where *X* is the type of the parameter, and `parameterIndex` is the index of the parameter in the statement. For example, the method `setString(int paramterIndex, String value)` sets a `String` value to the specified parameter. Table 13.6 contains a complete list of the methods in `PreparedStatement`.

The following statements pass parameters "Jack," "A," "Ryan" to the placeholder (?) for FIRSTNAME, MI, and LASTNAME in the `PreparedStatement` pstmt.

```
pstmt.setString(1, "Jack");
pstmt.setString(2, "A");
pstmt.setString(3, "Ryan");
```

TABLE 13.6   `PreparedStatement` **Methods**

Method Name	Description
clearParameters	Clears all the parameters in the statement
execute	Executes a prepared statement that may return multiple result sets
executeQuery	Executes a prepared statement that returns a single result set
executeUpdate	Executes a prepared INSERT, UPDATE, DELETE, or SQL DDL statement
setAsciiStream	Sets a parameter to an ASCII stream
setBigDecimal	Sets a parameter to a `java.lang.BigDecimal` value
setBinaryStream	Sets a parameter to a binary stream
setBoolean	Sets a parameter to a Java `boolean` value
setByte	Sets a parameter to a Java `byte` value
setBytes	Sets a parameter to a Java array of `byte` values
setDate	Sets a parameter to a `java.sql.Date` value
setDouble	Sets a parameter to a Java `double` value
setFloat	Sets a parameter to a Java `float` value
setInt	Sets a parameter to a Java `int` value
setLong	Sets a parameter to a Java `long` value
setNull	Sets a parameter to a SQL NULL value
setObject	Sets a parameter to a Java object
setShort	Sets a parameter to a Java `short` value
setString	Sets a parameter to a Java `String` value
setTime	Sets a parameter to a `java.sql.Time` value
setTimestamp	Sets a parameter to a `java.sql.Timestamp` value
setUnicodeStream	Sets a parameter to a Unicode stream

After setting parameters, you can execute the prepared statement by invoking execute(), executeQuery(), or executeUpdate(), depending on the type of SQL statement. The execute(), executeQuery(), and executeUpdate() methods are similar to the ones defined in the Statement interface except that they have no parameters, since the SQL statements are already specified in the preparedStatement() method when the object of PreparedStatement is created.

Example 13.3 Using PreparedStatement to Execute Dynamic SQL Statements

In this example, you will use dynamic SQL statements to select addresses and insert new addresses. A new menu, "Using Dynamic SQL Statements," will be added to the applet from the previous example. This new menu will bring up the same user interface as the menu "Using Static SQL Statements" with identical functions, but the dynamic SQL statements will be used to implement the SELECT and INSERT operations.

The example consists of two new classes: TestPreparedStatement and AddressBookUsingDynamicSQL. TestPreparedStatement adds a new menu item, "Using Dynamic SQL," to the previous example, and AddressBookUsingDynamicSQL extends AddressBook and uses the dynamic statements to override the select() and insert() methods.

Follow the steps below to complete the project.

1. Create a new project named PreparedStatementDemo.jpr, and copy TestStatement.java from the StatementDemo directory to the PreparedStatementDemo directory. Rename the file TestPreparedStatement.java in the Windows.

2. In the AppBrowser for PreparedStatementDemo, use the Add button to add TestPreparedStatement.java to the project. Replace StatementDemo with PreparedStatementDemo and TestStatement with TestPreparedStatement.

3. In the Menu Designer of TestPreparedStatement, add a menu item "Using Dynamic SQL Statements" in the Operation menu, and change the menu item's name to jmiDynamicSQL. Implement the menu item handler as follows:

```
void jmiDynamicSQL_actionPerformed(ActionEvent e)
{
  addAddressBookPanel(
    new AddressBookUsingDynamicSQL(
        dBConnectDialog1.connection));
}
```

4. Implement addAddressBookPanel method to add an instance of AddressBook to the applet.

```
// Add an address book panel to the center of applet
void addAddressBookPanel(AddressBook addressBookPanel)
{
  if (dBConnectDialog1.connection != null)
  {
    // Remove UI components from the applet
    this.getContentPane().removeAll();

    // Put the menubar back
    this.getContentPane().add(jMenuBar1, BorderLayout.NORTH);

    // Add AddressBook panel to the applet
    this.getContentPane().add(addressBookPanel,
      BorderLayout.CENTER);

    this.validate();
  }
  else
    System.out.println("Database not connected");
}
```

5. Modify the handler for the "Using Static SQL Statements" menu command to add the AddressBook panel for using static SQL statements:

```
void jmiStaticSQL_actionPerformed(ActionEvent e)
{
  // Add the AddressBook panel
  addAddressBookPanel(
    new AddressBook(dBConnectDialog1.connection));
}
```

6. Create a new class AddressBookUsingDynamicSQL that extends AddressBook and implements the select() and insert() methods using dynamic SQL statements, as shown in Listing 13.6.

7. Run TestPreparedStatement to test the program. The main frame is shown in Figure 13.13. When selecting "Using Dynamic SQL Statements," the same user interface as shown in Figure 13.12 appears in the frame for searching and inserting addresses.

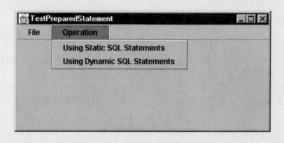

Figure 13.13   *The menu "Using Dynamic SQL Statements" was added to test* PreparedStatement.

continues

```java
package PreparedStatementDemo;

import java.sql.*;
import StatementDemo.AddressBook;

public class AddressBookUsingDynamicSQL extends AddressBook
{
  PreparedStatement pstmt1;
  PreparedStatement pstmt2;

  public AddressBookUsingDynamicSQL(Connection connection)
  {
    super(connection);

    // Create prepared SQL statements
    try
    {
      pstmt1 = connection.prepareStatement(
        "SELECT * FROM AddressBook WHERE FIRSTNAME = ?
        AND LASTNAME = ?");
      pstmt2 = connection.prepareStatement(
        "INSERT INTO ADDRESSBOOK VALUES (
        ?, ?, ?, ?, ?, ?, ?, ?, ?)");
    }
    catch (SQLException ex)
    {
      jlblStatus.setText(ex.getMessage());
    }

    jlblStatus.setText("Using dynamic SQL statements");
  }

  // Override the select() method defiend in AddressBook
  protected void select()
  {
    try
    {
      pstmt1.setString(1, jtfFirstName.getText().trim());
      pstmt1.setString(2, jtfLastName.getText().trim());
      ResultSet rs = pstmt1.executeQuery();

      if (rs.next())
      {
        jtfMI.setText(rs.getString(2));
        jtfStreet.setText(rs.getString(4));
        jtfCity.setText(rs.getString(5));
        jtfState.setText(rs.getString(6));
        jtfZip.setText(rs.getString(7));
        jtfTelephone.setText(rs.getString(8));
        jtfEmail.setText(rs.getString(9));
        jlblStatus.setText("Dynamic SQL selection succeeded");
      }
      else
      {
        jlblStatus.setText("no record found");
      }
    }
    catch (SQLException ex)
```

Listing 13.6   *AddressBookUsingDynamicSQL.java*

```
                    {
                      jlblStatus.setText(ex.getMessage());
                    }
                }

                // Override the insert() method defiend in AddressBook
                protected void insert()
                {
                  try
                  {
                    pstmt2.setString(1, jtfFirstName.getText().trim());
                    pstmt2.setString(2, jtfMI.getText().trim());
                    pstmt2.setString(3, jtfLastName.getText().trim());
                    pstmt2.setString(4, jtfStreet.getText().trim());
                    pstmt2.setString(5, jtfCity.getText().trim());
                    pstmt2.setString(6, jtfState.getText().trim());
                    pstmt2.setString(7, jtfZip.getText().trim());
                    pstmt2.setString(8, jtfTelephone.getText().trim());
                    pstmt2.setString(9, jtfZip.getText().trim());

                    pstmt2.executeUpdate();

                    jlblStatus.setText("Dynamic SQL Insertion succeeded");
                  }
                  catch (SQLException ex)
                  {
                    jlblStatus.setText(ex.getMessage());
                  }
                }
              }
          }
```

Listing 13.6   *Continued*

Example Review

AddressBookUsingDynamicSQL extends AddressBook created in Example 13.2. The select() and insert() methods in AddressBook were overridden to accommodate using the prepared statements pstmt1 and pstmt2, where pstmt1 can be used to select records from the ADDRESSBOOK table, and pstmt2 can be used to insert records into ADDRESSBOOK table in the database.

A new method addAddressBookPanel was created in TestPreparedStatement, which enables you to add an instance of AddressBook to the center of the applet's content pane. First, all the components in the applet's content pane were removed, using the removeAll() method. Then the menu bar and the AddressBook instance were added to the applet. You may use the remove() method to remove a specified component from a container, if you assign a name for an instance of AddressBook rather than use an anonymous instance.

PreparedStatement is more efficient than Statement in the project for viewing and inserting new records because the SQL statements are precompiled and reused without recompiling. Please refer to Exercise 13.1 for performance evaluations of using static SQL statements and dynamic SQL statements.

continues

> ■■■ **CAUTION**
>
> To override a method in the superclass, the method has to be declared exactly as in its superclass. It would be a mistake, for example, if you missed the `protected` keyword for the `select()` or the `insert()` method, because this keyword is used for declaring these methods in its superclass.

> ■■■ **NOTE**
>
> Due to driver limitations, dynamic SQL statements do not work with the current JDBC-ODBC driver. A dynamic SQL statement can be executed only once. An error would occur the next time.

CallableStatement

The `CallableStatement` interface is designed to execute SQL-stored procedures with OUT or IN OUT parameters. An OUT parameter returns a value after the procedure is completed, but it contains no value when the procedure is called. An IN OUT parameter contains a value passed to the procedure when it is called, and returns a value after it is completed. For example, the following procedure in Oracle PL/SQL has IN parameter p1, OUT parameter p2, and IN OUT parameter p3.

```
CREATE OR REPLACE PROCEDURE Sample
  (p1 IN VARCHAR, p2 OUT NUMBER, p3 IN OUT INTEGER) IS
BEGIN
  —doing something
  NULL;
END Sample;
```

> ■■■ **NOTE**
>
> The syntax of stored procedures is vendor-specific. Oracle PL/SQL is used for demonstrations of stored procedures in this book. PL/SQL is a procedural language extension of SQL. It is a fully functional programming language whose syntax is very similar to Ada.

A `CallableStatement` object can be created using the `prepareCall(String call)` method in the `Connection` interface. For example, the following code creates a `CallableStatement` cstmt on `Connection` connection for procedure `Sample`.

```
CallableStatement cstmt = connection.prepareCall(
  "{call Sample(?, ?, ?)}");
```

`{call Sample(?, ?, ...)}` is referred to as the *SQL escape syntax*, which signals the driver that the code within it should be handled differently. The driver parses the escape syntax and translates it into code that the particular database understands.

TABLE 13.7   `CallableStatement` **Methods**

Method Name	*Description*
getBigDecimal	Gets an OUT parameter as a `java.math.BigDecimal` object
getBoolean	Gets a `boolean` from an OUT parameter
getByte	Gets a `byte` from an OUT parameter
getBytes	Gets an OUT parameter as an array of `byte` values
getDate	Gets an OUT parameter as a `java.sql.Date` object
getDouble	Gets a `double` from an OUT parameter
getFloat	Gets a `float` from an OUT parameter
getInt	Gets an `int` from an OUT parameter
getLong	Gets a `long` from an OUT parameter
getObject	Gets an OUT parameter as a Java `Object`
getShort	Gets a `short` from an OUT parameter
getString	Gets a `string` from an OUT parameter
getTime	Gets an OUT parameter as `java.sql.Time` object
getTimeStamp	Gets an OUT parameter as `java.sql.TimeStamp` object
registerOutParameter	Registers an OUT parameter's data type.
asNull	Returns null if an OUT parameter is SQL NULL

For this case, Sample is an Oracle PL/SQL procedure. The call is translated to a string `"BEGIN Sample(?, ?, ?); END"` and passed to an Oracle database for execution.

You can call procedures as well as functions. The syntax to create a SQL callable statement for a function is as follows:

```
{? = call FunctionName(?, ?, ...)}
```

`CallableStatement` inherits `PreparedStatement`. Additionally, the `CallableStatement` interface provides methods for registering OUT parameter and for getting values from OUT parameters. These methods are listed in Table 13.7.

Before calling a SQL procedure, you need to use appropriate set methods to pass values to IN and IN OUT parameters, and use `registerOutParameter` to register OUT and IN OUT parameters. For example, before calling procedure Sample, the following statements pass values to parameters p1 (IN) and p3 (IN OUT) and register parameters p2 (OUT) and p3 (IN OUT).

```
cstmt.setString(1, "dummy");
cstmt.setLong(3, 1);
cstmt.registerOutParameter(2, java.sql.Types.DOUBLE);
cstmt.registerOutParameter(3, java.sql.Types.INTEGER);
```

You may use execute() or executeUpdate() to execute the procedure depending on the type of SQL statement, then use get methods to retrieve values from the OUT parameters. For example, the following statements retrieve the values from parameters p2 and p3.

```
double d = cstmt.getDouble(2);
int i = cstmt.getInt(3);
```

Example 13.4 Using CallableStatement to Execute SQL Stored Procedures

In this example, you will use a SQL stored function to check whether an address is already in the database before inserting a new address. The example is a continuation of Example 13.3. You will add a new menu, "Using Callable Statements," to demonstrate using stored procedures.

The following Oracle PL/SQL function returns 1 if an address with specified FIRSTNAME and LASTNAME already exists in the table ADDRESSBOOK; returns 0 otherwise.

```
CREATE OR REPLACE FUNCTION AddressFound
  (first VARCHAR2, last VARCHAR2)
  RETURN INTEGER IS
  s AddressBook%ROWTYPE;
BEGIN
  SELECT * INTO S
  FROM ADDRESSBOOK
  WHERE ADDRESSBOOK.FIRSTNAME = first AND
    ADDRESSBOOK.LASTNAME = last;

  RETURN 1;

  EXCEPTION
    WHEN NO_DATA_FOUND THEN
      RETURN 0;
END AddressFound;
```

Suppose table ADDRESSBOOK and function AddressFound are already created in the database. The example consists of two new classes: TestCallableStatement and AddressBookUsingStoredProc. TestCallableStatement adds a new menu item, "Using Callable Statements," to the previous example, and AddressBookUsingStoredProc extends AddressBookUsingDynamicSQL and overrides the insert() method to check whether an address for the given first name and last name is already in the database. If so, nothing is done; if not, the superclass's insert() method is invoked to insert a new record.

To see the development in action, follow the steps below:

1. Create a new project named CallableStatementDemo.jpr, and copy TestPreparedStatement.java from the PreparedStatementDemo directory to the CallableStatementDemo directory. Rename the file TestCallableStatement.java in the Windows.

2. In the AppBrowser for CallableStatementDemo, use the Add button to add TestCallableStatement.java to the project. Replace PreparedStatementDemo with CallableStatementDemo and TestPreparedStatement with TestCallableStatement.

3. In the Menu Designer for TestCallableStatement, add a new menu item, "Using Callable Statements," in the Operation. Change the menu name to jmiStoredProc. Generate and implement the code for handling the menu command as follows:

```
void jmiStoredProc_actionPerformed(ActionEvent e)
{
  addAddressBookPanel(
    new AddressBookUsingStoredProc(
      dBConnectDialog1.connection));
}
```

4. Create the class AddressBookUsingStoredProc that extends AddressBookUsingDynamicSQL with additional features that check whether an address already exists before executing insertion, as shown in Listing 13.7.

5. Run TestCallableStatement.java to test the program. The main frame is shown in Figure 13.14. When selecting "Using Stored Procedures," the same user interface as shown in Figure 13.12 appears in the frame for searching and inserting addresses.

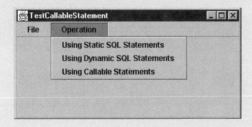

Figure 13.14 *The menu "Using Callable Statements" was added to test* CallableStatement.

Listing 13.7   AddressBookUsingStoredProc.java

```
package CallableStatementDemo;

import java.sql.*;
import PreparedStatementDemo.AddressBookUsingDynamicSQL;

public class AddressBookUsingStoredProc
  extends AddressBookUsingDynamicSQL
{
  CallableStatement cstmt;
```

continues

Listing 13.1   *Continued*

```java
     public AddressBookUsingStoredProc(Connection connection)
     {
       super(connection);

       try
       {
         // Create a callable statement
         cstmt = connection.prepareCall
           ("{ ? = call AddressFound(?, ?)}");
       }
       catch (SQLException ex)
       {
         jlblStatus.setText(ex.getMessage());
       }

       jlblStatus.setText("Using stored SQL procedures");
     }

     protected void insert()
     {
       try
       {
         if (addressFound() == 1)
           jlblStatus.setText("Address already exist");
         else
           super.insert();
       }
       catch (SQLException ex)
       {
         jlblStatus.setText(ex.getMessage());
       }
     }

     // Return true if an address matching the given firstname and
     // lastname is already in the database
     int addressFound() throws SQLException
     {
       cstmt.setString(2, jtfFirstName.getText().trim());
       cstmt.setString(3, jtfLastName.getText().trim());
       cstmt.registerOutParameter(1, Types.INTEGER);
       cstmt.execute();
       return cstmt.getInt(1);
     }
   }
```

Listing 13.1   *Continued*

Example Review

Since the syntax and capabilities of stored procedures vary among vendors, JDBC's escape syntax for invoking procedures is translated into vendor-specific code for invoking procedures. To see whether the database supports stored procedures, call supportsStoredProcedures() in the DatabaseMetaData interface.

Use preparedStatement or CallableStatement to process stored procedures with IN parameters. You must use CallableStatement to process stored procedures with OUT parameters. Before executing a stored procedure with the OUT parameter, you must use `registerOutParameter()` to register the OUT parameter with a data type specified in `java.sql.Types`.

■ TIP
A common mistake is to put a semicolon (;) at the end of the escape syntax for invoking stored procedure. This would cause a runtime error.

Chapter Summary

This chapter introduced JDBC metadata and creating and processing database statements. You learned how to use the `DatabaseMetaData` interface to obtain database-wide information and the `ResultSetMetaData` interface to obtain the information on the specific `ResultSet`. You also learned how to develop database projects using static SQL statements, prepared SQL statements, and callable SQL statements.

Chapter Review

13.1. Describe the methods for retrieving general information in the `DatabaseMetaData` interface.

13.2. Describe the methods for finding database capabilities in the `DatabaseMetaData` interface.

13.3. Describe the methods for getting database objects in the `DatabaseMetaData` interface.

13.4. How do you create an instance of `DatabaseMetaData`?

13.5. What is `ResultSetMetaData` for? Describe the methods in `ResultSetMetaData`. How do you create an instance of `ResultSetMetaData`?

13.6. Describe static statements, prepared statements, and callable statements and their relationship. How do you create instances of `Statement`, `PreparedStatement`, and `CallableStatement`? How do you execute these statements?

Programming Exercises

13.1. Write a program to insert 100 records into a table using static SQL statements, and another inserting the same 100 records into a table using dynamic SQL statements. Compare the two.

13.2. Modify Example 13.4 to create three tabs, "Static SQL," "Dynamic SQL," and "Callable SQL," instead of using menus.

Applications Using JBuilder DataExpress and Data-Aware Components

Objectives

- Understand the DataExpress API.
- Develop database applications using the DataExpress and data-aware dbSwing components.
- Create master-detail forms using DataExpress and dbSwing components.
- Use a data module to separate data from GUI.

Introduction

JDBC provides a generic, low-level SQL database access interface. It defines Java interfaces to represent database connections, SQL statements, result sets, database metadata, and so on. With the support of these interfaces, Java programmers issue SQL statements and process results. JDBC works well in this capacity and is easier to understand than ODBC, but it was designed to be a base upon which to build high-level interfaces and tools. JBuilder DataExpress API is a more user-friendly and convenient API built upon the JDBC API to provide powerful support for accessing and manipulating relational databases.

JBuilder also provides the data-aware version of Swing components known as db-Swing components that seamlessly bind to data sets defined in the DataExpress API. You can use these components to develop pure, powerful Java database applications with minimum coding.

■ NOTE

The DataExpress and dbSwing components are available in JBuilder 3 Professional Edition and JBuilder 3 Enterprise Edition.

DataExpress API

The DataExpress API consists of the following major classes contained in the `com.borland.dx.dataset`, `com.borland.dx.sql.dataset`, and `com.borland.data-store` packages. All the following classes are installed in the Data Express page of the Component palette.

- **Database**: This component installed in the Component palette encapsulates a database connection through JDBC to the SQL server and also provides lightweight transaction support. It combines the JDBC functions of loading driver and connecting database into one component.

- **DataSet**: This is an abstract class that provides basic editing, view, and cursor functionality for access to two-dimensional data. It supports the concept of a current row position, which allows for navigation of the data in the `DataSet`. The `DataSet` also manages a pseudo record — an area in memory that temporarily stores a newly inserted row or changes to the current row.

- **StorageDataSet**: This is an abstract class that extends the `DataSet` class by providing basic cursor functionality to structural changes to the `DataSet`. It supports storage of data using `MemoryStore` or `DataStore`.

- **QueryDataSet**: This component installed in the Component palette is a subclass of `StorageDataSet` for storing the results of a query string executed against a server database. It provides functionality to run a SQL query with or without parameters. This component works with the `Database` component to connect to database server and executes queries. Once the resulting data are stored in the `QueryDataSet`, you can manipulate them using the `DataSet` API.

■ `ProcedureDataSet`: This component installed in the Component palette is a subclass of `StorageDataSet`, which provides functionality to run a stored procedure against data stored in a SQL database, passing in parameters if the procedure expects them.

■ `TableDataSet`: This component installed in the Component palette is a subclass of `StorageDataSet` for importing data from a text file.

■ `DataSetView`: This component extends `DataSet` functionality by presenting an alternative view of the data in the `DataSet`. The `DataSetView` itself has no storage of data but sees all the unfiltered data contained in its `storageDataSet` property to which you can apply a different sort order and filter criterion than the original `StorageDataSet`. The navigation of the `DataSetView` data is separate from that of its `StorageDataSet`.

■ `DataStore`: This component provides high-performance data caching and compact persistence for `StorageDataSet`. By default, the `StorageDataSet` uses a `MemoryStore` if the `store` property of `StorageDataSet` is not set. The `MemoryStore` class defines in-memory storage behavior for data that have been loaded into a JBuilder `DataSet` component. This class is used internally by other JBuilder classes. You should never use this class directly.

When using JDBC API to create a database application, you load the appropriate driver, establish a database connection, create and execute statements, and process the execution results. A typical procedure for developing database applications using the DataExpress API is as follows:

1. Use the `Database` class to specify a driver and connect to the database.

2. Use the `QueryDataSet`, `TableDataSet`, or `ProcedureDataSet` class to create and execute queries.

3. Use the methods in the `QueryDataSet`, `TableDataSet`, and `ProcedureDataSet` classes to process the query results.

Example 14.1 Creating an Address Book Using the DataExpress Components

This example creates a program to manage an online address book similar to the one in Example 13.2, "Using `Statement` for Executing Static SQL Statements." The address book was developed with the JDBC API in Example 13.2. This example uses DataExpress components to create a new address book component named `DataExpressAddressBook` that extends the `StatementDemo.AddressBook` class and places the bean in an applet. Figure 14.1 shows a sample run of the applet.

continues

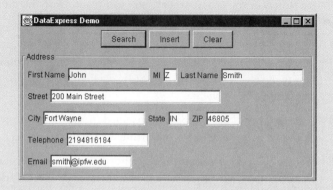

Figure 14.1 *You can search a record to match First Name and Last Name, insert a new record, or clear a record.*

Here are the steps to complete the project.

1. Create a new project named DataExpressDemo.jpr, and create a new class named `DataExpressAddressBook` that extends `StatementDemo.AddressBook` using the New Class Wizard.

2. Follow the steps below to establish a database connection.

   2.1. In the UI Designer of DataExpressAddressBook.java, drop a `Database` from the Data Express page of the Component palette to create `database1`. `database1` appears under the Data Access node in the Component tree.

   2.2. In the Inspector of `database1`, click the Ellipsis button in the value field of property `connection` to display the Connection dialog box, as shown in Figure 14.2.

   2.3. Click Choose URL to display the Choosing a Connection URL dialog box, as shown in Figure 14.3. Choose a data source that contains the AddressBook table, and click OK to close this dialog box.

NOTE

A new data source that has never been used in JBuilder will not appear in the list. You can find a new driver by clicking the Show Data Source button for an ODBC data source. Once the data source is used, it will appear in the list.

   2.4. Click Test connection in the Connection dialog box (Figure 14.2) to test the selected connection. Check Prompt user password, and click OK to close the Connection dialog box.

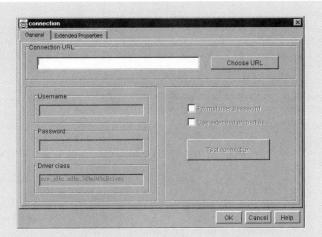

Figure 14.2   *The Connection dialog box gathers information about the database you want to connect.*

Figure 14.3   *You can choose a data source from the Choosing a Connection URL dialog.*

3. The Search button searches the address to match the specified first name and last name. These two names are parameters in the SQL SELECT statement. You need to use the `ParameterRow` class to define two parameters for first name and last name. Follow the steps below to create a `ParameterRow`.

3.1. Drop a `ParameterRow` from the Data Express page of the Component palette to create `parameterRow1`. `parameterRow1` appears under the Data Access node in the Component tree.

3.2. Expand `parameterRow1` by clicking the + button in front of `parameterRow1` in the Component tree. You will see <new column> under `parameterRow1`.

continues

607

3.3. Choose <new column>. In the Inspector of <new column>, set `caption` and `columnName` to firstname, and set `parameterType` to IN. You will see a new parameter named `firstname` appearing under `parameterRow1` in the Component Tree.

NOTE

If you don't see firstname in the Component tree, close the project and re-open it.

3.4. Choose <new column> again. In the Inspector of <new column>, set caption and columnName to lastname, and set parameterType to IN. You will see a new parameter named `lastname` appearing under `parameterRow1` in the Component tree.

4. Follow the steps below to create a `QueryDataSet`.

4.1. Drop a `QueryDataSet` from the Data Express page of the Component palette to create `queryDataSet1`. `queryDataSet1` appears under the Data Access node in the Component tree.

4.2. In the Inspector of `queryDataSet1`, click the Ellipsis button in the value field of `metaDataUpdate` to display the metaDataUpdate dialog box. Click None and click OK to close this dialog box. It is necessary to make this field None for the Insert and Update operation to work in this program.

4.3. In the Inspector of `queryDataSet1`, click the ellipsis button in the value field `query` to bring up the query dialog box, as shown in Figure 14.4.

4.4. Choose `database1` in the Database choice menu to associate the query to the `database1` data source. Type the following SQL statement in the text area:

```
SELECT * FROM AddressBook WHERE
    FirstName = :firstname and LastName = :lastname
```

4.5. Choose the Parameters tab in the query dialog box, select `parameterRow1`, and click OK.

4.6. Switch to the Query page in the query dialog box. You can also use SQL Builder to construct SQL statements instead of typing the statement manually, as shown in Figure 14.5. You can browse the tables by clicking the Browse tables button and test the query by clicking the Test query button.

4.7. Expand `queryDataSet1` in the Component tree to see the columns appearing under `queryDataSet1`. In the Inspector of FIRSTNAME

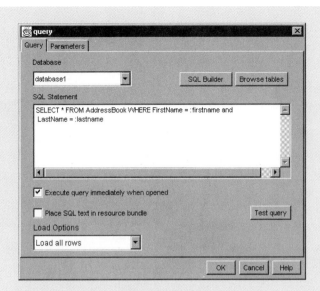

Figure 14.4   *The query dialog box lets you construct and test a query with or without parameters.*

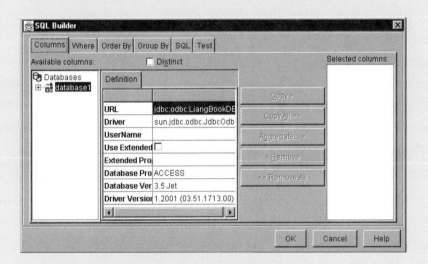

Figure 14.5   *The SQL Builder tool helps you build a SQL statement.*

and LASTNAME, set the `rowid` property to true. Thus, FIRST-NAME and LASTNAME together form the primary key. This is necessary to ensure the insert operations that work without the need to supply a row ID.

4.8. Set AddressBook in the `tableName` property of `queryDataSet1`. This property is needed to ensure that the table can be updated.

continues

5. Override the methods select(), insert(), and update() in the Address-Book class using queryDataSet1 and parameterRow1, as shown in Listing 14.1.

6. Run the program. When the program starts, a dialog box is displayed to prompt the user to enter the password, as shown in Figure 14.6. Enter username and password to enter database. If your database does not require a password, close the dialog box. Test the Search, Update, and Insert buttons, as shown in Figure 14.1.

Figure 14.6 *The Password dialog box prompts the user to enter a password to establish a database connection.*

```java
package DataExpressDemo;

import java.awt.*;
import java.awt.event.*;
import java.applet.*;
import javax.swing.*;
import StatementDemo.*;
import com.borland.dx.sql.dataset.*;
import com.borland.dx.dataset.*;

public class DataExpressAddressBook extends StatementDemo.AddressBook
{
  Database database1 = new Database();
  ParameterRow parameterRow1 = new ParameterRow();
  Column column1 = new Column();
  Column column2 = new Column();
  QueryDataSet queryDataSet1 = new QueryDataSet();
  Column column3 = new Column();
  Column column4 = new Column();

  public DataExpressAddressBook()
  {
    try
    {
      jbInit();
    }
    catch(Exception e)
```

Listing 14.1 *DataExpressAddressBook.java*

```
      {
        e.printStackTrace();
      }
    }

    // Component initialization
    private void jbInit() throws Exception
    {
      this.setSize(new Dimension(456, 226));
      database1.setConnection(
        new com.borland.dx.sql.dataset.ConnectionDescriptor(
          "jdbc:odbc:LiangBookDB_MDB", "", null, true,
          "sun.jdbc.odbc.JdbcOdbcDriver"));
      queryDataSet1.setMetaDataUpdate(MetaDataUpdate.NONE);
      queryDataSet1.setTableName("AddressBook");
      queryDataSet1.setQuery(
        new com.borland.dx.sql.dataset.QueryDescriptor(database1,
        "SELECT * FROM AddressBook
        WHERE FirstName = :firstname  and  LastName "
        + "= :lastname  ", parameterRow1, true, Load.ALL));
      column1.setCaption("firstname");
      column1.setColumnName("firstname");
      column1.setDataType(com.borland.dx.dataset.Variant.STRING);
      column1.setParameterType(ParameterType.IN);
      column1.setTableName("");
      column2.setCaption("lastname");
      column2.setColumnName("lastname");
      column2.setDataType(com.borland.dx.dataset.Variant.STRING);
      column2.setParameterType(ParameterType.IN);
      column3.setColumnName("FIRSTNAME");
      column3.setDataType(com.borland.dx.dataset.Variant.STRING);
      column3.setRowId(true);
      column4.setColumnName("LASTNAME");
      column4.setDataType(com.borland.dx.dataset.Variant.STRING);
      column4.setRowId(true);
      parameterRow1.setColumns(new Column[] {column1, column2});
      queryDataSet1.setColumns(new Column[] {column3, column4});
    }

    // Override the select() method in the AddressBook class
    protected void select()
    {
      try
      {
        parameterRow1.setString("firstname",
          jtfFirstName.getText().trim());
        parameterRow1.setString("lastname",
          jtfLastName.getText().trim());
        queryDataSet1.refresh();
        displayAddress();
      }
      catch (Exception ex)
      {
        System.out.println(ex);
      }
    }

    // Display address in the UI
```

continues

Listing 14.1   *Continued*

```
void displayAddress()
{
  try
  {
    jtfMI.setText(queryDataSet1.getString(1));
    jtfStreet.setText(queryDataSet1.getString(3));
    jtfCity.setText(queryDataSet1.getString(4));
    jtfState.setText(queryDataSet1.getString(5));
    jtfZip.setText(queryDataSet1.getString(6));
    jtfTelephone.setText(queryDataSet1.getString(7));
    jtfEmail.setText(queryDataSet1.getString(8));
  }
  catch (Exception ex)
  {
    jlblStatus.setText(ex.getMessage());
  }
}

// Override the insert() method in the AddressBook class
protected void insert()
{
  try
  {
    if (!queryDataSet1.isOpen()) queryDataSet1.open();
    queryDataSet1.insertRow(false);
    update();
  }
  catch (Exception ex)
  {
    jlblStatus.setText(ex.getMessage());
  }
}

// Update the record
void update()
{
  try
  {
    queryDataSet1.setString(0, jtfFirstName.getText());
    queryDataSet1.setString(1, jtfMI.getText());
    queryDataSet1.setString(2, jtfLastName.getText());
    queryDataSet1.setString(3, jtfStreet.getText());
    queryDataSet1.setString(4, jtfCity.getText());
    queryDataSet1.setString(5, jtfState.getText());
    queryDataSet1.setString(6, jtfZip.getText());
    queryDataSet1.setString(7, jtfTelephone.getText());
    queryDataSet1.setString(8, jtfEmail.getText());
    queryDataSet1.saveChanges();
  }
  catch (Exception ex)
  {
    jlblStatus.setText(ex.getMessage());
  }
}
}
```

Listing 14.1   *Continued*

Example Review

As you can see in the example, JBuilder provides easy-to-use and powerful property editors for many DataExpress components. You can create instances of these components and set their properties using the UI Designer with no coding. The code generated by JBuilder can be modified and maintained.

The connection property editor of the Database component lets you choose a database URL, set user name and password, and test the connection during design time. JBuilder generates a ConnectionDescriptor object to store the connection properties. You can connect several DataSet components to a Database component.

NOTE

The local InterBase server that is bundled in the Professional edition of JBuilder allows only one active concurrent connections. So is the MS Access database.

The query property editor of the QueryDataSet dialog box allows you to choose a database and construct a SQL statement with or without parameters. It also allows testing the query. Once a Database object is created, it automatically appears in the choice list of the database field in the query dialog box. A database must be chosen for a QueryDataSet object. JBuilder generates a QueryDescriptor object to store the query properties.

The ResultSet in JDBC is absorbed in QueryDataSet. The execution result of the query is stored in the QueryDataSet. This allows for much greater flexibility in navigation of the resulting data. The QueryDataSet inherits the maxRows property from StorageDataSet. This allows you to set the maximum number of rows that can be initially stored in the QueryDataSet from a query execution.

When you created the table AddressBook in Example 13.2, you did not specify the primary key. For the insert operation to work properly, you set the rowid property on the columns FIRSTNAME and LASTNAME to true so that they would form the primary key. If the primary key were declared in the table, the property field of the column would automatically set to true.

To ensure the QueryDataSet can be updated, set the tableName property to AddressBook and set the MetaDataUpdate property to MetaDataUpdate.NONE, in addition to having a rowid in the table.

QueryDataSet contains a variety of methods. Among these are open() for opening query, refresh() for refreshing query, addRow() for adding a new row, insertRow() for inserting a new row, delete() for deleting the current row,

continues

getXXX() for retrieving field of appropriate type, setXXX() for setting a new value in the field of appropriate type, and saveChanges() for saving changes in the table.

To assign parameter values in a parameterized query, you must first create a ParameterRow and add named columns that will be the placeholders for the values to be passed to the query. In this example, you created an instance parameterRow1 of ParameterRow and added columns firstname and lastname, which are the parameters used in the SQL query. ParameterRow is a subclass of ReadWriteRow, which contains one row of storage. You can get a parameter using a statement like this:

```
parameterRow1.getString("FIRSTNAME");
```

You can set the value of a parameter using a statement like this:

```
parameterRow1.setString("FIRSTNAME", aString);
```

Data-Aware Components

JBuilder provides many data-aware components to simplify creating data-aware user interface. These components are installed in the dbSwing, More dbSwing, dbSwing Models, and JBCL pages of the Component palette. Using these components greatly speeds up the Java database development process. The components in the dbSwing, More dbSwing, and dbSwing Models pages are referred to as *dbSwing components*. The JBCL (JavaBean Component Library) components were originally developed by Borland before Swing was introduced. Some of the JBCL components are heavyweight. JBCL components are completely replaced by the dbSwing components. You should avoid using JBCL components with Swing-based projects.

The dbSwing components are data-aware versions of the Swing components. They are capable of accessing database through DataExpress data sets. Most of the dbSwing components are subclasses of Swing components. For example, jdbTextField is a subclass of JTextField, jdbComoboBox is a subclass of JComboBox, and jdbTable is a subclass of JTable. The dbSwing visual components are named with the prefix jdb.

Most dbSwing data-aware components have a dataSet property and a columnName property. These properties bind the component to a specific DataSet, and a specific Column within that DataSet. (Some components work with all the columns of a DataSet, and therefore only have a dataSet property.) You should first choose a DataSet in the dataset property of the dbSwing component, then specify a column from the dataset.

The following dbSwing components are often useful:

- JdbCheckBox: A data-aware extension of the JCheckBox component. To make JdbCheckBox data-aware, set its dataSet and columnName properties so that it is linked to the desired column in the data set. Values in that column must denote a boolean value. If this is the case, a value that evaluates to true checks the check box, and a false value removes the checkmark. If the user checks the check box, a value that equates to true is entered in the column of the active record in the data set. Unchecking the check box puts a value that equates to false in the data set.

- JdbLabel: A data-aware extension of the JLabel component. To make JdbLabel data-aware, set its dataSet and columnName properties to link the text property to the data value for the column of the current row.

- JdbComboBox: A data-aware extension of the JComboBox component. To make JdbComboBox data-aware, set its dataSet and columnName properties to display the values in the specified column of the data set.

- JbdList: A data-aware extension of the JList component. To make JdbList data-aware, set its dataSet and columnName properties to display the values in the specified column of the data set.

- JdbTextField: To make JdbTextField data-aware, set its dataSet and columnName properties to display the data value for the column of the current row.

- JdbTextArea: A data-aware extension of the JTextArea component. To make JdbTextArea data-aware, set its dataSet and columnName properties to display the value for the column of the current row in the text area.

- JdbTable: A data-aware extension of the JTable component. To make JdbTable data-aware, set its dataSet. The table cells can be edited. To make JdbTable scrollable, you must place it inside an instance of TableScrollPane, which is an extension of JScrollPane designed specifically for use with a JdbTable.

- JdbNavToolBar: A data-aware control that contains multiple preset buttons for performing operations on the data, such as searching, inserting, deleting, posting changes, and refreshing data source.

- JdbStatusLabel: The JdbStatusLabel control displays custom messages. If its dataset property is set, it displays status messages generated by its associated DataSet. These include row position, row count, validation errors, and data update notifications.

- JdbNavField: A JTextField with built-in row locating functionality when its dataSet property is set. If its columnName property is set, it locates data in that column only. If the columnName property is not set, it locates data in the DataSet column that had focus last. If no column had focus, the first column in the DataSet that supports locate operations is chosen. Unlike JdbTextField, JdbNavField never writes to a DataSet column.

If the searched column is of the String type, the search occurs incrementally as characters are typed. If the search string is all lower case, then the search is case-insensitive. If the search string is mixed case, then the search is case-sensitive.

If the searched column is not of the String type, the search doesn't occur until the Enter key is pressed.

To search for prior and next matches, use the up and down arrow keys, respectively.

If a JdbStatusLabel is present, it displays usage information about the JdbNavField currently in use.

Example 14.2 Using dbSwing Data-Aware Components

In this example, you will develop a new address book (see Figure 14.7) using the dbSwing data-aware components JdbNavToolBar, JdbTable, JdbNavField, JdbTextField, and JdbStatusLabel.

You will use the same database as in Example 14.1. The query in the QueryDataSet is "SELECT * FROM AddressBook." You can use JdbNavToolBar to cruise through the QueryDataSet and to insert and delete the records in the

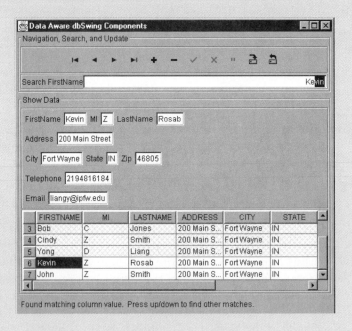

Figure 14.7   *You can display, search, and modify records in the AddressBook using the data-aware dbSwing components.*

QueryDataSet. The JdbTable displays all the records in the QueryDataSet, and the Show Data panel displays the current row in the QueryDataSet. You can search the record according to FIRSTNAME by entering a value in the Search Value field. The JdbStatusLabel displays the message indicating the status of the operations.

Here are the steps to complete the project.

1. Create a new project named dbSwingDemo.jpr, and create a new applet named TestdbSwing using the Applet Wizard.

2. With TestdbSwing.java selected in the Navigation pane, switch to the UI Designer.

3. Establish a database connection and create a query set as follows:

   3.1. Drop a Database from the Data Express page to create database1. In the Inspector of database1, double-click the Ellipsis button to bring up the Connection dialog box. Choose the same URL, username, and password as in Example 14.1. Close the Connection dialog box.

   3.2. Drop a QueryDataSet from the Data Express page to create queryDataSet1. In the Inspector of queryDataSet1, set the metaDataUpdate property to None, set the tableName property to AddressBook, and create "SELECT * FROM AddressBook" in the query property using the Query dialog box.

4. Create the user interface as follows (shown in Figure 14.7). The generated code is shown in Listing 14.2.

   4.1. Drop a JPanel to the north of the applet to create jpControl, drop a JPanel to the center of the applet to create jpData, and drop a JdbStatusLabel to the south of the applet to create jdbStatusLabel1. Set the border with title "Navigation, Search, and Update" on jpControl and the border with title "Show Data" on jpData. Set the dataSet property of jdbStatusLabel1 to queryDataSet1.

   4.2. Set the layout of jpControl to BorderLayout. Drop a JdbNavToolBar to the north of jpControl to create jdbNavToolBar1. Set the dataSet property of jdbNavToolBar1 to queryDataSet1.

   4.3. Drop a JPanel to the center of the jpControl to create jpSearchField with an Etched border and a BorderLayout. Drop a JLabel to the west of jpSearchField with text "Search FirstName." Drop a JdbNavField from the More Swing page of the Component palette to the center of jpSearchField to create jdbNavField1. Set the dataSet property of jdbNavField1 to queryDataSet1 and the columnName to FIRSTNAME.

continues

617

4.4. Set the `layout` of `jpData` to `BorderLayout`. Drop a `TableScrollPane` from the dbSwing page to the center of `jpData`, and drop a `JdbTable` to the scroll pane to create `jdbTable1`. Set its `dataSet` property to `queryDataSet1`. Drop a `JPanel` to the north of `jpData` to create `jpRecord`. Set its `layout` to `GridLayout` with five rows.

4.5. Use `JLabel` and `JdbTextField` to create user interface for displaying a single record in `jpRecord`. For each instance of `JdbTextField`, set its `dataSet` property to `queryDataSet1` and its `columnName` to an appropriate column. For example, for the text field for FirstName, set its `columnName` to FIRSTNAME.

```
package dbSwingDemo;

import java.awt.*;
import java.awt.event.*;
import java.applet.*;
import javax.swing.*;
import com.borland.dx.sql.dataset.*;
import com.borland.dbswing.*;
import com.borland.dx.dataset.*;
import javax.swing.border.*;

public class TestdbSwing extends JApplet
{
  boolean isStandalone = false;
  Database database1 = new Database();
  QueryDataSet queryDataSet1 = new QueryDataSet();
  TableScrollPane tableScrollPane1 = new TableScrollPane();
  JdbTable jdbTable1 = new JdbTable();
  JdbNavToolBar jdbNavToolBar1 = new JdbNavToolBar();
  JdbStatusLabel jdbStatusLabel1 = new JdbStatusLabel();
  Column column1 = new Column();
  Column column2 = new Column();
  JPanel jpControl = new JPanel();
  BorderLayout borderLayout1 = new BorderLayout();
  JdbNavField jdbNavField1 = new JdbNavField();
  JPanel jpData = new JPanel();
  BorderLayout borderLayout2 = new BorderLayout();
  JPanel jpRecord = new JPanel();
  JPanel jPanel1 = new JPanel();
  JdbTextField jdbTextField1 = new JdbTextField();
  GridLayout gridLayout1 = new GridLayout();
  JLabel jLabel1 = new JLabel();
  JLabel jLabel2 = new JLabel();
  JdbTextField jdbTextField2 = new JdbTextField();
  JLabel jLabel3 = new JLabel();
  JdbTextField jdbTextField3 = new JdbTextField();
  FlowLayout flowLayout1 = new FlowLayout();
  JPanel jPanel2 = new JPanel();
  JLabel jLabel4 = new JLabel();
  JdbTextField jdbTextField4 = new JdbTextField();
  FlowLayout flowLayout2 = new FlowLayout();
  JPanel jPanel3 = new JPanel();
```

Listing 14.2 *TestdbSwing.java*

```java
    JLabel jLabel5 = new JLabel();
    JdbTextField jdbTextField5 = new JdbTextField();
    FlowLayout flowLayout3 = new FlowLayout();
    JLabel jLabel6 = new JLabel();
    JdbTextField jdbTextField6 = new JdbTextField();
    JLabel jLabel7 = new JLabel();
    JdbTextField jdbTextField7 = new JdbTextField();
    JPanel jPanel4 = new JPanel();
    JLabel jLabel8 = new JLabel();
    FlowLayout flowLayout4 = new FlowLayout();
    JdbTextField jdbTextField8 = new JdbTextField();
    JPanel jPanel5 = new JPanel();
    JLabel jLabel9 = new JLabel();
    JdbTextField jdbTextField9 = new JdbTextField();
    FlowLayout flowLayout5 = new FlowLayout();
    TitledBorder titledBorder1;
    TitledBorder titledBorder2;
    JLabel jLabel10 = new JLabel();
    JPanel jpSearchField = new JPanel();
    BorderLayout borderLayout3 = new BorderLayout();

    // Construct the applet
    public TestdbSwing()
    {
    }

    // Initialize the applet
    public void init()
    {
      try
      {
        jbInit();
      }
      catch(Exception e)
      {
        e.printStackTrace();
      }
    }

    // Component initialization
    private void jbInit() throws Exception
    {
      titledBorder1 = new TitledBorder("");
      titledBorder2 = new TitledBorder("");
      queryDataSet1.setMetaDataUpdate(MetaDataUpdate.NONE);
      queryDataSet1.setQuery(
        new com.borland.dx.sql.dataset.QueryDescriptor(database1,
        "SELECT * FROM ADDRESSBOOK;\n", null, true, Load.ALL));
      database1.setConnection(
        new com.borland.dx.sql.dataset.ConnectionDescriptor(
        "jdbc:odbc:LiangBookDB_MDB", "", "", false,
        "sun.jdbc.odbc.JdbcOdbcDriver"));
      this.setSize(new Dimension(402, 392));
      jdbTable1.setDataSet(queryDataSet1);
      jdbNavToolBar1.setDataSet(queryDataSet1);
      jdbStatusLabel1.setText("jdbStatusLabel1");
      jdbStatusLabel1.setDataSet(queryDataSet1);
      column1.setColumnName("FIRSTNAME");
      column1.setDataType(com.borland.dx.dataset.Variant.STRING);
      column1.setPrecision(15);
```

continues

```
            column1.setRowId(true);
            column1.setTableName("ADDRESSBOOK");
            column1.setServerColumnName("FIRSTNAME");
            column1.setSqlType(12);
            column2.setColumnName("LASTNAME");
            column2.setDataType(com.borland.dx.dataset.Variant.STRING);
            column2.setPrecision(15);
            column2.setRowId(true);
            column2.setTableName("ADDRESSBOOK");
            column2.setServerColumnName("LASTNAME");
            column2.setSqlType(12);
            queryDataSet1.setColumns(new Column[] {column1, column2});
            jpControl.setLayout(borderLayout1);
            jdbNavField1.setText("jdbNavField1");
            jdbNavField1.setHorizontalAlignment(SwingConstants.RIGHT);
            jdbNavField1.setColumnName("FIRSTNAME");
            jdbNavField1.setDataSet(queryDataSet1);
            jpData.setLayout(borderLayout2);
            jdbTextField1.setColumnName("FIRSTNAME");
            jdbTextField1.setDataSet(queryDataSet1);
            jpRecord.setLayout(gridLayout1);
            jLabel1.setText("FirstName");
            jLabel2.setText("MI");
            jdbTextField2.setColumns(2);
            jdbTextField2.setColumnName("MI");
            jdbTextField2.setDataSet(queryDataSet1);
            jLabel3.setText("LastName");
            jdbTextField3.setColumnName("LASTNAME");
            jdbTextField3.setDataSet(queryDataSet1);
            jPanel1.setLayout(flowLayout1);
            flowLayout1.setAlignment(FlowLayout.LEFT);
            gridLayout1.setRows(5);
            jLabel4.setText("Address");
            jdbTextField4.setColumnName("ADDRESS");
            jdbTextField4.setDataSet(queryDataSet1);
            jPanel2.setLayout(flowLayout2);
            flowLayout2.setAlignment(FlowLayout.LEFT);
            jLabel5.setText("City");
            jdbTextField5.setColumnName("CITY");
            jdbTextField5.setDataSet(queryDataSet1);
            jPanel3.setLayout(flowLayout3);
            flowLayout3.setAlignment(FlowLayout.LEFT);
            jLabel6.setText("State");
            jdbTextField6.setColumnName("STATE");
            jdbTextField6.setDataSet(queryDataSet1);
            jLabel7.setText("Zip");
            jdbTextField7.setColumnName("ZIP");
            jdbTextField7.setDataSet(queryDataSet1);
            jLabel8.setText("Telephone");
            jPanel4.setLayout(flowLayout4);
            flowLayout4.setAlignment(FlowLayout.LEFT);
            jdbTextField8.setColumnName("TELEPHONE");
            jdbTextField8.setDataSet(queryDataSet1);
            jLabel9.setText("Email");
            jdbTextField9.setText("jdbTextField9");
            jdbTextField9.setColumnName("EMAIL");
            jdbTextField9.setDataSet(queryDataSet1);
            jPanel5.setLayout(flowLayout5);
            flowLayout5.setAlignment(FlowLayout.LEFT);
```

Listing 14.2 *Continued*

```
            jpControl.setBorder(titledBorder1);
            titledBorder1.setTitle("Navigation, Search, and Update");
            jpData.setBorder(titledBorder2);
            titledBorder2.setTitle("Show Data");
            jLabel10.setText("Search FirstName");
            jpSearchField.setBorder(BorderFactory.createEtchedBorder());
            jpSearchField.setLayout(borderLayout3);
            jpRecord.setBorder(BorderFactory.createEtchedBorder());
            this.getContentPane().add(jdbStatusLabel1, BorderLayout.SOUTH);
            this.getContentPane().add(jpControl, BorderLayout.NORTH);
            jpControl.add(jdbNavToolBar1, BorderLayout.NORTH);
            jpControl.add(jpSearchField, BorderLayout.CENTER);
            jpSearchField.add(jLabel10, BorderLayout.WEST);
            jpSearchField.add(jdbNavField1, BorderLayout.CENTER);
            this.getContentPane().add(jpData, BorderLayout.CENTER);
            jpData.add(tableScrollPane1, BorderLayout.CENTER);
            jpData.add(jpRecord, BorderLayout.NORTH);
            jpRecord.add(jPanel1, null);
            jPanel1.add(jLabel1, null);
            jPanel1.add(jdbTextField1, null);
            jPanel1.add(jLabel2, null);
            jPanel1.add(jdbTextField2, null);
            jPanel1.add(jLabel3, null);
            jPanel1.add(jdbTextField3, null);
            jpRecord.add(jPanel2, null);
            jPanel2.add(jLabel4, null);
            jPanel2.add(jdbTextField4, null);
            jpRecord.add(jPanel3, null);
            jPanel3.add(jLabel5, null);
            jPanel3.add(jdbTextField5, null);
            jPanel3.add(jLabel6, null);
            jPanel3.add(jdbTextField6, null);
            jPanel3.add(jLabel7, null);
            jPanel3.add(jdbTextField7, null);
            jpRecord.add(jPanel4, null);
            jPanel4.add(jLabel8, null);
            jPanel4.add(jdbTextField8, null);
            jpRecord.add(jPanel5, null);
            jPanel5.add(jLabel9, null);
            jPanel5.add(jdbTextField9, null);
            tableScrollPane1.getViewport().add(jdbTable1, null);
      }
   }
```

Listing 14.2   *Continued*

Example Review

The dbSwing package contains the components that extend the Swing components, such as `JdbTable` and `JdbTextField`, which are the extensions of
`javax.swing.JTabel`, `javax.swing.JTextField` with built-in database support.
The dbSwing package also contains additional components that complement
the standard Swing components, such as the `jdbNavToolBar` and `jdbNavField`.
To make these components data-aware, simply set the component's `dataSet`
property to bind the component to a `DataSet`, and set the `columnName` property
to the desired column name.

continues

All the data-aware components bound to a data set display or control data automatically. As in this example, a JdbTextField displays the value of the column of the current row. The buttons in the JdbNavToolBar are implemented to perform common database operations on the associated data set, the JdbTable displays all the records in the query set. The JdbNavField automatically searches for the value on the specified column.

The buttons on the JdbNavToolBar can be customized. You can hide a button; for instance, you can hide the Next button by setting the buttonStateNext property to HIDDEN.

JdbNavField performs an incremental search for string columns as each character is typed into the component. The search allows for a partial match. If the column is not a character column, such as a number or a time, no partial locate is performed as keys are typed. A non-string search is performed only when the Enter key is typed.

JdbTable is a powerful and sophisticated component. It displays data in a two-dimensional tabular form. This component contains many properties for customization. You can specify whether to display column headers and customize the headers. By default, the headers are shown using the column name. You can specify where grid lines are visible or not and whether column width can be changed at runtime or not, etc.

JdbStatusLabel is commonly used with a DataSet. It automatically displays status messages generated by the DataSet to provide valuable information on the status of the operations.

As you can see in this project, with the support of data-aware components, you can rapidly develop complete and comprehensive database applications with almost no coding. The project is easy to maintain and scalable.

Master-Detail Relationship

The projects presented thus far involve single tables. A practical database may have many tables storing interrelated data that represent an enterprise. In a relational database, all data are related whether they are in the same table or in different tables. Data in different tables are linked together through foreign keys. Loosely speaking, foreign keys are common columns shared by two or more tables. A master-detail relationship is usually a one-to-many type relationship based on foreign keys between two tables. For example, a table DEPARTMENT describing university academic departments consists of columns DEPTNO, DEPTNAME, and DEPTCHAIR, and a table EMPLOYEE representing employees consists of columns EMPNO, EMPNAME, OFFICE, and DEPTNO. The column DEPTNO is shared in both tables. You can create a master-detail relationship that will enable you to cruise through the DEPARTMENT table and display the employees in the current department.

Master-detail forms are common in database applications. JBuilder makes it easy to develop master-detail forms using the powerful DataExpress and dbSwing components. To create a master-detail form, you simply create two query data sets and link them together through the `masterLink` property in the query data set for the detailed table. You can then use components like `JdbTable` to control and display records in the master table and the detail table.

Example 14.3 Creating Master-Detail Forms

This example creates two tables, DEPARTMENT and EMPLOYEE, and develops a master-detail form to navigate through the DEPARTMENT to display all the employees in the selected department, as shown in Figure 14.8.

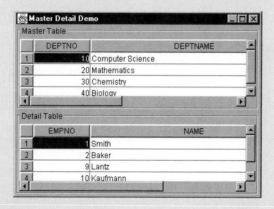

Figure 14.8   *You can select a department in the master table to display all the employees associated with the department in the detail table.*

Here are the steps to complete the project.

1. Create tables DEPARTMENT and EMPLOYEE in the database. The SQL statements for creating the tables are shown in Listing 14.3.

   ```
   CREATE TABLE DEPARTMENT
   (
     DEPTNO   INTEGER NOT NULL,
     DEPTNAME VARCHAR(50),
     DEPTCHAIR VARCHAR(50),
     PRIMARY KEY (DEPTNO)
   );

   CREATE TABLE EMPLOYEE
   (
   ```

continues

```
        EMPNO INTEGER NOT NULL,
        NAME VARCHAR(50),
        OFFICE VARCHAR(15),
        DEPTNO INTEGER,
        PRIMARY KEY (EMPNO)
    );
```

2. Create a new project named MasterDetailDemo.jpr, and create an applet named TestMasterDetail using the Applet Wizard.

3. Establish a database connection and create a query data set as follows:

   3.1. With MasterDetailApplet.java selected in the Navigation pane, switch to the UI Designer.

   3.2. Drop a Database from the Data Express page to the UI to create database1. In the Inspector of database1, click the Ellipsis button to display the Connection dialog box to connect to the Liang-BookDB_MDB.

   3.3. Drop a QueryDataSet twice from the Data Express page to the UI to create queryDataSet1 and queryDataSet2. queryDataSet1 will serve as the master table, and queryDataSet2 will serve as the detail table. In the query property editor of queryDataSet1, enter the following SQL statement in the SQL statement text box:

   SELECT * FROM DEPARTMENT

   3.4. In the query property editor of queryDataSet2, enter the following SQL statement in the SQL statement text box.

   SELECT * FROM EMPLOYEE

   3.5. In the Inspector of qeryDataSet2, double-click the value field of the masterLink property to bring up the masterLink dialog box, as shown in Figure 14.9. Choose queryDataSet1 in the Master DataSet choice menu. Since DEPTNO is shared by both queryDataSet1 and queryDataSet2, it automatically appears in the Master Link Columns and Detail Link Column. Press the Test button to test the link before clicking OK to close the dialog box.

4. Create the UI. Change the applet's layout to GridLayout with two rows. Drop a TableScrollPane twice into the applet, and set their border titles, "Master Table" and "Detail Table," respectively. Drop a JdbTable to the first scroll pane and another JdbTable to the second scroll pane. Set the dataSet property of the tables to queryDataSet1 and queryDataSet2, respectively.

5. Run the program. When selecting a department in the master table, you will see the corresponding employees in the department displayed in the in the detail table.

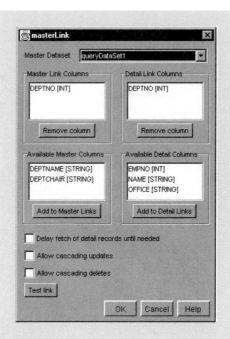

Figure 14.9   *The masterLink dialog box allows you to set the links.*

```
package MasterDetailDemo;

import java.awt.*;
import java.awt.event.*;
import java.applet.*;
import javax.swing.*;
import com.borland.dbswing.*;
import javax.swing.border.*;
import com.borland.dx.sql.dataset.*;

public class TestMasterDetail extends JApplet
{
  boolean isStandalone = false;
  TableScrollPane tableScrollPane1 = new TableScrollPane();
  TitledBorder titledBorder1;
  JdbTable jdbTable1 = new JdbTable();
  TitledBorder titledBorder2;
  Database database1 = new Database();
  QueryDataSet queryDataSet1 = new QueryDataSet();
  QueryDataSet queryDataSet2 = new QueryDataSet();
  GridLayout gridLayout1 = new GridLayout();
  TableScrollPane tableScrollPane2 = new TableScrollPane();
  JdbTable jdbTable2 = new JdbTable();

  // Construct the applet
  public TestMasterDetail()
  {
  }
```

continues

Listing 14.4   *Contains the code generated from the design.*

```
        // Initialize the applet
        public void init()
        {
          try
          {
            jbInit();
          }
          catch(Exception e)
          {
            e.printStackTrace();
          }
        }

        // Component initialization
        private void jbInit() throws Exception
        {
          titledBorder1 = new TitledBorder("");
          titledBorder2 = new TitledBorder("");
          this.setSize(new Dimension(400,300));
          this.getContentPane().setLayout(gridLayout1);
          tableScrollPane1.setBorder(titledBorder1);
          titledBorder1.setTitle("Master Table");
          titledBorder2.setTitle("Detail Table");
          database1.setConnection(
            new com.borland.dx.sql.dataset.ConnectionDescriptor(
              "jdbc:odbc:LiangBookDB_MDB", "", "", false,
              "sun.jdbc.odbc.JdbcOdbcDriver"));
          queryDataSet1.setQuery(
            new com.borland.dx.sql.dataset.QueryDescriptor(database1,
              "SELECT * FROM DEPARTMENT", null, true, Load.ALL));
          jdbTable1.setDataSet(queryDataSet1);
          queryDataSet2.setQuery(
            new com.borland.dx.sql.dataset.QueryDescriptor(database1,
              "SELECT * FROM EMPLOYEE", null, true, Load.ALL));
          gridLayout1.setRows(2);
          jdbTable2.setDataSet(queryDataSet2);
          tableScrollPane2.setBorder(titledBorder2);
          this.getContentPane().add(tableScrollPane1, null);
          this.getContentPane().add(tableScrollPane2, null);
          tableScrollPane2.getViewport().add(jdbTable2, null);
          tableScrollPane1.getViewport().add(jdbTable1, null);
          queryDataSet2.setMasterLink(
            new com.borland.dx.dataset.MasterLinkDescriptor(queryDataSet1,
            new String[] {"DEPTNO"},
            new String[] {"DEPTNO"}, false, false, false));
        }
      }
```

Listing 14.4   *Continued*

Example Review

This project was created without coding. JBuilder DataExpress components greatly simplify database application development. A complex project like this can be rapidly developed with little or no coding. Such a project is easy to maintain and highly scalable.

In a master-detail relationship, the values in the master fields determine which detail records will display. The records for the detail data set can be fetched all at once or for a particular master when needed. By default, the option "Delay fetch of detail records until needed" in the masterLink dialog box is unchecked to allow all the detailed records to be fetched.

By default, detail link columns are not displayed in a `JdbTable`, because they duplicate the values in the master link columns, which are displayed. You can insert, delete, and update records in both the master and the detail table. When a new record is inserted in the detail table, JBuilder uses the current value of the link columns. You can choose whether to allow cascading updates or cascading deletes in the masterLink dialog box.

Data Modules

Data modules, also known as *data models*, are specialized containers where data access components and their associated properties are collected into a reusable component. You define your data module once, then use it among various applications, or various frames within a single application.

Data modules can be used to separate database access logic and business rules from the application user interface. This enables you to modularize your code and maintain control over the use of data modules. The data modules can be put into a central location (a server, for example) so that the most recent version of the business logic is immediately available to the user without requiring changes of user applications.

To create a data module, you need to implement the `DataModule` interface, which declares the basic behavior of the data module. Since the `DataModule` interface does not contain any variables, properties, methods, or events, however, by implementing it you implicitly declare that your class is a data module.

Example 14.4 Using Data Modules

This example creates a project with three frames:

- A main frame, as shown in Figure 14.10, which contains two buttons that can be clicked to show or hide the other two frames.

- A frame, as shown in Figure 14.11, which contains a `JdbTable` to show the whole table.

- A frame, as shown in Figure 14.12, which contains a `JdbNavToolBar`, and a panel for displaying a single row in the table.

continues

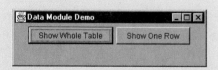

Figure 14.10   *The main frame contains two buttons for controlling two subframes.*

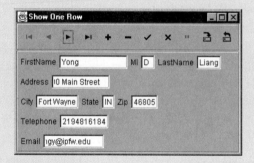

Figure 14.11   *The whole table is displayed in a* JdbTable.

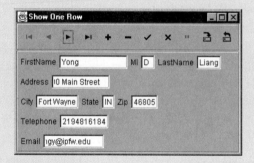

Figure 14.12   *The* JdbNavToolBar *navigates through the table to display the current row.*

The project can be divided into the following four tasks:

1. Create the main frame.

2. Create the data module to encapsulate the database information.

3. Create the frame for displaying the whole table.

4. Create the frame for displaying a row in the table.

1. Create the main frame.

    1.1. Create a new project named DataModuleDemo.jpr, and create DataModuleApplication.java and DataModuleFrame.java using the Application Wizard.

1.2. With DataModuleFrame.java selected in the Navigation pane, switch to the UI Designer. Change the layout of the frame to FlowLayout. Drop a JButton twice to the frame to create jbtShowTable and jbtShowRow.

1.3. Double-click jbtShowTable to generate the method jbtShowTable_actionPerformed() for handling the Show Whole Table button. Implement the method as shown in Listing 14.5.

1.4. Double-click jbtShowRow to generate the method jbtShowRow_actionPerformed() for handling the Show One Row button. Implement the method as shown in Listing 14.5.

```
package DataModuleDemo;

import java.awt.*;
import java.awt.event.*;
import javax.swing.*;

public class DataModuleFrame extends JFrame
{
  FlowLayout flowLayout1 = new FlowLayout();
  JButton jbtShowTable = new JButton();
  JButton jbtShowRow = new JButton();

  // Create two frames
  GridFrame gridFrame = new GridFrame();
  RowFrame rowFrame = new RowFrame();

  // Construct the frame
  public DataModuleFrame()
  {
    enableEvents(AWTEvent.WINDOW_EVENT_MASK);
    try
    {
      jbInit();
    }
    catch(Exception e)
    {
      e.printStackTrace();
    }
  }

  // Component initialization
  private void jbInit() throws Exception
  {
    jbtShowTable.setText("Show Whole Table");
    jbtShowTable.addActionListener(
      new java.awt.event.ActionListener()
    {
      public void actionPerformed(ActionEvent e)
      {
        jbtShowTable_actionPerformed(e);
      }
```

continues

Listing 14.5   *DataModuleFrame.java*

```
        });
        this.getContentPane().setLayout(flowLayout1);
        this.setSize(new Dimension(400, 300));
        this.setTitle("Frame Title");
        jbtShowRow.setText("Show One Row");
        jbtShowRow.addActionListener(new java.awt.event.ActionListener()
        {
          public void actionPerformed(ActionEvent e)
          {
            jbtShowRow_actionPerformed(e);
          }
        });
        this.getContentPane().add(jbtShowTable, null);
        this.getContentPane().add(jbtShowRow, null);
      }

      // Overridden so we can exit on System Close
      protected void processWindowEvent(WindowEvent e)
      {
        super.processWindowEvent(e);
        if(e.getID() == WindowEvent.WINDOW_CLOSING)
        {
          System.exit(0);
        }
      }

      // Handler for the Table button
      void jbtShowTable_actionPerformed(ActionEvent e)
      {
        if (jbtShowTable.getText().equals("Show Whole Table"))
        {
          jbtShowTable.setText("Hide Whole Table");
          gridFrame.pack();
          gridFrame.setVisible(true);
        }
        else if (jbtShowTable.getText().equals("Hide Whole Table"))
        {
          jbtShowTable.setText("Show Whole Table");
          gridFrame.setVisible(false);
        }
      }

      // Handler for the Row button
      void jbtShowRow_actionPerformed(ActionEvent e)
      {
        if (jbtShowRow.getText().equals("Show One Row"))
        {
          jbtShowRow.setText("Hide One Row");
          rowFrame.pack();
          rowFrame.setVisible(true);
        }
        else if (jbtShowTable.getText().equals("Hide One Row"))
        {
          jbtShowRow.setText("Show One Row");
          rowFrame.setVisible(false);
        }
      }
    }
```

Listing 14.5 *Continued*

2. Create the data module.

    2.1. Choose File, New to bring up the New dialog box. Double-click the Data Module icon in the New dialog box to display the New Data-Module dialog box, as shown in Figure 14.13. Uncheck the Option "Invoke Data Modeler." Type AddressBookDM in the Class Name field, and click OK to generate the data module AddressBookDM. java. If the option "Invoke Data Modeler" is checked, a Data Modeler Wizard will be displayed, which can be used to create a data module. See Exercise 14.4.

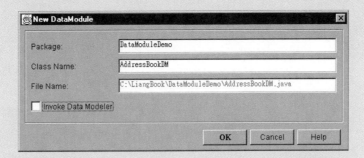

Figure 14.13 *The New DataModule dialog box creates a data module.*

    2.2. With AddressBookDM.java selected in the Navigation pane, switch to the UI Designer. Drop a Database from the Data Express page to the Data Access node in the Component tree. An object named database1 will appear in the component tree. Rename database1 as db. In the connection property editor, choose the URL of Liang-BookDB_MDB to connect db to the database.

    2.3. Drop a QueryDataSet from the Data Express page of the Component palette to the Data Access node in the Component tree. An object named queryDataSet1 appears in the component tree. Rename queryDataSet1 to qds. In the query property editor, select db in the Database choice menu and enter the following SQL statement. Set the rowID property True for the column FIRSTNAME and LAST-NAME. Set the metaDataUpdate property to None. The generated code for the data module is shown in Listing 14.6.

```
SELECT * FROM AddressBook
```

TIP

To create instances for Database and QueryDataSet in a data module, you need to drop them to the Access Node in the Component tree, rather than to the UI.

```
package DataModuleDemo;

import java.awt.*;
import java.awt.event.*;
import com.borland.dx.dataset.*;
import com.borland.dx.sql.dataset.*;

public class AddressBookDM implements DataModule
{
  private static AddressBookDM myDM;
  Database db = new Database();
  QueryDataSet qds = new QueryDataSet();
  Column column1 = new Column();
  Column column2 = new Column();

  public AddressBookDM()
  {
    try {
      jbInit();
    }
    catch (Exception e) {
      e.printStackTrace();
    }
  }

  private void jbInit() throws Exception
  {
    column2.setColumnName("LASTNAME");
    column2.setDataType(com.borland.dx.dataset.Variant.STRING);
    column2.setPrecision(15);
    column2.setRowId(true);
    column2.setTableName("AddressBook");
    column2.setServerColumnName("LASTNAME");
    column2.setSqlType(12);
    column1.setColumnName("FIRSTNAME");
    column1.setDataType(com.borland.dx.dataset.Variant.STRING);
    column1.setPrecision(15);
    column1.setRowId(true);
    column1.setTableName("AddressBook");
    column1.setServerColumnName("FIRSTNAME");
    column1.setSqlType(12);
    qds.setMetaDataUpdate(MetaDataUpdate.NONE);
    qds.setQuery(new com.borland.dx.sql.dataset.QueryDescriptor(db,
      "SELECT * FROM AddressBook", null, true, Load.ALL));
    db.setConnection(
      new com.borland.dx.sql.dataset.ConnectionDescriptor(
      "jdbc:odbc:LiangBookDB_MDB", "", "", false,
      "sun.jdbc.odbc.JdbcOdbcDriver"));
    qds.setColumns(new Column[] {column1, column2});
  }

  public static AddressBookDM getDataModule()
  {
    if (myDM == null)
      myDM = new AddressBookDM();
    return myDM;
  }
```

Listing 14.6   *AddressBookDM.java*

```
      public com.borland.dx.sql.dataset.Database getDb()
      {
        return db;
      }

      public com.borland.dx.sql.dataset.QueryDataSet getQds()
      {
        return qds;
      }
  }
```

Listing 14.6   *Continued*

3. Create the frame for displaying the whole table.

   3.1. Create a new frame named TableFrame.java using the Frame Wizard.

   3.2. With TableFrame.java selected in the Navigation pane, choose Wizards, Use Data Module to bring up the Choose a DataModule dialog box, as shown in Figure 14.14. Choose AddressBookDM in the DataModule class section, and check the radio button Share (static) instance of DataModule. Click OK to close the dialog box. You will see addressBookDM1 created in the source code.

   3.3. Drop a TableScrollPane from the dbSwing page to the center of the frame, and drop a JdbTable to the scroll pane to create jdbTable1. Set its dataSet property to addressDM1.

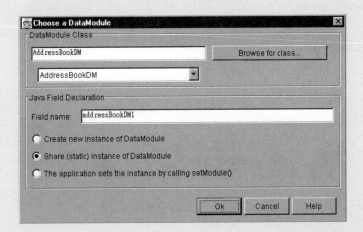

Figure 14.14   *The Choose a DataModule dialog box lets you choose a DataModule from the current project or from the library.*

continues

The generated code for TableFrame.java is shown in Listing 14.7.

```java
package DataModuleDemo;

import java.awt.*;
import javax.swing.JFrame;
import com.borland.dbswing.*;

public class TableFrame extends JFrame
{
  AddressBookDM addressBookDM1;
  TableScrollPane tableScrollPane1 = new TableScrollPane();
  JdbTable jdbTable1 = new JdbTable();

  public TableFrame()
  {
    try
    {
      jbInit();
    }
    catch(Exception e)
    {
      e.printStackTrace();
    }
  }

  private void jbInit() throws Exception
  {
    addressBookDM1 = DataModuleDemo.AddressBookDM.getDataModule();
    jdbTable1.setDataSet(addressBookDM1.getQds());
    this.setTitle("Show Whole Table");
    this.getContentPane().add(tableScrollPane1, BorderLayout.CENTER);
    tableScrollPane1.getViewport().add(jdbTable1, null);
  }
}
```

Listing 14.7 *TableFrame.java*

4. Create the frame for displaying a row in the table.

   4.1. Create a new frame named RowFrame.java using the Frame Wizard.

   4.2. With RowFrame.java selected in the Navigation pane, choose Wizards, Use Data Module to bring up the Choose a DataModule dialog box. Choose AddressBookDM in the DataModule class section, and check the radio button Share (static) instance of DataModule. Click OK to close the dialog box. You will see addressBookDM1 created in the source code.

   4.3. With RowFrame.java selected in the Navigation pane, switch to the UI Designer. Drop a JdbNavToolBar from the dbSwing page to the north of the frame to create jdbNavToolBar1. Set its dataSet property to addressDM1.

4.4. Drop a JPanel to the center of the frame to create jpRow. Set the layout property of jpRow to GridLayout with five rows. Drop a JPanel five times to jpRow to create five panels for containing the labels and text fields for records to display a row in the ADDRESS-BOOK table.

4.5. Add appropriate labels and text fields to the panels using JLabel and JdbTextField in the same way as in Example 14.2. Be sure to bind the text field's dataSet to addressBookDM1 and select the appropriate column names.

The generated code for RowFrame.java is shown in Listing 14.8.

```java
package DataModuleDemo;

import java.awt.*;
import com.borland.dbswing.*;
import javax.swing.*;

public class RowFrame extends JFrame
{
  AddressBookDM addressBookDM1;
  JdbNavToolBar jdbNavToolBar1 = new JdbNavToolBar();
  JPanel jpRow = new JPanel();
  GridLayout gridLayout1 = new GridLayout();

  JPanel jPanel1 = new JPanel();
  JdbTextField jdbTextField1 = new JdbTextField();
  JLabel jLabel1 = new JLabel();
  JLabel jLabel2 = new JLabel();
  JdbTextField jdbTextField2 = new JdbTextField();
  JLabel jLabel3 = new JLabel();
  JdbTextField jdbTextField3 = new JdbTextField();
  FlowLayout flowLayout1 = new FlowLayout();
  JPanel jPanel2 = new JPanel();
  JLabel jLabel4 = new JLabel();
  JdbTextField jdbTextField4 = new JdbTextField();
  FlowLayout flowLayout2 = new FlowLayout();
  JPanel jPanel3 = new JPanel();
  JLabel jLabel5 = new JLabel();
  JdbTextField jdbTextField5 = new JdbTextField();
  FlowLayout flowLayout3 = new FlowLayout();
  JLabel jLabel6 = new JLabel();
  JdbTextField jdbTextField6 = new JdbTextField();
  JLabel jLabel7 = new JLabel();
  JdbTextField jdbTextField7 = new JdbTextField();
  JPanel jPanel4 = new JPanel();
  JLabel jLabel8 = new JLabel();
  FlowLayout flowLayout4 = new FlowLayout();
  JdbTextField jdbTextField8 = new JdbTextField();
  JPanel jPanel5 = new JPanel();
```

continues

Listing 14.8   *Continued*

```java
    JLabel jLabel9 = new JLabel();
    JdbTextField jdbTextField9 = new JdbTextField();
    FlowLayout flowLayout5 = new FlowLayout();

    public RowFrame()
    {
      try
      {
        jbInit();
      }
      catch(Exception e)
      {
        e.printStackTrace();
      }
    }

    private void jbInit() throws Exception
    {
      addressBookDM1 = DataModuleDemo.AddressBookDM.getDataModule();
      jpRow.setLayout(gridLayout1);
      gridLayout1.setRows(5);
      jdbNavToolBar1.setDataSet(addressBookDM1.getQds());
      jdbTextField1.setColumns(10);
      jdbTextField1.setColumnName("FIRSTNAME");
      jdbTextField1.setDataSet(addressBookDM1.getQds());
      this.setTitle("Show One Row");
      this.getContentPane().add(jdbNavToolBar1, BorderLayout.NORTH);
      this.getContentPane().add(jpRow, BorderLayout.CENTER);

      jLabel1.setText("FirstName");
      jLabel2.setText("MI");
      jdbTextField2.setColumns(2);
      jdbTextField2.setColumnName("MI");
      jdbTextField2.setDataSet(addressBookDM1.getQds());
      jLabel3.setText("LastName");
      jdbTextField3.setColumnName("LASTNAME");
      jdbTextField3.setDataSet(addressBookDM1.getQds());
      jPanel1.setLayout(flowLayout1);
      flowLayout1.setAlignment(FlowLayout.LEFT);
      gridLayout1.setRows(5);
      jLabel4.setText("Address");
      jdbTextField4.setColumnName("ADDRESS");
      jdbTextField4.setDataSet(addressBookDM1.getQds());
      jPanel2.setLayout(flowLayout2);
      flowLayout2.setAlignment(FlowLayout.LEFT);
      jLabel5.setText("City");
      jdbTextField5.setColumnName("CITY");
      jdbTextField5.setDataSet(addressBookDM1.getQds());
      jPanel3.setLayout(flowLayout3);
      flowLayout3.setAlignment(FlowLayout.LEFT);
      jLabel6.setText("State");
      jdbTextField6.setColumnName("STATE");
      jdbTextField6.setDataSet(addressBookDM1.getQds());
      jLabel7.setText("Zip");
      jdbTextField7.setColumnName("ZIP");
      jdbTextField7.setDataSet(addressBookDM1.getQds());
      jLabel8.setText("Telephone");
      jPanel4.setLayout(flowLayout4);
```

Listing 14.8   *Continued*

```
        flowLayout4.setAlignment(FlowLayout.LEFT);
        jdbTextField8.setColumnName("TELEPHONE");
        jdbTextField8.setDataSet(addressBookDM1.getQds());
        jLabel9.setText("Email");
        jdbTextField9.setColumnName("EMAIL");
        jdbTextField9.setDataSet(addressBookDM1.getQds());
        jPanel5.setLayout(flowLayout5);
        flowLayout5.setAlignment(FlowLayout.LEFT);
        jpRow.setBorder(BorderFactory.createEtchedBorder());
        jpRow.add(jPanel1, null);
        jPanel1.add(jLabel1, null);
        jPanel1.add(jdbTextField1, null);
        jPanel1.add(jLabel2, null);
        jPanel1.add(jdbTextField2, null);
        jPanel1.add(jLabel3, null);
        jPanel1.add(jdbTextField3, null);
        jpRow.add(jPanel2, null);
        jPanel2.add(jLabel4, null);
        jPanel2.add(jdbTextField4, null);
        jpRow.add(jPanel3, null);
        jPanel3.add(jLabel5, null);
        jPanel3.add(jdbTextField5, null);
        jPanel3.add(jLabel6, null);
        jPanel3.add(jdbTextField6, null);
        jPanel3.add(jLabel7, null);
        jPanel3.add(jdbTextField7, null);
        jpRow.add(jPanel4, null);
        jPanel4.add(jLabel8, null);
        jPanel4.add(jdbTextField8, null);
        jpRow.add(jPanel5, null);
        jPanel5.add(jLabel9, null);
        jPanel5.add(jdbTextField9, null);
    }
}
```

Listing 14.8 *Continued*

Example Review

As you can see from this example, data modules offer the significant advantage of separating database connection and query information from the user interface, which enables multiple frames or applets to share the same application logic and business rules.

For example, suppose you wish to log the transaction for the delete record operation on the AddressBook table. All you need to do is to modify the Address-BookDM data module without requiring modifications of the other programs.

The data module does not need to be in the same directory with the application project. In fact, it can be stored on a server. Database applications based on data modules are easy to maintain, and clients can always get the latest version of the business logic from a centralized data module.

You can create a custom data module class manually, but the Data Module Wizard greatly simplifies the process of creating a data module. The wizard au-

continues

tomatically creates code that instantiates your data components at the data module class level. In addition, property settings made in the Inspector are reflected in a jbinit() method. Individual "getter" methods are also created that return each Database, DataSet, DataStore (and so on) in your data module. This allows DataSet components to be visible to the dataSet property of data-aware components in the Component Inspector when the data modules are used with data-aware components in the same application. As you can see in this example, addressBookDM1 appears in the dataSet property of jdbTable1 in TableFrame.java and also in jdbNavToolBar1 of RowFrame.java.

The property settings and business rules code you created in the data module cannot be overridden in the application that uses the data module. If you have rules that do not apply across all the applications that use this data module, you should create a separate data module to isolate the differences.

To reference your data module in your current application, select the Use Data-Module option from the Wizards menu to display the dialog box. This dialog box displays all the data modules in your project, allows you to browse to find other data modules in the library, and lets you choose the kind of constructor you want. In this example, you chose the option "Share (static) instance of DataModule." This option lets you access a single instance of your data module shared across your application instead of allocating memory for multiple instances. The static instance was automatically generated by the Data Module Wizard. If you create a data module manually, make sure to write the code to declare the static instance.

Chapter Summary

This chapter introduced the development of Java database applications using the JBuilder DataExpress API, dbSwing components, and data modules. You learned how to use the DataBase component to connect to a JDBC source and the QueryDataSet component to create queries. You also learned how to create applications using data-aware dbSwing components that link to QueryDataSet, how to create master-link forms, and how to create a data module to separate data from the GUI.

Chapter Review

14.1. Describe the DataExpress API. How do you connect to a data source using the Database component? How do you connect to a database and a query in QueryDataSet?

14.2. What properties do you have to set in the QueryDataSet to enable insertion and deletion of records in a table?

14.3. What properties do you need to bind a dbSwing component with a data source?

14.4. Describe the components `JdbNavToolBar` and `JdbNavField`.

14.5. Describe the process of creating a master-detail link between two instances of `QueryDataSet`.

14.6. What are the advantages of data modules? How do you create a data module?

Programming Examples

14.1. Modify Example 14.1 to add a new button to enable the user to update a record and add another button to enable the user to delete a record.

14.2. Modify Example 14.2 to add a `JComboBox` with values FIRSTNAME and LASTNAME. When FIRSTNAME is chosen, the search in the `JdbNavField` is based on the FIRSTNAME column of the table. When LASTNAME is chosen, the search is based on the LASTNAME column of the table.

14.3. Modify Example 14.3 to add a `JdbNavToolBar` and a `JdbStatusLabel` for each table, so that the user can manipulate the tables using the `JdbNavToolBar` buttons and get the message from the `JdbStatusLabel`.

14.4. Example 14.4 creates a data module without invoking the Data Modeler in the Data Module Wizard. Create the same data module using the data modeler.

PART V

DISTRIBUTED JAVA PROGRAMMING

The final part of the book introduces the development of distributed projects using Java. You will learn how to use Remote Method Invocation and CORBA to develop distributed applications.

CHAPTER 15   DISTRIBUTED PROGRAMMING USING JAVA REMOTE
              METHOD INVOCATION

CHAPTER 16   MULTI-TIER APPLICATION DEVELOPMENT USING CORBA

DISTRIBUTED PROGRAMMING USING JAVA REMOTE METHOD INVOCATION

Objectives

- @ Understand how RMI works.

- @ Learn the process of developing RMI applications.

- @ Know the differences between RMI and socket-level programming.

- @ Develop three-tier applications using RMI.

- @ Use callbacks to develop interactive applications.

Introduction

The Java language is superior for developing reusable software components, and the JavaBeans technology enables you to create Java applications by using a builder tool to assemble JavaBeans components during design time. The Remote Method Invocation (RMI) technology provides a framework for building distributed Java systems. Using RMI, a Java object on one system can invoke a method in an object on another system on the network. A distributed Java system can be defined as a collection of cooperative distributed objects on the network. This chapter introduces RMI basics. You will learn how to use RMI to create useful distributed applications.

RMI Basics

RMI is the Java Distributed Object Model for facilitating communications among distributed objects. RMI is a higher-level API built on top of sockets. Socket-level programming allows you to pass data through sockets among computers. RMI enables you not only to pass data among objects on different systems, but also to invoke methods in a remote object.

RMI is similar to Remote Procedure Calls (RPC) in the sense that both RMI and RPC enable you to invoke methods, but there are some important differences. With RPC, you call a standalone procedure. With RMI, you invoke a method within a specific object. RMI can be viewed as object-oriented RPC.

In many ways, RMI is an evolution of the client/server architecture. A *client* is a component that issues requests for services, and a *server* is a component that delivers the requested services. Like the client/server architecture, RMI maintains the notions of clients and servers, but the RMI approach is more flexible than the client/server paradigm.

- A RMI component can act as both a client and a server, depending on the scenario in question.

- A RMI system can pass functionality from a server to a client, and vice versa. A client/server system typically only passes data back and fourth between server and client.

How Does RMI Work?

For an object to be invoked remotely, it must be defined in a Java interface accessible to both the server and the client. Furthermore, this interface must extend the `java.rmi.Remote` interface. Like the `java.io.Serializable` interface, the `java.rmi.Remote` contains no constants or methods. It is only used to identify remote objects. The implementation of the remote object interface, referred to as *server implementation*, resides on the server machine and is registered with the RMI registry, as shown in Figure 15.1. A client looks through the RMI registry for the remote object. Once it is located, it can be used in the same way as a local object.

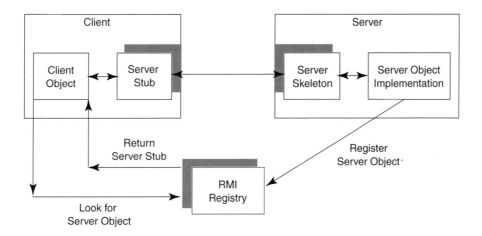

Figure 15.1 *Java RMI uses a registry to provide naming services for remote objects, and uses the stub and skeleton to facilitate communications between client and server.*

Obviously, invoking methods in a remote object on the server is very different from invoking methods in a local object on the client, since the remote object is in a different address space on a separate machine. The following steps are usually involved in invoking a remote method:

1. The client sends method parameters to the server.

2. The server receives the method parameter and executes the method.

3. The server sends the result back to the client.

4. The client receives the results.

Implementing this service is complicated, but the good news is that RMI provides a mechanism that liberates you from writing the tedious code for handling parameter passing and invoking remote methods. The basic idea is to use two helper classes known as *stub* and *skeleton* for handling communications between the client and the server, as shown in Figure 15.1.

The stub and the skeleton can be automatically generated from the server implementation using an RMI utility called `rmic`. The stub resides on the client machine. It contains all the reference information the client needs to know about the server object. When a client invokes a method on the server object, it actually invokes a method that is encapsulated in the stub. The stub is responsible for sending parameters to the server, and for receiving the result from the server and returning it to the client.

The skeleton communicates with the stub on the server side. The skeleton receives parameters from the client, passes them to the server for execution, and returns the result to the stub.

Passing Parameters

When a client invokes a remote method with parameters, passing the parameters is handled by the stub and the skeleton. Let us consider three types of parameters:

- ■ Primitive data type. A parameter of primitive type, such as char, int, double, or boolean, is passed by value like a local call.

- ■ Local object type. A parameter of local object type, such as java.lang. String, is also passed by value. This is completely different from passing an object parameter in a local call. In a local call, an object parameter is passed by reference, which corresponds to the memory address of the object. In a remote call, there is no way to pass the object reference because the address on one machine is meaningless to a different Java VM. Any object can be used as a parameter in a remote call as long as it is serializable. The stub serializes the object parameter and sends it in a stream across the network. The skeleton deserializes the stream into an object.

- ■ Remote object type. Remote objects are passed differently from local objects. When a client invokes a remote method with a parameter of a remote object type, the stub of the remote object is passed. The server receives the stub and manipulates the parameter through it. See Example 15.3, "The RMI TicTac-Toe Implementation," for details.

Developing RMI Applications

Now that you have a basic understanding of RMI, you are ready to write simple RMI applications. The steps in developing a RMI application are shown in Figure 15.2.

The following example demonstrates the development of a RMI application through these steps.

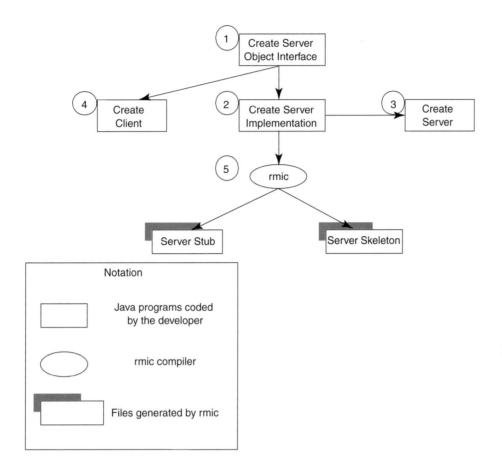

Figure 15.2 *The steps in developing RMI applications.*

Example 15.1 Retrieving Student Scores from a RMI Server

This example creates a client to retrieve student scores from a RMI server. The client, shown in Figure 15.3, displays the score for the specified name.

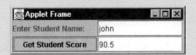

Figure 15.3 *You can get the score by entering a student name and clicking the Get Student Score button.*

continues

Here are the steps to complete this example:

1. Create a new project named RMIDemo.jpr.

2. Create the server interface named Student.java, as shown in Listing 15.1. The interface tells the client how to invoke the server's findScore() method to retrieve a student score.

3. Create StudentImpl.java (Listing 15.2) to implement the Student interface. The findScore() method simply returns the score for a specified student. This method returns -1 if the score is not found.

4. Create a server program named StudentServer that creates an instance of server implementation, and register it with the RMI registry. StudentServer.java is shown in Listing 15.3.

5. Now turn your attention to developing the client:

   5.1. Create an applet named StudentClient using the Applet Wizard.

   5.2. Create the user interface. In the UI Designer for StudentClient.java, change the applet's layout to GridLayout to create gridLayout1. Select gridLayout1 in the Component tree, and set columns and rows to 2. Drop a JLabel, a JTextField, a JButton, and a JTextField to the applet, and rename them to jlblName, jtfName, jbtGetScore, and jtfScore. Set the text property of jlblName to "Enter Student Name," and the text property of jbtGetScore to "Get Student Score."

   5.3. Create the method initializeRMI() for locating the Student server, as shown in Listing 15.4. Add the code to invoke this method from the jbInit() method.

   5.4. In the UI Designer, double-click jbtGetScore to generate the supporting code for the handler jbtGetScore_actionPerformed(). Implement this handler for finding and displaying the student's score, as shown in Listing 15.4.

6. At a DOS prompt, change the directory to c:\LiangBook, and type the following command to generate the stub and skeleton.

   C:\LiangBook>rmic RMIDemo.StudentImpl

   The stub named StudentImpl Stub.class and the skeleton named StudentImpl_Skel.class were generated. Move these two files to the RMIDemo directory where the class files for the client and servers are located.

7. Follow the steps below to run this example.

   7.1. Start RMI Registry by choosing Tools, RMIRegistry, if you use JBuilder 3 Enterprise Edition, or type "**start rmiregistry**" at a DOS prompt. By default, the port number 1099 is used by rmiregistry. To use a different port number, simply type the command "**start rmiregistry *portnumber***" at a DOS prompt.

7.2. Start StudentServer using the following command at C:\LiangBook directory:

java -Djava.security.policy=policy RMIDemo.StudentServer

The policy file is located at C:\LiangBook with the following contents to give global permission to anyone from anywhere:

```
grant
{
  // Allow everything for now
  permission java.security.AllPermission;
};
```

■ NOTE

You can modify the permission. For more information about the permission file, see www.javasoft.com/products/jdk/1.2/docs/guide/security/permissions.html

---

7.3. Run StudentClient as an application. A sample run of the application is shown in Figure 15.3.

7.4. Run RMIDemo.StudentClient.html from the appletviewer. A sample run is shown in Figure 15.4.

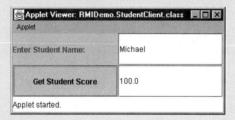

Figure 15.4 *You can run StudentClient as an applet.*

■ NOTE

You should have an active TCP/IP connection either by LAN or ISP, for otherwise the test will be very slow or will fail.

■ CAUTION

Every time you change the server implementation, you need to reapply the rmic utility to generate a new stub and skeleton.

---

continues

```
// Student.java: Student server interface
package RMIDemo;

import java.rmi.*;
import java.awt.*;

public interface Student extends Remote
{
  // Return the score for specified the name
  // Return -1 if score is not found.
  public double findScore(String name)
    throws RemoteException;
}
```

Listing 15.1   *Student.java*

```
// StudentImpl.java: implementation for Student.java
package RMIDemo;

import java.rmi.*;
import java.rmi.server.*;
import java.util.*;

public class StudentImpl extends UnicastRemoteObject
  implements Student
{
  // Stores scores in a dictionary indexed by name
  private Dictionary scores = new Hashtable();

  // Constructor
  public StudentImpl() throws RemoteException
  {
    // Initialize student information
    initializeStudent();
  }

  // Initialize student information
  protected void initializeStudent()
  {
    scores.put("John", new Double(90.5));
    scores.put("Michael", new Double(100));
    scores.put("Michelle", new Double(98.5));
  }

  // Return the score for specified the name
  // Return -1 if score is not found.
  public double findScore(String name)
    throws RemoteException
  {
    Double d = (Double)scores.get(name);

    if (d == null)
    {
      System.out.println("Student " + name + " is not found ");
```

Listing 15.2   *StudentImpl.java*

```
          return -1;
        }
        else
        {
          System.out.println("Student " + name + "\'s score is "
            + d.doubleValue());
          return d.doubleValue();
        }
      }
    }
  }
```

Listing 15.2   *Continued*

```
// StudentServer.java: register StudentImpl with the RMI registry
package RMIDemo;

import java.rmi.*;
import java.rmi.server.*;

public class StudentServer
{
  public static void main(String args[])
  {
    // Set RMI security manager
    if (System.getSecurityManager() == null)
    {
      System.setSecurityManager(new RMISecurityManager());
    }

    // Create and register the server implementation
    try
    {
      StudentImpl studentImpl = new StudentImpl();
      // To register the object on remote host, use
      // Naming.bind("//hostname:port#/Student Server", studentImpl);
      Naming.bind("Student Server", studentImpl);
      System.out.println("Server " + studentImpl + " registered");
    }
    catch(Exception ex)
    {
      System.out.println(ex);
    }
  }
}
```

Listing 15.3   *StudentServer.java*

```
// StudentClient.java: Student RMI Client
package RMIDemo;

import java.rmi.*;
import javax.swing.*;
import java.awt.*;
import java.awt.event.*;
```

continues

Listing 15.4   *StudentClient.java*

651

```java
public class StudentClient extends JApplet
{
  // Declare a Student instance
  Student student;

  boolean isStandalone = false;
  JLabel jlblName = new JLabel();
  GridLayout gridLayout1 = new GridLayout();
  JTextField jtfName = new JTextField();
  JButton jbtGetScore = new JButton();
  JTextField jtfScore = new JTextField();

  // Construct the applet
  public StudentClient()
  {
  }

  // Initialize the applet
  public void init()
  {
    try
    {
    jbInit();
    }
    catch (Exception e)
    {
    e.printStackTrace();
    }
  }

  // RMI initialization and Component initialization
  private void jbInit() throws Exception
  {
    // Initialize RMI
    initializeRMI();

    this.getContentPane().setLayout(gridLayout1);
    jlblName.setText("Enter Student Name:");
    gridLayout1.setColumns(2);
    gridLayout1.setRows(2);
    jbtGetScore.setText("Get Student Score");
    jbtGetScore.addActionListener(new java.awt.event.ActionListener()
    {
      public void actionPerformed(ActionEvent e)
      {
        jbtGetScore_actionPerformed(e);
      }
    });

    this.setSize(300,100);
    this.getContentPane().add(jlblName, null);
    this.getContentPane().add(jtfName, null);
    this.getContentPane().add(jbtGetScore, null);
    this.getContentPane().add(jtfScore, null);
  }

  // Main method
  public static void main(String[] args)
  {
```

Listing 15.4   *Continued*

```java
      // Omitted for brevity
    }

    // Initialize RMI
    protected void initializeRMI()
    {
      String url;

      if (isStandalone)
      {
        // System.setSecurityManager(new RMISecurityManager());

        url = "rmi:///";
        // Use rmi://hostname/ if the server is located on hostname,
        // i.e. rmi://liangy.ipfw.edu/
      }
      else
      {
        // Initialize RMI for an applet
        url = getCodeBase().getHost();
        if (url.equals("default")) url = "";
        url = "rmi://" + url + "/";
      }

      try
      {
        student = (Student)Naming.lookup(url + "Student Server");
        System.out.println("Server object " + student + " found");
      }
      catch(Exception ex)
      {
        System.out.println(ex);
      }
    }

    // Handler for the Get Student Score button
    void jbtGetScore_actionPerformed(ActionEvent e)
    {
      try
      {
      // Get student score
      double score = student.findScore(jtfName.getText().trim());

        // Display the result
        if (score < 0)
          jtfScore.setText("Not found");
        else
          jtfScore.setText(new Double(score).toString());
      }
      catch(Exception ex)
      {
        System.out.println(ex);
      }
    }
}
```

continues

653

Example Review

Any object that can be used remotely must be defined in an interface that extends the `java.rmi.Remote` interface. The `Student` interface defines the `findScore()` method that can be remotely invoked by a client to find a student's score. Each method in this interface must declare that it may throw a `java.rmi.RemoteException`. So your client code that invokes this method must be prepared to catch this exception in a try-catch block.

On the server side, the `StudentImpl` class implements the `Student` interface. This class must also extend the `java.rmi.server.RemoteServer` class or its subclass. `RemoteServer` is an abstract class that defines the methods needed to create and export remote objects. Often its subclass `java.rmi.server.UnicastRemoteObject` is used. This subclass implements all the abstract methods defined in `RemoteServer`.

`StudentImpl` contains the `findScore()` method. For simplicity, three students, John, Michael, and Michelle, and their corresponding scores are stored in an instance of `java.util.Dictionary` named `scores`. `Dictionary` is a superclass of `java.util.Hashtable` that makes it possible to search and retrieve a value using a key. Both values and keys are of `Object` type. The `findScore()` method returns the score if the name is in the dictionary, and returns -1 if the name is not found.

`StudentServer` is responsible for starting the server. It performs the following tasks:

1. Installing a RMI security manager to control the classes that are dynamically loaded with the following code:

   ```
   System.setSecurityManager(new RMISecurityManager());
   ```

2. Creating an instance of the server implementation and registering it in the RMI registry with the following code:

   ```
   Naming.rebind("Student Server", studentImpl);
   ```

`java.rmi.Naming` provides the bootstrap mechanism for locating remote objects. The server registers with the service, and the client retrieves the stub of the remote object through the service. The static method `bind()` binds the name to the specified remote object. You can also use the `rebind()` method to rebind the name to a new object and replace any existing binding associated with the name.

`StudentClient` invokes the `findScore()` method on the server to find the score for a specified student. The key method in `StudentClient` is the `initializeRMI()` method that is responsible for locating the server stub. The stub is specified in a RMI URL using the usual host name, port, and server name:

rmi://hostname:port/servername

where *hostname* is the host name of the RMI registry (defaults to current host), *port* is the port number of the RMI registry (defaults to the registry port number), and *servername* is the name for a remote object, such as "Student Server" in this example.

The `initializeRMI()` method treats standalone applications differently from applets. The hostname should be the name where the applet is downloaded. It can be obtained using the `Applet`'s `getCodeBase().getHost()`. For standalone applications, the hostname should be specified explicitly.

The `Naming.lookup()` method returns the remote object for the specified RMI URL. Once a remote object is found, it can be used just like a local object, although the stub and the skeleton are used behind the scenes to make the remote method invocation work.

If you run the client and the server on separate machines, you need to start RMIRegistry and run `StudentServer` on the server machine before running `StudentClient` on the client machine. To run `StudentClient` standalone, you need to deploy Student.class, StudentImpl_Stub.class, StudentClient.class on the client machine, and place Student.class, StudentImpl.class, StudentImpl_Skel.class and StudentServer.class on the server machine. To run `StudentClient` from a Web browser, you need to place Student.class, StudentImpl.class, StudentImpl_Stub.class, StudentImpl_Skel.class, StudentClient.class, and StudentClient.html on the server machine.

TIP

If you modify the remote object implementation class, you must regenerate updated stub and skeleton classes. You need to restart the server class to reload the skeleton to the RMI registry. In some old versions of rmiregistry, you may have to restart rmiregistry.

TIP

Uncheck the option "Synchronize output directory" in the Compiler page of the Project Property dialog so that the stub and skeleton files will not be deleted when you run the program from JBuilder. With this option checked, all the class files without the source code would be automatically removed by JBuilder. Note that the stub and skeleton files are created from a class for server object implementation. Therefore, the stub and skeleton files do not have Java source code.

RMI vs. Socket-Level Programming

Example 15.1 involves many files, but the stub and the skeleton were automatically generated by the rmic utility. These programs are easy to develop once you understand RMI. To appreciate the power and elegance of the RMI concept, this section rewrites Example 15.1 using socket-level programming so that you can compare RMI programming with socket-level programming.

Example 15.2 Retrieving Student Scores from a Server Using Socket-Level Programming

This example rewrites Example 15.1 using socket-level programming. The purpose is to highlight the differences between RMI and socket-level programming and to demonstrate the superiority of RMI for client/sever applications. If you are not familiar with socket-level programming, please refer to Chapter 16, "Networking," in my *Introduction to Java Programming with JBuilder 3.*

Here are the steps to complete the example.

1. Create a new project named SocketProgrammingDemo.jpr.

2. Create the server class named SocketStudentServer, as shown in Listing 15.5.

3. Create the client class named SocketStudentClient, as shown in Listing 15.6.

4. Start SocketStudentServer and then start SocketStudentClient. SocketStudentClient runs like StudentClient, as shown in Figure 15.4.

```
package SocketProgrammingDemo;

import java.io.*;
import java.net.*;
import java.util.*;

public class SocketStudentServer
{
  private Dictionary scores = new Hashtable();

  // Constructor
  public SocketStudentServer()
  {
    // Initialize scores hashtable
    initializeStudent();

    try
    {
      // Create a server socket
      ServerSocket serverSocket = new ServerSocket(8000);
```

Listing 15.5 *SocketStudentServer.java*

```
      // Server the clients
      while (true)
      {
        // Listen for a new connection request
        Socket connectToClient = serverSocket.accept();
        System.out.println(
          "Starting a new server thread for a new client");

        // Create a new thread for the connection
        ThreadHandler thread = new ThreadHandler(connectToClient);

        // Start the new thread
        thread.start();
      }
    }
    catch(IOException ex)
    {
      System.err.println(ex);
    }
  }

  public static void main(String[] args)
  {
    // Initialize SocketStudentServer
    new SocketStudentServer();
  }


  // Initialize student information
  protected void initializeStudent()
  {
    scores.put("John", new Double(90.5));
    scores.put("Michael", new Double(100));
    scores.put("Michelle", new Double(98.5));
  }

  // Get student score. Return -1 if score is not found.
  public double findScore(String name)
  {
    Double d = (Double)scores.get(name);

    if (d == null)
    {
      System.out.println("Student " + name + " is not found ");
      return -1;
    }
    else
    {
      System.out.println("Student " + name + "\'s score is "
        + d.doubleValue());
      return d.doubleValue();
    }
  }

  // The server for handling a client, an inner class
  class ThreadHandler extends Thread
  {
    private Socket connectToClient; // A connected socket
```

continues

```java
        public ThreadHandler(Socket socket)
        {
          connectToClient = socket;
        }

        public void run()
        {
          try
          {
            // Create data input and print streams
            BufferedReader isFromClient = new BufferedReader(
              new InputStreamReader(connectToClient.getInputStream()));
            PrintWriter osToClient =
              new PrintWriter(connectToClient.getOutputStream(), true);

            // Continuously serve the client
            while (true)
            {
              // Receive student name from the client in string
              String name = isFromClient.readLine();
              System.out.println(
                "Student name received from client is " + name);

              // Find score
              double score = findScore(name);

              // Send score back to the client
              osToClient.println(score);
            }
          }
          catch(IOException ex)
          {
            System.err.println(ex);
          }
        }
      } // End of the inner class
    }
```

Listing 15.5   *Continued*

```java
// StudentClient.java: Student Client
package SocketProgrammingDemo;

import javax.swing.*;
import java.awt.*;
import java.awt.event.*;
import java.io.*;
import java.net.*;
import java.util.*;

public class SocketStudentClient extends JApplet
{
  // Declare I/O streams
  protected BufferedReader isFromServer;
  protected PrintWriter osToServer;
```

Listing 15.6   *SocketStudentClient.java*

```java
boolean isStandalone = false;
JLabel jlblName = new JLabel();
GridLayout gridLayout1 = new GridLayout();
JTextField jtfName = new JTextField();
JButton jbtGetScore = new JButton();
JTextField jtfScore = new JTextField();

// Construct the applet
public SocketStudentClient()
{
  try
  {
    // Create a socket to connect to the server
    Socket connectToServer = new Socket("localhost", 8000);

    /* Create a buffered input stream to receive data
       from the server
     */
    isFromServer = new BufferedReader(
      new InputStreamReader(connectToServer.getInputStream()));

    // Create a buffered output stream to send data to the server
    osToServer =
      new PrintWriter(connectToServer.getOutputStream(), true);
  }
  catch (IOException ex)
  {
    System.err.println(ex);
  }
}

// Initialize the applet
public void init()
{
  try
  {
  jbInit();
  }
  catch (Exception e)
  {
  e.printStackTrace();
  }
}

// Component initialization
private void jbInit() throws Exception
{
  this.getContentPane().setLayout(gridLayout1);
  jlblName.setText("Enter Student Name:");
  gridLayout1.setColumns(2);
  gridLayout1.setRows(2);
  jbtGetScore.setText("Get Student Score");
  jbtGetScore.addActionListener(new java.awt.event.ActionListener()
  {
    public void actionPerformed(ActionEvent e)
    {
      jbtGetScore_actionPerformed(e);
    }
  });
```

continues

659

```
          this.setSize(300,100);
          this.getContentPane().add(jlblName, null);
          this.getContentPane().add(jtfName, null);
          this.getContentPane().add(jbtGetScore, null);
          this.getContentPane().add(jtfScore, null);
        }

        // Main method
        public static void main(String[] args)
        {
          // Omitted for brevity
        }

        void jbtGetScore_actionPerformed(ActionEvent e)
        {
          try
          {
            // Send student name to the server
            osToServer.println(jtfName.getText().trim());

            // Get score from the server as a string
            StringTokenizer st = new StringTokenizer(
              isFromServer.readLine());

            // Convert string to double
            double score = new Double(
              st.nextToken()).doubleValue();

            // Display the result
            if (score < 0)
              jtfScore.setText("Not found");
            else
              jtfScore.setText(new Double(score).toString());
          }
          catch (IOException ex)
          {
            System.err.println(ex);
          }
        }
      }
```

Listing 15.6 *Continued*

Example Review

The server class SocketStudentServer basically does the following things:

1. Initialize the scores in the hash table, which is the same as in Example 15.1.

2. Create an instance of java.net.ServerSocket named serverSocket, which is the base for listening to incoming connection requests from clients. The server socket is associated with a specific port. In this case, port 8000 is the server socket.

3. Create an instance of java.net.Socket for connecting to a client, and start a new server for handling the client on a separate thread. Since this server

(ThreadHandler) is an inner class, scores and the findScore() method defined in SocketStudentServer are accessible directly in this class. ThreadHandler continuously reads a name from the client, finds the score, and sends it to the client.

The client class SocketStudentClient is similar to StudentClient in Example 15.1 except it communicates with the server through socket I/O, as follows:

1. Create an instance of java.net.Socket for connecting with the server at port 8000. Instantiate the I/O streams for sending and receiving data from the server.

2. In the handler for button Get Student Score, write the code to send the name to the server and receive the score from the server.

Comparing Example 15.1 with Example 15.2, the advantages of using RMI against using the socket-level programming are clear:

- RMI enables you to program at a higher level of abstraction. It hides the details of socket server, socket, connection, and sending or receiving data. It even implements a multithreading server under the cover, while with socket-level programming you have to explicitly implement threads for handling multiple clients.

- RMI applications are scalable and easy to maintain. You can change the RMI server or move it to another machine without modifying the client program except for resetting the URL to locate the server. (To avoid resetting the URL, you can modify the client to pass the URL as a command-line parameter.) In socket-level programming, a client operation to send data requires a server operation to read it. The implementation of client and server at the socket-level is tightly synchronized.

- RMI clients can directly invoke the server method, whereas socket-level programming is limited to passing values.

As you can see, socket-level programming is very primitive. You should avoid using it to develop client/server applications. In an analogy, socket-level programming is like programming in assembly language, while RMI programming is like programming in a high-level language.

Developing Three-Tier Applications Using RMI

Three-tier applications have gained considerable attention in recent years, largely because of the demand for more scalable and load-balanced systems to replace traditional two-tier client/server database systems. A centralized database system not only handles data access but also processes the business rules on data. Thus, a centralized database is usually heavily loaded because it requires extensive data manipulation and processing. In some situations, data processing is handled by the client and business rules are stored on the client side. It is preferable to use a middle tier as a buffer between a client and the database. The middle tier can be used to apply business logic and rules, and to process data to reduce the load on the database.

A three-tier architecture does more than just reduce the processing load on the server. It also provides access to multiple network sites. This is especially useful to Java applets that need to access multiple databases on different servers, since applets can only connect with the server from which the applet is downloaded.

The following example demonstrates the use of RMI to create three-tier applications.

Example 15.3 Retrieving Student Scores on a Database Using RMI

This example rewrites Example 15.1 to find scores stored in a database rather than a hash table. In addition, the system is capable of blocking a client from accessing a student who has not given the university permission to publish his/her score. A RMI component is developed to serve as a middle tier between the client and the database; it sends a search request to the database, processes the result, and returns an appropriate value to the client.

For simplicity, this example reuses the Student interface and StudentClient class from Example 15.1 with no modifications. Here are the steps to complete the project.

1. Reopen project RMIDemo.jpr, which was created in Example 15.1.

2. Create Student3TierImpl to implement the Student interface for accessing a JDBC data source, as shown in Listing 15.7. This implementation retrieves a record from the SCORES table, processes the retrieved information, and sends the result back to the client.

3. At a DOS prompt, change to C:\LiangBook, and type the following command:

```
C:\LiangBook>rmic RMIDemo.Student3TierImpl
```

Copy Student3TierImpl_Stub.class and Student3TierImpl_Skel.class to the C:\LiangBook\RMIDemo directory.

4. Create Student3TierServer for creating an instance of Student3TierImpl and registering it with the RMI registry, as shown in Listing 15.8.

5. Start the RMI registry and Student3TierServer. Run StudentClient to find student scores.

```
// Student3TierImpl.java: implementation for Student.java
// for accessing JDBC source
package RMIDemo;

import java.rmi.*;
import java.rmi.server.*;
import java.sql.*;

public class Student3TierImpl extends UnicastRemoteObject
  implements Student
{
  // Use prepared statement for querying DB
  private PreparedStatement pstmt;

  // Constructor
  public Student3TierImpl() throws RemoteException
  {
    // Initialize student information
    initializeDB();
  }

  // Load JDBC driver, establish connection and create statement
  protected void initializeDB()
  {
    try
    {
      // Load the JDBC driver
      // Class.forName("oracle.jdbc.driver.OracleDriver");
      Class.forName("sun.jdbc.odbc.JdbcOdbcDriver");
      System.out.println("Driver registered");

      // Establish connection
      /*Connection conn = DriverManager.getConnection
        ("jdbc:oracle:thin:@sesrv00.ipfw.edu:1521:test",
          "scott", "tiger"); */
      Connection conn = DriverManager.getConnection
        ("jdbc:odbc:LiangBookDB_MDB", "", "" );
      System.out.println("Database connected");

      // Create the SCORES table and initialize it if necessary
      initializeTable(conn);

      // Create a prepared statement for querying DB
      pstmt = conn.prepareStatement(
        "SELECT * FROM SCORES WHERE name = ?");
    }
    catch (Exception ex)
    {
      System.out.println(ex);
    }
  }

  // Create the SCORES table and initialize it if necessary
  private void initializeTable(Connection conn)
  {
    try
    {
```

continues

Listing 15.7 *Student3TierImpl.java*

```java
              // Create a statement
              Statement stmt = conn.createStatement();

              // stmt.executeUpdate("DROP TABLE SCORES");

              // Create the table,
              // if already exists, an exception would be raised
              stmt.executeUpdate(
                "CREATE TABLE SCORES" +
                "(NAME VARCHAR(20), SCORE NUMBER, PERMISSION NUMBER)");

              // Insert three records into the SCORES TABLE
              stmt.executeUpdate(
                "INSERT INTO SCORES VALUES ('John', 90.5, 1)");
              stmt.executeUpdate(
                "INSERT INTO SCORES VALUES ('Michael', 100, 1)");
              stmt.executeUpdate(
                "INSERT INTO SCORES VALUES ('Michelle', 100, 0)");
            }
            catch (SQLException ex)
            {
              System.out.println(ex);
            }
          }

          // Return the score for specified the name
          // Return -1 if score is not found.
          public double findScore(String name)
            throws RemoteException
          {
            double score = -1;

            try
            {
              // Set the specified name in the prepared statement
              pstmt.setString(1, name);

              // Execute the prepared statement
              ResultSet rs = pstmt.executeQuery();

              // Retrieve the score
              if (rs.next())
              {
                if (rs.getBoolean(3))
                  score = rs.getDouble(2);
              }
            }
            catch (SQLException ex)
            {
              System.out.println(ex);
            }

            System.out.println(name + "\'s score is " + score);
            return score;
          }
        }
```

Listing 15.7   *Continued*

```
              // Student3TierServer.java: register Student3TierImpl
              // with the RMI registry
              package RMIDemo;

              import java.rmi.*;
              import java.rmi.server.*;

              public class Student3TierServer
              {
                public static void main(String args[])
                {
                  // Set RMI security manager
                  if (System.getSecurityManager() == null)
                  {
                    System.setSecurityManager(new RMISecurityManager());
                  }

                  // Create and register the server implementation
                  try
                  {
                    Student3TierImpl student3TierImpl = new Student3TierImpl();
                    Naming.rebind("Student Server", student3TierImpl);
                    System.out.println("Server " + student3TierImpl +
                      " registered");
                  }
                  catch(Exception ex)
                  {
                    System.out.println(ex);
                  }
                }
              }
```

Listing 15.8 *Student3TierServer.java*

Example Review

This example is similar to Example 15.1 except that the Student3TierImpl class finds the score from a JDBC data source instead from a hash table.

The table named SCORES consists of three columns, NAME, SCORE, and PERMISSION, where PERMISSION indicates whether the student has given permission to show his/her score. Since SQL does not support a boolean type, PERMISSION is defined as a number whose value of 1 indicates true and 0 indicates false.

The initializeDB() method loads the appropriate JDBC driver, establishes connections with the database, initializes the table if necessary, and creates a prepared statement for processing the query. If the table does not exist, the initializeTable() method creates a table and initializes it with three records.

The findScore() method sets the name in the prepared statement, executes the statement, processes the result, and returns the score for a student whose PERMISSION is true.

continues

665

> **NOTE**
> The JDBC prepared statement does not work properly with the JDBC-ODBC driver at this time. The first execution of the prepared statement can go through, but subsequent executions will fail. The Oracle JDBC Thin driver and InterClient driver work fine.

RMI Callbacks

In a traditional client/server system, a client sends a request to a server, and the server processes the request and returns the result back to the client. The server cannot invoke the methods on a client. One of the important benefits of RMI is that it supports *callbacks*, which enable the server to invoke the methods on the client. With the RMI callback feature, you can develop interactive distributed applications.

The following example demonstrates the use of the RMI callback feature to develop an interactive TicTacToe game.

Example 15.4 Developing a TicTacToe Game with RMI

This example creates a distributed application for playing TicTacToe. In a Tic-TacToe game, two players alternate turns by marking an available cell in a 3 × 3 grid with their token (X or O). One player is X, and the other is O. When one player places three tokens in a row on the grid (whether horizontally, vertically, or diagonally), the game is over and that player has won. A draw (no winner) occurs when all spaces on the grid have been filled with tokens and a win has not been achieved by either player. Figures 10.5 and 10.6 are representative sample runs of the example.

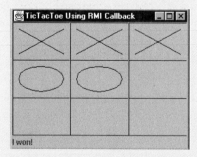

Figure 15.5   *This sample shows that player X has won.*

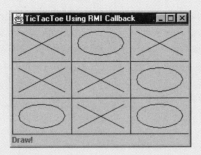

Figure 15.6 *This sample shows a draw with no winner.*

All the examples you have seen so far in this chapter have simple behaviors that are easy to model with classes. The behavior of the TicTacToe game is somewhat complex. To create the classes to model the game, you need to study and understand it and distribute the process appropriately between client and server.

Clearly the client should be responsible for handling user interactions, and the server should coordinate with the client. Specifically, the client should register with the server, and the server can take two and only two players. Once a client makes a move, it should notify the server; the server then notifies the move to the other player. The server should determine the status of the game, i.e., whether the game is won or drawn, and should notify the players. The server should also coordinate the turns, i.e., which client has the turn at a given time. The ideal approach for notifying a player is to invoke a method in the client to set appropriate properties in the client or to send messages to a player. Figure 15.7 illustrates the relationship between clients and server.

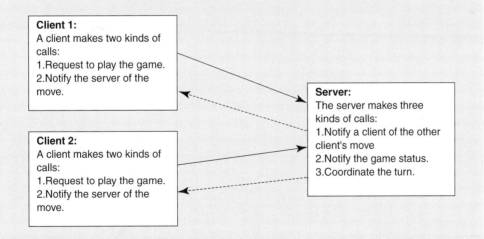

Figure 15.7 *The server coordinates the activities with the clients.*

continues

All the calls a client makes can be encapsulated in one remote interface named TicTacToe (Listing 15.9), and all the calls the server invokes can be defined in another interface named CallBack (Listing 15.10).

```
// TicTacToe.java: TicTacToe RMI interface, invoked by clients
package RMITicTacToe;

import java.rmi.*;

public interface TicTacToe extends Remote
{
  // Connect to the TicTacToe server and return the token
  // if the returned token is ' ', the client is not connected to
  // server
  public char connect(CallBack client) throws RemoteException;

  // A client invokes this method to notify the server of its move
  public void myMove(int row, int column, char token)
    throws RemoteException;
}
```

Listing 15.9 *TicTacToe.java*

```
// CallBack.java: CallBack RMI interface, invoked by the server
package RMITicTacToe;

import java.rmi.*;

public interface CallBack extends Remote
{
  // The server notifies the client for taking a turn
  public void takeTurn(boolean turn) throws RemoteException;

  // The server sends a message to be displayed by the client
  public void notify(java.lang.String message)
    throws RemoteException;

  // The server notifies a client of the other player's move
  public void mark(int row, int column, char token)
    throws RemoteException;
}
```

Listing 15.10 *CallBack.java*

What does a client need to do? The client interacts with the player. Assume that all the cells are initially empty, and that the first player takes the X token and the second player takes the O token. To mark a cell, the player points the mouse to the cell and clicks it. If the cell is empty, the token (X or O) is displayed. If the cell is already filled, the player's action is ignored.

From the preceding description, it is obvious that a cell is a GUI object that handles the mouse-click event and displays tokens. The candidate for such an object could be a button or a canvas. Canvases are more flexible than buttons. The token (X or O) can be drawn on a canvas in any size, but it only can be displayed as label on a button. `Canvas` is an AWT component, its Swing counterpart is `JPanel`. Therefore, a `JPanel` is used to model a cell in this example.

Let `Cell` be a subclass of `JPanel`. You can declare a 3×3 grid to be an array `Cell[][] = new Cell[3][3]` for modeling the game. How do you know the state of a cell (marked or not)? You can simply use a property named `marked` of the `boolean` type in the `Cell` class. How do you know whether the player has a turn? You can use a property named `myTurn` of `boolean`. This property (initially `false`) can be set by the server through a callback.

The `Cell` class is responsible for drawing the token when an empty cell is clicked, so you need to write the code for listening to the `MouseEvent` and for painting the shape for tokens X and O. To determine which shape to draw, introduce a variable named `marker` of the `char` type. Since this variable is shared by all the cells in a client, it is preferable to declare it in the client and to declare the `Cell` class as an inner class of the client so this variable is accessible to all the cells.

Now let us turn our attention to the server side. What does the server need to do? The server needs to implement the `TicTacToe` interface and to notify the game status to the clients. The server has to record the moves in the cells and check the status every time a player makes a move. The status information can be kept in a 3×3 array of `char`. You can implement a method named `isFull()` to check whether the board is full and implement a method named `coor(token)` to check whether a specific player has won.

Once a client is connected to the server, the server notifies the client which token to use, i.e., X for the first client, and O for the second. Once a client notifies the server of its move, the server checks the game status and notifies the clients.

Now the most critical question is how the server notifies a client. You know that a client invokes a server method by creating a server stub on the client side. A server cannot directly invoke a client, because the client is not declared as a remote object. The `CallBack` interface was created to facilitate the server's callback to the client. In the implementation of `CallBack`, an instance of the client is passed as a parameter in the constructor of `CallBack`. The client creates an instance of `CallBack` and passes its stub to the server, using a remote method named `connect()` defined in the server. The server then invokes the client's method through a `CallBack` instance. The triangular relationship of client, `CallBack` implementation, and server is shown in Figure 15.8.

continues

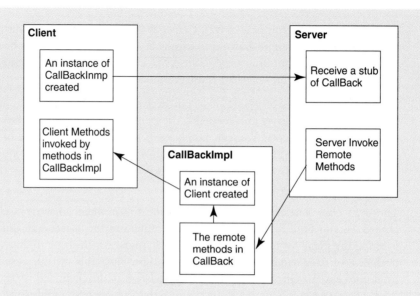

Figure 15.8 *The server receives a* CallBack *stub from the client and invokes the remote methods defined in the* CallBack *interface, which can invoke the methods defined in the client.*

Here are the steps to complete the example.

1. Create a new project named RMITicTacToe.jpr. Uncheck the option "Synchronize output directory" in the Compiler page of the Project Property dialog.

2. Create the TicTacToe interface and the CallBack interface, as shown in Listings 15.9 and 15.10.

3. Create TicTacToeImpl to implement the TicTacToe interface, as shown in Listing 15.11.

4. Create CallBackImpl to implement the CallBack interface, as shown in Listing 15.12.

5. Use the rmic utility to generate the stubs and the skeletons for TicTacToeImpl and CallBackImpl, and move the generated files to the directory C:\LiangBook\RMITicTacToe.

6. Create TicTacToeServer for creating and registering an instance of TicTacToeImpl, as shown in Listing 15.13.

7. Create TicTacToeClient for interacting with a player and communicating with the server, as shown in Listing 15.14.

8. Start a RMI registry and start TicTacToeServer. Start two TicTacToeClient to play the game.

```
// TicTacToeImpl.java: The TicTacToe RMI Server Implementation
package RMITicTacToe;

import java.rmi.*;
import java.rmi.server.*;

public class TicTacToeImpl extends UnicastRemoteObject
  implements TicTacToe
{
  // Declare two players, used to call players back
  CallBack player1 = null;
  CallBack player2 = null;

  // board records players' moves
  char[][] board = new char[3][3];

  // Constructor
  public TicTacToeImpl() throws RemoteException
  {
  }

  // Connect to the TicTacToe server and return the token
  // if the returned token is ' ', the client is not connected to
  // server
  public char connect(CallBack client) throws RemoteException
  {
    if (player1 == null)
    {
      // player1 (first player) registered
      player1 = client;
      player1.notify("Wait for a second palyer to join");
      return 'X';
    }
    else if (player2 == null)
    {
      // player2 (second player) registered
      player2 = client;
      player2.notify("Wait for the first palyer to move");
      player2.takeTurn(false);
      player1.notify("It is my turn (X token)");
      player1.takeTurn(true);
      return 'O';
    }
    else
    {
      // Already two players
      client.notify("Two players are already in the game");
      return ' ';
    }
  }

  // A client invokes this method to notify the server of its move
  public void myMove(int row, int column, char token)
    throws RemoteException
  {
    // Set token to the specified cell
    board[row][column] = token;
```

continues

Listing 15.11   *TicTacToeImpl.java*

```java
        // Notify the other player of the move
        if (token == 'X')
          player2.mark(row, column, 'X');
        else
          player1.mark(row, column, 'O');

        // Check if the player with this token wins
        if (won(token))
        {
          if (token == 'X')
          {
            player1.notify("I won!");
            player2.notify("I lost!");
            player1.takeTurn(false);
          }
          else
          {
            player2.notify("I won!");
            player1.notify("I lost!");
            player2.takeTurn(false);
          }
        }
        else if (isFull())
        {
          player1.notify("Draw!");
          player2.notify("Draw!");
        }
        else if (token == 'X')
        {
          player1.notify("Wait for the second player to move");
          player1.takeTurn(false);
          player2.notify("It is my turn, (O token)");
          player2.takeTurn(true);
        }
        else if (token == 'O')
        {
          player2.notify("Wait for the first player to move");
          player2.takeTurn(false);
          player1.notify("It is my turn, (X token)");
          player1.takeTurn(true);
        }
      }

      // Check if a player with the specified token wins
      public boolean won(char token)
      {
        for (int i=0; i<3; i++)
          if ((board[i][0] == token)
              && (board[i][1] == token)
              && (board[i][2] == token))
            return true;

        for (int j=0; j<3; j++)
          if ((board[0][j] == token)
              && (board[1][j] == token)
              && (board[2][j] == token))
            return true;
```

Listing 15.11   *Continued*

```
            if ((board[0][0] == token)
                && (board[1][1] == token)
                && (board[2][2] == token))
              return true;

            if ((board[0][2] == token)
                && (board[1][1] == token)
                && (board[2][0] == token))
              return true;

            return false;
          }

          // Check if the board is full
          public boolean isFull()
          {
            for (int i=0; i<3; i++)
              for (int j=0; j<3; j++)
                if (board[i][j] == '\u0000')
                  return false;

            return true;
          }
        }
```

Listing 15.11   *Continued*

```
        // CallBackImpl.java: The CallBack RMI interface implementation
        package RMITicTacToe;

        import java.rmi.*;
        import java.rmi.server.*;

        public class CallBackImpl extends UnicastRemoteObject
          implements CallBack
        {
          // The client will be called by the server through callback
          TicTacToeClient thisClient;

          // Constructor
          CallBackImpl(Object client) throws RemoteException
          {
            thisClient = (TicTacToeClient)client;
          }

          // The server notifies the client for taking a turn
          public void takeTurn(boolean turn) throws RemoteException
          {
            thisClient.setMyTurn(turn);
          }

          // The server sends a message to be displayed by the client
          public void notify(java.lang.String message)
            throws RemoteException
          {
```

continues

Listing 15.12   *CallBackImpl.java*

```
      thisClient.setMessage(message);
  }

  // The server notifies a client of the other player's move
  public void mark(int row, int column, char token)
    throws RemoteException
  {
    thisClient.mark(row, column, token);
  }
}
```

Listing 15.12   *Continued*

```
// TicTacToeServer.java: launch TicTacTorImpl
package RMITicTacToe;

import java.rmi.*;
import java.rmi.server.*;

public class TicTacToeServer
{
  public static void main(String args[])
  {
    System.setSecurityManager(new RMISecurityManager());
    try
    {
      TicTacToeImpl ticTacToeImpl = new TicTacToeImpl();
      Naming.rebind("TicTacToe Server", ticTacToeImpl);
      System.out.println("Server registered");
    }
    catch(Exception ex)
    {
      System.out.println(ex);
    }
  }
}
```

Listing 15.13   *TicTacToeServer.java*

```
// TicTacToeClient.java: TicTacToeClient applet
package RMITicTacToe;

import java.rmi.*;
import java.awt.*;
import java.awt.event.*;
import java.applet.*;
import javax.swing.*;

public class TicTacToeClient extends JApplet
{
  // marker is used to indicate the token type
  char marker;
```

Listing 15.14   *TicTacToeClient.java*

```
            // myTurn indicates whether the player can move now
            private boolean myTurn = false;

            // Each cell can be empty or marked as 'O' or 'X'
            private Cell[][] cell;

            // ticTacToe is the game server for coordinating with the players
            TicTacToe ticTacToe;

            boolean isStandalone = false;
            JLabel jlblStatus = new JLabel();
            JPanel jPanel1 = new JPanel();
            GridLayout gridLayout1 = new GridLayout();

            // Construct the applet
            public TicTacToeClient()
            {
            }

            // Initialize the applet
            public void init()
            {
              try
              {
              jbInit();
              }
              catch (Exception e)
              {
              e.printStackTrace();
              }
            }

            // Component and RMI initialization
            private void jbInit() throws Exception
            {
              // Create user interface
              this.setSize(400,300);
              jPanel1.setLayout(gridLayout1);
              gridLayout1.setRows(3);
              gridLayout1.setHgap(1);
              gridLayout1.setColumns(3);
              this.getContentPane().add(jlblStatus, BorderLayout.SOUTH);
              this.getContentPane().add(jPanel1, BorderLayout.CENTER);

              // Create cells and place cells in the panel
              cell = new Cell[3][3];
              for (int i=0; i<3; i++)
                for (int j=0; j<3; j++)
                  jPanel1.add(cell[i][j] = new Cell(i, j));

              // Initialize the CORBA enviornment
              initializeRMI();
            }

            // Initialize RMI
            protected boolean initializeRMI() throws Exception
            {
              String url;
```

continues

Listing 15.14 *Continued*

```java
      if (isStandalone)
      {
        // Initialize RMI for a standalone application
        // System.setSecurityManager(new RMISecurityManager());
        url = "rmi:///";
        // Use rmi://hostname/ if the server is located on hostname,
        // i.e. rmi://liangy.liangy.edu/
      }
      else
      {
        // Initialize RMI for an applet
        url = getCodeBase().getHost();
        if (url.equals("default")) url = "";
        url = "rmi://" + url + "/";
      }

      ticTacToe = (TicTacToe)Naming.lookup(url + "TicTacToe Server");
      System.out.println("Server found");

      // Create callback for use by the server to control the client
      CallBackImpl callBackControl = new CallBackImpl(this);

      if (
        (marker = ticTacToe.connect((CallBack)callBackControl)) != ' ')
      {
        System.out.println("connected as " + marker + " player.");
        return true;
      }
      else
      {
        System.out.println("already two players connected as ");
        return false;
      }
    }

    // Set variable myTurn to true or false
    void setMyTurn(boolean myTurn)
    {
      this.myTurn = myTurn;
    }

    // Set message on the status label
    public void setMessage(String message)
    {
      jlblStatus.setText(message);
    }

    // Mark the specified cell using the token
    void mark(int row, int column, char token)
    {
      cell[row][column].setToken(token);
    }

    //Main method
    public static void main(String[] args)
    {
      // Omitted for brevity
    }
```

Listing 15.14   *Continued*

```java
// Inner class Cell for modeling a cell on the TicTacToe board
public class Cell extends JPanel implements MouseListener
{
  // marked indicates whether the cell has been used
  private boolean marked = false;

  // row and column indicate where the cell appears on the board
  int row, column;

  // The token for the cell
  private char token;

  // Construct a cell
  public Cell(int row, int column)
  {
    this.row = row;
    this.column = column;
    addMouseListener(this);
  }

  // Set token on a cell (mark a cell)
  public void setToken(char c)
  {
    token = c;
    marked = true;
    repaint();
  }

  // Paint the cell to draw a shape for the token
  public void paintComponent(Graphics g)
  {
    super.paintComponent(g);

    // Draw the border
    g.drawRect(0, 0, getSize().width, getSize().height);

    if (token == 'X')
    {
      g.drawLine(10, 10, getSize().width-10, getSize().height-10);
      g.drawLine(getSize().width-10, 10, 10, getSize().height-10);
    }
    else if (token == 'O')
    {
      g.drawOval(10, 10, getSize().width-20, getSize().height-20);
    }
  }

  public void mouseClicked(MouseEvent e)
  {
    //TODO: implement this java.awt.event.MouseListener method;
    if (myTurn && !marked)
    {
      // Mark the cell
      setToken(marker);

      // Notify the server of the move
      try
      {
```

continues

Listing 15.14 *Continued*

```
                      ticTacToe.myMove(row, column, marker);
                  }
                  catch (RemoteException ex)
                  {
                      System.out.println(ex);
                  }
              }
          }

          public void mousePressed(MouseEvent e)
          {
              // TODO: implement this java.awt.event.MouseListener method;
          }

          public void mouseReleased(MouseEvent e)
          {
              // TODO: implement this java.awt.event.MouseListener method;
          }

          public void mouseEntered(MouseEvent e)
          {
              // TODO: implement this java.awt.event.MouseListener method;
          }

          public void mouseExited(MouseEvent e)
          {
              // TODO: implement this java.awt.event.MouseListener method;
          }
      }
  }
```

Listing 15.14   *Continued*

Example Review

The `TicTacToe` interface defines two remote methods, `connect(CallBack client)` and `myMove(int row, int column, char token)`. The `connect()` method plays two roles: one is to pass a `CallBack` stub to the server, and the other is to let the server assign a token for the player. The `myMove()` method notifies the server that the player has made a specific move.

The `CallBack` interface defines three remote methods, `takeTurn(boolean turn)`, `notify(String message)`, and `mark(int row, int column, char token)`. The `takeTurn()` method sets the client's `myTurn` property to `true` or `false`. The `notify()` method displays a message on the client's status label. The `mark()` method marks the client's cell with the token at the specified location.

`TicTacToeImpl` is a server implementation for coordinating with the clients and managing the game. The variables `player1` and `player2` are instances of `CallBack`, each of which corresponds to a client, passed from a client when the client invokes the `connect()` method. The variable `board` records the moves by the two players. This information is needed to determine the game status. When a client invokes the `connect()` method, the server assigns a token X for the first player and O for the second player, and only two players are accepted by the server. You can modify the program to accept additional clients as observers. See Exercise 15.4 for more details.

Once two players are in the game, the server coordinates the turns between them. When a client invokes the myMove() method, the server records the move and notifies the other player by marking the other player's cell. It then checks to see whether the player wins or whether the board is full. If the game should continue, the server gives a turn to the other player.

The CallBackImpl implements the CallBack interface. It creates an instance of TicTacToeClient through its constructor. The CallBackImpl relays the server request to the client by invoking the client's methods. When the server invokes the takeTurn() method, CallBackImpl invokes the client's setMyTurn() method to set the property myTurn in the client. When the server invokes the notify() method, CallBackImpl invokes the client's setMessage() method to set the message on the client's status label. When the server invokes the mark() method, CallBackImpl invokes the client's mark() method to mark the specified cell.

TicTacToeClient can run as a standalone application or as an applet. The initializeRMI method is responsible for creating the url for running as standalone application or as an applet, for locating the TicTacToe server stub, for creating the CallBack server object, and for connecting the client with the server.

Interestingly, obtaining the TicTacToe stub for the client is different from obtaining the CallBack stub for the server. The TicTacToe stub is obtained by invoking the lookup() method through the RMI registry, and the CallBack stub is passed to the server through the connect() method in the TicTacToe stub. It is a common practice to obtain the first stub with the lookup() method, but to pass the subsequent stubs as parameters through remote method invocations.

Since the variables myTurn and marker are defined in TicTacToeClient, the Cell class is defined as an inner class within TicTacToeClient in order to enable all the cells in the client to access them. Exercise 15.4 suggests alternative approaches that implement the Cell as a non-inner class.

Chapter Summary

RMI is a high-level Java API for building distributed applications using distributed objects. The key idea of RMI is its use of stub and skeleton to facilitate communications between objects. The stub and skeleton are automatically generated, which relieves programmers of tedious socket-level network programming. For an object to be used remotely, it must be defined in an interface that extends the java.rmi.Remote interface. In an RMI application, the initial remote object must be registered with the RMI registry on the server side and be obtained using the lookup() method through the registry on the client side. Subsequent use of stubs of other remote objects may be passed as parameters through remote method invocations. RMI is especially useful for developing scalable and load-balanced multi-tier distributed applications. RMI is a pure Java solution, and it cannot be used to develop a distributed system involving different programming languages. The next chapter introduces the CORBA technology, which can be used to develop distributed systems using C, C++, Ada, or other languages, as well as Java.

Chapter Review

15.1. How do you define an interface for a remote object?

15.2. Describe the roles of the stub and the skeleton.

15.3. How do you generate the stub and the skeleton?

15.4. What is the RMI registry for? How do you create a RMI registry?

15.5. How do you register a remote object with the RMI registry?

15.6. How does a client locate a remote object stub through the RMI registry?

15.7. How do you start a RMI registry and start a server from the DOS prompt?

15.8. Describe how parameters are passed in RMI. What is the problem if the connect() method in the TicTacToe interface is defined as

```
public boolean connect(CallBack client, char token)
    throws RemoteException;
```

or as

```
public boolean connect(CallBack client, Character token)
    throws RemoteException;
```

15.9. What is callback? How does callback work in RMI?

Programming Exercises

15.1. Modify Example 15.1 to limit the number of concurrent clients to 10.

15.2. Write an applet to show the number of visits made to a Web page. The count should be stored on the server side in a file. The applet should send a request to the server every time the page is visited or reloaded, and the server should increase the count and send it to the applet. The applet should then display the count in a message, such as You are visitor number: 1000. The server can read or write to the file using a random file access stream.

15.3. Use the three-tier approach to modify Example 12.4, "Using Borland Inter-Client Driver Accessing InterBase Servers," as follows:

   ■ Create an applet client to manipulate student information, as shown in Figure 12.16.

■ Create a remote object interface with methods for retrieving, inserting, and updating student information, and an object implementation for the interface.

15.4. Modify Example 15.4 as follows:

■ Allow a client to connect to the server as an observer to watch the game.

■ Rewrite the Cell class as a non-inner class.

MULTI-TIER APPLICATION DEVELOPMENT USING CORBA

Objectives

- Understand the concept of CORBA.
- Learn the process of developing CORBA applications using VisiBroker for Java.
- Know the similarities and differences between CORBA and RMI.
- Develop three-tier applications using CORBA.
- Use callbacks to develop interactive applications in CORBA.

Introduction

The *Common Object Request Broker Architecture*, known as *CORBA*, is a specification for creating interoperable distributed object systems. VisiBroker for Java is a product by Inprise that uses Java to implement the CORBA specification. The RMI technology introduced in Chapter 15, "Distributed Programming Using Java Remote Method Invocation," is for developing Java-only distributed systems. Realistically, we do not live in a Java-only world. Many other programming languages are currently used to develop software systems, and many legacy systems have been developed in COBOL. RMI is not suitable for integrating new systems developed in Java with existing systems developed in a language other than Java. CORBA is the answer to integrate systems developed in different programming languages.

CORBA is not a programming language. It is a language-neutral specification that enables applications written in diverse programming languages to interoperate. Java is the most popular programming language for developing Internet applications. Java and CORBA together provide a solid foundation for developing highly reusable and interoperable distributed software systems. This chapter introduces the basics of CORBA. You will learn how to use VisiBroker for Java to create useful distributed applications.

NOTE
To run the examples in this chapter, you need JBuilder 3 Enterprise Edition.

Introduction to CORBA

Software interoperability is a dominating issue facing the IT industry today. CORBA was proposed by the *Object Management Group* (OMG) to facilitate the specification for developing interoperable software systems. OMG is a nonprofit consortium that includes almost all computer companies except Microsoft, which promotes its own competing object request broker called the *Distributed Component Object Model* (DCOM). Microsoft was initially at odds with CORBA and OMG, but it has recently reconciled with OMG and supports the peaceful coexistence of CORBA and DCOM.

CORBA Is Distributed

CORBA is a standard for supporting interoperable distributed applications. In many ways, CORBA is similar to RMI. In fact, it was the model for RMI. CORBA is very complex and difficult to learn. For this reason, the folks at JavaSoft invented RMI to simplify the development of Java distributed systems. With RMI, you are limited to all-Java programs. CORBA enables you to build language-neutral distributed systems.

Like RMI, CORBA maintains the notions of clients and servers. A *client* is a component that issues requests for services, and a *server* is a component that delivers the requested services. Unlike RMI, CORBA objects are location-transparent. The client does not need to know where the server is located. The client requests services through a CORBA server, which then locates the server.

Interface Definition Language

CORBA clients do not need to know how servers are implemented, as long as they know what services the server provides. The services are defined in *Interface Definition Language* (IDL), which serves as a contract between the server and its potential clients. IDL separates object definition from implementation. A client sees a server object solely through the IDL interface.

IDL is language-neutral and purely declarative. It is essential to ensure CORBA interoperability. Interfaces written in IDL can be mapped to interfaces in any programming language. In other words, a client written in Java can communicate with a server written in C++, which in turn can communicate with a server written in Ada, and so forth.

Object Request Broker

At the heart of the CORBA specification is the *Object Request Broker*, known as *ORB*, which is a software component used to facilitate communications and interactions among objects. The client does not need to know the server's location in the network. ORB locates the server and enables clients to make requests and receive responses from the server transparently. ORB assumes the responsibilities of routing and passing method parameters.

Basic Object Adapter

The *Basic Object Adapter*, known as *BOA*, is a software component interfacing the server with ORB. BOA provides the runtime environment in which ORB and the server communicate with each other. Specifically, BOA is responsible for activating and deactivating server objects, assigning them object IDs and passing requests to them. BOA is not combined with ORB; rather, it is used to provide specialized services that have been optimized for a particular environment, platform, and server.

Internet Inter-ORB Protocol

The implementation of ORB is vendor-specific. The *Internet Inter-ORB Protocol*, known as *IIOP*, was introduced to address ORB interoperability. IIOP enables the objects of one vendor's ORB to communicate with the objects of another vendor's ORB. IIOP is only of concern for ORB vendors to make their products interoperable with other ORBs; developers are not directly involved with it.

Figure 16.1 demonstrates the interactions of objects with IDL, ORB, BOA, and IIOP.

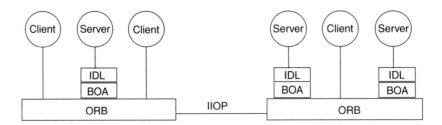

Figure 16.1   *The client accesses a server based on the server's IDL interface. BOA registers the server with ORB. ORB is responsible for locating the server upon a client's request. Communications among ORBs are handled through IIOP.*

The IDL Compiler and Its Generated Files

An IDL interface describes the resources provided by a server for use by its potential clients. These resources include data and methods. IDL is language-neutral and contains no implementation details. An IDL compiler translates the IDL definitions into definitions in a host language, such as Java, C++, Ada, or COBOL. The host language must provide the code for implementing the methods. The implementation is often referred to as *server implementation* or *object implementation*.

To understand IDL and know what files are generated by an IDL compiler, let us consider an IDL definition for a Student server, as shown in Listing 16.1. The interface defines a single method named findScore, which can be invoked by a client to find the score for a specified student.

```
// Student.idl
module StudentPackage
{
  interface Student
  {
    double findScore(in string name);
  };
};
```

Listing 16.1   *Student.idl*

IDL syntax is similar to Java. An IDL module is like a Java package, and an IDL interface is translated to a Java interface. Please refer to Chapter 3, "IDL to Java Mapping," in "VisiBroker for Java Reference" in JBuilder Help for complete coverage of IDL syntax.

The IDL compiler generates two sets of files for each interface in the IDL definition, as shown in Figure 16.2. One set, referred to as *client-side files*, makes a particular CORBA server interface available to a client. The other set, referred to as *server-side files*, provides server templates to be implemented by the server.

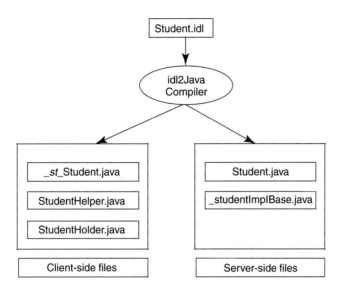

Figure 16.2 *The idl2Java compiler generates client-side files and server-side files.*

The file _st_Student.java (Listing 16.2), referred to as a *client stub*, implements the client-side operations for communicating with the server. Invoking a server method such as findScore() essentially involves the following operations:

1. Write the input arguments to an output stream for the server to receive.

2. Invoke the server method.

3. Read the result from an input stream sent by the server.

```
package StudentPackage;
public class _st_Student extends org.omg.CORBA.portable.ObjectImpl
  implements StudentPackage.Student {
  protected StudentPackage.Student _wrapper = null;
  public StudentPackage.Student _this() {
    return this;
  }
  public java.lang.String[] _ids() {
    return __ids;
  }
  private static java.lang.String[] __ids = {
    "IDL:StudentPackage/Student:1.0"
  };
  public double findScore(
    java.lang.String name
  ) {
    org.omg.CORBA.portable.OutputStream _output;
    org.omg.CORBA.portable.InputStream _input;
    double _result;
    while(true) {
      _output = this._request("findScore", true);
```

Listing 16.2 *_st_Student.java*

```
          _output.write_string(name);
          try {
            _input = this._invoke(_output, null);
            _result = _input.read_double();
          }
          catch(org.omg.CORBA.TRANSIENT _exception) {
            continue;
          }
          break;
        }
        return _result;
      }
    }
```

Listing 16.2   *Continued*

The file StudentHelper.java (Listing 16.3), referred to as a *client helper*, provides many helper functions for a client. One of these functions is the bind() method, which can be used to locate the server through the **VisiBroker Smart Agent**, a very useful and simplified naming service.

```
package StudentPackage;
abstract public class StudentHelper {
  public static StudentPackage.Student
    narrow(org.omg.CORBA.Object object) {
    return narrow(object, false);
  }
  private static StudentPackage.Student
    narrow(org.omg.CORBA.Object object, boolean is_a) {
    if(object == null) {
      return null;
    }
    if(object instanceof StudentPackage.Student) {
      return (StudentPackage.Student) object;
    }
    if(is_a || object._is_a(id())) {
      StudentPackage._st_Student result =
        (StudentPackage._st_Student)new StudentPackage._st_Student();
      ((org.omg.CORBA.portable.ObjectImpl) result)._set_delegate
        (((org.omg.CORBA.portable.ObjectImpl) object)._get_delegate());
      ((org.omg.CORBA.portable.ObjectImpl)
        result._this())._set_delegate
        (((org.omg.CORBA.portable.ObjectImpl) object)._get_delegate());
      return (StudentPackage.Student) result._this();
    }
    return null;
  }
  public static StudentPackage.Student bind(org.omg.CORBA.ORB orb) {
    return bind(orb, null, null, null);
  }
  public static StudentPackage.Student
    bind(org.omg.CORBA.ORB orb, java.lang.String name) {
    return bind(orb, name, null, null);
  }
  public static StudentPackage.Student
    bind(org.omg.CORBA.ORB orb, java.lang.String name,
```

Listing 16.3   *StudentHelper.java*

```
              java.lang.String host, org.omg.CORBA.BindOptions options) {
      return narrow(orb.bind(id(), name, host, options), true);
    }
    private static org.omg.CORBA.ORB _orb() {
      return org.omg.CORBA.ORB.init();
    }
    public static StudentPackage.Student
      read(org.omg.CORBA.portable.InputStream _input) {
      return StudentPackage.StudentHelper.narrow(_input.read_Object(),
true);
    }
    public static void write(org.omg.CORBA.portable.OutputStream _output,
      StudentPackage.Student value) {
      _output.write_Object(value);
    }
    public static void insert
      (org.omg.CORBA.Any any, StudentPackage.Student value) {
      org.omg.CORBA.portable.OutputStream output =
any.create_output_stream();
      write(output, value);
      any.read_value(output.create_input_stream(), type());
    }
    public static StudentPackage.Student extract(org.omg.CORBA.Any any) {
      if(!any.type().equal(type())) {
        throw new org.omg.CORBA.BAD_TYPECODE();
      }
      return read(any.create_input_stream());
    }
    private static org.omg.CORBA.TypeCode _type;
    public static org.omg.CORBA.TypeCode type() {
      if(_type == null) {
        _type = _orb().create_interface_tc(id(), "Student");
      }
      return _type;
    }
    public static java.lang.String id() {
      return "IDL:StudentPackage/Student:1.0";
    }
  }
```

Listing 16.3 *Continued*

The StudentHolder.java (Listing 16.4), referred to as a *client holder*, holds a public instance for the Student object. This class provides methods for reading and writing a Student object value.

```
package StudentPackage;
final public class StudentHolder
  implements org.omg.CORBA.portable.Streamable {
  public StudentPackage.Student value;
  public StudentHolder() {
  }
  public StudentHolder(StudentPackage.Student value) {
    this.value = value;
  }
  public void _read(org.omg.CORBA.portable.InputStream input) {
```

Listing 16.4 *StudentHolder.java*

```
      value = StudentPackage.StudentHelper.read(input);
    }
    public void _write(org.omg.CORBA.portable.OutputStream output) {
      StudentPackage.StudentHelper.write(output, value);
    }
    public org.omg.CORBA.TypeCode _type() {
      return StudentPackage.StudentHelper.type();
    }
  }
}
```

Listing 16.1   *Continued*

The file Student.java (Listing 16.5), referred to as a *server interface*, is a mapping of the Student IDL interface to the corresponding Java interface.

```
package StudentPackage;
public interface Student extends org.omg.CORBA.Object {
  public double findScore(
    java.lang.String name
  );
}
```

Listing 16.5   *Student.java*

The file _StudentImplBase.java (Listing 16.6), referred to as a *server skeleton*, implements the server-side operations for communicating with the client. Executing a server method such as findScore() essentially involves the following operations, which are the reverse of the client stub:

1. Read the arguments from an input stream sent by a client.

2. Execute the server method.

3. Write the result to an output stream for the client to receive.

```
package StudentPackage;
abstract public class _StudentImplBase
  extends org.omg.CORBA.portable.Skeleton
  implements StudentPackage.Student {
  protected StudentPackage.Student _wrapper = null;
  public StudentPackage.Student _this() {
    return this;
  }
  protected _StudentImplBase(java.lang.String name) {
    super(name);
  }
  public _StudentImplBase() {
  }
  public java.lang.String[] _ids() {
    return __ids;
  }
}
```

Listing 16.6   *_StudentImplBase.java*

```
        private static java.lang.String[] __ids = {
          "IDL:StudentPackage/Student:1.0"
        };
        public org.omg.CORBA.portable.MethodPointer[] _methods() {
          org.omg.CORBA.portable.MethodPointer[] methods = {
            new org.omg.CORBA.portable.MethodPointer("findScore", 0, 0),
          };
          return methods;
        }
        public boolean _execute(org.omg.CORBA.portable.MethodPointer method,
          org.omg.CORBA.portable.InputStream input,
          org.omg.CORBA.portable.OutputStream output) {
          switch(method.interface_id) {
          case 0: {
            return StudentPackage._StudentImplBase._execute(_this(),
              method.method_id, input, output);
          }
          }
          throw new org.omg.CORBA.MARSHAL();
        }
        public static boolean _execute(StudentPackage.Student _self,
          int _method_id, org.omg.CORBA.portable.InputStream _input,
          org.omg.CORBA.portable.OutputStream _output) {
          switch(_method_id) {
          case 0: {
            java.lang.String name;
            name = _input.read_string();
            double _result = _self.findScore(name);
            _output.write_double(_result);
            return false;
          }
          }
          throw new org.omg.CORBA.MARSHAL();
        }
      }
```

Listing 16.6 *Continued*

■■■ **NOTE**

An IDL module may contain many interfaces. The IDL compiler generates separate client-side files and server-side files for each interface.

Developing CORBA Applications

With a basic understanding of the key CORBA components and the IDL compiler, you can begin to write CORBA applications. This section introduces the development of CORBA applications using JBuilder 3 Enterprise Edition.

The steps in developing a CORBA application are shown in Figure 16.3.

The following example demonstrates the development of a CORBA application
through these steps.

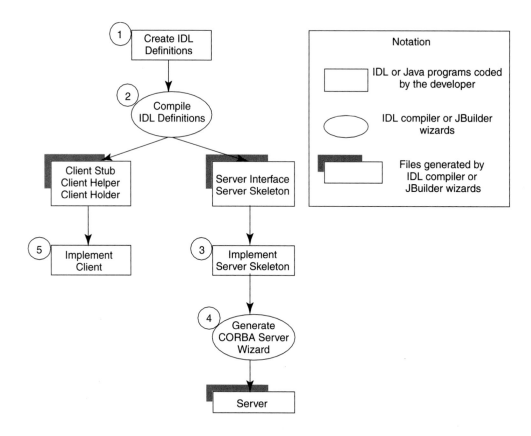

Figure 16.3   *The steps for developing CORBA applications.*

Example 16.1 Retrieving Student Scores from a CORBA Server

This example creates a client to retrieve student scores from the server. The example is the same as Example 16.1 except that it uses CORBA rather than RMI. The client, shown in Figure 16.4, displays the score for the specified name.

Here are the steps to complete this example:

1. Create a new project named CORBADemo.jpr, and create the IDL file named Student.idl, as shown in Listing 16.1. The IDL definition tells the client how to invoke the server's findScore() method to retrieve a student score. The IDL file name extension must be .idl.

2. Select Student.idl in the Navigation pane, and right-click the mouse to display a popup menu. Choose IDL Properties in the popup menu to display the VisiBroker IDL Properties dialog box, as shown in Figure 16.5. Uncheck all the options in the Generated code options section. Click OK to close the dialog box. In the Student.idl context menu, choose Make to compile the IDL file.

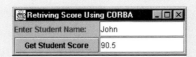

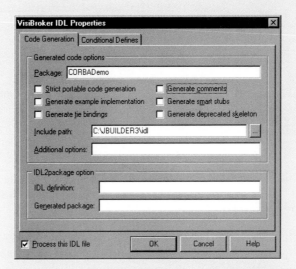

Figure 16.4   *You can get the score by entering a student name and clicking the Get Student Score button.*

Figure 16.5   *The IDL Properties dialog box enables you to set IDL compiler options.*

3. Create StudentImpl.java (Listing 16.7) to implement the server skeleton `_StudentImp1Base`. `StudentImpl` is the server implementation for the `Student` interface. Note that `_StudentImp1Base` is an abstract class that implements `Student`. The `findScore()` method is not implemented in `_StudentImplBase`. You must implement `findScore()` in `StudentImpl`. StudentImpl.java is often referred to as *server implementation*.

4. Select StudentImpl.java in the Navigation pane. Choose File, New to display the Object Gallery. Open the CORBA page and click the CORBA Server icon to display the Generate CORBA Server Wizard, as shown in Figure 16.6. Type or choose the values as shown in this figure, and click OK to generate StudentServer.java, as shown in Listing 16.8. This class contains a main method for starting the server implementation class `StudentImpl`.

5. Now turn your attention to developing the client:

   5.1. Create an applet named StudentClient.java using the Applet Wizard.

continues

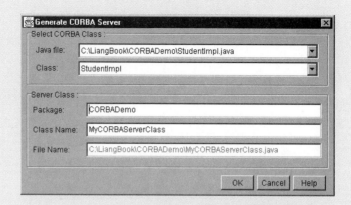

Figure 16.6   *The Generate CORBA Server Wizard enables you to generate the server class for starting the server implementation class.*

5.2. Create the user interface, which is the same as in Example 15.1.

5.3. Create the method `initializeCORBA()` for starting Student server, as shown in Listing 16.9. Add the code to invoke this method from the `jbInit()` method.

5.4. In the UI Designer, double-click `jbtGetScore` to generate the supporting code for the handler `jbtGetScore_actionPerformed()`. Implement this handler for finding and displaying the score for the student, as shown in Listing 16.9.

6. Run the example as follows:

6.1. Start **osagent** by choosing Tools, VisiBroker Smart Agent, or type c:\JBuilder3\bin\oagent at the DOS prompt. Smart Agent is introduced in the next section, "VisiBroker Smart Agent."

6.2. Start `StudentServer`.

6.3. Run `StudentClient` as an application. A sample run of the application is shown in Figure 16.4.

6.4. Start a Gatekeeper by typing c:\JBuilder3\bin\gatekeeper at the DOS prompt from the directory where the HTML file for `Student-Client` is located. In our example, StudentClient.html is located in c:\LiangBook. Gatekeeper is necessary for running `StudentClient` as an applet. Gatekeeper is introduced in the section "VisiBroker Gate-Keeper."

6.5. Run CORBADemo.StudentClient.html (Listing 16.10) from the appletviewer. A sample run is shown in Figure 16.7.

6.6. Run CORBADemo.StudentClient.html from Netscape. A sample run is shown in Figure 16.8.

6.7. Run CORBADemo.StudentClient.html from Internet Explorer. A sample run is shown in Figure 16.9.

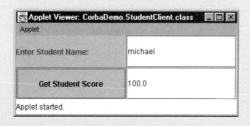

Figure 16.7   *Run the program from appletviewer.*

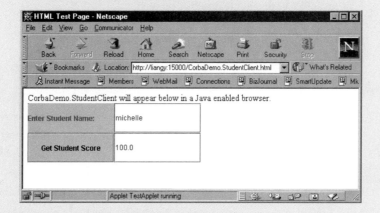

Figure 16.8   *Run the program from Netscape.*

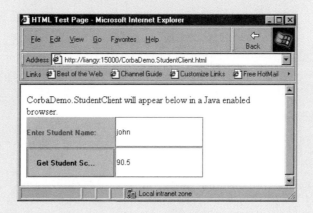

Figure 16.9   *Run the program from Internet Explorer.*

continues

```java
// StudentImpl.java: The Student Server Implementation
package CORBADemo;

import java.util.*;

public class StudentImpl extends StudentPackage._StudentImplBase
{
  private Dictionary scores = new Hashtable();

  // Constructors
  StudentImpl(String name)
  {
    super(name);
    System.out.println(name + " Created");

    // Initialize student information
    initializeStudent();
  }

  // Initialize student information
  protected void initializeStudent()
  {
    scores.put("John", new Double(90.5));
    scores.put("Michael", new Double(100));
    scores.put("Michelle", new Double(98.5));
  }

  // Get student score. Return -1 if score is not found.
  public double findScore(String name)
  {
    Double d = (Double)scores.get(name);

    if (d == null)
    {
      System.out.println("Student "+name+" is not found ");
      return -1;
    }
    else
    {
      System.out.println("Student " + name + "\'s score is "
        + d.doubleValue());
      return d.doubleValue();
    }
  }
}
```

Listing 16.7 *StudentImpl.java*

```java
// StudentServer.java: The Student Server
package CORBADemo;

import java.util.*;

public class StudentServer
{
  public static void main(String[] args)
  {
```

Listing 16.8 *StudentServer.java*

```
            try
            {
              // Initialize the ORB
              org.omg.CORBA.ORB orb =
                org.omg.CORBA.ORB.init(args,System.getProperties());

              // Initialize the BOA
              org.omg.CORBA.BOA boa =
                ((com.visigenic.vbroker.orb.ORB)orb).BOA_init();

              // Create the Student server object
              StudentPackage.Student implObject =
                new CORBADemo.StudentImpl("Student");

              // Export the server object to ORB
              boa.obj_is_ready(implObject);
              System.out.println(implObject+ " is ready.");

              // Wait for incoming requests from the clients
              boa.impl_is_ready();
            }
            catch (Exception e)
            {
              e.printStackTrace();
            }
          }
        }
```

Listing 16.8 *Continued*

```
        // StudentClient.java: Student Client
        package CORBADemo;

        import javax.swing.*;
        import java.awt.*;
        import java.awt.event.*;

        public class StudentClient extends JApplet
        {
          // Declare a Student instance, this object is an ORB server
          StudentPackage.Student student;

          // Arguments passed from the main method and used in the ORB init
          String[] args;

          boolean isStandalone = false;
          JLabel jlblName = new JLabel();
          GridLayout gridLayout1 = new GridLayout();
          JTextField jtfName = new JTextField();
          JButton jbtGetScore = new JButton();
          JTextField jtfScore = new JTextField();

          // Construct the applet
          public StudentClient()
          {
          }
```

continues

Listing 16.9 *StudentClient.java*

```java
      // Initialize the applet
      public void init()
      {
        try
        {
        jbInit();
        }
        catch (Exception e)
        {
        e.printStackTrace();
        }
      }

      // ORB initialization and Component initialization
      private void jbInit() throws Exception
      {
        // Initialize CORBA and bind server object
        initializeCORBA();

        this.getContentPane().setLayout(gridLayout1);
        jlblName.setText("Enter Student Name:");
        gridLayout1.setColumns(2);
        gridLayout1.setRows(2);
        jbtGetScore.setText("Get Student Score");
        jbtGetScore.addActionListener(new java.awt.event.ActionListener()
        {
          public void actionPerformed(ActionEvent e)
          {
            jbtGetScore_actionPerformed(e);
          }
        });

        this.setSize(300,100);
        this.getContentPane().add(jlblName, null);
        this.getContentPane().add(jtfName, null);
        this.getContentPane().add(jbtGetScore, null);
        this.getContentPane().add(jtfScore, null);
      }

      // Main method
      public static void main(String[] args)
      {
        StudentClient applet = new StudentClient();

        // Pass the main method arguments for initialize ORB when
        // running the client as an application
        applet.args = args;

        applet.isStandalone = true;
        JFrame frame = new JFrame();
        frame.setTitle("Retriving Score Using CORBA");
        frame.getContentPane().add(applet, BorderLayout.CENTER);
        applet.init();
        applet.start();
        frame.pack();
        Dimension d = Toolkit.getDefaultToolkit().getScreenSize();
        frame.setLocation((d.width - frame.getSize().width) / 2,
          (d.height - frame.getSize().height) / 2);
```

Listing 16.9 *Continued*

```
        frame.setVisible(true);
      }

      // Initialize ORB and bind the server object
      protected void initializeCORBA()
      {
        try
        {
          // Initialize the ORB
          System.out.println("Initializing the ORB");

          org.omg.CORBA.ORB orb;

          if (isStandalone)
          {
            // Initialize the ORB for a standalone application
            orb = org.omg.CORBA.ORB.init(args, null);
          }
          else
          {
            // Initialize the ORB for an applet
            orb = org.omg.CORBA.ORB.init(this, null);
          }

          // Bind the Student server object
          System.out.println("Locating Student Server" + orb);
          student = StudentPackage.StudentHelper.bind(orb, "Student");
        }
        catch (org.omg.CORBA.SystemException ex)
        {
          ex.printStackTrace();
        }
      }

      // Handler for the Get Student Score button
      void jbtGetScore_actionPerformed(ActionEvent e)
      {
        // Get student score
        double score = student.findScore(jtfName.getText().trim());

        // Display the result
        if (score < 0)
          jtfScore.setText("Not found");
        else
          jtfScore.setText(new Double(score).toString());
      }
    }
```

Listing 16.9   *Continued*

```
    <h1>VisiBroker for Java Client Applet</h1>
    <hr>
    <center>
      <applet
        codebase = "."
        code = "CORBADemo.StudentClient.class"
```

continues

Listing 16.10   *CORBADemo.StudentClient.html*

```
        width=200 height=80>
        <param name=org.omg.CORBA.ORBClass
         value=com.visigenic.vbroker.orb.ORB>
        <h2>You are probably not running a Java enabled browser.
        Please use a Java enabled browser (or enable your browser for
Java)
        to view this applet...</h2>
      </applet>
    </center>
    <hr>
```

Listing 16.10   *Continued*

Example Review

The IDL compiler generates three client-side files and two server-side files. These files can be seen in the Navigation pane by clicking the + sign in front of Student.idl. You can modify the IDL file, but do not modify the generated files. If the IDL file is modified, you need to remove the generated files by choosing Remove Generated Files from the idl file context menu before recompiling the IDL file.

StudentImpl is the implementation for Student. This class is almost the same as StudentImpl in Example 15.1, "Retrieving Student Scores from a RMI Server," except for two differences in coding.

- The CORBA StudentImpl extends StudentPackage._StudentImplBase, while the RMI StudentImpl extends UnicastRemoteObject and implements Student.

- The constructor of the CORBA StudentImpl invokes super(name) to register object's name, while invoking superclass's constructor in the RMI StudentImpl is not necessary.

StudentServer is responsible for starting the server. It contains the following functions:

1. Creating an instance of ORB by invoking the static init() method in org.omg.CORBA.ORB. The org.omg.CORBA.ORB class provides a way to initialize the org.omg.CORBA infrastructure.

2. Creating an instance of BOA by invoking the instance BOA_init() method in the org.omg.CORBA.ORB class. This method returns an instance of org.omg.CORBA.BOA, which can be used to register server implementation objects with ORB.

3. Creating an instance of the server implementation.

4. Registering the server implementation object with ORB by invoking the obj_is_ready() method on an org.omg.CORBA.BOA instance.

5. Notifying BOA that the server implementation object is ready for use by invoking the `impl_is_ready()` method on the `org.omg.CORBA.BOA` instance.

`StudentClient` invokes the `findScore()` method on the server to find the score for a specified student. The `initializeCORBA()` method is responsible for setting up the client-side infrastructure to enable `StudentClient` to access the server. The `org.omg.CORBA.ORB.init(args,null)` method creates an ORB instance for supporting a client application and the `org.omg.CORBA.ORB.init(applet, null)` method creates an ORB instance for supporting a client applet. Invoking `StudentHelper.bind(orb, "Student")` locates the `Student` server for use by a client.

To run this example, you have to first start osagent and then start the `StudentServer` class. To enable the client to run as an applet, the Gatekeeper must be used to bypass the applet security restrictions. Note that osagent.exe and gatekeeper.exe are located in \jbuilder3\bin directory. When the applet is run on a Web browser, the following applet parameter is needed in the HTML file to ensure that the Web browser uses VisiBroker ORB:

```
<param name=org.omg.CORBA.ORBClass
value=com.visigenic.vbroker.orb.ORB>
```

You started the Gatekeeper in the directory where the HTML file is located. The Gatekeeper is a Web server running at port 15000. You should use http://yourhostname:15000/CORBADemo.StudentClient.html as the URL to run the applet from the Web browser. This example works on either Netscape 4.5 or Internet Explorer 4.0.

VisiBroker Smart Agent

ORB Smart Agent, or *osagent,* is a very useful proprietary utility provided in VisiBroker. It is a dynamic directory service that enables a server to register with an agent and enables a client to locate a server through the agent. The osagent also provides fault-tolerance and load-balancing facilities.

Location Services

The osagent need not be on the same machine with the client or the server, but at least one osagent must be started on a host in the local network in the same subnet where the client and the server are running. There may be multiple instances of the osagent on different hosts; each osagent registers a set of server objects and communicates with other osagents to locate objects it cannot find.

A server implementation is registered with an osagent when the `obj_is_ready()` method on an `org.omg.CORBA.BOA` instance is invoked. To locate an osagent, a server sends a broadcast message, and the first osagent to respond will be used to register the server. When a client invokes the `bind()` method in the client helper class, it searches for an osagent by sending a broadcast message to all the hosts in the subnet, and the first osagent to respond carries out the tasks needed to locate the specified server object. If the server object is not registered with the current osagent, the osagent communicates with other osagent to locate the server object and obtain the object reference. The client then communicates with the server using the object reference.

Suppose a local network includes four hosts, as shown in Figure 16.10. Two osagents are started in Host 1 and Host 2. Consider the following scenario:

1. The server starts from Host 3, and the osagent on Host 1 responds first for registering the server.

2. The client requests the server, and the osagent in Host 2 responds.

3. Since the server is not registered with this agent, the agent communicates with the agent on Host 1.

4. The server object is found by the agent on Host 1. The sever object reference is obtained and passed back to the agent on Host 2.

5. The agent on Host 2 passes the server object reference to the client on Host 4.

6. The client sends the request to the server, using the server object reference.

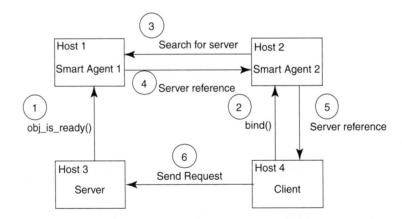

Figure 16.10   *The osagent facilitates communications of CORBA server objects.*

Fault Tolerance

The osagent supports two types of fault tolerance: osagent fault tolerance and server-object fault tolerance.

You can run multiple osagents on different hosts to support osagent fault tolerance. If one instance of the osagent becomes unavailable, all server implementations registered with it will be notified and will be automatically reregistered with other agents. No administration or coding is required. A client using an agent that is unavailable can be automatically switched to another agent by VisiBroker as long as one is still available.

You can start server objects on multiple hosts to support server-object fault tolerance. If one server object fails, ORB will automatically detect the lost connection between a client and the server, and will attempt to establish a connection with another server. The client request will be routed to a new server object by VisiBroker. The fault tolerance is transparent to the client and requires no administration.

Load Balancing

You can register multiple server objects with an osagent to gain load balancing as well as achieve fault tolerance. If there are multiple instances of server objects registered with an osagent, the agent uses a round-robin scheme to choose an instance to achieve load balancing.

Configuring osagent

There is no need to configure an osagent unless you need to run it on a specified port or connect it with another osagent in a different subnet.

Running osagent on a Specified Port

By default, an osagent uses port 14000 to communicate with clients, servers, and other agents. Occasionally, it is desirable to have separate sets of osagent running at the same time to avoid conflicts. For instance, students in a CORBA class may work the same project independently. To avoid conflicts, it is desirable for each student to use a separate osagent domain. The environment-variable OS-AGENT_PORT must be set on each host running as osagent, a server, or a client. On Windows 95 or Windows 98, use the following command to set the variable to 14001, for example:

SET OSAGENT=14001

You need to type this command for each MS-DOS session unless it is fixed in the autoexec.bat file.

With Windows NT, you can set the environment variable in the System dialog box accessible from the Control Panel.

Connecting Smart Agents on Different Subnets

Using UDP broadcast messages, osagents within the same subnet can automatically discover one other. To enable an osagent to communicate with an osagent in a different subnet, simply add the host name or IP address of the remote osagent in a file named localaddr. If a remote network has multiple osagents running, add the host name or IP address of each host in localaddr.

The osfind Utility

osfind is a useful lookup utility to find VisiBroker-related services and objects on a given network. To use it, simply type **osfind** at a DOS prompt, as shown in Figure 16.11. The osfind finds all the osgents running on the local network and the exact host on which each is running. The osfind also reports on all the object-activation daemons (OADs), all the server objects registered with OADs, and all the server objects that are currently running. For information on OAD, please refer to Chapter 6, "Activating objects and implementations," in *VisiBorker for Java Programmer's Guide* from the JBuilder Help.

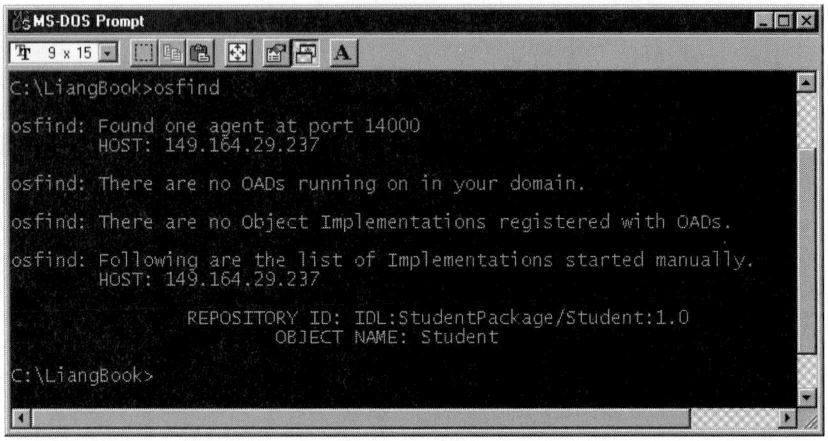

Figure 16.11   *The osfind command finds osagents, OADs, and objects registered with OADs or with osagents.*

VisiBroker Gatekeeper

You need the VisiBroker Gatekeeper to run Java applet clients. The Gatekeeper enables your applets to communicate with the servers while still conforming to the security restrictions imposed by Web browsers.

Three types of limitations are imposed on applets to prevent destructive programs from damaging the system on which the browser is running:

- Applets are not allowed to read from, or write to, the file system of the computer. Otherwise, they could cause damage to files and spread viruses.

- Applets are not allowed to run any programs on the browser's computer. Otherwise, applets might call destructive local programs and cause damage to the local system on the user's computer.

- Applets are not allowed to establish connections between the user's computer and another computer except for the server where the applets are stored. This restriction prevents the applet from connecting the user's computer to another computer without the user's knowledge.

The last limitation is prohibitive for a Java applet client seeking to access servers in the network. The Gatekeeper offers a way to circumvent this restriction by serving as a gateway between the client and the server. For any object server that is not running on the Web server, the ORB in the applet sends the service request to the Gatekeeper. The Gatekeeper then forwards the request to the server object.

Developing Three-Tier Applications Using CORBA

This section gives an example of the development of a three-tier application using CORBA.

Example 16.2 Retrieving Student Scores on a Database Using CORBA

This example rewrites Example 15.3, "Retrieving Student Scores on a Database Using RMI." It finds scores stored in a database through a CORBA middle tier instead of using RMI. For simplicity, the example reuses the Student interface and the StudentClient class from Example 16.1 with no modifications. Here are the steps to complete the project.

1. Reopen project CORBADemo.jpr, which was created in Example 16.1.

2. Create Student3TierImpl to implement the Student server IDL interface for accessing a JDBC data source, as shown in Listing 16.11. This implementation retrieves a record from the SCORES table, processes the retrieved information, and sends the result back to the client.

3. Select Student3TierImpl.java in the Navigation pane. Choose File, New to display the Object Gallery. In the CORBA page, double-click the CORBA Server icon to display the Generate CORBA Server dialog box. Type Student3TierServer in the Class Name field, and click OK to generate Student3TierServer.java, as shown in Listing 16.12.

4. Run the example as follows:

   4.1. Start osagent by choosing Tools, VisiBroker Smart Agent.

   4.2. Start the server by running Student3TierServer.java.

   4.3. Run StudentClient.java as an application.

   4.4. To run StudentClient.java as an applet, start Gatekeeper from c:\LiangBook at the DOS prompt, then run the applet.

continues

```java
// Student3TierImpl.java: The Student Server Implementation
package CORBADemo;

import java.sql.*;

public class Student3TierImpl extends StudentPackage._StudentImplBase
{
  //Use prepared statement for querying DB
  private PreparedStatement pstmt;

  // Constructors
  Student3TierImpl(String name)
  {
    super(name);
    System.out.println(name + " Created");

    // Initialize JDBC
    initializeDB();
  }

  // Load JDBC driver, establish connection and create statement
  protected void initializeDB()
  {
    try
    {
      // Load the JDBC driver
      // Class.forName("oracle.jdbc.driver.OracleDriver");
      Class.forName("sun.jdbc.odbc.JdbcOdbcDriver");
      System.out.println("Driver registered");

      // Establish connection
      // Connection conn = DriverManager.getConnection
      // ("jdbc:oracle:thin:@sesrv00.ipfw.edu:1521:test",
      //   "scott", "tiger");
      Connection conn = DriverManager.getConnection
        ("jdbc:odbc:LiangBookDB_MDB", "", "" );
      System.out.println("Database connected");

      // Create the SCORES table and initialize it if necessary
      initializeTable(conn);

      // Create a prepared statement for querying DB
      pstmt = conn.prepareStatement(
        "SELECT * FROM SCORES WHERE name = ?");
    }
    catch (Exception ex)
    {
      System.out.println(ex);
    }
  }

  // Create the SCORES table and initialize it if necessary
  private void initializeTable(Connection conn)
  {
    try
    {
```

Listing 16.11   *Student3TierImpl.java*

```java
      // Create a statement
      Statement stmt = conn.createStatement();
      //stmt.executeUpdate("DROP TABLE SCORES");

      // Create the table,
      // if already exists, an exception would be raised
      stmt.executeUpdate(
        "CREATE TABLE SCORES" +
        "(NAME VARCHAR(20), SCORE NUMBER, PERMISSION NUMBER)");

      // Insert three records into the SCORES TABLE
      stmt.executeUpdate(
        "INSERT INTO SCORES VALUES ('John', 90.5, 1)");
      stmt.executeUpdate(
        "INSERT INTO SCORES VALUES ('Michael', 100, 1)");
      stmt.executeUpdate(
        "INSERT INTO SCORES VALUES ('Michelle', 100, 0)");
    }
    catch (SQLException ex)
    {
      System.out.println(ex);
    }
  }

  // Get student score. Return -1 if score is not found.
  public double findScore(String name)
  {
    double score = -1;

    try
    {
      // Set the specified name in the prepared statement
      pstmt.setString(1, name);

      // Execute the prepared statement
      ResultSet rs = pstmt.executeQuery();

      // Retrieve the score
      if (rs.next())
      {
        if (rs.getBoolean(3))
          score = rs.getDouble(2);
      }
    }
    catch (SQLException ex)
    {
      System.out.println(ex);
    }

    System.out.println(name + "\'s score is " + score);
    return score;
  }
}
```

continues

Listing 16.11   *Continued*

```
// Student3TierImpl: for starting Student3TierServer
package CORBADemo;

import java.util.*;

public class Student3TierServer
{
  public static void main(String[] args)
  {
    try
    {
      org.omg.CORBA.ORB orb = org.omg.CORBA.ORB.init(args,null);
      org.omg.CORBA.BOA boa
        =((com.visigenic.vbroker.orb.ORB)orb).BOA_init();
      StudentPackage.Student implObject =
        new Student3TierImpl("Student");
      boa.obj_is_ready(implObject);
      System.out.println(implObject+ " is ready.");
      boa.impl_is_ready();
    }
    catch (Exception e)
    {
      e.printStackTrace();
    }
  }
}
```

Listing 16.12   *Student3TierServer.java*

Example Review

The Student.idl and StudentClient.java were created in Example 16.1 and reused with no modifications.

This example is identical to Example 15.3 except that it uses CORBA as a middle tier instead of RMI.

CORBA Callbacks

Like RMI, a CORBA server can invoke a client's method through callbacks. CORBA callbacks work in very much the same way as RMI callbacks. This section gives an example of the development of a CORBA application with callbacks.

Example 16.3 Developing a TicTacToe Game Using CORBA

This example rewrites Example 15.4, "Developing a TicTacToe Game Using RMI," to create a distributed application for playing TicTacToe using CORBA. The design of the example is the same as in Example 15.4. The client is responsible for handling user interactions, and the server coordinates with the clients. A client first needs to register with the server. Once the server receives two clients, the game starts. When a client makes a move, it notifies the server, the server then notifies the move to the other player. The server determines the status of the game, i.e., whether the game is won or drawn, and notifies the players. The server also coordinates the turns, i.e., which client has the turn at one time. The server notifies the client through a callback interface.

To see the development in action, follow the steps below:

1. Create a new project named CORBATicTacToe.jpr.

2. Create an IDL file named TicTacToe.idl (Listing 16.13), which contains two IDL interfaces named TicTacToe and CallBack.

3. Right-click TicTacToe.idl in the Navigation pane to display a context menu. Choose Make in the menu to compile this file. A set of files was generated. Among them are TicTacToe.java and CallBack.java, as shown in Listing 16.14 and 16.15, respectively.

4. Create the TicTacToeImpl class to implement the TicTacToe IDL interface, as shown in Listing 16.16.

5. Create the CallBackImpl class to implement the CallBack IDL interface, as shown in Listing 16.17.

6. Create the client named TicTacToeClient for the players, as shown in Listing 16.18.

7. Select TicTacToeImpl in the Navigation pane. Choose File, New to display the Object Gallery. Click the CORBA tab and choose the Generate CORBA Server Wizard to display the Generate CORBA Server dialog box. Type TicTacToeServer in the Class Name field, and click OK to generate TicTacToeServer.java, as shown in Listing 16.19.

8. Run the example as follows:

   8.1. Start osagent by choosing Tools, VisiBroker Smart Agent.

   8.2. Start TicTacToeServer by running TicTacToeServer.java.

   8.3. Run TicTacToeClient as an application.

   8.4. To run TicTacToeClient as an applet, start a Gatekeeper by typing gatekeeper at the DOS prompt from the directory where the HTML file for TicTacToeClient is located.

   8.5. Run CORBATicTacToe.TicTacToeClient.html from the appletviewer.

continues

709

```
// TicTacToe.idl
module TicTacToePackage
{
  interface CallBack
  {
    // The client can make a move
    void takeTurn(in boolean turn);

    // Notify the client with a message
    void notify(in string message);

    // Mark the specified cell in the client
    void mark(in long row, in long column, in char token);
  };

  interface TicTacToe
  {
    // The client requests connection with the server
    boolean connect(in CallBack client, inout char marker);

    // The client notifies the server of the move
    void myMove(in long row, in long column, in char token);
  };
};
```

Listing 16.13   *TicTacToe.idl*

```
package TicTacToePackage;
public interface TicTacToe extends org.omg.CORBA.Object {
  public boolean connect(
    TicTacToePackage.CallBack client,
    org.omg.CORBA.CharHolder marker
  );
  public void myMove(
    int row,
    int column,
    char token
  );
}
```

Listing 16.14   *TicTacToe.java*

```
package TicTacToePackage;
public interface CallBack extends org.omg.CORBA.Object {
  public void takeTurn(
    boolean turn
  );
  public void notify(
    java.lang.String message
  );
  public void mark(
    int row,
    int column,
    char token
  );
}
```

Listing 16.15   *CallBack.java*

```
// TicTacToeImpl.java: The TicTacToe Server Implementation
package CorbaTicTacToe;

public class TicTacToeImpl
  extends TicTacToePackage._TicTacToeImplBase
{
  // Declare two players, used to call players back
  TicTacToePackage.CallBack player1 = null;
  TicTacToePackage.CallBack player2 = null;

  // board records players' moves
  char[][] board = new char[3][3];

  // Constructor
  public TicTacToeImpl(String name)
  {
    super(name);
    System.out.println(name + " Created");
  }

  // Connect to the TicTacToe server, defined in the TicTacToe IDL
  public boolean connect
  (
    TicTacToePackage.CallBack client,
    org.omg.CORBA.CharHolder marker
  )
  {
    if (player1 == null)
    {
      // player1 (first player) registered
      player1 = client;
      marker.value = 'X';
      player1.notify("Wait for a second palyer to join");
      return true;
    }
    else if (player2 == null)
    {
      // player2 (second player) registered
      player2 = client;
      marker.value = 'O';
      player2.notify("Wait for the first palyer to move");
      player2.takeTurn(false);
      player1.notify("It is my turn (X token)");
      player1.takeTurn(true);
      return true;
    }
    else
    {
      // Already two players
      client.notify("Two players are already in the game");
      return false;
    }
  }

  // A client invokes this method to notify the server of its move
  // Defined in the TicTacToe IDL
  public void myMove
  (
```

continues

Listing 16.16   *TicTacToeImpl.java*

```
          int row,
          int column,
          char token
        )
        {
          // Set token to the specified cell
          board[row][column] = token;

          // Notify the other player of the move
          if (token == 'X')
            player2.mark(row, column, 'X');
          else
            player1.mark(row, column, 'O');

          // Check if the player with this token wins
          if (won(token))
          {
            if (token == 'X')
            {
              player1.notify("I won!");
              player2.notify("I lost!");
              player1.takeTurn(false);
            }
            else
            {
              player2.notify("I won!");
              player1.notify("I lost!");
              player2.takeTurn(false);
            }
          }
          else if (isFull())
          {
            player1.notify("Draw!");
            player2.notify("Draw!");
          }
          else if (token == 'X')
          {
            player1.notify("Wait for the second palyer to move");
            player1.takeTurn(false);
            player2.notify("It is my turn, (O token)");
            player2.takeTurn(true);
          }
          else if (token == 'O')
          {
            player2.notify("Wait for the first palyer to move");
            player2.takeTurn(false);
            player1.notify("It is my turn, (X token)");
            player1.takeTurn(true);
          }
        }

        // Check if a player with the specified token wins
        public boolean won(char token)
        {
          for (int i=0; i<3; i++)
            if ((board[i][0] == token)
                && (board[i][1] == token)
                && (board[i][2] == token))
```

Listing 16.16   *Continued*

```
                    return true;

              for (int j=0; j<3; j++)
                if ((board[0][j] == token)
                    && (board[1][j] == token)
                    && (board[2][j] == token))
                  return true;

              if ((board[0][0] == token)
                  && (board[1][1] == token)
                  && (board[2][2] == token))
                return true;

              if ((board[0][2] == token)
                  && (board[1][1] == token)
                  && (board[2][0] == token))
                return true;

              return false;
            }

            // Check if the board is full
            public boolean isFull()
            {
              for (int i=0; i<3; i++)
                for (int j=0; j<3; j++)
                  if (board[i][j] == '\u0000')
                    return false;

              return true;
            }
          }
```

Listing 16.16 *Continued*

```
          // CallBackImpl.java: The CallBack IDL implementation
          package CorbaTicTacToe;

          public class CallBackImpl extends TicTacToePackage._CallBackImplBase
          {
            // The client will be called by the server through callback
            TicTacToeClient thisClient;

            // Constructor
            CallBackImpl(Object client)
            {
              super();
              thisClient = (TicTacToeClient)client;
              System.out.println(client + " Created");
            }

            // The server notifies the client for taking a turn
            // Defined in the CallBack IDL
            public void takeTurn(boolean turn)
            {
              thisClient.setMyTurn(turn);
            }
```

continues

Listing 16.17 *CallBackImpl.java*

```
                  // The server sends a message to be displayed by the client
                  // Defined in the CallBack IDL
                  public void notify(java.lang.String message)
                  {
                    thisClient.setMessage(message);
                  }

                  // The server notifies a client of the other player's move
                  // Defined in the CallBack IDL
                  public void mark(int row, int column, char token)
                  {
                    thisClient.mark(row, column, token);
                  }
                }
```

Listing 16.17 *Continued*

```
            // TicTacToeClient.java: TicTacToeClient applet
            package CORBATicTacToe;

            import java.awt.*;
            import java.awt.event.*;
            import java.applet.*;
            import javax.swing.*;

            public class TicTacToeClient extends JApplet
            {
              // Arguments passed from the main method and used in the ORB init
              String[] args;

              // marker is a CORBA char holder, used to indicate the token type
              org.omg.CORBA.CharHolder marker = new org.omg.CORBA.CharHolder();

              // ticTacToe is the game server for coordinating with the players
              TicTacToePackage.TicTacToe ticTacToe;

              // myTurn indicates whether the player can move now
              private boolean myTurn = false;

              // Each cell can be empty or marked as 'O' or 'X'
              private Cell[][] cell;

              boolean isStandalone = false;
              JLabel jlblStatus = new JLabel();
              JPanel jPanel1 = new JPanel();
              GridLayout gridLayout1 = new GridLayout();

              // Construct the applet
              public TicTacToeClient()
              {
              }

              // Initialize the applet
              public void init()
              {
                try
```

Listing 16.18 *TicTacToeClient.java*

```
      {
      jbInit();
      }
      catch (Exception e)
      {
      e.printStackTrace();
      }
   }

   // Component and CORBA initialization
   private void jbInit() throws Exception
   {
      // Create user interface
      this.setSize(400,300);
      jPanel1.setLayout(gridLayout1);
      gridLayout1.setRows(3);
      gridLayout1.setHgap(1);
      gridLayout1.setColumns(3);
      this.getContentPane().add(jlblStatus, BorderLayout.NORTH);
      this.getContentPane().add(jPanel1, BorderLayout.CENTER);

      // Create cells and place cells in the panel
      cell = new Cell[3][3];
      for (int i=0; i<3; i++)
        for (int j=0; j<3; j++)
          jPanel1.add(cell[i][j] = new Cell(i, j));

      // Initialize the CORBA enviornment
      initializeCORBA();
   }

   // Initialize the CORBA enviornment
   boolean initializeCORBA()
   {
      // Initialize the ORB
      System.out.println("Initializing the ORB");

      org.omg.CORBA.ORB orb;

      try
      {
        if (isStandalone)
        {
          // Initialize the ORB for a standalone application
          orb = org.omg.CORBA.ORB.init(args, null);
        }
        else
        {
          // Initialize the ORB for an applet
          orb = org.omg.CORBA.ORB.init(this, null);
        }

        // Bind the TicTacToe server object
        System.out.println("Locating TicTacToe Server");
        ticTacToe = TicTacToePackage.TicTacToeHelper.bind
          (orb, "TicTacToe");

        // Create callback for use by the server
        // to control the client
        CallBackImpl callBackControl = new CallBackImpl(this);
```

continues

```
                    // Connect the object with the ORB
                    // This call is not necessary since the object is passed to
                    // the server
                    // orb.connect(callBackControl);

                    // Connect with the server
                    if (ticTacToe.connect(callBackControl, marker))
                    {
                      System.out.println("connected as "+marker.value+" player.");
                      return true;
                    }
                    else
                    {
                      System.out.println("already two players connected as ");
                      return false;
                    }
                  }
                  catch (org.omg.CORBA.SystemException ex)
                  {
                    System.out.println(ex);
                  }

                  return false;
                }

                // Set variable myTurn to true or false
                void setMyTurn(boolean myTurn)
                {
                  this.myTurn = myTurn;
                }

                // Set message on the status label
                public void setMessage(String message)
                {
                  jlblStatus.setText(message);
                }

                // Mark the specified cell using the token
                void mark(int row, int column, char token)
                {
                  cell[row][column].setToken(token);
                }

                // Main method
                public static void main(String[] args)
                {
                  TicTacToeClient applet = new TicTacToeClient();

                  // Pass the main method arguments for initialize ORB when
                  // running the client as an application
                  applet.args = args;

                  applet.isStandalone = true;
                  JFrame frame = new JFrame();
                  frame.setTitle("CORBA TicTacToe Client");
                  frame.getContentPane().add(applet, BorderLayout.CENTER);
                  applet.init();
                  applet.start();
```

Listing 16.18 *Continued*

```java
      frame.setSize(400,320);
      Dimension d = Toolkit.getDefaultToolkit().getScreenSize();
      frame.setLocation((d.width - frame.getSize().width) / 2,
        (d.height - frame.getSize().height) / 2);
      frame.setVisible(true);
    }

    // Inner class Cell for modeling a cell on the TicTacToe board
    public class Cell extends JPanel implements MouseListener
    {
      // marked indicates whether the cell has been used
      private boolean marked = false;

      // row and column indicate where the cell appears on the board
      int row, column;

      // The token for the cell
      private char token;

      // Construct a cell
      public Cell(int row, int column)
      {
        this.row = row;
        this.column = column;
        addMouseListener(this);
      }

      // Set token on a cell (mark a cell)
      public void setToken(char c)
      {
        token = c;
        marked = true;
        repaint();
      }

      // Paint the cell to draw a shape for the token
      public void paintComponent(Graphics g)
      {
        super.paintComponents(g);

        // Draw the border
        g.drawRect(0, 0, getSize().width, getSize().height);

        if (token == 'X')
        {
          g.drawLine(10, 10, getSize().width-10, getSize().height-10);
          g.drawLine(getSize().width-10, 10, 10, getSize().height-10);
        }
        else if (token == 'O')
        {
          g.drawOval(10, 10, getSize().width-20, getSize().height-20);
        }
      }

      public void mouseClicked(MouseEvent e)
      {
        // TODO: implement this java.awt.event.MouseListener method;
        if (myTurn && !marked)
        {
          // Mark the cell
          setToken(marker.value);
```

continues

```
                          // Notify the server of the move
                          ticTacToe.myMove(row, column, marker.value);
                      }
                  }

                  public void mousePressed(MouseEvent e)
                  {
                      // TODO: implement this java.awt.event.MouseListener method;
                  }

                  public void mouseReleased(MouseEvent e)
                  {
                      // TODO: implement this java.awt.event.MouseListener method;
                  }

                  public void mouseEntered(MouseEvent e)
                  {
                      // TODO: implement this java.awt.event.MouseListener method;
                  }

                  public void mouseExited(MouseEvent e)
                  {
                      // TODO: implement this java.awt.event.MouseListener method;
                  }
              }
          }
      }
```

Listing 16.18 *Continued*

```
      // TicTacToeServer.java: Register TicTacToeImpl with the ORB
      package CORBATicTacToe;

      import java.util.*;

      public class TicTacToeServer
      {

          public static void main(String[] args)
          {
              try {
                  org.omg.CORBA.ORB orb =
                      org.omg.CORBA.ORB.init(args,System.getProperties());
                  org.omg.CORBA.BOA boa =
                      ((com.visigenic.vbroker.orb.ORB)orb).BOA_init();
                  TicTacToePackage.TicTacToe implObject =
                      new CORBATicTacToe.TicTacToeImpl("TicTacToe");
                  boa.obj_is_ready(implObject);
                  System.out.println(implObject+ " is ready.");
                  boa.impl_is_ready();
              }
              catch (Exception e) {
                  e.printStackTrace();
              }
          }
      }
```

Listing 16.19 *TicTacToeServer.java*

Example Review

All the calls a client can invoke are encapsulated in one IDL interface named TicTacToe, and all the calls the server can invoke are defined in another interface named CallBack. Both interfaces are contained in the IDL module TicTacToePackage (Listing 16.13). Since the CallBack interface is referenced by the connect() method in the TicTacToe interface, CallBack must be declared before TicTacToe in the IDL module.

Note that the connect() method is different from the connect() method in the RMI version of the TicTacToe interface. In the RMI TicTacToe interface, the signature of the connect() method is

```
public char connect(CallBack client) throws RemoteException;
```

However, the signature of the connect() method in the CORBA TicTacToe inter-face is

```
boolean connect(in CallBack client, inout char marker);
```

You could redefine the connect method as

```
char connect(in CallBack client);
```

With appropriate modifications, the project should work fine. I deliberately made the change to demonstrate the use of the inout parameters in CORBA IDL.

CORBA IDL parameters can appear in three modes: *in, out,* and *inout.* You have used the in mode in the previous examples. An in mode basic IDL type can be directly mapped to an appropriate Java primitive type. For example, the IDL boolean is mapped to the Java boolan, the IDL char is mapped to the Java char, the IDL long is mapped to the Java int, and the IDL long long is mapped to the Java long. An out or inout mode basic IDL type cannot be mapped to a primitive Java type, because a Java primitive type parameter is passed by value.

To allow the parameters of IDL basic types to be used with out and inout modes, CORBA introduces holder classes. The holder class is named *Type*-Holder for a primitive Java *type.* For example, the holder class for char is CharHolder, for boolean is BooleanHolder, for int is IntHolder, and for double is DoubleHolder. An IDL compiler maps an out or inout IDL type to its corresponding holder class. For example, the IDL char parameter in the connect method was translated to CharHolder, as shown in Listing 16.14.

The holder classes are grouped in the org.omg.CORBA package. A holder class like org.omg.CORBA.CharHolder is similar to a Java wrapper class like java.lang.Character, but there is one critical difference. Each holder class has a public data member named value, which can be modified to change the contents of a

continues

719

holder object. However, you cannot change the contents of a wrapper object once it is created. A holder object provides a level of indirection. A client instantiates a holder object and passes it to the server. The server may then set or modify the `value` data field of the holder object.

Like RMI, the server CORBA remote object (`ticTacToe`) is located through ORB using the `bind()` method. The `CallBack` object is passed to the server through the `connect()` method in the `ticTacToe` object.

Chapter Summary

CORBA is a language-neutral approach for developing interoperable distributed applications. Interface Definition Language is the key to achieving language independence. You can develop clients using one language and implement servers using another language. In this chapter, you learned how to develop distributed Java applications using VisiBroker for Java. The naming service osagent makes it easy to locate the object on the network. The gatekeeper facilitates applet clients to communicate with CORBA objects.

CORBA and RMI have much in common; both are for developing distributed applications, and their programming features are comparable. The critical difference is that CORBA can support any high-level language, but RMI cannot be used to develop a distributed system involving different programming languages.

Chapter Review

16.1. Describe the differences between CORBA and RMI.

16.2. Describe the roles of the IDL interfaces.

16.3. How do you compile an IDL file? What files are generated by the IDL compiler?

16.4. What is the osagent for? How do you start an osagent? Can you have multiple osagents running on the same machine or different machines?

16.5. What is the gatekeeper for? How do you start a gatekeeper?

16.6. How do you register a remote object with ORB?

16.7. How does a client locate a remote object through ORB?

16.8. Describe the mapping of basic IDL types. Why are the holder classes used for the parameters of the out or inout mode?

16.9. How does callback work in CORBA?

Programming Exercises

16.1. Develop a chat application to enable two clients to exchange messages through a CORBA server.

16.2. Extend the previous exercises to develop a chat system that enables multiple clients to talk simultaneously.

16.3. Rewrite Example 16.3 using the following signature of the connect method in the TicTacToe interface.

```
char connect(in CallBack client);
```

INDEX

Abstract Window Toolkit (AWT), 162

ActiveX, 417

Anonymous inner class, 99

AppBrowser window, 7–10
Content pane, 8–10
Navigation pane, 8
Structure pane, 10

Applet Wizard, 27–30

Application class, 20, 21–22

Applications using JBuilder, DataExpress, and data-aware components, 603–639
data-aware components, 614–622
DataExpress API, 604–614
data modules, 627–638
master-detail relationship, 622–627

Basic Object Adapter (BOA), 685

Bean, 50

BeanBox, 401–408

Bean component, 50

Bean events, 75–107
custom event sets and source components, creating, 79–85
event adapters, 89–90
existing event sets, working with, 101–106
inner classes and anonymous inner classes, 97–101
Java event model, 76–79
event listener interface, 78
event objects, 77
JButton components, 78–79
listener components, 78
source components, 78
listener components, creating, 86–89
using adapters in JBuilder, 90–97

Bean information class, 462

BeanInsight Wizard, 475

Bean introspection, 55

Bean introspection and customization, 461–511
creating BeanInfo classes, 462–470
EventSetDescriptor class, 465
MethodDescriptor class, 465
PropertyDescriptor class, 464
specifying image icons, 465–466
creating component customizers, 501–509
creating GUI custom editors, 492–501
customizing property editors, 476–484
creaing property values, 477–484
displaying property values, 477
editing property values, 477
FeatureDescriptor class, 484–485

inspecting bean components, 470–475
using Bean Designer to create property editors and generate BeanInfo classes, 485–492
using BeanInsight Wizard, 475–476

Bean persistence, versioning, and using beans in other tools, 387–426
BeanBox, 401–408
bean versioning, 412–417
customizing serialization, 409–411
instantiating serialized beans, 396–400
JavaBeans bridge for ActiveX, 417–424
converting components, 417–424
object serialization and deserialization, 388–395
transient keyword, 395–396

BeansExpress Wizard, 112–124

BorderLayout, 222

Bound and constraint properties, 427–460
implementing, 428–437
implementing constraint properties, 445–449
implementing model-view components, 450–460
PropertyChangeSupport class, 437–438
using Bean Designer, 438–444

Bound property, 428

BoxLayout2, 227

BoxLayout and Box class, 225–227

CallableStatement, 596–601
methods, table, 597

Callbacks, 666

CardLayout, 222–223

CASE tool, 149

Client, 644

Client helper, 688

Client holder, 689

Client-side files, 686

Client stub, 687

Column model, 342, 351

Combo box, 332

Common Object Request Broker Architecture (CORBA), 684

Component customizers, creating, 501–509

Component Inspector, 55

Component palette, 7

Components, developing and using, 109–157
component development process, 111–112
developing beans *vs.* using beans, 110
developing components using model-view approach, 131–142
packaging and deploying Java projects in JBuilder, 149–153

manifest file, 151–152

running archived projects, 152–153

using Deployment Wizard, 150–151

Rapid Application Development (RAD) process, 142–149

using Bean Designer to create events, 124–131

using BeansExpress Wizard to create properties, 112–124

Component tree, 10

`Connection` **interface, 521**

Containers and layout managers

containers, definition of, 216–219

JApplet, 218

JFrame, 217–218

JPanel, 218–219

creating custom layout managers, 242–247

JSplitPane, 251–256

JTabbedPane, 247–251

layout manager, how it works, 240–242

layout managers, definition of, 219–221

layout managers, working with, 221–240

BorderLayout, 222

BoxLayout2, 227

BoxLayout and Box class, 225–227

CardLayout, 222–223

FlowLayout, 222

GridBagLayout, 223–225

GridLayout, 222

Null, 225

OverlayLayout, 228

PanelLayout, 228

VerticalFlowLayout, 229–240

XYLayout, 227–228

Context menu, 273

Controller, 132

Convenience listener adapter, 90

CORBA, 417

applications, developing, 691–701

callbacks, 708–720

three-tier applications, developing, 705–708

Data-aware components, 614–622

`DatabaseMetaData` **interface, 522**

finding database capabilities, table, 556

getting database objects, table, 557

retrieving general information, table, 555

DataExpress API, 604–614

Data models, 627

Data modules, 627–638

dbSwing components, 614

Delegation-based model, 77

Deployment Wizard, 150–151

Dialog box, 281

Display area, 223

Distributed Component Object Model (DCOM), 684

Distributed programming using Java Remote Method Invocation, 643–681

developing RMI applications, 646–655

developing three-tier applications using RMI, 661–666

RMI basics, 644–646

how it works, 644–645

passing parameters, 646

RMI callbacks, 666–679

RMI *vs.* socket-level applications, 656–661

Divider, 251

`Driver` **interface, 520**

`DriverManager` **class, 520–521**

`DriverPropertyInfo` **class, 521**

Event, 76

`EventDescriptor` **class, 465**

Event listener interface, 77

Event object, 76, 77

Event pair, 78

Event set, 78

Event source, 78

Example programs

2.1: Writing a Simple Java Bean Component, 51–55

2.2: Moving Message on a Panel, 63–65

2.3: Using Editors for Array, Enumerated, and Object Properties, 68–72

3.1: Creating a Custom Event Set and a Source Component, 80–85

3.2: Writing a Listener Component Manually, 86–89

3.3: Creating a Listener Component Using JBuilder, 91–97

3.4: Developing a Source Component Using Existing Event Sets, 101–106

4.1: Creating a Clock Component, 113–124

4.2: Creating an Alarm Clock, 124–131

4.3: Developing Model-View Components, 132–142

4.4: Developing a Mortgage Calculator, 144–149

5.1: Using JButton, JToggleButton, JCheckBox, JRadioButton and Border, 180–189

5.2: Using Labels and Scroll Panes, 191–195

5.3: Using JEditorPane, 197–200

5.4: Using Scroll Bars, 202–205

5.5: Using the Progress Bar, 208–211

6.1: Choosing Colors, 229–240

6.2: Creating a Custom Layout Manager, 242–247

6.3: Using JTabbedPane, 248–251

6.4: Using JSplitPane, 252–256

7.1: Using JBuilder Menu Designer, 266–273

7.2: Using Popup Menus, 273–277

7.3: Creating Toolbars, 278–280

7.4: Creating Standard Dialogs, 287–293

7.5: Creating Custom Dialogs, 293–299

7.6: Creating a Text Editor, 303–309

8.1: Simple List Demo, 316–319

8.2: List Model Demo, 320–324

8.3: List Cell Renderer Demo, 325–332

8.4: Combo Box Demo, 333–338

8.5: Editing in a Combo Box, 339–341

8.6: Testing Table Properties, 345–349

8.7: Using Table Models, 352–358

8.8: Using Predefined Table Renderers and Editors, 358–361

8.9: Using Custom Table Renderers and Editors, 363–365

8.10: Using Table Events, 366–370

8.11: Creating Custom Trees, 373–375

8.12: Adding and Removing Nodes, 376–379

9.1: Testing Object Serialization, 390–395

9.2: Instantiating Beans, 398–400

9.3: Using BeanBox, 403–408

9.4: Making the Clock Component Persistent, 409–410

9.5: Using the Externalizable Interface, 410–411

9.6: Testing Bean Versioning, 414–417

9.7: Using JavaBeans in Visual Basic, 421–423

9.8: Using JavaBeans in Word, 424

10.1: Beans Communication Through Bound Properties, 428–437

10.2: Using the Bean Designer to Create Bound Properties, 438–444

10.3: Using Constraint Properties, 445–449

10.4: Implementing Model-View Components Using Bound Properties, 450–460

11.1: Using the BeanInfo class, 466–470

11.2: Analyzing Components, 471–475

11.3: Providing Custom Property Editors, 479–484

11.4: Creating TimeZoneIDEditor and the BeanInfo Class for the Clock Component, 485–492

11.5: Creating GUI Property Editors, 493–501

11.6: Creating a Customizer for the Clock Component, 503–509

12.1: Testing the JDBC-ODBC Bridge Driver, 529–533

12.2: Using the JDBC OCI Driver, 534–536

12.3: Using the Oracle JDBC Thin Driver, 536–540

12.4: Using the Borland InterClient Driver Accessing Inter-Base Servers, 541–551

13.1: Discovering Databases, 558–578

13.2: Using Statement to Execute Static SQL Statements, 581–590

13.3: Using PreparedStatement to Execute Dynamic SQL Statements, 592–596

13.4: Using CallableStatement to Execute SQL Stored Procedures, 598–601

14.1: Creating an Address Book Using the DataExpress Components, 605–614

14.2: Using dbSwing Data-Aware Components, 616–622

14.3: Creating Master-Detail Forms, 623–626

14.4: Using Data Modules, 627–638

15.1: Retrieving Student Scores from an RMI Server, 647–655

15.2: Retrieving Student Scores from a Server Using Socket-Level Programming, 656–661

15.3: Retrieving Student Scores on a Database Using RMI, 662–666

15.4: Developing a TicTacToe Game with RMI, 666–679

16.1: Retrieving Student Scores from a CORBA Server, 692–701

16.2: Retrieving Student Scores on a Database Using CORBA, 705–708

16.3: Developing a TicTacToe Game Using CORBA, 708–720

FeatureDescriptor class, 484–485

Fillers, 226

FlowLayout, 222

Frame class, 20, 22–27

Generated applet class, modifying, 31–34

Getter method, 65

Glues, 226, 227

GridBagLayout, 223–225

GridLayout, 222

GUI custom editors, creating, 492–501

GUI property editor, 492

Handlers, 78

Heavyweight components, 162, 163

Image icons, 265

Inner class, 97

Interface Definition Language (IDL), 685

Internet Inter-ORB Protocol (IIOP), 685

JApplet, 218

Java applets, creating, 27

Java archive file format (JAR), 149

JavaBeans, 49–74

    bean properties, 65–67

        properties and data members, 66

        property naming patterns, 65–66

        property types, 66–67

    beans and objects, 50–55

    and Java Builder tools, 55–56

    property editors, 67–72

    using in JBuilder, 56–65

        adding bean to Component palette, 56–59

        beans, 59–65

Java database programming, introduction to, 515–552

    connecting to databases using JDBC drivers, 526–551

        JDBC URL naming conventions, 527–528

        using the JDBC-ODBC driver, 528–533

        using the middle-tier driver, 540–551

        using the native-API driver, 533–536

        using the native-protocol driver, 536–540

    JDBC API, overview of, 517–526

        Connection interface, 521

        DatabaseMetaData interface, 522

        developing JDBC applications, 518–520

        Driver interface, 520

        DriverManager class, 520–521

        DriverPropertyInfo class, 521

        JDBC drivers, 523–526

        JDBC support classes, 523

        ResultSet interface, 522

        ResultSetMetaData interface, 523

        SQL exception classes, 522

        Statement, PreparedStatement, and CallableState-ment interfaces, 521–522

Java style, 165

JBuilder3, 3–48
  creating and managing projects, 13–19
    new project, creating, 18–19
    project properties, setting, 13–18
  creating Java applications, 19–34
    Applet Wizard, using, 27–30
    application class, 21–22
    frame class, 22–27
      modifying, 24–27
    generated applet class, 31–34
  customizing JBuilder environments, 41–45
  designing user interfaces using UI Designer, 34–41
  online help, getting, 45–46
  starting, 5–13
    AppBrowser window, 7–10
    compiling and running projects, 10–13
    main window, 6–7
JBuilder environments, customizing, 41–45
JButton, 173–175
JCheckBox, 176
JColorChooser, 300–302
JComboBox, 332–341
JComponent class, 169–173
  action objects, 170
  JComponent properties, 170–172
  keystroke handling, 170
  SwingSet demo, 172–173
JDBC, 516
  classes, table, 517
  driver types, table, 523
  URL naming conventions, 527–528
JDBC-ODBC bridge driver, 524
JEditorPane, 197–200
JFileChooser, 302–303
JFrame, 217–218
JLabel, 189–196
  JScrollPane, 190–191
  JTextField, 195–196
JList, 313–332
JOptionPane dialogs
  confirmation dialogs, 283–284
  input dialogs, 284–286
  message dialogs, 282–283
  option dialogs, 286–287
JPanel, 218–219
JRadioButton, 176–189
  border, 177–180
JScrollBar, 200–205
JSlider, 205–211
  JProgressBar, 207
JSplitPane, 251–256
JTabbedPane, 247–251
JTable, 342–370
JTextArea, 196–197
JToggleButton, 175–176

JToolBar, 277
JTree, 370–381

Keyboard
  accelerators, 265–266
  mnemonics, 265–266

Layout manager, 216
Leaf, 371
Lightweight components, 162, 163
List, 313
List cell renderers, 325
Listener, 76
List models, 319–320
List-selection model, 324–325, 342

Main window, JBuilder 3, 6–7
Manifest file, 151–152
Master-detail relationship, 622–623
Menu bar, 6
Menu Designer, 266
Menu items, 262
Menus, toolbars, and dialogs, 261–312
  creating custom dialogs, 293–299
  JColorChooser, 300–302
  JFileChooser, 302–309
  JOptionPane dialogs, 281–293
    confirmation dialogs, 283–284
    input dialogs, 284–286
    message dialogs, 282–283
    option dialogs, 286–293
  JToolBar, 277–280
  menus, 262–266
    image icons, keyboard mnemonics, and keyboard accelerators, 265–266
  popup menus, 273–277
  using JBuilder Menu Designer, 266–273
Metadata, 554
Metadata and statements, 553–601
  CallableStatement, 596–601
  getting database metadata, 554–578
  PreparedStatement, 590–596
  Statement, 578–590
    execute(), executeQuery(), and executeUpdate() methods, 579–590
Metal style, 165
MethodDescriptor class, 465
Microsoft Component Object Model (COM), 417
Middle-tier driver, 525–526, 540–551
Minimum JavaBeans component requirements, 51
Model, 131
Model-view approach, 131–142
Motif style, 165
Multi-tier application development using CORBA, 683–721

CORBA callbacks, 708–720
developing CORBA applications, 691–701
developing three-tier applications using CORBA, 705–708
IDL compiler and its generated files, 686–691
introduction to CORBA, 684–686
   Basic Object Adapter (BOA), 685
   distributed, 684–685
   Interface Definition Language (IDL), 685
   Internet Inter-ORB Protocol (IIOP), 685–686
   Object Request Broker (ORB), 685
VisiBroker Gatekeeper, 704–705
VisiBroker Smart Agent, 701–704
   configuring osagent, *703*
   fault tolerance, 702–703
   load balancing, 703
   location services, 701–702
   osfind *utility, 704*

Native-API driver, 524–525, 533–536
Native-protocol driver, 526, 536–540
Null, 225

Object deserialization, 388
Object implementation, 686
Object Management Group (OMG), 684
Object Request Broker (ORB), 685
Object serialization, 388
Online help, JBuilder, 45–46
OpenDoc, 417
Option buttons, 176
ORB Smart Agent, 701
osagent, 701
   configuring, 703
osfind utility, 704
OverlayLayout, 228

PaneLayout, 228
Peers, 162
Pluggable look and feel, 164–167
Popup menu, 273
Popup property editor, 492
Popup trigger, 273
PreparedStatement, 590–596
   methods, table, 591
Project, 13
Project properties, 13–18
   Code Style page, 17
   Compiler page, 15–17
   Paths page, 15
   Run Debug page, 18
PropertyChangeSupport class, 437–438
PropertyDescriptor class, 464
Property editors, 67–72
   array, 67
   choice-menu, 67

   object, 67, 68
   simple, 67
Property editors, customizing, 476–484
   creating property editors, 477–478
   displaying property values, 477
   editing property values, 477
Property types, 66–67
   bound, 66, 67
   constraint, 66, 67
   indexed, 66, 67
   simple, 66, 67

Radio buttons, 176
Rapid Application Development (RAD), 142–149
   deployment, 143–144
   implementation, 143
   maintenance, 144
   requirements specification, 142–143
   system analysis, 143
   system design, 143
   testing, 143
Reflector, 55
Remote Method Invocation (RMI), 644
Remote Procedure Calls (RPC), 644
ResultSet interface, 522
ResultSetMetaData interface, 523
ResultSetMetaData interface, methods, table, 558
Rigid areas, 226–227
Root, 371
Runtime, 470

Scroll bar, 200
   horizontal, 200
   vertical, 200
Selection modes
   multiple-interval, 314
   single, 314
   single-interval, 314
Selection modes, TreeSelectionModel
   contiguous, 376
   discontiguous, 376
   single, 376
Serial/Version UID, 412
Server, 644
Server implementation, 644, 686
Server interface, 690
Server-side files, 686
Server skeleton, 690
Setter method, 66
Skeleton, 645
Socket-level programming, 656–661
Source object, 76
Statement, 578–590
   methods, table, 580
Statement, PreparedStatement, and

CallableStatement interfaces, 521–522
Status bar, 7
Struts, 226
Stub, 645
Swing components, 161–213
  JButton, 173–175
  JCheckBox, 176
  JComponent class, 169–173
    action objects, 170
    JComponent properties, 170–172
    keystroke handling, 170
    SwingSet demo, 172–173
  JEditorPane, 197–200
  JLabel, 189–196
    JScrollPane, 190–191
    JTextField, 195–196
  JRadioButton, 176–189
    border, 176–180
  JScrollBar, 200–205
  JSlider, 205–211
    JProgressBar, 205–211
  JTextArea, 196–197
  JToggleButton, 175–176
  lightweight component framework, 162–163
  overview of Swing classes, 167–169
  pluggable look and feel, 164–167
  Swing Model-View architecture, 163–164
Swing components, advanced, 313–384
  JComboBox, 332–341
    editing combo boxes, 338–341
  JList, 313–332
    list cell renderers, 325–332
    list models, 319–324
    list selection models, 324–325
  JTable, 342–370
    custom table renderers and editors, 362–365
    properties, 343–349

    TableColumn class, 351–358
    table column models, 351
    table events, 365–370
    table models, 350
    table renderers and editors, 358–361
  JTree, 370–381
    creating trees, 372–375
    processing tree nodes, 375–379
    tree events, 381
    tree node rendering and editing, 380–381
Swing Model-View architecture, 163–164

TableColumn class, 351–352
Table events, 365
Table model, 342, 350
Table renderers and editors, predefined, table, 358
Target, 89
Toolbar, 6
transient keyword, 395–396
Transparent Network Substrate (TNS), 536
Traversals, 375
Two-phase approach, 445

UI Designer, designing user interfaces using, 34–41

VerticalFlowLayout, 229
View, 131
VisiBroker Gatekeeper, 704–705
VisiBroker Smart Agent, 688, 701–704
Visual event design, 408

Windows style, 165

XYLayout, 227–228

END USER LICENSE AGREEMENT

You should carefully read the following terms and conditions before breaking the seal on the CD-ROM envelope. Among other things, this Agreement licenses the enclosed software to you and contains warranty and liability disclaimers. By breaking the seal on the CD-ROM envelope, you are accepting and agreeing to the terms and conditions of this Agreement. If you do not agree to the terms of this Agreement, do not break the seal. You should promptly return the package unopened.

LICENSE

Prentice-Hall, Inc. (the "Company") provides this Software to you and licenses its use as follows:

a.   use the Software on a single computer of the type identified on the package;

b.   make one copy of the Software in machine-readable form solely for back-up purposes.

LIMITED WARRANTY

The Company warrants the physical CD-ROM(s) on which the Software is furnished to be free from defects in materials and workmanship under normal use for a period of sixty (60) days from the date of purchase as evidenced by a copy of your receipt.

DISCLAIMER

THE SOFTWARE IS PROVIDED "AS IS" AND COMPANY SPECIFICALLY DISCLAIMS ALL WARRANTIES OF ANY KIND, EITHER EXPRESS OR IMPLIED, INCLUDING, BUT NOT LIMITED TO, THE IMPLIED WARRANTIES OF MERCHANTABILITY AND FITNESS FOR A PARTICULAR PURPOSE. IN NO EVENT WILL COMPANY BE LIABLE TO YOU FOR ANY DAMAGES, INCLUDING ANY LOSS OF PROFIT OR OTHER INCIDENTAL, SPECIAL OR CONSEQUENTIAL DAMAGES EVEN IF COMPANY HAS BEEN ADVISED OF THE POSSIBILITY OF SUCH DAMAGES.

SOME STATES DO NOT ALLOW THE EXCLUSION OF IMPLIED WARRANTIES OR LIMITATION OR EXCLUSION OF LIABILITY FOR INCIDENTAL OR CONSEQUENTIAL DAMAGES, SO THE ABOVE EXCLUSIONS AND/OR LIMITATIONS MAY NOT APPLY TO YOU.

LIMITATIONS OF REMEDIES

The Company's entire liability and your exclusive remedy shall be:

1.   the replacement of such CD-ROM if you return a defective CD-ROM during the limited warranty period, or

2.   if the Company is unable to deliver a replacement CD-ROM that is free of defects in materials or workmanship, you may terminate this Agreement by returning the Software.

GENERAL

You may not sublicense, assign, or transfer the license of the Software or make or distribute copies of the Software. Any attempt otherwise to sublicense, assign, or transfer any of the rights, duties, or obligations hereunder is void.

Should you have any questions concerning this Agreement, you may contact Prentice-Hall, Inc. by writing to:

Prentice Hall
Computer Science/ Engineering
One Lake Street
Upper Saddle River, NJ 07458
Attention: Mechanical Engineering Editor

YOU ACKNOWLEDGE THAT YOU HAVE READ THIS AGREEMENT, UNDERSTAND IT, AND AGREE TO BE BOUND BY ITS TERMS AND CONDITIONS. YOU FURTHER AGREE THAT IT IS THE COMPLETE AND EXCLUSIVE STATEMENT OF THE AGREEMENT BETWEEN US THAT SUPERSEDES ANY PROPOSAL OR PRIOR AGREEMENT, ORAL OR WRITTEN, AND ANY OTHER COMMUNICATIONS BETWEEN US RELATING TO THE SUBJECT MATTER OF THIS AGREEMENT.

Borland® JBuilder™3 University Edition

Authorized Book Publisher License Statement and
Limited Warranty for Inprise Products

IMPORTANT—READ CAREFULLY

This license statement and limited warranty constitutes a legal agreement ("License Agreement") for the software product ("Software") identified above (including any software, media, and accompanying on-line or printed documentation supplied by Inprise) between you (either as an individual or a single entity), the Book Publisher from whom you received the Software ("Publisher"), and Inprise International, Inc. ("Inprise").

BY INSTALLING, COPYING, OR OTHERWISE USING THE SOFTWARE, YOU AGREE TO BE BOUND BY ALL OF THE TERMS AND CONDITIONS OF THE LICENSE AGREEMENT. If you are the original purchaser of the Software and you do not agree with the terms and conditions of the License Agreement, promptly return the unused Software to the place from which you obtained it for a full refund.

Upon your acceptance of the terms and conditions of the License Agreement, Inprise grants you the right to use the Software solely for educational purposes, in the manner provided below. No rights are granted for deploying or distributing applications created with the Software.

This Software is owned by Inprise or its suppliers and is protected by copyright law and international copyright treaty. Therefore, you must treat this Software like any other copyrighted material (e.g., a book), except that you may either make one copy of the Software solely for backup or archival purposes or transfer the Software to a single hard disk provided you keep the original solely for backup or archival purposes.

You may transfer the Software and documentation on a permanent basis provided you retain no copies and the recipient agrees to the terms of the License Agreement. Except as provided in the License Agreement, you may not transfer, rent, lease, lend, copy, modify, translate, sublicense, time-share or electronically transmit or receive the Software, media or documentation. You acknowledge that the Software in source code form remains a confidential trade secret of Inprise and/or its suppliers and therefore you agree not to modify the Software or attempt to reverse engineer, decompile, or disassemble the Software, except and only to the extent that such activity is expressly permitted by applicable law notwithstanding this limitation.

Though Inprise does not offer technical support for the Software, we welcome your feedback.

This Software is subject to U.S. Commerce Department export restrictions, and is intended for use in the country into which Inprise sold it (or in the EEC, if sold into the EEC).

LIMITED WARRANTY

The Publisher warrants that the Software media will be free from defects in materials and workmanship for a period of ninety (90) days from the date of receipt. Any implied warranties on the Software are limited to ninety (90) days. Some states/jurisdictions do not allow limitations on duration of an implied warranty, so the above limitation may not apply to you.

The Publisher's, Inprise's, and the Publisher's or Inprise's suppliers' entire liability and your exclusive remedy shall be, at the Publisher's or Inprise's option, either (a) return of the price paid, or (b) repair or replacement of the Software that does not meet the Limited Warranty and which is returned to the Publisher with a copy of your receipt. This Limited Warranty is void if failure of the Software has resulted from accident, abuse, or misapplication. Any replacement Software will be warranted for the remainder of the original warranty period or thirty (30) days, whichever is longer. Outside the United States, neither these remedies nor any product support services offered are available without proof of purchase from an authorized non-U.S. source.

TO THE MAXIMUM EXTENT PERMITTED BY APPLICABLE LAW, THE PUBLISHER, INPRISE, AND THE PUBLISHER'S OR INPRISE'S SUPPLIERS DISCLAIM ALL OTHER WARRANTIES AND CONDITIONS, EITHER EXPRESS OR IMPLIED, INCLUDING, BUT NOT LIMITED TO, IMPLIED WARRANTIES OF MERCHANTABILITY, FITNESS FOR A PARTICULAR PURPOSE, TITLE, AND NON-INFRINGEMENT, WITH REGARD TO THE SOFTWARE, AND THE PROVISION OF OR FAILURE TO PROVIDE SUPPORT SERVICES. THIS LIMITED WARRANTY GIVES YOU SPECIFIC LEGAL RIGHTS. YOU MAY HAVE OTHERS, WHICH VARY FROM STATE/JURISDICTION TO STATE/JURISDICTION.
LIMITATION OF LIABILITY

TO THE MAXIMUM EXTENT PERMITTED BY APPLICABLE LAW, IN NO EVENT SHALL THE PUBLISHER, INPRISE, OR THE PUBLISHER'S OR INPRISE'S SUPPLIERS BE LIABLE FOR ANY SPECIAL, INCIDENTAL, INDIRECT, OR CONSEQUENTIAL DAMAGES WHATSOEVER (INCLUDING, WITHOUT LIMITATION, DAMAGES FOR LOSS OF BUSINESS PROFITS, BUSINESS INTERRUPTION, LOSS OF BUSINESS INFORMA-TION, OR ANY OTHER PECUNIARY LOSS) ARISING OUT OF THE USE OF OR INABILITY TO USE THE SOFTWARE PRODUCT OR THE PROVISION OF OR FAILURE TO PROVIDE SUPPORT SERVICES, EVEN IF INPRISE HAS BEEN ADVISED OF THE POSSIBILITY OF SUCH DAMAGES. IN ANY CASE, INPRISE'S EN-TIRE LIABILITY UNDER ANY PROVISION OF THIS LICENSE AGREEMENT SHALL BE LIMITED TO THE GREATER OF THE AMOUNT ACTUALLY PAID BY YOU FOR THE SOFTWARE PRODUCT OR U.S. $25; PROVIDED, HOWEVER, IF YOU HAVE ENTERED INTO A INPRISE SUPPORT SERVICES AGREEMENT, IN-PRISE'S ENTIRE LIABILITY REGARDING SUPPORT SERVICES SHALL BE GOVERNED BY THE TERMS OF THAT AGREEMENT. BECAUSE SOME STATES AND JURISDICTIONS DO NOT ALLOW THE EXCLU-SION OR LIMITATION OF LIABILITY, THE ABOVE LIMITATION MAY NOT APPLY TO YOU.

HIGH RISK ACTIVITIES

The Software is not fault-tolerant and is not designed, manufactured or intended for use or resale as on-line control equipment in hazardous environments requiring fail-safe performance, such as in the operation of nuclear facilities, air-craft navigation or communication systems, air traffic control, direct life support machines, or weapons systems, in which the failure of the Software could lead directly to death, personal injury, or severe physical or environmental dam-age ("High Risk Activities"). The Publisher, Inprise, and their suppliers specifically disclaim any express or implied warranty of fitness for High Risk Activities.

U.S. GOVERNMENT RESTRICTED RIGHTS

The Software and documentation are provided with RESTRICTED RIGHTS. Use, duplication, or disclosure by the Government is subject to restrictions as set forth in subparagraphs (c)(1)(ii) of the Rights in Technical Data and Com-puter Software clause at DFARS 252.227-7013 or subparagraphs (c)(1) and (2) of the Commercial Computer Software-Restricted Rights at 48 CFR 52.227-19, as applicable.

GENERAL PROVISIONS

This License Agreement may only be modified in writing signed by you and an authorized officer of Inprise. If any provision of this License Agreement is found void or unenforceable, the remainder will remain valid and enforceable according to its terms. If any remedy provided is determined to have failed for its essential purpose, all limitations of li-ability and exclusions of damages set forth in the Limited Warranty shall remain in effect.

This License Agreement shall be construed, interpreted and governed by the laws of the State of California, U.S.A. This License Agreement gives you specific legal rights; you may have others which vary from state to state and from country to country. Inprise reserves all rights not specifically granted in this License Agreement.